ISBN 978-1-334-27589-0
PIBN 10760808

This book is a reproduction of an important historical work. Forgotten Books uses
state-of-the-art technology to digitally reconstruct the work, preserving the original format
whilst repairing imperfections present in the aged copy. In rare cases, an imperfection in
the original, such as a blemish or missing page, may be replicated in our edition. We do,
however, repair the vast majority of imperfections successfully; any imperfections that
remain are intentionally left to preserve the state of such historical works.

1 MONTH OF
FREE
READING

at

www.ForgottenBooks.com

By purchasing this book you are eligible for one month membership to ForgottenBooks.com, giving you unlimited access to our entire collection of over 1,000,000 titles via our web site and mobile apps.

To claim your free month visit:

www.forgottenbooks.com/free760808

English
Français
Deutsche
Italiano
Español
Português

www.forgottenbooks.com

Mythology Photography **Fiction**
Fishing Christianity **Art** Cooking
Essays Buddhism Freemasonry
Medicine **Biology** Music **Ancient
Egypt** Evolution Carpentry Physics
Dance Geology **Mathematics** Fitness
Shakespeare **Folklore** Yoga Marketing
Confidence Immortality Biographies
Poetry **Psychology** Witchcraft
Electronics Chemistry History **Law**
Accounting **Philosophy** Anthropology
Alchemy Drama Quantum Mechanics
Atheism Sexual Health **Ancient History**
Entrepreneurship Languages Sport
Paleontology Needlework Islam
Metaphysics Investment Archaeology
Parenting Statistics Criminology
Motivational

THE CHRISTIAN MINISTRY;

WITH

AN INQUIRY INTO THE CAUSES OF ITS INEFFICIENCY

BY THE REV. CHARLES BRIDGES, A.M.,

V¹CAR OF OLD NEWTON, SUFFOLK, AND AUTHOR OF
'AN EXPOSITION OF PSALM CXIX.'

FROM THE SIXTH LONDON EDITION.

NEW YORK:
ROBERT CARTER, 58 CANAL STREET,
AND PITTSBURG, 56 MARKET STREET.
1847.

CONTENTS.

PART V.

THE PASTORAL WORK OF THE CHRISTIAN MINISTRY 307

PART VI.

PREFACE.

THE Work now presented to the Public originated in a letter to a beloved friend upon the interesting subject of Ministerial inefficiency; which, at his desire, and by the disinterested kindness of the Editor of the Christian Observer, was subsequently inserted with a few enlargements in that valuable Miscellany;[1] and an impression taken from thence for private circulation. Several applications having been made for its separate publication, the Writer was induced to reconsider the subject in a more extended range, and to avail himself of the suggestions of friends, until the small pamphlet has gradually swelled into its present extended dimensions.

As to the Work itself—the Writer desires to be with his brethren "in weakness, and in fear, and much trembling."[2] He is aware that his proper situation, both in authority and experience, is at the feet of many, who are thus constrained to listen to him; and it would be to him a subject of the most painful regret, if he were supposed to advance any pretensions to a standard of zeal, earnestness, or Ministerial attainment, above his brethren. He has not described what he is, but what he ought, and what he trusts he desires to be; and if, (after the model of the Country Parson) he has 'set the mark as high as he could;' it is, because ' he shoots higher that threatens the moon, than he that aims at a tree.'[3] He has endeavoured, however, to write in the first instance for himself; and to point every arrow of conviction at his own heart—"Thou that teachest another, teachest thou not thyself?"[4]

The Writer will be found to have dealt rather largely in illustration —not only, as being more suited to his relative situation with his brethren than didactic instruction; but as exhibiting that sympathy of care and anxiety, which gives to us a peculiar place in each other's remembrance, an interest in each other's prayers, and a witness in each other's hearts. "The same afflictions are accomplished in our brethren that are in the world."[5]

---

[1] Christian Observer, March, April, 1828.   [2] 1 Cor. ii. 3.
[3] G. Herbert's Preface to 'The Country Parson.'   [4] Rom. ii. 21.
[5] 1 Peter v. 9.

The materials for this work have been brought from different departments of the territory of the Church. Though the Writer has had a special regard to the Ministry of the Establishment (to which he is bound by the strongest and most endearing ties, and which occupies in his view the most commanding station in the Church of Christ); yet he would be sorry to refuse a cordial admission, and to neglect a diligent improvement of the acknowledged excellences of the honoured men of God in other communions.[1] If he should be thought to have been too large in his references, he can only apologize by his anxiety to shelter his own statements (which in themselves could possess but little weight) by the strength of accredited authority.

After all, he is deeply conscious, that this most responsible work has suffered—perhaps materially—from the unskilfulness of its treatment. He would desire, however, to be "accepted of his brethren,"[2] in a sincere attempt to subserve the grand cause, to which they, equally with himself, are consecrated; and he would beg to express his earnest desires to be favoured with private communications for the improvement of a second edition (should it ever be called for); for which purpose he subjoins his place of residence at full length.

For his work he has no other wish than that of the Country Parson: 'The Lord prosper the intention to myself, and others, who may not despise my poor labours; but add to those points, which I have observed, until the book grows to a complete pastoral.'[3]

For himself—he would be animated by the concluding exhortation of an eminent Minister to his Student and Pastor—' And now go thy way, O thou son greatly beloved; and work in thy lot lively, and prayerfully, and cheerfully to the end of thy days; and wait and look for what the glorious Lord will do for thee at the end of thy days; in those endless joys, wherein thou shalt shine as the brightness of the firmament, and as the stars for ever and ever.'[4]

Old Newton, Stowmarket,
June 22, 1829.

---

[1] The Christian spirit in one of the dignified advocates of our Establishment is truly admirable, which admitted the Life of Philip Henry (often referred to in these pages) into his collection of Ecclesiastical Biography—with the admission, that any Nonconformist of superior piety would also have found a place in his work. Wordsworth's Ecclesiastical Biography—Preface, p. xviii.

[2] Esther x. 3.   [3] Preface to 'The Country Parson.'
[4] Conclusion to Mather's 'Student and Pastor.'

ADVERTISEMENT TO THE FOURTH EDITION.

THE Writer has been induced to send out this New Edition in what will probably be considered a more convenient form. Feeling with the eminently learned, and modest Melancthon, that 'to be single-handed is to be weak,'[1] he thankfully acknowledges assistance derived from various sources of 'substantial profit. Though his work has swelled far beyond its original dimensions, he trusts that it may be a Manual of Ministerial responsibilities, privileges, and encouragements, illustrative of the elevated standard of our Ordination engagements, and stimulating to their more devoted and cheerful exercise. The time allowed him for revision enables him to bring out this Edition with far greater satisfaction to himself than any that have preceded it. He only entreats, that those who gain from it any instruction or interest, will follow it with their prayers, that it may conduce to the grand designs of the Christian Ministry. May the prayer of an old Writer[2] upon this subject be speedily and largely fulfilled, that our ' God would give unto his Church pious and faithful Pastors, and unite us together that we may be One in Him ; praising Him with heart, tongue, and *whole life*, so that in a blessed immortality freely vouchsafed to us, we may enjoy the presence of the Chief Shepherd, our Mediator Jesus Christ, throughout eternity.'

Old Newton Vicarage,
September 17, 1835.

[1] Scott's Continuation of Milner, ii. 180
[2] Nic. Hemmingii Pastor. Pref. As his book is little known, the Writer is tempted to transcribe the beautiful dedicatory prayer, in the spirit of which he has endeavoured to conduct his own more extended work—' Te, principem pastorem, Domine Jesu Christe invoco ; qui solus animam tuam pro ovibus dedisti, ut eas e faucibus lupi, qui est Diabolus, eriperes. Solus oves tuas in ovile tuum humeris tuis portasti. Solus sanguine tuo pretioso lavisti. Spiritu tuo sancto sanas, et pabulo æternæ vitæ pascis. Tibi supplico, ut mihi indignissimo servo tuo adesse tua gratia velis, et ea scribenti suggerere ex fontibus verbi tui digneris, quæ ad piam faciant instructionem eorum, quibus oves tuas pascendas commendasti, quibusque nomen quod tibi soli proprium est, communicasti; nempe ut dicantur ovium tuarum pastores, tuam solius vocem sonantes, quam solum ut oves tuæ agnoscunt ; ita te solum norunt, et sequuntur pastorem. Nam in te uno omnes sinceri pastores unum sunt; quia una est vox omnium, qua tu aggregas oves tibi, quaque pascis in amænissimis tuis pratis aggregatas, ac fontibus salutis liberalissime potas ac reficis. Ut igitur Ministris tuis, quos pastorum nomine dignaris, optimi vivendi, agendique modum præscribam, tu efficito: et simul da gratiam, ut ipse cum illis juxta disciplinæ præscribendæ normam, vitam totam peragam; donec, curriculo vitæ præsentis expleto, tibi, qui Episcopus animarum nostrarum es, tradam spiritum quem dedisti. Tibi pastori animarum nostrarum, ac soli Deo cum Patre et Spiritu Sancto, sit benedictio, et gloria, et sapientia, et gratiarum actio, honor et virtus, et robur in secula seculorum. AMEN. AMEN.

2

ADVERTISEMENT TO THE SIXTH EDITION.

THE Writer, not willing needlessly to extend the dimensions of his work, has refrained from much enlargement, except in one chapter—(Part v. Chap. v.) where the importance of the subject appeared to call for a more full consideration. This Chapter—for the use of the Purchasers of the former Editions, as well as from a desire to give a more comprehensive view than the limits of this work would admit—he has published in a separate and enlarged form.

Feeling as he does the circumstances of the times, to give a deepened tone of responsibility to our work, he has only to commend to his beloved —specially to his younger brethren—the two Apostolical determinations, as comprising all the principles of Ministerial efficiency:

"We will give ourselves continually to prayer, and to the Ministry of the Word." Acts vi. 4.

"I determined not to know any thing among you, save Jesus Christ and him crucified." 1 Cor. ii. 2.

Old Newton Vicarage,
March 20, 1844.

THE CHRISTIAN MINISTRY.

PART I.

GENERAL VIEW OF THE CHRISTIAN MINISTRY.

CHAPTER I.

THE DIVINE ORIGIN AND INSTITUTION OF THE CHRISTIAN MINISTRY.

THE Church is the mirror, that reflects the whole effulgence of the Divine character. It is the grand scene, in which the perfections of Jehovah[1] are displayed to the universe. The revelations made to the Church—the successive grand events in her history—and, above all—the manifestation of " the glory of God in the Person of Jesus Christ"—furnish even to the heavenly intelligences fresh subjects of adoring contemplation.[2]

The means also employed in the building of the Church are equally illustrative of the wisdom of their great Author. The exhibition of Almighty " strength made perfect in weakness" effectually secures the important end—" that no flesh should glory in his presence." A separate order of men were consecrated to the great work of laying the foundation, and raising the superstructure, of his Church. Twelve only were included in the original institution, with a commission, bounded at first within the scanty extent of " Immanuel's land ;" but afterwards enlarged with a tender of the promised blessing to " every creature."[3] As the work increased upon them, the necessity for a corresponding increase of labourers became apparent. To provide for this exigency, the Great Mediator had delegated the power of his own commission to

---

[1] See Ephes. iii. 10.   [2] See 1 Peter i. 12.
[3] Matt. x. 1—6; xxviii. 18—20. Mark xvi. 15. Luke xxiv. 47.

his faithful labourers.[1] Thus invested with plenary authority, they " ordained elders in every Church," (who were acknowledged to be " made overseers over the flock" by the appointment of the Holy Ghost"[2]) and entrusted the power of ordination successively to others,[3] for the continuance of the function—according to the special promise—" *unto the end of the world.*"[4] Not indeed that the Lord has transferred to men his supreme authority ; but he has exercised the right of the master workmen in the choice of his own instruments.   And as in fact no instrumentality was needed, his selection of the delegates of his commission, and the represent-atives of his person, is an act of grace ; exercising our humility in the submission to men of like infirmities with ourselves, and our love in this cementing bond of reciprocal interest.[5]   'Thus every step in the way of our salvation hath on it the print of infinite majesty, wisdom, and goodness ; and this among the rest, that men, sinful, weak men, are made subservient in that great work, of bringing Christ and souls to meet ; that by " the foolishness of preaching" (or what appears so to carnal wisdom) the chosen of God are called, and come unto Jesus, and are made wise unto sal-vation ; and that the life, which is conveyed to them by the word of life in the hands of poor men, is by the same means preserved and advanced.'[6]

The Great Head of the Church has ordained three grand reposi-tories of his truth.   *In the Scriptures* he has preserved it by his Providence against all hostile attacks.   *In the hearts of Christians* he has maintained it by the Almighty energy of his Spirit—even un-der every outward token of general apostacy.[7]   *And in the Chris-tian Ministry* he has deposited " the treasure in earthen vessels" for the edification and enriching of the Church in successive ages.

This sacred office is administered by agents, Divinely-called through the medium of lawful authority,[8] and entrusted with the most responsible and enriching blessing ;[9] rendering the highest possible service to their fellow-men, because *that* most nearly con-nected with the glory of the Saviour.   In the comprehensive view given of the office (Eph. iv. 7—16.) the grandeur of its introduction is shewn to have been prefigured by the glorious descent and as-cent of Jehovah upon Mount Sinai.[10]   This inestimable gift to the

---

[1] See John xx. 21.   [2] Acts vi. 1—6 ; xiv. 23 ; xx. 28.
[3] 2 Tim. ii. 2.   Titus i. 5.   [4] Matt. xxviii. 20.
[5] See Calvin's Instit. Book iv. c. iii. 1.   Compare Leighton's Exposition of Isaiah vi. 8. Works, Vol. ii. 406, 407, Jerment's edition.
[6] Leighton on 1 Peter v. 2.   [7] Compare 1 Kings xix. 18, with Rom. xi. 4, 5.
[8] Gal. i. 1.   Acts xiii. 2, 3.   [9] 1 Tim. i. 11.
[10] Compare Psalm lxviii. 7—18, with Ephes. iv. 8—10.

Church, in its original grant and institution, belongs to the mediatorial work of the Son of God, as the purchase of his humiliation, and the immediate result of his investiture with glory.[1] The high pre-eminence of this gift, as well as the efficiency of its operations, appears in its distributive variety of office.[2] The privileges communicated to the Church by its instrumentality, are union with her glorious Head, and the communion of the several members with others in their diversified relations, and mutual dependencies. Thus the body "cometh in the unity of the faith, and of the knowledge of the Son of God, unto a perfect man."[3] Each member contributes to the establishment of the system. That tossing instability of profession, which is connected with so much of doctrinal and practical error, is powerfully resisted. Party spirit melts away in the atmosphere of love.[4] The whole body, "growing up into its Head in all things," is enriched by the mutual impartation of the gifts severally distributed to the members, each of whom readily forgets his own proper individuality in a considerate regard to the general interest.[5] How decisively does this entire view of the Christian Ministry mark its Divine original! And surely it is not easy to conceive of a machine better adapted for the grand purposes which it was intended to subserve—the completion of the Church and the regeneration of the world. Suppose it to be in its full effective operation—how admirably is it framed to make the Church the most important blessing to the world! What an extensive medium of pouring forth the light and life of the Gospel upon a benighted world! What a vast and valuable body of moral influence would it spread throughout its widely expanded sphere ! How would its wise and kindly control of " the madness of the people" impose a check even upon the political convulsions of the earth ! And what an unlimited flow of national, social, and individual blessing would be communicated to our own, and to every land through this divinely-appointed channel !

We may remark in this great system of agency, the illustration of the Unity of the Divine will and purposes in the administration of the Church. From each of the Sacred Persons in the Godhead did this holy office originate : " *God hath given to us the Ministry of Reconciliation.*"[6] Yet was it also, as we have seen, *the gift of his exalted Son*—promised by him to the Church before his departure from the earth ;[7] communicated as the first act of his glorious power in " filling all things ;[8] and sealed in every instance

---

[1] Verses 8—10.   [2] Verses 11, 12.   [3] Verses 12, 13.
[4] Verse 14.   [5] Verses 15, 16.   [6] 2 Cor. v. 18.
[7] Matt. xxvii. 19, 20.   [8] Psalm lxviii. 18. with Eph. iv. 10, 11.

by his joint commission.[1]—At the same time is this office emphatically called " *the Ministration of the Spirit*."[2] It is his authority, that calls to the work[3]—his guidance, that directs in it[4]—and
his influence, that supplies the needful furniture of gifts and graces.[5] Thus do the institutions of the Gospel exhibit its deeper and
more mysterious doctrines.[6] The three adorable persons are severally and distinctly glorified. The ministry has an equal concern
and dependence upon each, and owes equal honour and service to
each. Tracing therefore this sacred ordinance to the footstool of
the eternal throne, with what prostration of soul should we bind
ourselves to its solemn obligations ! " Mine eyes"—saith the Evangelical prophet—" have seen the King, the Lord of Hosts—*Here
am I*"—was his answer to the sacred voice—" *send me*."[7]

Nor can we wonder to see " the chiefest of the Apostles" unable
to express his overwhelming sense of his responsibility—" Who is
sufficient for these things ?"[8] Who, whether man or angel, " is
sufficient" to open " the wisdom of God in a mystery"—to speak
what in its full extent is " unspeakable"—to make known that
which " passeth knowledge"—to bear the fearful weight of the care
of souls ? Who hath skill and strength proportionate ? Who has
a mind and temper to direct and sustain so vast a work ? If our
Great Master had not himself answered these appalling questions
by his promise—" My grace is sufficient for thee ;"[9] and if the experience of faith did not demonstrably prove, that " our sufficiency
is of God ;"[10] who, with an enlightened apprehension, could enter
upon such an awful service ; or, if entered, continue in it ?

But how solemn is the sanction—infinitely above all human
authority—stamped and engraven upon the sacred office ! And
how tremendous the guilt of rejecting its commission !—" He that
heareth you, heareth me ; and he that despiseth you, despiseth
me · and he that despiseth me, despiseth him that sent me."[11]

CHAPTER II.

THE DIGNITY OF THE CHRISTIAN MINISTRY.

THE Divine original of the Christian Ministry has already opened a view of its dignity far above any earthly honour or elevation,

[1] Gal. i. 1.   [2] 2 Cor. iii. 9.   [3] Acts xiii. 2.   [4] Ibid. xvi. 6, 7.
[5] 1 Cor. xii. 7—11. [6] See Ibid. 4—6.   [7] Isaiah vi. 5—8.   [8] 2 Cor. ii. 16.
[9] Ibid. xii. 9.   [10] Ibid. iii. 5.   [11] Luke x. 16.

and such as the infidel scoff can never degrade. An institution—introduced into the world, and confirmed to the Church, with such solemn preparation—conversant with the interests, and entrusted with the charge, of immortal souls—ordained as the main instrument for the renovation of the world, and the building up of the Church—cannot be of inferior eminence. The office of "fellow-worker with God"[1] would have been no mean honour to have conferred upon the archangel nearest the everlasting throne. It formed the calling, the work, and the delight of the Lord of glory during his last years of abode upon earth; and was established by himself as the standing ordinance in his Church, and the medium of the revelation of his will to the end of time. He has not indeed (as the judicious Calvin observed)—'called his ministers into the function of teaching, that, after they have brought the Church under, they may usurp to themselves the government; but that he may use their faithful diligence to associate the same to himself. This is a great and excellent thing, for men to be set over the Church, that they may represent the person of the Son of God.'[2] The dignity however of the sacred office belongs to a kingdom "not of this world."[3] It is distinguished therefore, not by the passing glitter of this world's vanity, but by eternal results, productive, even in their present influence, of the most solid and enduring happiness.[4] For surely it is 'the highest dignity, if not the greatest happiness, that human nature is capable of here in this vale below, to have the soul so far enlightened as to become the mirror, or conduit or conveyor of God's truth to others.'[5] The chastised apprehension of this high calling, so far from fostering a vain-glorious spirit, has a direct tendency to deepen self-abasement and reverence. For can we help recoiling from so exalted an office—from handling such high and holy things? What! We to convey life, who ourselves

[1] 1 Cor. iii. 9. 2 Cor. vi. 1. This association is evidently that of a Minister with God—and not, we think, (as Doddridge and Macknight have supposed)—of one Minister with another. Comp. Rom. xvi. 3, 9, 21. Phil. ii. 25, iv. 3. Philemon 1, 24. "Yet all is of God." For this co-operation is "God working in us to will and to do." The strength for the work is imparted—not natural; nor was there any "fellow-worker" in the first principles of strength, or in its subsequent increase. 'Eximium elogium Ministerii, quod, cum per se agere possit Deus, nos homunciones tanquam adjutores adsciscat, et tanquam organis utatur.' Calvin in 1 Cor. iii. 9.
[2] Calvin on John iii. 29.   [3] John xviii. 36
[4] Burnet beautifully illustrates the honourable designations of the holy office. Pastoral Care, ch. 1. Compare also, Chrysostom De Sacerdotio, book iii. Gregory Nazianzen's Oration, appended usually to Chrysostom, and Bowles' Pastor Evangelicus—1665. 12mo. Pref. An old writer expatiates upon no less than forty-three Scriptural appellations of its dignity and usefulness. Sal Terræ. cap. ii. by T. Hall. 12mo. Francof. 1658. Another writer counts sixty names, more or less applying to "the diversities of operations," in the Ministry. Hottingeri Typus Pastoris Evangelici. 12mo. Basil. 1741. The remark of one of the Reformers carries with it a valuable lesson,—'De nomine observandum—vocari Ministerium non Magisterium.' Buceri De Vi et Usu S. Min.
[5] Mather's Student and Pastor, p. 161.

are dead! We, so defiled, to administer a service so pure, so purifying! "Woe is me"—said one of old, when contrasting this honour with his personal meanness—"for I am undone; for I am a
man of unclean lips."[1] How can we think of this vast commission
—this momentous trust, but as an act of most undeserved favour?[2]

But let the *remembrance of this sacred dignity give a deeper
tone of decision* to our ministrations. 'A Pastor'—remarks Bishop Wilson—'should act with the dignity of a 'man, who acts by
the authority of God'[3]—remembering, that while we speak to men,
we speak in God's stead.' And this is the true Scriptural standard
of our work—"As we were allowed of God"—said the great Apostle—"to be put in trust with the Gospel," (the highest trust that
ever could be reposed in man) "*even so we speak;* not as pleasing
men, but God, which trieth our hearts."[4] Let it also connect itself
with its *most responsible obligations*—that we disgrace not the
dignity—that we live under the constraint—of our high calling—
"Ye are the salt of the earth. Let not the salt lose its savour.
Ye are the light of the world. Let your light shine before men"
—are the impressive exhortations of the Great Master.'[5] "Neglect
not"—said the great Apostle—"the gift of God that is in thee: stir
it up"[6] by the daily exercises of faith, self-denial, and prayer.
Quesnel observes—'What courage, what boldness, what freedom
ought the dignity of the Ministry to give a bishop or priest; not
for his own interests, but for those of the Church; not through
pride, but fidelity; not while he employs carnal means, but while
he makes use of the armour of God."[7] 'The moment we permit·
ourselves to think lightly of the Christian Ministry, our right arm
is withered; nothing but imbecility and relaxation remains.'[8] But
let the *weight of this dignity be relieved by Evangelical encouragement*—The ministration of the Spirit and of righteousness
constitutes the chief glory of the evangelical economy. "Therefore," says the Apostle, after an exhibition of its pre-eminent excellency—"seeing *we have this Ministry*"—so richly endowed, so
freely vouchsafed—"as we have received mercy, *we faint not.*"[9]

A sense of the dignity of our office—accurately formed, carefully
maintained, and habitually exercised—is therefore of the highest
importance. It elevates the standard of Christian consistency even
in the prospective consideration and choice of the work. For what

---

[1] Isa. vi. 5.   [2] See Eph. iii. 8. 1 Tim. ii. 12.
[3] Sacra Privata. Comp. 2 Cor. v. 20.   [4] 1 Thess. ii. 4.
[5] Matt. v. 13—16. See an awakening appeal in the conclusion of Bishop Taylor's
· first sermon on the Minister's duty in life and doctrine. Works, Vol. vi.
[6] 1 Tim. iv. 14. 2 Tim. i. 6.   [7] On 2 Cor. iii. 8. Comp. Daven. in Col. i. 1.
[8] Hall on the Discouragements and Supports of the Ministry, p. 51.   [9] 2 Cor. iv. 1.

is unsuitable to the Ministerial character is obviously unsuitable to the probationer for the Ministry. In the actual discharge also of duty, the mind will thus be excited to a more solid and devoted consecration; and the whole man will be gradually formed in this heavenly mould—exalted, not elated. Dignity of character will thus correspond with dignity of station. The "office" will be "magnified"[1] in perfect harmony with the lowliest personal humility—and, indeed, never more eminently displayed, than in the exercises of genuine humility; the man invested with these high responsibilities sinking in the dust as an "unprofitable servant."[2]

CHAPTER III.

THE USES AND NECESSITY OF THE CHRISTIAN MINISTRY.

'BECAUSE the nature of things consisting, as this doth, in action, is known by the object whereabout they are conversant, and by the end or scope whereunto they are referred; we must know that the object of this function is both God and men: God, in that he is publicly worshipped of his Church; and men, in that they are capable of happiness by means, which Christian discipline appointeth. *So that the sum of our whole labour in this kind is to honour God, and to save men.*[3]

The ministry of the word was ordained for the planting and watering[4] of the Church. The epistles were written to the respective churches, which had been planted by the preaching of the gospel—to supply the place of an oral ministry—to reduce them to church order and unity—to confirm them in Christian steadfastness, and to advance them to Christian perfection. The several individuals also addressed were the fruits of this ministry. Timo·

---

[1] See Rom. xi. 13.
[2] The views of Philip Henry were truly worthy of his high office. Thus he wrote on the day of his ordination—'I did this day receive *as much honour and work* as ever I shall be able to know what to do with. Lord Jesus! proportion supplies accordingly.' Two scriptures he desired might be written in his heart. 2 Cor. vi. 4, 5. and 2 Chron. xxix. 11. And so influential were these views in maintaining a course of deep-toned humility, 'that he laid himself out with as much diligence and vigour,' in a very contracted sphere, 'as if he had the oversight of the greatest and most considerable parish in the country.' P. Henry's Life, (Williams's Edition) p. 38; which Dr. Chalmers has justly characterized, as 'one of the most precious religious biographies in our language.' Oh! for a large supply of such Ministers in every department of the Church of God!
[3] Hooker, book v. 76. The Divine purpose respecting the Church most harmoniously combines these two ends—"I will place *salvation* in Zion for Israel *my glory*." Is. xlvi. 13.
[4] See 1 Cor. iii. 6.

thy, Titus, and Philemon appear to have been "begotten in Christ Jesus," through the ministry of Paul; as were probably "the elect lady and her children," and the beloved Gaius, "the seals of the apostleship" of John.[1]

Thus has this great ordinance of the Gospel regard to the continual progress of the Church, both in its collective body, and in the several states of its individual members. It was given "for the perfecting of the saints, for the edifying of the body of Christ."[2] There was not only a foundation to be laid, but a building to be raised. Elementary truths were to be carried to perfection.[3] Constant superintendence was needed even in the most flourishing churches. The administration of the word was the appointed remedy to "perfect that which was lacking in the faith" of the Thessalonians.[4] Peter wrote his second epistle to those that "were established in the faith;" yet "he would not on that account be negligent to put them *always* in remembrance of these things."[5] For the same reason the beloved disciple wrote to the Church; "not"— said he—"because ye know not the truth, *but because ye know it.*"[6]

The primary use, therefore, of this holy function is, as we have already observed, the channel of communication from the Head to the several members of the body. Its more specific uses may be readily collected from the various scriptural illustrations of the office—each bearing a relation to the nature of the ministration, and the necessities of the charge. If the Church be called a flock, the Minister is the pastor to "seek that which is lost—to strengthen the diseased—to heal the sick—to bring again that which was driven away;" in a word, to shepherd the flock in all the exercises of tenderness, consideration, and care, that belong to this endearing character.[7] If the family of Christ be an household, the Minister is "the faithful and wise steward,"[8] who dispenses the provision of the house according to the necessities of its several members. If the Church of God be a city, he is the watchman[9] to wake and warn slumberers of their peril. If it be a husbandry, he is the "labourer,"[10] to plant and water the soil—to cleanse the earth—to watch the growth of the plant—and instrumentally to bring forward the harvest. If it be a building, he is the "Master-builder,"[11] to build upon the "sure foundation" lively stones—a spiritual house —"growing into an holy temple of the Lord, builded together for an habitation of God through the Spirit."[12] If there be a treaty of

[1] See the inscriptions to the several epistles to those individuals, and Philemon 19.
[2] Eph. iv. 12.   [3] Comp. 1 Cor. ii. 6. Heb. vi. 1, 2.   [4] See 1 Thess. iii. 10, 11.
[5] 2 Peter i. 12.   [6] 1 John ii. 21.   [7] Ezekiel xxxiv. 4.
[8] Luke xii. 42.   [9] Ezek. xxxiii. 7.   [10] 1 Cor. iii. 9.
[11] Ibid. 10.   [12] 1 Peter ii. 5. Eph. ii. 20—22.

peace to be negotiated between the Majesty of heaven and a world of rebels, he is the ambassador, entrusted with "the Ministry of reconciliation;" and praying them in Christ's stead—"Be ye reconciled unto God."[1]

We do not limit the infinite extent and power of Divine grace, when we speak of the necessity of the Christian Ministry. These uses of the sacred institution are not and cannot be necessary to God, as if he were unable to work without them. But they are such as he has appointed and made necessary in the constituted order of means, for the accomplishment of his own purposes of mercy to the world.[2] His sovereign pleasure has ordained this office as a first link of means in the chain of salvation; so that without a Ministry there should be no hearing of the word—consequently no faith in the only Saviour of whom it speaks—no calling upon his name—no salvation.[3] It is not our province to prescribe what he might have done, but to mark the consummate wisdom of what he has done, and to exercise the humility of faith, when we cannot discern the reasons of his dispensations. Doubtless he might have instructed as well as converted Paul by a miracle; but it was his pleasure to direct him to a fellow-sinner for the explicit revelation of his will.[4] The angel also might have been an instructor to Cornelius; but, in order to maintain the order of the divine œconomy, the Ministry of the word was made the medium of conveying evangelical light to his soul.[5] This, therefore, is the ordained means of conversion, and of subsequent establishment in every stage of the Christian life; and its necessity must continue while there is a single sinner to be brought into the family of God, or a single grace in the heart of the saint to advance to perfection.[6]

---

[1] 1 Cor. v. 20. [2] Comp. James i. 18. Eph. iv. 12. 13.
[3] Rom. x. 13—16. 1 Cor. i. 21. Thus also the destitution of the Ministry is the dark sign of the departure of the presence of God from the Church. Compare 2 Chron. xv. 3. Hosea iii. 5.
[4] Acts ix. 10—17. [5] Ibid. x. 3—6.
[6] It is a weighty remark of Hooker's, that 'religion without the help of a spiritual Ministry is unable to plant itself. Which assertion,'—says he,—'needeth no further confirmation. If it did, I could easily declare, how all things which are of God, he hath by wonderful art and wisdom soldered as it were together by the glue of mutual assistance, appointing the lowest to receive from the nearest to themselves what the influence of the highest yieldeth. And therefore the church, being the most absolute of all his works, was in reason to be also ordered with like harmony, that what he worketh might, no less in grace than in nature, be effected by hands and instruments, duly subordinated to the power of his own Spirit.' Book v. 76. Mosheim observes to the same purport, that the best system of religion must necessarily either dwindle to nothing, or be egregiously corrupted, if it is not perpetually inculcated and explained by a regular and standing Ministry.' Eccles. Hist. Cent. i. part. ii. chap. ii. 'Not even,'—says Calvin,—'is the light and heat of the sun—not even is meat and drink, so necessary for the support and cherishing of our present life, as the Apostolical and Pastoral Office for the preservation of the church on earth.' Instit. lib. iv. c. iii. 3.

CHAPTER IV.

THE TRIALS AND DIFFICULTIES OF THE CHRISTIAN MINISTRY.[1]

OUR Lord's illustration of the necessity of a previous counting of the cost in important undertakings, forcibly applies to the Christian Ministry.[2] Too often has the neglect of serious and prayerful calculation given awful power to the temptation to draw back from so momentous a work. Indeed no previous contemplation can give just apprehensions of its difficulties, any more than a spectator of the field of battle can realize the intense anxiety of the actual conflict. Whatever general notions of a serious and intelligent character may be attained, much will yet be left, that experience alone can supply—much that will enforce the exhortation once given by a veteran to a young soldier—" Thou therefore, my son, be strong in the grace that is in Christ Jesus. Thou therefore endure hardness, *as a good soldier of Jesus Christ*."[3] Indeed the difficulties of this work to the considerate conscientious mind must exclude any expectation of temporal ease and comfort. Many other tracks in life offer a large promise of indulgence. But to this work is most especially linked the daily cross:[4] and in it must be anticipated severe and sometimes overwhelming trials—arising from *the professing church, the world, the power of Satan, and ourselves.*

Our *relation to the professing church* is associated with no common difficulties. How instructive are the deep views of the apostolical Eliot on this work! 'He looked upon the conduct of a church,' as his biographer (Cotton Mather) informs us, 'as a

---

[1] For some serious and important views of this subject we may refer to Scougal's Sermon on the Ministerial function.

[2] Luke xiv. 28—30. Erasmus justly laments the evil results of this inconsideration—' Verum ad conciones sacras admittuntur, interdum etiam assiliunt, adolescentes, leves, indocti, quasi nihil fit facilius, quam apud populum, exponere Divinam scripturam, et abunde sufficiat perfricuisse faciem, et abstersa pudore linguam volvere. Hoc malum ex eo fonte manat; *quod non perpenditur*, quid sit ecclesiastici concionatoris tum dignitas, tum difficultas, tum utilitas.' (Eccles. Lib. i. p. 1. Ed. 1535.) Thus also an excellent old writer reflects upon such thoughtless calculators—' Hi sane non tam soliciti quærerent onus, cui pares non sunt; si cogitarent qualis sit res ovile Christi; si perpenderent, quam pulchra et Deo grata sit ovium Christi societas; in cujus medio Dominus ille est, cui sol et luna famulantur, cui adsunt ministri ejus millia millium, et decies centena millia; si intelligerent, quantæ molis sit, Christianam condere gentem; hoc est, regnum Christi erigere, et Satanæ palatia demoliri.' N. Hemmingii Pastor. 12mo. Lips. p. 124. Comp. Bowles's Pastor, Lib. i. c. xiii.   [3] 2 Tim. ii. 1—3.

[4] ' Evangelium Christi sincere prædicantibus nunquam deest crux.' Erasm. The Apostle connects endurance of affliction with the work of an evangelist. 2 Tim. iv. 5. See Daven. in Col. i. 24, 29.

thing attended with so many difficulties, temptations, and humiliations, as that nothing but a call from the Son of God could have encouraged him unto the susception of it. He saw that flesh and blood would find it no very pleasant thing to be obliged unto the oversight of a number, that by a solemn covenant should be listed among the volunteers of the Lord Jesus Christ;[1] that it was no easy thing to feed the souls of such a people, and of the children and the neighbours, which were to be brought into the same sheep-fold with them; to bear their manners with all patience; not being by any of their infirmities discouraged from teaching of them, and from watching and praying over them; to value them highly, as the flock which God purchased with his own blood, notwithstanding all their miscarriages ; and in all to examine the rule of scripture for the warrant of whatever shall be done; and to remember the day of judgment, wherein an account must be given of all that has been done. It was herewithal his opinion (as the great Owen expresses it) that notwithstanding all the countenance that is given to any church by the public magistracy, yet whilst we are in this world, those who will faithfully discharge their duty as Ministers of the gospel shall have need to be prepared for sufferings; and it was in a sense of these things that he gave himself up to the sacred Ministry.'[2] We need scarcely remark, what dexterity of application, diligence of labour, " discerning of spirits,"[3] how large a portion of " the meekness and gentleness of Christ," of his yearning compassion, and persevering self-devotedness is here required! Except we realize a high estimation of the Church, the constraining influence of the Saviour's love, and the upholding prop of Almighty grace, what is there to preserve us from sinking in despondency?

But perhaps here our chief burden lies in the recollection, that, like our Divine Master, we are " set for the fall and rising again of many in Israel."[4] For if it be joyous to convert, how afflicting to harden, by our ministry !—specially in the fear, that the more lively is its energy for conversion, in the same proportion is its influence

[1] Alluding to the congregational form of church government and union, which was most prevalent in America in Eliot's time.

[2] Mather's Magnalia—History of New England, book iii. pp. 183, 184.

[3] Nunc si reputemus in eodum populo, quanta sit varietas sexuum, ætatum, conditionis, Ingeniorum, opinionum, vitæ, institutionis, consuetudinis, quantâ oportet esse præditum prudentiâ ecclesiastum, cui sit temperanda oratio!—Erasmi Ecclesiastes, Lib. i. p. 9.

[4] Luke ii. 34. 'Since I was ordained'—says Mr. Brown of Haddington—'I know not how often it hath been heavy to my heart to think how much this scripture (Isa. vi. 9, 10) hath been fulfilled in my ministry. Frequently I have had an anxious desire to be removed by death from becoming a plague to my poor congregation. Often, however, I have tasked myself, and have considered this wish as my folly, and begged of the Lord, that, if it was not for his glory to remove me by death, he would make me successful in my work.' Life and Remains, p. 18.

for judicial condemnation. And though even "in them that perish" we ourselves are unto God "a sweet savour of Christ;" yet under the sinking pressure we can but sympathize with the cry of the great Apostle—"Who is sufficient for these things?"[1] Truly our office is no negative institution. And who but one deeply conversant with the momentous realities of eternity can be duly furnished for it?

From the difficulties with the world, unfaithfulness to our Master furnishes the only "way of escape." The subject matter of our commission comes into immediate contact with latent and deep-rooted prejudices. The strongest feelings of a proud nature are brought into constant play against our unwelcome tale: so that we "become the enemy," instead of the friend of our fellow-sinners, "because we tell them the truth."[2] The sacrifice, which in our Master's name we demand, of the cherished objects of misplaced affections; the exhibition of heavenly pleasures, far nobler in their character, and more permanent in their enjoyment—yet most distasteful to the natural mind; the certain endurance of reproach in the service of the Gospel—these component parts of our commission, even from the voice of the most alluring charmer, excite the enmity of the carnal mind to our message, and to the messenger for his work's sake.[3] Does not our personal experience furnish recollections of the mighty influence of this innate indisposition to the Gospel, and of the peculiar wisdom, patience, and faithfulness needed for its subjugation?

But sometimes the difficulties from the world are of a different character. We come to them "as a lovely song of one that playeth well upon an instrument."[4] Their enmity, though not radically subdued, may be restrained, and even clothed with much of outward courtesy. To meet this aggravated difficulty with gentleness, and yet to detect and uncover the evil, requires a rare combination of firmness, wisdom, and consideration. To risk the almost certain consequence of a change of feeling towards us, demands the exercise of much prayer and faith. The kindness of the world is far more formidable than its enmity. Many, who were prepared to stem the torrent of its opposition, have yielded with compromising indulgence to its paralyzing kindness.

Difficulties must also be expected *from the restless and subtle*

---

[1] 2 Cor. ii. 15, 16.—Luther entered deeply into the feelings of the Apostle—'Etsi jam senex, et in concionando exercitus sum, tamen timeo, quoties suggestum conscendo.'
[2] Gal. iv. 16.
[3] Rom. viii. 7. John iii. 19, 20, with 1 Kings xxii. 8. 'Prædicare nihil aliud est, quam derivare in se furorem mundi.'—Luther.
[4] Ezekiel xxxiii. 32.

activity of the tempter. Apart from that baneful influence, by which, (as we shall afterwards show[1]) he obstructs the general efficiency of the work—his power over the tone of the minister's mind is most distressing. Often indeed does he succeed in unhinging his spirit and paralyzing his exertions, by diverting his mind from the main design, or by bringing the dark cloud of unbelief over his soul, so that the Ministration of the Church, as Calvin observes, 'is not an easy and indulgent exercise, but a hard and severe warfare, where Satan is exerting all his power against us, and moving every stone for our disturbance.'[2]

But, after all, the greatest difficulties *derive their origin and power from ourselves.* The spiritual character of our employment—no more than secular occupations—exempts us from the conflict with our corruptions. It is not easy to overcome our natural love of ease, our indisposition to self-denying devotedness, and our false tenderness in flinching from the declaration of unpalatable truths. Were we angels by nature as well as by office, the difficulty would be of little account. But, while we bear upon us the marks of our apostacy, we cannot advance without a constant, and sometimes most painful, effort.[3] Many circumstances, from this exciting tendency, materially increase the difficulty. We must labour, when our hearts are in a cold and languid state. Hence the danger, lest the powerful energy of the word should be weakened in its application to ourselves; lest we should gradually lose our relish for our work, excuse ourselves from its self-denying exercises, and sink into heartless despondency. A course of opposition also to our message may stir up a selfish, unhumbled spirit. Popularity is yet more dangerous: the few, who escape its influence unhurt, have been exercised in painful conflicts, such as have shown their deliverances from this fiery trial to have been nearly miraculous. Symptoms of success, unless tempered with personal abasement and habitual watchfulness, excite to self-confidence. The want of these tokens, on the other hand, is too often accompanied with impatience or despondency; so that—assaulted at the ex-

---

[1] Part. ii. chapter iv.   [2] Calvin on 2 Cor. xi. 28.
[3] 'When a Minister, deeply impressed with the important difficulty of his work, looks into his own heart, to explore the resources with which he is furnished for so difficult a service, there, alas! he meets with little that does not serve to increase his sense of weakness, and to confirm his fears. For it must be remembered, that he is a man of like passions with his flock, inheriting a body of corruption—that he is perhaps deficient in ability—perhaps unfortunate in the natural constitution of his mind—that at all events he has to struggle with infirmities, is exposed to temptations, has more to accomplish than others, as well as greater difficulties to surmount; and that, whilst more will be expected from him, in himself he may have no resources above those of his congregation.' Venn's Sermons, vol. i. p. 9.

treme points, and from opposite directions—we need "the armour of righteousness on the right hand and on the left."[1]

Perhaps with many of us the conscientious discharge of official duty furnishes the only anticipation of Ministerial difficulties. This want of acquaintance *with the real difficulties* in every part of the function, by failing to realize our entire helplessness, is one main cause of its unfruitfulness. None of us will find this "pleasure of the Lord to prosper in our hands," except every effort is grounded upon the practical conviction, that no strength but the arm of Omnipotence is sufficient for the work. Many of us, perhaps, had tasted in the prospect some of the delights and encouragements of the work; and in all the spring and freshness of . youth had calculated upon a steady and uninterrupted devotedness rising above all opposing obstacles. But scarcely had we passed the threshold, before the dream of confidence passed away. The chilling influence of the world, and the disheartening effect of unsuccessful pains, soon made us conversant with disappointment, and dispelled our sanguine expectation of a harvest proportioned to our industry. Our constancy and love have been often put to a severe and searching trial; and though we can never forget the dignity of character and the principles of encouragement connected with the Ministry, we are made to feel, that "if a man desires" the

[1] 2 Cor. vi. 7. The following extracts from the diaries of two excellent Ministers will give a graphical delineation of painful exercises, familiar to many of us. 'I almost constantly find the following temptations, the one or the other, assaulting me in the discharge of my office as a Minister. 1st. If I think that I am unsuccessful, I am in danger, through an unbelieving despondency, of being discouraged, of becoming remiss, and cold, and more indifferent respecting the success of my ministry. Though this should have a quite contrary effect, yet this is the use which the devil and my own corruptions try to make of it. 2ndly. If I am, or think I am, successful, this also hath a tendency to take me off my guard, and to make me less careful in watching against sin, and in mortifying universally its whole body. Spiritual pride, I suppose, comes in through my success and applause, by drawing a favourable comparison between me and others, as if I were better than they. And in proportion to my want of constant thoughts of my own vileness in the sight of God, and to the good opinion I have of myself, is always my remissness, and want of vigilance and exertion to press forward. I see now the wisdom of the caution which the Apostle gives to Timothy, not to admit "a novice," (1 Tim. iii. 6,) one who hath but little experience of the workings and deceit of sin, and hath made but little progress in the ways of God—not to admit such into the office of the Ministry, "lest he should be lifted up with pride, and fall into the condemnation of the devil." The Apostle himself was not without some danger from this quarter. (2 Cor. xii.) Considering the greatness of my danger, how should I "work out my salvation with fear and trembling?" None but the Lord can keep me.' Life of the Rev. T. Charles, of Bala, pp. 133, 134. 'I saw on the Sabbath four evils which attend me in my Ministry. First, either the devil treads me down by discouragement and shame; from the sense of the meanness of what I have provided in private meditations. Or, secondly, carelessness possesses me; arising because I have done well, and been enlarged, and been respected formerly; hence it is not such great matter, though I be not always alike. Thirdly, infirmities and weakness, as want of light, want of life, want of a spirit of power to deliver what I am affected with for Christ; and hence I saw many souls not set forward, nor God felt in my Ministry. Fourthly, want of success, when I have done my best.' From the diary of Mr. Shepard, of New England, author of several valuable treatises upon experimental divinity. —Mather's New England, book iii. p. 91.

office, he desires a toilsome and self-denying, as well as "a good work."[1] We must work, like Nehemiah and his men, with the trowel in one hand and the sword in the other.[2] The progress of the work would be stopped by the laying down of the trowel. The enemy would gain a temporary advantage by the sheathing of the sword. Nothing therefore remains but to maintain the posture of resistance in dependence upon our wise Master-builder, and the Captain of our salvation—waiting for our rest, our crown, our home.

We have, however, no reason to complain of a dispensation, so obviously fraught with important blessings to ourselves, and so subservient to the blessed ends of the Ministry. The discipline of the cross is most needful to repress the overweening confidence of presumption; to establish an habitual confidence in the divine promises; to prove the power of faith, the privileges of prayer, and the heavenly support of the word of God; and to furnish us with "the tongue of the learned;" that, from our own experience of the difficulties and supports of our Christian warfare, we "should know how," after the Master's example, "to speak a word in season to him that is weary."[3]

Yet in our contact with Ministerial difficulty the enlivening views of faith are most important. Conscious helplessness sinks under the depressing weight of responsibility. Faith links our weakness in immediate connexion with the promises of Almighty aid;[4] and enables us to say to the mountain of difficulty—"Who art thou, O great mountain? Before Zerubbabel thou shalt become a plain."[5] Thus discouragements, properly sustained and carefully improved, become our most fruitful sources of eventual encouragement; while love to our work bears us on above all our difficulties.[6]

---

[1] 1 Tim. iii. 1. 'Opus, non dignitatem; laborem, non delicias.'—Jerome. 'The sacred Ministry is not a state of idleness or of delight; but a holy warfare, in which there are always toils and fatigues to be endured. Whoever is not resolved courageously to maintain the interests of Jesus Christ, and to labour continually to enlarge his kingdom, is not fit for this warfare.'—Quesnel on 1 Timothy i. 18.
[2] Neh. iv. 17.   [3] Isaiah l. 4.
[4] Such as Exodus iv. 10—12. Jer. i. 6—10. Matt. xxviii. 20. 2 Cor. xii. 9.
[5] Zech. iv. 6.
[6] 'Magnum opus omnino et arduum conamur; sed nihil difficile amanti puto.' Cicero.

4

CHAPTER V.

THE COMFORTS AND ENCOURAGEMENTS OF THE CHRISTIAN MINISTRY.

IT is of the utmost importance to grasp the whole compass of the Christian Ministry. The view of one side only of the prospect (whichever side that may be) must necessarily give an imperfect and inaccurate representation. Painful and habitual experience constrains us to be with our people " in weakness, and in fear, and in much trembling."[1] The opposition of the world—the inconstancy of the wavering—the inconsistency of the mere professor—the difficulties that beset the inquirer's path—our frequent disappointments with the hopeful—combined with the recollection of what we are—what we ought to be—and what we ought to do—all this fearfully acts upon our weakness and depravity. Did we carry on " the warfare at our own charges,"[2] we should " be pressed out of measure, above strength."[3] But such are " the contradictions meeting in our work," that, though it is a sorrow, it is yet " a sorrow full of joy."[4] " Temptations" indeed " take us, besides such as are common to man." We have a painful pre-eminence above our fellow Christians in bearing a double share of " the burden and heat of the day." But if " the sufferings of Christ abound in us, our consolation also aboundeth by Christ."[5] This happy equipoise of conflict and support, of responsibility and privilege, invigorates every effort in the exercise of simple dependence and patient hope.

We must acknowledge that the grounds of support and encouragement are fully commensurate with the momentous difficulty of the work. *How cheering is the recollection of our office, as the ordinance of Christ, and as the standing proof of his love to his Church!* For will he not honour his own institution, and secure its appointed end, in the glory of his name and the prosperity of his Church? Will not he that sent us furnish us for our work? May we not plead his ordinance, as the ground of dependence upon him for all needful assistance and encouraging acceptance?

[1] 1 Cor. ii. 3.   [2] Ibid. ix. 7.   [3] 2 Cor. i. 8.
[4] See an exquisite hymn on Ministerial Experience in the Olney Collection, Book ii. 26. Compare also 2 Cor. vi. 6—10.
[5] 2 Corinthians i. 5.

How ample also are our sources of encouragement within the compass of our work![1] Did we depend upon the failing support of human agency, or upon the energy of mere moral suasion—we should cry out, prostrate in heartless despondency—"Who is sufficient for these things?"[2] But the instant recollection—that "our sufficiency is of God"—"lifts up our hearts in the ways" and work of the Lord. Added to this—"the character of our ministration—as that "of the New Testament, not of the letter, but of the Spirit,"—the cheering joys connected with the ministration of life and righteousness—together with our own personal interest in its blessings—all combine to invigorate our · faith and expectancy under all apprehended difficulties. Therefore, seeing we have *this Ministry* (so far exceeding in glory" the preceding dispensation) "*as we have received mercy*, we faint not."[3] We have the fullest assurance, that "the life-giving Spirit" employs our Ministry as the vehicle of conveying his heavenly influence "to open the blind eyes," and to quicken the spiritually dead. And to have his Divine seal to our work, as the honoured instrument of communicating the life of God, with all its attendant privileges, to the soul of man, cannot but bring with it a reflex delight of the most exalted character.[4]

The spiritual and permanent fruits of our Ministry must rank among our highest consolations. The repentance of a single sinner, is an event that causes rejoicing in heaven,[5] (the only recorded instance of heavenly interest connected with our lower

---

[1] Witsius' spirit on entering upon the duties of his professorship was full of encouragement—'Quidni ergo jucundissima mihi illa Domini verba applicem, quibus servum suum Josuam quondam affatus est? 'Nonne ego precepi tibi? Confirmare igitur et fortis esto; quia tecum est Dominus Deus tuus quocunque iveris.' Licet infirmitatis me meæ conscientia anxium reddat, reficit tamen Divinæ gratiæ, nunquam suos deserentis, ad sustentandum prompta facilitas—illius autem gratiæ, cui lubitum est virtutem suam in infirmitate confirmare, quæque abjectissimis sæpe et rei gerendæ minime idoneis instrumentis utitur, ut totius operis gloria in solidum ac illibata sibi remaneat.' Oratio De Vero Theologo. Misc. Sacra, ii. 851, 852.
[2] 2 Cor. ii. 16.   [3] Ibid. iii. 5—9; iv. 1.
[4] 'I will remind you,' says Cotton Mather,—'that one of the greatest personages (an Archbishop and a Lord-Keeper) in the English nation (Archbishop Williams) once uttered this memorable speech. 'I have passed through many places of honour and trust both in Church and State, more than any of my order in England for seventy years before: but were I assured, that by my preaching I had converted but one soul unto God, I should herein take more comfort, than in all the honours and offices that have ever been bestowed upon me.' You are entering upon a work, that will keep you continually in the way of this incomparable satisfaction; and I hope . . . . that the saving, or enlightening and edifying of one soul, at any time, will be a matter of more joy unto you than if all the wealth of Ophir should flow in upon you.' Mather's Student and Pastor, pp. 159, 160. It was a golden sentence of Dr. Hammond, well worthy to be recorded, 'Oh what a glorious thing—how rich a prize for the expense of a man's whole life were it, to be the instrument of rescuing one soul from ruin!' Indeed the Christian Pastor—as Bowles remarks—would readily make with the hireling the compact of the king of Sodom with Abraham,—"Give me the persons, and take the goods to thyself." (Gen. xiv. 21.) Lib. iii. c. 9.   [5] Luke xv. 10.

world); and therefore may well be conceived to bring no common pleasure to the Minister's heart. Indeed, one such instance is a spring of encouragement even in the sinking contemplation of the mass of ignorance and sin that surrounds us. The subsequent walk also of our people in the faith, hope, and love of the Gospel, forms our ground of unceasing thanksgiving to God, our chief joy, and the very life of our life. "We have no greater joy, than to hear that our children walk in truth."[1] We turn to them in the expression of parental anxiety and delight—" Now we live, *if ye stand fast in the Lord.*"[2]

The interest we possess in the affectionate sympathies of a beloved people is also a subordinate source of comfort and encouragement. Rich indeed, and heart-gladdening is "the consolation in Christ, the comfort of love, the fellowship of the Spirit,"[3] which we enjoy in communion with a flock, to whom God has owned our labours. In this love—the most touching love that this world affords—we find a full compensation for the scorn of an ungodly world, and the secret spring of many an hour of support and enjoyment, by which we are carried forward in our painful course. The Christian and intelligent part of our flock well know, that we are " men of like passions with themselves," that our path is strewn with snares, and our hearts are often keenly wounded with sorrow and temptation. Christian sympathy engages them to "communicate with our affliction." A sense of duty and privilege calls forth their exertions, and directs their conduct, so that, as far as possible, all just grounds of complaint or grief may be removed; and our labours for their sakes, and in their service, made consoling to our own souls.[4] Our debt of obligation to the secret expressions of their love at the throne of grace is reserved among the discoveries of the great day, to add dignity and emphasis to the acknowledgment now made "in part," and then to be more fully proclaimed; that " we are their rejoicing, even as they also are ours, in the day of the Lord Jesus."[5]

Another comfort and encouragement in our work, of a more individual character, deserves to be mentioned—*its special advantages for the cultivation of personal religion.*[6] Such is the

---

[1] 2 John 4.   [2] 1 Thess. iii. 7—9.   [3] Phil. ii. 1.
[4] Quesnel thus beautifully expresses the mutual relation between the Pastor and the people—' The latter ought to alleviate the troubles which attend the pastoral function, by a filial respect, " obedience and fear." The former ought to make a suitable return on all occasions by his care, and continually to cherish the flock by fresh testimonies of satisfaction, joy, and tenderness.' On 2 Cor. vii. 15, 16. Also on 2 Cor. ii. 3. Phil ii. 26.   [5] 2 Cor. i. 14.
[6] See this clearly illustrated by Bishop Burnet—Pastoral Care, ch. viii. Mr. Boston, the well-known author of 'The Fourfold State,' dates his earliest thoughts and desires of

deadening influence of secular callings upon the concerns of eternity, that without special exercises of watchfulness and prayer, the Christian cannot maintain his high elevation.[1] Often did the "man after God's own heart," when engrossed with the cares of his kingdom, seem to envy the Ministers of the sanctuary their peculiar privilege of a nearer approach to their God, and a constant abiding in his work.[2] And what exercised Christian does not mourn over the necessary secularities of his calling, as abridging him of his spiritual enjoyments : and distracting even those seasons, which, by the active habit of self-denial, he is enabled to consecrate to communion with his God ? It is so difficult to be *employed*, without being " *entangled*, with the affairs of this life ;"[3] there are so many weeds of a worldly growth and of a rank luxuriance, "choking the word," when it has given fair promise of fruit, and is even advancing " to perfection,"[4] that the comparative freedom from these embarrassing hindrances is not among the least of our privileges. Add to this—while secular occupations have a tendency to divert us from God, this holy employ naturally draws us to him. In calling us to the search of the rich mines of Scripture, to heavenly contemplation, and spiritual devotedness, it furnishes the appointed means for the salvation of our own souls ; so that "he that watereth is watered also himself."[5] And thus—the devotion of time, the concentration of attention, and the improvement of talents and opportunities—when applied in simplicity to that employment, which is the present and eternal rest of the soul, forms and matures the character for a richer supply of heavenly communications, and for more extensive usefulness in the Church of God.

We remark also the *confirmation, afforded to our own faith by the daily routine of a spiritual ministration.* The palpable display of the blindness and enmity of the natural man—the necessity of a radical change of heart and habit—the means by which this change is effected—its beneficial influence upon the whole character—its sustaining efficacy, as manifested in " the

---

the Ministry from the consideration—'because of all men ministers were most taken up about spiritual things.' 'Is it not our unspeakable advantage, beyond all the gainful and honourable employments of the world, that the whole work of our particular calling is a kind of living in heaven; and, besides its tendency to the saving of the souls of others, is all along so proper and adapted to the purifying and saving of our own!' Leighton's Letter to the Clergy of Dumblane. Compare also his Works, ii. 452. We shall afterwards (Part. iii. ch. viii.) be led to remark upon the peculiar hindrances arising from this source. Yet these—be it remembered—are the workings of temptation, acting upon a corrupt nature; while the direct tendency of a spiritual function must be the advancement of spiritual religion in the heart.

[1] Compare Psalm cxix. 25, with Isaiah xl. 31.
[2] Compare Psalm lxv. 4; lxxxiv. 4.   [3] 2 Tim. ii. 4.
[4] Luke viii. 14.   [5] Proverbs xi. 25.

patience and faith of the saints"—all meet us on every side in our closer and more familiar survey of man ; strengthening our own personal faith in the Scriptural revelation, and enabling us to set our seal with stronger confidence, that in our official testimony " we have not followed cunningly-devised fables."[1]

The certainty of success must not be forgotten (though the subject will hereafter come under consideration[2]) as one of the main-springs of Ministerial support.   All the covenanted engagements made to our great Mediator are mainly fulfilled through the instrumentality of the Christian Ministry.[3]   This, therefore, secures to us—that " the pleasure of the Lord shall prosper in *our* hand," and quickens us to be " steadfast, unmoveable, always abounding in the work of the Lord, *forasmuch as we know that our labour is not in vain in the Lord.*"[4]

But it is the *prospect of eternity*, that consummates our hopes and joys.   Then indeed will the inspired aphorism be fully illustrated—" He that winneth souls is wise"—when " they that be wise shall shine as the brightness of the firmament, and they that turn many to righteousness as the stars for ever and ever." " When the chief shepherd shall appear, they shall receive a crown of glory that fadeth not away."[5]   Our recompense is measured not " according to" our success, but " our labour,"[6] and as with our blessed Master, vouchsafed even in the failure of our ministration.[7] And though we be only the instruments of the Divine purpose, and the organs of Almighty agency—yet is it as rich and full, as if the glory of the work were our own.   What clearer proof is needed, that the rewards of the Christian dispensation are of " grace and not of debt"—the indulgence of free and sovereign mercy, wholly irrespective of man's desert—which, were its claims insisted upon, instead of exalting him to the favour of God, would cover him with " shame and everlasting contempt ?"

Admitting, therefore, that we are called to difficult and costly service ; yet have we abundant cause to be satisfied with the sustaining support and consolation provided for every emergency.   All indeed may be included in the single promise—" Lo, I am with you alway, even to the end of the world."[8]   ' The officers he employs in every age'—observes an excellent Minister addressing a

---

[1] 2 Peter i. 16.   See this point admirably drawn out in a somewhat varied view in the Bishop of Chester's interesting sermons on the Christian Ministry, pp. 37—44.
[2] Part ii. c. 1.   [3] Isaiah liii. 10—12, with 1 Cor. i. 21 ; 2 Cor. i. 20.   [4] 1 Cor. xv. 58.
[5] Prov. xi. 30.   Dan. xii. 3.   1 Peter v. 4.   For a magnificent view of the glory of the ministerial crown, see Hall's Sermon on the Discouragements and Supports, &c. pp. 51 —53.
[6] 1 Cor. iii. 8.   [7] 2 Cor. ii. 15, 16, with Isaiah xlix. 4.   [8] Matt. xxviii. 20.

brother—'are entitled to this treasure, as well as those of the first age.—Keep your mind'—he added—'believingly, attentive to this *"always"*—*Lo, I am with you*, to qualify and succeed you in whatever work I call you to. *" Lo, I am with you,"* to comfort you by my presence and Spirit, when your hearts are grieved. *" Lo, I am with you,"* to defend and strengthen you in trials, though all men forsake you. While he stands with you, there can be no just cause of fear or faintness. You need no other encouragement. This you shall never want, if you continue faithful : and hereupon you may conclude—'The Lord shall deliver me from every evil work, and will preserve me unto his heavenly kingdom.'[1]

Thus does every view of our office encourage us to increased exertion and devotedness ;[2] so that in the midst of many painful exercises of faith and patience, we can "thank God and take courage." None, who have devoted themselves in simplicity to the work, will hesitate in subscribing to Mr. Scott's testimony—'With all my discouragements and sinful despondency; in my better moments, I can think of no work worth doing compared with this. Had I a thousand lives, I would willingly spend them in it : and had I as many sons, I should gladly devote them to it.'[3]

CHAPTER VI.

THE QUALIFICATIONS OF THE CHRISTIAN MINISTRY.

MR. NEWTON'S important remark may be considered as an axiom—"None but he who made the world can make a Minister of the Gospel." He thus proceeds to *illustrate* his position (for it cannot be thought to need any *proof*)—"If a young man has capacity ; culture and application may make him a scholar, a philosopher, or an orator ; but a true Minister must have certain principles, motives, feelings, and aims, which no industry or endeavours of men can either acquire or communicate. They must be given from above, or they cannot be received."[4]

---

[1] D. Williams on the Ministerial Office, 1708. pp. 43, 44.

[2]. Ab humi repentibus curis erigat animum tuum considerata functionis dignitas: a prevaricatione deterreret delegantis dignitas: Socordiam excludat muneris difficultas. Industriam ac vigilantiam exstimulet præmii magnitudo, quod non ab hominibus, sed a Deo erit expectandum. Erasm. Eccles. p. 193.

[3] Scott's Life, pp. 343, 344.   [4] Newton's Works, Vol. v. p. 62.

These principles, wrought out and exhibited in their practical influence and application, will furnish a complete view of the necessary qualifications for the Christian Ministry. There is something so fearfully responsible in entering upon this work with incompetent abilities, that the man can scarcely have felt any serious concern for his own soul, for the immortal interests of his fellow-sinners, or for the welfare of the Church of God, whose mind has not been more or less exercised upon the ground of personal unfitness. When we see the most " able Minister of the New Testament" that the Church has ever known, deeply penetrated, and indeed well-nigh overwhelmed,[1] with the sense of the "necessity laid upon him"—we may well be ashamed, that with qualifications far inferior, our sense of obligation should be less accurate and constraining.

In our discussion of this subject we assume a suitable measure of natural and intellectual endowments, as well as their conscientious improvement of them. As to spiritual qualifications, we would be careful neither to lower, exceed, or deviate from, the Scriptural standard. It is obvious that all requisites (though none without bearing upon the efficiency of the Ministration) are not of equal moment. We must therefore distinguish between what is desirable and what is essential—between what is wanting from immaturity or inexperience, or in the substance and character of the man—and again, between that deficiency, which incapacitates for the work, and a comparative measure of unfitness, as contrasted with Ministers of acknowledged eminence.—"There are diversities of gifts," and " differences of administration" of the same gifts, under " the same Spirit and the same Lord."[2] But under all circumstances, the Divine call to this sacred office will be evidenced by a supply of competent qualifications for its discharge.

In "considering the Apostle and High Priest of our profession, Christ Jesus,"[3] we witness a most harmonious combination of seemingly opposite characteristics. The Ministry of our Lord was distinguished by the dignity of God, and the sympathy of a man and a brother—by the authority of the commissioned delegate of his Father, and yet by the humility of a servant, who "came not to be ministered unto, but to minister."[4] If " he taught as one having authority," yet were they " gracious words which proceeded out of his mouth,"[5] tempered with " the meekness of wisdom" and the

---

[1] 2 Cor. ii. 16.   [2] 1 Cor. xii. 4, 5.   [3] Heb. iii. 1.
[4] Matt. xx. 28.   [5] Ib. vii. 29, with Luke iv. 22.

"gentleness" of love. Indeed, the several features of his Ministerial character furnish the most accurate standard of our official
qualifications, and the explicit directory for every exercise of our
office, public or private. But, lest we should despond in our infinite remove from this standard of perfection, let us mark this high
function, as administered by "men of like passions with ourselves,"
and yet by the grace of their Great Master, following closely in his
steps. A rich treasure of instruction will be found in an attentive
perusal of the Acts of the Apostles. The Epistles will also furnish
a complete portraiture of the character, no less than a comprehensive system of the doctrines of the Christian Ministry. The different
traits of St. Paul's Ministry—as they break forth in the natural flow
of his writings, and the brief sketches which he occasionally inter-
sperses—embody the various particulars of his invaluable didactic
instructions. Quesnel has drawn out no less than thirty-three individualities of the sacred character from a single chapter.[1] The
incidental mention of Epaphroditus introduces some of the primary
qualifications for this holy work. Paul speaks of him as his "brother"—a sincere Christian. He marks his sympathy, diligence,
and perseverance, as his "fellow-soldier;" his "endurance of hardness" as his "fellow-labourer;" his tender attachment to his flock,
in longing to relieve them from needless anxiety on his account;
and his high estimation of his Master's service, as dearer to him
than life itself.'[2]

I. In taking a general view of Ministerial qualifications, we must
remark—that, if the ministry be a spiritual work, a corresponding
spiritual character seems to be required in its administrators.
Whatever be the value of human literature in a minister; unconnected with this prime qualification, its influence will prove unprofitable—if not prejudicial—to his work. The Scripture justly
insists—that Ministers should be "holy"[3]—in a peculiar sense men
of God—men taught of God[4]—men consecrated to God by a daily
surrender of their time and talents to his service—men of singleness of purpose—living in their work—living altogether but for one
end; and for the promotion of this end, "moved by none of the afflictions that await them; neither counting their life dear to them,

---

[1] 1 Thess. ii.; and again, twenty-one, from a part only of another chapter (2 Cor. vi.
1—12); ten from two verses in a third chapter (Col. i. 28, 29.) Indeed his commentary
throughout exhibits a deep study of the Pastoral Office, and an accurate exhibition in detail of its duties, obligations, and encouragements.
[2] Phil. ii. 25—30. Some beautiful touches are given also of the character of Timothy,
verses 19—22.
[3] Titus i. 8. Compare ii. 7. 2 Cor. vi. 4—6. 1 Tim. iv. 12, with Exodus xxviii. 36.
[4] It is excellently remarked by Erasmus—'Qui cupit juxta Paulum esse διδακτικος,
det operam, ut prius sit Θεοδιδακτος—i. e. Divinitus edoctus.' Eccles. Lib. i. pp. 4, 5.

5

so that they might finish their course with joy, and the Ministry
which they have received of the Lord Jesus, to testify the Gospel
of the grace of God." Such was the Apostle Paul, the living exemplar of his own instructions—as he drew them out in that charge
to the Elders of Ephesus,[1] which might serve as an admirable pattern for our episcopal charges; and of which Baxter truly observed,
'that it better deserveth a twelvemonth's study, than most things
that young students do lay out their time in.' 'O brethren,' (con-
tinues this earnest pleader for his Master) 'write it on your study
doors, or set it as your copy in capital letters, still before your eyes.
Could we but well learn two or three lines of it, what preachers
should we be! Write all this upon your hearts, and it will do yourselves and the Church more good than twenty years' study of those
lower things, which, though they get you greater applause in the
world, yet separated from these, will make you but sounding brass
and tinkling cymbals.'[2]

It is evident, however, that this Ministerial standard pre-suppo-
ses a deep tone of experimental and devotional character—habitually exercised in self-denial, prominently marked by love to the
Saviour, and to the souls of sinners; and practically exhibited in a
blameless[3] consistency of conduct. The Apostle justly pronounces
"a novice"[4] to be disqualified for this holy work. The bare existence of religion provides but slender materials for this important

---

[1] Acts xx. 17—35.   [2] Reformed Pastor.
[3] Some of Erasmus' terms are far too unmeasured—'In Ecclesiasta hæc imprimis
spectanda sunt, *ut cor habeat ab omnibus vitiis et cupiditatibus humanis mundum.*'—(He
goes on, however, in his best style of terseness and accuracy of description,) 'ut vitam
habeat non tantum a criminibus, sed et suspicione, specieque criminum, puram, inculpa-
tam; ut spiritum habeat adversus omnes Satanæ machinas firmum, adamantinum, incon-
cussum: ut mentem igneam, et ad bene merendum de omnibus flagrantem; ut animum
habeat sapientem ad condiendam populi stultitiam, cor habeat prudens et oculatum; ut
facile dispiciat quid silendum, quidve dicendum, et apud quos, quo tempore, quo modo,
temperanda oratio. Qui cum Paulo sciat mutare vocem, et omnia fieri omnibus, ut cun-
que viderit saluti auditorem expedire. Nam hunc unicum oportet esse scopum, ad quem
Ecclesiastes rationes suas omnes dirigat; a quo si deflecteris oculos, continuo fit, ut quo
magis instructus fueris ad dicendum eo majorem invehas perniciem in gregem Dominicam.'
Eccles. Lib. i. p. 10. We may compare with this, another finished portrait of the Christian Minister from the pen of the admirable Vitringa. 'Quanti igitur facias fidum
servum Christi, doctorem evangelii, animo rectum, gloriæ Divinæ et salutis hominum
studio flagrantem; non *quærentem quæ sint hominum, sed homines;* non quæ *sua* sunt,
sed quæ *Domini;* a Spiritu Sancto doctum, viarum Dei per experientiam peritum; castis
purisque moribus; virtutes pietatis, modestiæ, mansuetudinis, zeli, prudentiæ, gravitatis,
docentem exemplo; qui instar lampadis impositus candelabro, omnibus, qui in domo sunt
lucem præfert; omnibus salutis suæ cupidis, tum viam salutis demonstrat, tum ipsam
gratiam et salutem conditionibus evangelicis dispensat! Quoquo incedit, lux est. Quoquo
se vertit, salus est. Ubi aperit, sal est. Ubique carus, venerabilis, non minus solatii
aliis impertit, quam ipse sibi solatio est; post decursum vitæ ac laborum studium tandem
ausurus se Domino ac Judici suo sistere cum fiducia, et libero ore, administrationes suæ
reddere rationem, secundum formulam: 'Duo talenta a te accepi. Domine: totidem
lucratus cum sorte tibi reddo." Pref. animadv. ad method. Homil. A third striking
sketch will be found Chrysost. De Sacerd. Lib. iii. 16.
[4] 1 Tim. iii. 6. Comp. note 2, pp. 14, 15. Bowles' Pastor. Lib. i. c. 13.

function. A babe in grace and knowledge is palpably incompetent to become " a teacher of babes," much more a guide of the fathers. The school of adversity, of discipline, and of experience, united with study and heavenly influence, can alone give " the tongue of the learned." Some measure of eminence and an habitual aim towards greater eminence are indispensable for Ministerial completeness; nor will they fail to be acquired in the diligent use of the means of Divine appointment—the word of God and prayer.

II. *Spiritual attainments also must be combined with a spiritual character*—including chiefly a clear and comprehensive view of the evangelical system. However we may admire the simplicity of the Gospel, (consisting only of a few leading ideas, and included often in a single verse[1]) and admit an experimental acquaintance with its elementary principles, "as able to make wise unto salvation ;" yet the Scripture, in its comprehensive extent, is given for a variety of important purposes, and for this express intent ; " that the man," or the Minister, "of God" (who seems to be chiefly meant) " might be perfect, thoroughly furnished unto all good works."[2] The solid establishment of the people may be materially hindered by the Minister's contracted statement, crude interpretations, or misdirected Scriptural application. His furniture for his work must therefore include a store of knowledge far beyond a bare sufficiency for personal salvation. " The *priest's lips should keep knowledge*, and they should seek the law at his mouth ; for he is the messenger of the Lord of Hosts."[3] He must be the " householder—instructed into the kingdom of heaven, which bringeth forth out of his treasure things new and old."[4] Without this store he is incompetent for the great end of his work—" to speak unto men to

---

[1] Such as John iii. 16, or 1 Tim. i. 15.   [2] 2 Tim. iii. 16, 17.   [3] Malachi ii. 7.
[4] Matthew xiii. 52. 'The cursory perusal of a few books,' (as Dr. Owen well observes) 'is thought sufficient to make any man wise enough to be a Minister. And not a few undertake ordinarily to be teachers of others, who would scarcely be admitted as tolerable disciples in a well-ordered church. But there belongeth more unto this wisdom, knowledge, and understanding than most men are aware of. Were the nature of it duly considered, and withal the necessity of it to the Ministry of the Gospel, probably some would not so rush on the work as they do, which they have no provision of ability for the performance of. It is, in brief, such a comprehension of the scope and end of the Scripture, of the revelation of God therein; such an acquaintance with the system of particular doctrinal truths in their rise, tendency, and use; such a habit of mind in judging of spiritual things, and comparing them one with another; such a distinct insight into the springs and course of the mystery of the love, grace, and will of God in Christ, as enables them, in whom it is, to declare the counsel of God, to make known the way of life, of faith, and obedience unto others, and to instruct them in their whole duty to God and man therein. This the Apostle calls his "knowledge in the mystery of Christ," which he manifested in his writings. For as the Gospel, the dispensation and declaration which is committed unto the Ministers of the Church, is "the wisdom of God in a mystery;" so their principal duty is, to become so wise and understanding in that mystery, as that they may be able to declare it to others, without which they have no Ministry committed unto them by Jesus Christ.' Owen's Pneumatologia.

edification, and exhortation and comfort."[1]   For how can he, without an enlarged acquaintance with his own principles, exhibit them in their true light, or apply them to successive emergencies?

III. *But spiritual gifts must be connected with spiritual attainments.*   The rich variety of these gifts (the fruit of the ascension of Christ, and the furniture of his servants for their important work[2]) is a matter of equal admiration and praise.   There must be an ability to communicate and apply what has been imparted; else the highest attainments, however serviceable to their possessors, can never become the public benefit of the Church.   Yet here much discernment will be necessary, lest we confound the ready exercise of spiritual gifts with Divine influence, and thus foster self-delusion of a most fatal tendency.

The diligent student of the Epistles of St. Paul will readily observe, that they were written, as his brother Apostle reminds us, "according to the wisdom given unto him."[3]   With what admirable skill does he adapt his instruction to an almost infinite diversity of persons, occasions, and circumstances—to their strength or feebleness—their progress or decay—their mistaken or wilful abuses—their different capacities, advantages, or disadvantages!   With what exquisite address does he " change his voice," in meekness or in vehemence—in tenderness—or in sharpness—in reproof or in expostulation—thus in his administration, as in his personal conduct, " becoming all things to all men, if that by any means he might save some !"[4]   Thus spiritual wisdom is as important for the building up of the Church of God, as was the wisdom imparted to Bezaleel and Aholiab for the raising of the Levitical tabernacle.[5] Thus we " approve ourselves unto God, workmen that need not to be ashamed, rightly dividing the word of truth."[6]   Thus, as " stewards of the mysteries, and rulers over the household"[7] of God, we distribute the stores of provision to every member of the household, suited to their several wants, and answering to their Master's wise and gracious will.   Thus we take account of their individual state—the strength and exercise of their spiritual capacities—the kind of food, which they severally require for the nourishment of the Christian life, according to their infantine, growing, or adult state—their special hindrances or advantages—their advance, apparently stationary condition, or visible decay in the ways of God.   The treatment of these several individualities, demands a deep and well-digested acquaintance with the methods of the grace of God, in order

[1] Cor. xiv. 3.   [2] Compare Eph. iv. 8, 9, with 1 Cor. xii. 4—11.   [3] 2 Peter iii. 15.
[4] See the close of quotation from Erasmus, ut supra, p. 34, *note.*
[5] Exod. xxxv. 30—35.   [6] 2 Tim. ii. 15.   [7] 1 Cor. iv. 1. Luke xii. 42.

to administer a seasonable and effective distribution of the word. The Apostle marks also the gift of "utterance"[1] as a spiritual endowment in the dispensation of the word—enabling us to address our people with "opened mouth" and "enlarged heart;"[2] to "speak as the oracles of God"—in mode as well as in matter—in "sound speech" as well as in "sound doctrine;"[3] delivering our testimony with holy confidence, "not as the word of man, but in truth the word of God"—in a manner suitable to the dignity of the pulpit, and yet plain to the weakest capacity. The natural powers of clear thinking and arrangement of matter, of aptitude of expression, and of familiar and appropriate illustration, are often used as sanctified instruments of conveying the life-giving power of the Gospel with increasing acceptance and powerful application. Not, however, that these abilities are communicated by an extraordinary or sudden afflatus, or that they necessarily accompany in an equal measure the efforts of diligence.[4] The diligence of faith will ever receive its measure of encouragement in the growth, increase and improvement of Ministerial gifts. Yet we must not intrench upon the exercise of the Divine sovereignty; remembering, that "all these worketh that one and the self-same Spirit, dividing to every man severally as he will."[5]

'It is not to be supposed' therefore (to use the words of a sensible writer), 'that such an office can be easily filled. It demands not merely some, but many, nay, all excellences, in happy combination. A person may, in a general way, be said to be qualified for the Ministry, who has talents for preaching, though not fitted for profitable private intercourse, or the affairs of Church Government. But this is evidently not a complete adaptation to the work. It is, on the contrary, a very imperfect one, and one with which no man should be content. For, all the aspects of Ministerial labour are, if not equally, yet highly important; every one of them far too important to be trifled with. The right performance of each affords facilities for the rest, and gives additional beauty and efficacy to all. To be fit for only one department, cannot but greatly impede

---

[1] Eph. vi. 19.   [2] 2 Cor. vi. 11.   [3] Titus ii. 1, 7, 8.

[4] Bishop Sanderson observes—'It was Simon Magus' error to think, that the gifts of God might be purchased with money; and it has a spice of his sin, and so may go for a kind of simony, to think that spiritual gifts may be purchased with labour. You may rise up early and go to bed late, and study hard, and read much, and devour the marrow of the best authors; and, when you have done all, unless God give a blessing to your endeavours, be as lean and meagre in regard of true and useful learning, as Pharaoh's lean kine were, after they had eaten the fat ones. It is God, that both ministereth the seed to the sower, and multiplieth the seed sown: the principle and the increase are both his.' Sermon on 1 Cor. xii. 7.

[5] 1 Cor. xii. 11.

our activity, and diminish our success.   To fill the Ministerial office with a degree of satisfaction and benefit commensurate with its capabilities, or with the desire of a heart awake to its importance, we must be all that it demands—men of God, perfect, completely furnished to every good work.[1]   This is an elevated standard.   He that aims highest will most approximate to it.

CHAPTER VII.

PREPARATION FOR THE CHRISTIAN MINISTRY.

WE have already seen, that the weight of Ministerial responsibilities renders the work apparently more fitting to the shoulders of angels than of men.[2]   It is therefore a matter of the deepest regret, that any should intrude upon it, equally unqualified for its duties, and unimpressed with its obligations.   ' Fools rush in where angels fear to tread.'   But though many see little necessity for preparation ; here, if ever, labour, diligence, observation, and intelligence, are needful to produce a " workman that needeth not to be ashamed."[3]

The influence also of selfish or secular motives awfully blinds the conscience to the sense of the present necessity, and to the anticipation of the day of account; while young men of ardent feelings and promising talents, but with unfurnished minds and unrenewed hearts, are thrust forward by the persuasion of injudicious friends, or by the excitement of some momentary bias, into the sacred office.   The Church has severely suffered from this woeful inconsideration ; and the victims of this self-deluding impetus have felt to their cost its bitter fruit in the disappointment of their

---

[1] Hinton on Completeness of Ministerial Qualifications, pp. 11, 12.   ' It will not fail to be objected,'—remarks Mr. Ostervald—' that if none were to be admitted into holy orders, except those who are possessed of every necessary qualification, there could not possibly be procured a sufficient number of Pastors for the supply of our Churches.'   To which I answer, that a small number of chosen Pastors is preferable to a multitude of unqualified teachers.   At all hazards we must adhere to the command of God, and leave the event to Providence.   But in reality the dearth of pastors is not so generally to be apprehended.   To reject those candidates for holy orders, whose labours in the Church would be wholly fruitless, is undoubtedly a work of piety.   Others, on the contrary, who are qualified to fulfil the duties of the sacred office, would take encouragement from this exactness and severity ; and the Ministry would every day be rendered more respectable in the world.'   Ostervald on Sources of Corruption.
[2] Onus Angelicis humeris formidandum.—Augustine.
[3] Nulla ars doceri præsumitur, nisi intenta prius meditatione discitur.   Ab imperitis ergo pastoribus magisterium pastorale suscipitur in magna temeritate, quoniam ars est artium regimen animarum.   Greg. de Cura Pastor. cap 1.

Ministry, and the discomfort—if not the ruin—of their own souls. In other cases, the precious time for gathering in the store has been either wasted in feebleness and sloth; or misapplied in studies which have no direct tendency to form a solid, judicious, and experimental Ministry; so that, with every advantage of deliberation, but a slender stock of spiritual or intellectual furniture is ready to meet the successive and daily increasing demands.[1]

We may confidently anticipate an efficient Ministry, when the momentous cost has been considerately calculated: because then the work is contemplated,—not in the colouring of a self-indulgent anticipation, but in its true light, as warranted by Scripture, and confirmed by the experience of every faithful labourer—a work not of ease, but of self-denial—not of hasty effort, but of patient endurance—not of feeling and impulse, but of faith, prayer and determination.

A season of preparation—employed in storing the mind with Christian doctrine, and in directing it to devotional and practical purposes—in habits of self-communion and converse with God, and in the exercises of active godliness, will turn to most profitable account throughout the course of a protracted Ministry. We shall venture to offer a few suggestions on the subject under the divisions of—Habits of General Study—the Special Study of the Scriptures—Habits of Special Prayer—and employment in the cure of souls.

SECTION I.

HABITS OF GENERAL STUDY.

" Give attendance to reading"[2] is the Scriptural rule for Ministerial study. It is obviously of a general character; nor is there any reason for restricting its application to the Sacred Volume. " Paul the aged," in sending for his " books and parchments,"[3] (which, it may be presumed, he wanted for perusal) exemplified the comprehensive extent of his own rule. Indeed who can doubt, that the

---

[1] Quesnel's remarks are in his own style, but are well worthy consideration. 'The duties of an evangelical Preacher, before he begins his ministry, are, 1. To grow in piety, by feeding on the bread of prayer (gathered in by prayer.) 2. To give his zeal time to wax strong by reading the Holy Scriptures and Fathers. 3. To continue in silence and retirement, till God is pleased to bring him out, and show him to the world; men deceive themselves, when they imagine, that they ought to produce and employ their talents without delay, and that they cannot hide them without violating the command of God. On the contrary they violate it in not waiting his proper time, but making the wants of their neighbour alone a sufficient call.' On Luke i. 80.
[2] 1 Tim. iv. 13.　　　　　　　　　[3] 2 Tim. iv. 13.

Church is built up by the Ministry of the pen as well as of the mouth ; and that in both ways " the manifestation of the Spirit is given to every man *to profit withal ?*"[1] We cannot suppose that God would suffer the labours of his servants, in communicating the results of exercised, deep, and devotional study, to be in vain. The experience of men of God, like that of diligent travellers, is a public benefit ; and the fruit of it in successive ages is preserved as a most valuable store of important knowledge to the Church.

The Apostle's own practice again explains his rule to embrace the wide field of *General Study.*[2] His introduction of heathen aphorisms in the illustration or application of sacred truth[3] proves, that he apprehended no necessary debasement of its purity from an intermixture of human learning. Stephen mentions it to the honour, not to the discredit, of the Jewish Lawgiver, that he was " learned in all the wisdom of the Egyptians."[4] The illiterate owe a mighty debt to human learning, for a translation of the Scriptures, which otherwise would have lain by them as a dead letter in an unknown tongue. The intelligent reader is indebted to the same source for the explanation of its difficulties; and for many powerful defences of its authority, which enable him " with meekness and fear," but yet with confidence, to " be ready always to give an answer to every one that asketh him, a reason of the hope that is in him."[5]

At the Reformation, learning and religion revived together. The Reformers combined deep study with active Ministry. Erasmus's learning (notwithstanding its too great alliance with " philosophy and vain deceit"[6]) was a material assistance to Luther in his great work. ' We are taught by St. Paul's Epistles, that we may avail ourselves of every human aid to dispense the blessings of the Gos-

---

[1] 1 Cor. xii. 7.

[2] Mr. Scott refers this rule ' to the study of the Scriptures, or of *any other books which could add to his fund of profitable knowledge.*' His earlier notions on these subjects (he candidly confesses) ' were too contracted.' Mature consideration, however, formed his studious life upon more enlarged principles, which he never failed strongly to inculcate ; marking at the same time, the importance of a due subordination to the main end. ' The object of all your studies,' (he writes in one of his letters) ' should be, neither celebrity, advantage, nor knowledge, *for its own sake*, but furniture to enable you to serve God in your generation.' Life, pp. 102, 103, 330. A Minister of the present day said to a friend, who found him reading Gibbon's History—that ' he read every thing with a particular view to his Ministry, that he collected some materials for the pulpit from books of almost every description, and that he made all his readings contribute something towards what was needful for the Sunday.' Christian Observer, October, 1828, p. 608. Indeed, to restrict our reading to matters of immediate connection with our grand subject, would exclude us from much valuable collateral knowledge, and expose us to prejudice and misconception.

[3] Such as Acts xvii. 28. 1 Cor. xv. 33. Titus i. 12.   [4] Acts vii. 22.
[5] 1 Peter iii. 15.   [6] Col. ii. 8.

pel. All these human aids are valuable gifts of God, and only cease to be blessings by the abuse of them. It is true, that the Gospel may be preached with great energy by Ministers possessing very inconsiderable attainments in literature. It sometimes happens, that the most successful Ministrations are conducted by men of very moderate acquirements. And indeed the character of the Gospel seems to require, that in most cases (where the true doctrine is preached) it should give more honour to zeal and diligence than to genius and learning. But it is also true, that God is pleased to make himself known by the use of means. And when the means are used in subordination to his grace, he will honour the means. Let us then honour human learning. Every branch of knowledge, which a good man possesses, he may apply to some useful purpose. If he possessed the knowledge of an archangel, he might employ it all to the advantage of men, and the glory of God.'[1] Does not every expansion of the mind increase its range of power and general comprehension, and consequently render it more capable, under Divine teaching, of exploring those things, which angels desire to look into?"

As well might we suppose that the all-sufficiency of grace supersedes the importance of general knowledge, as that a child under the influence of grace is equally fitted for the Christian Ministry, with an intelligent adult under the *same* degree of this heavenly influence. But if knowledge is not to be despised, then neither is study as 'the means of obtaining it, to be neglected, specially as a preparation for publicly instructing others. And though having the heart full of the powerful influences of the Spirit of God may at some times enable persons to speak profitably, yea, very excellently without study ; yet this will not warrant us needlessly to cast ourselves down from the pinnacle of the temple, depending upon it, that the angel of the Lord will bear us up, and keep us from dashing our foot against a stone, when there is another way to go down, though it be not so quick.'[2]

May the Writer suggest in this view the importance of a conscien-

---

[1] Dr. Buchanan's Sermons, pp. 249—251. See some valuable remarks in Scott's continuation of Milner, vol ii. pp. 385, 386. 'I am confidently persuaded,'—says Dr. South, —'that there is no endowment, no natural gift whatever, with which the great Father of lights has furnished the mind of man, but may, in its highest operations, be sanctified, and rendered subservient to this great work of the Ministry. Real religion engages no man, *particularly no Minister*, to be dull, to lounge, and to be indolent; but on the contrary, it stirs up all the active powers of the soul in designing and bringing about great and valuable ends. Leighton declared—'that there could not be too much learning, if it were but sanctified.' At the same time pointing to his books, he said—'One devout thought is worth them all,'—meaning, no doubt, that no accumulation of knowledge is comparable in value to internal holiness.' Life by Rev. J. N. Pearson, p. cxx.
[2] Edwards's Works, Vol. viii. p. 589.

tious regard to the course of the University study ? Even where
academical distinctions are passed by, the habits of discipline and
self-denial, furnish an effectual safe-guard against the detrimental
influence of mental, and possibly also religious, dissipation. In the
theological department, we cannot but regret the want of a more
direct reference to the Christian Ministry. But—apart from this
deficiency—much store is laid in of important principles of knowledge—the studious habit is formed—and a tone of mind is acquired
or strengthened for the subsequent attainment of methodized, well-
digested, and comprehensive views.[1]

Professor Campbell remarks—'that, whatever in respect of knowledge supplies the materials necessary for edifying, comforting, and
protecting from all spiritual danger the people that may be committed to his charge, or is of use for defending the cause of his Master, must evidently be a proper study for the man who intends to
enter into the holy Ministry.' Again—'Whatever may enable
him to make a proper application of those acquisitions in knowledge, so as to turn them to the best account for the benefit of his
people, is not less requisite. To little purpose will it be to him
to be possessed of the best materials, if he have not acquired
the skill to use them. The former we may call the theory of the
profession ; the latter the practice. The first regards purely the
science of theology : the second the application of that science to
the purpose of the Christian Pastor.'[2]

'The science of theology' consists in whatever may tend to illustrate, confirm, enforce, or recommend Divine Revelation. However superficial our knowledge may be on some other subjects, here
at least it should be intelligent and comprehensive—including a
competent acquaintance with the Evidences of the Christian re-
ligion—the Holy Scriptures—and the History of the Church,
and especially of our own Church. In *regard to the Eviden-*
ces — Dr. Leland's volumes furnish a panoply for the defender
of the faith in the Deistical controversy ; as does Butler's Analogy in the close combat with the Infidel. In the more direct
track—Paley's masterly analysis of external Evidence—Doddridge's
popular survey of the whole field—the Bishop of Chester's original

---

[1] Perhaps some of us in the recollection of this important era may be led to make Philip
Henry's confession ; and would that it might be made with equal sincerity and tenderness of spirit ! 'What must needes bee done in college exercise, for disputations every
day in Term time, for theames and verses one a week, and for declamations; when it
came to my turn, I did as others of my standing, and sometimes had praise for it. But
as for that which we call hard study, giving myself to reading, late and early, and digest-
ing what I read by daily serious reviews, I was too much a stranger to it.'

[2] Lectures on Pulpit Eloquence—Lecture 1.

and satisfactory treatise (professedly confined to a single argument, but incidentally embracing the main points)—and the Lectures of the Bishops of Calcutta and Ohio[1] (equally addressed to the understanding and to the conscience)—these may well command our chief attention. The cold abstract metaphysics of Clarke—the evangelical and enlivening display of Bates and Charnock—and the popular and analogical proofs of Paley and Gisborne[2]—should be digested, as illustrative of the Divine character and perfections. Nor should Paley's Horæ Paulinæ be forgotten, as opening a new track of collateral evidence of Christianity, which has since been extended to a wider field with satisfactory reasoning.[3]

Reserving the subject of *acquaintance with the Scriptures* for the next section, we proceed to remark *the importance of Church History, as a component part of* Ministerial study. 'This will teach the student'—(as Dr. Dwight justly observes)—'the sins and virtues, the errors and sound doctrines, the prosperous and adverse circumstances, which have existed in the Church in its various ages ; together with the causes, by which they have been produced. Generally he will derive from this source the same advantages, in the ecclesiastical sense, which the statesman derives in a political sense, from civil history. He will learn what the church has been ; why it has thus been; and how in many respects it may be rendered better and happier.'[4] Mosheim will furnish the requisite information respecting the visible church, and Milner respecting the real church. A comparison of these two works in the prominent events of successive eras will open a field of most enlarged and interesting, but too often painful, contemplation. A work, combining the two in a comprehensive grasp, and with impartial but decided Christian views, remains yet to be supplied to the Church.[5]

The importance of an intelligent acquaintance with the grounds of his own church, seems to direct the candidate for the Established Ministry to a thoughtful study of Hooker's incomparable

[1] Course of Lectures delivered in New York by C. P. Mc Ilvaine, D. D. Bishop of Ohio.
[2] See Clarke on the Attributes. Charnock's Works, vol. i. Paley's and Gisborne's Natural Theology.
[3] The Veracity of the Gospels and Acts argued from undesigned coincidences. By Rev. J. J. Blunt, 8vo. 1828. Veracity of the Book of Moses, 8vo. 1828.
[4] Dwight's Theology, chap. v. p. 227.
[5] Weisman's Historia Sacra (2 vols. 4to. 1745, by a disciple of Dr. Spener's school) is considered by Mr. Conybeare to combine erudition and piety, but it is little known ; and, being shut up in Latin, is scarcely popular enough to supply the vacuum. Spanheim's Ecclesiastical Annals, from the creation of the world to the reformation (contained in the first volume of his works) is a store-house of valuable information. A translation of his own abridgment of this work has been given by the Rev. George Wright.

work. The power with which he has set forth the Apostolical foundation of our church, and its careful conformity to the Scriptural model, is at once above all praise, and proof against all attack. Nothing has since been added materially to strengthen the ground, on which he has fixed her—nothing indeed is needed. But the characteristic of the work—that which gives to it its peculiar dignity and interest, and in which it differs from many similar works of acknowledged ability is—*its holiness.* It not only exhibits the exquisite symmetry of the outward superstructure, but it views the interior of the temple with the eye of a man of God. The work is cast into the mould of the subject matter. It marks the genuine spiritual character of the church in its requirements and its privileges, and displays the " beauty of holiness" stamped upon the services of her sanctuary. We hesitate whether to admire more—the strength or the sanctity of his Fifth Book ; but it would be difficult to produce objections to the system or detail of our Ecclesiastical polity (the result either of prejudice or misconception,) that do not here meet with a satisfactory consideration.

Jewell's Apologies are highly deserving attention, as being of a kindred spirit and eloquence with Hooker. Comber will give an able and devotional exhibition of our public formularies. The doctrines of the Church are best known by a careful comparison of her Homilies and Articles with the word of God. Burnet's History of the Reformation furnishes most interesting details of their gradual formation upon the Scriptural basis. His Exposition of the Articles (if it does not always display the full and clear views of Evangelical truth, and if it occasionally errs in an excess of candour) contains a vast body of information, well worthy of the attention of the Ministerial student. Pearson on the Creed also must be especially named, as containing, in connection with the treatment of his great subjects, a large fund of the most valuable theology.

But after all, it is in the wide field of divinity, that the student, like David, must " prepare with all his might for the house of his God."[1] He had need be a man of store—" a scribe instructed unto the kingdom of heaven." His " lips must keep knowledge," that they may " seek the law at his mouth."[2] His course of reading therefore must embrace a comprehensive view of Scripture in its doctrinal light, practical obligation, and experimental influence. Robinson's Christian System and Dwight's System of Theology will furnish most valuable materials for digestion. As to details

---

[1] 1 Chron. xxix. 2.   [2] Mal. ii. 7, with Matt. xiii. 52.

of study—the Epistles nearest to the Apostolical era, as well as the works of the Christian Fathers—some of Augustine's Treatises especially—deserve attention; though of course in so wide a field and in such various degrees of Scriptural purity in their works, and of our own leisure of opportunity, much discrimination will be needed. In a brighter age of the Church, the writings of our Reformers open a rich treasure-house. From the mass of their writings the difficulty of selection is proportionably great.[1] Cranmer and Jewell however stand foremost for deep learning, large views of truth, and Christian wisdom and eloquence. Bradford's writings for their unction of spirit, and edifying and experimental matter, deserve the highest regard. Among the Foreign Reformers, Calvin, Luther, and Melancthon, indisputably are 'the first three.' Yet to select from upwards of thirty folios is no easy task. Calvin's Commentaries however (even in the judgment of Bishop Horsley, and others unfriendly to his peculiar dogmas) are among the most valuable illustrations of the Sacred Volume. His Institutes (apart from the system which they were intended to unfold) are full of admirable statements of the fundamental doctrines of the Gospel. His expositions of the Moral law, (always excepting his loose and unguarded views of the Christian Sabbath) and of the Sacraments, are eminently judicious and practical. Luther's Commentary on the Galatians exhibits the most full and enlivening display of the grand doctrine of justification probably ever given to the Church. His Diatribe against Erasmus (allowing for some hasty statements) is a powerful defence of the humbling doctrines of the Gospel against the pride of reason and self-sufficiency. Melancthon's Common Places (taking care to obtain the most matured expression of his sentiments) was one of the most important and influential works of the Reformation era, and abounds with solid and Evangelical statements. Indeed this school affords perhaps the most Scriptural model for the moulding of our system of Divinity. Its standard of theology is high and consistent; its statements of Christian doctrine are less encumbered with distinctions, less fettered by systematic accuracy, and more immediate and direct in their reference to the great object of our faith, than those of the subsequent school.[2]

The Divines of the Puritan School, however, (with due allow-

---

[1] The Parker Society promises to put the most important works of this School into extensive circulation.

[2] The Harmony of the Confessions, 4to. 1643, (of which a new and enlarged edition has lately been published by Rev. P. Hall,) and Corpus et Syntagma Confessionum, (4to. 1612), are well worthy of consideration in the Study of the School of the Reformers.

ance for the prevalent tone of scholastic subtleties) supply to the
Ministerial student a large fund of useful and edifying instruction.
If they be less clear and simple in their doctrinal statements than
the Reformers, they enter more deeply into the sympathies of
Christian experience. Profoundly versed in spiritual tactics—the
habits and exercises of the human heart—they are equally qualified to awaken conviction and to administer consolation ; laying
open the man to himself with peculiar closeness of application ;
stripping him of·his false dependencies, and exhibiting before him
the light and influence of the Evangelical remedy for his distress.
Owen stands pre-eminent among the writers of this school. 'His
scholars' (as Mr. Cecil observes) 'will be more profound and enlarged, and better furnished than those of most other writers.'
Among his voluminous works, we may mark his Exposition of the
Epistle to the Hebrews (with all its prolixity), as probably a most
elaborate and instructive comment upon a detached portion of
Scripture. His work on the Spirit (though discordant in some
particulars from the principles of our Church) embraces a most
comprehensive view of this vitally important subject. His exposition of Psalm cxxx. exhibits the most full and unfettered display
of Divine forgiveness, admirably suited to the perplexities of exercised Christians. His Tracts upon 'Understanding the Mind of
God in Scripture,' and 'The Reason of Faith,' manifest his usual
accuracy of spiritual discernment. His Treatises upon Indwelling
Sin, Mortification of Sin, the Power of Temptation, and the Danger of Apostacy—shew uncommon depths of exploring the secre-
cies of the heart. His view of Spiritual-Mindedness draws out a
graphic delineation of the tastes and features of the new character.
And indeed upon the whole—for luminous exposition, and powerful defence of Scriptural doctrine—for determined enforcement of
practical obligation—for skilful anatomy of the self-deceitfulness
of the heart—and for a detailed and wise treatment of the diversified exercises of the Christian's heart, he stands probably unrivalled.
The mixture of human infirmity with such transcendant excellence
will be found in an unhappy political bias—in an inveterate dislike
to episcopal government,[1] and (as regards the character of his Theology,) a too close and constant endeavour to model the principles of
the Gospel according to the proportions of human systems. But

---

[1] We refer not to his decided views of independency, but to his aggressive spirit in in-
terspersing animadversions upon the Establishment throughout his most spiritual and
discursive writings. Dwight has defended the principles of Dissent from Episcopacy
with equal power and determination; but in that spirit of Christian moderation which
conciliates respect, even when it fails of conviction.

who would refuse to dig into the golden mine from disgust at the base alloy, that will ever be found to mingle itself with the ore?[1]

Baxter must be mentioned in this School—though his views of the Gospel appear to the Writer not to partake of the fulness of Owen; nor (as Mr. Cecil remarks) 'is he to be named with him as to furnishing the Student's mind.' Yet is his 'Christian Directory' a most valuable work upon Casuistical Divinity. His 'Reasons for the Christian Religion' constitute a powerful defence of the bulwarks of our faith. His 'Saints' Rest' is a fine specimen of heavenly contemplation interspersed with most pungent addresses to the lukewarm and careless, though with too scanty infusion of the melting and attractive influence of evangelical motives. It were needless minutely to particularize more. R. Bolton, Howe, Charnock, are peculiarly distinguished by strength of genius and fund of matter (though—the first at least—with the occasional mixture of obscurity and bombast). Perhaps Flavel may be said to furnish the best model for the pulpit; his preaching being specially marked by an earnest and affectionate tenderness, by much unction of spirit, clearness of doctrine, and direct enforcement of practical obligations.

No department, however, of Ministerial study is of greater importance than Pastoral Theology. Chrysostom on the Priesthood, for its deep-toned solemnity of eloquence[2]—Herbert's Parson, for its primitive simplicity—Burnet, for its impressive detail of the Pastoral obligations—Bowles, for its excursive range throughout every department of the work—Baxter's Reformed Pastor, for its awakening apprehensions of Ministerial responsibility, realizing it as in the immediate presence of God and in the light of eternity—these are works for the Minister's first shelf. Close by their side may stand Ministerial Biography—the embodying of the deep-felt obligations in active and devoted operation. Such lives as those of

---

[1] Though his works will be the Minister's constant companion through his course, yet are they most valuable parts of his preparatory study, as exhibiting Scriptural doctrines in an experimental mould and in practical influence—a complete pattern of that form of Ministry, which equally adapts itself to the various purposes of our office.

[2] We must, however, remark upon the evident deficiency of Chrysostom's Treatise in those lively views and exercises of faith, which are the grand stimulants to our work. But for the characteristic we have mentioned, combined with practical expositions and an elevated standard of ministerial conduct and obligations, it is only to be equalled by Baxter's celebrated and invaluable work. His deficiency disables him indeed as a sustaining comforter to the desponding Minister. But the man, who could exclaim in fearful astonishment and hesitation—Θαυμαζω, εἰ τινά εστι των αρχοντων σωθῆναι (Homil. on Heb. xiii. 17.), and who declared that he was shaken as with an earthquake every time he read these words, (De Sacerd. vi. i.) must have much to teach us of more serious, self-abasing, and exciting views of our sacred work. We may also observe of Baxter's work, that his heart-stirring exhortations would have lost none of their pungency, had they flowed more fully and naturally from the enlivening and constraining principles of faith in the promises of God, and a realized apprehension of the love of Christ.

Archbishop Leighton, Alleine, P. Henry, M. Henry, Hallyburton, Cotton Mather, Eliot, Brainerd, Doddridge, Bishop Wilson, S. Walker, Martyn, Buchanan, Scott, Richmond, Oberlin and Neff, T. Lloyd, Thomason, and H. Venn—are of the highest value and consideration. More lessons of practical detail and encouragement may be learnt from this branch of study, than from whole treatises of abstract theology.

The Apostle enforces the habit of study upon his beloved son, as a means of preserving his youthful ministry from contempt.[1] And, indeed, (as Dr. Buchanan has observed,) 'in this age, when learning is general, an ignorant clergyman will be treated with contempt.'[2] The wide extension of knowledge proportionably increases our responsibility of storing our minds with subjects of general interest; as well to diversify our materials of sold instruction, as to protect our character and office from that contempt, to which a palpable inferiority to the intelligent part of our congregation would expose us. The Apostle's rule of study was not given to " a novice," but to a convert of many years' standing; who had been blest from his childhood with an excellent scriptural education;[3] who was endowed with good natural talents, spiritual gifts and pre-eminent religious advantages under the Apostle's personal tuition; and whose early elevation in the Church showed a satisfactory improvement of his privileges. Yet is he warned to instruct himself before he attempted to instruct others,—to " give attendance" first " to reading"—then " to exhortation, to doctrine." Such advice, given to an elder under such circumstances, and in an age of inspiration, carries the weight of authority, and serves as a rebuke for negligence under our comparative disadvantages.

Nor let it be thought, that studious habits must necessarily infringe upon our more active employments. What shall we say to the nine pondrous folios of Augustine, and the thirteen of Chrysostom—volumes not written, like Jerome's, in monastic retirement, but in the midst[4] of almost daily preaching engagements, and conflicting, anxious, and most responsible duties—volumes—not of light reading, the rapid flow of shallow declamation—but the results of deep and well-digested thinking? The folios also of Calvin—the most diligent preacher,[5] and of Baxter, the most laborious pastor of

[1] See 1 Tim. iv. 12. 13.
[2] Church Missionary Proceedings, Fourteenth Anniversary, p. 353, note.
[3] 2 Tim. iii. 15.
[4] ' Ye heard yesterday—ye shall hear to-morrow'—very commonly occurs in their Homiletical writings.
[5] ' What shall I say of his indefatigable industry, even beyond the power of nature, which being paralleled with our loitering, I fear will exceed all credit, and may be a true object of admiration, how his lean, worn, svent, and weary body could possibly hold out?

his day—full of thought and matter, bear the same testimony to the entire consistency of industrious study with devoted Ministerial diligence. The secret of this efficiency seems to have much consisted in a deep sense of the value of that most precious of all talents —*time;* and of an œconomical distribution of its minutest particles for specific purposes. Mr. Alleine would often say, ' Give me a Christian that counts his time more precious than gold.'[1] Mr. Cotton[2] would express his regret after the departure of a visitor—' I had rather have given this man a handful of money, than have been kept thus long out of my study.' Melancthon, when he had an appointment, expected, not only the hour, but the minute to be fixed, that time might not run out in the idleness of suspense. Seneca has long since taught us, that time is the only thing of which 'it is a virtue to be covetous.' But here we should be, like the miser with his money—saving it with care, and spending it with caution. It is well to have a book for every spare hour, to improve what Boyle calls the ' parenthesis or interludes of time : which, coming between more important engagements, are wont to be lost by most men for want of a value for them : and even by good men, for want of skill to preserve them. And since goldsmiths and refiners'—he remarks—' are wont all the year long to save the very sweepings of their shops, because they may contain in them some filings or dust of those richer metals, gold and silver ; I see not, why a Christian may not be as careful, not to lose the fragments and lesser intervals of a thing incomparably more precious than any metal—time ; especially when the improvement of them by our meletetics may not only redeem so many portions of our life, but turn them to pious uses, and particularly to the great advantage of devotion.'[3]

Bishop Burnet indeed has justly observed, ' that a great measure

He read every week in the year three divinity lectures, and every other week over and above; he preached every day, so that (as Erasmus saith of Chrysostom) I do not know, whether more to admire the indefatigableness of the man, or his hearers. Yea, some have reckoned up, that his lectures were yearly one hundred and eighty-six, his sermons two hundred and eighty-six, besides Thursday he sat in the presbytery,' &c. &c. Clark's Lives. Calvin's own account in one of his letters to Farel, thus speaks—' When the messenger called for my book (the Commentary on the Romans), I had twenty sheets to revise—to preach—to read to the congregation—to write forty-two letters—to attend to some controversies—and to return answers to more than ten persons, who interrupted me in the midst of my labours, for advice.'

[1] Alleine's Life and Letters, p. 94.

[2] The grandfather of Cotton Mather, an excellent scholar, formerly of Emmanuel college, and one of the first settlers in New England. One of his cotemporaries in New England (Mr. Norton) if he found himself not so much inclined to diligence and study, as at other times, would reflect upon his heart and ways, lest some unobserved sin should provoke the Lord to give him up to a slothful listless frame and spirit. In his diary he sometimes had these words—' Leve desiderium ad studendum : *ponam ex peccato admisso.*' Mather's History of New England, Book iii.

[3] Boyle's Reflections, pp. 9, 10.

of piety, with a very small proportion of learning, will carry one a great way.'[1]   Considerable latitude also is required in speaking of the high importance of study.   With some, the cord must be drawn tight—with others much may be left to the direction of their natural bias.   Yet Archbishop Secker's remark, must, we think, be generally admitted—'A point of great importance to Clergymen is, that they be studious.[2]   Far, very far, would we be from asserting the pre-eminence of theological study to spiritual-mindedness.   Yet we cannot expect to see a tone of healthful spirituality, without an industrious habit.   The religion of an idler is, to say the least, of a very questionable character ; nor can we doubt, that a diligent improvement of inferior talents by study, exercise, and prayer will be more profitable to their possessor, and serviceable to the Church, than the gift of superior abilities suffered to slumber for want of active use.[3]

Different qualifications, however, are required for the improvement of study.   Some need great patience.   Ardent minds wish, and seem almost to expect, to gain all at once.   There is here, as in religion, " a zeal not according to knowledge."—There is too great haste in decision, and too little time for weighing, for storing, or for wisely working out the treasure.   Hence arises that most injurious habit of skimming over books, rather than perusing them. The mind has only hovered upon the surface, and gained but a confused remembrance of passing matter, and an acquaintance with first principles far too imperfect for practical utility.[4]   The ore

---

[1] Pastoral Care, ch. vii.

[2] Secker's Charges.   Mather remarks upon the importance of habits of study—'There never was an eminent, who was not an industrious man.   You must be diligent in your business, if you hope to stand in any desirable circumstance before that Great King, unto whose service you are dedicated.'   Student and Pastor, pp. 195, 196.   'I have directed close attention to this subject,' (remarks a professor in an American Theological Seminary,) 'and the result without one solitary exception is, that I never knew an individual gain any considerable mass of really digested and valuable knowledge, *without unwearied industry.*'   Professor Miller's Letters on Clerical Habits addressed to a Student in the Seminary at Princeton, N. J. p. 256.   It was an excellent reply to a complaint of a bad memory as a discouragement from study ; *Lege, lege ; aliquid hærebit.*   That sentence in Prov. xiv. 13, deserves to be written in letters of gold upon your study table—" In all labour there is profit."   To another young Ministerial student it was said—' Abhor one hour of idleness, as you would be ashamed of one hour of drunkenness.'—Life of Mr. Thomas Shepard, in Mather's New England, Book IV.

[3] 'As it is in the body,'—observes Mr. Locke—'so it is in the mind, practice makes it what it is ; and most even of those excellences, which are looked on as natural endowments, will be found, when examined into more minutely, to be the product of exercise, and to be raised to that pitch by repeated actions'—Again—'The faculties of the soul are improved and made useful to us, just after the same manner that our bodies are.   Would you have a man write or paint well, or perform any other mechanical operation dexterously and with ease ? let him have ever so much vigour and activity, suppleness, and address, yet nobody expects this from him, unless he has been used to it, and has employed time and pains in fashioning and forming his hand or other parts to these motions. Just so it is in the mind—Would you have a man reason well ? you must use him to it betimes, exercise his mind in it.'—Conduct of the Understanding.

[4] 'Patient application is literally every thing.   Without it you may have a number of

of knowledge is purchased in the lump, but never separated, or applied to important objects.

Some again need discretion in the direction of their study. 'They study,' (as Bishop Burnet remarks in the conclusion of his history) 'books more than themselves.' They lose themselves in the multiplicity of books;[1] and find to their cost, that in *reading* as well as "*making* books there is no end ; and much study is a weariness of the flesh."[2] Bishop Wilkins observes,—'There is as much art and benefit in the right choice of such books, with which we should be most familiar, as there is in the election of other friends or acquaintances, with whom we may most profitably converse.[3] No man can read everything ; nor would our real store be increased by the capacity to do so. The digestive powers would be overloaded for want of time to act, and uncontrolled confusion would reign within.[4] It is far more easy to furnish our library than our understanding. A man may have read most extensively upon theological subjects, and yet be a tyro in theology. Professor Campbell remarks, in his forcible manner,—'It has been the error of many ages, and still is of the present age, that to have read much is to be very learned. There is not, I may say, a greater heresy against common sense. Reading is doubtless necessary ; and it must be owned, that eminence in knowledge is not to be attained without it. But two things are ever specially to be re-

half-formed ideas floating in your mind ; but deep, connected, large, and consistent views of any subject you will never gain. Impatient haste is the bane of deep intellectual work. If you are investigating any important doctrine, be not ready to leave it. Come to it again and again ; seeking light from every quarter ; and perusing with attention the best books, until you have entered, as far as you are capable, into its profoundest merits. And, if compelled by any circumstance to leave the subject before you have reached this point, hold it in reserve for another and more satisfactory examination. In short, let your motto, and, as far as practicable, your habit be, to leave nothing till you have thoroughly mastered it.' Professor Miller's Letters, pp. 256–258.

[1] Distrahit animum librorum multitudo. Itaque, cum legere non possis, quantum habueris, sat est habere quantum legas. Sed modo, inquis, hunc librum evolvere volo, modo illum. Fastidientis stomachi est, multa degustare ; quæ, ubi varia sunt et diversa, coinquinant, non alunt. Probatos itaque semper lege ; et si quando ad alios divertere libuerit, ad priores redi.' Seneca, Ep. i.

[2] Eccles. xii. 12.

[3] Wilkins, Eccl. p. 44. Dr. Watts has remarked,—'It is of vast advantage for improvement of knowledge and saving time, for a young man to have the most proper books for his reading, recommended by a judicious friend.'—On the Improvement of the Mind, ch. iv. This and ch. v. abound with most valuable instructions upon Christian study. Professor Franck accompanies the same advice to young students with the following admonitions. 'They should read little, but read that little well ; they should prefer those works, whose tendency is to lay a solid foundation, and prove them in a sedate and attentive manner ; never commencing any other book, until the subject of the former be perfectly understood and digested. If these monitions be neglected, they may become sciolists, but never men of learning ; sophists, but never truly wise ; the mind will be possessed with an intemperate thirst after "knowledge that puffeth up," and filled with unholy indifference' for "the wisdom that cometh from above." Franck's Guide to the Reading of the Scriptures, ch. iii.

[4] See quotation from Seneca, ut supra.

garded on this topic, which are these : First, that more depends on the quality of what we read, than on the quantity.[1] Secondly, more depends on the use, which, by reflection, conversation, and composition, we have made of what we read, than upon both the former.'[2] Mr. Fisk's remark upon Missionary qualifications applies—' More knowledge of languages should be acquired: I say, *more knowledge* of languages—rather than a knowledge of *more languages*.'[3] The accuracy of study is of far greater importance than its extent. ' A little study, *well digested in a good, serious mind*, will go a great way, and will lay in materials for a whole life.'[4] This intellectual process incorporates the subjects of thought with our own minds; and thus, instead of weakening their energies by an unnatural pressure, enlarges their capabilities of receiving and retaining their treasures. Massillon well distinguishes the main requisites of this digestive habit, to be—' love of study; a desire of becoming useful to our parish ; a conviction of the neces-

---

[1] Lectures on Systematic Theology, lect. i. Mr. Locke speaks most excellently to this point—' There are fundamental truths, which lie at the bottom, the basis upon which a great many others rest, and in which they have their consistency. These are teeming truths, rich in store, with which they furnish the mind, and like the lights of heaven, are not only beautiful and entertaining in themselves, but give light and evidence to other things, that without them could not be seen or known. These, and such as these, are the truths we should endeavour to find out and store our minds with.' Conduct of the Understanding, § 43.

[2] This has always been the view of the most judicious masters of study. Dr. Watts again observes,—' A well furnished library and a capacious memory are indeed of singular use toward the improvement of the mind; but if all your learning be nothing else but a mere amassment of what others have written, without a due penetration into its meaning, and without a judicious choice and determination of your own sentiments, I do not see what title your head has to true learning above your shelves.' On the Improvement of the Mind, ch. i. Thus again Mr. Locke—' Reading furnishes the mind only with materials of knowledge; it is thinking makes what we read ours. We are of the ruminating kind, and it is not enough to cram ourselves with a great load of collections.—There are indeed in some writers instances of deep thought, close and acute reasoning, and ideas well pursued. The light these would give would be of great use, if their reader would observe and imitate them—but that can be done only by our own meditation.' Conduct of the Understanding, § 43. Lord Bacon's directions on this matter, are replete with admirable wisdom:—' Read not to contradict and refute, nor to believe and take for granted, nor to find talk and discourse; but to weigh and consider. Some books are to be tasted, others to be swallowed, and some few to be chewed and digested; that is, some books are to be read only in parts; others to be read, but not curiously; and some few to be read wholly, and with diligence and attention. Some books also may be read by deputy and extracts of them made by others. Reading maketh a full man; conference a ready man: and writing an exact man: and therefore if a man write little, he had need have a good memory; if he confer little, he had need of much cunning, to appear to know what he doth not.' Mason observes—' that some books better deserve to be read over ten times, than others once, and recommends the examination of important discussions within the book, as a test of its solid or superficial character.'—Perhaps the periodicals of the present day may prove ensnaring to the studious mind. Though many of them are replete with valuable matter, yet from their slight and discursive character, they should be connected with hours of relaxation rather than with hours of study.

[3] Life of Pliny Fisk, Missionary to Palestine; a most valuable piece of Missionary, and indeed of Ministerial Biography, p. 25. Mr. Fisk was one of the instances of subsequent conviction of the mistake, that industrious study is inconsistent with ardent practical religion.

[4] Burnet's Conclusion to the History of his own times.

sity of deriving from prayer that knowledge which study does not afford ; of being impressed with a desire of salvation, and of applying all the means of advancing in evangelical wisdom, to inspire our flock with a love of their duty, in order that they may the more easily be induced to practice it : in a word, a sincere desire to fulfil our Ministry.'[1]

It is of great moment, that the habit of study should, as far as possible, be maintained through life. For the most part—the ground work only has been laid. Let our early attainments excite, not satisfy, our thirst for information—divert, not bound, our investigations. If useful habits are gained, they are probably far from being matured. St. Paul's instructions so often alluded to, were given (as we have hinted) to an elder of some years' standing in the Church. Mr. Scott to the last combined the student with the Minister.[2] 'If we live only on old stores,' (as a beloved brother has observed) ' we shall never enlarge our knowledge. It is allowed, that it is not easy diligently to pursue a course of persevering study. Our families and our daily duties must not be neglected. It requires fixed plans, vigorously followed up. Our natural indolence, and the love of society, must be broken through. Cecil says—' Every man, whatever be his natural disposition, who would urge his powers to the highest end, must be a man of solitary studies.'[3]

Yet, after all, the solidly-learned, the studious, and well-furnished man is but the unshapen mass, from which the Christian Minister is formed. The plastic energy—the quickening influence of the Almighty Spirit—is still needed to put light, life, and motion into the inert substance, to mould it into the Divine image, and to make it a " vessel of honour meet for the Master's use." Nor must we deny, that studious habits are attended with ensnaring temptations.[4] The tree of knowledge may thrive, while the tree of life is languishing. Every enlargement of intellectual knowledge has a natural tendency to self-exaltation. The habit of study must be

[1] Massillon's Charges, p. 222.
[2] Scott's Life, pp. 600, 601. Mr. Richmond's advice to his son looking forward to the Ministry was—'From the day that a youth on Christian principles is devoted to the Ministry, he ought to become a Divinity Student, and all his studies should bend to the one great object.'
[3] Bickersteth's Christian Hearer, pp. 243, 244. The whole chapter is replete with valuable thought upon Christian study. 'How few read enough to stock their minds? and the mind is no widow's cruse, which fills with knowledge as fast as we empty it. Why should a clergyman labour less than a barrister? since, in spiritual things as well as temporal, it is "the hand of the diligent which maketh rich." Does the conscience, in fact, never whisper upon any topic in theology—" Art thou a master in Israel, and knowest not these things?"' Christian Observer, 1828, p. 420.
[4] See some valuable remarks on this subject in Bickersteth's Christian Student, ch. viii.

guarded, lest it should become an unsanctified indulgence ; craving to be fed at the expence of conscience or propriety ; employed in speculative enquiries, rather than in holy and practical knowledge ; preoccupying the time that belongs to immediate duties ; or inter- fering with other avocations of equal or greater moment.   A sound judgment and a spiritual mind must be exercised, in directing these studies to the main end of the Ministry.   Let none of them intrench upon these hours, that should be devoted to our study of the Bible, or our preparation for the pulpit.   And wheresoever we find our in- clination too much attached to ány particular human science, let us set a guard upon ourselves, lest it rob us of Divine studies, and our best improvement.   A Minister should remember, that himself with all his studies is consecrated to the service of the sanctuary. Let every thing be done therefore with a view to one great end ; and let us pursue every part of science with a design to gain better qualifications thereby for our sacred work.'[1]

This section cannot be better concluded than with Quesnel's ex- position of the text, which has formed its basis.—' Not to read or study at all is to tempt God : to do nothing but study, is to forget the Ministry : to study, only to glory in one's knowledge, is a shameful vanity : to study, in search of the means to flatter sinners, a deplorable prevarication : but to store one's mind with the knowl- edge proper to the saints by study and by prayer, and to diffuse that knowledge in solid instructions and practical exhortations,— this is to be a prudent, zealous, and laborious Minister.'[2]

---

[1] Watts' Humble Endeavour for a Revival, pp. 17, 18.   How closely did Henry Mar- tyn live in the spirit of this caution—' May I be taught to remember, that all other studies are merely subservient to the great work of ministering holy things to immortal souls ! May the most holy works of the Ministry, and those which require most devotedness of soul, be the most dear to my heart !'   Martyn's Life, p. 269.

[2] It may be important to add to this Section the course of study for proficiency in the Christian Ministry, pursued by one of the most profound Theologians of his or of any age.   ' My method of study' (President Edwards informs us,) 'from my first beginning the work of the Ministry, has been very much by writing; applying myself in this way to improve every important hint; pursuing the clue to the utmost, when anything in reading, meditation? or conversation has been suggested to my mind, that seemed to pre- mise light in any weighty point; thus penning what appeared to me my best thoughts on innumerable subjects for my own benefit.   The longer I prosecuted my studies in this method, the more habitual it became, and the more pleasant and profitable I found it. The further I travelled in this way, the wider the field opened; which has occasioned my laying out many things in my mind to do in this manner, (if God should spare my life,) which my heart hath been much set upon.'   Life, Works, vol. i. pp. 79, 80.   Cecil's rule must, however, be carefully regarded,   ' Every man should aim to do one thing well.   If he dissipates his attention on several objects, he may have excellent talents intrusted to him, but they will be intrusted to no good end.   Concentrated on his proper object, they might have vast energy; but dissipated on several, they will have none.   Let other ob- jects be pursued indeed; but only so far as they may subserve the reader's purpose.   By neglecting this rule, I have seen frivolity and futility written on minds of great power; and by regarding it, I have seen very limited minds acting in the first rank of their pro- fession.   I have seen a large capital and a great stock dissipated; and I have seen a small capital and stock improved to great riches.'

SECTION II.

SPECIAL STUDY OF THE SCRIPTURES.

THE connection of this section with the preceding, is peculiarly important. Habits of General study, however well regulated and perseveringly maintained, will reflect no light or spiritual apprehension of the Gospel, independent of the special study of the sacred volume. Nor is it sufficient merely to combine these courses of study. Their connexion is not that of *equality*, but of the direct *subserviency* of General study to this specific purpose—a more enlightened and fruitful study of the word of God.[1] The intellectual excitement of literary or even theological study needs much watchfulness, lest it should deaden the freshness of our mind to the more spiritual study of the Scriptures.[2] We must be careful also, that our studies draw us to the Bible, and that we draw our studies to the Bible; instead of merely drawing the Bible to our studies, in which case they will be worse than unprofitable. ‘When *commencing the study of Divine truth*, amid all the jarring opinions of human authors, it is of inexpressible moment to begin with studying the pure word of God, and to go regularly through the whole of that word before we prepossess our minds with human opinions. *While continuing the study of Divine truth*, it is also of vast moment to keep up the daily reading of considerable portions of the pure word of God, and so to keep Scriptural truth (as it has been observed) continually revolving in the mind. It will be the only

---

[1] ‘I wish him,’—said Mr. Richmond respecting his son—‘to be diligent in his studies; but the Bible is the proper library for a young man entering into the Church.’ Life, p. 602. ‘I read other books,’ (P. Henry would say,) that I may be the better able to understand the Scripture.’ Again—‘Prefer having eyes to read the Scripture, and be blind to every thing else, rather than to read every thing else and neglect the Bible.’ Life, p. 24. 206. ‘Study close,’ (said his excellent son, addressing young Ministers) ‘study close: especially make the Bible your study. There is no knowledge, which I am more desirous to increase in, than that. Men get wisdom by books; but wisdom towards God is to be gotten out of God’s book; and that by *digging*. Most men do but walk over the surface of it, and pick up here and there a flower. Few dig into it. Read over other books to help you to understand *that book*. Fetch your prayers and sermons from thence. The volume of inspiration is a full fountain, ever overflowing, and hath always something new.’ Life, p. 293. ‘Scripturarum ea est profundior altitudo, quæ nunquam exhauritur; ea impervia difficultas, quæ, utcunque indies indagatur, nunquam tamen plene eruitur; ea perennis efficacia, quæ multitoties repetita, de novo semper operatur in cordibus fidelium. Nec id quisquam miretur, cum infinitus sit spiritus, qui in iis loquitur, his præ aliis adest, et per has suam præcipuii exserit ενεργιαν.’ Bowles. lib. i. c. 18.

[2] Martyn appears to have been most tenderly susceptible upon this point. ‘So deep was his veneration for the word of God, that, when a suspicion arose in his mind, that any other book he might be studying, was about to gain an undue influence on his affections, he *instantly* laid it aside; nor would he resume it, till he had felt and realized the paramount excellence of the divine oracles. He could not rest satisfied, till all those lesser lights, that were beginning to dazzle him, had disappeared before the effulgence of the Scriptures.’ Life, p. 59.

effèctual preservative against the taint and deterioration, which the mind might otherwise receive from reading human authors.'[1]

The Bible then must be, in a true Protestant sense, the *Liber Sacerdotalis.* 'The chief and top of the knowledge of the Country Parson consists in the Book of Books—the storehouse and magazine of life and comfort—*the Holy Scripture.*'[2] As no one can pretend to be a Christian without a competent acquaintance with it ; so no one can be qualified for the sacred office without such an accurate and spiritual insight into its contents, as shall prove him to be, like Ezra, " a ready scribe in the law,"—not only "a faithful man," but "able to teach others also."[3] 'It is of the Gospel,' (Archbishop Secker reminded his clergy) 'that you are Ministers ; all other learning will leave you essentially unqualified ; and this alone, (the doctrine and precepts of the Gospel,) comprehends every thing that is necessary.' With this end he recommends a diligent perusal of the Holy Scriptures.[4] Indeed, if the Bible be the fountain of light and truth, it is impossible to distinguish light from darkness, or truth from error in human writings, without an enlightened and enlarged apprehension of the word of God. By this touchstone we must " prove all things," so as to " hold fast that which is good."[5]

But we want a study—a searching into the Scriptures—the patient investigating spirit of the miner, digging into hidden treasure.[6]

[1] Bickersteth's Christian Hearer, p. 232. The following remarks of a valuable Puritan writer are well worthy attention—'When scholars furnish themselves with stores of other writers, besides the Scriptures, draw the Scriptures to the authors whom they most affect, and not their authors to the Scriptures, their divinity proves but humanity, and their Ministry speaks to the brain, but not to the conscience, of the hearer. But he that digs all the treasures of his knowledge and the ground of religion out of the Scripture, and makes use of other authors, not for ostentation of himself, nor for the ground of his faith, nor for the principal ornament of his Ministry, but for the better searching out of the deep wisdom of the Scriptures, such an one believes what he teaches, not by an human credulity from his author, but by a divine faith from the word; and because he believes, therefore he speaks; and speaking from faith in his own heart, he speaks much more powerfully to the begetting and strengthening of faith in the hearer.' Hildersham's Address prefixed to his Exposition of John iv.

[2] Herbert's Parson, chap. iv. 'A book,' (as Isaac Walton remarks in his characteristic style) 'so full of plain, prudent, and useful rules, that the Country Parson that can spare twelve pence, and yet wants it, is scarcely excusable; because it will both direct him what he ought to do, and convince him for not having done it.'

[3] Ezra vii. 6. 2 Tim. ii. 2. 'The capital error' (as Burnet observes in the conclusion to the History of his own times) 'in men's preparing themselves for that sacred function is, that they read divinity more in other books than in the Scriptures.' It is needless to allude to the great advantage resulting from the knowledge of the original languages of Scripture, and to the powerful motives that urge us to the study of them. Apart from the interest of this study—it is most desirable amidst the conflicting opinions of commentators to arrive at an intelligent and satisfactory judgment from our own resources.

[4] Secker's Charges, p. 267.

[5] 1 Thess. v. 21. 'I find,' (said President Edwards,) 'it would be very much to my advantage to be thoroughly acquainted with the Scriptures. When I am reading doctrinal books, or books of controversy, I can proceed with abundantly more confidence, and can see upon what foundation I stand.' Life, Works, vol. i. p. 24.

[6] Prov. ii. 4. John v. 39. See Matthew Henry's Counsel *ut supra,* and compare the account of Zwingle's diligent study of the Scriptures in Scott's Continuation of Milner,

Some with good intentions and competent capacities, are in danger of becoming crude and inexperienced throughout their course, by substituting warm impressions of Scripture for that close study of its sacred contents, which can alone form a solid and efficient Ministry. 'In general,' (Mr. Scott remarks) 'I have found it advantageous sometimes to read the Scriptures with such exactness, as to weigh every expression, and the connexion, as if I were about to preach upon every verse ; and then to apply the result to my own case, character, experience, and conduct, as if it had been directly addressed to me—in short—to make the passages into a kind of sermon, as if about to preach to others, and then to turn the whole application on myself, as far as suited to my case. At other times I have read a passage more generally, and then selected two or three of the most important observations from it, and endeavoured to employ my mind in meditation on them, and consider how they bore on the state of my heart, or on my past life, or on those things which I heard or observed, in the world or the Church, and to compare them with the variety of sentiments, experiences, conducts, or prominent characters, with which we become gradually more and more acquainted.'[1] It is most important also, that our research should compass, as far as possible, the whole extent of the mine. The wise scattering of the truth over the whole surface of Scripture is far more adapted to the ends of instruction, than would have been a compression of its component parts within their several departments. None of us probably are wholly free from undue partialities ; and, had our favourite doctrines been concentrated in particular divisions of the volume, an exclusive or disproportioned attention to those parts would have contracted our views of the whole system. The present disposition of truth, however, compels us to study the entire volume ; and thus, by considering the whole mind of God, our views are extended to the length and breadth of the land, while we insensibly imbibe more of the enlarged spirit of the Divine revelation.

Perhaps the Pentateuch, the Prophecies, and the Epistles, may be marked out as the peculiar subjects of study. *On the Pentateuch*—Dean Graves's Lectures may be referred to for much valuable criticism and information, equally illustrative of the wisdom and of the difficulties of the Mosaic code. Faber's Horæ Mosaicæ opens a diversified, instructive, and Christian view of this sacred

Vol. ii. Part ii. Upon the whole subject of this section the writer begs to recommend a most valuable volume—'Remarks on Clerical Education.' By the Rev. Henry Raikes, Chancellor of the Diocese of Chester.

[1] Life, p. 328, 329.

field. *On the Prophecies*—Mede stands foremost as the Prince
among the Interpreters of this mysterious revelation. Bishop Newton's Dissertations also are full of important illustration respecting
fulfilled Prophecy. Davison's Lectures lay open the scope with
much solid, serious, and original contemplation. After all that has
been written in the present day upon unfulfilled prophecy, upon
different principles of interpretation, (and not always with suitable
humility, forbearance, and patience,) a dark cloud still hangs over
the development of the prospects of the Church. Faber's " Sacred
Calendar of Prophecy," must however be deemed on all sides
worthy of an attentive perusal, though serious doubts will be entertained on particular parts of his system. Mr. Bickersteth's "Practical Guide to the Prophecies," though it throws out some uncertain
views, is fraught with glowing Scriptural motives and valuable
information. Comparison of the different chains of prophecy in the
sacred volume in a simple, dependent, investigating spirit opens a
most interesting and profitable course of study, to which indeed the
signs of the present times imperiously call us. *The Epistles*, in
some respects, may be considered the most important portion of
Scripture to the Minister, in order to obtain a connected and comprehensive system. Perhaps Scott's Commentary—*with as large
a selection of his references as may be practicable*—may be regarded upon the whole as the best source of solid and spiritual
instruction upon the grand subjects discussed by the different inspired writers.

Our obligation to "keep back nothing that is profitable"[1] to the
people, sufficiently marks the importance of this research. Adults
must be fed as well as babes. Those that have successfully exercised the diligence of faith, must not be hindered in their advance
to higher attainments by being bound up in the same line and
measure with others, who from the neglect of the same advantages
have come short. The main design of the Ministry is to carry our
people forward—to " present every man perfect in Christ Jesus."[2]
The reverent exposition, therefore, of " the deep things of God," is
included in our commission, and demands a deep and accurate
study of the sacred volume. Difficulties indeed will remain to the
end ; most profitably exercising our subjection to the authority of
Scripture, and our habitual dependence upon Divine teaching.[3]

1 Acts xx. 20.   2 Comp. Eph. iv. 12. Col. i. 28.
   3 Profesor Francks's Guide to the Reading of the Scriptures gives most admirable rules
for the intelligent, devotional, and practical study of the Scriptures. Mr. Horne's Introduction also furnishes a valuable digest of thoughtful matter. Vol. ii. Part ii. Mr. Dod-
well judiciously recommends to make the Bible the common-place book for all our other
studies. (Letters of Advice, p. 235.) Philip Henry in his preparatory Ministerial study

Indeed, this spirit of humble submission to the word, is the requisite preparation for admittance in every part of this heavenly treasure; where the lowest possessor of this Christian spirit will not fail to realize a most valuable blessing.

In *speaking of Commentaries*—the value of Scott's Commentary, as exhibiting a matured knowledge of Scripture, sound principles of interpretation, and a body of solid practical instruction—is generally acknowledged. Henry's Commentary (though inferior to Scott in luminous view of doctrine) may be said to excel him in simplicity of style and fertility of illustration. Yet for that exegetical and critical explanation necessary for the elucidation of Scriptural difficulties, we must go to Calvin's Commentaries—Poole's Synopsis—or Patrick, Lowth, and Whitby in a lower and (as respects Whitby,) an unscriptural standard of theology.

It is, however, most important to remember, that the service or disservice of commentaries wholly depends upon the place which they occupy in the system of study. Let them not be discarded as utterly useless; for many of them comprise the labours of men, who had a far deeper insight into the word of God than those who despise them are generally likely to attain. But let them not be placed before the word, nor be consulted (habitually at least), until the mind has been well stored with the study of God's own book. Professor Campbell speaks most admirably upon this point—'I would not have you at first' (says he) 'recur to any of them. Do not mistake me as though I meant to signify, that there is no good to be had from commentaries. I am far from judging thus of the commentaries in general, any more than of systems. But neither are proper for the beginner, whose object it is impartially to search out the mind of the Spirit, and not to imbibe the scheme of any dogmatist. Almost every commentator has his favourite system, which occupies his imagination, biases his understanding, and more or less tinges all his comments. The only assistances which I would recommend, are those, in which there can be no tendency to warp your judgment. It is the serious and frequent reading of the Divine oracles, accompanied with fervent prayer; it is the comparing Scripture with Scripture; it is the diligent study of the languages in which they are written; it is the knowledge of those histories and antiquities, to which they allude. These indeed will not tell you what you are to judge of every passage: and so much

___

used an interleaved Bible for short notes upon Scripture—a plan, which he recommended to his young men; adding, that such expositions and observations are more happy and considerable sometimes than those that are found in the professed commentators. 'I profess' (he would say) 'to teach no other learning but Scripture learning.' Life, p. 206.

the better.—God has given you judgment, and requires you to exercise it.   "And why even of yourselves judge ye not what is right?" '   In answer to the question—'when it is proper to recur to systems and commentators'—the Professor. replies—'after you have acquired such an insight into the spirit and sentiments of sacred writ, that you are capable of forming some judgment of the conformity or contrariety of the doctrine of these authors to that infallible standard.   With the examination of such human compositions, the *studies of the theologian ought in my judgment to be concluded, and not begun.*"[1]   This appears to be the only profitable and safe use of commentaries.   We thus avail ourselves freely of all the store of wisdom within our reach : while at the same time our " faith does not stand in the wisdom of men, but in the power of God."[2]

To illustrate the importance of this principle—Suppose a Theological student of ardent mind, but with uninformed or unfixed biblical principles, to sit down to Poole's invaluable Synopsis, or even to make it a book of frequent reference; this digest of Critici Sacri would soon prove to him a Sylva Critica.   He would find opinions successively overthrown, which had passed before him with more or less conviction.   Or—more frequently, two conflicting sets of opinion would demand his attention, while—having no umpire to decide between them—his judgment (if indeed he were able to form any under such circumstances) would be formed with hesitation, or taken up with haste or partiality, rather than as the result of deliberate and enlightened conviction.   Or suppose him to have heard much commendation of Mr. Scott's Commentary, or his general views of Theology.   He knows them to have given an influential tone to the religion of his day.   He reads them with avidity; he receives them as the standard of orthodoxy, and feels himself impregnably entrenched in the strong positions of Divine truth.   But he may hear Mr. Scott's principles controverted with

[1] Campbell on Systematic Theology, Lecture ii.   This was Dr. Doddridge's Plan from the commencement of his studies.   Orton's Life: Chap. i.   Bishop Spratt mentions the instance of a Bishop in the troublous times, confined nearly twenty years in the Tower, plundered of his library, and applying himself to the exclusive study of the Scriptures, as the faithful companion of his solitude, and solace of his afflictions.   ' But what was very remarkable, (observes the Bishop in giving this history) 'and for which I am bold to produce him as an instance worthy your imitation—I know he was often heard to profess solemnly, that in all his former studies, and various readings and observations, he had never met with a more useful guide, or a surer interpreter to direct his paths in the dark places of the lively oracles, to give information to his understanding in the obscure passages, or satisfaction to his conscience in the experimental truths of them, than when he was thus driven by necessity to the assiduous contemplaton of the Scripture alone, and to weigh it by itself, as it were, in the balance of the sanctuary.'—Charge to the Diocese of Rochester—Clergyman's Instructor, pp. 265, 266.

[2] 1 Cor. ii. 5.

considerable force and subtlety of argument, and *apparently* upon an equal basis of Scriptural authority. Now, if his mind has not been exercised in the field of Holy Writ, he will be incompetent to bring the opposing dogmas to an infallible standard, by comparing them respectively with the analogy of faith; and therefore (though from partiality, respect, or hesitating conviction he may still maintain his ground) his basis of truth—not having been fixed upon the sole and immoveable rock of the Bible—will be materially shaken. His standard (if he should be "a standard-bearer") will be lifted up with a feeble and trembling hand; and the indecisive character of his ministerial system will preclude any sanguine prospect of efficiency.[1]

We may trace many of the differences subsisting in the Church, to a feeble, uninfluential recognition of the supreme authority of Scripture. Different tracts are taken at the commencement of the inquiry—'What is truth?' The mind is controuled by the bias of some human system. And thus the unity of truth is destroyed: and the clear and heavenly light of scriptural revelation is darkened by the prejudices of men, conflicting with each other, instead of bowing implicitly to the obedience of faith. In fact, from the constitution of the human mind, genuine independence is a matter of extreme difficulty and of rare occurrence. Attachment to some particular system is a spiritual self-indulgence, which too often guides our Scriptural reading, and gives an individual character to it, rather than receives a complexion from it.

The book of God is indeed the living voice of the Spirit. To be

[1] The principle of this course of biblical reading is excellently illustrated by the habit of the venerable writer just referred to—' Having perhaps heard or read the opinions of different men on any disputed subject, I have, in my daily reading of the Scriptures, constantly kept those opinions in view, that I might at length form my judgment on which side truth lay. In doing this, I have always aimed to keep my mind from the two extremes—on the one hand, of giving up my own opinion, from a kind of false humility, and deference for men, without being previously convinced that I had been mistaken; and, on the other hand, of assuming my opinion to be truth, so as to exclude light, especially if it came from an enemy, or a person not entitled to much deference. So that I have always aimed to be open to conviction; to bring every man's probable opinion to the touchstone, and to give it a fair trial, if not tried before; but not to receive it, without plainly perceiving its agreement with the Scripture; and at the same time to aim, that my heart might be suitably affected with the conclusions of my understanding—in which I have principally failed.' Scott's Life, pp. 329, 330, and some valuable remarks of his son in enforcing this peculiar feature of his father's example, pp. 667, 668.

Upon the same principles Archbishop Usher gave the following wise instructions to young Ministers:

' 1. Read and study the Scriptures carefully, wherein is the *best learning, and only infallible truth.* They can furnish you with the best materials for your sermons; *the only rules of faith and practice;* the most powerful motives to persuade and convince the conscience; and the strongest arguments to confute all errors, heresies, and schisms.

' 2. *Take not hastily up with other men's opinions without due trial; nor vent your own conceits; but compare them first with the analogy of faith, and rules of holiness, recorded in the Scriptures, which are the proper tests of all opinions and doctrines.'* Life of Usher, by his Chaplain, Dr. Parr, prefixed to his valuable Collection of Letters, p. 87.

intent therefore upon the study of it, must result in a clear apprehension of the mind of God.   Hence the maxim—'*Bonus textuarius, bonus Theologus.*'   Most beautifully does Witsius set out the value of this primary Ministerial qualification—"mighty in the Scriptures."   'Let the Theologian ascend from the lower school of natural study, to the higher department of Scripture, and, sitting at the feet of God as his teacher, learn from his mouth the hidden mysteries of salvation, which "eye hath not seen, nor ear heard ; which none of the princes of this world knew;" which the most accurate reason cannot search out ; which the heavenly chorus of angels, though always beholding the face of God, "desire to look into." In the hidden book of Scripture, and no where else, are opened the secrets of the more sacred wisdom.   Whatever is not drawn from them—whatever is not built upon them—whatever does not most exactly accord with them—however it may recommend itself by the appearance of the most sublime wisdom, or rest upon ancient tradition, consent of learned men, or the weight of plausible argument—is vain, futile, and, in short, a very lie.   "To the law and to the testimony.   If any one speak not according to this word, it is because there is no light in them."   Let the Theologian delight in these sacred oracles : let him exercise himself in them day and night ; let him meditate on them ; let him live in them ; let him derive all his wisdom from them ; let him compare all his thoughts with them ; let him embrace nothing in religion which he does not find here.   Let him not bind his faith to a man—not to a Prophet —not to an Apostle—not even to an Angel himself, as if the dictum of either man or angel were to be, the rule of faith.   Let his whole ground of faith be in God alone.   For it is a Divine, not a human faith, which we learn and teach ; so pure that it can rest upon no ground but the authority of God, who is never false, and never can deceive.   The attentive study of the Scriptures has a sort of constraining power.   It fills the mind with the most splendid form of heavenly truth, which it teaches with purity, solidity, certainty, and without the least mixture of error.   It soothes the mind with an inexpressible sweetness ; it satisfies the sacred hunger and thirst for knowledge with flowing rivers of honey and butter ; it penetrates into the innermost heart with irresistible influence ; it imprints its own testimony so firmly upon the mind, that the believing soul rests upon it with the same security, as if it had been carried up into the third heaven, and heard it from God's own mouth ; it touches all the affections, and breathes the sweetest fragrance of holiness upon the pious reader, even though he may not perhaps comprehend the full extent of his reading. We can scarcely say, how strongly we are opposed to that preposterous method of study, which, alas! too much prevails among us—of forming our views of Divine things from human writings, and afterwards supporting them by Scripture authorities, the result either of our own inquiry, or adduced by others too rashly, and without further examination or bearing upon the subject; when we ought to draw our views of Divine truths immediately from the Scriptures themselves, and to make no other use of human writings, than as indices marking those places in the chief points of Theology, from which we may be instructed in the mind of the Lord.' This exquisite Master of Theology proceeds in the same strain to remark the importance of the Student giving himself up to the inward teaching of the Holy Spirit, as the only mean of obtaining a spiritual and saving acquaintance with the rule of faith; 'it being needful that he that is a disciple of Scripture should also be a disciple of the Spirit.' But the whole Oration De Vero Theologo, and its accompaniment, De Modesto Theologo, are so intrinsically valuable for the elegance of their Latinity, the beauty of their thoughts, and most of all for the heavenly unction that breathes throughout the compositions, that nothing further seems needed, than to commend them to the earnest consideration of the Ministerial Student.[1]

The serious exhortation of our Ordination Service—referring *generally to study*, and *specifically to the study of the Scriptures*, will fitly sum up this section in connection with the preceding— 'You will apply yourselves wholly to this one thing, and draw *all your cares and studies* this way; continually praying to God the Father by the mediation of our only Saviour Jesus Christ, for the heavenly assistance of the Holy Ghost; that *by daily weighing of the Scriptures*, you may wax riper and stronger in your Ministry.'

SECTION III.

HABITS OF SPECIAL PRAYER.

LUTHER long since has said—'Prayer, meditation, and temptation, make a Minister.' No one will hesitate to admit the importance of the first of these qualifications, who has ever realized the weight of Ministerial responsibility, who has been led to know

---

[1] See Witsii Misc. Sacra, vol. ii. Compare also similar thoughts, expressed with the same spiritual holiness, in Vitringa Typus Doctr. Prophet. pp. 106–108. Some valuable quotations are given from the Fathers in Du Pin's Method of Studying Divinity, chap. xiii.

that his "sufficiency is of God," and that prayer is the appointed channel of heavenly communications. The student's conscious need of wisdom, humility and faith, to ascertain the pure simplicity of his purpose, his necessary qualifications, and his Divine call to the holy office—will bring him a daily suppliant to the throne of grace. In his General Studies, abstracted from this spirit of prayer, he will find a dryness—a want of power to draw his resources to this one centre of the Ministry—or perhaps a diversion from the main object into some track of self-indulgence.[1] And even in this special duty of the Scriptures he will feel himself, (as Witsius says) 'like a blind man contemplating the heavens,'—or as when the world in its original confusion " was without form and void, and darkness was upon the face of the deep." God must speak to his heart—"Let there be light;" and " for this he will be inquired of to do it unto him."

Wickliff's judgment of the main qualification of an expositor of Scripture is equally striking and accurate. He should *be a man of prayer—he needs the internal instruction of the primary Teacher.*[2] Dr. Owen observes with his usual impressiveness— ' For a man solemnly to undertake the interpretation of any portion of Scripture *without invocation of God,* to be taught and instructed by his Spirit, is a high provocation of him ; nor shall I expect the discovery of truth from any one, who thus proudly engages in a work so much above his ability. But this is *the sheet anchor* of a faithful expositor in all difficulties ; nor can he *without this* be satisfied, that he hath attained the mind of the Spirit in any Divine revelation. When all other helps fail, as they frequently do, this will afford him the best relief. The labours of former expositors are of excellent use : but they are far from having discovered the depth of this vein of wisdom ; nor will the best of our endeavours prescribe limits to our successors ; and the reason why the generality go in the same track, except in some excursions of curiosity, is—not giving themselves up to the conduct of the Holy Spirit in the diligent performance of their duty.'[3]

---

[1] The Life of Dr. Andrew Willet furnishes us with an important and encouraging hint—' As he applied his heart to know, and to search, and to seek out wisdom, and to that end, according to that Apostolical direction, " gave attendance to reading :" so likewise he followed that godly advice of Cyprian to Donatus, Epist. lib. ii. Epist. 2, to mingle frequent prayer with diligent reading : ' Sometimes,' (he saith,) ' speak to God— and sometimes let God speak to thee ;' and he *professed to his friends how much he had thereby improved his talent.'*

[2] Milner's Church Hist., iv. 134.

[3] See his work on the Spirit. Mr. Scott bears the same testimony—Speaking of his Scriptural studies remarks—' A spirit of continual prayer, mixed with reading, has been my practical help in all these things.' Life, p. 330. Quesnel, speaking of the importance of the study of the Scriptures to the Christian Minister, adds—' He must learn them

Let the probationer then seriously calculate the cost of the work. Many are the painful exercises of faith and patience superadded to the daily difficulties of the Christian life. Need we therefore remind him, what an awakening call there is for prayer, for additional supplies of heavenly influence—that his knowledge may grow " unto all the riches of the full assurance of understanding" —that his heart may be constrained to a cheerful and ready obedience—that all his powers may be consecrated to this sole object —and that the whole work of preparation may be sealed by an abundant blessing ? George Herbert justly remarks of ' some in a preparatory way,' that their ' aim and labour must be, not only to get knowledge, but to subdue and mortify all lusts and affections, and not to think, that, when they have read the fathers or schoolmen, a Minister is made, and the thing done. *The greatest and hardest preparation is within.*[1] And indeed *hic labor—hoc opus est.* To bring the heart to the work, and to keep it there—to exchange the indulgence of ease for labour and self-denial, the esteem of the world for the reproach of Christ and of his cross—to endure the prospect of successive disappointment and discouragement—this it is that raises within the " evil spirit" of despondency : "which kind can come forth by nothing *but by prayer* and fasting."[2]

The first Ministers of the Gospel were prepared for their work (unconsciously indeed to themselves) by their Master's retirement for the continuance of a whole night of prayer to God.[3] With the same holy preparation the first Missionaries to the Gentiles were sent forth ;[4] and thus—instead of "returning (like the nobles of Judah) with their vessels empty, ashamed and confounded, and covering their heads"[5]—they gladdened the hearts of their brethren with tidings of the great things " that God had done with them."[6] Indeed an entrance upon this great work without the spirit of prayer, would be to " go a" most fearful " warfare at our own charges." The kingdom of Satan would have little to apprehend from an attack of literature, or from any systematic mechanism of external forms. The outworks might be stormed, but the citadel would remain impregnable. " The prey" will never be " taken from the mighty, nor the lawful captures delivered," by any other

otherwise than by study. The unction of the Spirit is a great master in this science: and it is by prayer that we become his scholars. Much prayer and little study advance the work of God, more than abundance of study without prayer.' On John vii. 17. ' Januas Scripturarem custodit Spiritus Sanctus: non datur aditus, nisi propriæ cæcitatis conscius, hujus opem imploraris.' Bowles, Lib. i. c. 18.

1 Country Parson, chap. ii.   2 Mark ix. 29.   3 Luke vi. 12—16.
4 Acts xiii. 2, 3.   5 Jeremiah xiv. 3.   6 Acts xiv. 27; xv. 3, 4.

power than the Ministry of the Gospel clothed with Almighty energy.[1] By this means the first attack was made by the servants of Christ, waiting in earnest prayer for the fulfilment of the faithful promises.[2] The Christian Ministry is a work of faith; and, that it may be a work of faith, it must be a work of prayer. Prayer obtains faith, while faith in its reaction quickens to increasing earnestness of prayer. Thus spiritual, enlightened, and encouraging views of the Ministry flow from the habit of diligent waiting on God. We may therefore safely conclude with Bernard,—'Utilis lectio,—utilis eruditio—sed magis necessaria unctio, quippe quæ docet de omnibus.'

If then the candidate for the sacred office should never bow his knee, without making the momentous work before him a subject of large supplication, he will do well. But if he should add to his customary times of prayer seasons of retirement, consecrated to the sole purpose of contemplating the work, and separating himself to its service, he will do better. A man of special prayer will be a man of special faith : and faith enables " the worm to thresh the mountains," and, in holy triumph, to cast them down before him —"Who art thou, O great mountain? before Zerubbabel thou shalt become a plain."[3]

SECTION IV.

EMPLOYMENT IN THE CURE OF SOULS.

" EXERCISE thyself unto godliness"[4]—was one of the wise rules of the Apostle to his beloved son, for the course of his Ministry ; a rule, which bears with most important application to the noviciate. Its connexion with the rule of study in the succeeding context is worthy of remark. " Giving attendance to reading," without active energy, would form a most incomplete and inefficient ministry. The want of exercise is as hurtful to the spiritual as to the bodily system ; nor will "reading" communicate any benefit, except its results are operative in Christian activity. Equally important is the combination with prayer. In fact, study, prayer, and exercise, may be said to form the minister. *Study* stores the mind, *prayer* infuses a divine influence, *exercise* carries out the resources into effective agency.

The Apostle insisted upon a period of probation, even for the

[1] Comp. John xii. 32. 1 Cor. i. 21—24.   [2] Acts i. 8, 14, with ii. 1.
[3] Isaiah xli. 14, 15. Zech. iv. 7.   [4] 1 Tim. iv. 7.

lowest department of the ministry ; adverting to natural gifts and spiritual qualifications, as well as personal consistency.[1] Now, though no man taketh this honour unto himself, until he be solemnly called to it by the Church ; yet there is much subordinate occupation in the cure of souls, that may legitimately employ the natural capacities of the young probationer, increase his store of experience, and impart considerable benefit to the Church, and reciprocal advantage to himself. *From the superintendence of a Sunday-school* many have drawn most valuable lessons of practical utility in the future exercise, and during the whole course, of their Ministry. *The instruction of the poor* (whether in the way of casual intercourse, or with more or less of system) may be conducted with humility, perseverance, and love, without infringement on the holy function ; and perhaps with more preparation for future usefulness, than could have been gathered from many months of contemplative study. An insight into the real condition of the future subjects of the parochial Ministration, and the acquaintance with their modes of expression, their peculiar difficulties and temptations, the causes of their ignorance, the wisest and most successful avenues of approach to them—this is knowledge, in which it would be well to be initiated, before the solemn obligation is undertaken ; and the defect of which gives a *general* and *therefore unimpressive* character to the early ministrations of many excellent pastors. The best sermons composed in the study, must, under such circumstances, necessarily fail in adaptation to the wants and circumstances of their people ; as exhibiting a want of sympathy in their distresses—a want of consideration of their ignorance—a want of accuracy in drawing the lines of character, and consequently in directing our " doctrine, reproof, correction, and instruction in righteousness" to the precise cases of just application. The *visitation of the sick* also, in the exercise of Christian sympathy, is of the highest importance to the probationer for the Ministry. Lessons are learned here, that could never be learned in the study. *There* the importance of the Gospel may be described or contemplated— *here* it is realized. *There* recollections may be digested with seriousness and accuracy of the vanity of the world, the nearness and prospects of eternity, the danger of delay, the blessedness of preparation, the deceitfulness of the heart, the power of Satan, the grace and love of the Saviour ; *here* the scenes are before the eye. Oh ! how much " better is it to go to the house of mourning than to the house of feasting !"[2] How important is the observant study of the

---

[1] 1 Tim. iii. 10, with Acts vi. 3. [1] Eccles. vii. 2.

sick chamber! How responsible is a frequent attendance upon it! How fruitful are the instructions connected with it! How varied and direct their bearing upon every department of public and private Ministration! Many have been trained for important usefulness in the Church by frequent, and, in many instances, painful attendance, upon this school of instruction.[1]

The Ministry is not (like some branches of natural science,) a work of contemplation, but of active, anxious, devoted, employment. The spirit, business, and delight of doing good must therefore form an essential part of Preparation for the work. It would be well indeed, if the disciple of the Ministry was never obliged to say—'perdidi diem.' It would probably be wise to act as much as possible upon system grounded upon a deep sense of personal neglect, strengthened by incessant prayer, and maintained by a course of persevering effort. Let him begin with his own family. Let him place their individual cases before him for distinct consideration and prayer; then pass on to neighbours, friends, societies, with which he may be more or less connected, and with all of whom his connection is most responsible. The diligent cultivation of the most contracted sphere will furnish abundant employ for his exertions. There are neighbours to be instructed—the sick to be visited —the young to be won over to the ways of God. Opportunities daily press before him, which are as "the price in the hands of a fool that hath no heart" to improve them: but which to him are treasures of inestimable price, and talents of most solemn account. The circle of influence, and the field of opportunity, will probably extend in proportion to the pains bestowed upon them; while, even within the smallest limits, there will be sufficient exercise of faith, prayer, and labour to serve the great purpose of Ministerial preparation; and "he that is faithful in that which is least, will be faithful also in much."[2]

The present subject suggests the remark, that a very rapid transition from the studies of the University to the services of the Sanctuary, does not appear desirable. At least, where these studies have been vigorously pursued, surely some interval of active (*not monastic*) retirement is needed to divert the mind from its former

---

[1] 'One of the best universities, and one far too much unvisited, is the retired apartment of suffering poverty, the cottage or the garret of the afflicted; and one of the best lectures in divinity, and most fruitful of Christian conferences, is conversation on the things of God with those "poor of this world," whom "God hath chosen rich in faith." Many a Minister has there first learned the lesson of saving knowledge for his own soul, and thence has carried the best lessons, which he could give to his people.' *Bickersteth's Christian Student*, p. 37.
[2] Luke xvi. 10.

course into a more observant and consecrated habit of action. The schools of Plato and Newton discipline the mind into most useful Ministerial habits, and furnish many lessons of instruction; but their general influence is far too remote for immediate practical purposes. They supply no *direct* materials, whether of observation or of experience, for the rudiments of the Ministry. A preparatory course of probation upon a spiritual system, would be a most valuable appendage to our National Establishment. In defect of this advantage, an interval of inspection or initiation into the routine of the work under the superintendence of a judicious Pastor, might prove a commencing era of Ministerial fruitfulness. The opportunities of learning would form the best preparation for teaching. Converse with experienced and exercised Christians would offer many advantages.[1] The habit of religious conversation would contribute, even more than private study, to the enlargement of the mind; and much would be acquired in this field of observation and incipient engagements, which no other medium could adequately supply.[2]

Experience enables the writer to speak upon this subject with decision. From this initiatory system (during a short residence in a country village under the affectionate instruction of a venerable relative,[3]) he conceives himself to have gained his first interest in this hallowed and blessed work, and sufficient insight into its diversified character and solemn obligations, to acknowledge a debt of gratitude to the end of his course.

Upon the whole, it is most important to mark the combination of these three Sections of Ministerial preparation—Study, Prayer, and Exercise. The omission of one of these, whichever it may be, weakens the practical influence of the rest. *Study* furnishes the materials—*Prayer* sanctifies them—*Exercise* makes a suitable distributive application of them to the several cases brought before us. Nor let them be supposed to be necessary for the probationer

[1] Amongst which Dr. Doddridge enumerates—1. Increase to our own stock of knowledge: 2. Excitement to our own spirits: 3. The conciliation of respect among our people: 4. The forming of an experimental strain of preaching. See his Lectures on Preaching.

[2] President Edwards remarks in his Diary,—' More than ever convinced of the usefulness of religious conversation. I find by conversing on natural philosophy, I gain knowledge abundantly faster, and see the reason of things much clearer than in private study. Wherefore, resolved earnestly to seek at all times for religious conversation, and for those persons that I can with profit, delight, and freedom, so converse with.' Works, i. 25.

[3] The late Rev. Dr. Bridges, Vicar of Willoughby, Warwickshire. 'Recommend this to Henry,'—was Mr. Richmond's earnest dying counsel respecting his son—'as the very best preparation for the Ministry. Tell him, his poor father learnt his most valuable lessons for the Ministry, and his most useful experience in religion, in the poor man's cottage.' Life, pp. 602, 603.

only. The Christian Minister will realize their value and their fruitful advantage throughout every department of his work.

But let every prospective view of the Ministry realize it as *an absorbing work*—as a high and holy vocation; involving results, which eternity alone can disclose, and therefore demanding the entire consecration of health, time, energy, and life itself to the accomplishment of its vast designs. If the soul be really engrossed with the mighty project of "saving souls from death," and *instrumentally* fixing them in the Redeemer's crown—how will every other object fade as a mere transient emotion—how will this great work of Preparation deepen in the sense of the responsibility! The one self-annihilating desire will be, that, whether our course be long or short—in joy or sorrow—in honour or dishonour—"we may so labour, that we may be accepted"[1] of our Gracious Master.

[1] 2 Cor. v. 9.

PART II.

GENERAL CAUSES OF THE WANT OF SUCCESS IN THE CHRISTIAN MINISTRY.

THE prophet's complaint—"Who hath believed our report?"[1] —has applied to every successive Ministry in the Church. It was echoed in reference even to the Ministry of Him, who "spake as never man spake;" who retained a listening multitude hanging upon his lips, and "wondering at the gracious words that proceeded out of his mouth."[2] It was again repeated under the Apostolic dispensation, clothed as it was "with the demonstration of the Spirit and with power."[3] And it has ever since been expressive of the experience of faithful labourers in the Lord's harvest. A young Minister indeed—speaking his message from the feeling of a full heart, and without an accurate calculation of the cost—may anticipate a cordial conviction and reception of the truth, as the almost immediate result. But painful experience will soon correct such unwarranted expectations. The power of Satan, the current of sin, and the course of this world—all combine to impress our work with the character of a special conflict. But, as complaint should lead to inquiry (and surely no inquiry can be more important), we will proceed to mark a few of the more general causes, that operate unfavourably upon our work.

[1] Isa. liii. 1.   [2] John vii. 37, 38.   [3] Rom. x. 16.

CHAPTER I.

THE SCRIPTURAL WARRANT AND CHARACTER OF MINISTE-
RIAL SUCCESS—TOGETHER WITH THE SYMPTOMS OF WANT
OF SUCCESS.

A FEW remarks upon these preliminary topics will introduce the
discussion of the general subject.

I. It may be laid as the ground of our inquiry—*that the warrant of Ministerial success is sure.* This indeed is involved in
the character of our work, while it supplies the spring to diligence
and perseverance in it.[1] In the spiritual, as in the temporal harvest, the field is prepared for the reaper's sickle. The providential
dispensations, also, appointing to the several labourers their work,
have the same security of successful results[2]—grounded—not upon
any efforts of human wisdom, zeal, or suasion, but upon the "word
for ever settled in heaven." Indeed every fertilizing shower is the
renewed symbol and pledge of the Divine promise.[3] Thus fruitfulness ever attended the labours of the Old Testament Ministers.[4]
It was the end of the ordination of the first Christian Ministers.[5]
It is the seal affixed to Ministerial devotedness.[6] The terms of the
promise are most express.[7] The day of Pentecost exhibited a large
display of its faithfulness;[8] and the apostles ever afterwards (whether preaching to persecuting Jews, or to blind idolaters) found the
same seal of their apostleship,[9] so that, wherever the Gospel was
sent, and so long as it was continued, the work of success invariably proceeded.

Now, as bearing the same commission, we have the same warrant of success—the sure foundation of "the word of the Lord,"
which "endureth for ever." The Divine Sovereignty (to which
we would bow with the most implicit and adoring subjection) is
the righteous government of a faithful God. We must not therefore place his sovereignty in opposition to his faithfulness. A measure of success is assured to our work. Some seed shall fall on the
good ground, as well as by the way-side, or upon the stony or

[1] See Luke i. 17.   [2] Acts xviii. 9, 10.   [3] See Isa. lv. 10, 11.
[4] See Mal. ii. 6. Compare Jer. xxiii. 22.   [5] See John xv. 16.
[6] See 1 Tim. iv. 16.   [7] Matt. xviii. 20.   [8] Acts ii. 37—47.
[9] At Antioch, Acts xi. 21; xiii. 48. Philippi, xvi. 14, 34. Thessalonica, xvii. 4, 5.
Athens, 32—34. Corinth, xviii. 8. 1 Cor. xi. 2. 2 Cor. iii. 1—3. Ephesus, xix. 17—
20. Rome, xxviii. 24. The edification of the Churches, xvi. 4, 5.

thorny soil.[1] " There shall" at least " be an *handful* of corn in
the earth on the top of the mountains."[2] The purpose is beyond
all the powers of earth and hell to defeat—"All that the Father
giveth me *shall come* to me."[3] The promise is sealed to the exercise of faith ; though the distribution of it *in measure* is often
marked by an unsearchable, but infinitely wise and gracious, appointment.

II. In marking the specific *character of this warranted success*,
we may observe that *visible success is various.* There are some
that plant—others that water;[4] some that lay the foundation—
others that build upon it.[5] Some are designed for immediate—
some for ulterior, work. Yet all have their testimony and acceptance in the Lord's own time and way. Success is not limited to
the work of conversion.[6] Where therefore the Ministry fails to
convert, we may still be assured, that it convinces, reproves, exhorts,
enlightens, or consoles, some one in some measure at all times. It
never " returns to God void," when delivered in the simplicity of
faith ; nor will it, under the most unpromising circumstances, fail
of accomplishing his unchangeable purpose.

But we must remember also, that present success is not *always
visible.* Apparent must not be the measure of the real result.
There is often an under-current of piety, which cannot be brought
to the surface. There may be solid work advancing under ground,
without any sensible excitement;[7] as we observe the seed that
produces the heaviest grain, lies the longest in the earth. We are
not always the best judges of the results of our Ministry. Mr. Scott
thus encourages a clergyman from his own Ministerial experience :
'My prevalent opinion is, *that you are useful, but do not see the
effect.* Even at Ravenstone, I remember complaining in a New
Year's Sermon, that for a whole twelvemonth I had seen no fruit
of my preaching ; yet it appeared within the course of the next
twelvemonth, that not less than ten or twelve had been brought to
" consider their ways" during that discouraging year ; besides others, I trust, that I did not know of.'[8] The sick and death-bed often
gladden our heart with the manifestation of the hidden fruit of our
work. And though something is graciously brought out for our
encouragement, yet much more probably is concealed to exercise
our diligence, and from a wise and tender regard to our besetting

---

[1] Matt. xiii. 3—8.   [2] Psalm. lxxii. 16.   [3] John vi. 37.
[4] 1 Cor. iii. 6.   [5] Ibid. 10.
[6] St. Paul longed to impart to his Roman and Thessalonian Churches spiritual establishment and consolation. Rom. i. 11, 12. 1 Thess. iii. 10.
[7] See Mark iv. 26. Luke xvii. 24.   [8] Scott's Life, p. 387.

temptations. Indeed who of us may not detect the principle of self mingling itself alike with depression and exultation, greatly needing our Master's rebuke for our more valuable effectiveness? Under all our trials therefore, we must be careful, that no present apparent failure weaken our assurance of the ultimate success of faithful and diligent perseverance.

Symptoms of success are also frequently mistaken. They are at best but doubtful signs—if our people crowd to hear the word[1]—if they love our persons[2]—admire our discourses[3]—and are brought to a general confession of sinfulness,[4] or to a temporary interest in our message.[5] Nor must we on the other hand too hastily conclude upon their apparent want of diligence in the means of grace, or of interest in our parochial system. Family hindrances or outward crosses may restrain the improvement of Christian privileges. The want of tact, the influence of retired habits, or the necessary demands of the domestic sphere, may impede communications with our plans; so that often "the kingdom of God," may be established in real "power," yet with little of outward "observation." The complaint of inefficiency may therefore sometimes be unwarranted, as the disappointment of a too sanguine mind; as the failure of efforts, calculated upon in our own wisdom, and attempted in our own strength; or the blast of expectations, indulged without due consideration of a Scriptural basis, or of individual or local difficulties.

Adverting also to subordinate benefits—"Our manifestation of the truth, commends itself to every man's conscience in the sight of God."[6] Here is a Christian standard of morals opposed to the principles of the world. Here is a Divine rule taking cognizance of the heart, charging guilt upon numberless items that before had passed as harmless, and thus laying the foundation for more evangelical conviction. Here is therefore the restraint and counteraction of much positive evil, and a large infusion of wholesome moral obligation, throughout the mass. Besides—as regards the Gospel—the constant dwelling on the Saviour's name and work familiarizes him with our people, as a refuge, a friend in trouble. It is no small advantage in the storm to know where to seek for safe anchorage; and who can tell how many have found such a refuge in distress from the recollections of the Gospel hitherto neglected, but now applied with sovereign power to their hearts?

More directly also—Ministerial success must be viewed, as *ex-*

---

[1] See Matt. iii. 5.   [2] Gal. iv. 14—16.   [3] Ezek. xxxiii. 32.
[4] Matt. iii. 6, 7.   [5] John v. 35.   [6] 2 Cor. iv. 2.

tending beyond present appearances. The seed may lie under the clods till we lie there, *and then spring up.* Of the prophets of old "that saying was true ; One soweth, and another reapeth ;" they sowed the seed, and the Apostles reaped the harvest. As our Lord reminded them—"Other men laboured, and ye are entered into their labours." And is it no ground of comfort, that our work may be the seed-time of a future harvest ? Or, should we neglect to sow, because we may not reap the harvest? Shall we not share the joy of the harvest, even though we be not the immediate reapers of the field ?[1] Is it not sufficient encouragement to "cast our bread upon the waters," that " we shall find it *after many days ?*" ' In the morning" (as the wise man exhorts us,) "sow thy seed, and in the evening withhold not thine hand; for thou knowest not whether shall prosper, either this or that ; or whether they both shall be alike good."[2]

It has been admirably observed on this subject—' In order to prevent perpetual disappointment, we must learn to extend our views. To seek for the real harvest produced by spiritual labours only in their immediate and visible results, would be not less absurd, than to take our measure of infinite space from that limited prospect, which the mortal eye can reach ; or to estimate the never-ending ages of eternity by a transitory moment of present time—It often happens, that God withholds his blessing for a time, in order that, when the net is cast in " on the right side," it may be clearly seen, that " the multitude of fishes" inclosed are of the Lord's giving ; lest men should attribute their success to a wrong cause, and should " sacrifice unto their own net, and burn incense unto their own drag."[3] We may add to this the recollection of the extensive results from " the day of small things." Only two souls appear as the immediate fruit of the vision of " the man of Macedonia ;" but how fruitful was the ultimate harvest in the flourishing Churches of that district ![4] Our plain and cheering duty is therefore to go forward—to scatter the seed—to believe and wait.

[1] See John iv. 36—38.   [2] Eccles. xi, 1, 6.
[3] Bishop of Winchester on the Ministerial Character of Christ, pp. 544—550. (2nd Edit.) Thus Calvin remarks on the parable of the seed cast into the ground—' Christ seemeth earnestly to apply his speech to the Ministers of his word, lest they should wax cold in their offices, because their fruit doth not presently appear. Therefore he setteth before them the husbandmen to follow, which in a hope of a time to reap do "cast the seed into the earth," and are not vexed with greediness which never is at quiet ; but they go to rest, and rise again; that is, they do ordinarily apply their daily labour, and refresh themselves with their nightly rest, until the corn wax ripe at length in the due time. Therefore though the seed of the word lie hid for a time, as if it were choked or drowned, yet Christ commandeth the godly teachers to be of good comfort, lest distrust should abate their diligence.' On Mark iv. 26.
[4] See Acts xvi. With Epist. to Philippians and Thessalonians.

Yet must there be expectancy as well as patience. The warrant of success is assured—not only as regards an outward reformation—but a spiritual change of progressive and universal influence. The fruit of Ministerial labour is not indeed always visible in its symptoms, nor immediate in its results, nor proportioned to the culture. Faith and patience will be exercised—sometimes severely so. But after a pains-taking, weeping seed-time, we shall bring our sheaves with rejoicing, and lay them upon the altar of God, " that the offering up of them might be acceptable, being sanctified by the Holy Ghost."[1] Meanwhile we must beware of saying— " Let him make speed, and hasten his work that we may see it."[2] The measure and the time are with the Lord. We must let him alone with his own work. Ours is the care of service—His is the care of success.[3] " 'The Lord of the harvest" must determine, when, and what, and where the harvest shall be.

III. But notwithstanding this justly warranted expectation, the *want of Ministerial success* is most extensively and mournfully felt. We are sometimes ready to believe, and to complain, that none labour so unfruitfully as ourselves. Men of the world expect their return in some measure proportioned to their labour. Alas! with us, too often, " is our strength labour and sorrow ;" and at best attended with a very scanty measure of effect; and we are compelled to realize the awful sight of immortal souls perishing under our very eye ; dead to the voice of life and love, and madly listening to the voice that plunges them into perdition !

It may be well to state a few of the most decisive symptoms of this unfruitfulness. When our public services are unprofitable ;[4] when " iniquity abounds," and the mass of our people continue in an impenitent and ungodly state ;[5] when there is an unconcern among us for the honour and cause of God :[6] when there is a general want of appetite for the " sincere milk of the word,"[7] and the public worship of the Sabbath, and the weekly lecture (if there be any,) are but thinly attended ; when there are no instances of conversion in our Sunday Schools, and but few of our young people are drawn into the " ways of pleasantness and peace ;" when the children of deceased Christian parents, instead of being added spiritually to the Church, continue in and of the world :[8] when small addition[9] is made to the select flock, who *truly* commemorate the

[1] Psalm cxxvi. 5, 6. Rom. 15, 16.   [2] Isa. v. 19.
[3] In cælo cathedram habet, qui corda movet. Augustine.
[4] Isa. lxiv. 7. Matt. xiii. 14, 15.   [5] Isa. lix. 1—15. Jer. v. xxiii. 10, &c.
[6] Hag. i. 4—10.   [7] Numb. xxi. 5. 2 Tim. iv. 3.
[8] 2 Chron. xviii. 1; xix. 2. Ezra. ix. 2.   [9] Acts ii. 47.

death of their Saviour in the Holy Sacrament—these and similar appearances may well agitate the question with most anxious concern—" Is the Lord among us or not ?"[1] Symptoms so dark and discouraging loudly call for increasing earnestness of supplication —" Oh ! that thou wouldest rend the heavens ; that thou wouldest come down, that the mountains might flow down at thy presence ! O Lord, revive thy work !"[2]

Among the more general causes of this failure, we may mark the withholding of Divine influence—the enmity of the natural heart—the power of Satan—local hindrances—and the want of clearness in the Ministerial call. Each of these will now come before us.

CHAPTER II.

THE WITHHOLDING OF DIVINE INFLUENCE, THE MAIN CAUSE OF THE WANT OF MINISTERIAL SUCCESS.[3]

THE Scriptural warrant leads us to entertain high expectations from the labours of the Christian Ministry. And yet, in every sphere of labour, these bright prospects are more or less overcast ; as if a sanguine temperament had unduly heightened our anticipations. Much cultivation, as we have lately observed, is sometimes bestowed upon the soil with little proportionate success. The same means and instruments, that had been formerly productive of important benefits, fail in their accustomed effect. Now who would cultivate his lands at considerable and disappointed cost, without inquiring into the causes of the failure of his just expectations? And must not we ask—What is wanting to give effect to that order of means, the power of which has been often exhibited, and which we know to be constituted in the purpose of God for the renovation of the world ? Mr. Cecil has remarked—' There is a manifest want of spiritual influence in the Ministry of the present day. I feel it in my own case, and I see it in that of others.'[4] This remark sufficiently explains the symptoms of that barrenness which prevails among us. For not more needful are the influences of heaven to fertilize the soil, and promote vegeta-

[1] Exodus xvii. 7.   [2] Isaiah lxiv. 1.   Hab. iii. 2.
[3] For some striking views on this subject—see Dr. Chalmers' Sermon on the necessity of the Spirit to give effect to the Preaching of the Gospel.
[4] Cecil's Remains.

tion, than is this heavenly influence to give quickening power to the word. In vain therefore do we plough and sow, if the Lord " command the clouds, that they rain no rain "[1] upon the field of the spiritual husbandry.

Let us advert to *Scriptural testimony.* To this source is traced the want of effect produced by the first promulgation of the will of God, (confirmed as it was by signs and wonders) together with the unbelief of Israel in the prophetic report, and even in the Ministry of the Son of God.[2] Our Lord insists upon the necessity of Divine influence in order to come to him,[3] and to abide in him.[4] The want of this influence rendered his public Ministry comparatively inefficient. Though his doctrine was from God—though his character was perfect—and though daily miracles attested his mission, yet little appears to have been done; while Peter, a poor fisherman, endued with this almighty power, becomes the instrument of converting more under a single sermon, than probably his Master had done throughout his whole Ministry.[5] The other Apostles preached both in collective and individual instances, with the same "demonstration of the Spirit and power." At Antioch, "*the hand of the Lord was with them,* and *a great number believed and turned unto the Lord.*"[6] Lydia " attended unto the things that were spoken of Paul—not because Paul was an eloquent preacher, or she an attentive hearer (though in this disposition alone can the blessing be expected)—but because "*the Lord opened her heart.*"[7] Thus does the uniform tenor of the sacred records mark the power of the Spirit, as the seal and confirmation of the word, and as the life-giving influence, diffused throughout the church, from the time that the first lively stone was laid upon the foundation of God. And therefore the withholding of this blessing must necessarily be attended with proportionate painful symptoms of Ministerial inefficiency.

The *reason of the thing* confirms this view of the subject. Admitting the Scriptural statements of man's natural condition—

---

[1] Isaiah v. 6.   [2] See Deut. xxix. 4, 5. Isaiah liii. 1. John xii. 39, 40.
[3] See John vi. 44, 65.   [4] Ibid. xv. 1—5.
[5] Acts ii. See this accounted for John vii. 39; and indeed promised John xiv. 12. 'I once said to myself in the foolishness of my heart, ' What sort of a sermon must that have been, which was preached by St. Peter, when three thousand souls were converted at once!' What sort of sermon! Such as other sermons. There is nothing to be found in it extraordinary. The effect was not produced by his eloquence, but by the mighty power of God present with his Word. It is in vain to attend one Minister after another and to have sermon after sermon, unless we pray that the Holy Spirit may accompany his Word.'—Cecil's Remains. Who will not join with a pious old writer in ardent longing for another Pentecost! 'O si hisce pessimis et ultimis temporibus consimili rore vespertino (ut illi matutino) sicca Ecclesiæ Christi pomeria irrigarentur ac fæcundarentur!' T. Hall's Sal. Terræ.
[6] Acts xi. 21.   [7] Ibid. xvi. 14.

" dead in trespasses and sins "—" having his understanding darkened "—his mind the very principle of enmity to the truth even under its most attractive form—and his stony heart insensible to its blessings[1]—how palpable is the need of power from on high ! ' Can a well-composed oration,' (Charnock asks) ' setting out all the advantages of life and health, raise a dead man, or cure a diseased body? You may as well exhort a blind man to behold the sun, and prevail as much. No man ever yet imagined, that the strewing a dead body with flowers would raise it to life ; no more can the urging a man spiritually dead with eloquent motives ever make him to open his eyes, and to stand upon his feet. " The working of mighty power " is a title too high for the capacity of mere moral exhortations. A mere suasion does not confer a strength, but supposes it in a man ; for he is only persuaded to use the power which he hath already.'[2] The clearest instructions may furnish the understanding, but they have no power to sway the will, except to what is suitable and connatural to its native suggestions and habits. Whenever therefore the gospel successfully influences the heart, it is "not by might, nor by power, but by my Spirit, saith the Lord of Hosts."[3]

And does not *observation and experience* add further confirmation to this subject ? Do we not know accomplished and devoted Ministers, who are less honoured in their work than others of their brethren of far inferior qualifications ? And do we not find differences of effect under the same Ministry, and even under the same sermons, which can only be explained by the sovereign dispensation of divine influence ? Has not personal experience shewn us, that the same motives operate in the same service with very different measures of influence ? And do we not realize the same difference in our Ministerial experience—in our pastoral as well as in our pulpit work ; that sometimes a single sentence is clothed with Almighty power—at other times it is only the feeble breath of a worm ? ' Have you never' (Charnock again asks in his usual terseness) ' discoursed with some profane loose fellow so pressingly, that he seemed to be shaken out of his excuses for his sinful course, yet not shaken out of his sin : that you might as soon have persuaded the tide at full sea to retreat, or a lion to change his nature, as have overcome him by all your arguments ? So that it is not the faint breath of man, or the rational consideration of the mind, that are able to do this work, without the mighty

[1] Compare Eph. ii. 1; iv. 18; Acts xxvi. 18. Rom. viii. 7. John iii. 19, 20. &c.
[2] Charnock on Regeneration, Works, vol. ii. 200.   [3] Zechariah iv. 6.

pleadings and powerful operations of that great Paraclete or Advocate, the Spirit, to alter the temple of the soul.'[1] This, then, is the main source of Ministerial success. "Until the Spirit be poured upon us from on high,"[2] the wilderness, notwithstanding the most diligent cultivation, must remain a wilderness still.

But why is this promised blessing[3] withheld?—"Even so, Father; for so it seemeth good in thy sight."[4] Yet we must not slumber in acquiescence without self-inquiry. Do we fervently seek and cherish this influence? Do we actively "stir up the gift of God which is within us?"[5] Above all, does our pulpit set out that full exhibition of our Divine Master, which alone commands this heavenly blessing?[6] The encouragement of prayer and faith are always the same. God is indeed absolutely sovereign in the distribution of his blessing; but by his command to seek, he has pledged himself, that we shall not seek in vain. Having freely promised, he will faithfully perform. Let all means be used in diligence, but in dependence—in self-denial, but in self-renunciation. Let not ministers be unduly exalted among their people. We are only instruments "*by whom* they believe,"[7] and a dependence on our labour may provoke the grand Agent—who "giveth not his glory to another"—to wither the most effective Ministry, that these idolaters may "know that we are but men." We may be reduced to ask—"Where is the Lord God of Elijah?"[8]—who can accomplish more by one feeble sentence from the feeblest instrument, than we can do without him by the most powerful preaching.

---

[1] Charnock on Regeneration, vol. ii. 201. 'Alas!' (exclaims Mr. Howe) 'what would preaching do, if we could suppose it never so general, while the Spirit of the living God restrains and withholds his influences! We may as well attempt to batter strong walls with the breath of our mouths, as to do good upon men's souls without the Spirit of God.' Sermon xiv. on the Work of the Spirit in the Church. Works, v. 356. 'Spiritus sanctus operetur oportet intrinsecus, ut valeat aliquid medicina, quæ adhibetur extrinsecus; nisi hic cordi adsit audientis, otiosus est sermo loquentis.' Augustine.

[2] Isaiah xxxii. 15. 'In preaching,'—said Mr. Cecil—'I have no encouragement, but the belief of a continued Divine operation. To bring a man to love God—to love the law of God, while it condemns him—to loathe himself before God—to tread the earth under his feet—to hunger and thirst after God in Christ—*with man this is impossible.* But God has said—*It shall be done*—and bids me go forth and preach, that *by me, as his instrument, he may effect these great ends: and therefore I go.*' Remains.

[3] Compare Isaiah xliv. 3—5. Joel ii. 28.   [4] Matt. xi. 26.   [5] 2 Tim. i. 6.

[6] John xvi. 45, with Acts ii. 36, 37, x. 43, 44.   [7] 1 Cor. iii. 5—7.   [8] 2 Kings ii. 14.

CHAPTER III.

THE ENMITY OF THE NATURAL HEART A MAIN CAUSE OF THE WANT OF MINISTERIAL SUCCESS.

THE office of the Christian Ministry might seem to command a successful issue of the work. It is "the Ministry of reconciliation:" where the offended party stoops to make the first overtures of peace, and sends his ambassadors to "beseech by them," and pray the rebels "in his stead—Be ye reconciled to God."[1] Such a display of disinterested condescension, infinite humility, and compassionate tenderness, might have been expected to give resistless efficacy to the message. The rich fruits of everlasting love are brought to the door of those, who are most deeply interested in it, and whose need of the blessing is inexpressibly great. Such a promulgation of mercy, given to men in guileless ignorance and urgent need, would meet with a ready and universal welcome. But here it meets with a resisting medium. The avenues of approach are barred against its entrance, and the success is limited within comparatively narrow bounds.

By the terms of the commission, it is "preached to every creature;"[2] but the disproportionate effect reminds us of the solemn and sententious declaration—" Many be called, but few chosen."[3] If indeed we were " as many, which corrupt the word of God"—if we would lower its requisitions to a worldly standard, or to a corrupt heart, we should "have our reward" (purchased indeed at an infinite cost[4]) in the praise of men. But if " as of sincerity, as of God, in the sight of God, we speak in Christ:"[5] renouncing the hidden things of dishonesty ; not walking in craftiness, nor handling the word of God deceitfully; but by manifestation of the truth, commending ourselves to every man's conscience in the sight of God,"[6] —we must not wonder to hear it repeated—" I hate him, for he doth not prophecy good concerning me, but evil."[7] Nor is this opposition confined to the world—so called. In the professing church —a revulsion against the truth of God *as a whole*—such as Mr. Scott found manifested in rejecting the practical enforcement of Christian doctrine[8]—marks the same principle of resistance. And

---

[1] 2 Cor. v. 18—20.   [2] Mark xvi. 15.   [3] Matt. xx. 16.
[4] See Gal. i. 7—10.   [5] 2 Cor. ii. 17.   [6] Ibid iv. 2.
[7] 1 Kings xxii. 8.   [8] Life, p. 232—237.

indeed 'whoever pricks the conscience of his hearers closely, without producing repentance, will soon find them either absentees from his ministry, or unwilling listeners, if not open opponents.'[1] Thus our whole course is a struggle against the mighty current of sin— flowing out of that restless bias of the natural heart, which upon the highest authority is declared to be "enmity against God."[2]

This hindrance therefore to the reception of the Gospel must not be placed to the Minister's account. Ignorance, eccentricity, inconsistency, want of conciliation and address, will indeed be *an occasion* of calling forth this enmity. A defective exhibition of the spirit of the cross greatly aggravates the offence of the cross. But it must be remembered, that the Ministration of the Gospel from an angel's mouth would stir up the natural principle of degenerate man. What could be conceived more attractive than the combination of dignity, humility, patience, and love, that marked the Ministry of the Son of God? Yet was it universally despised and rejected. His doctrine was most offensive to the natural prejudices of the unhumbled heart. His general statements were listened to with the interest of curiosity, and the desire of "hearing some new thing;" but their personal application to the consciences of his hearers—the certain reproach of his cross—the relinquishment of all that was held dear for his service—the prostrate submission required for the reception of his truth—all combined to produce the "murmuring among themselves;" the complaint of the intolerable "hardness of his sayings," and the resolution to abandon their temporary profession.[3]

The innate opposition, existing between the substance and the objects of our Ministry, offers therefore a material impediment to our success. We speak to those, whose attention is already preoccupied, whose affections have been long pre-engaged, and whose "hearts are hardened through the deceitfulness of sin." The truth therefore never comes into contact with a sincere and honest heart. Enmity is the concentrated essence of man's depravity. It is at once the cause and the effect of that moral or spiritual darkness, which shuts out the entrance of light, and offers difficulties to the process of "enlightening the eyes of the understanding," unconquerable by any force short of heavenly influence. The power that "slays the enmity," opens the heart to the perception, obedience, and love of the truth, and to a full possession of the inestimable blessings of our office.

[1] Bishop of Winchester's Ministerial Character of Christ, p. 552, 553.
[2] Romans viii. 7.
[3] John vi. 24—66.

CHAPTER IV.

THE POWER OF SATAN A MAIN HINDRANCE TO MINISTERIAL SUCCESS.

THE active power and unsearchable subtlety of Satan are always directed against the Christian Ministry, as the engine "mighty through God to the pulling down of his strong holds."[1] This is his grand point of attack upon the Redeemer's kingdom. Indeed we could scarcely expect, that "the devouring lion"[2] would quietly submit to have his prey wrested from his teeth; or that "the strong man armed"[3] would resign his spoils without a severe conflict.

The nature and extent of his unceasing opposition are less difficult to conceive than accurately to define. It meets us however in every sphere. *In the world* his influence is palpable, in a general listless inattention to the word of God, and an immediate transition from thence into the very vortex of the world[4]—in the awful blindness of men to the glory of the Saviour,[5] in their thoughtless unconcern for eternity,[6] and in his captivating dominion over such vast multitudes,[7] unable to "deliver their souls," or to say—"Is there not a lie in my right hand ?"[8] 'The course of this world' (or what is elsewhere called "the lust of the flesh, the lust of the eye, and the pride of life"[9]) is distinctly identified with the power of "the spirit which now worketh in the children of disobedience."[10] The same enemy stirs up the natural enmity of the heart to the followers of Christ, and employs with incessant malignity tongues, pens, and influence against the cause of God[11]—thus illustrating and sustaining his Scriptural character—as the "prince and the god of this world"—"the father of lies,"—"the old serpent, which deceiveth the whole world."[12]

In the professing church—this restless enemy works his artful leaven with "all deceivableness of unrighteousness ;" covering his spiritual wiles with some new and pleasing doctrines, adapted to the taste of the times ; and thus poisoning the bread of life by the adulteration of man's devices. His subtlety is peculiarly marked in the accommodation of the forms of deception to the different tem-

---

[1] 2 Cor. x. 4, 5. [2] 1 Peter v. 8. [3] Luke xi. 21, 22. [4] Matt. xiii. 19.
[5] 2 Cor. iv. 4. [6] Luke xi. 21. [7] 2 Tim. ii. 26. [8] Isa. xliv. 20.
[9] 1 John ii. 16. [10] Ephes. ii. 2. [11] Compare Gen. iii. 15. Rev. xii. 17.
[12] John xii. 31. 2 Cor. iv. 4. John viii. 44. Rev. xii. 9.

peraments of his victims. Carnal security suits with the world, and succeeds to the utmost of his desires in keeping "his goods in peace.". But such schemes would be ineffectual with a nominal recognition of serious religion. In the Church he "transforms himself into an angel of light"[1]—exhibiting either the attractive idol of self-righteousness—or that most inveterate form of antichrist—the dependence on the profession of a pure doctrine.

The Apostle intimates, that the general symptoms of Ministerial ineffectiveness may be traced to this source.[2]   And indeed his active influence is discoverable in every point of detail.   The explanation of the growth of the tares among the wheat, is—"An enemy hath done this."[3]   The serpent, that beguiled Eve though his "subtlety" still "corrupts" the minds of the weak "from the simplicity that is in Christ."[4]   The Ministerial hindrances from divisions and want of love among professors,[5] and the successful opposition sometimes made to schemes of Ministerial usefulness—are traced to the secret operation of the same active cause.[6]   The hypocrisy of professors within the Church,[7]—or their apostacy from her communion ;[8] all the successive vicissitudes of her history ; all the drawbacks to the full energies of our work—flow from this "fountain" of evil, continually "sending forth bitter waters."

Individual experience discloses the constant exercise of the same agency.   To this source the Christian traces his subtle workings of unbelief[9]—his wanderings of heart in prayer[10]—his occasional indulgence of self-confidence,[11] spiritual pride,[12] and worldliness[13]—the injection of blasphemous thoughts[14]—the power of evil tempers[15]—and the general commission of sin ;[16]—all which, according to their prevalency, are positive hindrances to the holy and blessed influence of our labours.   The appalling conflict between the powers of darkness and light is therefore exhibited before us —" the god of this world blinding the eyes of them that believe not"—while the Ministry of the gospel exhibits ".Christ Jesus the Lord," as the medium, by which "God, who commandeth the light to shine out of darkness, shines into the hearts" of his people with the revelation of his "glory."[17]   Thus, while the active agency of the Evil Spirit by his direct and instrumental operation,[18] is counteracting the progress of our work, we may be said indeed to

---

[1] 2 Cor. xi. 14.   [2] 1 Thess. iii. 5. .   [3] Matt. xiii. 24—28.   [4] 2 Cor. xi. 3.
[5] Ibid. ii. 10.   [6] 1 Thess. ii. 18.   [7] Acts v. 1—5.   [8] Luke xxii. 3.   Rev. xii. 3, 4.
[9] Gen. iii. 1—3.   [10] Job i. 6.   [11] 1 Chron. xxi. 1.   Luke xxii. 31.
[12] 2 Cor. xii. 7.   [13] Matt. xvi. 23.   [14] Eph. vi. 16.   [15] Ibid. iv. 27.
[16] 1 John iii. 8.   [17] 2 Cor. iv. 6.
[18] 'Homines instrumentaliter, mundus materialiter, Satanas efficienter'—was the pithy distinction of an old writer.

" wrestle not against flesh and blood, but against principalities and powers, against the rulers of the darkness of this world, against spiritual wickedness in high places."[1]

CHAPTER V.

LOCAL HINDRANCES TO MINISTERIAL SUCCESS.

WE have already incidentally glanced at some of the main drawbacks upon the Christian Ministry ; and others in a more minute detail will hereafter come under consideration. Our present business is with those impediments, that depend not so much upon the personal or official character of the Minister, as upon extrinsic causes, connected with the circumstances of his individual sphere. Thus a town presents many hindrances, which in the same degree do not belong to the superintendence of a country parish. The moral impossibility of penetrating the dense mass of the population, and of insulating the several component parts, originates a want of that personal application of the word to individual consciences, which is so powerfully effective for the great purpose of the Pulpit. The course also of public instruction is necessarily of a more general complexion. The character and exercises of the Minister's own mind may indeed give an individual mould to his system ; but his want of particular acquaintance with his people must proportionably preclude the adaptation of his Ministry to the specialities of their respective cases. *Local habits and circumstances also* tend materially to counteract the direct power of our work. Large congregated bodies, (as in manufacturing districts) are usually most corrupting pests—" hand joining in hand ;" and " every man helping his neighbour " in the way of sin, " and saying to his brother—Be of good courage."[2] Then again—the state of trade in the parish—the population unemployed, or uncivilized, or distressed—these are matters that often affect our results. There are also *local hindrances* connected *with the constitution of the Ministry.* A co-partnership in the sacred work often excites most painfully the Corinthian heresy of a party spirit among the people. Mutual jealousies are fomented (which it is well if they do not reach the bosom of the labourers themselves.) Men " are puffed up for one against another;" they learn to "glory in men;" and with the highest advantages of a spiritual administration, their Pastors are constrained still to speak unto them not as unto spiritual, but as unto carnal, even as unto babes in Christ "walking as men."[1] The *rise and progress of various heresies* may also be strengthened by local combinations not immediately under our controul. The want of insight into the several departments of the flock in an extensive. sphere, gives occasion for the watchful enemy to cast in his leaven, which, with a deadly influence, threatens to "leaven the whole lump." The Ministrations of some of the most eminent servants of God[2] have suffered severely from this source; though it was probably as needful a trial of faith, patience, and humility in the midst of their successful energy, as was "the thorn in the flesh" to the great Apostle, to save him from the impending danger of being "exalted above measure."[3]

Other hindrances, also, of this local character, belong more immediately to the Ministry of the Establishment, and often act unfavourably even upon faithful and laborious exertions. The ground may have been pre-occupied by one or more of the organized systems of dissent, recognizing the grand principles of the Gospel, but under a form in many particulars opposed to the framework of our own system. This, under the most favourable circumstances, must be regarded as an evil;[4] inasmuch as the want of Christian unity diminishes proportionably from the native power of the Gospel. Even if the respective Ministers are men of forbearance and brotherly love, and in the true spirit of their commission lay far more stress upon their points of agreement than upon their points of difference—it is not likely, that the same spirit should universally spread through their congregations; and the defect of this mutual forbearance, often called forth by comparative trifles, reminds us in its baneful consequences—"how great a matter a little fire kindleth!"[5]

The faithful labourer may also find *many hindrances rooted in the soil,* before it passed under his hands for cultivation. The rank and luxuriant weed of profession may have choked the growth of much, that might otherwise have sprung up with a prospect of bearing "fruit unto perfection." He may suffer also from the effects of prejudice superadded to the natural enmity to

[1] See 1 Cor. i. iii. iv.
[2] Cecil's Life of Cadogan. (Works, i. 252.) Vaughan's Life of Robinson, pp. 188—195.
[3] 2 Cor. xii. 7.
[4] See some valuable remarks on this subject by Mr. Budd, in his work on Baptism, pp. 282, 283. Compare also Bickersteth's Christian Student, p. 290.
[5] James iii. 5.

the Gospel, arising from the inexperience, imprudence, or inconsistency of his predecessor.

Lay influence also, often hangs a weight upon the effectiveness of the work. Particular individuals in the parish, in the lowest or even the highest ranks, are a frequent bar to usefulness. The contempt also of the Sabbath—the predominant character of pleasure, dissipation, and the general inattention or opposition to religion in the heads of the parish—too often present a hostile front to our course of effort and instruction. And, where the influence of the higher classes is of a less decided character, or even where it is exercised on the side of the Church, yet it is rarely unattended with material drawbacks. The respect for religion and for the ordinances of God does not always regulate the arrangements of the house, the general style of appearance, or the deportment of the lower members of the household. It may also be not wholly divested of a love of power ; a reluctance to be controlled by spiritual restraints, or to depart from the indulgent course of neutrality, when a more full sway of influence on the side of the Gospel might incur inconvenience or reproach.

Now these hindrances, in their origin, are irrespective of personal responsibility, but most detrimental in their consequences. It would be obviously impossible to prescribe any specific course of procedure, applicable to every form of resistance. The general principles of the Ministry, well directed against the several points of attack, will be, however, of immense service in this warfare. The combined power of the diligence of faith, "the meekness of wisdom," and "the patience of hope"—if they do not wholly counteract the evil —will materially retard its aggressive operation. Nor are the difficulties attached to extensive spheres insurmountable. Much may be done—much has been done—by bending general systems to more minute applications. Methodized habits have been more effective under the greatest disadvantages, than an undisciplined course of exercise, assisted by much local superiority. District systems of visiting have enabled laborious ministers to pass over a wide extent of ground with far more particularity and fruitfulness. And above all, the wise superintendence of the great Head of the Church has been signally displayed in a suitable adaptation of his chosen instruments for their specific work. Men are not all alike qualified for all situations. But "he that holdeth the seven stars in his right hand,"[1] appoints unto each its place in the spiritual firmament, as shall be most suited for the honour of his name, for the

---

[1] Revelation ii. 1.

purpose of his will, and for the edification of his Church. The hindrances, however, to which we have alluded, must impede our progress ; so that our success will often consist, not so much in any *prominent* outward change in our sphere, as in the silent and effectual opposition to the current of evil ; in the raising up of a band of witnesses to co-operate with us in our labour ; and in the steady perseverance with which the ground is maintained in the midst of conflict and discouragement.

CHAPTER VI.

THE WANT OF A DIVINE CALL A MAIN CAUSE OF FAILURE IN THE CHRISTIAN MINISTRY.

WE may sometimes trace ministerial failure to the very threshold of the entrance into the work. Was the call to the sacred office clear in the order of the church, and according to the will of God ? This question bears with vast importance upon the subject. Where the call is manifest, the promise is assured.[1] But if we run unsent, our labours must prove unblest. Many, we fear, have never exercised their minds upon this inquiry. But do not we see the standing ordinance of the church written upon their unfruitful Ministrations—" I sent them not, nor commanded them ; *therefore they shall not profit this people at all, saith the Lord ?*"[2] The blast was not, that their doctrine was unsound, but that they preached unsent.

Under the old dispensation, intrusion into the priestly office was marked as the most dangerous presumption.[3] Nor is it a less direct act of usurpation to take unwarranted authority in the

---

[1] See Exod. iii. 10—12. Jer. i. 4—19.

[2] Jer. xxiii. 21, 32. Comp. Article xxiii. Luther's language is very strong—' Expecta vocantem; interim esto securus; imo si esses sapientior ipso Salomone et Daniele; tamen, nisi voceris, plus quam infernum fuge, ne verbum effundas. Si tui eguerit, vocabit te. Si non vocabit, non te rumpat scientia tua.—Nunquam enim Deus fortunat laborem eorum, qui non sunt vocati; et quanquam quædam salutaria afferant, tamen nihil ædificant. E regione, magna semper fecerunt, qui, Deo vocante, docuerunt.' Quoted in Sal Terræ, ut supra. Comp. Scott's Conti. of Milner, i. 156. ' I wish it were well considered by all clerks, what it is to run without being called or sent; and so to thrust one's self into the vineyard, without staying till God by his providence puts a piece of his work into his hands. This will give a man a vast ease in his thoughts, and a great satisfaction in all his labours, if he knows that no practices of his own, but merely the directions of providence, have put him in a post.' Burnet's Past. Care, ch. vii. ' The Ministry is a matter of pure grace and favour; who then will dare to enter into it without a Divine call? There is nothing in which a king would willingly be more absolute than in the choice of his Ministers. And shall we dare to contest, and take away this right from the King of kings?' Quesnel on Ephes. iii. 2. Col. i. 1.

[3] See Numb. xviii. 7. 2 Chron. xxvi. 16—20.

Church of Christ. Our great Head himself appeared with *delegated, not with self-commissioned authority.* Prophetically he had declared his call to his great work.[1] It was manifested to the world, at the commencement, as well as during the course of his public Ministry.[2] Often did he appeal to it as the credentials of his commission.[3] Those who "entered into the fold," without his authority, he stamps as "thieves and robbers;" and he only, who "entered in by the door" of his divine commission, "was the Shepherd of the sheep."[4]

The Scriptural terms of Ordination imply a direct controlling influence upon the agents.[5] The various illustrations also of the office tend to the same point. We cannot conceive of a herald—an ambassador—a steward—a watchman—a messenger—an angel—with self-constituted authority. The Apostle asks, with regard to the first of these—"How shall they preach, except they be sent?"[6] They may indeed preach without a mission, but not as the messengers of God. No one can be an ambassador, except he be charged *expressly* with instructions from his Sovereign (else would he deliver the fruit of his own brain, not his Sovereign's will and commands); nor can any one legitimately come in the name of God to confirm the revelations of his will, except by his own express appointment. God will seal his own ordinance, but not man's usurpation.

As *to the entrance to the sacred function*—having no extraordinary commission, we do not expect an immediate and extraordinary call. Our authority is derived conjointly from God and from the Church—that is, originally from God—confirmed through the medium of the Church. *The external call* is a commission received from and recognized by the Church, according to the sacred and primitive order; not indeed qualifying the Minister, but accrediting him, whom God had internally and suitably qualified. This call communicates therefore only official authority. *The internal call* is the voice and power of the Holy Ghost, directing the will and the judgment, and conveying personal qualifications. Both calls, however—though essentially distinct in their character and source—are indispensable for the exercise of our com-

---

[1] Isa. xlviii. 16. lxi. 1.   [2] Matt. iii. 16, 17, also xvii. 5. John xii. 28—30.
[3] John viii. 16, 42.   [4] Ibid. x. 1, 2.
[5] Such as *called*, Heb. v. 4. *Separated*, Acts xiii. 2. Rom. i. 1. *Sent*, John xx. 21; with Isa. vi. 8. *Made*, Acts xx. 28. *Thrust out*, Matt. ix. 38. (Gr.) &c. Hooker admirably observes—'They are therefore Ministers of God, not only by way of subordination, as princes and civil magistrates (whose execution of judgment and justice the supreme hand of Divine Providence doth uphold); but Ministers of God, as from whom their authority is derived, and not from men. For in that they are Christ's ambassadors and his labourers, who shall give them their commission, but He whose most inward affairs they manage?' Book v. c. lxxvii. 1, 2.
[6] Romans x. 15.

12

mission. Both therefore unite in His government, who "is not the Author of confusion, but of peace, as in all churches of the saints ;"[1] and whose unction, of a rational, holy, and orderly character, harmoniously combines with the constituted appointment of his will. How plainly do the superscriptions of St. Paul's Epistles, (with one or two exceptions,) stamp his instructions to the churches with the seal of his heavenly commission! 'He is never weary of inculcating on us this truth—that the will of God is the sole rule of any man's call, and the only gate by which he can enter into the Ministry. The Mission is divine in its fountain and institution—human in its channel and way of communication.'[2] It is therefore in this combined authority that we " serve God with our spirit in the gospel of his Son ;"[3] that we have the confidence that he will stand by us, and own our work ; and that we " thank Christ Jesus our Lord, who hath enabled us, for that he counted us faithful, putting us into the Ministry."[4]

The *external call*, though necessary and authoritative in its character—yet, as being the mere delegation of man, is evidently not of itself a sufficient warrant for our work. *The inward call* is the presumptive ground, on which our Church delegates her authorized commission. Nothing can be more explicit than her solemn question to us—' Do you trust that you are inwardly moved by the Holy Ghost to take upon you this office ?' 'Certainly,' (as Bishop Burnet remarks with his usual seriousness) 'the answer that is made to this ought to be well considered ; for if any says— ' *I trust so*'—that yet knows nothing of any such motion, and can give no account of it, he lies to the Holy Ghost, and makes his first approach to the altar with a lie in his mouth, and that not to men, but to God.'[5] Now if there be any meaning in terms as illustrative of things, an inward movement by the Holy Ghost must imply his influence upon the heart—not indeed manifested by any enthusiastic impulse ; but enlightening the heart under a deep impression of the worth of souls ; constraining the soul by the love of Christ to " spend and be spent for him ;" and directing the conscience to a sober, searching, self-inquiry ; to a daily study of the word : to fervent prayer in reference to this great matter ; and to a careful observation of the providential indications of our Master's will.

However, ' that which no man ought to do, almost every man

---

[1] 1 Cor. xiv. 33.
[2] Quesnel on 2 Cor. i. 1. Gal. i. 1. 'In times past,' observes Luther, 'when I was but a young Divine, methought Paul did unwisely in glorying so oft of his calling in all his Epistles; but I did not understand his purpose; *For I knew not that the Ministry of God's word was so weighty a matter.*' On Gal. i. 1.
[3] Rom. i. 9.   [4] 1 Tim. i. 12.   [5] Pastoral Care, chap. vi.

does, in making himself the sovereign judge of his own calling.'[1]
A misguided bias, constitutional propensity, or worldly considerations, often perplex the path, and obscure the tokens of the Divine
guidance. May a man presume that he is thus "inwardly moved
by the Holy Ghost," because his inclination leads him to the Ministry—or he has been educated for it—or he is thrust into it by the
wishes of friends, or even by parental counsel or authority? It
would indeed open a wide door for enthusiasm, to suppose, that a
bias of the mind was a sufficient warrant for this most solemn undertaking. Motives and feelings, individual character and capacities, are so often viewed through the medium of self-complacency,
that we are forcibly reminded of the sacred aphorism—"He that
trusteth to his own heart is a fool."[2] What would survive the fervour of the bias, beside the melancholy exhibition of an unfurnished mind; or such a low standard of Ministerial obligation, as
would bring the office into utter contempt? Nor must we admit
parental interference in the choice of a work, that wholly depends
upon what Burnet calls 'a Divine vocation.' 'The national
Church' (as has been truly and feelingly stated by one, who had a
deep personal interest in the subject) 'groans and bleeds from the
crown of its head to the sole of its feet from the daily intrusion of
unworthy men into the Ministry' from this source.[3] 'The will of
man' must be in subserviency—not in forwardness—on a point so
deeply connected with the interests of the Church, and where the
will of God should govern the sole and ultimate decision. 'Happy
that person, who can say with the Apostle, that it is "through the
will of God," and not *through his own, or that of his parents*,
that he is in the sacred Ministry.'[4]

Nor should personal and consistent piety (irrespective of other
considerations) form our determination. 'No man,' indeed, (as
Bishop Burnet remarks,) 'ought to think of this profession, unless
he feels within himself a love to religion, with a zeal for it, and an
internal true piety, which is chiefly kept up by secret prayer and
reading the Scriptures. As long as these things are a man's burden, they are infallible indices, that he has no inward vocation, nor
motion of the Holy Spirit to undertake it.'[5] Yet, on the other

---

[1] Quesnel on Heb. v. 4. [2] Prov. xxviii. 26.
[3] Life of Legh Richmond, p. 475. The whole letter is worthy the deep consideration
of Christian parents, in the ultimate designation of their children for the Christian Ministry. The pious Quesnel puts up a prayer in reference to this deadly evil—'Lord,
vouchsafe to put a stop to the torrent of this carnal love in parents. *Thou seest how thy
church is almost overwhelmed with it.*' On John vii. 5. [4] Quesnel on 1 Cor. i..1.
[5] Conclusion to the History of his Own Times. See also Past. Care, chap. vii. Even
for the charge of the poor—probably connected with the preaching of the Gospel—spiritual
qualifications were requisite. Acts vi. 3. Comp. 1 Tim. iii. 8—10.

hand, every Christian is not ordained to be a Minister. The examples of Aquila and Priscilla,[1] and the various helpers of the primitive church called over by name in the Apostolical salutations,[2] clearly prove, that devotedness to the cause of God is a component and acceptable part of Christian obligation. In this wide field of service, laymen may exhibit the spirit of the Ministry in perfect consistency with their secular employ, and without an unauthorized intrusion upon the express commission of the sacred office ;—the entrance into which, without a Divine call, the greatest talents, the most elevated spirituality, and the most sincere intentions, cannot justify.

The two grand combining requisites for this "Divine vocation" may be determined to be, *a desire, and a fitness, for the office.*

I. *The desire of the work* was a prominent feature in the Ministerial character and qualifications of Christ. While in the bosom of the Father, and in the anticipation of his work, " his delights were with the sons of men."[3] " When he cometh into the world," for the accomplishment of his work, the same earnest desire distinguished him.[4] On one occasion of bodily need, he told his disciples, that " he had meat to eat that they knew not of;" bidding them to understand, that his delight in his Father's work was to him " more than his necessary food."[5] The Apostle strongly marks *a constraining desire* as a primary Ministerial qualification ;[6] something far beyond the general Christian desire to promote the glory of God—a special kindling within—in character, if not in intensity, like " the burning fire shut up " in the prophet's bosom, and overcoming his determination to go back from the service of his God."[7] This constraint rises above all difficulties, takes pleasure in sacrifices for the work's sake, and quickens to a readiness of mind, that (were it not restrained by conscious unfitness and unworthiness) would savour of presumption. The sense of defilement almost shuts the mouth ; but the sense of mercy fills the heart, and it " cannot stay."[8] The work is more desirable than the highest earthly honours ; so that, even under the most desponding anticipations it cannot be relinquished.[9] This desire will be

---

[1] Acts xviii. 25.   [2] Phil. iv. 3.   Rom. xvi. &c.   [3] Prov. viii. 31.
[4] Comp. Psalm xl. 8. with Heb. x. 5—9.   [5] John iv. 32—34.
[6] ' *This is a true saying*,'—(his peculiar mark of emphasis—1 Tim. i. 15; iv. 9; 2 Tim. ii. 11, with 1 Tim. iii. 1'), Ὀρεγομαι, Appeto. It signifies an earnest desire, *quasi porrectis manibus prehendere et arripere*, 1 Tim. vi. 10. Heb. xi. 16. *Quo verbo vehementior appetitus ac desiderium significator.* Estius ad locum. Orexis apud Plinium desiderium.' Leigh's Critica Sacra. καλου εργου επιθυμει. The lusting of the spirit.
[7] Compare Jer. xx. 9. Thus Moses separated the Divinely-appointed builders of the tabernacle, Exodus xxxv. 21.   [8] Compare Isaiah vi. 5—8.
[9] It is difficult to allude to the experience of Henry Kirke White on this subject, with-

most enlivening, when the mind is most spiritual, and will connect the communication of the blessing, with ardent prayers for a large reciprocal benefit.

It should also be a *considerate desire*—the result of matured calculation of the cost. This, we fear, has been sometimes lost sight of, in the exchange of secular professions, (more especially the army and navy,) for the service of the altar. But seldom is the declaration more important—" He that believeth shall not make haste."[1] Waiting time is of the utmost moment to scrutinize the real principles of the heart, which have dictated an abandonment of the calling originally, (as it was presumed) suggested by the Providence of God ; and in which ordinarily it is the. will of God that we should " abide."[2] The relinquishment of a secular calling for the sacred office, can never be justified *in foro conscientiæ*, or be productive of ultimate advantage either to the individual or to the Church—without the clearest providential light—the most watchful caution against the influence of natural inclination, as the interpreter of Providence—the most earnest and persevering prayer —and the most satisfactory evidence of abstraction from all motives of personal ease, indulgence, or interest. Under these circumstances, where the call is not evidently of God, a due contemplation of the difficulties in prospect, combined with a trembling sense of his own weakness, will probably direct the mind of the candidate to some less responsible undertaking. This *inconsiderate desire* will gradually weaken and die away ; or, if it should act presumptuously in pushing forward to the work, it will issue (unless the Lord should open his eyes) in bitter and unavailing fruits of repentance.[3]

It must also be a *disinterested* desire. Pure intention is indispensable to the meanest service in the Lord's work. Much more important therefore is it—that our choice of the service of his sanctuary should be uninfluenced by the love of literature, or the op-

out some feeling of regret at his (to us) premature dismission.—' Since the time I was awakened to a true sense of religion, I have always felt a strong desire to become useful in the church of Christ— a desire which has increased daily, and which it has been my supplication might be from God. It is true, before I began to be solicitous about spiritual things, I had *a wish to become a clergyman ; but that was very different.* I trust I may now say, that I would be a Minister, that I may do good; and although I am sensible of the awful importance of the Pastoral Charge, I *would sacrifice every thing* for it, in the hope, that I should be strengthened faithfully to discharge the duties of that sacred office. I think I have no other reason to offer but this—the hope of being an instrument in the hands of God to the promotion of his glory is my chief motive.' See his Remains.
[1] Isaiah xxviii. 16.   [2] 1 Cor. vii. 20.
[3] Matthew Henry admirably warns against intrusion into the sacred office. 'We must not' (said he) 'be *forward* to put forth ourselves in the exercise of spiritual gifts. Pride often appears in this, under the pretence of a desire to be useful. If the motive be correct, it is good; but *humility will wait for a call.*' Life, p. 294.

portunities of indulgent recreation—that we should guard against desires of professional elevation—that we should be divested of the selfish motives of esteem, respectability, or worldly comfort—that we should "seek not great things for ourselves"—that we should aim at nothing but souls, rather willing to win one to Christ than a world to ourselves—and that we should exhibit a devoted consecration of all our talents to the service of God.[1] 'He who is called to instruct souls' (said Bernard) 'is called of God, and not by his own ambition; and what is this call, but an inward incentive of love soliciting us to be zealous for the salvation of our brethren? So often as he, who is engaged in preaching the word, shall feel his inward man to be excited with Divine affections, so often let him assure himself, that God is there, and that he is invited by him to seek the good of souls.'[2] To the same purpose Quesnel observes— 'One of the most certain marks of the Divine call is, where it is the purpose of a man's heart *to live, to labour, and to possess nothing,* but for Jesus Christ and his Church.'[3] Where the heart is

---

[1] The following Scripture references may employ secret and serious self-inquiry:—1 Sam. ii. 36. Micah iii. 11. Phil. ii. 20, 21. 1 Tim. iii. 8. Titus i. 7—11. The command of God—Jer. xlv. 5. The appeal of his faithful servants—1 Sam. xii. 3. Acts xx. 33. 1 Thess. ii. 4—9. 'Ask yourselves often'—said Bishop Burnet—'would you follow that course of life, if there were no settled establishment belonging to it, and if you were to preach under the cross, and in danger of persecution? For till you arrive at that, you are yet carnal, and come into the priesthood for a piece of bread.' Conclusion to the History of his own times.

[2] Milner's Church History, Vol. iii. 409.

[3] Quesnel on Rom. i. 1, and John x. 1, 2. Calvin gives the same view—'Est autem bonum cordis nostri testimonium, *quod neque ambitione, neque avaritia, neque ulla alia cupiditate,* sed sincero Dei timore, et ædificandæ Ecclesiæ studio oblatum munus recipiamus. Id quidem unicuique nostrum (ut dixi), si volumus Ministerium nostrum Deo approbare, necessarium est.' Instit. Lib. iv. c. iii. 11. Comber supposes, that our Reformers had this definition in their view in framing the important question in the Ordination Service, which was written a few years after the publication of the Institutes. Philip Henry gave a most beautiful exposition of this desire, in answer to the question put to him at his Ordination.—'As far as upon search and inquiry I can hitherto find, though there be that within me, that would seek great things for myself (if indeed they were to be found in this calling), yet with my mind I seek them not. But the improvement of the talent, which I have received in the service of the Gospel, for the glory of God, and the salvation of souls, I hope is in my eyes. If there be any thing else, I own it not—I allow it not. While so many "seek their own," it is my desire, and it shall be my endeavour, to "seek the things of Jesus Christ,"' Life, p. 34—Matthew Henry's self-inquiry at the same sacred season was of a similar spirit. '1. *What am I?*' Have I been convinced of my condition, and been humbled for my sin? Have I heartily given myself to Christ? Have I a real hatred of sin, and love of holiness? 2. *What have I done?* Time trifled! opportunities lost! engagements broken! conversation unprofitable! forgetfulness of God and of duty! 3. *From what principles do I undertake this work?* I trust from a persuasion of the Divine institution of the Ministry, of the necessity of a Divine call, and of my call to the work: from zeal to God, and love to precious souls. 4. *What are my ends in this work?* Not taking it as a trade to live by; not to get myself a name, or to maintain a party; but aiming at the glory of God, and the good of souls. 5. *What do I want?* That God would fix my heart in dedication to the work; that he would be with me at my Ordination; that he would fit me for my work with the gifts of knowledge, utterance, and prudence; and with all Ministerial graces, especially sincerity and humility; and that he would open a door of opportunity to me. 6. *What are my resolutions?* To have nothing to do with sin; to abound in gospel obedience; to consider my Ordination Vow in the employment of my talents, the maintenance of the

freed from selfishness, and purely acted upon by the will of God, and the readiness to labour for him, there is much encouragement to advance toward this holy function. The importance and purity of this desire are strongly marked, as the grand qualifications to " feed the flock of God."[1] " If I do this thing willingly," (says the Apostle) " I have a reward."[2]—'But if you do not feel in your-selves' (as the eloquent Massillon addresses his clergy) ' *a desire* of being employed as the ambassadors of God—judge ye yourselves, *whether ye are called into the Lord's vineyard.* God implants a love in the heart for the service to which he calls ; and better would it have been for you to have felt, that it was not the Ministry for which you were intended, than that you should possess a want of inclination for the performance of its duties. *It is not necessary,* that a voice from heaven should say to you in secret—" The Lord hath not sent you." Your judgment, enforced by the dictates of your conscience, tells you so.'[3]

II. But to this desire must be added *a competent measure of Ministerial gifts.* Our Lord was furnished with this evidence of his call, and endowment for his work.[4] The Apostle distinctly connects this ability with our commission, which he directs to be consigned not to " faithful men" generally—but to those among them, *" which shall be able to teach others also."*[5] But as this subject has already come before us,[6] we shall only observe, that the ability for the sacred office is very distinct from natural talent, or the wisdom and learning of this world. These—*though subordi-nately most useful and important*—are no where mentioned as constituting the essentials of Ministerial qualifications. A man of ordinary natural gifts, and under Divine teaching, may be able to pray, to preach the Gospel, to administer the sacraments, and to save immortal souls. And such a one has a far better claim to the title of a Minister of Christ, than an erudite scholar or accomplished theologian, *destitute of spiritual qualifications.* In directing the ignorant in the way of heaven—in awakening the careless and in-sensible—in subduing the rebellious—in dealing with the entangle-ments of tempted consciences—how inefficient would be all the force of philosophical or historical illustration ! One simple decla-

truth, the charge of my family, the superintendence of my flock, and the endurance of opposition. Abridged from M. Henry's Life, p. 34—44.
  [1] See 1 Peter v. 2.   [2] 1 Cor. ix. 17.   [3] Massillon's Charges, p. 60.
  [4] Compare Psalm xlv. 7. Isaiah xi. 2—4; xlii. 1; lxi. 1. His own messenger exhib-ited these credentials to the people—John iii. 34.
  [5] 2 Tim. ii. 2. Elsewhere he marks this qualification by a word, which our trans-lators have given with sufficient accuracy—" apt to teach "—διδακτικος—1 Tim. iii. 2. 2 Tim. ii. 24. Compare 2 Cor. iii. 6.
  [6] Part I. chapter vi. On Ministerial Qualifications.

ration of the Gospel,[1] on the other hand, would, with the **Lord's** blessing, remove the darkness, melt away the stubbornness, and bring in all the consolation of heavenly light and peace. We doubt not but the true Christian Minister, well-furnished with human learning—*without casting away this valuable gift*—yet makes far more use of, and estimates at a far higher value, that learning which he has obtained " in the secret place of the Most High."[2] This is the fitness *mainly, though not exclusively*, to be sought for. Let the noviciate be found in the daily habit of prayer, in the conscientious improvement of his natural gifts, in a diligent increase of his intellectual as well as spiritual stores—and he will find the promise made good—" Whosoever hath, to him shall be given, and he shall have more abundantly."[3] In this course he may largely encourage his desire to be duly admitted into the sacred office, soberly anticipating the results according to the will and word of God, but not regarding them as the warrant of his preparation or desire for the work.

So important, however, is the combination of desire and capacity, that neither, separated from the other, can be deemed sufficient. The desire (though correctly answering to the standard of intensity, consideration, and purity) does not of itself attest a Divine vocation. We cannot suppose the Lord to send unqualified labourers, *however willing*, into his vineyard :[4] and none but he can qualify them. The servant of God, therefore, may be called to yield his most ardent wishes in the conscious inability to set forth the truth in an intelligent and effective form. Yet may he in this self-renouncing sacrifice console himself with the most gracious acceptance of his desires,[5] though his services be not required. Nor will the richest furniture of Ministerial gifts, without a special desire and interest in the work, (though it may qualify the Christian for important usefulness as a helper of the Church) evidence a movement by the Holy Ghost for this high and important service. But when the Lord constrains the heart of his servant with a desire, and furnishes him with competent ability—when in the clear apprehension of the labour, pain, and difficulty of the work, he can yet say—*None of these things move me*[6]—then may he seek to be set apart by the instrumentality of man, having the witness

---

[1] Such as Matt. xi. 28· John iii. 16, &c.   [2] See Philippians iii. 7. 8.
[3] Matt. xiii. 12; xxv. 29.
[4] In common life, " he that sendeth a message by the hand of a fool, cutteth off the feet, and drinketh damage "—Prov. xxvi. 6. Could we then suppose, that Divine wisdom would commit the administration of the Church to capacities inadequate to the responsibility of that most important trust?
[5] 1 Kings viii. 18.   [6] Acts xx. 24.

within him that he has been called by God. And such a call will be duly authorized by the presbyters of the Church, and will doubtless be yet more clearly attested by the Divine blessing upon his work.[1]

The Providence of God, as we have before hinted, will probably afford more or less confirmation of this call. For this is "the wheel within a wheel," moving in harmonious conjunction, but in direct subserviency to his purposes respecting his Church. If therefore these arrangements direct the choice of a secular calling, much more may we expect him thus to guide the inward call to his own work—a matter so deeply connected with the interests of his kingdom. The providential disposing, therefore, of a person's circumstances, thoughts, inclinations, and studies, to this main end—the disappointment of his plans for a future course in life—the unexpected and repeated closing up of worldly avenues—unlooked-for openings in the Church (in the *way of usefulness, not of preferment*)—some particular crisis in the individual sphere—some change or influence of family circumstances—one or more of these may prove the "word behind him, saying—This is the way, walk ye in it."[2] Direction, however, will probably be given rather in opposition to indulgence of a constitutional propensity—damping a sanguine temperament, and rousing an indolent habit. Wise and tender discipline will form the pliable spirit, ready to discern and follow our Father's will. The Lord usually trains his servants to waiting, and to much conflict in their way to his immediate service. But in humble patient confidence, their "path will be as the shining light."[3]

The *judgment of Christian friends, and specially of experienced Ministers*, might be useful in assuring the mind, whether or not the desire for the work be the impulse of feeling rather than of principle, and the capacity be self-deceiving presumption. The

---

[1] This view of the subject is nearly identical with Bishop Burnet. His application is too striking to be omitted. ' *This man*' (remarks the Bishop with a solemnity truly episcopal), '*and this man only—so moved and qualified, can in truth and with a good conscience* answer, that he trusts he is inwardly moved by the Holy Ghost. And every man that ventures on the saying it without this, is a sacrilegious profaner of the name of God, and of his Holy Spirit. He breaks in upon his church, not to feed it, but to rob it; and it is certain, that he who begins with a lie may be sent by the father of lies; but *he cannot be thought to* " *enter in by the door*," *who prevaricates in the first word that he says in order to his admittance.*'—Pastoral Care, ch. vi.

[2] Isaiah xxx. 21.

[3] I must add this to the encouragement and comfort of such as can resolve to deliver themselves up to the conduct and direction of Providence, that I never knew any one of those few, who have followed this maxim exactly, that have not found the fruit of it even in this world—as if there had been a secret design of heaven, to encourage others to follow their measures—to depend on God, to deliver themselves up to his care, and to wait till he opens a way for their being employed and settled in such a portion of his husbandry, as he shall think fit to assign them." Pastoral Care, ch. vii.

late pious and learned Dr. Leland took this satisfactory view of his own case—' God has been graciously pleased ', (said he,) ' to *give me some talents*, which seem capable of being improved to the edification of the Church. He hath *disposed and inclined my heart to a willingness* to take upon me the sacred Ministry, and that not from worldly, carnal ends and views, but from a sincere intention and desire of employing the talents he has given me in promoting the salvation of souls, and serving the interests of truth, piety, and righteousness in the world. And I have been encouraged by the judgment and approbation of several learned and pious Ministers, who, after a diligent course of trials, carried on for a considerable time, judged me to be properly qualified for that sacred office, and animated me to undertake it. Upon seriously weighing all these things, I cannot but think, I have a clear call to the work of the Ministry ; and I verily believe, that, if I rejected it, I should sin against God, grieve many of his people, counteract the designs of Divine providence towards me, and alienate the talents he has given me to other purposes, than those for which they seem to have been intended.'[1]

The importance of this discussion will be generally allowed. To labour in the dark, without an assured commission, greatly obscures the warrant of faith in the Divine engagements; and the Minister, unable to avail himself of heavenly support, feels his " hands hang down, and his knees feeble " in his work. On the other hand, the confidence that he is acting in obedience to the call of God—that he is in his work, and in his way—nerves him in the midst of all difficulty, and under a sense of his responsible obligations, with almighty strength. Yet under no circumstances is there a warranted ground for distress in a simple consecration to the service of God. Let the Minister in seasons of anxiety cast himself upon the mercy of God, and doubt not of acceptance.

But in closing our consideration of this subject, we cannot forget, that the inward call has not always accompanied the public investment with Ministerial authority. With many of us it is a painful recollection, that we entered into this sacred office with hearts unenlightened with Christian doctrine, and unimpressed with Ministerial obligations.[2] Yet let the remembrance of this sin be in hu-

---

[1] See Leland's Life, prefixed to his sermons. ' Vocantur, quibus data facultas, voluntas, et locus. Omnia tria Dei dona tamen requirunt nostrum studium. Oratio et diligentia poscitur, quo discas quod doceas. Voluntas etiam petenda a Domino est. Locus docendi item quærendus est; nec tacendum, nisi ubi nemo velit audire.' Bucer. De vi et usu S. Min.

[2] See Scott's affecting reference to his own case—Force of Truth, and Practical Observations on Numbers xvi. 1—19. Also the same confession from Mr. Walker of Truro, a

miliation—not in despondency. Let us be afflicted indeed for our unhallowed approach to the sacred altar : yet not " swallowed up with overmuch sorrow." There is with our gracious God mercy for this, as well as for any other sin ; and we shall not apply to him for it in vain. Doubtless we should bear this sin in special remembrance to the end of our days ; both as an occasion of magnifying the grace of God,[1] and as an incentive to redoubled exertions throughout our future course. In order to generate in our hearts this deepened contrition, it will be well to bring frequently before our minds, and especially at the annual return of the season of our ordination, the vows, which we then took upon us : and in a new perception of their responsibility, to consecrate ourselves to God afresh, with a full determination of heart through grace to fulfil them. Thus receiving, as it were, a second commission, with shame and self-reproach, and yet with thankfulness ; we shall be given to it ; we shall have an evidence in our own souls, that, though at the time of ordination we were not " moved by the Holy Ghost," we are so now ; and if our conscience bear witness to us, that we are now cordially renouncing whatever is inconsistent with our high and heavenly calling, we need not doubt of God's merciful acceptance in all our labours of love, and (in confirmation of his own word) of a blessing to be conferred also on our own souls according to our labour.

minister of peculiar simplicity and most honoured devotedness to his Master's work. See his valuable collection of Tracts, entitled Practical Christianity, pp. 190, 191. Compare also ' Humbling Recollections of my Ministry'—(Seeley's) an edifying Memorial by a devoted Minister lately removed from his labours.

[1] See 1 Tim. i. 11—16.

PART III.

CAUSES OF MINISTERIAL INEFFICIENCY CONNECTED WITH OUR PERSONAL CHARACTER.[1]

THE Writer is well aware of the extreme delicacy, consideration, and tenderness, which the treatment of this part of his subject requires of him. He can, however, truly state, that, though for his personal profit he has diligently observed the Ministrations of his brethren, yet the material for remark which will now be detailed, is drawn rather from a painful acquaintance with his own deficiencies and temptations, than from a censorious scrutiny of others ; and he trusts that it will be remembered, that there is a wide difference between exposing the defects of his brethren in the pride of self-gratulation, and observing their failures in connection with a deep searching into his own heart, and for the purpose of bringing all into a condensed view for the common good.

The important influence, favourable or unfavourable, of our personal habits upon the Ministerial work, is obvious. The character of the individual must have a prominent part in forming the Minister ; and therefore the causes, that operate in the declension of the Christian life, must belong to this department of the subject. Particulars will now be specified.

[1] For some valuable papers on this division of our subject, the reader is referred to the Christian Observer, 1822.

CHAPTER I.

WANT OF ENTIRE DEVOTEDNESS OF HEART TO THE CHRISTIAN MINISTRY.

THE paragraph (1 Tim. iv. 13—16.) condenses in the smallest compass the most important body of appropriate instruction, and encouragement to Ministerial devotedness—" *Give thyself wholly to these things, that thy profiting may appear to all.* Take heed unto thyself and unto the doctrine; continue in them; for in *doing this thou shalt both save thyself, and them that hear thee.*" The effect of the Apostles' resolution to "*give themselves* to prayer, and *to the Ministry of the word,*" exhibited the influence of Christian devotedness upon Ministerial success.[1] The great Shepherd, indeed, who gave himself for, gave us to, the flock;[2] and there is no more responsible thought connected with our work, than the obligation of giving ourselves to our people, so that they shall be led to prize us as a gift from Christ. Oh! that we might be able to tell them 'We belong to Christ, and he has given us to you; we owe our whole selves entirely to you;[3] we are "your servants for Jesus' sake;"[4] we have given ourselves to the work, and we desire to be in it, as if there was nothing worth living for besides: it shall form our whole pleasure and delight. We will consecrate our whole time, our whole reading, our whole mind and heart to this service.' We cannot suppose it to be less necessary for us than for Archippus, to "take heed to the Ministry which we have received in the Lord, that we fulfil it,"[5] or that the Apostolical exhortations to unremitted diligence are less applicable to us than to the beloved Timothy.[6] Do the privileges and immunities of our admirable Establishment furnish a plea for self-indulgence? Or shall we be satisfied with a routine of outward service, sufficient to justify us in the eyes of our Diocesan; while, as respects any painful exercises of self-denial, we are "serving the Lord with that which doth cost us nothing?"[7] We are to be labourers, not loiterers, in the Lord's vineyard; not doing his work with a reluctant heart, as if we did it not, as if we feared being losers by him, or giving him more than

---

[1] Acts vi. 4—7. Mark this resolution exemplified in a faithful Minister of the primitive Church, equally given to prayer, and the more toilsome work of the Lord, Col. i. 7; with iv. 12. Phil. ii. 30.
[2] Comp. Eph. iv. 8—12.   [3] Rom. i. 14.   [4] 2 Cor. iv. 5.
[5] Col. iv. 17.   [6] 2 Tim. iv. 1, 2.   [7] 2 Sam. xxiv. 24.

he deserved. 'The pastoral dignity is really the condition of a servant. It obliges a man to *devote himself entirely* to Jesus Christ, and to his Church. Both the Minister and the Ministry are only for the Church. He who in this state does not apply himself entirely to the service of the Church, will be treated as a thief, and a sacrilegious person. Whoever has not the spirit of his Ministry, renders all the talents and advantages useless, which he has received to serve the Church. A pastor ought to have nothing at heart but the work of God and the salvation of souls. This ought to be his delight, his meat, and his life.'[1] Let us remember, that, as Ministers, we are not only, like our fellow-Christians, "bought with a price," but we are set apart, yea, devoted, to this work. We have, therefore, no right "to entangle ourselves with the affairs of this life," so as to hinder our entire consecration to the Church. So strongly was this obligation felt in the primitive age, that Cyprian gives the judgment of the Church, that a presbyter should not entangle himself with the office of an executor. If, however, they unadvisedly made an absolute rule, still the principle was excellent —that the Minister's constant employment in spiritual affairs, precluded him from giving the necessary attention even to important secular duties.[2]

Our responsibilities demand an entire devotedness of spirit to every soul, as if it were the sole object of our care. 'It ought therefore to be our solemn and cheerful determination, to refrain from studies, pursuits, and even recreations, that may not be made evidently subservient to the grand purpose of our Ministry. The Apostle would remind us, in our visits, journeys, the common intercourse of life, never to forget, not only our *Christian* but our *Ministerial* character. All must be stamped with its holiness : all must be a part of a system strictly adhered to, of being constantly learning, and waiting the opportunity of imparting what we have learned in the things of God.'[3] Mr. Cecil used to say, that the

---

[1] Quesnel on Rom. i. 1. Ephes. iii. 1. John iv. 34.

[2] 2 Tim. ii. 4. Cypr. Epist. i. See Burkitt on Luke ix. 61, 62. 'Facile unusquisque intelligat, sacrum ministerium a nemine posse ulli ecclesiæ, quamvis exiguæ, qui non huic procurando ministerio se totum addicat et impendat.' Bucer de Ordinat. Legit. Minist. Eccles.

[3] Scott's Letters and Papers, pp. 307, 308. In another place he writes to a friend in the same spirit of fervid and habitual devotedness—'My conscience is never quiet or joyful; but when I am busy in some Ministerial employment; not merely in acquiring, but in communicating, the knowledge of Divine things by my tongue and pen : not only by meditation endeavouring to affect my own heart, but by some method or other endeavouring to affect others, and stir them up to seek, trust, love, and serve the Lord. And after a multitude of thoughts about pride, ambition, &c. influencing me to be active, (and they will insinuate themselves,) I am persuaded Satan would have me while away my life in inactivity, under pretences of modesty, diffidence, and humility ; and he never is wanting to furnish me with excuses for delaying or shifting services.'—Life, p. 213.

devil did not care how ministers were employed, *so that it was not in their proper work.* Whether it was hunting or sporting, cards and assemblies, writing notes upon the classics, or politics, it was all one to him. Each might please his own taste. In contrast to this mind, how manly was Nehemiah's repeated answer to his subtle enemies, when they would have diverted him from the immediate service of his God—" I am doing a great work, so that I cannot come down !"[1]—And does not the building of the spiritual temple require the same concentrated devotedness of heart, the same sense of primary obligation? And are we, in a similar spirit, ready to answer the suggestions of a corrupt heart, of pride, indolence, love of ease, worldliness, and unbelief—'I may not—I must not—I dare not—" I cannot—come down?"' In the true spirit of our work we shall " let the potsherd strive with the potsherd of the earth "—yea, even " let the dead bury their dead," rather than allow the business of this life to detain us from the present and imperative duty—" Go thou, and preach the gospel of God."[2]

Bishop Burnet adverts to ' the great notion of the Pastoral care, which runs through our Ordination Service—that it is *to be a man's entire business,* and is to possess both his thoughts and his time.' ' What greater force or energy '—the Bishop asks—' could be put in words, than in these? Or where could any be found, that are more weighty and more express, to show the *entire dedication of the whole man, of his time and labour, and the separating himself from all other cares, to follow this one thing with all possible application and zeal?* There is nothing in any office, ancient or modern, that I ever saw, which is of this force—so serious and so solemn.'[3] The Clergy ' have a double account to settle—an account with God, as well as an account with man; and it may happen, that, although the latter party have nothing to object against them, yet their functions may not have been adequately discharged in the sight of the great High-Priest of the Church. Even if their engagement be not exactly in the nature of a conditional contract, as far as man is concerned, yet there are certain *extra-official obligations—certain undefined, though not less binding, duties, which every man set apart for the Ministry has undertaken to fulfil.*[4] His work must not be looked upon as

---

[1] Neh. vi. 3, 4. ' Minister verbi es. Hoc age '—was the quickening stimulus of the holy and learned Mr. Perkins.

[2] Isaiah xlv. 9. Luke ix. 59, 60.   [3] Pastoral Care, chap. vi.

[4] See Burnet's Past. Care, ch. viii. Mr. Richmond's Ministry may furnish a specimen of these ' undefined extra-official obligations.' Besides two complete services on the Sabbath—it consisted of a Sunday evening lecture for the young—Cottage lectures on Tuesday, and latterly, also, on Thursday evenings—a lecture in the church on Friday,

an ordinary profession, to be conducted on that principle of reciprocity, which governs the common dealings of mankind.   He dese-
crates his high calling, when he considers it in the light of a mere
commercial transaction, in which a bargain is struck for a certain
return of services upon the payment of a certain price.   Like his
heavenly pattern, he will be constantly about his Master's business;
he will avail himself of times and seasons and topics, and present
the truths of which he is the depository, in so judicious and pertinent a manner, that his "speech" may at all times "be seasoned
with salt, and that no man may be able to accuse him of neglect,
or inquire, like Esau, in the tone of mingled regret and reproach—
"Hast thou not a blessing for me also ?"[1]

Our "heavenly pattern" did indeed furnish a striking illustration
of the true spirit of the Christian Ministry—"doing with our
might."   His whole soul was in it—intent upon one thing—subordinating relative obligations,[2] personal convenience,[3]—and even
present necessity,[4] to the main business.   No time was wasted upon
trifles.   Such unblushing activity !   Never was an opportunity of
usefulness lost.   Even the common courtesies[5] of life—public occasions[6]—were improved as vehicles of the most important instruction.   The thought of relinquishing his work was intolerable.[7]
Through most sinking reproach and tribulation, he persevered to
the end.[8]   The labours of single days were unprecedented in Ministerial annals ;[9] and a lengthened course was compressed within
the contracted space of three years.

with weekly instruction at the workhouse, and a monthly lecture before the sacrament.
Combined with this system of public instruction was the constant fulfilment of the Apostolical injunction, of going from house to house.   See his Life, pp. 114, 115, 588, 589.
Many devoted Ministers would be "pressed out of measure, above strength," and would
shortly "have the sentence of death in themselves" from such incessant demands; and
'Christ' (as an excellent Minister said to his brother) 'is too great a Master to need,
and too good a Master to require, his servants to kill themselves in his service.'   Some,
however, profess to be retained from these 'extra-official' labours by the fear of entail-
ing heavy burdens upon their successors.   But the Lord will not require of them the
same portion of work with diminished physical resources; while he justly demands of
all his servants, that, as their strength, so their work shall be.   While the higher, and
most reasonable, demands of many of our Diocesans, are stimulating us to increasing
exertions, let us be careful, that prospective considerations do not paralyze our present
.energies, and that we grudge not to expend a healthful constitution in a service, in which
angels might think it an honour to be engaged.   Where health, strength, talents, and
opportunities are vouchsafed, who will say, that such labours are uncalled-for by the
exigency of the case, by the voice of conscience, by the constraining influence of our Master's love, (John xxi. 15—17.) or by those solemn Ordination engagements, which we
have voluntarily undertaken ?
    [1] Bishop of Winchester's Ministerial Character of Christ, pp. 232, 233.
    [2] Luke ii. 49.   Matt. xii. 46—50.   [3] Mark vi. 34—50.   [4] John iv. 6—14.
    [5] Luke vii. 36—50; xi. 37; xiv. 13—24.   [6] John vii. 37.
    [7] Matt. xvi. 23.   [8] Isaiah l. 5, 6.   John xvii. 4.
    [9] Compare Mark i. 32—38.   The parables, Matt. xiii. seem to have been delivered in
the afternoon of a day, that had been previously spent in the work of instruction.   Doddridge remarks on another occasion, that 'no one of the prophets that we read of in

In a large measure of the same spirit did the great Apostle follow his blessed exemplar. His very soul and spirit were set upon his work. Never did any hireling long for preferment, as did he to be made the organ of spiritual blessings[1] to the church. He had a heart and tongue to speak, wherever there was an ear to hear— even at Rome itself.[2] His account of one of his courses informs us, that he commenced his work the very " first day he came into Asia "—" publicly and from house to house "—" declaring the whole counsel of God "—" keeping back nothing that was profitable" —" warning every one night and day for three years "—outwardly exposed to the " temptations" of his enemies, and inwardly " pressed in his spirit " by a tenderness, fervour, and compassion, which could find no vent but in " tears "—and determined at whatever cost to pursue his course with undaunted perseverance.[3] Thus could he testify—" God is my witness, whom *I serve with my spirit* in the Gospel of his Son."[4]

And might we not ask—Is " God our witness?" Does he mark in us—we say not any particular frequency of preaching, but—the purpose, frame of heart, and stamp of a faithful Ministration of the Word—the spirit of a " pastor after God's own heart ?"[5] A devoted Minister feels, that there is sufficient employment for his whole life in his work ; that so far as he lives in the spirit of it, it is his highest pleasure ; and that he can never rightly perform its duties except he be wholly given to it. He will there-

the Old Testament, appears to have wrought so many beneficial miracles in his whole life as our Lord did on this one afternoon.' Family Expositor on Matt. ix. 33. Section lxxii.

[1] Rom. i. 11, 12. 1 Thess. iii. 8—11.   [2] Rom. i. 15.

[3] Compare Acts xx. 18—36. Other courses of considerable extent are described Rom. xv. 18—28.

[4] Rom. i. 9. Brainerd shows the nearest approximation to this spirit. He could scarcely give expression to the full glow of his love for his Master's work.—' I longed to be'—he would sometimes say—' as a flame of fire, continually glowing in the Divine service, preaching and building up Christ's kingdom to my latest, my dying hour.'

[5] Jer. iii. 15. Let us listen to Latimer's plain and faithful exhortations. Speaking of " the Shepherds abiding in the field, keeping watch over their flock by night,"—he adds—' I would wish that all clergymen, the curates, parsons, and vicars, the bishops and all other spiritual persons would learn this lesson by these poor shepherds ; which is, to abide by their flock, and by their sheep—to tarry among them—to be careful over them—not to run hither and thither after their own pleasure, but to tarry by their benefices, and feed their sheep with the food of God's word, and to keep hospitality, and so to feed them both soul and body. For I tell you, these poor unlearned shepherds shall condemn many a stout and great learned clerk ; for these shepherds had but the care and charge over brute beasts, and yet were diligent to keep them and to feed them ; and the others have the care over God's lambs, which he bought with the death of his Son, and yet they are so careless, so negligent, so slothful over them ; yea, and the most part intendeth not to feed the sheep, but they long to be fed by the sheep: they seek only their own pastimes, they care for no more. But saith Christ to Peter—What said he ? " Peter, lovest thou me ?" Peter made answer, Yes. " Then feed my sheep." And so the third time he commanded Peter to feed his sheep, &c. Luke ii. 8—12. Compare Quesnel on Luke xiii. 22.

fore find time for nothing, but what is more or less connected with this main end.

The want of Divine influence on our work should therefore suggest a close and searching scrutiny—Is the whole heart in singleness of purpose consecrated to the Christian Ministry? Mr. Brown's death-bed has given a most encouraging testimony on this subject—the result of forty years' experience—' Oh! labour, labour,' (said he to his sons) ' to win souls to Christ. I will say this for your encouragement—When the Lord led me out to be most earnest in this way, he poured in most comfort into my own heart, so that he gave me my reward in my bosom.'[1] To the same purport was the earnest exhortation of the excellent Bishop Beveridge —' As for those, who come to take upon them the office of deacon or priest, in the Church of Christ—let me now beseech them in the name of the Lord Jesus Christ, whose servants they are now to be, that from this day forward they look upon him as their great Master, and lay out themselves wholly in the service to which he calls them. And, whatsoever difficulties they meet with in it, let them follow the Apostle's example—faint not, nor be discouraged, but go on with cheerfulness and alacrity, as remembering, that they serve the best Master in the world; one that will not only stand by them and assist them, but reward them at last with a crown of righteousness.'[2]

CHAPTER II.

CONFORMITY TO THE WORLD.

As members of society, some intercourse with the world is a matter of necessity; or we " must needs go out of the world."[3] Some measure of communication is also indispensable for the due discharge of our Ministerial responsibilities. It is, however, most important to ascertain the Scriptural limits and principles of this intercourse, lest we deviate from our Divine Master's rule, transgress its requirements, lower its standard, or substitute other principles in the regulation of our conduct. Now if the prohibition of conformity to the world, and the call of God to " come out and be

---

[1] Brown's Life and Remains, p. 267.
[2] See his Sermon on the Institution of Ministers, quoted in Bishop Mant's notes on the Ordination Service.   [3] 1 Cor. v. 10.

separate,"[1] have any meaning at all, they must be supposed to warn the Minister of the sanctuary from the sports of the field or the chace,[2] from the theatre, the ball-room, the card-table, and the race-course ; and from that unprofitable, sensual life of folly, which un-consciously hurries us on from social intercourse to the ensnaring pleasures of sin. 'A life, in which the love of the world is predom-inant, is incompatible with that dignified and edifying piety, which should be the distinguishing characteristic of the sacred Ministry. It is this spirit of piety alone, that can insure to us utility.'[3] For what aptness to teach can be exercised or nourished, where the taste, time, talents, and activity are devoted to secular and self-in-dulgent engagements ?

Many shades of worldly conformity, most detrimental to our spir-itual influence, attach themselves peculiarly to the Clergy of the Establishment. Their rank in society, their education, their mode of living, and the necessity which is commonly felt for keeping up appearances—all are circumstances, which need the control of a heavenly and mortified mind, lest they should prove offences in our great work.[4] Perhaps few of us are aware of the keen eye, with which our dress, furniture, tables, and household are scrutinized, and the minuteness of comparison instituted between our Ministra-tion and personal habits. Mr. Scott's observations upon this sub-ject, are entitled to great consideration. After remarking upon the inconveniences and temptations of Ministers indulging an affecta-tion of appearance beyond their legitimate station, he adds,—' If we form our judgment on this subject from the Holy Scripture, we

[1] Rom. xii. 2. 2 Cor. vi. 17.
[2] Could Jerome, if he lived in our day, have written thus—' *Venatorem nunquem legi-mus sanctum ?*' The following sentiments delivered *ex cathedra* have the weight of au-thority as well as of intrinsic excellence. 'To speak my sentiments plainly,' (said the late Bishop Jebb at his Primary Visitation,) 'I do not see how a clergyman, consistently with the sacredness and separation of his character and office; consistently with the edification of the flock committed to his charge ; or consistently with the vows which he has made at his ordination, can pursue the sports of the mountain or the field ; can re-sort to the race-ground or the theatre ; can be found at the card-table or in the ball-room. In avowing these sentiments, I avow the sentiments, which from the earliest ages of the church have been maintained alike by the old Catholic bishops and fathers, and by the most distinguished and illustrious churchmen of modern times.' The body of our own Ecclesiastical Law, compiled by thirty-two commissioners, in the time of Edward the Sixth, and published under his royal authority, bearing date, April, 1571, gives an accu-rate and elevated standard—' Non sint compotores, non aleatores, non aucupes, non ve-natores, non sycophantæ, non otiosi aut supini ; sed sacrarum literarum studiis, et prædi-cationi verbi et orationibus pro Ecclesia ad Dominum diligentur incumbant.'
[3] Massillon.
[4] Jerome's Letter to Nepotian, though scanty in Christian Doctrine, contains some important hints on the general subject of Clerical conduct. It may be found appended to ' Bennet's Directions for the Study of Divinity and the Articles of the Church,' 12mo. 1715. An abstract is given by Burnet, Pastoral Care, chap. iv. Professor Campbell has some forcible remarks upon the same subject. On the Pastoral Character, Sect. ii. Com-pare also Secker's Charges, pp. 242, 243.

shall not think of finding the true ministers of Christ among the higher classes of society *in matters of external appearances or indulgence.* If a Minister thinks, that the attention of the great and noble requires him to copy their expensive style of living, he grievously mistakes the matter. For this will generally forfeit the opinion before entertained of his good sense and regard to propriety ;[1] and his *official* declarations concerning the vanity of earthly things, and the Christian's indifference to them, will be suspected of insincerity ; while it is observed, that he conforms to the world, as far, or even further than his circumstances will admit; and thus respect will often be changed into disgust.' At a later period of life he writes thus—' I am sorry to say, that worldly prudence, and the desire of making provision for families, not only for necessary things, but for *gentility and affluence,* is, in my opinion, eating up the life of spirituality, and simple trust in the Lord, even among those who preach scriptural doctrines. I believe these are *clogged in their Ministry*—nay, sink in general estimation, and are *excluded from usefulness more than they are aware of.*'[2] Admitting even that our income allows this indulgence of expensiveness, yet is it not a point of Christian forbearance to refrain? Is it not most important to show, that our heart is not set upon these things; that Christian plainness and simplicity are our deliberate choice; and that it is a matter of conscience, and of privilege, to devote to the service of God the expenditure, that might have been wasted upon "ceiled houses,"[3] or other useless decorations.

Social intercourse with our neighbourhoods often presents serious hindrance to our work. Not that religion inculcates any breach of good breeding, habits of moroseness, or declaiming with contemptuous severity against the follies of the world. This is neither the spirit of the Gospel of love, nor the spirit that should distinguish its professors, and much less its Ministers ; and what is said or done in this temper, had far better have been forborne, than exhibited in a garb of such unkindly roughness. Courtesy is an obligation, fully consistent with the exercise of Christian faithfulness ;[4] and, under decided Scriptural restraint, often melts down prejudice, and conciliates good-will. But *latet anguis in herbâ.* The double guard

---

[1] Jerome's Tract just alluded to may convey a useful hint. ' Facile contemnitur clericus, qui, sæpe vocatus ad prandium, ire non recusat. Nunquam petentes, raro accipiamus rogati.' Comp. Quesnel on Luke xi. 37.

[2] Scott's Remarks on the Character of Demas, in his notes on Pilgrim's Progress. Life, pp. 395, 396. And compare Letters and Papers, pp. 476—482. Works, x. 224, 225. ' The world is a deadly enemy to spiritual attainments. You cannot too soon see the high importance of being less conformed to it in all its vanities, vices, follies, and unprofitable waste of time, gifts, and talents.' Legh Richmond. Life, p. 105.

[3] See Hag. i. 4.   [4] 1 Peter iii. 8.

of watchfulness and prayer is most needful to preserve the single eye, and the heart devoted in simplicity to God. It is enchanted ground. A prudent Christian dares not walk on it without a special call. The late excellent Mr. Hervey resolved—'Never to go into any company, where he could not obtain access for his Master.' And at least we should determine to venture into no society, but where we *sincerely desire and endeavour*, to introduce our Master. There is indeed " a time for keeping silence,"[1] and " keeping our mouth with a bridle," in the presence of the ungodly; lest, by "giving that which is holy unto dogs, and casting our pearls before swine,"[2] we should provoke a needless excitement of enmity against the Gospel. But (as Dr. Watts has well observed)—'I doubt this caution has been carried much further by our own cowardice and carnality of spirit, than David ever practised it in the thirty-ninth Psalm, or than Jesus Christ meant it in the seventh of Matthew.'[3] Certainly if we are " dumb with silence, and hold our peace even from good," without feeling, like David under these circumstances, our " sorrows to be stirred ;"[4] it is but too plain, that we have lost that distinction of " the servants of Christ," which it would have been our honour to have preserved ; that our Christian prudence has degenerated into worldly cowardice ; and that our conversation with the world has been regulated by the fear of man, fleshly indulgence, and practical unbelief of the most solemn warnings of the Gospel.[5]

Our Divine Master never intended, that we should confine our religion to the services of the sanctuary. As men of God, we should have it at heart and in hand, spreading a spiritual savour over the common walks of society, and stamping us with the mark of confessors of Christ in the midst of a world, who hold him still in the same contempt, as when eighteen centuries since they nailed him to the cross. There must be some defect if we do not bring an atmosphere with us, which is more or less instantaneously felt.

[1] Eccles. iii. 7.   [2] Matt. vii. 6.
[3] Watts's humble attempt towards a revival, pp. 88, 89.
[4] Psalm xxxix. 2. See his Appeal. Psalm xl. 9.
[5] Such as Mark viii. 38. Archbishop Secker remarks, that 'we are apt to fail in not always appearing, in the common intercourse of life, sufficiently penetrated with the importance of our function, or sufficiently assiduous to promote the ends of our mission.' He warns us also, that 'talking with great earnestness about worldly affairs, or with great delight about diversions and trifles, betrays a mind over-much set upon them. Nay, our being only in a very peculiar degree good judges of such matters, or of any that are unconnected with our office, will, (unless we have some special call to them) be commonly thought to imply, that we have studied and love them beyond what we ought, to the neglect of our proper business.—If practical Christian piety, and benevolence, with constant zeal to promote them, are not the first and chief qualities which our parishioners and acquaintance ascribe to you; if they speak of you, as noted on other accounts, but pass over these articles, and, when asked about them, be at a loss what to say, excepting possibly that they know no harm of you; all is not right, nor can such a Clergy answer the design of its institution any where.' Charges, pp. 229, 236, 237.

It is the want of this high tone of character, that makes our private Ministrations so pointless and ineffective.[1] For when parochial visits have been unaccompanied with one searching inquiry respecting the state of the soul, it is easily supposed, that, as no suspicion was thrown out, none was entertained; and that, if there was not quite so much religion as with some others, yet that there was no ground for alarm, nor had the solemn statements of the pulpit any specific reference to them.

The importance of studying urbanity of behaviour in our intercourse with the world, is sometimes pleaded as an excuse for avoiding the direct offence of the cross. But let it be remembered, that God never honours a compromising spirit. The character of our profession with the world must not be merely negative. It must be marked by a wise, tender, but unflinching, exhibition of the broad line of demarcation, which, under the most favourable circumstances of mutual accommodation, still separates the world and the church from real communion with each other. Did the Apostle mean by that emphatic term—"*the course of this world*"[2]— no more than the round of giddy dissipation or vicious pleasure? Had this prohibition of worldly conformity, no regard to the principles, the standard, the taste, the external decency of worldliness? Does not his warning against even contact with the world[3]—(deduced from the reason and fitness of things, as well as from the express declaration of God)—directly apply to all the sources of interest, the fellowship, the habit of mind and conversation, which by the Scriptural standard are proved to be "not of the Father, but of the world?"[4] Or will an evangelical accuracy of doctrine, and correctness of outward deportment, be sufficient to stamp our profession with the broad seal of conformity to our Master's image?—"*They are not of the world, even as I am not of the world.*"[5] 'Doubtless' (as Archbishop Secker reminds us)—'we should endeavour to make religion agreeable; but not to make ourselves agreeable by leading our company to forget religion. We should, 'every one of us, please his neighbour for his good;' but not so 'please men,' as to fail in the character of 'Servants of

---

[1] Perhaps a profitable recollection may be gathered from the diary of a late excellent Minister—'Pardon me, O Lord, that I do not meet my friends more like a Minister of Christ.' Jay's Life of Winter. It was the opinion of the heavenly Leighton,—'that nothing takes off more from the authority of Ministers, and the efficacy of their message, than a custom of vain and frivolous conversation.' Pearson's Life, cxxvi. 'I perceive too much compliance with worldly company and conversation. Oh my soul, if I give way to this, my usefulness will be much diminished. '*Let me often remember, that I renounced the world at baptism.*' Diary of Legh Richmond. Life, p. 71.
[2] Ephesians ii. 2.
[3] "Touch not the unclean thing." 2 Cor. vi. 17, with 14—16.
[4] 1 John ii. 16.   [5] John xvii. 14, 16.

Christ.'[1] We should be made in a *fitting sense and measure,*
" all things to all men, that we may by all means save some ;" but
we shall lose ourselves, not save others, if we are quite different
persons in the pulpit and out of it.'[2] These admirable sentiments
fix the precise character and Scriptural limits of Christian courtesy, bounding it by the line of Christian edification, and distinguishing it by an entire disregard of our own interest, and
a single devotedness to the main object of the salvation of immortal souls.[3]   Indeed a successful attempt to ingratiate ourselves
with the world, should rather afford matter for godly jealousy,
than anticipation of advantage.   To have attached the world by
adventitious accomplishments to ourselves, while the Master, whom
we profess to venerate, is still with them a " despised and rejected "
Saviour, to a mind, reflecting upon Scripture principles, is a matter
of far greater alarm than of self-complacency.[4]   If they could not
endure the conciliating attractiveness[5] of the Son of God, even
whilst devoting himself to their service at an infinite cost to himself[6]—if they could count the great Apostle—(endued with so large
a portion of his Master's loveliness of deportment)—" as the filth
of the earth, and the offscouring of all things,"[7] they can only
court our society upon the perception, that we approximate to their
own standard rather than to these heavenly models.

Sometimes however this Ministerial association with the world is
justified upon principle.   It is said to operate as a restraint upon
unbecoming conversation or dissipated recreation.   It is even conceived to promise positive advantage, in recommending religion
to more general acceptance.   Yet surely the transgression of a
plain command, having a primary reference to Ministers,[8] can be
nothing less than wilful sin ;[9] while the motive pleaded in its ex-
tenuation, marks the character of the sin,—" doing evil that good
may come."   The best-intentioned motives can never justify the
infringement of a Divine obligation, even if (what in the present
case is contrary to fact and experience) the prospect of eventual
benefit were both assured and satisfactory.   But who does not
know, that the awe and restraint of our presence cannot reach to
the root of the evil ?   Its temporary and inefficient influence there-

---

[1] Gal. i. 10.   [2] Charges, p. 235.   [3] Compare Rom. xv. 2. 1 Cor. ix. 22. x. 33.
[4] See Luke vi. 22.   [5] See Matt. xi. 16, 17.
[6] Compare John xv. 18, with 13, 14.   [7] Compare 1 Cor. ix. 20—22, with 1 Cor. iv. 13.
[8] The reference 2 Cor. vi. 17. is to Isaiah lii. 11—a prophetic address to the Ministers
of the sanctuary on their return from Babylon, though subsequently extended under the
sanction of infallible authority, as a general rule of conduct under the Christian Dispensation. Poli Synopsis, in Isaiah liii. 11, and Comp. Ezra viii. 24—30.
[9] 1 John iii. 4.

fore has been dearly purchased, by a lowering of the tone of the Ministerial character, by a yielding conformity to the taste, habits and conversation of the world, and by a virtual sanction of an erroneous standard of conduct.[1] Would the Levitical high-priests have descended from their sacred elevation of immediate intercourse with God, to participate in the frivolities even of decorous worldliness? And why should we, under a more spiritual dispensation, be less separate, or our standard less heavenly? If indeed this connexion with the world should recommend us to their kindly consideration, yet no additional regard to our Master accrues from it; since we have usually been unable to mention his name with any glow of interest, nor has any feature of his holy image been illustrated or embodied in the spirituality of our conversation.[2]

It is allowed indeed, that our Divine Master occasionally associated with men decidedly adverse to his doctrine. But he could breathe a polluted atmosphere with perfect security, and therefore might venture, where common prudence would forbid those to follow, whose constitutions are predisposed to contagion. Besides, his intercourse with the world was uniformly that of an Instructor, not of a Conformist; and he accomplished his important designs, not by accommodating his conversational subjects to their taste (except indeed when illustrating his instructions from the topics and circumstances of the day,) but by chaining down their wondering attention to " the gracious words, which proceeded out of his mouth."[3] But is our intercourse with the world thus conformed to our Master's pattern? Are we ready to do " the hard and rough work of

[1] 'I fell into a mistake, when a young man,' (observes Mr. Cecil) 'in thinking, that I could talk to men of the world on their own ground, and could thus win them over to mine. I was fond of painting, and so I talked with them on that subject. This pleased them: but I did not consider, that I gave a consequence to their pursuits, which did not belong to them; whereas I ought to have endeavoured to raise them above these, that they might engage in higher. I did not see this at the time, *but I now see it to have been a great error.*' Cecil's Remains—a work abounding with most important thoughts upon the subject of the Christian Ministry. 'That man is mistaken,' (observes Quesnel) 'who thinks to prevail upon the world, by conforming himself to its fashions and manners. The world will much sooner corrupt the heart which opens itself thereto.' On Matt. xi. 8.

[2] Massillon warned his clergy most pointedly against this species of self-indulgent delusion.—'We often,' (he observes) 'persuade ourselves, that we ought to adopt or acquiesce in the taste, the language, and the manners of the world, that we may not be unacceptable companions; but when the world courts, adopts, and is delighted with a . Minister of the Gospel, *that Pastor gives a decisive proof,* that he ceases to regard the decorum of his station, and the respectability of his character. "If ye were of the world" —said our Lord to his disciples—"the world would love his own; but because ye are not of the world, therefore the world hateth you." No, my brethren, the *world does not run after a holy and respectable Pastor. Let us not deceive ourselves.* To purchase the friendship and esteem of the world, we must sacrifice a certain part of the dignity and gravity of our Ministry. *The world does not give up in the smallest degree its baneful prejudices and dangerous maxims, in order to unite itself with us. No! we must give up our consistency of character, to be admitted into its societies.'* Charges.

[3] See p. 105.

bringing God into his own world?"[1] Or are we not too easily satisfied with the influence of outward restraints, while no plain testimony has been delivered for him, "whose we are, and whom we"
profess to "serve?" It has been justly remarked, that "a worldly
state of mind is not less destructive of true holiness than gross sin."[2]
The example of Demas, the fellow-labourer of the Apostle, stands
as a beacon at the close of the Ministerial Epistles, to remind us—
even while invigorated by the glorious prospects of eternity[3]—of the
need of watchful carefulness against this baneful snare of our Ministry.[4]

Upon the full consideration of the subject, the Writer is constrained to express his decided conviction, that a very large proportion of
our inefficiency may be traced to the source of worldly conformity.
This needs no proof in the too frequent cases of decided love of
pleasure and dissipation. 'For' (as Massillon asks his clergy) 'after
having fully mixed in the diversions and follies of the world, can
you appear in a Christian pulpit, impressed with a sense of the importance of the Gospel and zealous for its success?' Of such Ministers we would speak "even weeping," that they are the sores of
the church—that they have given more strength to the cause of
separation, than the most powerful objections either to our established formularies or government—and (what is far more fearful)—
that they are charged with the awful responsibility of dragging

---

[1] Cecil's Remains. 'Examine, when you mix with the world, if duty calls you—if it
is for the good of men, and the glory of God—if it is his work you are going to do.
Look up, and you will find, it was so with your Master. If he manifested himself in a
village of Jewry, it was to do the work of his father; if at a marriage, it was to shew his
power and to command authority to his doctrine; if in the house of a publican, it was to
save a child of Abraham: if at Jerusalem on the feast-day, it was to purge the temple.'
Massillon.

[2] Bishop of Winchester's Ministerial Character of Christ, p. 289. 'Consider this also
—which is a great truth—that every degree of love to the world is so much taken from
the love of God.' Bishop Taylor's Advice to his Clergy.

[3] Compare 2 Tim. iv. 10. with verses 6—8.

[4] Not wishing to interrupt the direct line of argument in the text—we throw into the
form of a note the suggestion (applying with equal decision to Ministers in every department of the Church)—whether an engrossing interest in worldly politics does not canker
the spirituality of Christian Ministrations? 'Politics and party' (Bishop Burnet observed
of his day) 'eat out among us not only study and learning, but that which is the only
thing that is more valuable—a true sense of religion, with a sincere zeal in advancing that
for which the Son of God lived and died, and to which those who are received into holy
. orders have vowed to dedicate their lives and labours —These remarks—important in
themselves—derive additional weight from being found in the preface to the last edition
of the Pastoral Care, written only three years before the Bishop's death, when we may
hope that the remembrance of his own course, (far too political for the sanctity of his
office) suggested the caution. It is not meant, that the clergy should neglect the exercise of their civil privileges, or the enforcement of civil obligations. But surely the Minister of a "kingdom not of this world" ought to be ready to say of his own interest in the
politics of this world—"Let the potsherd strive with the potsherd of the earth." The
more we are of politicians, and of party men, the less we are of Ministers; and the less
of unction, fruitfulness, and comfort will be found in our work.—See some useful hints
to ministers in Scott's Life, pp. 306, 307.

with them immortal souls down to perdition by their negligence, or by the positive influence of their example.

But is not also the lax, indulgent approximation to the spirit of the world—either in our general habit and appearance—or in our intercourse with the world—a leading, though not always a tangible, cause of failure? Even the faithful exhibition of the cross must be materially weakened by a want of the corresponding exhibition of its power, in crucifying its Ministers to the lusts and affections of the world. A connexion with the world beyond the point of clear duty, (or even within these narrow bounds, without a heavenly temper) must bring us into a worldly atmosphere, which deadens the vigorous actings of a spiritual life, till, like the torpedo, we benumb every thing we touch. Conscience in a tender and susceptible state, might almost determine the question— What is the effect of such connexions upon the spiritual frame? Has there not been in this atmosphere a closer communion with the world than with God? Has not the spirit of prayer been well nigh extinguished, and delight in *the more spiritual exercises* of our work fearfully lost? And does not our Ministry thus become (perhaps unconsciously to ourselves) weak, general, and indefinite upon the main point of separation from the world? Or, even if our exhortations reach the Scriptural standard of decision, must not their power be wholly counteracted by this compromising spirit?

Accurate and earnest statements of truth, combined with sociable conformity to the world, will give no offence, and bring no conviction.[1] Cowper's line—'If parsons fiddle, why may'nt laymen dance?'—has at least as much truth as wit in it. If we go one step into the world, our flock will take the sanction to go two; the third will be still more easy, and the atmosphere more enticing, till at last it proves, "as a bird hasteth to the snare, and knoweth not that it is for his life."[2] 'The Minister, therefore, who would not have his people give in to worldly conformity such as he disapproves, must keep at a considerable distance himself. If he walks near the brink, others will fall down the precipice.'[3] 'A preacher who enjoys the smiles of the world, can hope for little success from

---

[1] 'The "way is still narrow," and "the gate is" yet "strait." The world will allow us to say this officially, to read it in the lesson of the day, and to amplify the solemn saying in a sermon. But if we *mean* what we preach, and awaken men's belief of our sincerity in the interval between one Sunday and another, then begins the debate between a Minister and his flock. So long as he is not missing in the circles of pleasure, he may deliver without suspicion the most fearful warnings of God against a slumbering world; and none will molest him. But the moment his own example comes in aid of his doctrine, and irritates the consciences of those around, his creed is discovered to be false and foolish."—Antichrist. By the Rev. J. Riland. Pp. 49, 50.

[2] Prov. vii. 23.   [3] Scott's Life, p. 122.

God ;' but 'a Minister of the Church, who is entirely disengaged from the love of earthly things, is a great treasure, and a great " consolation " to her.'[1]

CHAPTER III.

THE FEAR OF MAN.

WHAT conscientious Minister is not painfully reminded of the truth of the inspired aphorism—" The fear of man bringeth a snare ?"[2]   Perhaps no temptation is more specious in its character, or more subtle and diversified in its operation.   Its connection with worldly conformity is sufficiently evident from the recollection of his paralyzing influence upon Ministerial boldness.   Mr. Scott, in his early Ministry, appears to have suffered severely from this temptation.   ' This,' (he observes) ' is the last victory the Christian gains —Here I find my own deficiency, as much or more than in any other respect : and often I feel an inward timidity, when about to preach upon an unpopular doctrine, or expose a foible, which some one of my congregation, whom I otherwise love and esteem, is remarkable for : and in every instance I feel the greatest reluctancy to resign the good opinion, or act contrary to the judgment of those for whom I have esteem.   It is true, I am peculiarly bound to strive against this, by reason of my Ministerial office.   I am to speak boldly, " not as a man-pleaser, but as the servant of God "— and therefore I endeavour to master all these fears, to act implicitly as my conscience suggests, without respect of persons.   Conformity to others in things unchristian, the fear of man, a servile spirit of time-serving, &c., are the faults of Ministers, *and effectually hinder even those* that desire it from performing the most important parts of their Ministry, both in public preaching, and by private application.   But this kind of spirit goeth not out, but by a very spiritual and devout course of life.   Indeed its expulsion is the gift of God, and is especially to be sought for from him.'[3]

---

[1] Quesnel on 1 Cor. ii. 3.   Acts iv. 36.   See some striking thoughts on the subject of this Chapter, in the Bishop of Calcutta's Prefatory Essay to Baxter's Reformed Pastor, p. liii.

[2] Prov. xxix. 25.

[3] Scott's Life, pp. 117, 118.   Mr. Walker writes very feelingly upon this point, mentioning among his principal trials 'a most abominable fear of men's faces, especially in personal conference.   I have been forced to fight every inch of my way against this, and not without repeated advantage on its part, and a perpetual consciousness of not having

There are few of us of Lavater's self-observant stamp, but will have some sympathy with this graphical delineation. *In our public ministrations*—as with Mr. Scott—conviction of duty is often almost sacrificed to it. Subjects uncongenial to the taste and habits of influential men in our congregation are passed by, or held back from their just and offensive prominence, or touched with the tenderest scrupulosity, or expanded with wide and undefined generalities; so that the sermons (like letters put into the post-office without a direction) are addressed to no one. No one owns them. No one feels any personal interest in their contents. Thus a minister under this deteriorating influence chiefly deals in general truths devoid of particular application—more in what is pleasing than what is direct and useful. Many other subjects may be equally necessary, or indeed more important; but these are more conciliating. There is thus a continual conflict between conscience and the world —'I ought to speak for conscience' sake; but I dare not speak, for fear of the world.' The offensive truth must be smoothed, disguised, and intermixed, until it is attenuated into an insipid, pointless, and inoperative statement. The spirit of cold refinement, which gives occasion to this compromising Ministration, is one of the most baneful hindrances to our efficiency. Whether in or out of the Church, it is the real spirit of the world. It will tolerate and even approve a modified system of Evangelical truth, while the entire and unflinching presentment of the Gospel in its native simplicity and spirituality is unacceptable. Mr. Cecil remarks—' There is too much of a low, managing, contriving, manœuvering temper of mind, among us. We are laying ourselves out, more than is expedient, to meet one man's taste, and another man's prejudices. The Ministry is a grand and holy affair; and it should find in us a simple habit of spirit, and a holy but humble indifference to all consequences.'[1]

Our general Ministration is also ' sore let and hindered' by this principle. Indeed the subterfuges of cowardice and self-deception are endless, when " the wisdom of this world " has begun to prevail against the simplicity of faith. How seldom do the rich and poor

acted up to duty. I have hardly courage to this day in that private way, to act on the offensive. This was evidently from a love of esteem, supported by a constitutional timidity.' Life, p. 453. Second Edition. Comp. pp. 342, 343. The apostle appears to intimate the power of this Ministerial hindrance, in exhorting Timothy to "stir up all his gifts" of " power, love, and of a sound mind" (which—and not the " *spirit of fear*"—had been given him by the imposition of hands) to resist its influence. 2 Tim. i. 6—8.

[1] Cecil's Remains. Luther's rule was—' When one cometh into the pulpit he is much perplexed to see so many heads before him; when I stand there, I look upon none; but imagine, they are all blocks that are before me.' Table Talk, chap. 22. See some discriminating remarks in Bishop of Winchester's Ministerial Character of Christ, pp. 433 —438.

share alike in the faithfulness of Ministerial reproof! How hard is it, instead of "receiving honour one of another," to seek the honour that cometh from God only![1] How ready are we to listen to cautions from influential quarters against excessive zeal! How much more afraid are we of others going too far, than of coming short ourselves of the full requisitions of the Scriptural standard!—sometimes preferring intercourse with our brethren of a lower standard, or even with the world, rather than with those, whose Ministry most distinctly bears the mark of the cross! In how many cases of conviction is the "light hid under a bushel," or exhibited only to the friends of the Gospel! How many shrink from "witnessing a good confession," except under the shelter of some great name! How often are opportunities of usefulness neglected! and the "endurance of afflictions" in "making full proof of our Ministry"[2] avoided from the fear of the cross! 'We cannot' (we say) 'do all at once. We hope to gain our point by little and little. We dare not, therefore, by taking a bold step upon the impulse of the moment, close the avenues of distant and important advantage.' But does our conscience clear us of a desire to follow our Master, without "taking up *the daily cross*?" Are we not afraid of "being fools for Christ's sake?" Do we not sometimes "become all things to all men," when we ought to remember, that, "if we yet please men, we cannot be the servants of Christ?"[3] Christian prudence indeed is most valuable in its own place, connection, and measure; and the want of it brings with it great inconvenience. But except it be the exercise of faith, combined with boldness, and encircled with a warm atmosphere of Christian love,[4] it will degenerate, and become the time-serving spirit of the world. "The fear of man" often assumes the name of prudence, while a worldly spirit of unbelief is the dominant, though disguised, principle.

But *the fear of the professing church* is also a serious part of this temptation. We are afraid to exhibit the doctrines of grace in their fulness and prominence, lest we should be thought unmind-

, [1] John v. 44. 'A man sometimes suffers himself to be lulled asleep by the agreeable noise of a flattering world, which praises a Pastor for performing one half of his duty, while God condemns him for the neglect of the other.' Quesnel on 2 Tim. iv. 5.
[2] 2 Tim. iv. 5.
[3] Gal. i. 10. 'Jesus begins his preaching, not by flattering men in their inclinations, but by that which is most necessary for them.' Quesnel, on Matt. iv. 17. 'How sweet it is to have this testimony in our conscience, that one has not been afraid of men, when it was necessary to serve God.' Ib. on 1 Thess. 2. 'What!' said John Welsh (a fervent Scotch Minister, son-in-law to the celebrated John Knox,) 'that I should regard or fear the face of any man, when I remember and assure myself that I am standing before that sacred and Glorious Majesty, whose word, in his very sight, I am preaching to his servants and creatures! Believe me, when this thought enters my mind, I could not pay any regard to the face of any man, even if I wished ever so much to do so.'
[4] Compare 2 Tim. i. 7.

ful of the enforcement of practical obligation. The freeness of the Gospel invitations, and the unreserved display of Evangelical privileges, are often fettered by the apprehension of giving indulgence to Antinomian licentiousness. The fear of the imputation of legality restrains the detailed exposition of relative duties. What further proof need we of the baneful influence of this temptation, than the recollection of two Apostles beguiled for a short moment to deny the faith of the Gospel?[1] "With me," (said another Apostle to his people, whose determined resistance to the weakness of his brethren was the honoured means of their restoration) "it is a very small thing that I should be judged of you, or of man's judgment. He that judgeth me is the Lord."[2] Indeed the want of singleness of aim obscures the work of grace in our own hearts; nor can we maintain our peace of mind, except we feel, that we *have but One to please*—that "One is our Master, even Christ."[3] Nor is this supreme regard to our great Master less important, as insuring the success of our work. Where "the truth is imprisoned,"[4]—if not "in unrighteousness"—yet in unbelief, there must be a want of power upon Ministration.

The direct violation of Christian integrity has a necessary tendency to enfeeble exertion, by diverting our mind from that main object, which should be always directing our whole time and energies, and compared with which every other object is utterly unimportant—the edification and salvation of our people. The voice of conscience and duty speaks with a weaker tone in a worldly atmosphere. The habits of self-indulgence are strengthened, and the exercises of self-denial proportionably diminished in frequency and effectiveness. Thus, as the heart is more in the world, it is less in our work; our duties are consequently performed with reluctance, and unproductive in their results. Though we would by no means advocate indiscretion, yet well-intentioned imprudence is far better than the frigid wisdom of this world; and it will invariably be found, that those that act openly with an honest freedom (though they may probably commit mistakes) will be generally borne out, and find their path ultimately smoothed; while the temporizing spirit, that aims to please both God and man, will meet with disappointment from both. Where God is not honoured, he will not honour. And in defect of becoming Christian boldness, our people, under the influence of our example, will sink into the same benumbed spirit, while their confidence in us will be materially weakened by the manifest evidence of our inefficiency and unfruitfulness.

[1] Gal. ii. 11—14.   [2] 1 Cor. iv. 3.   [3] Matt. xxiii. 8.   [4] Rom. i. 18. in the Greek.

No less than four times in a single verse does God warn his prophet against this besetting temptation.[1] At another time he threatens his timid messenger with utter confusion.[2] Yet let the servant of God gird himself with his Christian panoply, and he will find ample provision made for his complete success. Let him study more deeply the high dignity of his glorious Ministry.[3] Let him seek to realize the presence of his heavenly Master " walking in the midst of the golden candlesticks," to direct, invigorate, and uphold " the angels of his Churches."[4] Let him associate himself with those Ministers, who are delivered from this degrading bondage, and " professing a good profession before many witnesses."[5] Let him call out his Christian principles into more uniform and active operation. The fear of God will subjugate the fear of man ; and, however strong the " confederacy," if he " sanctify the Lord of Hosts, he will be a sanctuary to him."[6] Faith exercised in simplicity will bring to view an invisible and present God—a covering, in the endurance of the cross, even from " the wrath of the King."[7] Thus—while " the fear of man bringeth a snare " it is written—" whoso trusteth in the Lord shall be safe."[8]

CHAPTER IV.

THE WANT OF CHRISTIAN SELF-DENIAL.[9]

It may be generally remarked, that, unless our work exhibit the self-denying character of the cross of Christ, it is the Christian Ministry in the letter only, not in the spirit ; it is not the work, that God has engaged to bless. The motives to this Ministerial principle (were it not for the strong counteracting current) would be irresistible. The impressive solemnity of Ordination (in which we voluntarily bound ourselves to ' *lay aside the study of the world and the flesh*[10]) might be thought to give at the very outset an impulse

---

[1] Ezek. ii. 6.   [2] Jer. i. 19.   [3] See 2 Cor. iv. 1.   [4] Rev. i. 13—20.
[5] 1 Tim. vi. 12.   [6] Isa. viii. 12—14.   [7] Heb. xi. 27.   [8] Prov. xxix. 25.
[9] On this subject see a most valuable chapter in the Bishop of Winchester's Ministerial Character of Christ—' *The self-denial of the Ministry of Christ.*'
[10] Exhortation to Priests: that is (as Archbishop Secker expounds it) ' not making either gross pleasures, or more refined amusements, even literary ones unconnected with your profession—or power, or profit, or advancement, or applause, your great aim in life; but labouring chiefly to qualify yourselves for doing good to the souls of men, and applying carefully to that purpose whatever qualifications you attain.'—Instructions to Candidates for Orders, appended to his Charges. Every thing, however refined, that has not the glory of God for its object, must be included in these terms.

to a course of habitual self-denial in our consecration to the service of God. But the continual struggle with natural self-indulgence, and the influence of old habits (perhaps the habits of our former unconverted state) fearfully operate to lower the Scriptural standard of exertion. The cultivation, therefore, and exercise of *this habit*, are the springs of the most beneficial activity; and the want, or the enervation of it, proportionably relaxes the operation of our high motives and encouragements. Archbishop Leighton admirably sets forth John the Baptist, as an example to Ministers of the gospel—' to live, as much as may be in their condition and station, disengaged from the world—not following the vain delights and ways of it—not bathing in the solaces and pleasures of earth, and entangling themselves in the care of it; but *sober and modest, and mortified in their way of living;* making it *their main business not to please the flesh,* but to do service to their Lord, to walk in his ways, and prepare his way for him in the hearts of his people.'[1] The Apostle sets before us the habitual temperance of the wrestler, as the illustration of his own Ministerial exercises, and as the safeguard to preserve his own stedfastness;[2] the necessity for which was in no respect diminished by his high Christian attainments. The missionary Eliot is said to have ' become so nailed to the cross of the Lord Jesus Christ, that the grandeurs of this world were unto him just what they would be to a dying man. He persecuted the lust of the flesh with a continual antipathy; and when he has thought that a Minister had made much of himself, he has gone to him with that speech—' Study mortification, brother; study mortification.' '[3] We might indeed apply the Apostle's remark on a subject not wholly dissimilar—" If a man know not how to rule *his own*" self, "how shall he take care of the Church of God?"[4] Fidelity to God requires the abridgment or relinquishment of whatever is inconsistent with " giving himself continually

[1] Lectures on Matt. iii. Works, vol. iii. 25.   [2] 1 Cor. ix. 25—27.

[3] Mather's Life of Eliot. His biographer, in the same spirit, on his entrance on the Ministry, having met with the remark—'that the want of mortification in a Minister is very often the cause of the unsuccessfulness of his Ministry, resolved to read over Dr. Owen's valuable Treatise on Mortification, with some other books for instruction and direction on the same subject—Life of Cotton Mather, by his son—an excellent abridgment of which may be found among an admirable system of Christian Biography, now publishing by the Religious Tract Society. See some hints on the subject, in the Life of Owen Stockton, republished in the same series. Henry Martyn appears to have deeply felt the incalculable value of this Ministerial habit—'A despicable indulgence in lying in bed' (he writes soon after his Ordination) 'gave me such a view of the softness of my character, that I resolved on my knees to lead a life of more self-denial; *the tone and vigour of my mind rose rapidly: all those duties, from which I usually shrink, seemed recreations.* I collected all the passages from the four gospels that had any reference to this subject. It is one, on which I need to preach to myself, and mean to preach to others.' Life, p. 68.
[4] 1 Tim. iii. 5.

to prayer, and to the Ministry of the word." He may "escape," indeed, "the pollutions that are in the world through lust;" but the subtle indulgence of sloth or levity still besets him with an influence as injurious as worldly dissipation.[1]

But to illustrate this important habit more in detail—*It should be visible in our manners and communication with our people.* The ordinary remove of a young Minister from the University to a country parish brings him into a new world. His intercourse, hitherto conducted with men on his own level—men of good breeding, education, and intelligence—must now be exchanged for contact with men of unfurnished minds, and engaged in pursuits utterly uncongenial with taste and refinement. Nor is he at liberty (as in the common walks of life) to decline their intercourse. He has bound himself by the deepest responsibility to live for them and with them, on terms not only of consideration and respect, but of mutual confidence and love. He must therefore deny himself, to "condescend to men of low estate." He must acquaint himself with their manners, their modes of thinking and expression, and their connections with one another, in order to bring them under the direct influence of pastoral instruction. The dignified condescension of our Divine Master's Ministry furnishes the best pattern for his servants. He "spake the words unto" the people—not as in his infinite wisdom he was able to speak—but "as they" in their infantine state of intelligence "were able to hear;"[2] and he invited them to "learn of him," in the assurance; that he was "meek and lowly in heart."[3] The want of conformity to this pattern shuts up the avenues of confidence, and consequently the prospects of success. It gives a force of repulsion rather than of attraction to Ministerial intercourse. The "rough places," instead of being "made smooth," are made more rough and impervious.[4]

The duties of the Ministry will constantly exercise Christian

---

[1] It was a most important remark of Œcolampadius, animadverting, in his celebrated Epistle to the Waldenses, upon the injunction of the celibacy of priests—'It is not marriage that spoils priests, but *sloth, self-indulgence, and the fear of the cross.*' Scott's Continuation of Milner, vol. i. 147. Dr. Watts's caution will explain this remark with valuable minuteness: 'Guard' (says he to his young Minister)—'against a love of pleasure, a sensual temper, an indulgence of appetite, an excessive relish of wine or dainties; this carnalizes the soul, and gives occasion to the world to reproach but too justly.'—Humble Attempt, pp. 80, 81.

[2] Mark iv. 33.   [3] Matt. xi. 29.

[4] Bishop Wilson's sentiments on this point were those of one who had deeply imbibed his Master's spirit.—'The greatest prelate in the Church is he, who is most conformable to the example of Christ, by humility, charity, and care of his flock, and who for Christ's sake, will be a servant to the servants of God.' And again—'God give me a true and prudent humility; to have nothing of the secular governor—to attend the flock of Christ as a servant—to look back upon him as my pattern—to study his conduct and spirit—to spend and be spent for my flock, and that I may never strive to live at ease, in plenty, in luxury, repose, and independence.' Sacra Privata.

self-denial.[1] Thus it was with our Master. His food and rest were even foregone or forgotten in his absorbing delight in saving souls.[2] Seasons of necessary retirement were interrupted without an upbraiding word.[3] Hunger, thirst, cold, or fatigue set no bounds to the determined forgetfulness of himself. How uniformly also did the great Apostle prefer the spiritual advantage of his people to his own personal comfort![4] a pattern for us in the daily sacrifice of our ease, convenience, and legitimate indulgence. *As regards the visitation of the sick*—it was said of Mr. Grimshaw, (could it be said of many of us?) that 'night and day were the same to him. He has been known *to walk several miles in the night, in storms of snow, when few people would venture out of their doors, to visit a sick person.*'[5] We must be the pastors of the whole flock, not of a select few; not indulging ourselves with the most hopeful and interesting, but labouring for those, whose urgent need cries loudly for our instruction—like the good shepherd—bestowing our primary attention upon the lost sheep.[6] In detail—we shall often have much to bear from their ignorance and weakness; sometimes also from their impertinence and unreasonable demands. But the grand object of winning their souls will restrain even the appearance of harshness or petulance, which might " turn the lame and diseased out of the way," when " rather it ought to be healed."[7] The meanest of our people must have his full share of our consideration. Let him have free access to us at proper or even at inconvenient times. Let us carefully weigh his every scruple and difficulty. What seems trifling to us, may be important to him. His doubts and perplexities are sacred to him, and require the same tender sensibility of treatment, as if they were sacred to us. This exercise of sympathy will not only tell on the success of our Ministry, but will also form us into a style of experimental preaching, which ' will be a far more effective part of our furniture, than any classical learning, or even than the critical knowledge of the Scripture itself.'[8]

[1] To a person, who lamented to Dr. Johnson, that he had not been a Clergyman, because he considered the life of a clergyman to be an easy and comfortable life—he replied—' The life of a conscientious clergyman is not easy. I have always considered a clergyman as the father of a larger family than he is able to maintain. No! sir; I do not envy a clergyman's life as an easy life; nor do I envy the clergyman who makes it an easy life.'

[2] Compare John iv. 6, 31—34.   [3] Compare Mark i. 35—38; vi. 31—34.

[4] As, for example, sending Tychicus to the Church at Ephesus, and Epaphroditus to Philippi; choosing rather himself to want a soothing attendant in prison, than that the Churches should want a comforter! Eph. vi. 21, 22. Phil. ii. 25, 28.

[5] Newton's Life of Grimshaw, p. 102. For similar instance of Ministerial self-denial —compare Memoir of Oberlin, p. 216—of Neff by Dr. Gilly, pp. 133—136 (third edition) —of Rev. T. Thomason, p. 117.

[6] See Luke xv. 4.   [7] Heb. xii. 13.

[8] Doddridge's Sermons on the Power and Grace of Christ, on Is. xl. 11.

There is also the imperceptibly growing tendency of old age to abated vigour and activity, which brings a chilling frost or damp upon our energies, and in various ways gives advantage to the ever-watchful enemy to counteract or paralyse a course of usefulness. Massillon speaks to this point with much impressiveness— 'Never' (says he) 'consider your Ministry, at any period of it, as a situation of honourable repose. *Think not of appropriating any time to yourself, if you can by a different application of it preserve only one soul from perdition.* Content not yourselves with going through your public and ordinary duties, after which we are ready to persuade ourselves, that we are discharged from every other. Let not age itself, let not the long and active discharge of your Ministerial avocations, in which you have grown old, suggest to you a legitimate reason for ceasing from the combat, and of at length enjoying the repose, to which, after so many years of labour, you may seem to be entitled. Rather let your "youth be renewed like the eagle." Zeal may supply powers, which nature may in appearance refuse. These precious remains of decay are honourable to the Ministry. Let not old age become a motive to any indulgence, which may not be strictly consistent at the close of a life dedicated to the discharge of the pastoral obligations. Continue to abound in the work of the Lord.'[1]

Self-denial must also controul our *Ministerial study.* The importance of the habit of study has been already noticed.[2] But no less important is its controul. From the literary education of clergymen, 'it will easily be perceived, that an ardour for extra-professional studies is a temptation exactly fitted to their situation or previously-formed habits, and one by which they are more likely to be seduced, than by others of a less specious appearance:' and thus 'the literary pursuits of a Minister will in many cases afford a strong evidence of his religious character. Secular studies, however congenial to a person's taste, or necessary for his recreation, cannot possibly be the *chief object* of any Minister who is conscientiously devoted to his pastoral engagements.'[3] These remarks place the subject in a just light. The usefulness of these studies entirely de-

---

[1] Charges, pp. 122, 123. '*Rest,*' (said the Apostolical Bishop Wilson, speaking of himself) '*is a crime in one, who has promised to labour all the days of his Life.*' Sacra Privata. It was a frequent and important petition of Mr. Whitfield, 'that the Lord would keep me from growing slack in the latter stages of my journey.' Mr. Scott alludes to his own need of this petition. (Life, p. 280.) But who does not need it in reference to the *early* as well as 'the latter stages of the journey?' Yet even here the voice of self-denial may sometimes be—'Spare thyself,'—see Mr. Venn's affecting allusion to his own case. Correspondence, pp. 176, 185, 487.

[2] Part 1. Chap. vii. Sect. 1.

[3] Wilkes's Essay on Signs of Conversion or Unconversion in Christian Ministers, p. 45.

pends upon their subordination to the main purpose. Holding the principal place, they tend to secularize our spirit, to engross our time, and to divert our attention from a primary regard to our people, who, in the lack of our watchful superintendence, are in danger of perishing in ignorance and sin. The ' "vows of God" ' (as Mr. Scott reminds us) ' "are upon us." All our reading ought to be subservient to the immediate object of instruction. We may read any book, ancient or modern, sacred or profane, infidel, heretical, or what not; *but always as Ministers*, to note such things, as may the better enable us to defend and plead for the "truth as it is in Jesus;" never merely for amusement or curiosity, or love of learning, simply for its own sake, or for the credit or advantages derived from it.'[1]

No one attains remarkable eminence or success, without a resolute and habitual self-denial in subordinating every secondary point to the primary object. Perhaps the highest praise for a Minister of the Gospel was given by Dr. Johnson, when he remarked of Dr. Watts, that, 'whatever he took in hand, was, by his incessant solicitude for souls, converted to theology.' And indeed this determined singleness of purpose is indispensable to a conscientious discharge of Ministerial obligations. How fearful would be the responsibility of a soul passing into eternity unregarded and uninstructed, while our minds were engaged in some pursuit of literature, taste, accomplishment, or even abstract theology! How self-convicting would be the confession—" *While thy servant was busy here and there, the man was gone !*"[2] It is always dangerous to prefer the indulgence of study to the active exercises of the Ministry; or at least to "give ourselves to reading," so as to neglect the work of pastoral instruction.[3] These avocations are legitimate in

[1] Scott's Letters and Papers, pp. 309, 310. 'I wish every clergyman'—said Mr. Richmond—'to have a mind stored with useful literature, every particle of which should be consecrated to the study of the Bible and the souls of men.' 'I abhor'—said Baxter (Narrative of his Life) 'the folly of those unlearned persons, who revile or despise learning, because they know not what it is; and I take not any piece of true learning to be useless. And yet my soul approveth of the resolution of holy Paul, who determined to know nothing among his hearers (comparatively to value no other wisdom but the knowledge of a crucified Christ).' 'I carried along with me in all my studies this great design; namely, of improving them and the knowledge acquired by them for the honour of God's name, and the greater discovery of his wisdom, power, and truth; and so translated my secular learning into an improvement of Divine knowledge. And had I not practised this design in my acquests of human learning, I had concluded my time misspent: because I ever thought it unworthy of a man that had an everlasting soul, to furnish it only with such learning, as either would die with his body, and so become unuseful for his everlasting state, or that in the next moment after death would be attained, without labour or toil in this life.' Judge Hale's account of the Good Steward. Many of us might profitably sit at the feet of this distinguished Christian layman.
[2] See 1 Kings xx. 40.
[3] 'The Divine, who spends all his time in study and contemplation on objects ever so sublime and glorious, while his people are left uninstructed, acts the same part the eagle

their character, but criminal in their over-indulgence. An engross-ing attachment, preventing an entire self-devotedness of heart, though less scandalous, may prove eventually little less prejudicial to our usefulness, than the palpable love of money or of pleasure. And therefore—'as to the waters which are drawn from these springs, how sweetly soever they may taste to the curious mind, that thirsts for the applause which they sometimes procure, I fear there is often reason to pour them before the Lord with rivers of penitential tears, as the blood of souls which have been forgotten, while these trifles have been remembered and preserved.'[1] Such (as we have already remarked) was the godly jealousy of Henry Martyn, lest his literary and theological pursuits (for even *theology, except it be made a spiritual study,* may be a secularizing indul-gence) should deaden his soul to his more holy exercises.[2] The solemn ordination engagement impels us—if not to put away—yet at least to restrain within very contracted limits, many matters of legitimate Christian interest : under the conviction, (to use again the forcible words of Doddridge, who on this subject cannot be suspected of prejudice,) that they employ a very large portion of our retired time, and are studied rather as polite amusements to our own mind, than as things which seem to have an apparent subserviency to the glory of God, and the edification of our flock ; and consequently, I fear they will stand as *articles of abatement,* (if I may so express it) in our final account ; and, when they come to be made manifest, will be found " works that shall be burnt," as being no better in the Divine esteem than " wood, hay, or stubble," (1 Cor. iii. 12, 15.) how beautifully soever they may have been garnished or gilded over.[3] The best prospect of Ministerial fruitfulness is, with the heavenly view of Leighton, to '*count the whole world in compar-ison with the cross of Christ one grand impertinence :*' and to be brought to the mind of Professor Franck at the period of his con-version—'Whereas I had but too much idolized learning, I now

---

would do, that should sit all day staring at the sun, while her young ones were starving in the nest.' Bishop Horne's Essays, p. 71. 'Can any thing be more opposed' (asks an eloquent Presbyter of his brethren) 'to the simple character of an herald of Christ, than a mere taste for elegant literature, the mere labour of a scientific student, the mere ardour of the philosopher or the historian? Was it for this you undertook the cure of souls? Is it for this you desert your closet, your sick chambers, your private devotional duties ? A literary spirit in a Minister of Christ is direct rebellion against the first claims of his high office.' Bishop of Calcutta's Prefatory Essay to Baxter, p. 55.
  [1] Doddridge's Sermon on the neglect of souls. Works, vol. iii. 258.   The sermon is also given in ' Williams's Christian Preacher.'   [2] 49 note, 51 note.
  [3] Doddridge's Sermon, *ut supra.* Compare also his Family Expositor—Note on 1 Cor. iii. 15, and some important hints especially addressed to young Ministers, in his Observa-tions on the Childhood of the Saviour—On Luke ii. Sect. xiv. See also Bishop Horne's Considerations on John the Baptist, Sect. v. and Coleridge's advice to the young Parish Priest.

perceive, that all attainments at the feet of Gamaliel are to be val-ued like dung, in comparison of the excellency of the knowledge of Jesus Christ our Lord.'[1]

Christian self-denial must also be extended to *Clerical amuse-ments and recreations.* The amusements of gardening accom-plishments need a watchful subordination. Mr. Cecil cut the strings of his violin, and threw aside his painting brush, when he detected his indulgence diverting his mind from present duty.[2] Again—The recreation of farming, *pursued as a business,* is sure-ly an inconsistent "entanglement with the affairs of this life."[3] 'Let the ministry' (as Mr. Scott exhorts us) 'have our *whole time.* Let even recreation and animal refreshment be so regulated, mod-erated, and subordinated, that they may not interfere with our grand employment, or unfit us for it; but rather recruit and pre-pare us for it, that they may all become subservient to our main object.'[4] Neither mind nor body, indeed, can be sustained without moderate relaxation. But what spiritual self-observer does not feel the need for incessant watchfulness, lest the love of ease and pleas-ure should abate the relish for heavenly employments, and consume that precious time which ought to have been industriously devoted to our high calling? Archbishop Secker justly remarks—'Not all things that are lawful are expedient; and certainly these things,' (speaking of worldly amusements,) 'further than they are in them-selves requisite for health of body and refreshment of mind, or some really valuable purpose, are all a misemployment of our leisure hours, which we ought to set our people a pattern of filling up well. A Minister of God's word, *attentive to his duty, will neither have leisure for such dissipations, public or domestic, nor liking to them.'*[5]

---

[1] Preface to Professor Franck's 'Christ the Sum and Substance of Holy Scripture,' p. xvii. 'We are to pursue our principal study at the feet of Jesus Christ. The Son of God declared to the world what he had received from his Father; and his Ministers are to teach the faithful what they have first learned from the Son of God. The Apostle professes himself to "know nothing, but Jesus Christ, and him crucified." And, indeed, he who knows this truth well, knows all others; and he arrives at this knowledge in a degree proportionable to his own needs, and those of the church, who studies with a crucified spirit.' Pastoral Instructions to his Clergy, by Anthony Godeau, Bishop of Grasse and Vence, translated from the French, 1703.
[2] See Mark ix. 47.   [3] See 2 Tim. ii. 4.   [4] Scott's Letters and Papers, p. 309.
[5] Charges, p. 238. It is no breach of charity to suppose, that to some of us Massillon would have spoken, as he did to his own clergy—'What is the most unreasonable, is, that the clergy, who plead the necessity of amusements, are ordinarily those who have the least need of them, who most neglect their duty, and the employment attached to their vocation. Their life consists in habitual indolence. We see in them nothing serious, not even in the discharge of their professional obligations, which are often hurried over with an air of fatigue, of reluctance, and of indecency. What ought to be their consolation is their trouble. They hasten into the world, where they may forget their profession and themselves together.' Charges, p. 142.

And may not this self-denial apply to Clerical attendance upon oratorios,[1] musical festivals, and similar exhibitions? If our worldly parishioners, who hear our pulpit remonstrances against the pursuit of this world's vanities, should express surprise or pleasure at meeting us at such places, ought not our consciences to whisper a wholesome doubt respecting *the expediency*[2] (to say the least) of our attendance? Much more, according to the rule just referred to, if our presence should give pain to a tender, or indeed, (as in the case alluded to by the apostle) a *scrupulous conscience*,[3] ought we not to restrain? Admitting the legitimacy of the indulgence abstractedly; yet forbearance is the present duty; the neglect of which is a "sin against our weak brethren, and therefore a sin against Christ."[4] In doubtful cases, Christian love and self-denial dictate the strait and the safest path. Restraint is the natural and direct expression of "love to the brethren." It saves us from the *possible hazard* of becoming stones of stumbling to those, whom we ought to guide in the way of the cross. As an act of violence to our own inclination, at the supposed call of duty, it is also in the true spirit of our Divine Master's injunction—"Deny thyself:"[5] and an exemplification of the practical rule—"Brethren, ye have been called unto liberty; only use *not liberty for an occasion to the flesh : but by love serve one another.*"[6] Upon this principle, clergymen have been led to relinquish the amusement of shooting. Without attaching moral evil to this recreation, yet surely it does not exhibit the Minister in his proper Levitical habits. Would not the transition be deemed somewhat violent, to visit the sick and dying in the way home from shooting? Could we leave the dog and gun at the threshold, and expect to realize in the sick chamber the nearness of eternity in its unspeakable horrors or its everlasting joys? Would not a shooting dress rather repel than invite a tempted conscience, seeking for spiritual counsel at our mouth ; or

[1] The Writer begs to refer to some letters from the pen of a most enthusiastic lover of music, written under the influence of this habit, which enabled him to subjugate his most favourite pursuits to the designs of his office. Life of Rev. Legh Richmond, pp. 397—404.

[2] Comp. 1 Cor. vi. 12. Cecil's Remains, p. 117.   [3] Comp. Ib. viii. 10.

[4] Ib. 12. This point is powerfully argued by Professor Campbell, Lecture iii. on the Pastoral Character, and by Archbishop Secker; Sermons, vol. iii. A respectable body of Christians (the Society of Friends) find it easy to deny themselves such recreations. Ought then a minister of the Gospel, whose character should embody the principles of self-denial, to complain of these restrictions, which many tender as well as scrupulous consciences deem necessary to maintain the consecrated sanctity of our office ? How paltry after all is this sacrifice, compared with the worldling's daily exercise of self-denial —"rising up early, sitting up late, to eat the bread of sorrows;" in pursuit of a shadow —a bubble—a nothing!

[5] Matt. xvi. 24.

[6] Gal. v. 13. See some excellent remarks in Coleridge's Advice to the Young Parish Priest.

an awakened soul, anxious for an answer to the infinitely momentous question—"What must I do to be saved?" These holy employments—which seem peculiarly to call for an unction from above, or to suppose an habitual frame of spiritual aspiration—carry to the mind so manifest an incongruity with such a recreation, that it is difficult to place its abandonment upon any less ground than of positive duty.

It may be asked—'What virtue is there in abstaining from things indifferent? Why, if convinced of their innocence, may we not act according to our own convictions, rather than according to the superstitions of others?' But "no man"—especially no Minister—"liveth to himself?"[1] The "strong ought to bear the infirmities of the weak, and not to please themselves."[2] Will not an honest self-scrutiny detect a criminal fondness for pleasure? For what other principle could allow the habit of self-gratification at so serious a cost to the interests of others? To affect, by our conduct, to despise what appears to us weakness, scrupulosity, or prejudice, is the way rather to confirm, than to cure, the evil; while the sacredness of the Ministerial standard is lowered, with equal injury to ourselves, and to the dignity and blessing of our work.

The sum of what is offered for consideration is simply this—Whatever experience has proved to chill our fervour, to dissipate our mind, to divert our attention, or to occupy a large portion of time or interest, is the "right eye," that we are called to "pluck out and cast from us."[3] Far be it from the Writer to advocate ascetic austerity. He would not render the bow useless by keeping it always bent. He would not forget, that we are men as well as ministers; servants, and not slaves. But do we not warn our people, that the love of any created object, interfering with our Saviour's claims to supreme affection, ruins their hopes of salvation for eternity? And ought not we to remind ourselves, that the attraction of mind to any one subject of interest, which diverts our minds from our consecrated employment, involves it in the positive guilt of unfaithfulness to our Master, must bring a curse instead of a blessing upon our Ministry, and may well lead us to tremble for our ultimate safety? The devoted servant of God will find a measure of relaxation in turning from the more painful to the more soothing exercises of his work. Some total diversion will however occasionally be needed. And let

---

[1] Rom. xiv. 7. [2] Ib. xv. 1.
[3] Matt. v. 29. 'He that is appointed to minister in holy things must not suffer secular affairs, or sordid arts, to eat up a great portion of his employment. It was a great idleness in Theophylact, the patriarch of Constantinople, to spend his time in his stable of horses, when he should have been in his study, or in his pulpit, or saying his holy offices.' Bishop Taylor.

him not suppose, that his Master requires labour, when both his body and spirits demand rest. A wise management of diversion will tend rather to strengthen, than to enervate, the tone of his spiritual character, and the power of his Ministry.

CHAPTER V.

THE SPIRIT OF COVETOUSNESS.

COVETOUSNESS in Ministers has almost grown to a proverb. Judas is an awful example of its consistency with the highest Ministerial gifts. It is not the fault of any Ecclesiastical system, but the natural principle of a corrupt and selfish heart. It readily appended itself to Popery, from the transfer of the aggrandizing spirit of the system to individuals. But Judas and Demas had been its victims, long before "the Man of sin" sprang up in the Church. It has attached itself to Protestant Establishments, in the higher departments, from the influx of wealth : and in the lower departments, from the want of sufficient means to meet the present demands, and future exigencies. In this latter view especially, it allies itself to every system of Protestant dissent, with an influence as habitual and destructive, as in any Ecclesiastical Establishment.

The frequent Scriptural connexions of this selfish principle with the sacred office,[1] were doubtless intended to warn the servant of God of a most prevalent temptation. Our Church, without any express mention, has pointedly alluded to it in each of her Ordination services. She warns her deacons from the word of God, that they be "not greedy of filthy lucre." She exhibits to her priests the awful picture of "an hireling ;"[2] at the same time instructing them "how they ought to forsake and set aside (as much as they

---

[1] See the description of the Jewish teachers, Isaiah lvi. 11. Jer. vi. 13. Ezekiel xxxiv. 1—3. Micah iii. 11. Matt. xv. 5, 6; xxiii. 14—the contrast of Timothy with the Christian teachers, (Phil. ii. 20, 21.) the frequent warnings of Ministers against "filthy lucre"—1 Tim. iii. 3, 8; vi. 9—11. Titus i. 7; 1 Peter v. 2; also 2 Peter ii. 3; Jude 11. ' He enters not by Jesus Christ (into the sheepfold), who enters with a prospect of any other interest besides that of Christ and his Church. Ambition, avarice, love of ease, or desire to be distinguished from the crowd, to enjoy the conveniences of life, or to promote the interests of our family, and even the sole design of providing against want—these are all ways, by which *thieves and robbers* enter—and whoever enters in by any of these ways, or by simony, craft, &c., he deserves no better name.' Quesnel on John x. 1.

[2] ' Hireling, not one who performs the office or duty of a Minister for hire or reward, (for the Apostle, or rather our blessed Lord himself says—The labourer is worthy of his hire, or reward, 1 Tim. v. 18; Luke x. 7.) but one who endeavours to make a gain of godliness,' &c. Brewster, quoted in Bishop Mant's Prayer Book. ' He is not *an hire-*

may) *all worldly cares* and studies ;" and questioning them again more closely, upon their diligence and readiness in "laying aside the study *of the world and the flesh*." She deems it necessary to give to her highest order of Ministers this solemn charge—"Be to the flock of Christ *a shepherd, not a wolf; feed them; devour them not.*"[1] It was a blot upon the celebrated heathen moralist,[2] that, while he vehemently declaimed against covetousness, he was, throughout his life, a slave to the base traffic of usury. And how discreditable is earnest preaching against this besetting sin, if our personal habits, or family appurtenances, should exhibit its pollution ! When we warn our people against "the love of money, as the root of all evil,"[3] they will look into our own garden for this destructive weed ; which may possibly be growing there, even while we are seeking to root it out of every garden in our parish.

Covetousness is very distinct from frugality, which is a real duty —implying a well-directed and moderate use of the things of this life—"owing no man any thing"—"using the world, as not abusing it,"—like a good steward, making such provision for the present necessity, as shall prevent our families from becoming burdensome to the church. This, with Christian contentment, forms a right character. But covetousness is an inordinate thought of, desire after, and employment in, the care of this world. Its palpable exhibition is seen in a *habit of saving*—or a watching too closely over what we have, and a rooted reluctance to part with it. This is generally connected with a want of consideration and sympathy for the calls of distress, and of a very limited consecration of our substance to the extension of our Redeemer's kingdom. The reports of our Religious Societies often mark a somewhat unaccountable average of subscriptions from those, whose capabilities are so widely disproportionate. This may often arise from the great variety of channels into which the benevolent fund is distributed ; but does it in no cases originate in a want of economy, in self-indulgence, or covetousness?

---

ling, who, faithfully feeding the flock, is maintained by his Ministry : but he to whom the "filthy lucre" is the great object or inducement.' Scott in loco. Pluralities, (with some disinterested, and some necessary exceptions) have, to say the least, a plausible connexion with this hateful character.

[1] See the Ordination and Consecration services. 'Colligimus, neminem probum verbi Ministrum, quin non idem sit pecuniæ contemptor.' Calv. in Acts xx. 33. 'The moment a strong and governing desire of accumulating property takes possession of a Minister's mind—preach with orthodoxy, and some degree of animation, he may—visit his parishioners to a certain extent, he may—but a devoted labourer in the vineyard, who has one object in view—the extension and glory of his Master's kingdom—and who makes all his pursuits subservient to that object, he will not be. It is just as impossible for a man to be a great accumulator of property, and at the same time a faithful devoted Minister of Christ, as it is to establish a fellowship between light and darkness, Christ and Belial.' Professor Miller's Letters, pp. 433, 434.

[2] Seneca.   [3] 1 Tim. vi. 10.

Specious forms of this principle often belong to those who are highly connected in the world ; and the injury—unconscious perhaps to the individuals themselves—is generally exhibited in a lowered standard of separation from the world, in an unspiritual cast of mind, walk, and conversation, and in a straitened Divine influence upon their work.   In Mr. Cadogan, the dignity of the Ministerial character rose superior to the adventitious circumstances of elevated rank, without any degradation of his personal claim to respect : and the spirit of simplicity and holiness maintained throughout his course, was honoured with peculiar tokens of his Master's approbation.[1]

In the more ordinary walks of the Ministry we may discern "the cloak of covetousness "—in a mean attention to small matters—in the motives that influence our plans of economy—in carefulness to maintain present appearances—in contrivances to shift off expenses upon others—in the pleasurable excitement from the prospect of gain—in an undue depression from the disappointment of it—in the natural current of our thoughts in the direction of the world— in the readiness in lesser matters to put it upon a level with religion.   All or any of these actings of · this detestable principle. must deaden the exercises of the Christian life and of Ministerial energy.

We may advert also to a rigorous enforcement of ecclesiastical claims—a litigious and unconciliating spirit, ending in a fatal loss of our most important influence.   Without any fair ground for the charge of injustice or extortion—there may be a want of tenderness and recollection of the main ends of our office, and of the sole purpose, for which a maintenance is secured to us.[2]   Whatever consideration may belong to the due support of our family, yet the no-

---

[1] Massillon has a remarkable sermon on the temptation of Christ, which he transfers to the temptations of the Ministry.   It is hoped that the instruction (unsuitable indeed to the gravity of the pulpit) will not be rejected on account of the eccentric form of deduction in which it is given.   I. A scheme to live like gentlemen—"Command these stones to be made bread."   This danger belongs to the first entrance of the Ministry. II. Presumption to aspire after preferment—" He set him on a pinnacle of the temple." This belongs to an aspiring Minister: the second degree.   III. A boundless desire of riches and honour in elevated stations, by which a man is induced to submit to abject services for the sake of elevation—" All this will I give thee, if thou wilt fall down and worship me."

[2] Mr. Grimshaw is said to have been ' not rigorous in his exacting his dues, but contented with what his parishioners brought him.'   He would say to them—'I will not deserve your curses when I am dead for what I have received for my poor labour among you.   I want no more of you than your souls for my God, and a bare maintenance for myself.'   Newton's Life of Grimshaw, p. 124.   If he carried this principle beyond its legitimate bounds, yet the spirit of it is admirable.   The truth of Archbishop Secker's remark will be generally admitted—' A due measure of disinterestedness is one main requisite for the success of a Clergyman's labours.'   Charges, p. 248.   "I seek not your's, but you." 2 Cor. xii. 13, 14.   See Scott on 1 Cor. ix. 13—18.

ble spirit of the ministry rises above selfish considerations, and fixes upon the great trust committed to us.[1] In prospectively regarding also the rites of our successors, we may keep in mind Bishop Taylor's wholesome caution—"*Let not the name of the church be made a pretence for personal covetousness*—by saying, you are willing to remit many things, but you must not wrong the Church; for though it be true, that you are not to do prejudice to successors, yet many things may be forgiven upon just occasions, from which the Church shall receive no incommodity; but be sure, that there are but few things, which thou art bound to do in thy personal capacity, but *the same also, and much more,* thou art obliged to perform as thou art a public person.'[2] Even a heathen has remarked, that 'there is no more plain sign of a narrow and little mind, than the love of riches.'[3] And what need is there for a constant guard against those inclinations and occasions of temptations, that feed the power of this subtle principle! How hard is it habitually to maintain a practical belief of the Scriptural declarations of the fearful influence of riches upon our spiritual interests, and, *by consequence,* upon our Ministry!—"Thou, O man of God," (is the fatherly counsel to a young Minister) "*flee these things.*"[4] In the return of Apostolical simplicity, self-denial, and ove, we may anticipate a Pentecostal effusion of the spirit upon our Ministrations.

Covetousness is far more specious than worldly conformity. It has much to plead under the cover of necessity, justice, prudence, and economy. Yet we may detect its real character under all its deceptive garbs. Is not the straitness of means often an excuse from the exercise of Christian charity, while little or no restraint is laid upon the expensiveness of the dress, the table, furniture, or mode of living? Is not the charitable fund sometimes, in seasons of depression, the first that is curtailed? And do we not continue to "dwell," as before "in ceiled houses, while the house of God lies waste?"[5]

Self-denial in the family œconomy must also exercise a whole-

---

[1] The following memorandum of Bishop Wilson, for the use of his children, is in the most elevated spirit of primitive disinterestedness—'If I do not live to tell you, why I have saved no more for you out of my bishopric, let this satisfy you—that the less you have of goods gathered from the church, the better the rest that I leave you will prosper. Church livings were never designed to raise families, or to make portions out of them, but to maintain our families, to keep up hospitality, to feed the poor, &c. and one day you will be glad that this was my settled opinion, and God grant, that I may act accordingly.' Stowell's Life, pp. 58, 59.
[2] Advice to his Clergy. It may be found in Bishop Randolph's Enchiridion Theologicon, vol. i. or in the Clergyman's Instructor.
[3] Nihil est tam angusti tamque parvi animi, quam amare divitias. Cic. de Officiis. Lib: i.
[4] 1 Tim. vi. 11. [5] Compare Hag. i. 4.

some restraint. The pupilizing system, (when engaged in principally for keeping up appearances, or the worldly advantage of children,) and the adoption of worldly maxims in the education and disposal of our families, (which in Mr. Scott's judgment 'constitutes a considerable part of the *sins of the church* in the present day') come under this animadversion. It is also but too plain that the families of Clergymen are sometimes brought up to worldly expectations, rather than as disciples of the cross, and citizens of heaven. Too much weight can scarcely be given to Mr. Scott's inestimable instructions, as the embodied and most successful principles of his domestic system. 'We are to live' (he remarked) 'at the altar; but a living, a bare decent maintenance, *without any avaricious or ambitious views of advancing ourselves or our families,* should content us.' It was upon this principle (his son informs us) 'he acted through life—not that he in any way reflected upon clergymen who were born to wealth, or on whom Providence otherwise conferred it, if only they made a proper use of it. *Aspiring after it* was what he condemned.' His favourite maxim was—'what is best for the soul is really best for us,' and 'he ever looked upon worldly possessions with a jealous eye, *for his family* as well as for himself.'—'The grand secret of his success,' (that which gave him, as he tells us, the most satisfaction in the retrospect at the close of his life), appears to have been this —'that I always "sought" *for my children as well as for myself,* in "*the first place,* the kingdom of God and his righteousness."' 'This view,'—his son observes—'would extend to the value, practically and evidently set upon eternal in preference to temporal things: and very particularly to the disposal of his children in life, the places of instruction to which they should be sent, the families they should visit, the connections which they should form, and the openings which should be embraced or rejected for them.'[1]

Covetousness in all its varied forms is more easily detected in a Minister than in private Christians. The sources of his clerical income, being drawn from his people, are generally known; and consequently its capabilities and disposal are matters of public animadversion. Besides, "as a city set upon a hill, he cannot be hid."[2] Any marks of vicious indulgence upon the appearance of his house-

---

[1] Scott's Life, pp. 591, 611—614. Compare pp. 91, 396—398. Works, pp. 225, 226. Luther's dying prayer breathes the spirit of a man who had trampled the world under his feet—Domine Deus, gratias ago tibi, quod volueris me esse pauperem super terram,.et mendicum. Non habeo domum, agrum, possessiones, pecuniam, quæ relinquam. Tu dedisti mihi uxorem et filios. Tibi reddo. Nutri, doce, serva—ut hactenus me—O Pater pupilorum et judex viduarum.' Adam in Vita Lutheri. See also similar testimonies respecting Calvin, and the conviction produced upon the mind of the infidel Bayle. Scott's Contin. of Milner, iii. 486—488.   [2] Matt. v. 14.

hold will be "known and read of all men." The Apostle's appeal to God on this point[1] doubtless opens to us one of the grand main-springs of his success. On the other hand, there is no more fatal hindrance to the Ministry, none that makes our person and labours more contemptible in the eyes of the world, than this idolatrous principle. It counteracts the grand design of our office, which is to draw men from earth to heaven. It cankers many sources of our usefulness—such as simple devotedness to the work, charity and hospitality, according to the extent of our means. It hinders the spiritual elevation of the soul, and defiles the consecrated character of our office.[2] George Herbert's primitive Parson, therefore, 'labours most in those things, which are most apt to scandalize his parish. He is very circumspect in avoiding all covetousness; neither being greedy to get, nor niggardly to keep, nor troubled to lose, any worldly wealth; but in his words and actions slighting and disesteeming it; even to a wondering that the world should so much value wealth, which in the day of wrath hath not one drachm of comfort for us.'[3] The most effectual preventions of this corroding passion are—to have but few wants—to learn from our poor Christian day-labourers to cultivate faith for the future—to live not for men or for time, but for eternity—to have the glory of God, and the good of our fellow-creatures constantly in view—to study our Master's life and example—to obtain by habitual eyeing of the cross a gradual conformity to its spirit—and to remember, as Ministers, that an earnest desire to gain continually more souls to God is the sole avarice permitted to a pastor.[4]

[1] See 1 Thess. ii. 5. Compare also Acts xx. 33—35.
[2] Comp. Gregory de Cura Past. Part. i. ch. xi. Mr. Scott states the impression on his own mind on perusing the memoirs of Luther and Melancthon, of the disinterested spirit common to most of the eminent men, employed in the great work of the Reformation. His own applicatory remarks are well deserving of attention—Yes, and if we would aspire to be employed with success on such high and holy services, we must become detached more than we are from the interests of this life. Oh! are we not become too much given to contrive the means of a good provision, and of maintaining a handsome style of living? This was never the spirit, which wrought great things in the Church of God. Let us beware, lest we fall under the sentence, though in somewhat varied sense —"Ye have your reward"—in improved circumstances, but in blighted labours.' Continuation of Milner, vol. ii. pp. 181, 182. The closeness and accuracy of observation of the heathen on this point is very remarkable. They consider freedom from the love or care of money the strongest proof of the influence of Christianity. It was remarked by one of the most intelligent among them, of a native teacher—'There was only one flaw he discerned—in every thing else he was perfectly brought under the power of the gospel —he was not covetous; *but he had a degree of reluctance in parting with his money.*' Swartz's remarkable usefulness was manifestly connected with his high and uniform standard of personal disinterestedness. See Dean Pearson's interesting Life of Swartz.
[2] Herbert's Country Parson, chap. iii.
[4] Quesnel on Tit. i. 7. The subject of this Chapter suggests the notice of the opposite spirit of *improvidence.* Distressing embarrassments have often arisen from imprudent marriages, from wasteful wives, or from personal habits of negligence; by which Ministers have been degraded before their people, in the loss of their respectability, the true dignity and independence of their office, and their usefulness in the church. Whether

CHAPTER VI.

NEGLECT OF RETIREMENT.

IN the midst of the incessant, pressing, and active avocations of the Christian Ministry, how seasonable is the considerate advice of our gracious Master—" *Come ye yourselves apart into a desert place, and rest awhile.*"[1] The spirit of prayer cannot breathe freely in the atmosphere of constant and exciting employment. Not that we would seek retirement, like the contemplative monk, for the purposes of abstraction ; but to recruit our spiritual energies for renewed exercises of self-denial and perseverance. St. Paul's journey to Arabia immediately subsequent to his conversion (of which no mention is made in the inspired record of his Ministerial travels) was probably not to exercise his Ministry, but to ' receive further revelations.'[2] Secret prayer and meditation were doubtless the channels of Divine revelation to his soul ; while the more accurate and undisturbed study of his own heart, and the calculations of the fearful cost before him, must have been a most profitable occupation for this interval of comparative privacy.[3] The spirit of Brainerd's advice to a young candidate for the Ministry was in

---

these difficulties were incurred without rational prospect of deliverance ; or whether charitable assistance was contemplated, as opening a way of escape ; either case is most unworthy of our heavenly calling. Poverty, after the example of Christ and his apostles, can never be a disgrace : but liberality and wastefulness with the resources of others, (attended too often with crooked devices for our own personal interests), must bring the Ministry into contempt. The strict economy which the Ministerial income often demands, is a Providential appointment ; nor can we overstep the bounds, (except perhaps under peculiar dispensations) without equal discredit to ourselves and to our office. The aggravation of the evil is, that the embarrassments often arise not from actual necessity, but from needless expenditure. And therefore while we would deprecate the pitiful savings of meanness, we would seriously recommend a wise economy in maintaining the strict balance between our resources and our wants ; and a liberal spirit, within the bounds of those resources, to be attained by habits of plainness, simplicity, and self-denial. Restraint in our own indulgences, liberality to our friends, largeness of heart and sympathy with the poor—and consecration of all to the service of God—would fully exhibit the high spirit of the Christian Ministry.

[1] Mark vi. 31.   [2] Macknight on Gal. i. 17.

[3] Mr. Fletcher, when regret was expressed at his limited sphere, upon his first entrance into the Ministry, remarked with his characteristic piety—' If God does not call me to so much public duty, *I have the more time for study, prayer and praise.*' Cox's Life of Fletcher, p. 24. Compare also Quesnel on Gal. i. 17—19.—' The primitive Bishops had places of retirement near their cities, that they might separate themselves from the world ; lest teaching others, they should neglect themselves ; lest they should lose the spirit of piety themselves, while they were endeavouring to fix it in others.' Bp. Wilson's Sacra Privata. Indeed this appears to be the ordinary course of Ministerial preparation. Moses in Midian—(Exod. ii. 15 ; iii. 1.) John the Baptist in the desert, (Luke i. 80 ; iii. 2.)—Jesus in Nazareth, (Matt. ii. 23.) were trained in retirement for their public work.

his own holy character—'The way' (said he) 'to enjoy the Divine presence, and be fitted for distinguishing service for God, is to live a life of *great devotion and constant self-dedication* to him: observing the motives and dispositions of our own hearts, whence we may learn the corruptions that lodge there, and our constant need of help from God for the performance of the least duty: and, oh! dear sir, let me beseech you frequently to attend to the precious duties of secret fasting and prayer.'[1] The few amongst you, who are *necessarily* public men, deserve the sympathy and prayers of the church. If their habits of life were not very clearly appointed for them, their peculiar temptations (as we trust) sensibly felt, and their watchfulness and simplicity of faith habitually exercised; their own souls must suffer loss, whatever advantage might accrue to the church through their disinterested labours. Probably a strict adherence to Eliot's quaint but excellent rule to his young students is of great service to them—'I pray you look to it, that you be early birds:' meaning, we conclude, not merely early risers, but early Christian students, and above all, early worshippers.

The cultivation of habits of retirement is of the highest moment. Popular engagements must not interfere with our own personal interests, or Ministerial store. An experienced father with a well furnished mind, and intellectual habits, can afford to make sacrifices of time for the public cause, which would cost a young Minister the hazard of his permanent usefulness. *He* must at all events secure for himself time for Biblical attainments; else will his course of instruction be inefficient for the grand purposes of his office. Dr. Paley wisely recommended *retirement* to the younger Clergy, 'as the foundation of almost all good habits.' 'Learn' (said he) 'to live alone. Half your faults originate from the want of this faculty. It is impatience of solitude, which carries you continually from your parishes, your home, your duty, makes you foremost in every party of pleasure and place of diversion, dissipates your thoughts, distracts your studies, leads you into expense, keeps you in distress, or puts you out of humour with your profession.'[2] Indeed, the happiness of the Minister's life, and the effectiveness of his work, depend upon a judicious combination of retired habits with public or social exercises.

[1] Letter ix. appended to his Life. 'How great is the difference' (observes Quesnel) 'between a preacher formed gradually by the hand of God in retirement, fasting, and prayer; and those ordained in haste, who have no other school but the world, no other masters but themselves, and no other preparation than human studies, interrupted by worldly conversations, diversions!' &c. On Luke iii. 2. Compare Bishop of Winchester. pp. 62—66.

[2] Advice to the Younger Clergy of Carlisle.

But far more important is retirement for the Minister's communion with his God. We fear thăt Luther's custom to give his three
best hours of the day to this work, and Bradford studying on his
knees, are more often alluded to than followed. Yet the diligent
pastor will feel the importance, both to himself and to his people, of
living in his study as well as in his parish; not oṅly for the necessary digestion of the subject-matter of his Ministrations, but most
chiefly for the cultivation of a nearer and more habitual access to
God.[1] How delightful is it to us, and how edifying to our people,
to bring forth that Scripture as food to their souls, which the Spirit
of God hath opened to our own heaits![2] Truths that are thus obtained and wrought out in prayer have a peculiar unction. "Waiting on the Lord" will never be an encouragement to indolence. In
the habit of it, the weakest Ministrations will be efficient—in the
neglect of it the most powerful will be paralyzed. Indeed, the
'spirit of our Ministry' (as Massillon admirably observes) 'is a spirit
of prayer. Prayer is the ornament of the priesthood, the leading
feature of our character. Without prayer, a Minister is of ṅo use
to the church, nor of any advantage to mankind. He sows; and
God gives no increase. He preaches; and his words are only like
"sounding brass, or a tinkling cymbal." He recites the praises
of God; while "his heart is far from Him." It is prayer alone,
then, that gives the whole strength and efficacy to our different
administrations; and that man ceases, if I may use the expression,
to be a public Minister from the time he ceases to pray. It is
prayer, which supplies him with consolation in all his labours; and
he celebrates the ordinances of religion, as the hireling performs
his work—he considers them as a heavy task, or a 'severe imposition, if prayer doth not assuage its troubles, or console him for
want of success.'[3] If Solomon felt his need of heavenly wisdom

[1] Bishop Buṛnet's advice on the subject is truly episcopal—'To give the studies of the
clergy their full effect; a priest that is much in his study ought to employ a great part of
his time in secret and fervent prayer, for the direction and blessing of God in his labours,
for the constant assistance of his Holy Spirit, and for a lively sense of Divine matters,
that so he may feel the impressions of them grow deep and strong upon his thoughts.
*This, and this only, will make him go on with his work, without wearying, and be always
rejoicing in it. This will make his expressions of these things to be happy and noble, when
he can bring them out of the good treasure of his heart, that is ever full, and always warm
with them.'* Pastoral Care, chap. viii.
[2] Thus Cyprian speaks of his own Ministry—'Non solum proferimus verba, quæ de
Scripturarum sacris fontibus veniunt, sed cum ipsis verbis preces ad Dominum et vota
sociamus.' De bono pudicitiæ.
[3] Charges, pp. 24, 25. In the same impressive language he addresses his clergy in another place—'My brethren—a pastor who does not pray, who does not love prayer, does
not belong to that Church, which "prays without ceasing;" he is a dry and barreṅ tree,
which cumbers the Lord's ground; he is the enemy, and not the father of his people; he
is a stranger, who has usurped the pastor's place, and to whom the salvation of the flock
is indifferent. Wherefore, my brethren, be faithful to prayer, and your functions will be

to discriminate amongst his "great people," and to devise and execute the best-conducted measures for their prosperity, do not we "go out and come in" before our people with far deeper responsibilities, and yet with the ignorance of "a little child" to "discern between good and bad?" The most eminent Minister will be most ready to cry out—"Give therefore thy servant an understanding heart."[1] For of how little avail are the most splendid talents, the most mighty eloquence, and the most devoted diligence, except the unction be brought down from heaven by frequent and fervent supplication!

Prayer therefore is one half of our Ministry ;[2] and it gives to the other half all its power and success. It is the *appointed medium of receiving spiritual communications for the instruction of our people.* Those who walk most closely with God are most spiritually intelligent in "the secret of his covenant."[3] Many can set their seal to Luther's testimony, that he often obtained more knowledge in a short time by prayer, than by many hours of study. It will also *strengthen our habitual devotedness to our work, as well as our natural capacities for it.* Living near to the fountain-head, we shall be in the constant receipt of fresh supplies of light, support, and consolation—to assist us in our duties, to enable us for our difficulties, and to assure us of our present acceptance, and a suitable measure of ultimate success. The same heavenly resource will furnish us *with matter for experimental intercourse with our people*—giving us a clear insight into the workings of nature and grace, of sin and holiness ; and enduing us with a spiritual ability to counterwork the wiles of Satan and the deceitfulness of sin in their incessant and fatal influence. Thus also we shall be enabled to adapt *our Ministrations under the influence of Divine wisdom, to the several cases of our flock*—speaking with power to the unawakened—with compassion to the hardened—binding up "the bruised reed"—and "strengthening," by solemn admonitions and expostulations, "the things that remain" among us, "that were ready to die."[4] Nor is it the least advantage flowing from this habit, that it *fits us to advocate the cause of our people before God*, as well as to sympathize with their difficulties, and to lay ourselves out in their service. Probably the laborious fervency of Epaphras' secret exercises[5] were as fruitful

more useful, your people more holy, your labours will prove much sweeter, and the Church's evils will diminish.' Disc. Synod.
[1] Comp. 1 Kings iii. 7—9.   [2] Comp. Acts vi. 4.
[3] See Psalm xxv. 14. Comp. 2 Cor. iii. 5, 6.
[4] Rev. iii. 2.   [5] See Col. iv. 12.

as his public work; and who knoweth, but we shall find that our most successful efforts for our people were the hours—not when we were speaking to them from God, but when we were speaking for them to God?[1] In this view it is most important to *associate our own interests with those of our people*. The help we may thus be able to afford them in their difficulties, trials, and weakness, is intimately connected with the spiritual temperament of our own minds, acquired and maintained through the same organ of heavenly communication, which we recommend for their daily use and encouragement. The success of this operation is so certain, that an eminent divine has laid it down as a general rule—' that when we would have any great things to be accomplished, the best policy is, to work by an engine which the world sees nothing of.'[2] Our blessed Master's example is here much to be observed. As man, he had most responsible concerns to transact with God. Nothing important was done without prayer. His entrance on his Ministry was with prayer.[3] His ordination of his first Ministers was preceded by a whole night of prayer.[4] After a day spent in works of instruction and mercy, (such as would have included a week of our ordinary labour) time was redeemed from sleep for this sacred employment.[5]

The most effectual hindrances, therefore, to our work are those which impede our personal communion with the Lord. When the great enemy thus successfully intercepts our spiritual supplies, the work of God in our hearts, and connected with it, the work of God in our hands, languishes from the want of its accustomed and needful support. We have great need to watch, lest public activity should be considered to atone for neglect of private intercourse with God; and thus our profession should become a snare to ourselves, and divested of all spiritual savour to our flock. Henry Martyn had occasion to lament, that ' want of private devotional reading and shortness of prayer, through incessant sermon-making, had produced much strangeness between God and his own soul.' And in

[1] ' The kingdom of heaven must suffer violence, and the people will not ordinarily be brought into it without some violence: but let me tell you, it is not so much the violence of the pulpit, that doeth the deed, as the violence of the closet.' Bp. Sanderson's Sermon on Rom. xv. 5.

[2] Dr. Preston: formerly Master of Emmanuel College, Cambridge. Thus Archbishop Secker gave this valuable and encouraging advice to his clergy—' Form yourselves thoroughly by devout meditation and fervent prayer to seriousness of heart, and zeal for the eternal welfare of souls; *for then every thing else that you are to do will follow of course.'* Charges, p. 267.

[3] Luke iii. 21.   [4] Ibid. vi. 12.

[5] Mark i. 21—35. We cannot contemplate too closely this pattern of intermingling seasons of heavenly communion with active labour. Will not a spiritual pastor delight in the shade as well as in the sun-shine, and love to be alone with God, while he is most closely engaged in his work?

the review of the first year of his Ministry, 'he judged, that he had dedicated *too much time to public Ministrations, and too little to private communion with God.*'[1] Mr. Scott gives a most wholesome caution on this point—'The principle that made the Apostle determine not to "serve tables," though a good work in itself, should render Ministers in this day very careful not so to give their services, even to the most useful Societies, and to attending the meetings of them, as to *prevent their "giving themselves continually to the word of God and prayer."* A danger at present seems to arise on this side.'[2] The Writer would therefore wish to draw his own mind and his brethren habitually to this recollection, that nothing will enrich or console us in the neglect of intimate communion with God. We must "walk with God" *at any rate*, or our souls will die. Even Christian communion will form an empty substitute for this hallowed intercourse. The command is—"Enter into thy closet, and shut thy door."[3] Shut out not only vanity and the world, but even *for a time* "the communion of Saints." The soul may lose its spiritual vigour in any company but that of God—in the best as well as in the worst—in the Church, as well as in the world—in the active engagements of the Ministry, as well as in secular employments.

It was said of Fletcher, that 'his deepest and most sensible communications with God *were enjoyed in those hours, when the door of his closet was shut against human creatures, as well as human cares.* His closet was his favourite retirement, to which he constantly retreated, whenever his public labours allowed him a season of leisure. His public labours (astonishing as they were) bore but little proportion to those internal exercises of prayer and supplication, to which he was wholly given in private. The former of necessity were frequently discontinued; but the latter were almost uninterruptedly maintained from hour to hour. He lived in the spirit of prayer.'[4] Was not this the secret of the extraordinary power that rested upon his ministrations? The out-pouring of the Spirit of supplication would revive our work, and enlarge our success. We know who hath said—"Ask me of things to come concerning my sons; and *concerning the work of my hands command ye me."*[5]

---

[1] Martyn's Life, pp. 60, 62.   [2] Scott's Letters and Papers, p. 313.
[3] Matt. vi. 6.   [4] Gilpin's notes on Fletcher's Portrait of St. Paul, pp. 50, 51.
[5] Isaiah xlv. 11.

CHAPTER VII.

THE INFLUENCE OF SPIRITUAL PRIDE.

ONE of the most profound observers of the heart has remarked, that spiritual pride offers to Satan his main advantage over the Christian.[1] And indeed many circumstances (trifling in themselves, but gathering fearful strength from incidental causes) add fuel to the secret flame ; and in the destructiveness of the issue we are left to exclaim—"Behold ! how great a matter a little fire kindleth !"[2] An affectionate and devoted Minister is honoured of God, and acceptable to his flock.   Some regard him as an oracle ; and are almost ready, as at Lystra,[3] to "do sacrifice unto him."   What a large share of humility, what unceasing supply of Divine grace, is needed to resist a temptation, that falls in so powerfully with the selfish principle of the natural heart !   'Great care must be taken, while we are endeavouring to destroy external idols, or those of vice in others, that we do not insensibly substitute ourselves in their place.'[4]   Successful fishermen need especial watchfulness, "lest they sacrifice to their net, and burn incense unto their drag."[5]   We must indeed labour and pray unceasingly for enlarged success.   And yet in this prayer we sometimes "know not what we ask."   A season of remarkable prosperity will probably prove an hour of fearful temptation to our souls.

Cotton Mather appears to have been severely exercised on this subject, on his first entrance into the Ministry.   We must refer to his life for a most searching scrutiny, in substance as follows :—
'Apprehensions of pride—*the sin of young ministers*—working in my heart, filled me with inexpressible bitterness and confusion before the Lord.   I found, that, when I met with enlargement in prayer or preaching, or answered a question readily and suitably, I was apt to applaud myself in my own mind.   I affected pre-eminence above what belonged to my age or worth.   I therefore endeavoured to take a view of my pride—as *the very image of the Devil*, contrary to the grace and image of Christ—as an offence against God, and grieving of his Spirit—as the most unreasonable

[1] President Edwards' Thoughts on the Revival in New England.
[2] James iii. 5.   [3] Acts xiv. 13.
[4] Quesnel on Acts xiv. 15.   Sæpe sibi de se mens ipsa mentitur, et fingit se de bono opere amare quod non amat: de mundi autem gloria, non amare quod amat.   Gregor. de Curâ Pastor.   Comp. Bowles. Lib. i. c. 8.   [5] Hab. i. 16.

folly and madness for one, who had nothing singularly excellent, and who had a nature so corrupt—as infinitely dangerous, and ready to provoke God to deprive me of my capacities and opportunities. I therefore resolved to carry my distempered heart to be cured by Jesus Christ, that all-sufficient· Physician—to watch against my pride—to study much the nature and aggravations of it, and the excellence of the contrary grace.'

There is weighty truth in the remark, that spiritual pride is '*the sin of young Ministers*'—the enemy, with which 'incessant conflict must be maintained. Like Melancthon, they do not quickly learn the strength of 'old Adam.' The excitement of novelty gives a powerful energy to their work. Perhaps an atmosphere of popularity surrounds them. All this tends to blind their perception of "the mystery of iniquity" within, and to excite self-confidence, until they seem almost to aspire to a partnership with God in the salvation of souls; or at least conceive, that their services are of high importance in the Divine dispensations. *Vox populi*, is their secret motto. The breath of the multitude is their life. "Good report" is therefore a far closer test of the internal principle than "evil report." There is great knowledge of character in that sacred aphorism—"As the fining pot for silver, and the furnace for gold, so is a man to his praise."[1] How few of us could say with Henry Martyn—'Men frequently admire me, and I am pleased; *but I abhor the pleasure that I feel!*'[2]

[1] Prov. xxvii. 3. 'It is a very uncommon thing for men not to receive at least one part of the glory that is offered them. This is the touchstone, by which the fidelity of the Minister of Christ is tried. We value ourselves upon rejecting gross commendations, and extravagant flattery, because we would not make ourselves ridiculous. But when the praise is fine and delicate, and the incense prepared with art, how seldom is it, that we do not suffer ourselves to be intoxicated thereby!'—Quesnel on Acts xiv. 13. 14. 'Si minister verbi, laudatur, versatur in periculo.' Augustine.—'They are not our best friends, that stir the pride of our hearts by the flattery of their lips. The graces of God in others (I confess) are thankfully to be owned, and under discouragements and temptations to be wisely and modestly spoken of; but the strongest Christians do scarcely show their own weakness in any one thing more than they do in hearing their own praises. Christian! thou knowest thou carriest gunpowder about thee.—Desire those that carry fire, to keep at a distance from thee. It is a dangerous crisis, when a proud heart meets with flattering lips. Faithful, seasonable, and discreet reproofs are much more safe to us, and advantageous to the mortification of sin in our souls.' Flavel. Mr. Walker mentions among 'the things principally to lament—the workings of conceit, especially in talking or hearing of what was done by me, which has cost me a deal of self-condemnation, and needed much fear and watchfulness to oppose. In the beginning I saw little of it, and less of its evil; and though now it is but rarely that I experience what I call a sensible conceit, the pleasing tickling of the heart, yet I have cause to fear a worse thing, a more settled self-opinion, which would receive commendation as its due, and expect submission in others.' Life, p. 453.
[2] Life, p. 43. The same Christian tenderness and self-suspicion appeared upon the report of his Ministerial success—'I was encouraged and refreshed beyond description, and could only cheerfully and gratefully offer up myself to God's service: but it was at the same time a check to my mind to reflect, that, though God might in his sovereignty bless his word by my mouth, I was not on that account less sinful in my Ministrations.'

Selfishness is indeed the peculiar character of this sin. It is, as if we could take no comparative interest in the conversion of sinners through other instrumentality than our own; or as if we measured our regard to the glory of God by the opportunities afforded for the display of our own glory. We wish for eminence rather than for usefulness. We want to stand alone. Instead of rejoicing in the spiritual acquirements of others, we are reluctant to admire superior talents, even when they are consecrated to the cause of their Great Master. We cannot bear any thing that shines too near us, and will probably eclipse our own brightness, either in the higher excellence of gifts, or in their more diligent improvement of them. How different was. the spirit of the Jewish Lawgiver, who was willing that all the people should share in his extraordinary gifts![1] How different was the temper of the Great Apostle, who could rejoice in the extension of the Gospel even from unchristian motives, and by the mouth of those who were ranging themselves in unprovoked opposition to his disinterested labours![2] And can we anticipate any measure of heavenly influence upon our work, except as we are resisting this unchristian jealousy, and the consciousness of our secret disposition to its indulgence covers us with self-abasement before our God? For let none of us conceive ourselves beyond the reach of the snare. Human nature can never be raised to distinction without being tempted to vanity. A subtle pestilential influence breathes around the pulpit steps, and in the purest atmosphere of holy consecration.

The hindrance of this sin to the progress of our work *may be argued à priori* from the character of a jealous God, who " giveth not his glory to another ;"[3] and who therefore will blast all assumptions to the honour of Divine agency, as encroachments upon his sovereign prerogative. It may also be *practically evinced* by the testimony of conscience, observation, and experience. Is not the " axe" powerless, when it dares to " boast itself against him that heweth therewith ?"[4] Have not we uniformly found, that those Ministrations, which have brought us most honour with men, have been scantily favoured with the tokens of our Master's presence and power? It is never likely to be so well with us, as when we are content to appear, like Paul at Corinth, " fools for Christ's sake, weak and despised ;"[5] and ready " most gladly to glory in our infirmities, that the power of Christ may rest upon us."[6] It is of little comparative moment, that our Ministry should bear the

---

[1] Numb. xi. 29. [2] Phil. i. 15—18. [3] Isa. xlii. 8.
[4] Isa. x. 15. [5] 1 Cor. iv. 10. [6] 2 Cor. xii. 9.

stamp of talent, erudition, or pathos. But if it should be characterized by the savour of humility and love, it would be best adapted
to display the glories of Immanuel, and most honoured with the
manifestations of his Spirit.

CHAPTER VIII.

ABSENCE OR DEFECT OF PERSONAL RELIGION.

IT was surely not without reason or meaning, that the Apostle,
charging first the elders, and afterwards the Bishop of the Church
of Ephesus, places a personal caution first in order—" Take heed
to yourselves—to thyself."[1] For how awful is it to appear as a
Minister, without being really a Christian ! to have a competency,
and. even (by continual exercise) an increase of Ministerial gifts,
while our real character is only, that we "have a name that we
live, but we are dead !" How difficult ! how dreadful ! to preach an
unknown Saviour !   Our Lord's prayer that his servants might be
" sanctified through the truth "[2]—strongly sets out personal holiness
as the basis of public usefulness.   All the Ministerial appellations
—such as the " salt of the earth "—" the light of the world "[3]—imply the same responsibility.   And indeed *it is this that gives power
and unction* to the commission, which we profess to deliver from
the mouth of God.   The Roman orator hath told us, that no man
can be truly eloquent on a subject with which he is unacquainted.[4]
Nor indeed can the exhibition of unknown and unfelt truth be expected to be productive of permanent effect.   Even Mr. Locke reminds
us—' He is very unfit to convert others, who was never converted
himself.'[5]   Baxter remarks with his characteristic solemnity—' Verily, it is the common danger and calamity of the Church, to have
unregenerate and unexperienced Pastors, and to have so many men
become preachers, before they are Christians ; to be sanctified by
dedication to the altar as God's Priests, before they are sanctified by
hearty dedication to Christ as his disciples ; and so to worship an
unknown God, and to preach an unknown Christ, an unknown
Spirit, an unknown state of holiness and communion with God,
and a glory that is unknown, and likely to be unknown for ever.

[1] Acts xx. 28. 1 Tim. iv. 16.   [2] John xvii. 17.   [3] Matt. v. 13, 14.
[4] Cic. de Orat. lib. 1.   [5] Letter on Toleration.

He is like to be but a heartless preacher, that hath not the Christ and grace that he preacheth in his heart.'[1]

Though indeed the blessing is in the institution, not in the instrument; yet a deficiency in the instrument ordinarily weakens the power of the institution. The want of personal religion is therefore a most serious hindrance to Ministerial efficiency. In the *general work of instruction*, the experience of the power of the Gospel is necessary to direct our treatment of the different cases of our Ministry.[2] The recollection of the means, by which we were enlightened, and subsequently confirmed and established in the truth, is most important to connect the perplexities of our people. In the work of *conviction*, what but an experimental perception of our own sinfulness can enable us to expose the deformity and deceitfulness of sin? Or how can we exhibit the exceeding breadth and spirituality of the law of God, except we have ourselves felt its condemning, killing power? In the more *delightful work of encouragement*, the power of administering the consolations of the Gospel is connected with the reception of them in our own hearts.[3] The love of the Saviour, the faithfulness of his word, the beauty of holiness, the prospect of eternity, will of course be most effectually exhibited by those who can say—" *We also believe, and therefore speak.*"[4]

Little fruitfulness can be expected in our *pulpit department*, in the absence or defect of heart-felt religion. ' I will be sure to live well,' (said George Herbert on the day of his induction to Bemerton) ' because the virtuous life of a clergyman is the most powerful eloquence to persuade all that see it to reverence and love, and at least to desire to live like him.'[5] Indeed, what persuasiveness can there be in the wearisome task of speaking of Divine things without Divine affections? A man who cannot persuade himself to be holy, will have little hope of succeeding with the

---

[1] Reformed Pastor. ' No theological erudition, as such, can answer the question— " What must I do to be saved?" He who furnishes the reply, must have something better—the possession of the same religion, which he can then only satisfactorily explain to others. Otherwise he will be either struck dumb by the enquiry, or be a blind leader of the blind, confident in his own wisdom, and in that wisdom liable to perish everlastingly.' Antichrist, by the Rev. J. Riland, p. 118. ' Neque enim aliorum salutem sedulo unquam *curabit, qui suam negligit.*' Calvin on Acts xx. 28. ' Unless Christ be learned spiritually and really, Divines shall speak of the word of God, as men speak of riddles, and as priests in former times said the matins, when they hardly knew what they said.' Perkins on Gal. i. 15.

[2] Brainerd remarked to his brother on his death-bed—' When Ministers feel these gracious influences on their hearts, it wonderfully assists them to come at the consciences of men, and as it were, handle them with their hands; whereas without them, whatever reason or oratory we make use of, we do but make use of stumps instead of hands.' See Appendix to his Life—a choice piece of Ministerial Biography.

[3] 2 Cor. i. 4—6.   [4] Ib. iv. 13.   [5] Walton's Life of George Herbert.

consciences of others. ' I would advise such preachers' (says Baxter) ' to go to the congregation, and there preach over Origen's sermon on Psalm 1. 16, 17 ;[1] and, when they have read this text, to sit down, and expound, and apply it by their tears ; and then to make a free confession of their sins ; and lament their case before the assembly ; and desire their earnest prayers to God for pardoning and renewing grace ; and so to close with Christ in heart, that before admitted him no further than into the brain ; that hereafter they may preach a Christ whom they know, and may feel what they speak, and may commend the riches of the Gospel by experience.[2]   Neither genius, nor the eloquence of the schools, nor oratorical declamation are required for public effect ; but that Christian eloquence of feeling and of love, which marks the impression of the spirit as well as the letter of the Bible—that genuine pathos and simplicity, with which ' a good man out of the good treasure of the heart bringeth forth that which is good.'[3]   This ' rhetoric of the life ' Leighton justly pronounces, to ' give to the instructions of the pulpit an energy, far beyond the reach of the loftiest strains of unhallowed oratory.'   To obtain this most desirable qualification, we must ourselves taste the word, before we distribute it to our people.   We must carefully connect it with our devotional reading.   A sermon, however well digested, can never be well preached, until it has been first preached to ourselves.[4]   It is the present experience, nourishment, and enjoyment, that gives a glow

---

[1] Referring to an affecting incident in Origen's history, when soon after his excommunication for having sacrificed to the idols, he was requested, and in a manner constrained, to preach at Jerusalem.   He opened his Bible, Psalm 1. 16.   " Unto the wicked saith God ; why dost thou preach my law ?" and was so overcome by the remembrance of his sin, that he closed the book with tears, and melted the whole congregation in sympathy with his sorrow—Clark's Marrow of Eccles. Hist. where are given his own most striking expressions of grief and contrition on the occasion.   Pp. 20—23.

[2] Reformed Pastor.   ' To preach of regeneration, of faith, when a man has no spiritual understanding of these things, is to talk of the sweetness of honey, when we never tasted it ; or of the excellence of such a country, which we were never in, but know by maps only.   If thou knowest the truths of God but by books, by authors only, and thy own heart feeleth not the power of these things ; thou art but as the conduit, that letteth out wine or refreshing water to others, but thou thyself tasteth not of it ; or like the hand that directeth the passenger, but thou thyself standest still.'   Anthony Burgess's Funeral Sermon for Rev. T. Blake.

[3] Matthew xii. 34.

[4] This was Doddridge's custom.—See Life, chap. ii.   Do not we thus penetrate into our subject with more depth and spiritual discernment, than mere thought or critical study could furnish ?   For may not these be employed *even upon our pulpit exercises,* without any of that tender seriousness and compassion for perishing souls, and sense of Ministerial obligation, which become the public discharge of our office ?   Mr. Robert Bolton, (one of the most eminent divines in the seventeenth century) professed on his death-bed, ' that he never taught any godly point, but he first wrought it on his own heart.'   Mr. Shepard of New England gave the same testimony.   How confidently, when we have thus proved our armour, may we venture to recommend it !   It was the neglect of this watchfulness that made a late eminent Minister remark, that in preparing sermons for others he had sometimes been in danger of destroying his own soul.

of unction far beyond the power of adventitious accomplishment; and makes us not only edifying to our people but (what is more rare and difficult) profitable ministers to ourselves. To bear our message written upon our hearts, is the best method of conveying to our people deep and weighty impressions of the things of God. We must bring them not only—" that which we have seen with our eyes, which we have looked upon," but something—" which our hands have handled of the word of life," if we desire them to have " joint fellowship with the Father, and with his Son Jesus Christ."[1] Like John the Baptist,[2] we should point out the Saviour to our people from our own perception of his glory and love.

We observe again the importance of personal religion—*in confirming our testimony with a Christian example.*[3]—' Men judge things more fully by the eye than by the ear; consequently Ministers' practice is as much regarded, if not more than their sermons. So that—suppose in the pulpit they should resemble Holy Angels, yet if in conversation they be found but very ordinary, carnal men; ''tis not a thousand elaborate discourses, which will be able, either solidly to impress their hearers with the faith of reality in religion, or any way engage their souls practically to fall in love with the same.'[4] Fenelon well observes, in his Dialogue on Eloquence—' that moral instructions have no weight nor influence, when they are neither supported by clear principles, nor good examples. Whom do you see converted by them? People are accustomed to hear such harangues, and are amused by them, as with so many fine scenes passing before their eyes. They hearken to such lectures, just as they would read a satire, and they look on the speaker as one that acts his part well. They believe his life more than his talk, and when they know him to be selfish, ambitious, vain, given to sloth and luxury, and see that he parts with none of those enjoyments, which he exhorts others to forsake; though for the sake

---

[1] 1 John i. 1—3.   [2] John i. 36.

[3] The judgment of the ancient church was most concurrent on this particular. 'Non possunt quæ doces habere firmitatem, nisi ea prior feceris.' Lactan. Instit. Lib. 4. c. 24. 'Non confundant opera tua sermonem tuum: ne, cum Ecclesia loqueris, tacitus quilibet respondeat, cur ergo hæc quæ dicis, ipse non facis? Sacerdotis Christi os, mens, manusque concordent.' Hieron. ad Nepot. The council of Trent also exhibited an elevated standard of Ministerial consistency—' Nihil est, quod alios magis ad pietatem et Dei cultum assidue instruat, quam eorum vita et exemplum, qui se Divino Ministerio dedicarunt, &c. Quapropter sic decet omnino clericos in sortem Domini vocatos, vitam, moresque suos omnes componere, ut habitu, gestu, incessu, sermone, aliisque omnibus rebus nil nisi grave, moderatum, ac religione plenum præ se ferant, &c.' Concil. Trid. Sess. 22. c. 1. Care however must be taken to distinguish between the self-righteousness of a mere external gravity, and that spirituality of character, which results from evangelical principles, and influences the heart to Ministerial devotedness.

[4] Blackwell's Methodas Homiletica, 1712—a valuable work.

of custom and ceremony they hear him declaim, they believe and act as he does. But what is worst of all, people are too apt to conclude, that men of this profession do not believe what they teach. This disparages their function; and when others preach with a sincere zeal, people will scarce believe this zeal to be sincere.'[1] We must build up with both hands—with our doctrine and our life. We must be what we preach; exhibiting the pattern, the motives, and the principles of godliness to our people: 'not only putting the copy before them, and leaving them to write; but taking the pen, and showing them how to form each letter.'[2] The minister is a continual—not a periodical character. "The beauty of holiness" must not be merely the appurtenance of the Sabbath. A holy sermon is but for an hour. A holy life is his perpetual sermon—a living, practical commentary of his doctrine—the gospel to the senses. Thus, (as one of the Fathers[3] observed of our Divine Master) he will often 'preach, when he does not open his mouth,'—like a faithful shepherd—who, "when he putteth forth his own sheep, *goeth before them;* and the sheep follow him, for they know his voice."[4] It was truly, though quaintly, remarked by the old divines, that a Minister's life is the life of his Ministry. For (as Bishop Horne observes) 'he who undertakes to reprove the world, must be one, whom the world cannot reprove.'[5] We should each of us consider ourselves as the appointed luminary in our respected spheres—placed as the centre of the system—the source of light and warmth to all within our circle. We should thus be "burning" as well as "shining lights."[6] We need not always blaze; but we must always burn. There must be love as well as light—the light of holy love.'[7]

---

[1] 'The Priest,' (observes Bishop Bull) 'who is not clothed with righteousness—though otherwise richly adorned with all the ornaments of human and divine literature, and those gilded over with the rays of seraphic prudence—is yet but a naked, beggarly, despicable creature, of no authority, no interest, no use, no service in the Church of God.' Sermon in Clergym. Instruct. p. 286. The inscription—'Holiness to the Lord'—upon the costly dress of the High Priest strongly marks the adorning of the profession of the ministers of the sanctuary. Exod. xxviii. 28—30. with xxxix. 30, 31. Compare Lev. xxi. 21.

[2] Scott's Sermon. Compare 1 Timothy iv. 12.   [3] Theophylact on Matt. v. 2.

[4] John x. 3, 4. The minister who would win his people must not only *Doctorem virtutis se præbere, sed ducem*—as Lactantius; 'ut si præcipientem sequi nolint, sequantur antecedentem.' Bp. Reynold's Works, p. 1061. The inscription which Herodotus mentions on the tomb of an Egyptian king, should be the Minister's motto—'Εις εμε τις ορεων, ευσεβης εστω.' What Cicero applied to the Senate, ought to be said here—'Is ordo vitio careto: cæteris specimen esto.' De Leg. Lib. iii.

[5] Considerations on John the Baptist, p. 84.   [6] John v. 35.

[7] 'You may be innocent, and yet not "zealous of good works:" but if you be not this, you are not good ministers of Jesus Christ. You must be excellent, not *tanquam unus de populo*, but *tanquam homo Dei*—not after the common manner of men, but "after God's own heart"—not only pure, but shining—not only blameless, but didactic, in your lives; that as by your sermons you preach "in season"—so by your lives you may

How painfully has this subject been illustrated in the deep wounds of the church from ungodly ministers ! " The sin of Eli's sons was very great before the Lord; *for men abhorred the offering of the Lord.*"[1] The successors of these young men are found in men pressing the Gospel upon others, while neglecting it themselves—in profession the servants of God ; in principle serving themselves—" building again" with their lives " the things which they had destroyed" by their doctrine, and making "themselves transgressors" with a guilty load of responsibility ?[2] On the other hand how *convincing is the power of a consistent Ministry !* When Levi had " the law of truth in his mouth, *he did turn many away from iniquity.*"[3] The holiness of the faithful ministry of John struck awe even into wicked Herod ; added to which " many for a season," and many probably for more than a season, " rejoiced in his light."[4] The Apostle's success in Thessalonica is mainly attributed to the same cause.[5] 'Happy those labourers in the Church, the secret savour of whose life and conversation attracts people after Christ.'[6]

The Missionary Eliot 'imposed a law upon himself, that he would leave something of God, and heaven, and religion, with all that should come near him ; so that in all places his company was attended with majesty and reverence. We cannot say, that we ever saw him walking any whither, but he was therein walking with God; and it might be said of him, as was said of Origen,— ' *Quemadmodum docet, sic vixit :* and *quemadmodum vixit, sic docet.*'[7] Now such an habitual Ministry, spreading the atmosphere of heaven over the secular employments, proves the stamp of a Divine impression, and in " manifestation of the truth commends itself to every man's conscience in the sight of God." It is like the " angel standing in the sun"—the undoubted representative of the Divine Majesty.

preach " out of season," that is—at all seasons, and to all men; that " they seeing your good works, may glorify God on your behalf" and on their own.' Bishop Taylor's Sermon on the Minister's duty in life and doctrine, Works, vol. vi. ' When prejudices are to be overcome, or ignorance to be removed, it is necessary to show, that the man, who labours to introduce new modes of feeling and thinking, is not only the convert of his own opinions, but an example of their practical influence in forming a spiritual character.' Bishop of Winchester's Ministerial Character of Christ, p. 285.

[1] 1 Sam. ii. 17.   Mark the Lord's judgment, Jer. xxiii. 15.   Lev. x. 1—3.
[2] Nisi ipsi sacerdotes in omnibus virtutibus Christianis fidelium exemplaria sint—plus improba vita destruunt, quam sana doctrina ædificant: dedecori sunt sanctissimæ religioni ; de veritate eorum, quæ prædicant addubitare docent: atque ita libertinismo et atheismo latam portam pandunt. Wits. de Vero Theologo. Hence the severe sarcasm against inconsistent Ministers—' That, when in the pulpit, they ought never to come out: and, when out, they ought never to go in again.'
[3] Mal. ii. 5, 6.
[4] Mark vi. 20.   John v. 35.   Comp. Acts xi. 24, and Doddridge, on John viii. 30.
[5] See 1 Thess. i. 5, 9.   [6] Quesnel on Mark vi. 33.   [7] Mather's Life of Eliot.

We might further remark the power of Ministerial godliness—
as enabling us to water the seed sown with fervent prayer.
For as prayer is the life of spiritual religion, it follows of necessity,
that a spiritual Minister will be a man of prayer. But having
already expanded this point of detail,[1] we only now advert to it, to
mark the mutual relations and bearings of every department of the
sacred office.

But it may be asked—Do we sufficienrly consider, how much
our personal religion is endangered from the very circumstance of
religion being our profession? The decorous restraint induced by
a regard to our sacred office is essentially distinct from vital religion. While on the other hand the continual exercise of our gifts,
both in their excitement and acceptance, may be only a shadowy
exhibition of the true substance. Great indeed is the danger of
resting in a professional piety—in public religion. Awful indeed is
the reflection—how much of the fervid animation of the pulpit is
purely mechanical!—impulse rather than spirituality! In going
therefore through the duties, putting on the appearances, speaking
the language, and exhibiting the feelings of religion—what care!
what watchfulness! what tenderness of heart! what earnest prayer! is required to preserve the spirit of religion. Have none of us
cause to complain—" They made me keeper of the vineyards;
but mine own vineyard have I not kept?"[2] Does not the cultivation of the wilderness lead us sometimes unconsciously to overlook
the growth of the weeds within our own garden? Are we never
satisfied with being the instruments of grace, without being habitually the subjects of it? Yet of how little moment is it to " minister grace to our hearers," if we minister it not to ourselves! Is not
conscience often rebuked by the assumed identity of our personal
and official character? For, though the concentration of our employments in Divine things has clothed us officially with a spiritual garb;[3] yet who of us can have failed to discover, that spirituality of doctrine is not always connected with corresponding spirituality of heart or conduct? The best of us probably are far more
spiritual in our pulpits than in our closets, and find less effort required to preach against all the sins of our people, than to mortify
one of them in our own hearts. Oh! how much more easy is it to
preach from the understanding than from the heart! to expound
the truth with satisfactory clearness to our people, and with delusive complacency to ourselves; than to be ourselves so moulded
into its spirit, as to enjoy a holy preparation of heart in the previous

[1] See Chap. vi.   [2] Can. i. 6.   Comp. 1 Cor. ix. 27.   [3] See Hosea ix. 7.

study of it, its heavenly savour at the time of the delivery, and its experimental and practical influence in the after recollection.

This difficulty springs out of the peculiar self-deception, by which we are apt to merge our personal in our professional character, and in the Minister to forget the Christian. But time must be found for the spiritual feeding upon Scriptural truths, as well as for a critical investigation of their meaning, or for a Ministerial application of their message. For if we should study the Bible more as Ministers than as Christians—more to find matter for the instruction of our people, than food for the nourishment of our own souls; we neglect to place ourselves at the feet of our Divine Teacher; our communion with him is cut off; and we become mere formalists in our sacred profession. Mr. Martyn seems to have been tenderly conscious of this temptation—'Every time' (he remarked) 'that I open the Scriptures, my thoughts are about a sermon or exposition; so that even in private I seem to be reading in public.'[1] We cannot live by feeding others; or heal ourselves by the mere employment of healing our people; and therefore by this course of official service, our familiarity with the awful realities of death and eternity may be rather like that of the grave-digger, the physician, and the soldier, than the man of God, viewing eternity with deep seriousness and concern, and bringing to his people the profitable fruit of his contemplations. It has been well remarked—that, 'when once a man begins to view religion not as of personal, but merely of professional importance, he has an obstacle in his course, with which a private Christian is unacquainted.'[2] It is indeed difficult to determine, whether our familiar intercourse with the things of God is more our temptation or our advantage. For what accurate self-observer has not verified Butler's remarks on the repetition of passive impressions;[3] and found the effect of formal Ministerial repetition to be of a rapidly and powerfully hard-

[1] Martyn's Life, p. 60. How instructive was his godly jealousy in watching against this subtle temptation! 'I see' (he observes at a later period) 'how great are the temptations of a Missionary to neglect his own soul. Apparently outwardly employed for God, my heart has been growing more hard and proud. *Let me be taught, that the first great business on earth is the sanctification of my own soul; so shall I be rendered more capable also of performing the duties of the Ministry in a holy solemn manner.*' pp. 263, 264. The same incessant watchfulness was exercised in the work of translations—'May the Lord in mercy to my soul save me from setting up an idol of any sort in his place; as I do by *preferring even a work professedly for him, to communion with him!* "To obey is better than sacrifice; and to hearken than the fat of rams." Let me learn from this, that to follow the direct injunctions of God about my own soul, is more my duty, than to be engaged in other works, under pretence of doing him service.' p. 272.

[2] Wilkes's Essay on Conversion and Unconversion in Christian Ministers, p. 14.

[3] Analogy, Part i. ch. 5. Paley mentions among the chief impediments to the Christian Ministry—'the insensibility to religious impressions, which a constant conversation with religious subjects, and, still more, a constant intermixture with religious offices, is wont to induce.' He remarks more justly—'that the consequence of repetition will be

ening character !¹ As the natural consequence of going through the daily and Sabbath routine without renewed fire from the altar, the doctrines of the Gospel will be maintained, while the assimilation of our character to their heavenly spirit will be totally neglected. And in the absence of this spiritual character—what is our Ministry more than a beautiful and lifeless mechanism, unvisited by the Spirit of God, and unblest with the tokens of its acceptance ?

Upon the whole, therefore, we observe the weighty influence of personal character upon our Ministrations. "Simplicity and godly sincerity," disinterestedness, humility, and general integrity of profession—are an "epistle known and read of all men." Indeed character is power. The lack of it must therefore blast our success, by bringing the genuineness of our own religion, and the practical efficacy of the Gospel, under suspicion. Apart also from the natural effect of our public consistency, there is also a secret but penetrating influence diffused by the habitual exercise of our principles. Who will deny, that—had he been a more spiritual Christian—he would probably have been a more useful Minister ? Will not he, who is most fervent and abundant in secret prayer, most constant in his studies, most imbued with his Master's spirit, most single in his object, most upright and persevering in the pursuit of it—be most honoured in his work ? For is not he likely to be filled with an extraordinary unction ? Will not he speak most " of the abundance of his heart ?" And will not his flock " take knowledge of him," as living in the presence of his God ; and "receive him" in his pastoral visits and pulpit addresses, " as an angel of God—even as Christ Jesus ?"

felt more sensibly by us, who are in the habit of directing our arguments to others; for it always requires a second, a separate, and an unusual effort of the mind, to bring back the conclusion upon ourselves. In all the thoughts and study, which we employ upon our arguments, what we are apt to hold continually in view, is the effect, which they may produce upon those who hear or read them. The further and best use of our meditation (their influence upon our own hearts and consciences) is lost in the presence of the other.' Sermon on the dangers of the Clerical Character, Works, viii. 137—142.

¹ Massillon speaks with awful solemnity of the case of a formal Minister—' He contracts a callousness by his insensible way of handling Divine matters ; by which he becomes hardened against them, and by which he is so far put out of the reach of conviction, in all the ordinary means of grace, that it *is scarce possible he can ever be awakened, and by consequence, that he can be saved.*' Not less awful is the language of Dr. Owen— ' He that would go down to the pit in peace, let him obtain a great repute for religion ; let him preach and labour to make others better than he is himself, and in *the mean time neglect to humble his heart to walk with God in a manifest holiness and usefulness : and he will not fail of his end.*' Sermons and Tracts, folio. p. 47. ' It is shocking ' (as an old writer pointedly remarks) ' to fall into hell from under the pulpit—how much more so from out of the pulpit ! Is it supposed, that a holy office makes us holy ? Let it be remembered, that those who from their earliest childhood were fed with consecrated food, and breathed the air of incense, " *were sons of Belial—they knew not the Lord* " (1 Sam. ii. 12.) Can we forget, that Judas " *fell from his Apostleship, that he might go to his own place ?*" Acts i. 25. Does not every unconverted Minister carry about with him in his very commission his own sentence of condemnation ? Mark xvi. 16.

20

CHAPTER IX.

THE DEFECT OF FAMILY RELIGION; AND THE WANT OF CON-
NEXION OF THE MINISTER'S FAMILY WITH HIS WORK.

THE qualifications of a Christian Bishop apply to the lower orders of the Ministry. And not among the least important are those,
which mark the Minister in his family. 'A family' (as Quesnel
beautifully observes) 'is a small diocese, in which the first essays
are made of the Episcopal· and Ecclesiastical zeal, piety, and prudence.'[1] If therefore "a man know not how to rule his own house,
how shall he take care of the Church of God?"[2] For he cannot
reasonably expect to perform in his parish the work, which he has
not cared to accomplish at home. The mark set upon Eli's family
illustrates the necessity of the regulation, that an elder must be one
"having faithful children."[3] Though he cannot convey grace to
his children, at least he can enforce restraint, and acquit himself of
the guilt of "honouring his sons before God."[4] He can inculcate
upon them the responsibility of promoting his Ministry by a consistent conduct—thus 'adorning not only their Christian profession, but
their parent's principles; and shewing, that the principles of their

[1] Quesnel on 1 Tim. iii. 12.
[2] 1 Tim. iii. 5. Our Church fully recognizes the importance of this subject, in demanding of each of her candidates for the holy office a distinct pledge of family godliness.—
'Will you be diligent to frame and fashion your own selves *and your families* according
to the doctrine of Christ, and to make both yourselves, *and them,* as much as in you lieth,
wholesome examples, and patterns to the flock of Christ? I will apply myself thereto,
the Lord being my helper.' Service for Ordination of Deacons. 'This is the injunction
of the Apostle, 1 Tim. iii. 12. And the same command was enforced by the ancient laws
of the church, which were much stricter concerning Clergymen's wives, children, and
servants, than those of the laity. The houses of Ministers should be the schools of virtue, little emblems of a church, and patterns for all their parishioners, of peace and good
order, sobriety, and devotion.' Comber. Compare also Dr. Nicholls, in Bishop Mant's
notes on the service.—It was a frequent petition of the excellent Philip Henry in his
family worship 'That we might have grace to carry it, as a Minister, and a Minister's
wife, and a Minister's children, and a Minister's servants, should carry it; *that the Ministry might in nothing be blamed.*' Life, p. 81. The testimony on this point of one of
the most determined enemies of Christianity, is also remarkable. The emperor Julian,
in endeavouring to re-establish Paganism—and accounting (as he declares) 'the strictness and sanctity professed by Christians never be seen at the public games and spec-
their faith—gives directions (unquestionably copied from the injunctions to the primitive
priesthood) that the heathen priests should be men of serious temper and deportment
that they be neither expensive nor showy in their dress—go to no entertainments, but
such as are made by the worthiest persons never be seen at the public games and spec-
tacles—and *take care that their wives and children and servants be pious as well as themselves.*' *Fas est et ab hoste doceri.* Archbishop Secker thus briefly applies this testimony,
'Let not (I entreat you) this apostate put you to shame.' Jul. Epist. 49, ad Arsac, pp.
430, 431. Fragm. Epist. pp. 301—305. Secker's Charges, pp. 244, 245.
[3] 1 Sam. ii. 17. iii. 13, with Tit. i. 5, 6.   [4] 1 Sam. ii. 29.

father's house and Ministry are the rule of their conduct, and their real delight.'[1]

Mr. Herbert's 'Country Parson[2] is very exact in the governing of his house, making it a copy and a model for his parish. His family is a school of religion.' This opens a wide field; including daily family worship—the whole circle of family instruction—the principles of education, essentially upon a scriptural basis—the regulation of conversational habits—all bearing a concurrent testimony to the doctrine of the pulpit *in its fullest detail*. *Habits of order* also form an important part of this Christian model—doing every thing at its proper time—keeping every thing to its proper use—putting every thing in its proper place. Regularity in the payment of bills, and a strict avoiding of debts—are here worthy of high consideration. With respect to children—we must be careful to exhibit a clear practical illustration of the rules of order, submission, and indulgence, which we give to our people. How many of us in this point are wise for others, and yet unwise for ourselves! Perhaps nowhere are we so liable to self-deception, or so little open to conviction, as in the management of children. The importance of order also in the regulation of our servants is most obvious. Let them not be overburthened. A trifle. spent in procuring additional help will often prevent irritation, confusion, and what is more than all, the necessary loss of the private duties of religion. Let conscientious attendance upon these duties be encouraged—allowance be made for infirmities—patience and forbearance be constantly maintained—sympathy be shown in all their trials and difficulties—family reading be followed with individual instruction. Thus let our Ministry pervade the lower departments of the household, considering every member of the house as if interested in their temporal welfare, and responsible for the care of immortal souls.

Bishop Hooper's palace was as if we ' entered into some church or temple. In every corner thereof there was some smell of virtue, good example, honest conversation, and reading of Holy Scripture.'[3] Of Mr. Joseph Alleine (an admirable pastor) it is said—' that, as he walked about the house, he would make some spiritual use of every thing that did occur, and his lips did drop like the honey-comb to all that were about him.[4] Philip Henry's family œconomy exhibited the most beautiful display of patriarchal godliness, simplicity,

[1] Richmond's Life, p. 294, 295. The Mosaic law severely punished the transgression of the Priest's daughter, for the disgrace which she thus brought upon the holy office. Lev. xxi. 9. [2] Chap. x.
[3] Clark's Marrow of Ecclesiastical History, p. 222, and Fox's Acts and Monuments, vi. 644.
[4] Alleine's Life and Letters, pp. 97—100.

and order—"commanding his children and household after him, that they should keep the way of the Lord, to do judgment and justice."[1]   These are fine models of a domestic Minister—the pastor of "the Church in his own house."

A Minister is indeed "a city set upon an hill, that cannot be hid." He must expect not only his personal character, but his household arrangements—the conduct of his wife, the dress and habits of his children and servants, his furniture, and his table—to be the subject of a most scrutinizing observation.   Thus the correctness of our family system becomes to a great extent the standard of our parish; while its inconsistencies too often furnish excuse for the neglect of duty, or the positive indulgence of sin.   The detail of family religion is also a component part of our Ministry; inculcating principles of parental restraint and dutiful subjection—of constant instruction and superintendence—of precept illustrated by example—and of the daily exercise of Christian self-denial, holiness, cheerfulness, and love.   Now, (as men are influenced much more by what they see, than by what they hear) if the parsonage does not show the pattern as well as the doctrine, exhortations from thence will only excite the ridicule of the ungodly, and confirm them in their habits of sin.   How different must be our parochial influence, where the several members of our families appear as servants of God, or the children of this world!   Often has a worldly stamp upon the domestic œconomy utterly paralyzed the power of a faithful Ministration, even with the seal of personal consistency.[2]   It is therefore of great moment to repress all expensiveness of habits, studied attention to ornament, and every mark of "the course of this world's" pleasure or vanity—not only or chiefly upon the ground of pecuniary inconvenience, but from their injurious impressions upon our people.

The Apostle notices the example of the Minister's wife in gravity,

[1] Gen. xviii. 19.   Compare Philip Henry's Life, pp. 82—86.   Cotton Mather's family picture is less known.   He prayed for each of his children distinctly, and interested them early with engaging stories from Scripture, as the vehicle of inculcating lessons of practical usefulness.   He had always a word for them, when they fell in his way.   Their habits of secret prayer were early formed, and often brought to mind—'Child, don't forget every day to go alone and pray, as you have been taught.'   He endeavoured to enlarge their minds in Christian love, by engaging them daily in some 'essay to do good' for one another.   He encouraged and commended them, when he saw them take pleasure in it; and let them know, that a backwardness to it was highly displeasing to him.   When they were old enough, he would take them alone, one by one; and after many affectionate and solemn charges, to fear God, to love Christ, and to hate sin, he would let them witness his earnest melting prayers on their account.   He catechised them on every part of the Gospel, turning every truth into a question; as the best way of gaining their attention,.of informing their minds upon it, and applying it to their hearts.   It is no wonder, that such diligence in the domestic Ministry were associated with uncommon power in his public work.   The pattern expounded the doctrine with irresistible force of application and encouragement.

[2] See some striking matter of conviction on 'suspicious appearances in a Minister's Family,' in 'Negative Rules given to a Young Minister.'—Cecil's Remains.

self-control, sobriety of deportment, and faithful exhibition of relative and public duties, in connexion with our great object.[1] And of such importance is this considered, that, 'in the Protestant churches of Hungary, they degrade a pastor, whose wife indulges herself in cards, dancing, or any other public amusements, which bespeak the gaiety of a lover of the world rather than the gravity of a Christian matron. This severity springs from the supposition, that the woman, having promised obedience to her husband, can do nothing but what he either directs or approves. Hence they conclude, that—example having a greater weight than precept—the wife of a Minister, if she is inclined to the world, will preach worldly compliance with more success by her conduct, than her husband can preach the renunciation of the world by the most solemn discourses.'[2]

But—besides this domestic consistency—there is a superadded obligation of direct subserviency to our great work. It was well said by one, whose completeness of Ministration gave just weight to his remark—that '*a clergyman's family*, house, occupations, and every thing connected with him, should be consistent; and *all family arrangements made subordinate to his parochial duties*,'[3] —(of course with due regard to prudential considerations) so as to allow the largest scope for the various exercises of his pastoral work.

How momentous therefore is the responsibility of the Minister's married choice ! Apart from the Scriptural rule of a Christian's decision—" Only in the Lord "[4]—there are motives of a less selfish character, that should influence his determination. The tone of his Ministry will be formed, or moulded, by this critical change of circumstances. He will not be the man he was : he will be under the constraint of new inclinations and principles of action.[5] 'Many immortal souls'—as an aged Minister reminded a younger brother on this matter—'are deeply interested in the step which you are now taking.' And in truth—if his flock is not benefited by this new relation, it must suffer loss. Even a godly connexion without

---

[1] 1 Tim. iii. 11.

[2] Fletcher's Portrait of St. Paul, p. 129, note—' A Minister's public labours are intimately connected with his private and domestic consolations. A Minister's wife may be a main-spring of encouragement or discouragement to her husband in all his arduous and anxious occupations for the good of his flock. On her example and demeanour very much may often depend.'—Letter of Rev. L. Richmond to his daughter, on the day of her marriage to a Clergyman. Life, p. 511.

[3] The late excellent Rev. H. C. Ridley's ' Parochial Duties practically illustrated '— (Seeleys and Hatchard,)—a most interesting and exciting sketch of Ministerial devotedness.

[4] 1 Cor. vii. 39.   [5] Ibid. 32, 33.

experience, sympathy, or helpfulness, (whether arising from natural, adventitious or spiritual causes) must cripple his energies ; and he will be less of a Minister than before—less excited, less interested, less unfettered, less efficient.[1]   Surely therefore, if he should stamp his *every act* not only with the impress of a Christian, but with the high dignity, singleness, and elevation of his sacred office—how much more *this act*—the crisis of his course, the grand momentum of his future operations !   If the sense of his awful responsibility has ever awakened the complaint—" I am not able to bear all this people *alone*, because it is too heavy for me," may he not expect in the course of Providence, and in answer to prayer, the gift of one, who may stand to him as the seventy elders of Israel to Moses— endued with his spirit, for the express purpose of " bearing the burden of the people with him, that *he bear it not himself alone ?*"[2] There is, or ought to be, this difference between a Christian and a Ministerial choice.   A Christian wants a helpmeet for himself— a Minister wants *besides* a yoke-fellow in his work : he wants for his people as well as for himself.   It cannot be doubted, that our work has been greatly weakened by the dissociation of the Minister's wife from the service of God.   In every sphere there are departments peculiarly fitted for her.   Circumstances of propriety often (as in the female department of instruction) hinder the Minister from embracing the whole extent of his sphere.   Added to which, a press of labour, and the distraction of a multitude of interfering engagements, demands the counsel and active services of a true yoke-fellow.   A mistake therefore made in the original choice of a partner, and a want of sense of female responsibility,[3] leaves much

---

[1] ' It is scarcely to be calculated,' (remarks Mr. Cecil) ' what an influence the spirit of a Minister's wife will have on his own, and on all his Ministerial affairs.   If she come not up to the full standard, she will so far impede him, derange him, unsanctify him.   If there is such a thing as good in the world, it is in the Ministerial office.   The affairs of this employment are the greatest in the world.   In prosecuting these with a right spirit, the Minister keeps in motion a vast machine ; and such are the incalculable consequences of his wife's character to him, that, if she assist him not in urging forward the machine, she will hang as a dead weight upon its wheels.'—Cecil's Remains.

l. [2] See Numb. xi. 11—17, with Prov. xviii. 22 ; xix. 14.   Mr. Baxter thus solved the question—' Ought a clergyman to marry ?'   ' Yes ; but *let him think, and think, and think again before he does it.*'   ' Quod statuendum est semel, deliberandum est diu.'   Adherence to this rule, acted out in prayer for Divine direction, will be not less instrumental to personal comfort than to ministerial usefulness.

[3] Let us mark the female obligations of the Ministry, at once confirmed and encouraged by a death-bed testimony—' When eternity was full in view, and when she expected to stand shortly before the bar of God, she could and did say—' I have laboured for the parish : yes, I have laboured for the parish ; and, if the Lord spare my life, I will *labour more for it than I have ever yet done.*'   Funeral Sermon for Mrs. Bolland, wife of Rev. W. Bolland, Swinehead, Lincolnshire.   This instance, among many others, may show, that, if there is no express letter of Scripture requirement upon the subject, the obligation is acknowledged, and felt to be legitimately inferred from the post, which the Minister's wife officially and relatively occupies in the Church of Christ.   Another instructive in-

of the ground unbroken, or imperfectly cultivated; and much promise of an abundant harvest is blighted. Over maternal responsibility there is indeed no control. But may not time (the extent of which indeed conscience must determine) be redeemed for the work of the Lord, without intrenching upon other most imperative claims? Should not the wife aspire to the honour of being a spiritual as well as a natural mother? Should she have no connexion with her husband's spiritual family? Should she not desire to be a partner of his Ministry, as well as of his life? Is she content, by withdrawing from his public work, to share but *half his sympathy*, to bear but a *very small portion of his burdens?* Her characteristic should be that main feature of the gospel—*a disciple of the cross.* In uniting herself to a Christian Minister, she has bound herself to his work and to his cross; and must expect—*as far as she appears by her husband's side*—not only to sympathize, but actually to share, in the double measure of hardness, misrepresentation, and reproach, portioned out to the faithful servant of God: trials, that will exercise all that love, humility, patience, and self-denial that constitute the spirit of the cross. Nothing connected with her can be neutral. A cold indifference to the advancement of her husband's Ministry, or to the line of conduct best adapted to strengthen his interest—or even a weariness of his work, must clog the wheels of the machine, instead of supplying oil, for its accelerated progress. Any lack also of kindness or consideration on her part widens the distance between the pastor and his flock; and restrains much Ministerial communication, which would have been productive of mutual advantage. On the other hand, a natural spirit of conciliation and flow of sympathy draws out with freedom much, that otherwise had been restrained;[1] and an additional bond of reciprocal attachment is thus formed between the father and his numerous family. Thus is the confidence of the female part of our charge obtained—opening to us a most interesting medium of pastoral intercourse, and a most valuable pledge of permanent and extensive fruit. Indeed the weight of female responsibility has sometimes sustained the dignity and usefulness of the office, even where the Minister's personal character has been under a cloud; and in some instances it may be doubted,

stance may be seen in Memoirs of Mrs. J. Bickersteth, Acton, Suffolk—by her beloved partner. A small work—'Hints to a Clergyman's Wife,' will supply many valuable suggestions.

[1] Cotton Mather mentions an interesting instance of this in a Minister's wife—that the women would freely 'open their griefs' to her; 'who, acquainting her husband with convenient intimations thereof, occasioned him in his public Ministry more *particularly* and profitably to discourse on those things that were of everlasting benefit.' Mather's New England, Book iii. p. 17.

whether the pastor or his wife[1] were more useful in their respective labours.   It is however important, that in the general system each should keep to their own department.   Interference hurts the independence, and weakens the influence of both.   But happy indeed is the pastor, whose partner is thus the mother of his people, as well as the director and guardian in his family.   Happy indeed must he be, in offering his grateful acknowledgment for this special mercy to himself and to his flock.

May the Writer be permitted further to suggest, that the pastor's family worship—like the edifying exercises of Philip Henry[2] and Mr. Scott,[3] should bear the character of a daily Ministration?   A spiritual habit of prayer and meditation is however needed to render this social worship an enriching means of instruction.   We must guard against formality.   We must keep alive faith and expectation as the spring of life.   An occasional mixture of catechetical instruction will give an useful variety to the course.   Large portions of Scripture also would encourage and direct a more diligent and extended search of the sacred field.   A large heart in intercessory prayer—embracing the universal church, and the necessities of a fallen world—is of the highest moment.   The full expansion of this exercise of love inculcates upon our families important practical obligations, and introduces them into a sphere of privileged usefulness.

This Ministration, however, obviously includes something beyond the formal routine—familiar, close, and affectionate exhortation—a circle of instruction, that might profitably extend beyond the bounds of the parsonage, to any who were willing to improve the advantage.   The mere reading of an exposition, however excellent, scarcely rises to the responsibility of this service ; nor is it. likely to be impressive in effect.   For no foreign aid can supply, in the manner or matter of address, that adaptation to the different shades of character, and the ever-varying circumstances of the family, which seems necessary to give interest to the daily repetition of the social worship.   The family use of Mr. Scott's Commentary was probably intended chiefly for the assistance of the laity, or (in the clerical use of the work) to supply solid and useful materials for *free exposition*.   The Ministerial qualification—" apt to teach," and the character of " a scribe instructed unto the kingdom of heaven,"

---

[1] When the late Bishop Turner was a parish priest, no less than eleven instances of decided conversion crowned the self-denying labours of a minister's wife.

[2] Philip Henry's Life, pp. 72—81.   Mr. Wesley, in recommending Philip Henry's Life to his people, pointed out his mode of conducting family worship as a pattern.

[3] Scott's Life, pp. 71—76.

suppose an ability to "bring forth out of our treasure things new and old," for daily as well as Sabbath Ministrations.[1] Oh! how do we need the spirit of prayer, and the active habit of faith, to maintain our watchfulness in "neglecting not," and our diligence in "stirring up," for daily use, " the gift of God, that is in us by the putting on of hands!"[2] Every fresh exercise links us to our people with "a cord" of reciprocal feeling, that "is not quickly broken:" and opens their hearts to the reception, and the more established enjoyment, of the truth. Every sphere of parochial labour thus becomes an overspreading "shadow," inviting our people to "dwell under it;"[3] so that, in the recollection of its enlivening refreshment, they are ready to adopt Philip Henry's exclamation at the close of the Sabbath—'Well; if this be not the way to heaven, I do not know what is.'[4]

CHAPTER X.

WANT OF FAITH.

THE Baptist Missionary Society was raised upon two simple ideas, suggested by Dr. Carey, in a sermon upon Isaiah liv. 2, 3, shortly before his embarkation for India—'Expect great things; attempt great things.' This expectation is the life of faith—the vitality of the Ministry—that which honours God, and is honoured by God. All our failures may be ultimately traced to a defect of faith. We ask but for little, we expect but little, we are satisfied with little; and therefore we gain and do but little.[5] Our Saviour called this principle into exercise in almost all his miracles, and his almighty power appeared (so to speak) to be fettered by the influence of unbelief.[6] This power of faith in outward miracles seems intended to encourage its exercise with respect to the greatest of all miracles—the conversion of the soul. Indeed no limit, except the

---

[1] 1 Tim. iii. 2. Matt. xiii. 52. An American divine encouraged his son to these familiar exercises with the assurance, that he had found as much advantage by them as by most of his other studies in divinity: adding, that he looked upon it as the Lord's gracious accomplishment of that word—"Shall I *hide any thing* from Abraham? For I know Abraham, that he will command," &c. Mather's New England, iii. 15.

[2] 1 Tim. iv. 14. 2 Tim. i. 6.　　　　　[3] Alluding to Hos. xiv. 7.
[4] Philip Henry's Life, p. 192.
[5] Mr. Scott remarks, in a letter to his son—'I must be allowed to think, that we *have not* success, because we *ask not*, and do not stir up others to expect and ask the blessing from God only.' Life, p. 303.
[6] Comp. Matt. viii. 2, 3. ix. 2. Mark xi. 22, 23, with Matt. xiii. 58. Mark vi. 5, 6.

sovereign will of God, bounds the warranted expectation of believing prayer.[1] The dispensations of grace are established upon this rule—"According to your faith be it unto you."[2] The life of faith, therefore, is the life of the Minister's work, and the spring of his success.

A confidence, indeed, that has no foundation in the Divine promise, is not faith, but fancy. But the ground of Ministerial faith is the engagement, purpose, and promise of God—" *The zeal of the Lord of Hosts shall perform this.*"[3] Much would be expected from this determined and fervid principle in human hearts, though so often misguided, disproportionate, and uncertain. But how overwhelming is the thought of this affection possessing the heart of God—of the deep interest of his infinite mind in the progress of the kingdom of his dear Son—his thoughts engaged in it—his unsearchable plans embracing it, and controlling all the mighty movements of the world to subserve this main design! How solid therefore is the rock, on which the Christian Ministry rests as the grand engine for the accomplishment of the purposes and promises of God![4]

The extreme difficulty of the exercise of faith is not however readily apprehended. Sometimes we see a faint and sinking heart, where better things might have been expected. Jeremiah's case is most instructive to young Ministers—bold in public, but giving way in secret; full of compassionate weepings over the misery of his people, but "pressed above measure" under the power of his unbelief.[5]

Self-dependence is the grand hindrance to our efficiency. Our glorious Head "hath the residue of the Spirit," as the fountain and grand repository for his Ministers.[6] But, apart from the constant supply from his fulness, who are we, to call the dead to arise to a new and spiritual life? Where is the quickening virtue innate in our agency? To lean upon human instrumentality, instead of the Almighty power—is like Elisha trusting in his staff, instead of his Master[7]—presumption, which will bring us under the humbling rebuke of our jealous God. Again, a lack of godly simplicity shews itself in a trust to hopeful appearances, rather than to the full and faithful promises of our God. We are ready to say of some bright momentary prospect—"This same shall

---

[1] Comp. Matt. xxi. 22. 1 John v. 14, 15.   [2] Ibid. ix. 29.   [3] Isaiah ix. 7.
[4] Calvin remarks on this ground, that Ministers should go up into the pulpit to preach the word of God in his name, with that strength of faith as to be assured, that their doctrine can no more be overthrown than God himself. Comment on 2 Cor. iii.
[5] Compare Jer. ix. with xx. &c.
[6] Mal. ii. 15. Compare Col. i. 19, with John i. 14, 16. iii. 34.   [7] See 2 Kings iv. 31.

comfort us concerning our work :"[1] so that, when "we see not our signs :"[2] or when, "as the morning cloud and the early dew," they have "gone away," we are on the verge of despondency. Now if the promises were the *ground*, and favourable appearances only *the encouragements* of our hope, our minds would be preserved in an equipoise of faith ; dependent and sustained under every variation of circumstance : "rejoicing in hope" amid the withering blasts of disappointment ; and even "against hope believing in hope, strong in faith, giving glory to God." But the want of a due recollection makes it more easy to exercise a personal than a Ministerial faith, though the warrant in both cases is the same ; though the principle of faith is of equal power of application to every exigency ; and though the training for the discipline of the Ministerial warfare is the fruitful result of our personal trials.

The main difficulty, therefore, is not in our work, but in ourselves; in the conflict with our own unbelief, in the form either of indolence or of self-dependence. When faith is really brought into action, the extent and aggravation of the difficulty (even were it increased an hundred-fold) is a matter of little comparative moment. Difficulties heaped upon difficulties can never rise to the level of the promise of God. To meet the trembling apprehensions—"Who is sufficient for these things?" the answer is ready —"Our sufficiency is of God."[3] There is a link in the chain of moral causes and effects, which connects the helplessness of the creature with the Omnipotence of God, and encourages the creature to attempt every thing in the conscious inability to do any thing : and thus "in weakness" thoroughly felt, Divine "strength is made perfect."[4] It is equally important to feel our abasement, and to maintain it with a corresponding and proportionate exercise of faith. Let us lie low, but let us look high ; let us realize our weakness and strength at the same moment; let there be a remembrance, as well as a present exercise of faith. The Apostle supported his mind under the pressure of his responsibilities, not merely by his general interest in his Master's all-sufficiency, but by the recollection of what it had wrought in him.[5] This recollection will assure us of the sufficiency of Almighty grace ; and that, though the work immensely exceeds all human resources, the power and promise of God are fully equal, and faithfully pledged, to the exigency. No difficulty is therefore insurmountable. Our Lord has

---

[1] Gen. v. 29. [2] Psalm lxxiv. 9. [3] 2 Cor. ii. 16. iii. 4.
[4] 2 Cor. xii. 9. [5] Ibid. iii. 5, 6—"who also *hath made us,*" &c.

invested the principle of faith with his own Omnipotence.[1] The least grain will remove a mountain from its place.[2] What then would not a large grain—what would not many grains—do ? If the weakest exercise is so mighty, what might not be expected from the habit of faith ? May we be always sending up the disciples' prayer—" Increase our faith !"[3]

But to apply its operations to the different departments of our work—If the Ministry be a spiritual employment, it must be conducted on spiritual principles. Faith, therefore, belongs to every part of it. It is the mainspring and the regulator : it enters into every wheel and pivot of the machine. The power or the want of it is felt at every single point, enlivening or paralyzing the work. Thus *in preaching*—how encouraging are the recollections, that we are nothing, but we hold the rod of God's power in our hand— that his presence is pledged to bless our word—and that our poor Ministrations of his all-powerful Gospel are the appointed means of gathering and edifying his Church![4] It is faith also, that gives a tone of boldness to our public addresses.[5] We cease to fear the face of man, when we realize the power and presence of God. Men of faith are the most successful preachers. Whitfield is said to have seldom preached without the seal of conversion to his message—Such is the effect of a simple reliance on the power of God ! On the other hand, a formal preaching of Evangelical truth, being without faith, is wholly unproductive. And may we not also trace the barrenness even of an earnest Ministry to the same source—a want of practical conviction that the work is of God ? Does not sometimes a dependence upon our accurate expositions, forcible illustrations, or powerful and persuasive arguments, lead us to forget, " that the excellency of the power is of God, and not of us ?"[6] Do we never feel as if our light *must* open our people's eyes—as if they *must* see, be convinced, and persuaded ? *The use of means* honours the work of the Spirit. But *dependance upon means* obscures his glory, and therefore issues in unprofitableness. Again—*in our parochial visitation*—how much more natural is it to speak from our own mouth than from God's ! How hard to maintain the habitual simplicity of faith—looking for the " wisdom that is profitable to direct ;" for the word of seasonable doctrine, reproof, or consolation to the several cases of our

---

[1] Mark ix. 23.

[2] Compare Matt. xvii. 20. ' There are perhaps, but few Ministers of Christ,' (observes Quesnel on this verse) ' to whom, on their addresses to him in prayer, he might not answer: that the weakness of their faith is an hindrance to the conversion and improvement of souls.'   [3] Luke xvii. 5.   [4] See 1 Cor. i. 21.

[5] Compare 2 Peter ii. 5. with Heb. xi. 27. Acts iv. 24, 31.   [6] 2 Cor. iv. 7.

people ! *In our Sunday Schools also*—how soon do our hands hang down " in the work !" We "cast our bread upon the waters," with but faint hope of " finding it after many days."[1] We are ready to think, that nothing is done, because we do not see all that we want—in immediate fruit, visible progress, or thankful returns. *In discouraging instances in our visitation of the sick* —how grievously do we fail in the recollection of the sovereign freeness of Divine grace, to resist despondency, and keep alive expectation ; to go on waiting—pleading—hoping to the last ! And is not here the secret of our want of success ? As we " walk" —so must we work,—" by faith, not by sight ;" in diligence improving what is already given, in expectation looking for a larger blessing.

Of some departments of our work, however, (such as the visiting of the sick, or the instruction of the young) we are apt to say—' I have no gift, no talent for it.' But surely dependance upon the promise of heavenly wisdom would obtain a competent measure to meet the demand.[2] Or should it even be withheld, how profitable would be that humbling exercise of faith—" most gladly to glory in our infirmities, that the power of Christ may rest upon us !"[3] But nothing is more paralyzing to faith—nothing more clogs the wheels of exertion, than repining indolence indulged under the cover of humility. Sometimes in seasons of despondency we feel, as if we had been of no use in the work, because no present fruit springs up before us. But does not the promise of God warrant us to make the greatest attempts with the fullest assurance of ultimate success ? The thought of the breath of a worm instrumentally saving an immortal soul, (a work of far higher consideration in the eye of God than the temporal welfare of the universe) proves the Divinely-appointed means (independent of Almighty agency) to be as inadequate to the proposed effect, as were the rod of Moses, the brazen serpent, the trumpets of Joshua, the pitchers of Gideon, or the prophesying of Ezekiel in the valley of dry bones. But their very weakness was the display of the power of God, and the excitement to the exercise of faith : and the neglect of the means in the cases referred to, would have been fatal to their effects. The Scripture therefore speaks of discouragements as " the trials of faith." And when has God ever put honour upon the faith which he has not first tried ? Or when has he failed to honour it in, or after the trial.[4] And thus—as mementos of our weakness, and excitements

---

[1] Eccles. xi. 1.   [2] James i. 5.   [3] 2 Cor. xii. 9.
[4] It is specially "*the trial of faith*" that will be " found to praise, and honour, and glory at the appearing of Christ."—1 Peter i. 7.

of our faith—discouragements properly sustained, proved the channels of spiritual strength to ourselves, and of abundant spiritual blessings to our people.

It is most important habitually to contemplate our work in its proper character as a " work of faith." As such, it can only be sustained by the active and persevering exercise of this principle. This it is that makes it a means of grace to our own souls, as well as a grand medium of exalting our Divine Master.

It is faith that enlivens our work with perpetual cheerfulness. It commits every part of it to God, in the hope, that even mistakes shall be overruled for his glory ; and thus relieves us from an oppressive anxiety, often attendant upon a deep sense of our responsibility. The shortest way to peace will be found in casting ourselves upon God for daily pardon of deficiencies and supplies of grace, without looking too eagerly for present fruit. Hence our course of effort is unvarying, but more tranquil. It is peace—not slumber, rest in the work—not from it. Faith also supports us under the trials of our Ministerial warfare with the clear view of the faithfulness of the covenant, and the stability of the church. And indeed, as all the promises are made to faith, or to the grace springing from it, this is the only spring of Christian courage, and Christian hope. Unbelief looks at the difficulty. Faith regards the promise. Unbelief therefore makes our work a service of bondage. Faith realizes it as a "labour of love." Unbelief drags on in sullen despondency. Faith makes the patience, with which it is content to wait for success, " the patience of hope."[1] As every difficulty (as we have hinted,) is the fruit of unbelief; so will they all ultimately be overcome by the perseverance of faith. To gain therefore an active and powerful spring of renewed exertion, we must strike our roots deeper into the soil of faith. For the work will ever prosper or decline, as we depend upon an Almighty arm, or an arm of flesh.[2] Few, probably, even of the most devoted servants of God, had *duly* counted the cost before they put their hand to the plough ; and from the want of these preparatory exercises of faith, arises that oppressive faintness which gives the enemy

---

[1] 1 Thess. i. 3.

[2] Many of us can feelingly enter into Brainerd's experience, both in his depressions and subsequent elevations.—'Oh! how heavy' (says he) 'is my work, when *faith* cannot take hold of an *Almighty arm* for the performance of it! Many times have I been ready to sink in this case. *Blessed be God, that I may repair to a full fountain.*' 'I stagger along under the burden'—writes another exercised Minister—'like the poor travellers cast away in the desert, ready every step to sink under it. But when it seems as if I could not take another step, but must lie down and die, some spring opens to my view, and I get strength and courage to drag on a little further.' Memoir of Dr. Payson of America.

such an advantage in distressing our peace, and enfeebling our exertions. But after all, the grand secret is habitually to have our eye upon Christ. Peter—looking at the waves instead of the Saviour—'began to sink."[1] We too—if we look at the difficulties of our work, and forget the upholding arm of our ever-present Head—shall sink in despondency. Believe—wait—work—are the watchwords of the Ministry. Believing the promise, gives the power to wait. Waiting supplies strength for work, and such working "is not in vain in the Lord."

We remark also the supreme importance of the *Ministerial exercise of faith in its own character and office*, as substantiating unseen realities to the mind. The grand subjects of our commission have an immediate connection with the eternal world. The soul derives its value from its relation to eternity.[2] The gift of the Saviour opens and assures to the Christian a blissful prospect of eternity.[3] The sufferings of this present time are supported by an habitual contemplation of " things not seen,"[4] and by an estimate of the preponderating "glory that shall be revealed in us."[5] We realize the vanity of this transitory scene only by an accurate comparison with the enduring character of the heavenly state.[6] Daily experience reminds us of the extreme difficulty of maintaining spiritual perceptions of eternal things. The surrounding objects of time and sense spread a thick film over the organs of spiritual vision, and the indistinct haziness, in which they often appear, is as if they were not. Now a vivid apprehension of truth is the spring of a " full assurance of faith," such as will infuse a tenderness, seriousness, and dignity into our discourses, far beyond the power of the highest unassisted talents. ' Faith is the master-spring of a Minister. Hell is before me, and thousands of souls are shut up there in everlasting agonies. Jesus Christ stands forth to save men from rushing into this bottomless abyss. He sends me to proclaim his ability and his love. I want no fourth idea ! Every fourth idea is contemptible. Every fourth idea is a grand impertinence.[7]

We must also remark the *personal assurance of faith* as a

---

[1] Matt. xiv. 30.   [2] Matt. xvi. 26.   [3] John iii. 16.
[4] 2 Cor. iv. 17, 18.   [5] Rom. viii. 18.   [6] 1 John ii. 15—17.
[7] Cecil's Remains. ' He spake,' (observes Dr. Bates and Dr. Manton) ' as one, that had a living faith within him of divine truth.' ' We are so weak in the faith—is the greatest impediment of all. Hence it is, that, when we should set upon a man for his conversion with all our might, if there be not the stirrings of unbelief within us, whether there be a heaven and a hell—yet at least the belief of them is so feeble, that it will scarcely excite in us a kindly, resolute, constant zeal; so that our whole motion will be but weak, because the spring of faith is so weak. O what need therefore have Ministers for themselves and their work, to look well to their faith; especially that their assent to the truth of Scripture, about the joys and torments of the life to come, be sound and lively.'—Reformed Pastor.

spring of our effectiveness. "We are confident" (says the Apostle); "*wherefore* we labour."[1] The assured "knowledge" of Him, "whom he had believed," was at once his support under sufferings, and his principle of perseverance.[2] The persuasion "whose he was"—enabled him to confess with greater confidence—"Whom I serve."[3] And who does not find, that "the joy of the Lord"—the joy of pardon, of acceptance, of communion, and of expectation—"is our strength"[4] for our work in simple, affectionate, and devoted faith? The "spirit of adoption" converts toil into pleasure. What to a slave would be drudgery, to a child is privilege. Instead of being goaded by conscience, he is acted upon by faith, and constrained by love. "*Labor ipse voluptas.*" Thus faith is the principle, love is the enjoyment, and active devotedness is the habit of the work.

Upon the whole, then, we may conclude this subject with the consolatory remembrance of the character of our gracious and faithful Master. Every faithful Minister has fellowship with Polycarp's ground of support—'that he, who was constituted an *overseer* of the church, was himself overlooked by Jesus Christ.' Our Blessed Master will make us sensible of our weakness; but he will not suffer us to faint under it. Our store of sufficiency is treasured up in his inexhaustible fulness; while our insufficiency is covered in his compassionate acceptance. He engages to supply not only rules and directions, but ability and grace, for our momentous work. And if he enables us with a dependent spirit, a single eye, and a single heart, to make an unreserved surrender of ourselves and our talents to his service, he will overcome for us every apprehended difficulty, and we shall "go on our way rejoicing" in our work. But the power of unbelief will be matter of daily conflict to the end. We shall probably find it our chief hindrance. It will induce a faintness under want of success, or self-confidence under apparent usefulness; in either case inverting the Scripture order of life and comfort, and leading us to "walk" by sight, not "by faith;" so that the Saviour, (as we before hinted) cannot do *many* mighty works among us, *because of our unbelief.*[5]

The Writer submits this extended detail to his brethren, with painful self-conviction, and with a deep sense of the injury resulting from the hindrances which have been specified. The most Scriptural church is materially weakened by mal-administration.

[1] 2 Cor. v. 8, 9.   [2] 2 Tim. i. 12.   [3] Acts xxvii. 23.
[4] Neh. viii. 10.   [5] Matt. xii. 58.   Mark vi. 5, 6. ut supra.

Even the Jewish church, though framed by the hands of God, was paralyzed by the unfaithfulness of its Ministers. And who can tell · the injury that our own admirable Establishment may sustain, from hirelings entering into her service, as the way to respectability or emolument, instead of being inwardly "moved by the Holy Ghost," and supremely seeking the honour of their Master, and the interests of his church? The main secret of success doubtless is, to bring the spirit and unction of the Gospel into our public and private Ministrations. Let each of us, therefore, follow the excellent advice of Bishop Burnet—'more particularly to examine himself, whether he has that soft and gentle, that meek and humble, and that charitable and compassionate temper, which the Gospel does so much press upon all Christians; that shined so eminently through the whole life of the blessed Author of it; and which he has so singularly recommended to all his followers; and that has in it so many charms and attractives, which do not only commend those who have these amiable virtues; but (which is much more to be regarded) they give them vast advantages in recommending the doctrine of our Saviour to their people.'[1] Indeed the want of this Christian consistency obscures to our people the credentials of our commission. It is of little avail confidently and successfully to vindicate to them the lawfulness of our ecclesiastical call; except our faithfulness, humility, constancy, self-denial, and tenderness, lead them "*so to account of us*, as the Ministers of Christ, and Stewards of the mysteries of God."[2] It is vain to insist upon the Apostolic succession of our Ministry; except we enlighten it with the combined glory of Apostolical doctrine and example. *In this uniform consistency, not in any sacred antiquity, independent of this confirming seal—lies our spiritual power.* The Bodies of Dissent, making no pretensions to Apostolical descent—yet preaching Apostolical doctrines, will maintain a moral influence in the land, which we can never hope to acquire, except our public and private work is cast into the same Scriptural mould. The church cannot now accredit "the blind, and the halt, and the lame." The lives of her ministers must have the moral weight of holiness.

[1] Pastoral Care, chap. vii.
[2] 1 Cor. iv. 1. Bishop Burnet mentions the wise counsel given to him at an early period of his Ministry—to combine with the Ecclesiastical study of the primitive church, a view of the solemn sense of Ministerial obligation, almost universally entertained at that time; conceiving, 'that the argument in favour of the Church, however clearly made out, would never have its full effect upon the world, till we could show a primitive spirit in our administration, as well as a primitive pattern for our constitution.' 'This advice' (adds the Bishop) 'made even then a *deep impression on me; and I thank God the sense of it has never left me in the whole course of my studies.*'

Our people naturally " seek this proof of Christ speaking in us,"[1] to draw them to us with the impression, with which " A Master in Israel " approached his Divine Teacher—" *We know* that thou art a Teacher come from God."[2]   Those Ministers whom we observe specially honoured in their work, we shall mark generally to be distinguished by a consistent standard of profession and conduct.   And doubtless with more spiritualized affections, with greater abstraction from the world, with more fervent love to the Saviour and zeal for his cause, with a higher estimate of the value of souls, and with a more habitual determination to live with and for God—we shall have a clearer and more effective testimony in the hearts of our people.   We shall " magnify our office "[3] among them ; and they will gladly " receive us as angels of God, even as Christ Jesus."[4]

[1] Pastoral Care, chap. iv.   Comp. Preface.   Nearly to the same purpose he remarks in another place—' Maintaining arguments for more power than we have, will have no effect unless the world see, that we make a good use of the authority already in our hands.   It is with the Clergy as with Princes.   The only way to keep the prerogative from being uneasy to their subjects, and being disputed, is to manage it wholly for their good and advantage.   Then all will be for it, when they find it is for them.   Let the Clergy live and labour well, and they will feel as much authority will follow, as they will know how to manage well.   They will never be secured or recovered from contempt, but by living and labouring as they ought.'   Conclusion of the History of his own times.   2 Cor. xiii. 3.

[2] John iii. 2.   [3] Rom. xi. 13.   [4] Gal. iv. 14.

PART IV.

THE PUBLIC WORK OF THE CHRISTIAN MINISTRY.

THE Public Ministry of the word is the most responsible part of our work—the grand momentum of Divine agency—the most extensive engine of Ministerial operation—acting—not, like parochial visitations, upon individual cases—but with equal power of application to large numbers at the same moment. Baxter therefore justly remarks it to be 'a work, that requireth greater skill, and especially greater life and zeal, than any of us bring to it.'[1] It well deserves therefore a prominent and detailed consideration in passing over the Ministerial field, though a full discussion of its several particulars would furnish ample materials for a volume. We need hardly remark, that this description is more than ever important at the present time, when this Divine ordinance has been degraded from what we shall see to be its true Scriptural elevation.

[1] Reformed Pastor.

CHAPTER I.

THE INSTITUTION AND IMPORTANCE OF THE ORDINANCE OF PREACHING.

' BECAUSE therefore want of the knowledge of God is the cause of all iniquity amongst men, as contrariwise the ground of all our happiness, and the seed of whatsoever perfect virtue groweth from us, is a right opinion touching things Divine ; this kind of knowledge we may justly set down for the first and chiefest thing, which God imparteth unto his people ; and our duty of receiving this at his merciful hands, for the first of those religious offices, wherewith we publicly honour him on earth. For the instruction therefore of all sorts of men unto eternal life it is necessary, that the sacred and saving truth of God be openly published unto them. Which open publication of heavenly mysteries is by an excellency termed preaching.'[1]

The incidental notices of Enoch and Noah connect this institution even with the Ante-diluvian era.[2] In the Patriarchal ages public instruction was probably vested in the heads of families.[3] In the Jewish œconomy Moses received his commission immediately from God ; subsequently assisted by seventy elders associated with him.[4] Often did Joshua, like his predecessor, collect the people to hear the message of God.[5] Lower down the history—we read of the schools of the Prophets—the repositories of public teaching for the land.[6] After the captivity, the ordinance seems to have been received nearly according to the present simple, solemn, well-conducted ceremonial : with an established course of exposition and interpretation.[7] Our Lord—the great Preacher of righteousness—was anointed to this office,[8] and constantly employed in it.[9] He ordained his Apostles as his successors in office,[10] and sealed their commission with the gift of his own Spirit.[11] Invested with this authority they stretched their efforts, publicly and privately, to preach the Gospel to the utmost compass of their commission—

---

[1] Hooker, Book v. 18.   [2] Exod. xiv. 15. 2 Peter ii. 5.
[3] Gen. xiv. 14. marg. xviii. 19.   [4] Exod. xxiv. 12. Numb. xi. 16, 24, 25.
[5] Compare whole Book of Deuteronomy, with Joshua xxii.—xxiv.
[6] 1 Sam. x. 5, 6. Scott in loco.
[7] Compare Neh. viii. 4—8. with Acts xiii. 14, 15. xv. 21.
[8] Isa. lxi. 1, 2, with Luke iv. 16, 21, 43.   [9] Ps. xl. 9, 10, with Luke xix. 47.
[10] Mark iii. 14.   [11] Matt. xxviii. 18—20. Mark xvi. 15, with Luke xxiv. 47—49.

" unto every creature which is under heaven."[1]   No congregation in the Primitive Church separated without being ' fed ' (as Tertullian writes) ' with holy sermons.'[2]   And though for ages the preaching office was suspended in the papal, as indeed it is still in some branches of the Greek Church ; yet it is now generally acknowledged to be the primary instrument in the Divine appointment for the conversion of the world.[3]

An able writer of our day admirably illustrates the power of this grand institution—' Of all methods for diffusing religion, preaching is the most efficient.   It is to preaching that Christianity owes its origin, its continuance, and its progress : and it is to itinerating preaching (however the ignorant may undervalue it) that we owe the conversion of the Roman world from Paganism to primitive Christianity ; our own freedom from the thraldom of Popery, in the success of the Reformation ; and the revival of Christianity at the present day from the depression which it had undergone, owing to the prevalence of infidelity and of indifference.   Books, however excellent, require at least some previous interest on the part of the person, who is to open and to peruse them.   But the preacher arrests that attention, which the written record only invites ; and the living voice, and the listening numbers heighten the impression by the sympathy and enthusiasm which they excite ; the reality, which the truths spoken possess in the mind of the speaker, is communicated to the feelings of the hearers ; and they end in sharing the same views, at least for the moment, and in augmenting each other's convictions.'[4]

[1] Acts v. 20, 21, 42. xx. 20, 21, with Rom. xv. 19 ; Col. i. 23.

[2] The Homilies (or popular discourses—ὁμιλία, from ὅμιλος, a multitude) of the ancient fathers twice—occasionally if not frequently—three times on the Sabbath, are sufficient evidence on this point.   Compare Bingham and Cave.   Mosheim marks the simplicity of preaching in the second century, and its subsequent declension in the time of Origen.   In later ages, the corruption assumed another form not less darkening to the light of God—when the public instructions were drawn not from the Scriptures, but from the writings of the fathers ; and the Church sunk into darkness by her implicit faith in these most fallible guides.

[3] Compare 1 Cor. i. 17, 18, 21.   Rom. x. 14—17.   'Prædicatio verbi est medium gratiæ divinitus institutum, quo res regni Dei publice et explicantur et applicantur populo ad salutem et ædificationem.'   Bowles' Past. Evang. Lib. ii. c. i.   Archbishop Grindal in his celebrated remonstrance to Queen Elizabeth, upon her restraint upon his preaching exercises, well points out the supremacy of preaching in the Christian Ministry—' Public and continual preaching of God's word is the ordinary means and instrument of the salvation of mankind.   St. Paul calls it " the Ministry of reconciliation " of man unto God.   By preaching of God's word, the glory of God is enlarged, faith is nourished, and charity is increased.   By it the ignorant is instructed, the negligent exhorted and incited, the stubborn rebuked, the weak conscience comforted, and to all those that sin of malicious wickedness, the wrath of God is threatened.'   The whole of this admirable letter is given in Fuller's Church History, Book ix. and in Strype's Life of Grindal.

[4] Douglas's Advancement of Society in Knowledge and Religion.   A yet more excursive view is thus forcibly given by an anonymous writer—'The Pulpit, whether we view it with the eye of a Legislator, watching for the welfare of the state ; of the Learned,

This ordinance has always been held in the *highest honour.*
Gregory Nazianzen insists upon it, 'as the principal thing that belong to us Ministers of the Gospel.'[1] St. Augustine marks it as the
proper office of a Bishop.[2] Even in the dark ages of Popery, we
find an edict of the reign of Henry III., at a provincial synod, en-
joining all parish priests ' to instruct the people committed to their
charge, and to feed them with the food of God's word ;' the synod
styling them, in the event of their neglecting this duty, 'dumb
dogs.'[3] Erasmus gives a high pre-eminence to preaching—'The
Minister is then in the very height of his dignity, when from the
pulpit he feeds the Lord's flock with sacred doctrine.'[4] Mr. Thorn-
dike (a writer of some authority on ecclesiastical matters) justly remarks—' that preaching in respect of personal performance, is the
most excellent work bishops and presbyters are able to do in the service of God.'[5] Hooker's judgment is to the same purport—' So
worthy a part of Divine service we should greatly wrong, if we did
not esteem preaching as the blessed ordinance of God—sermons as
keys to the kingdom of heaven, as wings to the soul, as spurs to
the good affections of man, unto the sound and healthy as food, as
physic unto diseased minds.'[6] ' Certainly there is no employment
more honourable ; more worthy to take up a great spirit; more requiring a generous and free nurture, than to be the messenger and
herald of heavenly truth from God to man, and by the faithful
word of holy doctrine to procreate a number of faithful men, making a kind of creation like to God, by infusing his likeness into
them to their salvation, as God did into him ; arising to what cli-
mate he may turn him, like the Sun of righteousness that sent him,
with healing in his wings, and new light to break in upon the chill
and gloomy hearts of hearers, rising out of darksome barrenness a
delicious and fragrant spring of saving knowledge and 'good

jealous for public science and taste; of the Moral Philosopher, anxious for the virtue of
the community; or of the devout Christian, weighing every thing in the balance of eternity—the Pulpit must, in every light, appear an object of vast importance.' Eclectic Review. We may add, that so powerful is the influence of the Pulpit upon the Church,
that the general state of the Church at any given period may be correctly estimated by
the prevalent style of preaching.

[1] προοίμιον τῶν ἡμετέρων. Orat. I.

[2] De Offic. 1. c. 1. Thus the Council of Trent designates this office—*præcipuum Epis-
coporum munus.* Sess. iv. c. 2.

[3] Bishop Stillingfleet's Duties and Rights of the Parochial Clergy, p. 15. The Coun-
tess of Richmond (mother of King Henry the Seventh) ' had such a sense of the necessity of the office in those times, that she maintained many preachers at her own charges,
and employed Bishop Fisher to find out the best qualified for it.' Ibid. p. 206.

[4] Erasm. Eccles. Lib. i. Elsewhere he observes, that the sense of religion grows very
cold, without preaching.

[5] See his Due Way of composing Differences. The Primitive Bishops (Augustine,
Gregory, Chrysostom, Ambrose, &c.) were the greatest preachers of their time.

[6] Book v. 22.

works.'[1] All our diversity of means and machinery must subserve, and their energy depend upon a faithful exercise of the preaching commission. All the work done, or to be done, must be connected with "the foolishness of preaching," as God's chosen and chief ordinance.[2]

The sacred history connects this ordinance with national blessing, and the extension of scriptural religion. National distress and "vexation" marked the destitution of "a teaching priest" in Asa's reign.[3] In the subsequent reign of Jehoshaphat, great public prosperity was combined with the mission of Levites and Priests throughout all the cities.[4] The comparative disuse of preaching was a concomitant mark of the dark ages of Popery, while its revival was coeval with the era of the Reformation.[5]

George Herbert, therefore, might justly call his Country Parson's pulpit 'his joy and his throne'[6]—as, indeed, invested with a dignity, solemnity, and efficiency peculiar to itself.

CHAPTER II.

PREPARATION FOR THE PULPIT.

How honourable was the spirit of "the man after God's own heart," who could not endure the thought of offering unto the Lord his God "of that which did cost him nothing :"[7] and who, in contemplating the greatness of the work, and the majesty of his God, "prepared with all his might, for the house of his God !"[8] Nor did

[1] Milton.
[2] See 1 Cor. i. 21, 23, 24. Mark xvi. 15. Rom. x. 14—17. Yet in despite of these plain Scriptural declarations, we are now told—"that the Sacraments—*not preaching*— are the sources of Divine Grace," (Advert. Tracts for the Times, Vol. 1.) Again—'We would not be taught entirely to depreciate preaching as a mode of doing good. It may be necessary in a weak and languishing state: but it is an instrument, *which Scripture, to say the least, has never much recommended !*' Tract 89. Thus openly does proud man in his self-sufficiency contradict the testimony of God! How truly according to the mind of God was the view of Mr. Robinson—justly considering the commission—"Preach the word," as his main work, which the nearest of the rest followed at a long interval. 'It is well' (he would say) 'to visit: it is well to show kindness; to make friendly; to instruct at home; to instruct at their own houses; to educate the children; to clothe the naked. But the pulpit is the seat of usefulness; souls are to be converted and built up there; no exertion must be allowed, which may have the effect of habitually deteriorating this; whatever else is done should be with the design and hope of making this more effective.' Life, p. 297.
[3] 2 Chron xv. 3, 5.   [4] Ibid. xvii. 5—12.
[5] The object of the Reformers in the Book of Homilies was to remove the obstructions to preaching from the disuse of the office, and the ignorance of the Clergy.
[6] County Parson, ch. vii.   [7] 2 Sam. xxiv. 24.   [8] See 1 Chron. xxix. 1—5.

his illustrious son devote less preparation of heart and consecration
of service to the building of the spiritual temple, than to that magnificent material temple, which was the glory of his nation, and the
wonder of the world.   To the one he devoted all the treasures of
his kingdom ; to the other, all the riches of his mind—" large
and exceeding much, even as the sand that is on the sea-shore."[1]
" Because the Preacher was wise, he still taught the people knowledge ; yea, *he gave good heed*, and *sought out*, and set in order
many proverbs."[2]   His whole soul was engaged in the discovery of
the best mode, as well as the best substance, of instruction ; that
his thoughts might be clothed in language, worthy of the great
subject and its Divine Author.   He evidently considered the advantages of " study " to overbalance its " weariness to the flesh ;"
and " the words of this wisest " of men—the fruit of labour and
study—were as " goads " to quicken the slothful.   They not only
gained the ears, and moved the affections ; but they fixed upon the
memory, conscience, and judgment, " as nails fastened by the master of assemblies."[3]

Such an example of devoted preparation for public instruction it
well becomes us to follow.   For, indeed, to maintain a constant
recollection of the specific necessities of our people ; to decide upon
the most suitable course of Scriptural doctrine, exhortation, and
comfort ; to select the most appropriate vehicles for the presentment
of the truth—these are exercises of laborious and persevering diligence.   Yet with some, confidence supplies the place of premeditation.   A Bible and Concordance, with a few sermon-notes, or
even the impulse of the moment, with the gift of tolerable fluency
—these are thought a sufficient warrant to stand up in the name
of the great God.   But what is solid will alone be permanent.   No
powers of imagination, natural eloquence, or vehement excitement,
can compensate for the want of substantial matter.   The " pastors
according to God's heart will feed the people *with knowledge
and understanding*."[4]   But except there be a gathering proportionate to the expenditure, there can be no store of " knowledge
and understanding " for distribution to the people.

Preachers of this stamp are known by their general want of va-

[1] 1 Kings iv. 29.   [2] Eccles. xii. 9.   [3] Ib. xii. 10—12.
[4] Jer. iii. 15.   See the conclusion of Fenelon's First Dialogue on Eloquence. ' Preaching' (says an old writer) ' is not a labour of the lips, and an idle talk of the tongue from
a light imagination of the mind ; but is indeed an uttering of God's truth from a serious
meditation of the heart, in sound judgment, acquired through God's blessing by diligent
labour and study to profit God's people.   This preaching is of worth, deserves esteem,
procures credit to God's ordinance, will work upon the hearers, and will pierce deeply
as being spoken with authority.'   Bernard's Faithful Shepherd, 12mo. 1621.

riety. It is substantially not only (what it ought always to be) the same doctrine, but nearly the same sermon. If a new text may be expected, yet it is the repetition of the same thoughts, attenuated with regular but most wearisome uniformity—*semper eadem.* They are "householders," but without a "treasure." The "old" indeed they can readily "bring forth;" but where is "the new?"[1] This poverty of thought cannot be justly chargeable upon their resources. For there is no characteristic of Scripture more striking, than the diversified aspects and relations, in which it presents the same truths, fraught with fresh interest and important instruction. These monotonous exercises, even upon the highest of all subjects, are powerless in impression. Either this sterile sameness spreads a torpor over the congregation ; or the more intelligent part of them give vent to their dissatisfaction.[2]

It is indeed a "neglect of the gift of God that is in us," to trifle either in the study or in the pulpit. God will bless our endeavours —not our idleness. Our Master, and our people for our Master's sake, have a just claim to our best time and talents, our most matured thoughts, and most careful studies. To venture upon this infinite work of God with slender furniture, proves a guilty unconcern to our high responsibility. Admitting that some gifted Ministers may preach effectively without study; yet reverence for our Master's name, and a due consideration of the dignity and solemn business of the pulpit, might well serve to repress a rash and undi-

---

[1] Comp. Matt. xiii. 52.

[2] See Bishop of Winchester's Charge, 1837, p. 39. The example of Bishop Jewell offers much instruction to this class of preachers. His biographer writes—'The more eminent he was in dignity, the more diligent in the work of the Ministry—not so much in frequent as in exquisite teaching. For, though his sermons were very frequent, yet they were always rare for the matter and manner of his delivery. The Roman orator tells us of ' *negligentia quædam diligens* '—a certain negligent diligence and learned ignorance when the speaker carefully shunneth all affectation of art, and laboureth that his speech may not seem elaborate. But the sober and discreet hearer hath often cause to complain, of a *diligentia quædam negligens*—a negligent kind of diligence, in many popular preachers, who ascend frequently into the pulpit, but with extemporary provision ; are often in travail, but without pain ; and delivered of nothing for the most part but empty words : as if sermons were to be valued by the number and not by the weight. These men's sermons, though they exceed the hour in length, and the days of the week in number, yet they themselves lie open to the curse of the prophet, denounced against all those "that do the work of the Lord negligently." From all the danger of which malediction Jewell was freest of all his parts and place. For though he might best of any presume in this kind upon his multiplicity of reading, and continual practice of preaching, yet never would he preach in the meanest village, without precedent meditation, and writing also the chief heads of his sermons.' Featley's Life of Bishop Jewell. Compare Mr. Cecil's own account of the manner of commencing his Ministry—in his Life, prefixed to 'Remains.' This was the complaint in Jerome's time—' Sola Scripturarum ars est, quam sibi passim omnes vendicant. Hanc garrula anus, hanc delirus senex, hanc sophista verbosus, hanc universi præsumunt, lacerant, docent antequam discunt.' Epist. ad Paulin. Even the heathen epigrammatist remarked

' Si duri puer ingeni videtur,
Præconem facias.' Mart. Lib. 5. Epig. 56.

gested exercise of this holy function. How unequal to the exigency is the gathering of a few abstract and unconnected truths, without weighing the most forcible modes of application to the consciences and varied circumstances of our people![1] The Scriptural model gives no countenance to loose statements—the result only of inexcusable indolence. The diligence of faith will always meet with acceptance; wilful neglect with the merited recompence of our presumption.

The style, arrangement, and substance of the sermons of the most eminent preachers prove their diligence in pulpit preparation. President Edwards' high reputation as a preacher arose from his great pains in composition, especially in his early Ministry.[2] Philip Henry latterly would say—'that he might now take a greater liberty to talk, as he called it, in the pulpit, that is, to speak familiarly to the people. Yet *to the last he abated not in his preparation for the pulpit*'[3]—like the royal preacher in Jerusalem, who in the decline of life "*still* taught the people knowledge."[4] It is, however, yet more important, to cultivate a spiritual and experimental tone of our pulpit studies. The materials drawn from intellectual sources, or from a lowered standard of orthodox theology, only bring into the outer courts of the sanctuary. We must take a coal from the altar, that the "hearts" of our people may "burn within them."

---

[1] 'We must' (as Baxter reminds us) 'study how to convince and get within men, and how to bring each truth to the quick, and not leave all this to our extemporary promptitude, unless in cases of necessity. Experience will teach, that men are not made learned or wise without hard study, and unwearied labour and experience.' Reformed Pastor.

[2] See his Life prefixed to his Works, vol. i. 49.

[3] Life, p. 192. His excellent son's preparation for the pulpit was equally unremitting. 'To that leading object every other was subordinate. All he said, and all he saw, as well as the things he heard, were regarded by him with less or with more attention, as they bore upon *that*. Nothing crude or indigested found its way through his agency into the solemn assembly. 'Take heed' (he would say) 'of growing *remiss* in your work. Take pains while you live. Think not that after a while you may relax, and go over your old stock. The scripture still affords new things to those who search them. Continue searching. How can you expect God's blessing on your people's observance, if you are careless?'—Life, p. 112, 113. Eliot's view of the importance of preparation is admirable—'He liked no preaching, but what had been well studied for; and he would very much commend a sermon, which he could perceive had required some good thinking and reading in the author of it. I have been present,' (says his biographer) 'when he thus addressed a preacher just come home from the assembly with him—'Brother, there was oil required for the service of the sanctuary, but it must be beaten oil; I praise God, that I saw your oil so well beaten to-day. The Lord help us always by good study to beat our oil, that there may be no knots in our sermons left undissolved, and that there may be a clear light thereby given in the house of God.' And yet he likewise looked for something in a sermon beside and beyond the mere study of man. He was for having the Spirit of God breathing in it and with it; and he was for speaking those things, from those impressions and with those affections, which might compel the hearer to say—'The Spirit of God was here'—I have heard him complain—'It is a sad thing, when a sermon shall have that one thing—the Spirit of God—wanting in it.' Mather's Life of Eliot.   [4] Eccl. xii. 9.

There will be, however, great injury in slavishly following any popular pattern. It is useful to observe the diversities of gifts in our brethren; but our chief business is with the discernment and cultivation of our own gifts, and the sedulous endeavour to acquire a competent measure of all Ministerial gifts, at least so as not in any part *wholly* to come short. Many young Ministers have crippled their effectiveness, by a vain attempt to exercise the higher qualifications of their more favoured brethren; instead of improving the more humble, but perhaps equally useful capabilities, which had been distributed to them.[1]

Yet does fruitful pulpit preparation depend more upon our spirituality than even upon our diligence. It is an improving and industrious habit, flowing from the heart penetrated with a sense of the love of Christ, the value of souls, the shortness of time, and the supreme concerns of eternity. And when it is intelligently fixed upon the subject-matter, clear views of Scriptural truth are beautifully unfolded, flowing in perspicuous and natural order, and no less subservient to personal edification than to public instruction. Thus the Christian's operative principle realizes an accurate perception of the main object, and concentrates all the powers of the mind upon it; so that, without this habit, the most diligent Ministerial student becomes a mere trifler in his momentous work.

But the importance of this subject calls us to consider it more in detail, under the three particulars of—Composition of Sermons—Habit of Meditation—and Special Prayer.

I.—COMPOSITION OF SERMONS.

How much responsibility attaches to our pulpit addresses! It cannot be of light moment, whether our people are "fed with knowledge and understanding," or with ill-prepared and unsuitable provision. The pulpit is the ordinary distribution of the bread of life; and much wisdom indeed is required, "rightly to divide the word of truth,"[2] that each may be ready to say—" A word spoken in season, how good is it!"[3]

In the selection of our subjects, the Sacred Volume opens a field of almost infinite extent. We can only seize the most suitable points of present interest, without pretending to occupy the whole field. The Apostle gives us some wise cautionary rules respecting

---

[1] See some valuable remarks in Raikes on Clerical Education, p. 221.
[2] 2 Tim. ii. 15.   [3] Prov. xv. 23.

our choice of subjects—marking with equal distinctness " the things that are good and profitable to men," and " the things that are un‐ profitable and vain."[1] He warns us against curious or speculative matters, as inconsistent with our office, and hurtful in their results.[2] He would have us " affirm constantly" the doctrine of man's ruin and recovery, as the sole efficient spring of practical godliness ;[3] and, after his own example,[4] bend all subjects naturally to Christ, and concentrate them all in the full exhibition of his cross. The mate‐ rials for this system of instruction occur in the daily course of read‐ ing, in secret retirement with God, in the habit of family inter‐ course, in unlooked for, or even ordinary, providences ; and thus ris‐ ing before us, they will always find a responsive interest in their adaptation to the present wants and sympathies of our people. Cases also in our parochial intercourse—of ignorance, of hardened obstinacy, of perplexity, or of awakened conviction—furnish some of the best matter for our Sabbath Ministrations.[5]

The meaning and object of a text is a definite passage from the word of God, as the ground-work of some statement of truth, drawn from the word. This is natural and obvious. But we question the propriety of selecting texts merely as mottos for pul‐ pit dissertations. Instead of the sermon being made from the text, the text is made from the sermon. It is read as a customary intro‐ duction. It furnishes the occasion of the discursive inquiry, but its component parts, or its connexion with the context, are left un‐

---

[1] Comp. Tit. iii. 8, 9.

[2] 2 Tim. ii. 15, 16, 23. Bishop Reynolds guards us against a danger closely allied to this—' the vain affectation of finding something new and strange in the plainest texts, which shows pride and wantonness much more than solid learning or judgment.' Ser‐ mon on self-denial, Works, p. 810. The Minister's office in the pulpit—let it be re‐ membered—is that of " an Interpreter," to expound the mind of God—not to show what the text may be made to speak, but what there is good reason to believe the Holy Ghost intended it to speak. Hence we may give a Scriptural statement, and *at the same time*, a false exposition of Scripture. This Ministration enervates the most forcible matter by an uncertain dependence upon Divine authority, and builds our faith upon human fancy and imagination. In the gratification of fancy and conceit, the true prac‐ tical instruction is overlooked : Scripture is treated as if it had no definite meaning : ' making of any thing ' (as Hooker says, v. c. 59,) ' what it listeth, and bringing in the end all truth to nothing. On the subject of texts, see Claude's Essay, edited by Mr. Simeon, with many valuable improvements. Whatever may be thought of some of his minuter points of detail, no work will be found more useful in assisting a clear diges‐ tion, and a lucid arrangement of our subject matter. Some excellent hints also may be gathered from Lectures on Homiletics and Preaching, by E. Porter, D. D., Theo‐ logical President of the Seminary at Andover, United States. Compare Bowles, Lib. ii. c. 1, 2.

[3] Titus iii. 8, ινα—in order that—to the end that, &c.   [4] See 1 Cor. ii. 2.

[5] Blackwell notices, and profitably enlarges upon, the following particulars in refer‐ ence to the choice of subjects. 1. The spiritual state of the people. 2. Their capacity for hearing the Gospel. 3. Their predominant sins. 4. Providential occasions. Meth. Evang. pp. 48—58. Cotton Mather's rule was to ' consider the case and circumstance of his hearers, as his means of direction to his subjects ; and to have some particular design of edification in every sermon that he preached. Bowles adds the main rule for constant recollection—' *Salus populi inter concionandum suprema lex esto.*' Lib. ii. 1.

touched. This method—besides that it loses the office of the expositor—seems scarcely to acknowledge due reverence to the word of God. And though it may sometimes afford opportunities for useful discussion, yet it tends to 'divert the mind from the inspection, meditation, and weighing of sacred scripture, which is the true food of the soul, and the treasury of Divine wisdom : and to which alone the converting grace of the Holy Spirit is annexed.'[1]

Some of Cotton Mather's rules for his student's *treatment of texts* are excellent ; such as—If possible—to read the text in the original and consult commentators before he composed his sermon—to study a scriptural style in his sermons, and to confirm his several heads of discourse with some Scripture proof or illustration—to have much of Christ in all his sermons, as knowing that the Holy Ghost loves to glorify Christ ; and hoping, that if he followed this rule, the Holy Spirit would favour him with much of his influence in the exercise of his Ministry—to crowd every sermon as full of matter as possible without obscurity.[2]

A remark on some of these rules may be allowed. The use of commentators is well, before we compose our sermons, but not before *we have considered and arranged them*. This was Mr. Cecil's plan of preparation ; not to forestall his own views by the use of commentaries ; but first to talk over the subject to himself, writing down whatever struck his mind ; and *after having arranged* what he had written, settled his plan, and exhausted his own resources—to avail himself of all extrinsical help.[3] There is no greater hindrance to solid learning, than to make such use of other men's resources, as to neglect our own. The use of helps *generally*, and especially '*Helps for Composition*' in the form of '*Skeletons*'—needs great discretion, discrimination, and diligence, lest, by restraining the active energy of our native powers they do not rather prove *serious hindrances* to composition. Mr. Simeon's well-known and most useful work, may be said to give precisely that measure of help which is required—encouragement to inexperienced diligence, and at the same time a fair scope for

[1] Vitri. Methodus Homiletica, cap. iii.   [2] See his Life.
[3] See his Life, prefixed to his 'Remains.' The following are noticed by a valuable writer as among the important advantages arising from foreign research, as supplementary—not preliminary—to home resources—'It will give excitement to the mind, and rouse it to a state of higher energy and activity—It will present ample materials for thought and reflection ; and should the mind fix, with a vigorous grasp, only on some one interesting thought, that single idea may be the first of a train, which will give a character and a value to the whole discourse—It will give additional amplitude, richness, and vividness to many of the illustrations, which your own mind might have suggested in part, but with much less power of exciting interest and impression. It will also serve to give additional confidence in the expression of your own opinion.' Mental Discipline, by the Rev. H. F. Burder, p. 85.

the exercise of talent. For the care and thought requisite to produce from his volume, a complete and well-proportioned discourse, are fully equal to the labour of an original composition; so skilfully are the breaks contrived, to exercise the judgment in suitable filling up of the vacuum, and in the accurate arrangement of the scriptural matter.[1] Perhaps the highest commendation of the work is, that a mere copyist would exhibit the Skeletons like the bones in the prophetic vision, *very dry;* whereas a thoughtful mind would find ample and profitable employment in clothing them with solid matter, in the form of symmetry and strength.[2]

As to Cotton Mather's rule of *crowding his sermons with matter*—It would be well, that our discourses should be like Elihu's, "full of matter;"[3] and we must regret, that a good man is not always a wise or a full man. Yet we must remember our people's capabilities, the limited nature of their digestive powers, and the serious injury of stretching them beyond their natural exercise. The principle of our Lord's instruction was, to "speak the word unto the people, as they were able to hear it."[4] Had he said all that he could have said, it would have been infinitely more than they would have been able to have received; and consequently the grand end of his instruction would have been lost. It needs much prudence to select the most appropriate instruction, rather than by sweeping over too large a surface, to weaken distinctness of impression. Mr. Cecil justly remarks, that 'it requires as much reflection to know what is not to be put in a sermon, as what is.'[5] It is not, how much can be said; but what can best be said. Let us not aim

[1] This remark applies with less force to the Horæ Homileticæ of this revered writer; which, being constructed for the use of the laity as well as the clergy, came from the author's hands with more substance and completeness.

[2] Ezek. xxxvii. 2. We might take an illustration—Mr. Martyn's Sermon on Psalm ix. 17; which is the filling up of Mr. Simeon's Skeleton on that text. It was worked out (as we incidentally learn from his Life) under circumstances of peculiar disadvantage and mental agitation. But the life that is infused throughout, the variety of its enlargements, the accuracy of the proportions of its several parts, the skill with which the breaks are completed, and the warm and strong colouring given to the whole—all combine to give to it the power and effect of an original and talented composition. See his Life, pp. 130—132, and compare his volume of Sermons (v) with Helps to Composition, Skel. 387.

[3] Job xxxii. 18. Archbishop Usher used to call Dr. Manton a voluminous preacher—not from the tedious length of his discourses, but from his art of compressing the substance of volumes of Divinity into a narrow compass.

[4] Mark iv. 33.

[5] Cecil's Remains—'Verbum sic populo Dei dispensandum, ut multum, non multa. Prurit quandoque concionatoris animus, ut multa doctrinæ capita percurrat; sylvam materiæ in concione accumulet. At nec hoc est ritè concionari; nec sic populus ædificatur. Maxima pars vulgi, quâ est ingenii hebetudine, multitudine, rerum, quæ varii generis, potius obruitur, quàm instruitur. Non tam itaque refert, quot poteramus doctrinæ capita percurrere, quam, quid auditoribus commodum.' Bowles' Pastor, Lib. ii. c. 10—'Qui docet, vitabit omnia verba, quæ non docent'—was Augustine's sensible rule. De Doctr. Christian Lib. iv. 10.

at exhausting ourselves at every point of our subject. Let our thoughts be select, solid, naturally flowing out of the discussion, without breaking into the unity of our scheme.

The Writer feels that he can add nothing of importance to the rules of more practised writers. The great matter to keep in mind is *the opening of Scripture—expounding the mind of God—* not opening our subject *abstractedly*, but through the medium of Scripture, beaten out, and laid full and large before our people. In order to this primary end of preaching; every text should contain a complete sense. The selection of materials in beating out and applying this sense, requires much care. In avoiding the technical plan, which would reduce all subjects into one precise form, we must, however, carefully apply those fixed rules and principles, which belong to the science of preaching as a science, in giving to it the best method and expression. The subject probably should be digested previous to the arrangement of the sermon. This will best secure unity of design, combined with interesting variety of method. It will also guard us against the common evil of dissecting rather upon the principle of verbal than logical analysis; distributing the words, rather than the materials of discussion, under their several heads; thus obscuring the primary topics; amplifying secondary points: and bringing much irrelevant matter into the scheme. The exordium opens no sphere for artificial structure or for studied ornament, or generally even for fervid appeals. We might introduce he text naturally to view by some brief exposition of the context or of the subject in hand.[1] The clearness of the discussion materially depends upon 'having no more heads than can be sufficiently amplified within the bounds of the discourse, so as to be rendered sensible to the hearers. They should be quite distinct from one another, at the same time that they all concentre on the main point.'[2] This assists the hearer in the survey and retention of truth—'method being a chain, in which, if a man should let slip any one part, he may easily recover it again, by that relation and dependence which it hath with the whole.'[3] Some of the best pul-

---

[1] 'Exordium est ingressus quidam, quo ceu viam sternimus ad rem, quam tractaturi sumus; et quo de rebus non levibus, sed necessariis et salutaribus dicturos nos significamus, ad attentionem nobis conciliandam; quo etiam, in continuato textu præuntis loci cum præcedenti connexionem ostendimus.' Bucani Methodus Concion. vide p. 12. 12mo. Groning. 1645.

[2] Fordyce's Eloquence of the Pulpit.

[3] Bishop Wilkins's Ecclesiastes, p. 6. 'A clear division,' says Reybaz, 'is the handle of a vase; in the taking hold of which, every thing it contains goes with it.' 'Method raises a lively and beautiful composure out of a chaos of complicated and disorderly materials; and from a disorderly concourse and dark confusion of ideas calls forth light, order, and harmony. This assigns to every part its proper magnitude, figure, and situation, with so much judgment, that all stand in need of one another, and each con-

pit talents—such as fluency of utterance, richness and variety of illustration—without an orderly distribution, fail in arresting the attention, or fixing permanent impression.   There may be indeed a danger even on this side of a mode too artificial, and of fettering even the Divine Spirit (who "bloweth where he listeth") by the restriction of canons, sometimes too accurate for the free and popular flow of Scripture.[1]   It is however most desirable to avoid that habit of running away from our text, which has gained for some of us the name of ' fugitive preachers.'   The best matter loses its interest by an unnatural connection.   The simplest subjects are obscured by the introduction of irrelevant detail.

Bishop Wilkins states the three component parts of a sermon to be method, matter, and expression.   ' Each of these' (he observes) 'do contribute mutual assistance to each other.   A good method will direct to proper matter; and fitting matter will enable for good expression.'[2]   The method is seen in laying down the scheme—the matter in filling it up—and the expression in clothing it with an appropriate garb.   We have already adverted to *method*.   A sermon, in order to edification, must be rich in *matter*.   At least any deficiency of substance proportionably diminishes its usefulness. The primary sources of matter are found in a close analysis of every important word in the text, and of the design of the whole ; illustrated by the examination of the parallel references, by an attentive ruminating inspection of the context, and by a clear reference to the analogy of faith.[3]   Any historical circumstance connected with the text—the clear exposition of the meaning (not however needlessly distracting the mind with jarring interpretations) the scope of the sacred writer—the successive steps, and consecutive reasoning, by which he arrives at his point—must all be noticed.   The consideration also of the speaker, the occasion, the person addressed—the tracing of the principles developed in the text to their consequences, or the consequences referred back to their original principles—the connexion and suitableness of means to

---

tributes gracefulness and strength to the whole.   Three things are especially necessary—distinction of the parts—their mutual dependence on one another, and the perspicuity of the whole contexture.'   Sir Richard Blackmore's Accomplished Preacher. 8vo. 1731.

[1] Augustine excellently observes—' Periculum est, ne fugiant ex animo quæ sunt docenda, dum 'attenditur, ut arte dicantur.'—Lib. iv.—ut supra.   See some admirable thoughts on this subject in Hall's Sermon on the Ministry, pp. 25, 26.

[2] Bishop Wilkins's Ecclesiastes, p. 5.

[3] 'Concionem paraturus—textum ante omnia legat, relegat, perlegat; phrases seu locutiones, vocumque, tum singularum, tum complexarum, significationes accurate examinet; idque faciat, vel consultis ipsis fontibus, vel saltem omnium optimis laudatissimisque versionibus, unde sensum germanum eruat cum περιστασει loci, fidei analogia, et aliis Scripturæ locis convenientem.'—Bucan. ut supra. p. 10.

their end—these points will furnish instructive substance with practical and experimental application. Collateral matter may be found, diversified in the form of parallelism, contrast, illustration—the pursuit of the object in direct inference, objections, or hypothetical suppositions,[1] &c. The effective use of these helps obviously requires a sound judgment, and a mind stored with active intellectual furniture, such as enlarges our capabilities for communicating instruction.

But after all,—as an old man remarked to Musculus, one of the Swiss reformers—'*Si vis fieri bonus concionator, da operam, ut sis bonus Biblicus.*' The Scripture is the inexhaustible store-house of our most valuable materials—whether of clear instruction ; convincing argument; powerful or melting address; or even the higher strokes of eloquence—' thoughts that breathe in words that burn.' Any just complaint therefore of the barrenness or sameness of our preaching, must arise (as we have hinted) from want of industry in our research, not from the want of opulence of our resources. Augustine rightly estimates ' the preacher's wisdom, according to his proficiency in the diligent and intelligent search of the Scriptures. The more he sees the poverty of his own store, the more needful is it, that he should enrich himself in these treasures.'[2] Not that we would recommend a long string of texts, or what Burnet calls ' a bare concordance exercise,' (for ill-digested quotations even from the sacred treasury, may be very unprofitable); but an express reference to Scripture in confirmation of the distinct points of our discourses : not overcharging our sermons,[3] but yet at the same time giving a full prominence to the Divine testimony. To dilute our proofs in the natural flow of our own style, proportionably weakens the impression—*Thus God hath spoken ;* whereas a distinct reference to the authority of Scripture, confirms our statements with the stamp of God, and brings our hearers, like the camp at Sinai, prostrate before his awful majesty. On this account the Apostle's

---

[1] Mr. Sturtevant has pertinently illustrated Mr. Claude's detail of these various sources of matter. See his " Conversations and Letters upon Preaching," and " The Preacher's Manua."

[2] Augustine, ut supra—Lib. iv. 5. Dr. Watts reminded his Minister, that he was a Minister of the Word of God, a Professor and Preacher of the Bible; and not a mere Philosopher upon the foot of reason, nor an orator in a Heathen school. Humble Attempt, p. 64.

[3] It was Mr. Robinson's sensible judgment, 'that one or two texts were as good as one hundred.' A valuable old writer observes the defects on both sides—of loading sermons with a mass of Scripture, and leaving them wholly destitute. He remarks, that a judicious selection of Scripture proof (seldom more than one to a single point) was the practice of Christ and his apostles, though they could have produced multiplied testimonies of Scripture in defending themselves against their enemies. Zepperi Ars Conscion. Lib. II. chap. vi. Compare Bowles, Lib. ii. 2. Burnet's Past. Care, ch. ix.

"speech and preaching was not with enticing words of man's wisdom ;" but "in the words which the Holy Ghost teacheth," "that the faith of his people should not stand in the wisdom of man, but in the power of God."[1]

Generally speaking — the discussion should be comprehended within two or three divisions, the matter so clearly arranged, as to fall in readily under the several main heads ; the principal points strengthened and illustrated by Scriptural testimony, and closely applied to the respective cases of our congregation.[2] If the discussion were likely to extend beyond its due bounds, it would be better to sketch a short outline in the introduction, or to seize the most prominent points, rather than to be constrained to press its personal interest upon minds ill-prepared by weariness to receive a deep and permanent impression. It is not enough that the sermon should contain striking or good thoughts. The materials must be arranged so as to produce an effect upon the whole—a growing interest, conducting to a clear and powerful conclusion. We must beware, however, of fixing our minds upon the mechanism of the sermon, so as to forget that which alone can infuse life and power into it. We may produce a skeleton clothed with flesh, and exhibiting the most exact proportion of its several parts; yet still may it be, like the dry bones lately referred to, without the quickening breath of heaven. A spiritual, as well as an intellectual habit, is essential both to the composition and the delivery of our discourses.

With regard to the *style of our sermons*—simplicity and point seem to be the most important characteristics—simplicity, without undignified familiarity—point and energy, without unnatural labour to produce effect. Archbishop Whately admirably warns us against the two extremes of conciseness and prolixity connected with this style. 'It is obvious' (he observes) 'that extreme conciseness is ill-suited to hearers, whose intellectual powers and cultivation are small. The usual expedient, however, of employing a prolix style, by way of accommodation to such minds, is seldom successful.—They are likely to be bewildered by tedious expansion, and being unable to maintain a steady attention to what is said, they forget part of what they have heard, before the whole is completed. Add to which, that the feebleness produced by excessive di-

---

[1] 1 Cor. ii. 4, 5, 13. Chrysostom well remarks—'If any thing be spoken without Scripture, the knowledge of the hearers halteth.' On Psalm lxxxvi. To the same purport Augustine, 'Non valet—hæc ego dico, hæc tu dicis, hæc ille dicit; sed hæc dicit Dominus.' Ad Vincent.
[2] Three brief rules have been given by an eminent Master in composition—'Get the subject into your mind—Throw yourself into it—Pour both yourself and it into the bosoms of your hearers.'

lution, will occasion the attention to languish ; and what is imperfectly attended to, however clear in itself, will usually be but imperfectly understood. Young writers and speakers are apt to fall into a style of pompous verbosity, from an idea that they are adding both perspicuity and force to what is said, when they are only encumbering the sense with a needless load of words. It is not indeed uncommon to hear a speaker of this class mentioned, as having 'a very fine command of language ;' when perhaps it might. be said with more correctness, that 'his language has a command of him'—that is, that he follows a train of words rather than of thought.'[1]

The Bible furnishes unquestionably the perfect model of this clear, natural, and vigorous style. We see therefore the propriety of Cotton Mather's rule—to mould even the garb of our sermons after the Scriptural pattern. The phraseology dictated by the Holy Ghost is peculiarly calculated for public preaching.[2] There is no book so intelligible as the book of God ; no book that so clearly reveals man to himself ; or that has such inexpressible power over his heart ; or that connects itself so naturally with his popular feelings and interests. The savour of Divine truth is sensibly diminished, by passing under the conceptions or expressions of men. No language—whether of exposition, address, or illustration—is so generally acceptable as that of the inspired volume. Few readers of Saurin and French Divines of his class (orthodox in their views, and forcible in their statement of Scriptural truth), but have felt a lack of unction, warmth, and spiritual excitement, arising from their scanty infusion of the sacred dialect into their writings—a deficiency for which no powers of genius or eloquence can compensate to a spiritual mind.[3] The matter and manner, that is drawn fresh from the spring, will always be most enlivening.

---

[1] Whately on Rhetoric.   [2] See 1 Cor. ii. 13.
[3] 'The Bible' (as the late Mr. Hall admirably observed)—'being intimately associated in the mind with every thing dear and valuable, its diction more powerfully excites devotional feelings than any other ; and, when temperately and soberly used, imparts an unction to a religious discourse, which nothing else can supply. For devotional impression, we conceive that a very considerable tincture of the language of Scripture, or at least such a colouring, as shall discover an intimate acquaintance with these inimitable models, will generally succeed best.' Review of Foster's Essays. Vitringia speaks excellently to the same purport—'Non in sententiis tantum et doctrinis, verum etiam in dictis et phrasibus Scripturæ S. tantam vim et pondus esse, ut nullum verbum qualecumque aliud ei, in exponendis rebus spiritualibus sive *simplicitatis*, sive *proprietatis* et nativa, significationis respectu, comparari queat. Vocabula et dictiones Spiritus S. nudæ, et nullis permixtæ lenociniis orationis aut exegesios humanæ, passim sic afficiunt et illustrant mentem, ut quicquid iis admiscetur, insipidum videatur.' Method. Homil. Cap. iii. In the same spirit Witsius remarks—'Res Dei commodius explicari non possent quam verbis Dei. Male putat, quisquis presumit, se accuratius, vel clarius, vel efficacius, vel ad intelligendum aptius Theologiæ arcane explanaturum, quam iis terminis et phrasibus, quibus post Prophetas Apostoli usi sunt, ab eo dictatis, qui homini os et linguam forma-

We need scarcely animadvert upon the pitiful practice of a copyist in preaching. Mr. Addison (a name of far higher authority in accomplished literature, than in theology,) commends Sir Roger de Coverley's Chaplain for having his list of sermons from the best divines, ready drawn up in course for the whole year, adding—' I would heartily wish, that more of your country Clergymen would follow this example; and, instead of wasting their spirits in laborious compositions of their own, would endeavour after a handsome elocution, and all those other talents, which are proper to enforce, what has been penned by greater masters. This would be not only more easy to themselves, but would edify their people.'[1] Such a system of idleness would doubtless be 'more easy to ourselves.' But the results of edification are most questionable. No merely passive agent can make a solid or useful Minister. The talent entrusted to him, thus "hid in a napkin," instead of being put out to daily use, awfully stamps him as an "unprofitable servant."[2] Where " the gift is neglected," instead of "stirred up,"[3] what blessing can the Spirit, thus grieved and dishonoured, be expected to assure? Mr. Addison's conception of the power of a sermon was probably rather the magical effect of eloquence, or of moral suasion, than that fruit of faith and prayer, which the Divine pleasure has ordinarily connected with " the weak,"—not with the wise things of this world.[4] George Herbert justly replies to the objection— ' that where there are so many excellent sermons in print, there is no excuse for preaching bad ones.'—' Though the world is full of such composures; *yet every man's own is fittest, readiest, and most savoury to him.*'[5] Indeed, it may be questioned, whether

vit, qui fingit singulorum corda, et idcirco omnium optime novit, qua ratione cor instrui et moveri debeat.' De Vero Theologo. Mr. Brown of Haddington, though a man of considerable theological learning, said of himself, God hath made me generally to preach, as if I had never read another book but the Bible. I have essayed to preach Scriptural truths in Scriptural language. Life and Remains, p. 20. Dr. Watts, however, speaks of preachers, who ' have such a value for elegancy, and so nice a taste for what they call polite, that they dare not spoil the cadences of a period to quote a text of Scripture in it.' Improvement of the Mind, Part II. chap. vi. sect. iii.
[1] Spectator, No. 106. [2] Matt. xxv. 25—30.
[3] 1 Tim. iv. 14. 2 Tim. i. 6. [4] See 1 Cor. i. 26—29.
[5] Country Parson, ch. v. Bishop Sprat strongly reprobates this practice. Bishops Bull and Burnet however recommend it to the younger and uninformed clergy. The former suggests the use of Tillotson's sermons, the Homilies, or a section of the Whole Duty of Man. Clergym. Instructor, pp. 249—251, with 297, 298. Burnet, Past. Care, ch. ix. The Homilies indeed, as we have observed, were compiled with some reference to this purpose; and as the genuine expression of the sentiments of our Reformers, they may be considered (with some allowance for the phraseology of the times) the best substitute for original composition. Bishop Wilson recommends, as a part of academical instruction for Ministerial Students, the abridgment of some of the best practical sermons, marking the manner of handling the subjects, the ways of discussion, arguments, &c. adding however in character with our remark, that ' few discourses are nicely proper for any other place or circumstance, than those for which they were composed.' Works, iv. pp. 381—383. Perhaps compilation may be allowed in extreme cases, but not as the

any course of sermons can be framed for general use. For, according to the different shades of ignorance or knowledge in different spheres, it would be too elementary—or too full and enlarged—or not sufficiently systematic or detailed, and therefore in a greater or less degree inapplicatory. Yet this animadversion on the slavish use of foreign resources does not imply that every sentiment or sentence of our sermon must be (strictly speaking) original. The habit of reading will furnish many illustrations and trains of thought, which are insensibly moulded into our minds, and become our own by our individual method of application. Thus while we learn from all, we may almost be said to borrow from none. The Ministerial student will find this exercise both useful to his mind, and a means of grace to his soul. The fruits of his own study and acquaintance with his people's wants, consecrated to the Lord in the simplicity of faith, prayer, and love, (*though perhaps not according to rule, and of very inferior substance*) will be honoured; while human dependence, sloth, and indifference, will be unblest. We cannot tell to what extent the meanest gifts might have been cultivated with success. At all events the weakest effort of our own mind is more acceptable, than the indolent use of the most talented exercises of another. While, therefore, we would aim high, and keep the best rules before us, we are encouraged to "stir up the gift that is in us," (*however little it may be in our own eyes*) and the excuse of want of ability is disallowed.

Mr. Cecil remarks on deliberate preparation for the pulpit—'If it is driven off late, accidents may occur, which may prevent due attention to the subject. If the latter days of the week are occupied, and the mind driven into a corner, the sermon will usually be raw and undigested. Take time to reject what ought to be rejected, as well as to supply what ought to be supplied.'[1] Dr. Hammond always had a subject in hand, and no sooner had he finished one sermon, than he commenced another.[2] Though perhaps it would not be desirable to follow this constant routine, yet the habit of turning our studies to present account, is of the first moment. A lively imagination may indeed serve an itinerant; but the sermons of a stationary Minister, preaching twice or thrice in the week to

---

established rule. For where is the evidence of a Divine call to the sacred office in *a total destitution* of an important Ministerial qualification '*apt to teach?*' Until a man (to use Bishop Burnet's illustrations) 'is able to go without crutches, and work without patterns,' had he not better remain in the important character of a Christian student, until by prayer and study he should be able to 'purchase to himself a good degree' in the Christian Ministry?

[1] See his Life, prefixed to the ' Remains.'
[2] See Fell's Life of Hammond, an instructive piece of biography.

the same congregation, will, without a store, be insipid, tautological, and unedifying—keeping back as babes, in elementary instruction, those, who, under a more digested administration, might have been "fathers in Christ." The minister's life must, to the end, be a life of holy meditation and study. No man who neglects the apostle's exhortation to "give attendance to reading," will long continue a profitable preacher to an intelligent congregation. The native resources even of the most powerful minds need to be replenished; and therefore the preacher 'must not merely *have been* a man of reading; he must read . still; or his sermons will be trite and barren of thought.'[1] He had better however bring his old stores into fresh service, than trust to the impulse of the moment of duty, or draw imprudently upon the resources of a mind already too scantily stocked. At all events to suffer the week to draw to a close without ready furniture for our Sabbath work, is the mark of indolence and presumption, and promises a very inadequate and unfruitful performance of this weighty responsibility.'[2]

II.—HABITS OF MEDITATION.

'LECTIO inquirit—oratio postulat—meditatio invenit—contemplatio disgustat'—is Augustine's distinction of the relative departments of pulpit preparation.[3] The two last may illustrate the ruminating habit, without which, the results of study and composition, like undigested food lying upon the stomach, clog and weaken the powers of action. No mental compartment can be a storehouse for the reception of a confused mass of unshapen materials, unfitted for practical purposes. Composition, therefore, without a meditative mind, will present only what has been tersely called 'a mob of ideas.'

Meditation is essential to intellectual vigour. Without it, we

---

[1] Dr. Porter's Lectures on Homiletics, p. 215.

[2] Mr. Dod (an excellent old Divine) would say, that he had rather preach an old sermon ten times, than mount the pulpit without preparation. 'God will curse that man's labours, that is found in the world all the week, and then upon Saturday, in the afternoon, goes to his study; whereas God knows, that time were little enough to pray in, and weep in, and get his heart into a fit frame for the duties of the approaching Sabbath.' Preface prefixed to Shepherd's Subjection to Christ. See also Philip Henry's Life, p. 61. Dr. Owen animadverts upon some 'good men, so addicted to their study, that they thought the last day of the week sufficient to prepare for their Ministry, though they employ all the rest of the week in other studies.' Sermon on 1 Cor. xii. 11. Of Mr. Strong, (an eminent Puritan Divine) it is told—that, he made preaching his work, and was so much taken up in it, that he was often in watchings a great part of the night, besides his pains in his day studies.' Preface to Strong's Sermons, by Dr. Henry Wilkinson, Dean of Christchurch. ·

[3] Augustine, quoted in Bishop Wilkins.

may indeed acquire a foreign store of knowledge, but we shall never make it our own. It is important also to cultivate this habit in the bent of our own work—that is, that a Preacher should think as a Preacher—marking every thing (like any other man of business) with the eyes of his own profession. This course of drawing all the objects around him into connexion with his great work, enriches him with much valuable material for Christian instruction, and gives to his sermons great richness and variety of illustration. Habit of thought also is the best means of obtaining a good style, when the mind has the full controul of its own powers. Without the discipline of patient and accurate thinking, words are applied in an unmeaning and faulty arrangement. We may spend hours in this way without any mental exercise.

The want of this meditative habit is one cause of superficial religious knowledge. Valuable books are turned over, and the most striking and instructive passages noted down : but without the digested analytical study of the subject-matter; and consequently without conveying substantial food to the mind. Every intelligent Christian must be conscious of loss in the relaxation of this habit. The mind is occupied only in notions, not in thinking ; and therefore it presents all the difference between the power of truth passing lightly over it, or leaving a deep and practical impression. In the one case, the surface is barely swept. In the other, the bottom principles have been touched and called into action. The sudden flash of light leaves no influence. There is no movement from the heart, till the truth is clearly exhibited to the mind, set strongly and constantly in view, deeply pondered, and closely applied. This reflective habit often supplies the deficiency of extrinsical help ; constant excitement increases intellectual fertility ; the mind is brought to know the extent of its capabilities : and being strengthened and supported by frequent exercise, (to use Luther's words) ' suggests more, much more, than all our commentators united.' A mind thus invigorated, stamps its own character on all its exercises. It instinctively turns over and over again the matter presented to it ; apprehends it in its connexion and dependencies with other trains of thought and principles of action, and thus successfully adapts it to present circumstances.

No part of pulpit preparation ought to be merely intellectual employ. The habit of meditation (to which we now refer) is the exercise of the mind on spiritual objects for spiritual purposes, fixing a clear and permanent impression of truth. Our Divine Master inculcates this habit as the immediate preparation for our public work.[1] Indeed, one of the difficulties (might we not add—one of the privileges?) of the ministry is this; that it requires the continual revolving of spiritual subjects, in order to cast our minds into the mould of those truths, which we set forth before our people. The cultivation of this habit has a most important bearing upon our general efficiency,[2] forming "the man of God" into the character of "a good Minister of Jesus Christ, nourished up in the words of faith and of sound doctrine."[3] For (as Quesnel observes) 'how shall any one be able to nourish others with the word, who does not first nourish himself therewith? It is one thing for a man to enlighten his understanding, to fill his imagination, and to load his memory; and another, to nourish his heart with it. A man nourishes himself with it, if he lives upon it; and he lives upon it, if he changes it as it were into his own substance; if he practises it himself; if he renders it proper and familiar to himself, so as to make it the food and nourishment, with which he ought to feed others.'[4]

It is most important, that our successive pulpit preparations should increase our store of matter, strengthen our tone of thinking, and direct us to the most effectual mode of communication. The solid study of our best Scriptural Divines will be of essential service; at the same time remembering, that the sermons which are drawn from other books than from God's book, will be poor and unspiritual. Let the substance of our text be *first* beaten out from the pure word of God, and then digested in meditation and prayer—let our matter gather clearness of arrangement, force and spirit, from human resources. This sacred exercise will bring rich results, in the enlarged strength, activity, intelligence, and joy of our faith. The superficial student indeed (if student he should be called) has read only for the exercise of his memory, and neglected the investigation of the meaning. 'Much to be preferred' (saith Augustine) 'are those, who have had little care of retaining the words, and yet with the eyes of their hearts have beheld the very heart of Scripture.'[5]

---

[1] Ezekiel iii. 1, 2.   [2] 1 Timothy iv. 15. Comp. 2 Tim. ii. 7.   [3] 1 Timothy iv. 6.
[4] Quesnel on 1 Tim. iv. 6. Owen Stockton remarks as one of his chief encouragements for the Ministry, 'the benefiting of his own soul in his meditations for preaching. Whilst he was studying for others, the Lord made it a word of instruction for himself. And he found it the best means of growth, to be watering of others.' See his Life.
[5] Aug. de Doctr. Christian. iv. 5. 'In the plainest text' (as a good old writer observes) 'there is a world of holiness and spirituality; and if we in prayer and dependence upon God did sit down and consider it, we should behold much more than appears to us. It may be, at once reading or looking, we see little or nothing, as Elijah's servant: he went out once, he saw nothing; therefore he was commanded to look seven times. What now? says the prophet. "I see a cloud arising, like a man's hand;" and by and by the whole surface of the heavens was covered with clouds. So you may look lightly upon a Scripture and see nothing; look again and you will see a little; but look seven

Nor is this habit of meditation less important, in the imme-diate discharge of our public Ministry. It much assists our freedom, self-possession, and personal comfort in the act of deliv-ering our message, to have our subject-matter inwrought, as it were, both in our head and heart. It also enables us pertinently to avail ourselves of any ready suggestions for the moment, and to engraft them into their proper place without hurry and confusion. Thus every way, the devoted concentration of the powers of our mind to the service of God will prove us to be " vessels unto honour, sancti-fied and meet for the Master's use, and prepared unto every good work."[1] 'Suffer me therefore,' (wrote Brainerd to a Ministerial student) 'to entreat you earnestly to give yourself to prayer, to reading, and *meditation on Divine truths ;* strive to penetrate to the bottom of them, and never be content with a superficial know-ledge. By this means your thoughts will gradually grow weighty and judicious; and you hereby will be possessed of a valuable treasure, out of which you may produce " things new and old " to the glory of God.[2]

III.—SPECIAL PRAYER.

WE cannot feel too deeply the importance of this part of pulpit preparation. To study and meditate much, and to pray little, par-alyses all. On the other hand (as Dr. Doddridge found by experi-ence) 'the better we pray, the better we study.'[3] Therefore (as Augustine admirably exhorts) 'let our Christian orator, who would be understood and heard with pleasure, pray before he speak. Let him lift up his thirsty soul to God, before he pronounce any thing. For since there are many things which may be said, and many modes of saying the same thing ; who, but the Searcher of all hearts, knows what is most expedient to be said at the present hour? And who can make us speak as we ought, except he, in whose hands we and our words are; and by these means he may learn all that is to be taught, and may acquire a faculty of speak-ing as becomes a pastor. At the hour of speaking itself, the Lord's

times upon it; *meditate often upon it,* and there you shall see a light, like the light of the sun.' Caryl on Job.
[1] 2 Tim. ii. 21.   [2] Letter ix. appended to his Life.
[3] Orton's Life, ch. viii. Sect. 8. Again—' So it is, though it may seem a riddle, that when I pray and meditate most, I work most.'—Ib. Bishop Sanderson, speaking of prayer and study going hand in hand, observes—' omit either; and the other is lost la-bour. Prayer without study is presumption; and study without prayer atheism. You take your books in vain into your hand, if you turn them over, and *never look higher;* and you take God's name in vain within your lips, if you cry—' Da, Domine'—and *never stir farther.'* Sermon on 1 Cor. xii. 7.
25

words will occur to a faithful spirit—" Think not how or what ye shall speak; for it is not ye that speak, but the Spirit of your Father, which speaketh in you." If the Holy Spirit speaks in those, who are delivered to their persecutors for Christ, why not also to those, who deliver Christ to learners. But if any say, that, if the Holy Ghost make men teachers, they need know no rules; it might be said also, men need not pray, because the Lord saith—" Your Father knoweth what ye have need of, before ye ask him ; and St. Paul's rules to Timothy and Titus might be superseded.[1]

The most valuable results of meditative study are essentially defective without prayer. They are the effusions of the head rather than of the heart—cold, spiritless, dead. However important it may be, that the preacher's head should be well furnished ; it is of far higher moment that his heart should be deeply affected. He must himself draw nourishment from his subject in fervent prayer, that he may bring it out to his people in fulness, simplicity, and love. Indeed his success in composition mainly depends upon the state of his own soul. He cannot make an edifying sermon, when his heart is motionless. None but God can teach him to teach his people. Converse with Him in the study will give its own stamp of sanctity and energy upon his preparations for the pulpit. Our object is not to set off our talents or eloquence ; but to excite and strengthen an habit of holy sensibility. Our very employment, therefore, in the word and work of God especially binds us to study our sermons in a devotional spirit ; and thus only can we receive from above a blessing to impart to our people. Our message is applied with life and interest—not when it is set forth in human eloquence—but when the spirituality and unction of its delivery savours of real communion with God.

We may suggest a few distinct subjects for supplication, in reference to preparation for our public work.

Direction in the choice of texts and topics should be sought from above. This was Cotton Mather's general rule ; making more solemn supplication, before he entered upon extended discursions, or undertook a large course of Scripture. This spiritual habit ena-

---

[1] De Doctr. Christian. Lib. iv. c. 15, 16. See also a beautiful quotation given in the Bishop of Winchester's work, p. 100, n. The following is the excellent advice of an eminent writer, who has never been suspected of enthusiasm—' Sub horam concionis ecclesiastes det se profundæ deprecationi, et ab eo postulet sapientiam, linguam, et orationis eventum, qui linguas infantium facit disertas. *Incredibile dictu,* quantum lucis, quantum vigoris, quantum roboris et alacritatis hinc accedat ecclesiastæ.'—Erasm. Eccles. Pericles is said never to have ascended the rostrum without imploring a blessing from his gods. Are there no Christian orators who may stand condemned by this celebrated Athenian ?

bles us to receive direction from circumstances of Providence, or the secret guidance of the Spirit, to suitable and edifying subjects.

Much matter for supplication offers itself in *entering upon and pursuing our subject.* Cotton Mather's rule was, to stop at the end of every paragraph, in prayer and self-examination, and endeavour to fix upon his heart some holy impressions of the subject. Thus the seven hours, which he usually gave to a sermon, proved so many hours of devotion to his soul, and a most effectual means of infusing life, warmth, and spirituality into his compositions.[1] By this rule we shall never preach a sermon to our people, which, has not been previously made a blessing to our own souls.

The *frame of our own minds in the pulpit* is another matter for distinct supplication—that we may "speak as the oracles of God"—that "a door of utterance may be opened unto us"—that we may have a special message to our people—that our hearts may be tenderly affected by their state—that our preaching may flow from love to their souls, and from hearts powerfully excited by zeal for our Master's glory—that we may be assisted to deliver our sermons in a suitable frame; preserved from the influence of the fear of man, and with a simple, earnest dependence on the Divine blessing—and that the Lord may preach our sermons to our own hearts, both in the study, and in the moment of delivering them.[2]

We must not forget the main end of our labour, *in the power of our Ministry upon the hearts and consciences of our people.* We need to pray for them, as well as to preach to them—to bring our Ministry on their account before God, and to entreat for them; that their attention may be engaged, and their hearts opened to receive our commission; that all hindrances of prejudice, ignorance,

---

[1] This practice he strongly recommended to his Student and Pastor. Math. Stud. p. 191.—'Orabit Ecclesiastes pro se, ut in suo ipsius animo vivam illam efficacem et penetrantem verbi Divini vim experiatur, et sentiat; ne videlicet ad ignem, quam aliis exsufflat et accendit, ipse frigeat; sed ignis ardens in suo ipsius corde verbum prædicatum fiat. Zepperi Ars Concion. Lib. iv.

[2] While adverting to the importance of prayer for assistance in the pulpit, may we not remind ourselves, that the same assistance is equally needed in the desk? No uninspired service contains so much mind or spirituality as the Liturgy. As the service both of our understanding and of our heart, it requires the *energy* as well as the *devotion* of the spiritual habit. Mr. Cecil considered, that 'the leading defect in Christian Ministers was the want of a devotional habit'—a remark, that is too often illustrated by the contrast of the monotonous formality of the desk with the fervid energy of the pulpit; as if the exercise of communion with God in supplication, intercession, and thanksgiving, in penitential self-abasement and faith, were less spiritual than the delivery of a discourse to our fellow-sinners. We wonder not, *under such circumstances,* at the listlessness and want of response in our Liturgical worshippers. The *mere reading* of the prayers has little power of exciting a spirit of prayer throughout the congregation. It is when they *are felt and prayed,* that the chord of sympathy vibrates from the heart of the Minister to the hearts of his congregation—"Arise, O Lord, into thy rest. *Let thy priests be clothed with righteousness, and let thy saints shout for joy.*" Psalm cxxxii. 8, 9.

indifference, worldliness, and unbelief, may be removed; that the spirit of humility and simplicity, sanctification and faith, may be vouchsafed unto them; in a word—(to use the beautiful language of our church) 'that it may please thee to give to all thy people increase of grace, to hear meekly thy word, and to receive it with pure affection, and to bring forth the fruits of the Spirit.'

Nothing will give such power to our sermons, as when they are the sermons of many prayers.[1]   The best sermons are lost, except they be watered by prayer.   But if, like the ancient prophet, we " stand upon our watch, and watch to see what he will say unto us,"[2] we shall have a word to speak from his mouth; commending it in prayer, faith, and expectation for his blessing.   It is easy to bring to our people the product of our own study; but the blessing belongs to the message delivered to them, as from the mouth of God.   And waiting on God renews this commission from time to time, supplies our present need, strengthens our confidence; and obtains for us that παρρησια—that flowing unction of grace, which gives life and power to our preaching, and unites our stammering tongues to "speak boldly, as we ought to speak."[3]

This spirit of prayer implies the renunciation of all dependence upon our best preparations, ministerial gifts, or spiritual habits ; an acknowledgment of their insufficiency to qualify us for the discharge of our commission; and a simple dependence upon our Glorious Head for his present influence.   This is " simplicity and godly sincerity ;" not as if we were seeking, with Saul, to be "honoured before our people," but desiring only " by manifestation of the truth to commend ourselves to every man's conscience in the sight of God."[4]   Mr. Scott speaks of the great assistance in preaching, which he derived from this spirit—' The degree, in which, *after the most careful preparation for the pulpit*, new thoughts, new arguments, animated address, often flow into my mind, while speaking to a congregation, even on very common subjects, makes me feel as if I was quite another man, than when poring over them in my study.   There will be inaccuracies : but generally the most striking things in my sermons are unpremeditated.'[5]   This testimony

---

[1] 'Your work (said Mr. Shepard of New England, on his death-bed, to some young ministers) is great, and requires great seriousness. *For my own part, I never preached a sermon which in the composing of it did not cost me prayers with strong cries and tears.*'
[2] Hab. ii. 1.
[3] Eph. vi. 19, 20.   This was granted to the first apostles in an extraordinary measure, in answer to waiting and prayer.   Acts i. 14, with ii. 1—13.
[4] 1 Sam. xv. 30, with 2 Cor. iv. 2.
[5] Life, pp. 393, 394.   We would here suggest the importance of a special reference to our work in the prayer before the sermon.   If extempore prayer should be deemed inexpedient, yet several petitions might be collected into a short form, expressive of our entire

is familiar with the experience of many of our brethren, who *in this frame*, have often thus found luminous and affecting views of truth almost instantaneously presented to their minds. This however, being realized only in the use of the appointed means, does not countenance a relaxed system of preparation ; while it encourages the exercise of faith for present assistance, gives additional liveliness to our ministry, and brings down from heaven the warmest matter of our sermons at the time of their delivery.

The highest style of a preacher therefore is—that *he gives himself to prayer*.[1] On this account some inferior preachers are more honoured than others of their more talented brethren.[2] For sermons obtained chiefly by meditation and prayer, "are weighty and powerful;" while those of a far higher intellectual character, by the neglect of prayer, are unblest. It is therefore upon good grounds, that the most eminent servants of God have given the pre-eminence to this part of pulpit preparation.[3]

dependence upon the Spirit of God for the expected blessing upon our work. This distinct and solemn honouring of the Spirit would command the Divine influence upon our service ; while the sympathy excited throughout the Christian part of our congregation would give a large encouragement and warrant to faith. See Matt. xviii. 19; and Scott's Life, pp. 392, 393.

[1] See Acts vi. 4.

[2] 'Vera ecclesiæ ædificatione administrandis nulla eruditio, eloquentia, et diligentia (quæ interim tamen Divinissimæ hujus provinciæ omnibus modis necessaria sunt adminicula et instrumenta) sufficit; sed nauclero hic et præside opus est Spiritu Sancto, qui intellectum illuminet, cor et linguæ plectrum gubernet, atque ignitum reddat, et animum viresque addat.' Zepperi Ars Concion. Pref. 4, also Lib. ii. c. i. 16—18.

[3] It is stated of Mr. Bruce (one of "the excellent of the earth," in the troublous times of Scotland) that, though he was known to take much pains in searching the mine of God in Scripture, and though he durst not neglect the diligent preparation of suitable matter for the edification of his people, yet *his main business was in the elevation of his own heart into a holy and reverential frame, and in pouring it out before God ' in wrestling with him, not so much for assistance to the messenger as the message*.' The effect fully proved, that in his earnest endeavour to "present every man perfect in Christ Jesus, he laboured thereunto, striving according to his working, which worked in him mightily." Col. i. 28, 29. See an interesting account of Mr. Bruce, given in Fleming's Fulfilment of Scripture.

Mr. Spencer, of Liverpool, (a young Minister of extraordinary promise, prematurely, as we are led to think, though doubtless in mercy to himself, snatched away from the church) is stated invariably to have passed from secret communion with God to what he describes as 'that awful place'—a pulpit. Preface to a volume of posthumous sermons published by the Religious Tract Society. The uncommon interest and effect, which appeared to rest upon his Ministrations, were doubtless drawn more directly from his heavenly habit of mind, than from those powers of pulpit eloquence, which commanded universal admiration. For—as Bishop Jebb remarks—' let it not be deemed enthusiasm to say, that fervent prayer will make a more impressive preacher than all the rules of rhetoric; and that he who "speaks what he doth know," and testifies what he doth feel, as in the presence of his gracious God, will win more souls to heaven, than if he wielded at will all the eloquence of men and angels.'

Once more to revert to the practice of one, stamped by Mr. Southey with the name of 'saintly Fletcher.' Mr. Gilpin informs us, that ' his preaching was perpetually preceded, accompanied, and succeeded by prayer. Before he entered upon the performance of this duty, he requested of the Great "Master of assemblies" a subject adapted to the conditions of his people, earnestly soliciting for himself wisdom, utterance, and power; for them a serious frame, an unprejudiced mind, and a retentive heart. This necessary preparation for the profitable performance of his Ministerial duties was of longer or shorter

Massillon—after remarking the want of prayer, as the cause of the ineffectiveness even of conscientious Pastors—adds, ' The Minister, who does not habituate himself to devout prayer, will speak only to the ears of his people ; because the Spirit of God, who alone knows how to speak to the heart, and who, through the neglect of prayer, not having taken up his abode within him, will not speak by his mouth.'[1] Philip Henry thus wrote upon a studying day—' I forgot explicitly and expressly, when I began, to crave help from God ; and *the chariot wheels drove accordingly.* Lord, forgive my omissions, and keep me in the way of duty.'[2] Indeed, as an old divine observes—' If God drop not down his assistance, we write with a pen that hath no ink. If any in the world need walk dependently upon God more than others, the Minister is he.'[3] We need also much prayer in respect to the delivery, as well as in the composition of our sermons—especial consideration of the heart, *before we go into* the congregation. ' For,'—as Mr. Baxter observes—' if it be *then* cold, how is it to warm the hearts of the hearers ? Go therefore' (he recommends) ' especially to God for life.'[4]

Nor must we forget the work of subsequent as well as preparatory prayer—like our Master, who, when he had taught the multitude, and sent them away, " departed into a mountain to pray."[5] Our work is not over, when our people are dismissed from the house of God. While in the pulpit, there was one as active as ourselves, and much more powerful, incessantly employed in turning aside our every word from its destined object. Nor will he be less diligent in seeking to undo what had been done in spite of his efforts, and what will easily be undone by his persevering subtlety, except we are diligently counterworking in watchfulness and prayer. Dr. Owen reminds us—' to preach the word, and not to follow it with prayer constantly and frequently, is to believe its use, neglect its end, and cast away all the seed of the gospel at random.'

We want to be as deeply concerned after the conclusion, as at

duration, according to his peculiar state at the time; and frequently he could form an accurate judgment of the effect that would be produced in public by the languor or enlargement he had experienced in private. The spirit of prayer accompanied him from the closet to the pulpit; and while he was outwardly employed in pressing the truth upon his hearers, he was inwardly engaged in pleading that last great promise of his unchangeable Lord—" I am with you always, even unto the end of the world." ' Gilpin's Notes on Fletcher's Portrait of St. Paul, p. 52.

[1] Charges, pp. 207—209.   [2] Life, pp. 60, 61.
[3] Gurnal. ' There must be the labour of study before Ministers preach' (as he elsewhere observes) ' the labour of zeal and love in preaching—the labour of suffering after preaching—and *always the labour of prayer, to crown the whole with success.*' Mr. Walker enumerates among his many hindrances—' not enough committing my work to God by prayer: *this is a capital fault.*' Life, p. 454.
[4] Reformed Pastor.   [5] Mark vi. 34—46.

the commencement, of our work. Have not some convictions been probably awakened or strengthened by the stroke of the hammer that had just been uplifted ? May not some cases of transient impression be charged upon our secret neglect of labour to drive in the nail further, when it had once entered? May not some soul have now received its first impress of Divine grace ? These cases need all the power and unction of our prayer combined with Ministerial counsel. On all accounts, therefore, 'a systematic delivery of the doctrines of the Gospel is essentially requisite to the formation and gradual development of Christian principles; but it must be accompanied by many an earnest prayer for the effusion of some portion of that Divine grace, which, in primitive times, added to the church in one day three thousand souls.'[1] This exercise of prayer, though *subsequent* to the delivery of the word, yet is truly a part of *pulpit preparation ;* as keeping the mind in the spirit of prayer, and ready for action upon the next preparatory occasion—Besides, the connection of the prospect with the retrospect is so natural, that every supplication for a blessing upon the past would be accompanied with earnest desires, and assured expectations of a continued and necessary supply. 'Be much in prayer to God,' (was the direction of an excellent Minister) ; 'thereby you shall find more succour and success in your ministry, than by all your study.'[2]

We conclude the subject of Pulpit Preparation with a few remarks upon the combined effect of the several detailed parts, and upon the precise measure of warranted assistance.

Mather thus details the practice of Mr. Mitchel, an American divine—'In the writing of his discourses for the pulpit, he did (as they say, Aristotle did, when he wrote one of his famous books) '*dip his pen into his very soul.*' When he was going to compose a sermon, he *began with prayer :* thinking ' *Bene orasse est bene studuisse.*' He then read over the text in the original, and weighed the language of the Holy Ghost. If any difficulty occurred in the interpretation, he was wary, how he ran against the stream of the most solid interpreters, whom he still consulted. He was then desirous to draw forth his *doctrines*, and perhaps *other heads* of his discourse, at the beginning of the week, that so his occasional thoughts might be useful thereunto. And he would ordinarily improve his *own meditations* to shape his discourse, before he would consult any other authors who treated on the subject, that *so their notions might serve only to adorn and correct his*

[1] Bishop of Winchester, pp. 284, 285. [2] Mather's New England, iii. 138.

own. Lastly, having finished his composure, he concluded with a thanksgiving to the Lord his helper.'[1]

This example aptly illustrates our view of the completeness of pulpit preparation—including careful study, close meditation, and fervent prayer, that we may set aside all crude and indigested matter, and bring forth from our treasure-house solid and edifying food. However we may expect extraordinary assistance in emergencies, yet in the ordinary course, to produce what we have neither weighed in our minds, nor compared with the word of truth— is to " offer offerings unto the Lord of that which doth cost us nothing ;"—nay more—it is to " offer the blind, the lame, the sick," and even " a corrupt thing for sacrifice."[2] Yet with the most accurate study of Divine truth, except we realize its holy impression, are delivered into its mould, and speak from heart to heart, we shall lose our own interest in our labour—*the edification of our own souls.* How delightful is our public work, when we taste a heavenly sweetness in our message ! In the power of this enjoyment (alas ! too seldom fully realized) we might almost take up Elihu's words—" I am full of matter ; the spirit within me constraineth me ; behold my belly is as new wine which hath no vent ; it is ready to burst like new bottles. *I will speak, that I may be refreshed.*"[3] This is something far above study, and artificial means of excitement or improvement. It is the exercise of faith, the fruit of earnest persevering prayer, and accompanied with mighty energy upon our Ministry—enabling us "so to speak, that many believe."[4] Such sermons 'have the blood of our Saviour sprinkled on them, and his good Spirit breathing in them.'[5]

Pulpit preparation is therefore every way the great ordinance both for ourselves and for our people. It embraces our glorious Master as the grand centre of our subjects. It spiritualizes our soul in prayerful as well as intellectual meditation. It concentrates the mind to definite points, and to fixed apprehensions of these points, instead of wandering vaguely and unprofitably upon the field of infinite space. This brings solid knowledge with warm feelings—statements condensed, yet simple and enlarged—full of light as well as matter—of power as well as interest. We cannot but see, therefore, the necessity ' that Ministers should attend to the direction of conscience ; that they should mark the workings and convictions of the Holy Spirit, their exercises of mind, and the effects resulting from them ; that they should give their attention

---

[1] Mather's New England, iv. 205.   [2] 2 Sam. xxiv. 24.   Mal. i. 8, 13, 14.
[3] Job xxxii. 18—20.   [4] Acts xiv. 1.   [5] Mather's Student and Pastor, p. 178.

to the different changes in Christian experience, utterly unknown to men in their natural state; that they should maintain constant communion with God by meditation and prayer, in order to obtain an intimate knowledge of " the mysteries of the kingdom of heaven," and be apt to administer to the consciences of others, that they may escape the severe censure, with which the Lord rebuked Nicodemus—"Art thou a master in Israel, and knowest not these things?"[1] The consciences of serious Christians discover the value of a judicious and experimental Ministry. They feel themselves more soundly comforted by one discourse, woven and wrought out of a feeling heart, spiritually schooled in the ways of God and the methods of Satan, supported and sinewed by the solid expositions of the word of God, and enforced 'with the evidence and demonstration of the Spirit,' than from cold and abstract Scriptural statements. A high relish of sacred truth naturally gives a great insight into human character; and enables the Minister skilfully to set out his commission for the conviction of the judgment, the awakening of the conscience, and the solid instruction of the heart. This direct application will find a response in the consciences of the ungodly, and in the sympathies of sincere Christians.

The maxim of practical religion applies in full force to our subject. Labour in the preparation for the pulpit, as if our whole success depended on it. Pray, and depend wholly upon Christ; as feeling, that "without him we can do nothing." In neglecting preparation, we tempt God to depart from his ordinary course; in trusting to our preparation, we make a God of our gifts. It is more curious than important, to inquire into the modes of Divine assistance in the composition or delivery of our sermons; or to endeavour to determine the precise boundaries between the result of our own thought, and the efflux from a higher source. But it will be safe to ascribe all the honour of the success to the Heavenly agent, and to attribute to ourselves all the infirmities attendant upon the work. We are warranted to expect assistance to the utmost extent of our necessity; and we must lay our whole stress upon it as the only source of *effective* meditation, composition, or delivery. But such a dependence as supersedes the necessity of preparation, is unscriptural and delusive. Not that we must expect aid in the way of mechanical sufficiency, as purchased by a certain quantum or routine of preparation. After we have preached with power and acceptance for successive years, we are as dependent as at the first for present help. The supply is only continued in the renewed acting

1 Vitr. Method. Homilet. cap. 10.

of faith, replenishing our souls from the overflowing fountain of life.

Mr. Cecil, however gives the sum of all that need be said upon this subject.—'I have been cured' (he remarks) 'of expecting the Holy Spirit's influence without due preparation on our part, by ob. serving how men preach, who take up that error. We must combine Luther with St. Paul.—' *Bene orasse est bene studuisse*'— must be united with St. Paul's—' *Meditate upon these things ; give thyself wholly to them, that thy profiting may appear unto all.*' One errs who says—' I will preach a reputable sermon ;' and another errs who says—' I will leave all to the assistance of the Holy Spirit,' while he has neglected a diligent preparation.'[1]

CHAPTER III.

THE SCRIPTURAL MODE OF PREACHING THE LAW.

THE mark of a minister "approved unto God, a workman that needeth not to be ashamed," is, that he "rightly divides the word of truth." This implies a full and direct application of the Gospel to the mass of his unconverted hearers, combined with a body of spiritual instruction to the several classes of Christians. His system will be marked by Scriptural symmetry and comprehensiveness. It will embrace the whole revelation of God, in its doctrinal instructions, experimental privileges, and practical results. This revelation is divided into two parts—the Law and the Gospel—essentially distinct from each other ; though so intimately connected, that an accurate knowledge of neither can be obtained without the other. The preaching of the Law is therefore a main part of our subject. We shall consider it separately ; and in its connexion with the Gospel.[2]

---

[1] Cecil's Remains. Most of us will subscribe to the following humbling confessions—'In the preparation of our sermons, alas ! how cold, how formal have we often been ! Prayer has been the last thing we have thought of, instead of the first. We have made dissertations, not sermons ; we have consulted commentators, not our Bibles ; we have been led by science, and not by the heart : and therefore our discoveries have been so tame, so lifeless, so uninteresting to the mass of our hearers, so little savouring of Christ, so little like the inspired example of St. Paul.' Bishop of Calcutta's Essay to Baxter's Reformed Pastor, p. xiii.

[2] See Mr. Simeon's Sermons on Gal. iii. 19, in his Horæ Homileticæ, for a most luminous exhibition of the Scriptural preaching of the law. Comp. Daven. on Col. i. 28. on the duty and importance of preaching the law.

THE PREACHING OF THE LAW—ITS CHARACTER—USES—AND OBLIGATIONS.

THERE can be no question, that the preaching of the law in its true charater and connection forms a constituent part of the Ministry of the Gospel. Some indeed, most inaccurately identify the preaching of the law with legal preaching. Others preach the law independently of the Gospel. Others again narrow its exceeding breadth, by bringing character and conduct to the criterion of some lower rules and inferior standard—such as expediency, the opinion of the world, prudence, and consequences. But, as there is a legal mode of preaching the Gospel, so there is an evangelical mode of preaching the Law. Luther's indignation was roused by propositions brought to him, against the preaching of the law, because it could not justify. 'Such seducers' (said he) 'do come already among our people, while we yet live ; what will be done when we are gone? Never' (observes he) 'was a more bold and harsh sermon preached in the world, than that which St. Paul preached, wherein he quite abolisheth and taketh away Moses, together with his law, as insufficient for a sinner's salvation. Nevertheless, we must drive on with the ten commandments in due time and place. When we are not in hand with justification, we ought greatly and highly to esteem the law. We must extol and applaud it in the highest degree, and (with St. Paul) we must count it good, true, spiritual, and Divine, as in truth it is.'[1]

The Apostle combines his view of the character and obligations of the law with his most expanded views of evangelical truth. He defines its character to be "holy, just, and good."[2] He informs us that its lawful use is " good"[3] for us. The exposition of this character, and the enforcement of this use, must therefore be involved in the terms of the Ministerial commission.

The *character of the law of God*, as the transcript of the mind and image of God, is " *holy*," as presenting to man the love of God, and at the same time exhibiting that most glorious proof of God's love to man, which is the essence of his holiness ;—"*just*," as being conformable to, and deduced from, the first, most simple and clear principles of justice between God and his creature ;—"*good*," such a law as conscience tells us is suitable to the character of God, is most useful for the accomplishment of the Divine purpose, of uniting man to God by a happy discipline of obedience ; and the

---

[1] Luther's Table Talk, ch. xii.　　[2] Rom. vii. 12.　　[3] 1 Tim. i. 8.

constant obedience to which will bring him to that consummation
of bliss, which is ordained as the end and recompense of his work."[1]
Thus in its Author—in its matter—and in its end, it demands our
highest regard.

The uses of the law are various and important. *The world* are
indebted to it for many wholesome results. It discovers to them
the holy nature and character of God ; it informs them of their duty,
and binds them to the performance of it. But for the bridling restraint of the law, the world would become "a field of blood." It
condemns also those who cast off its yoke.[2] Even the heathen are
brought in guilty by "the work of the law, written in their hearts."[3]
It is also the *medium of conviction of sin.* Those indeed, who
dispense with the law from their Ministry, acknowledge no medium
of conviction but the cross. But did not our Lord employ the moral
law with the young Ruler, for this express purpose?[4] Was it not
also the appointed means of bringing the Apostle to the spiritual
apprehension of his sin?[5] Its cognizance of every thought, imagination, desire, word, and work, and its uncompromising demand of
absolute and uninterrupted obedience, upon pain of its everlasting
penalty—convince the heart of its guilt, defilement, and wretchedness, and leave the sinner without excuse and without help; under
the frown of an holy and angry God ; prepared to welcome a Saviour,
and lost for ever without him. Thus is the prayer—"God be
merciful to me a sinner"—forced even from him, whose external
deportment had been, "touching the righteousness which is in the
law, blameless."[6] He now sees in himself the very character of
sinfulness and misery to which the Gospel addresses itself; and,
stretching out the hand of desire and faith, he receives the free gift
of Christ. And now he feels the advantage of the law too well, to be
willing, with the Antinomian, to cast it off, because it has lost its
justifying power.[7] For its *covenant form* enlarges his apprehension
of the necessity, character, and excellency of the gospel ! The en-

---

[1] Vitr. Obs. Sacr. Lib. vi. cap. xvii. 11.   [2] See 1 Tim. i. 9.
[3] Rom. ii. 14, 15.   [4] Matt. xix. 16—21.
[5] Rom. vii. 7—9. Comp. his general assertion, iii. 20. Again—he informs us (v. 20.)
that "the law entered, *that the offence might abound*"—not in the transgression of *the
heart* (as the direct fruit of the law) but in *the conviction of the conscience*, awakened by a
strong display of the spirituality of the law, and of the denunciations of its righteous curse.
If "sin be the transgression of the law" (1 John iii. 4. Comp. iv. 15.) a just apprehension of the law must be the medium of conviction of sin. Nor indeed can we conceive
of conviction without it; since obliquity is only discovered by a reference to a given standard. Even the cross of Christ, as a *means of conviction, ultimately resolves itself into the
law*, the breach of which constituted the sin—the cause of his death. The law therefore
is of standing and indispensable use, bringing us to Christ—not always with terror, but
always with conviction.
[6] Phil. iii. 6.   [7] Comp. Rom. viii. 3.

tervention of a Surety, a Redeemer, and an atonement, was the effect of the Divine determination to magnify the law, and make it honourable ;"[1] that God might honourably pardon, justify, and save, the transgressors. The precept and penalty of the law explain therefore the necessity for the sufferings and death of Immanuel. Thus "the glory of the Ministration of condemnation" commends the " exceeding glory of the Ministration of life and righteousness."[2] This glass exhibits to us *indirectly*, what the Gospel shows us in *direct terms*—our infinite obligation to the love of Christ for what he has become, done, and suffered in our place. This is our constraining bond to his service, whose obedience has answered all the demands, suffered all the penalties standing against us, and "brought in everlasting righteousness" as our ground of acceptance before God.

As a rule of life also, the Law is of the utmost importance to the Christian. It comes to him 'as the chief perfection of righteousness,'[3] with the authority of God, as his Creator, his Sovereign, and his Judge. It is doubly enforced, as the law of his Redeemer ; for though he is " not without law to God," yet he is especially " under the law to Christ."[4] This is his course of cheerful obedience in his Master's yoke of love ; which is his highest earthly privilege, as it will be the consummation of his heavenly enjoyment.[5]

The uses of the law as a rule of life are most efficient means of promoting stedfastness and consistency. Being " written in the heart," it affords to the Christian a *continual touchstone of sincerity*. He has " the testimony of his conscience,"[6] that he " consents to the law that it is good ;" that he "delights in it after the inward man ;" that he " esteems all God's commandments concerning all things to be right ;" that he counts his want of perfect conformity to it the sin of every moment ; that he is satisfied with no attainment short of being " holy, as he that hath called him is holy," and " perfect, as his Father which is in heaven is perfect."[7]

The rule of the law also furnishes a *daily standard of self-examination*. The servant of God laments his natural, and often unconscious, spring of self-exaltation ; to which, however, the law, as the standard of perfection, operates as a constant and timely check. It lays him low in the dust; it confounds him for the sins of his services, as well as for his open transgressions ; that he may " count all but dung and dross" in comparison of Christ ; that he may be

---

[1] Isaiah xlii. 21.   [2] 2 Cor. iii. 7—9.   [3] Calv. on Luke x. 26.   [4] 1 Cor. ix. 21.
[5] Comp. Matt. xi. 29, 30. with Rev. vii. 15, xxii. 3.   [6] See 2 Cor. i. 12.
[7] See Rom. vii. 16, 22.   Psalm cxix. 128.   1 Pet. i. 15.   Matt. v. 48.

simple in his dependence on His cross, and quickened to renewed applications for pardon, acceptance, and supplies of grace.

The obligation of this law upon the Christian is immutable as the throne of God. What can annul the necessary relation of a creature to his Creator? The additional bond of redemption strengthens—not annihilates, the original obligation. Do we cease to be creatures by becoming new creatures? And are we not therefore still bound to personal obedience by the sovereign authority of God? Or does the obligation of the law lose its force by being conveyed to us through the hands of Christ—himself Lord of all, and standing to us in the most endearing and authoritative relation? Why, we may ask, do men wish to be rid of this rule? But for some latent enemy to the holiness of the Divine character, the thought of escaping from the directive force of the law would be intolerable. So far from " gendering unto bondage," it is " the perfect freedom" of evangelical service; so that it is hard to say, whether we are more indebted for deliverance from the law as a covenant, or for subjection to the law as a rule. The proof of our love to the Saviour is the " keeping of his commandments;"[1] which are none others than the precepts of the moral law, bound upon the Christian's heart with chains of the most powerful and attractive obligation. The first desire of the awakened sinner is—" Lord, what wilt thou have me to do?"[2] His constant prayer is—" that his love may abound yet more and more, in knowledge and in all judgment;" that he may " not be unwise, but understand what the will of the Lord is."[3] It cannot therefore, be legal bondage, or indeed otherwise than evangelical privilege, thus to receive the law from the Saviour's hands, stripped of its condemning power, and regulating our affections, temper, and conversation to his glory.

Some of our people, however, are so excited and enlivened by the promises of the Gospel, that the inculcation of the Law is depressing to them. But, in cases of sincerity, this arises from a narrow misconception of the design and uses of the Law: while looseness of conduct in many other cases too plainly proves their unconscious need of its wholesome restraints and directions. Some also of our brethren seem afraid of enforcing the obligations of the law, lest they should be thought to be teachers of Moses rather than of Christ. But our Lord had no hesitation in establishing the obligations of the old dispensation,[4] or in leading his disciples to confess them as their bounden duty.[5] Following, therefore, his example,

---

[1] John xiv. 15. [2] Acts ix. 6. [3] Phil. i. 9. Eph. v. 17.
[4] See Matt. v. 17. and Calvin in loco. [5] Luke xvii. 10.

we might much more easily bear the imputation of legality for enforcing the sanctions of the law, than the reproaches of our conscience for passing them by.

The leaven of Antinomianism is indeed most congenial with the corruption of the heart; and its deadly influence is but too apparent in the inconsistent lives of its professors. To substitute the law of love for the rule of the decalogue, is to put the main-spring of the watch in the place of the regulator; and to exchange a stable directory of conduct for a principle subject to incessant variations, and readily counterfeited by the delusions of a self-deceiving heart. The disciples of this school rarely, if ever, attain to stedfastness of profession; while in the too frequent defect of Christian sincerity, immortal souls perish as the melancholy victims of delusion.

Glancing for a moment at the relative aspects and uses of the law, we remark—As *a covenant,* it excites "the spirit of bondage unto fear;" humbling, alarming, convincing, and leading to despondency. As *a rule of life,* under Divine conduct, it exercises in the Christian "the spirit of adoption"—his habitual desire, and delight in conformity to it, witnessing his interest in the family of God. As *a covenant,* the law brings men to Christ for deliverance from its tyranny. Christ returns them to *the law as their rule:* that, while they are delivered from its dominion, ("that being dead wherein they were held,") they "might serve in newness of spirit, and not in the oldness of the letter."[1] And thus they show their gratitude to him for his *perfect obedience to it as a covenant* in their stead, by their *uniform obedience to it as a rule* in his service.

We cannot indeed have too much of the Gospel; but we may have too little of the Law. And a defect in the Evangelical preaching of the Law is as clear a cause of inefficient ministration, as a legal preaching of the Gospel. In such a Ministry there must be a want of spiritual conviction of sin *generally*—of spiritual sins *most particularly*—and—flowing directly from hence—a low standard of spiritual obedience. Indeed, all the prevalent errors in the Church may be traced to this source. We should never have heard of Methodist perfection—Mystic dependence upon the inward light—Antinomian delusion—inconsistent profession of orthodoxy—Pharisaical self-righteousness—or Pelagian and Socinian rectitude of nature—if the spiritual standard of the law had been clearly displayed, and its convincing power truly felt. In the want of this conviction,

[1] Rom. vii. 6.

the fullest perception of Evangelical views must fail in experimental and practical effect.

But there are Antinomian errors on the opposite side. If Antinomianism be the relaxation of obedience from the perfect standard of the law of God, is not *mere moral preaching* a refined species of this unhallowed leaven? Equally with the professed Antinomian, the standard of the law of God is exchanged for some indefinite and ever-varying standard of inclination or caprice. The notions of mercy and salvation, as in the other case, are here used as the palliation of sin. All hope; and no fear—is the character of this preaching. How frightful to think of deluded souls sliding into eternity in this golden dream ! And of what vast importance is it for the resistance of error, and for an effective exhibition of Divine truth—that our Ministry should be distinguished by a full display of the spiritual character, and unalterable obligations, of the law of God !

II.—THE CONNEXION OF THE LAW WITH THE GOSPEL.

Mr. Newton admirably remarks upon the importance of this subject—'Clearly to understand the distinction, connexion, and harmony between the Law and the Gospel, and their mutual subserviency to illustrate and establish each other, is a singular privilege, and a happy means of preserving the soul from being entangled by errors on the right hand or the left !'[1] Some in the Apostle's time "desired to be teachers of the law; understanding neither what they said, nor whereof they affirmed."[2] This seems to imply the importance, in a Christian teacher, of a clear understanding of the law in all its connexions. And indeed the momentous matter, of a sinner's acceptance with God cannot be accurately stated without a distinct view of the subject. The Judaizing teachers of the Galatian Church, from misconception of this point, had "darkened the counsel" of God "by words without knowledge ;" "bewitched" their "foolish" hearers from the simplicity of the Gospel ; and—instead of establishing them "in the liberty, wherewith Christ had made them free," had well nigh "entangled them again with the yoke of bondage."[3]

I. The subject embraces an explicit statement of the difference between the *law and the Gospel*. It was an axiom in the old schools of divinity—'Qui scit bene distinguere inter Legem et

[1] Newton's Works, i. 322.   [2] 1 Tim. i. 7.   [3] Gal. iii. 1. v. 1.

Evangelium, Deo gratias agat, et sciat se esse Theologum.'[1] There is much difference in the *original revelation*. The law, *partially at least*, (as in the case of the heathens,) is discoverable by the light of nature ;[2] whereas the Gospel is "the hidden mystery of God," which could only be known by the light of revelation.[3] We find, therefore, man in his natural state partially acquainted with the law ; but wholly unacquainted with the Gospel. There is also a difference in their *respective regards to man*. The law contemplates man as the creature of God, as he was at the period of its first promulgation—"standing perfect and complete in all the will of God." The gospel contemplates man as he is—a sinner, equally unable to obey, or to offer compensation for disobedience ; guilty, condemned, helpless, lost. They differ also *in the power of their sanction*. They both inform us what we ought to be and do. But the Gospel alone provides the necessary resources, in union with the Son of God, and participation of a heavenly life derived from him. Command is the characteristic of the law ; as promise and encouragement is of the Gospel. In the one case, obedience is required on the penalty of death ; in the other case it is encouraged by the promise of life. A promise is indeed attached *to the obedience* of the law,[4] but placed beyond our reach, upon terms far more difficult than those of Adam's covenant ; inasmuch as he was endued with sufficient strength for perfect obedience, while we are entirely helpless for the lowest spiritual requirements. The Gospel on the other hand gives the promise freely, *in order to obedience*, as the principle and motive of it.

In its condemning power also, the law is widely different from the Gospel. As a valuable writer tersely observes—' the law condemns, and cannot justify, a sinner ; the Gospel justifies, and cannot condemn, the sinner that believes in Jesus. In the law, God appears in terrible threatenings of eternal death ; in the Gospel, he manifests himself in gracious promises of life eternal. In the former he curses, as on Mount Ebal ; in the latter he blesses, as on Mount Gerizim. In the one, he speaks in thunder, and with terrible majesty ; in the other, with soft whispers, or "a still small voice." By the trumpet of the law he proclaims war with sinners ; by the jubilee-trumpet of the Gospel he publishes peace—"peace on earth, and good-will toward men." The law is a sound of terror to con-

---

[1] Some valuable remarks on this subject, together with Melancthon's sentiments (of whom Luther testified—'he teacheth exceeding well and plainly of the right difference, use, and profit of the Law and the Gospel') will be found in Scott's Continuation of Milner, Vol. II., pp. 230—237.
[2] See Rom. ii. 14, 15.   [3] Ibid. xvi. 25.   [4] Gal. iii. 12.

vinced sinners; the Gospel is a joyful sound, "good tidings of great joy." The former represents God as a God of wrath and vengeance; the latter as a God of love, grace and mercy. The one presents him to sinners as "a consuming fire;" the other exhibits the precious blood of the Lamb, which quenches the fire of his righteous indignation. That presents to the view of the sinner a throne of judgment; this "a throne of grace." Every sentence of condemnation in Scripture belongs to the law; every sentence of justification forms a part of the Gospel. The law condemns a sinner, for his first offence; but the Gospel offers him the forgiveness of all his offences.'[1] Thus in every point of difference, "that which was made glorious had no glory in this respect, by reason of the glory that excelleth."

II. The *harmony of the law with the Gospel* is also a most important subject of our Ministration. Though distinct, they are not opposite. As coming from the same source, they must ultimately meet in the same plan, and subserve the same end. Like the seemingly opposite perfections of their glorious Author, they harmonize in mutual subserviency in the Christian system. The provisions of the Gospel are fully commensurate with the demands of the law. Its righteousness fulfils the law as a covenant; its grace obeys it as a rule. Both have a commanding and condemning power. Both combine to "bring the sinner to Christ"— "the law *indirectly*—as a school-master," showing his need of him: the Gospel *directly*, exhibiting him in all points suitable to his need. In this centre of everlasting love, the "mercy" of the Gospel "and the truth" of the law "meet together." The "righteousness" of the law and the "peace" of the Gospel here "embrace each other."[2] Both unite to endear the ways of God to us—the law, as the instrument of conviction, teaching us to prize the grace of the Gospel; the Gospel, as the principle of holiness, exciting us "to delight in the law of God after the inward man."

The *directive* power of the law is in equal consonance with the spirit and end of the Gospel. The grace of the Gospel regulates our heart and life by the rule of the law. "Love," which is "the fulfilling of the law," is also the great end of the Gospel. The

---

[1] Colquhoun on the Law and Gospel, pp. 166, 167. Thus also Patrick Hamilton, the Scotch reformer, writes—'The law showeth us our sin—the gospel showeth us a remedy for it. The law showeth us our condemnation—the gospel showeth us our redemption. The law is the word of ire—the gospel is the word of grace. The law is the word of despair—the gospel is the word of comfort. The law is the word of disquietude—the gospel is the word of peace.' Patrick's Places—with a short preface by the martyr John Frith. See also Bradford's view of this subject. Fathers of English Church, vi. 389, 390.

[2] Psalm lxxxv. 10. See Calvin on Matthew v. 17.

Gospel dwells, only " where the law of God is written in the heart."
Thus, as they are both parts of the same revelation, they unite in
the same heart; and, though the offices of each are materially distinct, neither will be found separate from the other.   As both are
transcripts of the Divine mind and image, both must be hated or
loved together.   The hatred is the radical principle of the carnal
mind; the love is the mind of Christ, and the commencement of
the service of heaven.

III. *The law as a preparation for the Gospel,* is also a part of
our Ministry.   The preaching of John—*partaking· mainly of the
character of the law*—was ordained to *prepare the way for* Christ.
The Epistle to the Romans—the most systematic scheme of Ministerial instruction—clearly sets forth this order of "dividing the
word of truth."[1]   The Apostle speaks of us, " before faith came, as
being under the law"—*not left in imprisonment*—but " *shut up
unto the faith which should afterwards be revealed.*"   Thus
" the law is our schoolmaster, to bring us unto Christ, that we
might be justified by faith;" which Luther explains to mean—
'that the *law must be laid upon those that are to be* justified, that
they may be shut up in the prison thereof, until the righteousness
of faith come—that—*when they are cast down and humbled by
the law*, they should fly to Christ.   The Lord humbles them, not
to their destruction, but to their salvation.   *For God woundeth,*
that he may heal again.   He killeth, that he may quicken again.'[2]

This appears to have been the uniform opinion of the church.
Augustine remarks—'The conscience is not to be healed, if it be
not wounded.   *Thou preachest and pressest the law,* comminations, the judgment to come, with much earnestness and importu-
nity.   He which hears, if he be not terrified, if *he be not troubled,
is not to be comforted.*'[3]   The Reformers were evidently of this
judgment.   Tindal writes thus—'It becometh the preacher of
Christ's glad tidings, first, *through the opening of the law*, to
prove all things sin, that proceed not of the Spirit, and of faith in
Christ; and thereby to bring them unto the knowledge of himself,

[1] See the Gentile convicted by the law (i. 18—32; ii. 14, 15); then the Jew (ii.); then
the whole world collectively. (iii. 9—19.) The desperate condition of the world by
the law being proved, (20) *the Gospel is now* introduced in all its fulness and glory. (21
—31; iv. v. &c.) The instances adduced however forbid us ever to *preach the law unconnected with the Gospel.* Even John's ministry (Matt. iii. 1—11; John i. 29; iii. 25—
36; Luke i. 76, 77)—much more that of his Master—(Mark i. 15) linked the revelation
of the Gospel with the more severe exhortations of the law. The sermon on the Mount
combines the *most searching exposition of the spirituality of the law* with many encouraging declarations of the Gospel. The early chapters of the Epistle to the Romans were
the introduction only to that full exhibition of the Gospel Ministration, which is subsequently developed in that most important portion of Scripture.
[2] Gal. iv. 23, 24. and Luther in loco.   [3] Comment. in Psalm lix.

and of his misery and wretchedness, that *he might derive help.'*
Again—' Expound the law truly'—he writes to John Frith—' to
condemn all flesh, and prove all men sinners, and all deeds under
the law, before mercy have taken away the condemnation thereof,
to be sin, and damnable; and *then, as a faithful Minister,* set
abroad the mercy of our Lord Jesus, and let the wounded consciences drink of the water of life. ⸱ *And thus shall your preaching be with power, and not as the hypocrites. And the Spirit
of God shall work with you ; and all consciences shall bear record unto you that it is so.'*[1] Luther has been already referred to.
Calvin observes—' that the *law is nothing else but a preparation
unto the Gospel.'* And elsewhere—' The faithful cannot profit in
the Gospel, until they shall be first humbled; which cannot be,
until they come to the knowledge of their sins. It is the *proper
function of the law,* to call the consciences into God's judgment,
and to *wound them with fear.'*[2] Beza remarks briefly, but to the
point—' Men are ever to be *prepared for the Gospel, by the preaching of the law.'*[3] Archbishop Usher, in reply to the question before us—' What order is there (in the Ministry) used in the delivery of the word, for the begetting of faith?' answers—' First, the
covenant of the law is urged, to make sin, and the punishment
thereof, known; whereupon the sting of conscience pricketh the
heart with a sense of God's wrath, and maketh a man utterly to
despair of any ability in himself to obtain everlasting life. *After
this preparation the promises of God are propounded ;* whereupon the sinner, conceiving a hope of pardon, sueth to God for
mercy.'[4] The ablest of the Puritan divines took this view of the
subject. Mr. Perkins (one of the most systematic of them) speaks
of the influence of the work of the law, as making way for the
Gospel. ' *And then,'* (says he) ' succeeds seasonably and comfort-
ably, the work of the Gospel.'[5] Mr. Bolton (one of the most eloquent and experienced Ministers of his day) observes—' Let the
power of the law first break and bruise, which is *a necessary preparative* for the plantation of grace: and then pour in (and spare
not) the most precious oil of the sweetest Evangelical comfort.
But many, very many, mar all with missing this method ; either from want of sanctification in themselves, or skill to manage
their Master's business.'[6] Mr. Rogers of Dedham, (a most experi-

[1] Prologue to the Epistle to the Romans, and Fox's Book of Martyrs. 1533.
[2] Calvin on John x. 8. xvi. 10.   [3] Beza on 2 Cor. iii. 11.
[4] Usher's Body of Divinity, p. 399.
[5] Perkins on the Nature and Practice of Repentance, chap. iii. on Rom. viii. 15.
[6] Bolton's Discourse on True Happiness, p. 176.

mental Divine) speaks strongly on this view—'Let none speak *against the preaching of the law; for it is the wholesome way, that God himself and his servants in all ages have taken. The Law first humbles; then the Gospel comforts.* None can prove that faith was wrought in an instant at first, *without any preparation going before.*'[1]   Greenham, (of the same school, highly esteemed in his day) briefly writes—'When the word is administered in any power and sincerity, *there doubtless the preaching of the law strikes in,* and the preaching of the Gospel bringeth us unto. Christ.'[2]   Another writer of consideration observes—'Such is the nature of man, that *before he can receive a true justifying* faith, he must as it were, *be broken in pieces by the law.*'[3]   Gurnal expresses this view with his characteristic familiarity of illustration—'The sharp point of the law must prick the conscience, before the creature by the promises of the Gospel be drawn to Christ. The field is not fit for the seed to be cast into it, till the plough hath broken it up; nor is the soul prepared to receive the mercy of the Gospel, till broken with the terrors of the law.'[4]   We conclude this series of quotations with the full and decided testimony of Dr. Owen, not more remarkable for his powerful defence of Christian doctrine, than for his deep insight into every part of experimental godliness—'Let no man think' (says he) 'to understand the Gospel, who knoweth nothing of the Law. God's *constitution and the nature of things themselves have given the law the precedency* with respect to sinners; "for by the law is the knowledge of sin." And Gospel faith is the soul's acting according to the mind of God, for deliverance from that state and condition, which it is cast under by the law. And all those descriptions of faith, which abound in the writings of learned men, which do not at least include in them a virtual respect unto this state and condition, or *the work of the law on the consciences of sinners,* are all of them vain speculations. There is nothing in this whole doctrine that I will more firmly adhere unto, than the necessity of the *conviction* mentioned, *previous unto true believing;* without which not one line of it can be understood aright; and men do but beat the air in their contention about it.'[5]

These preparative operations of the law do not act in all cases with the same intensity. Yet some impression of guilt, as in the case of our fallen parents,[6] seems necessary to excite the desire, and

---

[1] Roger's Doctrine of Faith, pp. 99, 66.   [2] Greenham's Works, p. 139.
[3] Yates's Model of Divinity, Book ii. chap. 26.   [4] Gurnal on Ephesians vi. 19.
[5] Owen on Justification, chap. ii.   [6] Compare Genesis iii. 9—15.

to make way for the reception of the Gospel. We must, however, be careful not to load the sinner with threatenings, from an apprehension of a superficial work of contrition. The genuine spirit of humiliation is not the separate work of the law, but of the law preparatory to, and combined with, the Gospel—the sense of sin and misery connected with the hope of mercy. Still less must we insist upon these preparatory exercises as meritorious, or as entrenching in any degree upon the unconditional freeness of the Gospel. They are needful, not as qualifications to recommend us, but as pre-dispositions to draw us, to Christ. We must come.to him, if at all, upon the terms of his own gracious invitation, "without money and without price."[1] But the sense of misery is the preparative for the remedy. "The whole need not a physician, but they that are sick."[2] As Calvin remarks—'Christ is promised only to those, who are humbled and confounded with the sense of their own sins.'[3] The invitation is specially addressed to those "that labour and are heavy laden;" and none but such will "incline their ear and come."

Mr. Newton observes, in the case of Mr. Grimshaw, 'that a Minister walking with God in a conscientious improvement of the light received, deeply convinced under the law, and but imperfectly acquainted with the Gospel, is peculiarly qualified to preach with effect to ignorant and wicked people, whose habits of sin have been strengthened by a long disregard of the Holy Law of God, and who have had no opportunity of hearing the Gospel. They cannot at first receive, or even understand, that accurate and orderly statement and discussion of Evangelical truth, which renders Ministers, who are more advanced in knowledge, acceptable to judicious and enlightened hearers. But they feel a close and faithful application to their consciences, and are "persuaded," by "the terror of the Lord" to "consider their ways," before they are capable of being much influenced by the consideration of his tender mercies. The Minister is sufficiently before them to point out the first steps in the way ; and as he goes gradually forward, "growing in grace, and in the knowledge of the Saviour," they gradually follow him. Thus many of our most eminent Evangelical modern preachers were led.'[4]

IV. *We must not forget the establishment of the law by the Gospel.* The Apostle thus anticipates a feasible objection against his statement of justification—"Do we then make void the law

---

[1] Isaiah lv. 1.   [2] Matt. ix. 12.   [3] Calvin on Isaiah lxv. 1.
[4] Life of Grimshaw. The early history of Mr. Scott (see his 'Force of Truth,') will illustrate these valuable remarks.

through faith? God forbid! *Yea, we establish the law.*[1] *The faith or doctrine* of the Gospel "establishes the law" *in its covenant form,*—exhibiting a Divine Suretyship of obedience to the law, as the price for justification ; *and in its directive form,*—inculcating practical obligations upon a stronger foundation, and fulfilling them by the power of an heavenly life, and the impulse of evangelical motives. Thus the offices of Christ delightfully combine. As our Surety, he delivers us from the curse of the law. As our King, he brings us under its rule. This Scriptural faith saves us from its condemnation, and enables us for its requirements. Take away this principle, and we are under the full penalty of the broken law ; nor is there any root, on which to engraft a corrupt tree, that it might bring forth good fruit.

Thus also, the *grace of the Gospel* "establishes the law" in its two-fold character. What the doctrine of faith reveals, the grace of faith applies ; both for acceptance, as exposed to the penalty of the covenant ; and for ability to exercise that " love, which is the fulfilling of the law." Here, therefore, *believing and doing*, though opposed as light and darkness in the matter of justification, yet agree in the life and conduct of the justified sinner.

Indeed, if " the law" be the transcript of the Divine image, and a perfect rule of righteousness ; and if conformity to its precepts be the essence of holiness ; how could the Gospel, as a subsequent revelation, " make void" its authority and obligation ? But which part of the law does the Christian desire to " make void ;" whether that, which inculcates love to God, or the corresponding obligation of love to his neighbour ? Does he not rather wish both parts to be confirmed by additional obligations ? And do not the doctrines and motives of the Gospel establish his cheerful habit of obedience ?

The whole discussion will remind us of the importance of *accurately distinguishing in our Ministry between the Law and the Gospel ;* ' that we, through the misunderstanding of the Scriptures, do not take the Law for the Gospel, nor the Gospel for the Law ; but skilfully discern and distinguish the voice of the one

---

[1] Rom. iii. 31. The expositions of many of the Christian Fathers on this text prove their defective views of the law. Origen expounds the establishment of the law by faith —'Quia Christus inquit: " Moses de me scripsit." ' Ambrose—' Quia ceremonalia scripturaliter implentur, et quod minus in moralibus lex continebat, in Evangelio additur : et quod tunc promittebatur futurum, fides advenisse testatur.' Jerome—'Quia fide probamus verum esse, quod lex dicit, testamentum testamento, legem legi . . . . successuram.' As Parè remarks—' *Aliquid dicunt, non totum.*' Augustine entered far more clearly into the Apostle's meaning—' Lex non evacuatur, sed statuiter per fidem ; quia fides impetrat gratiam, quà lex impleatur.' De Spir. et Lit. c. 29. Again—' Literâ jubetur, spiritu donatur.' Epist. 200.

from the voice of the other.'[1] This distinction is confounded, when the law is preached as *in any measure* the efficient cause of salvation;[2] or when its requirements are inculcated, as if to be performed in our own strength. This unevangelical confusion of statement blocks up the way of free and immediate access to God, by interposing legal qualifications, as indispensable for the reception of the Gospel. Even sincere Christians sometimes look for their comfort more from obedience to the law than from the righteousness of the Gospel ; and the continual disappointment brings them under " the spirit of bondage unto fear ;" instead of rejoicing, and " standing fast in the liberty, wherewith Christ hath made us free."[3] Thus does this preaching " another Gospel"[4] encourage a self-righteous temper, bring perplexity and distress to awakened consciences, and hinder consistency and establishment in the Gospel.

But while we preserve *the distinction of the two*, let us also maintain their *mutual dependence and connexion*. ' Worldly epicures and secure mammonists, to whom the doctrine of the law doth properly appertain, do receive and apply to themselves most principally the sweet promises of the Gospel.'[5] And therefore to preach the Gospel without the Law, would encourage self-delusion. On the other hand (as Luther beautifully observes)—' As thunder without rain did more harm than good ; so Ministers, that preach the terrors of the law, but do not, at the same time, drop in the dew of gospel instruction and consolation, are not " wise masterbuilders ;" for they pull down, but build nothing up again.' Our commission directs us to preach the Gospel under the solemn sanctions of the law, and to preach the law under the gracious encouragements of the Gospel.

In fine—' This shows the ignorance and absurdity of those men, who cry down preaching the law, as a course leading to despair and discontentment, though we find by St. Paul, that it leadeth to Christ. To preach the law alone by itself, we confess, is to pervert the use of it : neither have we any power or commission so to do ; for we have " our power for edification, and not for destruction." It was published as an appendant to the Gospel, and so must it be preached. It was published "in the hand of a mediator," and must be preached in the hand of a mediator. It was published *evangelically*, and it must be so preached. But yet we must preach the law, and that in its own fearful shapes ; for, though it was published in mercy, it was published in thunder, fire, tempests, and

---

[1] Patrick's Places, ut supra.   [2] See Gal. ii. 21.   [3] Gal. v. 1.
[4] Ibid. i. 6—9.   [5] Patrick, ut supra.

darkness, even in the hand of a Mediator ; for this is the method of the Holy Ghost, to convince first of sin, and then to reveal righteousness and refuge in Christ. The law is the forerunner, that makes room, and prepares welcome in the soul for Christ.'[1]

CHAPTER IV.

THE SCRIPTURAL PREACHING OF THE GOSPEL.

THIS subject opens to us the master-spring of the effectiveness of the Ministry. The Writer desires to conduct the discussion with a decided standard of truth, combined with due exercise of Christian forbearance. The Scriptural rule for preaching is—" If any man speak, let him speak as the oracles of God ;"[2] forming all our discourses according to the sacred model, " as Moses was ordered to make all things according to the pattern showed him in the mount."[3] This rule implies great care to give to every point in the system, its just weight and proportion. Every man takes his own view of the truth of God. The bias of individual constitution or of circumstances, unconsciously places him in imminent danger of preaching either a defective or a disproportioned Gospel. Our rule will however frame itself into the determination of the Apostle—" not to know any thing among our people, save Jesus Christ, and him crucified."[4] This is the one mode of preaching that God has promised to bless : when ' all our sermons' (according to the admirable injunction of Herman, Archbishop of Cologne) are ' made to *set forth and magnify Christ the Lord.*'[4] Uniformity of sentiment upon this cardinal point has always marked the labour of faithful Ministers,[5] and secured the Divine blessing upon their work ; while

---

[1] Bishop Reynolds' Works, p. 149.
[2] 1 Peter iv. 11. Beza's note on 2 Tim. ii. 15, is an excellent exposition of this rule—' ορθοτομυντα—id est, qui primum omnium, quod ad doctrinam ipsam attinet, nihil prætermittat, quod dicendum sit; nihil etiam adjiciat de suo, nihil mutilet, discerpat, torqueat ; deinde spectet diligenter, quid ferat auditorum captus, quicquid denique ad ædificationem conducit.' [3] Hebrews viii. 5.
[3] 1 Cor. ii. 2. We might refer, by the way, to this context, as giving a complete summary of the ministry—in its character, *the testimony of God*—1, in its doctrines, *Christ crucified* :—2, in its spirit, *conscious weakness and humility* :—3, in its form, *not with human wisdom :* 1—4. in its power, the *demonstration of the Spirit,* 4. in its end, *the establishment of faith upon God's foundation,* 5.
[4] Religious Consultation for a Christian Reformation. Herman, Archbishop of Cologne and Prince Elector, 1548. Some notice of this scheme of Reformation, drawn up under the direction of Bucer and Melancthon, is given in Scott's Continuation of Milner, i. 377—379.
[5] The Missionary Eliot's word to young Ministers was—' Let there be much of Christ

a deficiency in this particular (as will presently be proved) is attended invariably with proportionate inefficiency.

Not that we would chime upon a name, as if it would operate with the magic of a charm. 'Some men think, that they preach Christ' gloriously, because they name him every ten minutes in their sermons. But this is not (necessarily) preaching Christ."[1] There is sometimes also a fastidious spirit, that would stamp as un-evangelical every sermon, that has not Christ for its *immediate* subject. Now every part of the Bible contains the Gospel *substantially, but not formally*. We must not therefore force unnatural interpretations on Holy Writ for the purpose of constantly introducing the name of Christ. As all the principles and duties of the Gospel bear a relation more or less direct to Him, their enforcement *upon the round of this relation*, is as strictly conformed to the Apostolic pattern, as would be the most complete exhibition of his sufferings and death.[2] Only let us be careful, that his name throws life and glory upon all our Ministrations, and that· every sermon tends to draw sinners to him, and to establish Christians in their consistent profession. The Acts furnishes the model of preaching in popular addresses—the Epistles in more didactic instruction.

But let not this exclusive scheme be supposed to cramp our system within the narrow range of a few points in theology. We might as well speak of a village that has no road to the metropolis, as of a point of Christian doctrine, privilege, or practice, that has no reference to Christ crucified. How does the first chapter to the Ephesians endear this beloved name, as the medium of " all spiritual blessings !"[3] How does every heavenly doctrine and privilege throughout the Epistle—every personal and relative obligation—draw its quickening influence from this source ! How naturally do the Apostles introduce their Master in the midst of discussions apparently the most irrelevant ![4] So clearly does this point form

in your Ministry. (Mather's Life.) ' Exhibit,' said Mather to his Student and Pastor, (p. 180) ' as much as you can of a glorious Christ: yea, let the motto upon your whole Ministry be—" Christ is All." Let your Sermons be dyed in the blood of the Redeemer,' was the strong language of a celebrated Divine. (Skelton.) 'Persons,' as Mr. Romaine once observed to a friend of the Writer, ' wonder that we are always preaching Christ; but the truth is, that we have nothing else to preach about.' 'Preach Christ,' said a venerable Minister to a young brother. 'I have,' was the reply. 'Then preach him again. Be always on it. Let every thing be in connection with it.'

[1] Cecil's Remains.

[2] If Eph. iv, v, vi, are not a component part of the preaching of Christ crucified, the Apostle was inconsistent with his own rule—1 Cor. ii. 2.

[3] Verses 3—14.

[4] Such as the duties of husbands, Eph. v. 25; servants, 1 Peter ii. 18—25; the sin of evil speaking, Titus iij. 2—6; matters of Ecclesiastical discipline, 1 Cor. v. 7. The impetuosity of feeling in the sacred writers was so skilfully controlled, that their transitions are equally unexpected, natural, and graceful. 'Let the serious Christian observe the exquisite skill, which here and every where conducts the zeal of our inspired writer.

the centre of a widely extended circle[1]—embracing all that is honourable to God, and profitable to man—all the delightful ways of Divine faithfulness and love, and all that concerns our character, our professions, our privileges, our obligations, our hopes and prospects for eternity! The resolution, therefore, to know nothing—to preach nothing—and to glory in nothing else, marks a mind equally enlarged in its compass, and scriptural in its apprehensions. It sets forth Christ to our people, as a remedy commensurate with the evil —enough for all, and proposed to all. And skilfully to accommodate all our various topics to this one point, is a lesson we must be learning all our lives. And truly is it worth all our labour to learn it more perfectly, and to practise it more effectually.

An appeal to facts will prove the beneficial and permanent results from this exclusive Ministry. It was this, which so eminently attested the Apostolic commission, "with the demonstration of the Spirit, and with power,"[2] and which, during the successive ages of the Church, kept the light burning in the candlesticks, like the sacred fire upon the altar, never wholly extinct. Popery was successfully resisted at the era of the Reformation with the same weapon. When the Moravian Missionaries first explained to the sottish Greenlanders the nature and perfections of God, and his just claims upon his creatures, the poor heathen were bound up and frozen, like their own icy mountains. But in reading to them the affecting scenes of Gethsemane and Calvary, their hearts began to melt in tenderness, contrition, faith, and love. They begged to have the story repeated, and it was to them as "life from the dead."[3]

The odes of Pindar are celebrated for their fine transitions, which, though bold and surprising, are perfectly natural. We have in this place (1 Cor. v. 7.) a very masterly stroke of the same beautiful kind. The Apostle, speaking of the incestuous Corinthian, passes, by a most artful digression, to his darling topic—a crucified Saviour. Who would have expected it on such an occasion? Yet, when thus admitted, who does not see and admire both the propriety of the subject, and the delicacy of its introduction?' Hervey's Theron and Aspasio, Dialogue III.

[1] Matthew Henry, speaking on the importance of preaching Christ, beautifully remarks—Though 'the scriptures are the circumference of faith, the round of which it walks, and every point of which compass it toucheth; yet the centre of it is Christ. That is the polar star, on which it resteth.'—Williams' Life, p. 119. In fact this is the true teaching of the solar system, beginning with the Sun. Nothing is understood till the great centre of light is set forth and brought to our apprehensions.

[2] Compare 1 Cor. ii. 2. ut supra, with Acts of the Apostles, passim.

[3] Crantz' History of Greenland. In North America the same effects were produced upon widely different subjects. The following was the touching account given of himself by the first convert—' Brethren,' (said he) 'I have been a heathen, and have grown old among the heathen; therefore I know how heathens think. Once a preacher came and explained to us that there was a God: We answered—' Dost thou think us so ignorant as not to know that?' Another preacher began to teach us—'You must not steal, lie, nor get drunk,' &c.: We answered, 'Thou fool, dost thou think that we don't know that?' And thus we dismissed him. After a time, brother Christian Henry Rauch, came into my hut, and sat down by me. He spoke to me nearly as follows: 'I come to

Brainerd gives the same account of the special Divine influence upon the simple exhibition of this all-powerful subject to the heathen Indians. 'This was the method of preaching, which was blessed of God for the awakening, and, I trust, the saving conversion, of numbers of souls, and was made *the means of producing a remarkable reformation among the hearers in general.*'[1] So true is it, that we must preach the Gospel, in order to reform the world.

The valuable lives of Mr. Walker of Truro,[2] and Mr. Milner of Hull,[3] nearer to our own time, and in our own Church, speak to the same point. Their diligent, conscientious, and exemplary labours, grounded on an erroneous scheme of Christian doctrine, were wholly unproductive ; while with a subsequent more enlightened Ministration, the most happy success attended them. The late Dr. Conyers also, when labouring in an extensive manufacturing parish in Yorkshire, was reported to the Society for propagating the Gospel, 'as the most perfect example of a parish priest, which this nation, or perhaps this age, has produced.' Yet his utmost success was a restraint upon outward irregularities. But under a new character of preaching, the root of sin was attacked ; and principles of life, holiness, and love, hitherto unknown, were displayed. His people were not only reformed, but converted. Multitudes were "the seal of his Apostleship in the Lord,"[4] and united themselves to his church ; and 'the unlearned and the unbeliever reported, that God was in him of a truth.'[5]

Nothing but the truth of the Gospel can be instrumental to the conversion of souls. Any wilful suppression—or any compromising statement of truth, dishonours the Holy Spirit in his own special office,[6] and therefore restrains his quickening influence. Many ear-

you in the name of the Lord of heaven and earth. He sends me to let you know, that he will make you happy, and deliver you from the misery in which you lie at present. To this end he became a man, gave his life a ransom for man, and shed his blood for us.' I could not forget his words. Even while I was asleep, I dreamt of that blood which Christ shed for us. I found this to be something different from what I had ever heard, and I interpreted Christian Henry's words to the other Indians. *Thus, through the grace of God, an awakening took place among us.* I say, therefore, brethren—Preach Christ our Saviour, and *his sufferings and death,* if you would have your words to gain entrance among the heathen.'—Loskiel's Missions to the North American Indians.
[1] Appendix I. to Brainerd's Life—a most important document for the Christian Minister or Missionary.
[2] Prefixed to his Lectures on the Church Catechism, pp. xxiv. &c. &c. See also a more full and interesting life lately published by the Rev. Edwin Sidney.
[3] Prefixed to his Sermons, pp. xxiii. &c.   [4] 1 Cor. ix. 2.
[5] Comp. Ibid. xiv. 23—25; and see an interesting sketch in Newton's Works, i. 562. 563. 'We have long been endeavouring to reform the nation by moral preaching. With what effect? None—We must change our voice. We must preach "Christ and him crucified." Nothing but the Gospel is the power of God unto salvation. Bishop Lavington's Charges.   [6] See John xvi. 14, 15.

nest, affectionate, and diligent Ministers, are mourning over the palpable unfruitfulness of their work ; without at all suspecting, that the root of the evil lies within themselves. Sincerity, earnestness, conscientiousness, and self-denial, when connected with a wrong or defective standard of doctrine or practice, are means utterly disproportioned to produce this moral miracle of a radical change. Bishop Horsley remarked—'It too often happens, that Ministers lose sight of that which is their proper office, *to publish the word of reconciliation.*'[1] And indeed, without this Ministry of reconciliation,[2] it is of no avail to appear before our people. We might beseech them with tears—"Be ye reconciled unto God." We might work upon their self-love. We might reason with them upon their folly. We might convince them by our arguments. They might listen to us, as to the sound of " one that playeth well upon an instrument."[3] But no abiding impression would be made. The drunkard, the swearer, and the devoted follower of the world would be alike uninfluenced.[4] But in lifting up the cross of Christ in our Ministrations, how does the Spiritof God, acting in his own office, delight to unveil the face of Christ, and to shed his animating glow upon this magnificent subject ! Thus—*thus only*—by his Almighty agency applying the doctrine to the heart—do our people live, grow, and flourish. Thus do they become crucified to sin, separate from the spirit of the world ; conformed to the image, and consecrated to the service, of God ; brought to the present enjoyment of Christian privileges, and "made meet for the inheritance of the saints in light."[5]

[1] Charges, p. 7.　　　[2] Cor. v. 19.　　　[3] Ezek. xxxiii. 32.
[4] This point is forcibly illustrated by our exquisite Christian poet, Cowper. Task, Book v. The result of this experiment, actually, but undesignedly tried by a master-mind, is most candidly and explicitly stated in Dr. Chalmers' Address to the inhabitants of Kilmany, pp. 40—43. See some valuable remarks in Bishop of Winchester's Min. Char. of Christ. pp. 442, 443.
[5] 'Were all these talents and excellences' (alluding to the classic sages and orators,) 'united in one man; and you were the person so richly endowed; and could you employ them all in every sermon you preach; yet you could have no reasonable hope to convert and save one soul, while you lay aside the glorious Gospel of Christ, and leave it intirely out of your discourses. Let me proceed yet further, and say—Had you the fullest acquaintance, that ever man acquired, with all the principles and duties of natural religion, both in its regards to God and your fellow-creatures—had you the skill and tongue of an angel to range all these in their fairest order, to place them in their fullest light, and to pronounce and represent the whole law of God with such force and splendour, as was done to the Israelites at Mount Sinai; you might perhaps lay the consciences of men under deep conviction (" for by the law is the knowledge of sin"); but I am fully persuaded, you would never reconcile one soul to God, you would never change the heart of one sinner, nor bring him into the favour of God, nor fit him for the joys of heaven, without this blessed Gospel which is committed to your hands.
The great and glorious God is jealous of his own authority, and of the honour of his Son Jesus. Nor will he condescend to bless any other methods for obtaining so Divine an end, than what he himself has prescribed. Nor will his Holy Spirit, whose office is to " glorify Christ," stoop to concur with any other sort of means for the saving of sinners, where the name and office of his Son, the only appointed Saviour, are known,

Would we then set aside the inculcation of practical obligations? We shall soon take occasion to shew, that the Scriptural enforcement of moral duties is no less necessary than doctrinal statements, for the completeness of our public Ministrations.[1]   The Gospel is irradiated with Divine holiness, as it is enriched with the glory of Divine grace.   Some however, 'preach the icy morality of Plato, Seneca, and Aurelius, and plainly declare by their practice, that they think Cicero and Socrates better preachers than the Saviour and his Apostles.'[2]   We must therefore maintain the spiritual inefficacy of mere lectures on morality, irrespective of the Gospel.   If they convert the brute into the man, they will never accomplish that higher and indispensable change, of converting the man into the saint.   All morality, not engrafted upon the stock of faith, is the futile attempt to improve the fruit, without "making the tree good."   No man ever preached more morality than St. Paul; but it was always upon the basis of Evangelical doctrine.   It is the man grafted into Christ, that "blossoms and buds, and fills the face of the" little "world" in which he moves "with fruit."

' Christ crucified is God's grand ordinance.'[3]   No souls, therefore, can be won to him, except by setting forth his name, work, and glory.   Christian stedfastness is, when our flock have so "received him, as to walk in him, rooted and built up in him, and established in the faith."[4]   Archbishop Secker warned his Clergy—' We have in fact lost many of our *people to sectaries* by not preaching in a manner sufficiently Evangelical;[5] and shall neither recover them from the extravagancies into which they have run; nor keep more from going over to them, but by returning to the right way—" *declaring all the counsel of God;* and that principally, "not in the words which man's wisdom teacheth, but which the Holy Ghost teacheth." '   And again—'If you have preached a considerable

---

despised, and neglected.   It is the Gospel alone, that is the power of God to salvation. ' If the Prophets will not stand in his counsel, nor cause the people to hear his way, they will never be able to turn Israel from the iniquity of their ways, nor from the evil of their doings—Unless, therefore, you have such an high esteem for the Gospel of Christ, and such a sense of its Divine worth and power, as to take it along with you in all your efforts to save souls, you had better lay down your Ministry, and abandon your sacred profession; for you but spend your strength for nought, and waste your breath in empty declamation.'   Watts's Humble Attempt, pp. 30, 31, 38.

[1] Sect. iii.   [2] Dwight's Sermons.   Vol. ii. 452.
[3] Cecil's Remains.   [4] Col. ii. 6, 7.
[5] Bishop Horne remarked to the same purport—'Many well-meaning Christians of this time thirst after the doctrine of the gospel, and think they have heard nothing unless they have heard of salvation by Jesus Christ, which is what we properly call the Gospel; and if they do not hear it in the discourses from our pulpits, where they expect to hear it, *they are tempted to wander in search of it to other places of worship.*'   Qu. Is the defalcation of our people to sectaries, however to be lamented, *the whole, or even the chief responsibility* connected with a defective tone of preaching?   "*My people are destroyed for lack of knowledge.*"   Hosea iv. 6.

time in a place, and done little or no good, there must in all probability be some fault, not only in your hearers, but in you, or your sermons. " For the word of God," when duly dispensed, is to this day, as it was originally, "powerful, and sharper than a two-edged sword." Inquire then where the fault may be.'[1]

The correct view of Scripture Preaching implies that it be full and distinct in its statements, unctional in its tone, popular in its mode of address, experimental in its sympathies, direct and practical in its enforcement—in fine—deeply impregnated with the very language and spirit of Scripture, so that we may be able to turn to our people with a warranted confidence, and say,— *We have the mind of Christ.* Let a man so account of us, as of the " Ministers of Christ, and stewards of the mysteries of God."[2] We will now pursue this subject in some of its more important details.

I.—DOCTRINAL PREACHING OF THE GOSPEL.

WE have shown, that " Christ crucified" is the soul of the Christian system. We now remark, that our preaching of this doctrine should be *full and explicit.* Let it comprehend within its circle the whole mystery of Christ, in his person, offices, and work ; connected with the love of the Father, and the work of the Spirit, in every department of privilege, duty, promise, and hope. We do not always observe this large compass in Christian Ministrations. Many are confined to favourite doctrines, neglecting others of at least equal importance. Some are continually employed in detecting the delusions of a false profession ; others, in fulminating the terrors of the law ; others, in painting the awful condition of the unconverted ; others, in general invitations to Christ ; or in dispensing indiscriminately the promises and consolations of the Gospel ; or in an abstract exposition of practical obligations. Some seem to forget, that the Church as well as the world needs a quickening Ministry. They withhold " the deep things of God, searched and revealed by the Spirit"[3]—if not altogether from their system— at least from their Scriptural prominence. Now in all these cases, there is a want of that *entireness,* so strongly bound up in our office—as angels, to keep close to our message ; as ambassadors, to discharge our commission ; as depositories, to be faithful to our

---

[1] Charges, pp. 276, 296. The Charges of the late Bishops Porteus and Barrington distinctly advert to the same point.
[2] 1 Cor. ii. 16. iv. 1.   [3] 1 Cor. ii. 10.

trust. Learning, wisdom, eloquence, gifts, make not a minister. *"It is required of stewards, that a man be found faithful."*[1] We must declare our testimony without concealment—not indeed forcing offensive truths into undue prominence ; yet not daring to withhold them in their Scriptural proportion—adapting our statements to the spiritual capacities of our people ;[2] yet jealous, that we omit nothing from our own or our hearers' disgust to particular doctrines ;—"not handling the word of God deceitfully ; but by manifestation of the truth commending ourselves to every man's conscience in the sight of God."[3]

The guilt, corruption, and ruin of man by the fall—his free and full justification through faith in the atoning blood and meritorious obedience of the Redeemer—his adoption by faith into the family of God—the holy nature and evidences of this faith—the immediate agency of the Holy Spirit in the work of regeneration, progressive sanctification, and in all his offices of holy and heavenly consolation[4]—the harmonious working of the three Sacred Persons, each in his specified office, in the œconomy of redemption—these are cardinal points in the Ministration of every "scribe instructed unto the kingdom of heaven."

But important and glorious as are these views of the Gospel ; yet to affirm, that they comprise the *entire Gospel,* is to put a part (though indeed a very considerable part) for the whole. To stop here, is to withhold much of the Divine revelation from our people, and to lower our statement from the Scriptural standard of truth. We ought to trace this river of infinite mercy to its source in the depths of eternity—in the bosom of God ; "who hath called us, according to his own purpose and grace given unto us in Christ Jesus before the world began."[5] This eternal purpose is not only an integral part of the scheme of salvation, but the fountain, from which all springs—the foundation, on which all rests and turns—

---

[1] 1 Cor. iv. 2. vii. 25. Mark the instances of Joshua, (viii. 35.)—Jeremiah's commission, (xxvi. 2. with xlii. 4.)—our Lord's appeals concerning his public Ministry, (Psalm xl. 9, 10. John xv. 15. xvii. 8.)—the angel's message to the apostles, (Acts v. 20.) Paul's testimony before the church, (Acts xx. 26, 27.) 'Who is a true and faithful steward ?' (asks Latimer in his honest "plainness of speech")—'He is true, he is faithful, that coineth no new money, but seeketh it ready coined of the good man of the house; and neither changeth it, nor clippeth it, after it is taken to him to spend, but spendeth even the self-same that he had of his Lord; and spendeth it, as his Lord commanded him.' Sermon on Luke xvi. 1, 2.
[2] Comp. Mark iv. 33. with 1 Cor. iii. 1—3. Heb. v. 11—14.
[3] 2 Cor. iv. 2. with ii. 17.
[4] Is the Gospel always set forth in its true character, as *"the Ministration of the Spirit?"* (2 Cor. iii. 6—8.) Are the offices of the Spirit—especially as the efficient cause of a believing reception of Christ—generally exhibited in their full Scriptural glory and necessity ? In giving due honour to this Blessed Person, we may hope that he will honour us, by exerting that power, which we have distinctly and dutifully ascribed to him.
[5] 2 Tim. i. 9.

the assurance by which all is confirmed. All the rest, however desirable and however desired, present nothing to secure their attainment, but the mutable will of the creature—the will of a mind
that is "enmity against God"—to secure reconciliation with him
and happiness in him. Our blessed Lord adverted to this primary
source of grace, not only in his more confidential discourses with
his disciples, *but also in his public general instructions;* referring the effectual application of his gospel to the Sovereign dispensation of his Father.[1] The apostles in their system of didactic instruction to the Churches, set forth the same views with greater
clearness of detail.[2] After this pattern, therefore, and in accordance with these statements, in declaring the freeness of the invitations of the Gospel, we must not hide the basis of our effectual
calling.[3] In displaying the riches of grace, we must not forget to
trace them to the sovereign pleasure of God.[4] We must enforce
the obligations of holiness as connected with, and resulting from,
the eternal designs of God.[5] We need not fear but the tendency
of these doctrines will be sound and holy, when we bring them
forth in their due place and order, and with that strength and distinctness of statement, in which we find them in the sacred volume; avoiding forced and needless repetition, yet not shrinking
from the manly tone of Scriptural decision ; connecting these
truths with every link in the chain of salvation ; yea—with every
step of Divine mercy, from its first origin in the mind of God, to
its final eternal consummation, in order that God may be glorified in all.

As to the mind of our Church upon this subject—Let any one
study the Seventeenh Article ; and he will find in it a full picture of electing love, as the source of our calling[6]—of our obedience to the call[7]—of our justification[8]—our adoption[9]—our holiness[10]—our Christian walk[11]—and our final happiness.[12] Surely
she must have given this elaborate and accurate—this cautious
but uncompromising statement, as a model to her Ministers for
the presentment of this high and holy doctrine. And if it be
(as she has described it) ' full of sweet, pleasant, and unspeakable
comfort to godly persons,' will not the exhibition of it be connected

---

[1] John vi. 24—65; x. 24—30.
[2] See Epistles to the Romans and Ephesians. Throughout the former Epistle—and
especially in the chapter of Christian privilege (viii.) electing love is exhibited in its full
and prominent proportion.
[3] John iv. 37.   [4] Eph. i. 3—6. 2 Tim. i. 9.
[5] Rom. viii. 29. Eph. i. 4. 2 Thess. ii. 13. 1 Pet. i. 2.
[6] 2 Tim. i. 9.   [7] 1 Peter i. 2.   [8] Rom. viii. 30.   [9] Eph. i. 5.
[10] Rom. viii. 29. Eph. i. 4. 2 Thess. ii. 13.   [11] Eph. ii. 10.
[12] John vi. 39: x. 28, 29; xvii. 24; Rom. viii. 30.

with a large influence of Christian privilege and holy devotedness,[1] flowing from its reception? And will not the want of its
cheering beams and enlivening principles in our Ministry be sensibly felt—if not in the work of conversion, yet in a more languid growth in Christian sanctification, and especially in the want
of that frame of mind, which above all others characterizes the
felicity of heaven—an adoring view and acknowledgment of sovereign grace?[2]

Nothing so little deserves the character of a judicious statement, as to refrain from the full and distinct declaration of the
mind and word of God. It is the folly of preferring our foolishness
to his unerring and infinite wisdom. ' I dare not'—said Mr. Richmond—' omit what God hath revealed to his Church ; or call that
useless or dangerous, which he requires me to believe and teach.'[3]
Indeed, we are bound to explain to our people, according to the
light afforded us, every part of that book, which was designed for
general instruction, and of which we are the ordained interpreters.
The commission entrusted to us at our Ordination—' Take thou
authority to preach the word of God,'[4] comprehends within its terms
the full extent of the Evangelical system. Judicious preaching
therefore implies a clear display *of every Doctrine of the Gospel*
—in the statement, in the order, according to the proportion, and
for the ends, in which we conceive it to be set forth in Scripture.
If our imperfect apprehensions (for such are the most enlightened
of them) prevent us from "declaring all the counsel of God ;" let
our sermons at least show that we " *do not shun* to declare it"[5]—
that we keep it in view—that nothing is *wilfully* concealed. In
this grand field of knowledge there is interminable range for perpetual progress.[6] Let it therefore be our aim, study, and prayer, so
to " grow in grace and in the knowledge of Christ," that our preaching may not only be true, but the truth—the whole truth—" the
truth as it is in Jesus." A correct system will lead us to set forth
every truth bearing the stamp of Divine authority ; connecting every part of it with some valuable end. A defective system will
show itself in a restraint upon Christian doctrine or practical exhortation. Yet on the other hand, we must guard against over-
statements, or an undue partiality for individual points, which is
equally unscriptural with an undue concealment.[7] Inferences, ap-

---

[1] See the prominent place, which this doctrine seems to occupy in that magnificent
passage, Rom. viii. 33—39.
[2] See Rev. v. 9—14.   [3] Life, p. 139.   [4] Ordination of Priests.
[5] Acts xx. 27.   [6] Compare Phil. iii. 10 ; with Eph. iii. 18, 19.
[7] See some important remarks in the application of Mr. Scott's Sermon on Election
and Perseverance.

parently legitimate, must be received with holy caution, except as they are supported by explicit Scripture declarations. 'Let us ever stop' (as Professor Campbell reminds us) 'where revelation stops; and not pretend to move one inch beyond it.'[1]

The study of the Apostolical Epistles will show, whether our course of instruction includes every "jot and tittle" of Scriptural truth, (casuistical questions excepted[2]) delivered to the primitive churches. It will teach us, what to bring forth, and in what mode —to form alike the doctrine, the statement, and the terms, upon the inspired model—not giving abstract views of the doctrines of grace, but combining with them, after the example of the sacred writers,[3] practical enforcement. It will mark also the error of avoiding the use of the terms, in which holy inspiration has clothed these deep and mysterious doctrines, (and in which our people find them in their own Scriptures) probably from the fear of exciting disgust, misconception, or licentiousness; a well-intentioned, but unevangelical spirit, which adulterates the purity of the Gospel with man's carnal wisdom.[4] It has been justly observed, that 'a

[1] On Systematic Theology, Lect. ii. Calvin's statements upon this subject are sometimes marked by special wisdom and sobriety. Instit. Lib. iii. c. 21. § 3, 4. In the same spirit Bishop Ridley writes to his fellow-martyr—Bradford—'In those matters' (referring to election, on which Coverdale informs us, he wrote an excellent treatise) 'I am so fearful, that I dare not speak further, yea, almost, none otherwise, than the very text doth, as it were, lead me by the hand.' Fathers of the English Church, vol. iv. 249. The Writer desires to state his own views in the spirit of forbearance to his brethren. He is aware that difference must be expected to exist upon these deep and mysterious subjects, until the plenary effusion of the Spirit of light and love. He conceives, however, that none of us should suppose ourselves to be *so entirely possessed of the whole truth*, as to be satisfied with present attainments. Every part of "the faith delivered to the saints," is not equally distinct to every spiritual apprehension. More study and prayer may be expected to bring clearer views of truth, and increasing fulness, simplicity, and unction in the exposition of them. Much prejudice against these particular doctrines has doubtless arisen from a controversial and repulsive mode of statement, unconnected with that humility, watchfulness, holy devotedness, and enjoyment of Christian privileges, in which the Church rises to a higher tone of spirituality, and a fuller unction of the Divine Spirit is poured out. At the same time, the danger of attachment to human systems should make us scrupulously careful, that we "call no man" Master "upon the earth." On the other hand, we must be equally careful not to oppose what we do not understand. We must watch against repugnance to the study of any particular portions of Scripture; which is the sure indication of a wrong temper of heart—of a want of "trembling at the word"—and of a disposition even to cancel what our proud hearts cannot receive. The Writer would therefore impress both upon his Calvinistic and Arminian brethren, the obligation of full and explicit statements of truth, as they are given in the Holy Scriptures. The bias of their own mind will indeed after all introduce some diversity of statement. But God's word will be honoured: they will be delivered from the guilt of the wilful suppression of truth; whatever difference may appear will not savour, as it too often does, of controversy; and while their respective views will more nearly approximate, their minds will be brought more into an harmonious and brotherly agreement. They will also be led to concede to each other that liberty, which, from a sense of fidelity to God, they severally claim for themselves; and, in conformity to the Apostolic rule, "whereto they have already attained," they will learn to "walk by the same rule, and mind the same thing." (Phil. iii. 16.)

[2] Such as Romans xiv. 1 Cor. vii. viii.

[3] See Deut. vii. 6; x. 15, 16; Rom. viii. 29; Eph. i. 4; ii. 10; 2 Thess. ii. 13; 1 Peter i. 2.

[4] Bishop Davenant remarks on this point—'Hoc adversatur huic libertati, quæ requi-

fixed deference to any other example leads insensibly to partial representations of the Gospel, if not to absolute error.'[1] We can only gain the confidence of our people, by embodying all the statements of their own Scriptures in our public Ministrations.

We sum up this point with Bishop Horsley's forcible exhortation —'Pray earnestly to God to assist the Ministration of the word, by the secret influence of the Holy Spirit in the minds of your hearers: and nothing doubting that your prayers are heard, however *mean and illiterate* the congregation may be, in which you exercise your sacred functions, fear 'not to set before them the *whole counsel of God. Open the whole of your message without reservation*, that every one of you may have confidence to say, when he shall be called upon to give an account of his stewardship —"Lord, I have not hid thy righteousness within my heart; I have not concealed thy lovingkindness and truth from the great congregation." '[2]

Our doctrinal statements must also be simple. Our materials of instruction are sufficiently simple—sin and salvation—ruined man recovered by Christ. But it is of main importance, that the sinner's way to Christ, like those to the cities of refuge, should be made plain. The "stumbling-blocks" of unbelief and self-righteousness must be "taken up out of the way of God's people."[3] The necessity of previous attainments of holiness must be discountenanced; an instant application to Christ upon the warrant of his word encouraged; the freeness of the invitations of the Gospel, and the willingness and sufficiency of the Saviour must be displayed: and finally, the certainty of acceptance to all that are willing to "repent and believe the Gospel," must be assured. "Repent and be converted." "Believe and be saved." "Look and live." "Whosoever will, let him come."[4] We are not to commence with the outskirts of the Gospel, and so reason on step by step till we come to Christ—thus keeping the sinner waiting in the dark. He wants to see the king. There needs no long ceremonial of approach from a distance. Let the great object be placed in immediate view. Every thing short of this is a grand impertinence.

ritur in Ministris Christi: quos oportet, non modo ipsam substantiam (ut ita loquar) et possessionem veritatis retinere; sed *extremos etiam limites, et quasi confinia ejusdem defendere*—in Col. iv. 4.

[1] Bishop of Chester's Apostolical Preaching, pp. 257, 258. Some valuable thoughts may be found in Macknight's Esay I.—Prefatory to his Commentary on the Epistles.

[2] Charges, p. 16. Need we remark how clearly this important advice and this divine example are opposed to the doctrine of Reserve, lately promulgated in 'The Tracts for the Times,' (Tract 80.) a doctrine that fearfully obscures the glory and paralyzes the influence of the glorious gospel of the grace of God?

[3] Isaiah lvii. 14.   [4] Acts iii. 19. xvi. 31: John iii. 14, 15. Rev. xxii. 17.

The sinner is dying, he is in instant, urgent, need of the physician and the remedy.   The brazen serpent must be lifted up before him —*not because he believes: but because he needs, and that he may believe.*

This is the Gospel in its freeness and suitableness.   And this Scriptural simplicity in our instructions, will preserve us from paralyzing our Ministrations by tame and subordinate topics; like men, whom Bishop Reynolds aptly describes—'of an Athenian temper, "who spend all their time in nothing else, but either to tell or to hear some new" Theology; not contenting themselves with the wholesome form of sound words, and the general harmony of orthodox doctrine—who direct all the studies and navigations of their minds unto *Theologia incognita,* to practise new experiments, and to make new discoveries.   In things doctrinal to cry up new lights, and to amuse the people with metaphysical fancies, as if they were deep and heavenly mysteries; and in the mean time to neglect the preaching of duty, and the savoury and saving principles of repentance and new obedience, is a far readier means to make men question the truth of all that they learned before, than ever to attain any certain knowledge of the things which are newly taught them.'[1]

This spirit of simplicity will also preserve in us a holy reverence for every tittle of Scripture, and a holy jealousy of perverting a single particle.   In expounding Scripture, we shall be led to adopt that interpretation, which seems most naturally to flow from Divine teaching; and which, if we belonged to no party in the Church, would appear to us to be the genuine meaning.

Our *doctrinal instructions must also be connected.*   No sermon can give the whole Gospel in detail.   Yet it should give its subject, as a part of a connected whole, and in distinct relation to the whole system.   Many important truths of the Gospel may be preached in a disjointed manner; and yet the Gospel itself, truly speaking, not be preached.   The perfections of God, without a view of their harmony in the work of Christ—the purposes of God,

---

[1] Sermon on Self-denial, Works, pp. 809, 810.   After warning against 'affectation of new senses and meanings of Scripture, and picking exceptions at the pious and solid expositions of other learned men'—he adds this admirable advice—' Whenever we judge it needful to interpose any opinion or sense of our own, let us—First—do it with humility and reverence, and with reservation of honour and reverence unto others from whom we differ; not magisterially with an ευρηκα, as if we spake rather oracles than opinions. Secondly, let us take heed of departing from "the analogy of faith," and that "knowledge which is according to godliness," into diverticles of fancy and critical curiosity; but let us resolve ever to judge those expositions best and soundest, which are most orthodox, practical, and heavenly, and most tending unto the furtherance of duty and godliness.'

unconnected with the freeness and holiness of the Gospel—the glories of heaven, without a reference to Christ as the way thither—the power, defilement, guilt, and condemnation of sin, separated from the doctrine of salvation through Christ—the work of the Holy Spirit, unconnected with the atonement—holiness irrespective of union with Christ—his imputed righteousness disunited from his imparted righteousness—the reception of him by faith, without its active working in the renewal of the heart—the exhibition of the promises, separated from the duties; or of the duties, independent of their constraining motives—these may be severally portions of the Gospel; but, being broken off from their Scriptural connexion, they do not constitute the preaching of the Gospel. These broken fragments of truth cannot produce that solid foundation and superstructure of Christian doctrine, by which the temple of God is raised. Misplacing of the truths of the Gospel, like confusion in the machinery of clock-work, makes the whole system go wrong. Disconnecting the operation of the Gospel from its principles, paralyzes all quickening influence. Important statements of practical truth, without a direct and immediate reference to Christ, produce, instead of " the pleasant fruits of the Spirit," only " wild grapes," or "dead works." For as " faith without works is dead," so works without faith are dead also.

It is possible therefore to preach much valuable truth essentially belonging to the Gospel, and yet not to preach the Gospel—to preach about Christ, yet not to preach Christ. There may be a want of that vital connection which links every part of the Divine system to the whole. Thus again we may forcibly set forth the importance of religion, without showing its true and spiritual character. Or we may be clear upon the point of the sinner's ruin, and indefinite in explaining the remedy, and not constantly combining the one with the other. These defective statements (generally attributable to youth, inexperience, to an early bias, or to imperfect apprehensions,) mar the beauty and completeness of the Gospel, and enervate its heavenly power and demonstration. But we must not mutilate, suppress, or disconnect truth, because others have perverted it. We must not deny to the children their bread; because some may have adulterated it, or others (to use our Lord's image) " cast it unto the dogs."[1] We must not withhold the " strong drink from him that is ready to perish," or the " wine" of heavenly consolation from " those that be of heavy hearts,"[2] because some have intoxicated themselves by unseasonable mixtures. If

[1] Matt. xv. 26.   [2] Prov. xxxi. 5.

some poison their people, others may be in danger of starving them. How few, comparatively, are "pastors according to God's heart, feeding his people with knowledge and understanding !"[1] Revulsion is one of the indirect evils of unscriptural schemes. We forget that *opposition to error*, may be error ; that (as has been wisely observed) 'heresy is not to be cured by heresy, but by truth ;'[2] and that truth (as for example—the doctrine of election) may be so distorted in its statement, and dissevered from its connexion, as to become positive error. Half-statements also on either side are mis-statements ; and it is of little moment to speak on some points "with the tongues of men and of angels," if on other points of considerable, if not of fundamental, importance, we speak indecisively, or under misconception.

We should be careful also, that *our doctrinal statements be unfettered.* In order to this, we must not be satisfied with a human medium of perception. We must search for ourselves. It is "in God's light that we must see light."[3] And yet, in attempting to embrace the whole Scripture, and to aim at Bible preaching, it is extremely difficult to escape the bias of some theological system.[4] No such system however grasps the entire compass of truth ; nor indeed can it be arranged without the smoothing of many rough edges, and the omission of many texts from fear of inconsistency. Christian integrity, therefore, will labour to state the doctrines of the Gospel, as they lie unfettered, though not unconnected, in the sacred volume. The system of Scripture (for doubtless there is a system of scriptural truth) embraces the sovereignty of God in perfect consistency with his universal equity, and the free agency of man untouched by his total depravity. And if our reason cannot discern or adjust the consistency of these seemingly opposite points, yet faith will receive them both with equal simplicity, and state them both in the most unmeasured terms ; leaving the harmonizing of them to the infinite wisdom of God. If God as a Sovereign "worketh all things after the counsel of his own will ;" yet does his mercy flow freely, according to the faithful engagements of his covenant. He "divideth unto every man severally as he will." He may give, or he may refuse. Yet he hath said—"Seek, and ye shall find ;" and by this promise he hath engaged, that none "shall seek his face in vain."[5] In the work of regeneration,

---

[1] Jer. iii. 15. [2] Cecil's Life of Cadogan. [3] Psalm xxxvi. 9. .
[4] Witsius thus solemnly warns his modest Divine—' Ea (Dei oracula) quovis, vel levissimo torquere modo, ut præjudicatis respondeant hypothesibus, *nefas ac propemodum scelus est.*' De Theologo Modesto.
[5] Matt. vii. 7, 8, with Isaiah xlv. 19.

God is the only efficient mover. Man is entirely passive. Hence it seems to follow, that he is acted upon as a machine. Yet is he "drawn with the cords of a man."[1] No constraint is put upon his will.[2] Salvation is offered, not forced upon him. His free agency therefore is preserved, while the whole work from first to last is the grace of God.[3] All is of God, who works in setting us to work,[4] and whose rule of procedure is—" He that hath, to him shall be given."[5] Man is addressed as a rational agent. Though paralytic, he is commanded to walk. Though dead, he is called to "rise from the dead."[6] He may come to Christ. He is invited to come. He is bound to come ; and it is his sin, if he does not come; while at the same time his selfish unhumbled heart chains him under a moral inability to come, and leaves him without excuse. For it cannot be supposed, that his inability cancels his obligation ; or that God will compromise with carnal men, by requiring any thing less than his just and absolute claim. But thus man is urged to acts, for which he has no inherent power. He is pressed with topics, which have a moral suitableness to interest his faculties, and move his natural affections: and in this constituted order of means, the sovereignty, grace, and power of God give life to the dispensation of his word. We deal with rational beings, capable of apprehending our message, and answerable for their reception of it. Let it be therefore *comprehensive, simple, connected, and unfettered ;* and " the Lord will give testimony unto the word of his grace."[7]

We have enlarged upon this subject from the decided conviction, that a Scriptural standard of .doctrine is indissolubly connected with a corresponding elevation of holiness and privilege. To accommodate our statement to the philosophy of the hman mind in the hope of conciliating regard, is to forget the native enmity of the heart to the Gospel,[8] and the determined opposition manifested to the Ministry of the wisest and most attractive of all preachers.[9] On this principle the Apostle would never have stumbled the Jew and the Greek by " the foolishness of the cross"—that is, he would never have brought " the power and wisdom of God" for their conversion to the Gospel.[10] Indefinite and indecisive statements may

---

[1] Hosea xi. 4.   [2] See Psalm cx. 3.

[3] Augustine well remarked—' Si non sit liberum arbitrium, quomodo damnabitur mundus ? Si non sit gratia, quomodo servabitur ?' Nearly identical was Bernard's language —' Si non sit liberum arbitrium, non est quod salvetur ; si non sit gratia, non est unde salvetur.' Epist. 46.

[4] See Phil. ii. 12, 13.   [5] Mark iv. 25.

[6] Eph. v. 14. See this subject illustrated in the parable of the dry bones. Ezek. xxxvii. 1—10.   [7] Acts xiv. 3.

[8] John i. 5; iii. 19, 20; Rom. viii. 7.   [9] Matt. xi. 16—19; John xii. 37—40.

[10] 1 Cor. i. 22—24.

quiet the enmity of the heart, and may even bring our people to a certain stage of conviction; but they will never carry them to the main point, and will be dependent upon human energy alone for their success. 'In these truths which we have ventured to present,' (as Mather reminds his Student) 'there are the articles, which the church either stands or falls withal. They will be the life of your Ministry, nor can the power of godliness be maintained without them. The loss of these truths will render a Ministry insipid and unfruitful; and procure this complaint about the shepherds—" The diseased ye have not strengthened, neither have ye brought again that which was driven away." '[1] " Simplicity, and godly sincerity"—not talent or eloquence—are the principles of our agency. One short sentence describes our system—" Christ is all, and in all."[2] He is not only exhibited in the picture, but in the foreground—as the principal figure—where every part of the picture is subordinated, to give him that prominence and effect, which attract the eye and the heart exclusively to Him.[3]

The striking exhortation of Bishop Reynolds will fitly conclude the subject—' Studiously and conscientiously apply yourselves to this heavenly skill of spiritual preaching. *So convince of sin*— the guilt, the stain, the pollution of it, the curse and malediction, whereunto the soul is exposed by it—that your hearers may be awakened, and humbled, and effectually forewarned " to flee from the wrath to come." So convince of the all-sufficient righteousness and unsearchable riches of Christ, the excellency of his knowledge, the immeasurableness of his love, the preciousness of his promises, " the fellowship of his sufferings, the power of his resurrection," the beauties of his holiness, the easiness of his yoke, the sweetness of his peace, the joy of his salvation, the hope of his glory—that the hearts of your hearers may burn within them, and they may " fly, like doves unto their windows," for shelter and sanctuary into the

---

[1] Mather's Student and Pastor, p. 185.   [2] Col. iii. 11.

[3] Bowles gives some cogent reasons for this full exhibition of Christ in our Ministry.— 1. Because in him is our only hope of salvation, Acts iv. 12; John xiv. 6. 2. Because he is the scope of the whole Scripture, the whole range of truth being employed—either (like the Mosaic œconomy,) " to bring us to him"—or to describe him as if before our eyes—or to lead us to communion with him by the outward and inward means—or lastly, that we might walk worthy of him. 3. Because all the first Ministers of the Gospel unite in giving him the pre-eminence in their Ministrations—John the Baptist, (John i. 29.) Philip, (Acts viii. 5.) Paul, (Acts ix. 20. 1 Cor. ii. 2. Eph. iii. 8.) 4. Because all our works except they be grafted on him, are no better than splendid sins. (John xv. 4, 5.) Lib. ii. c. 8. Again, 1. From the dignity of his person, (Col. ii. 3, 9. Cant. v. 9—16.) fitting him, as God and man, to be our Redeemer and the ground of our faith. 2. From his office as Mediator between God and man on our account. 3. From the inestimable blessings that flow from him. c. 13. ' Christum illi soli annunciant vere, et uti oportet, qui in illo solo docent omnem spem salutis humanæ repositam, qui per illum solum agnoscunt divitias gratiæ Divinæ ad nos derivari.' Dav. in Col. i. 28.

arms of such a Redeemer, who " is able" and willing " to save to the uttermost those that come unto God by him"—that they may with all ready obedience, and by the constraining power of the love of Christ, yield up themselves to the government of this Prince of Peace, by whom " the Prince of this world is judged and cast out," his " works destroyed," and we for this end " bought with a price," that we should " not be our own," but his that bought us ; nor " live any longer unto ourselves," but unto him that " loved us, and died for us, and rose again."

" *Preach Christ Jesus the Lord*." " Determine to know nothing among your people, but Christ crucified." Let his name and grace, his spirit and love, triumph in the midst of all your sermons. Let your great end be, to glorify him in the heart, to render him amiable and precious in the eyes of his people, to lead them to him, as a sanctuary to protect them, a propitiation to reconcile them, a treasure to enrich them, a physician to heal them, an advocate to present them and their services to God, as wisdom to counsel them, as righteousness to justify, as sanctification to renew, as redemption to save. Let Christ *be the diamond to shine in the bosom of all your sermons.*[1]

II.—EXPERIMENTAL PREACHING OF THE GOSPEL.

' PERHAPS the theory of the Gospel was never better understood since the Apostles' day, than it is at present. But many, *who preach it*, or who profess it, seem to lay too much stress upon a systematical scheme of sentiments, and too little upon that life and power, that vital, experimental, and practical influence, which forms the character, and regulates the conduct, of an established Christian.'[2] Our statements may be full and simple, connected and unfettered ; but without an application of the didactic system to the sympathies of the heart, they will impart only a cold and uninfluential knowledge.   We would not indeed be always dealing with certain trains of spiritual exercises ; but to enter with minuteness into the varied feelings, difficulties, conflicts, and privileges, belonging to what Scougal aptly calls ' the life of God in the soul of man,' is most important.

[1] Works, pp. 1039, 1040.   An uniform edition of his works has been lately presented to the public, dedicated to the present Bishop of London.   The Christian Remembrancer justly ranks Bishop Reynolds as ' one of the most eminent among the Divines of the seventeenth century ;' and marks this edition of his works, as ' forming a most valuable accession to our stores of sound and masculine theology.'   November, 1826.
[2] Newton's Life of Grimshaw, p. 65.

The connection of this section with the preceding is obvious. Christian experience is the influence of doctrinal truth upon the affections. Except therefore we exhibit the principles of the truths of God, we cannot excite those exercises which connect the heart with him. That preaching, however, which is merely descriptive of Christian feelings, irrespective of their connection with Scriptural doctrine, is unsubstantial and defective ; whereas an intelligent statement of truth from the preacher's heart, naturally flows with experimental sympathy to the hearts of his people.

Much wisdom is required, to adopt this style of preaching with advantage. It includes the various degrees of religious impression ; the power of conviction ; the danger of stifling it ; and the best method of cherishing, deepening, and directing its influence. The power of Satan also—"taking" the multitude "captive at his will,"[1] and his active and too successful influence over the servants of God—the incessant working of native principles of corruption, combining with, and aiding, the grand designs of the enemy—all need to be most correctly delineated. Some important rules for the assurance of sincerity, and for a Scriptural "trial of the spirits, whether they be of God,"[2] will be appended to these discussions. The different offices of the Holy Spirit—"helping infirmities" in prayer ; convincing, enlightening, consoling, strengthening every part of the soul ; imprinting the Divine image, and bearing witness to his own work—these also will form full and interesting subjects for detailed exposition. The connexion of his work with the love and offices of Christ, and the mutual interest and communion subsisting between Him and his church, in every part and in every member ; will present the grand subject of the atonement in its vivid application, and in all its experimental consolations. This view of the scheme of the Gospel widely differs from the dry and abstract doctrinal statement. Its life consists not in the exposition, but in the application of the doctrine to the heart for the sanctification and comfort of the sincere Christian. Subjects of this character may occasionally form entire subjects of our pulpit discourses ; though perhaps it is better, that they should give a general tone and character to our Ministry. Scriptural exhortations, however, to caution and watchfulness, must be judiciously introduced, in order to obviate the just imputation of enthusiasm in ourselves, and the real danger of it in our people.

We need scarcely remark, that this interesting style of preaching presupposes a personal acquaintance with these exercises, and an

[1] 2 Tim. ii. 26.   [2] 1 John iv. 1.

individual interest in their privileges. It is experience alone that qualifies the Minister for usefulness, by enabling him to touch the tender strings of the heart, and to suit his instruction to the different cases, trials, and circumstances of his people.[1] 'When he has,' (as Witsius beautifully observes) 'not only heard something ; but seen, and handled, and tasted of the word of life, and has been taught, not by mere speculation, but by actual experience, what he has thus found out ; he safely inculcates, from the assured persuasions of his mind, and applies to every case, from his own knowledge of what is suitable to each.'[2] He must therefore expect. his full portion of painful exercises ; not only for his own humiliation, (a most needful preparation for his success); but also—like his Divine Master—to "give him the tongue of the learned, that he may know how to speak a word in season to him that is weary."[3] His taste of the innumerable trials, fears, complaints, and temptations of private Christians, will alone enable him to prescribe the specific remedy for each varying complaint, and to exercise the sympathy of membership with them all.[4]

The Apostle in his letters to the churches, introduces occasional reference to his own experience with considerable effect.[5] And when we can tell our people—'We have passed with you through the same tribulations, conflicted with the same difficulties, fallen into the same snares, and overcome the same temptations'—this excites a reciprocity of interest ; and in the midst of present distress they "thank God" for us, "and take courage" for themselves. Addresses of this character flow directly to the heart with a warmth and impressiveness, like the enlivening glow of the sun, as contrasted with the cold clearness of moon-light. The way-post directs the traveller, but itself remains unmoved : but the living guide becomes a companion to sympathize with, enliven, and uphold his fellow. The frequency and suitableness, however, of these references must be cautiously regulated ; lest we " preach ourselves" instead of " Christ Jesus the Lord," and set up our own experience as a standard for our people—thus putting the servant in the Master's place—a worm in the place of God.

Our Pastoral Ministry will here supply much valuable assistance. In commenting upon the Epistle to the Galatians, we might present a faithful portraiture of the sin and danger of self-

[1] 'Any little knowledge of my own heart, and of the Lord's dealings with my own soul, hath helped me much in my sermons ; and I have observed, that I have been apt to deliver that which I had experienced, in a more feeling and earnest manner, than other matters.' Brown's Life and Remains.
[2] De Vero Theologo.   [3] Isaiah l. 4.   [4] 2 Cor. i. 3—7.
[5] Rom. vii. Phil. iii. 1 Tim. i. 12—15. et alia.

righteousness. Yet an observation of the diversified workings of this subtle principle in our people would furnish the materials of a more close and individual application. The features of the different classes of our hearers, drawn from the most experimental divines, will have far less of reality and conviction, than those which we have sketched from life in the routine of pastoral intercourse.

The advantages of this style of preaching are various and important. Not to speak of the echo that it finds in the hearts of our people—*it gives a peculiar flexibility to our Ministry*, and enables us to speak distinctly to the varying .exigencies of people. *It enables us also to make the proper use of our own experience;* not making it the standard of our Ministry; nor on the other hand regarding it as the cabinet of curiosities for private inspection—but working it up as useful materials for our ordinary addresses. *This character of Ministry is also usually attended with a peculiar blessing.* 'I always find' (said the late Mr. Richmond) 'that, when I speak from the inward feelings of my own heart, with respect to the workings of inbred corruption, earnest desire after salvation, a sense of my own nothingness, and my Saviour's fulness; the people hear, feel, are edified. and strengthened. Whereas, if I descend to mere formal or cold explanation of particulars, which do not affect the great question—"What must I do to be saved"—my hearers and I grow languid and dull together, and no good is done.'[1] The study of the Apostolical Epistles will fully illustrate this style of preaching. What interesting details of lively experience are brought before us in Rom. viii. ! How widely different is that wonderful portion of Holy Writ from a dry statement of abstract truth ! It is the direct influence of Evangelical doctrine and precept, in the speaking testimony of the love, peace, holy fellowship, conflict, joy, and triumph of the consistent believer.

Another use of this mode of preaching, is, *its suitableness to all Christians alike.* " As in water face answereth to face, so doth the heart of man to man."[2] As the features of the human countenance, (though so varied, that each may be considered an original) in all leading particulars are invariably the same ; so in Christian experience identity of character is preserved in the midst of an endless diversity of feature. All being the " children," under the same Divine teaching,[3] will be taught substantially the same lessons. And though the course of human instruction, or incidental circumstances, will individualize the several cases in their different

---

[1] Richmond's Life, p. 184.   [2] Prov. xxvii. 19.   [3] Isa. liv. 13.

degrees of proficiency ; yet the same system of experimental instruction will equally apply to all.   The young and the more
advanced will be alike profited by the detailed sketch of the ways
and means, in which the principles of the heavenly life are im-
planted, cherished, and maintained.   Conviction also may flash
even upon the unbeliever's mind—' If this be Christianity, I have
yet to learn it, to feel it, and to enjoy it.'   Who knoweth, but such
a thought may give birth to a desire, and form itself into a prayer,
which may prove the commencing era of a new life, such as will
find its full scope and influence only in the boundless expanse of
eternity !

III.—PRACTICAL PREACHING OF THE GOSPEL.

THE Gospel may be preached in all the accuracy of doctrinal
statement, and in all the richness of experimental comfort ; and
yet may be only as " a very lovely song of one that hath a
pleasant voice."[1] Its practical details are often a ground of offence, where its doctrinal expositions have been listened to with
interest, and even its spiritual enjoyments been tasted with self-
delusive delight.[2]   It is more easy to deal with a darkened understanding, and with excitable feelings, than with a corrupt will.
And if the work of God were to end with the understanding and
affections, without any corresponding practical obligations, the
message would be far less offensive to the natural heart.   But
the Minister will feel, that the " declaration of all the counsel of
God" would be as incomplete without a direct and detailed enforcement of practical obligation,[3] as in the absence of all reference to
doctrine or experience.   Let these three departments of preaching
be exhibited in their mutual connexion, dependence, and use ; and
the head, heart, and life, will be simultaneously influenced.

The connection of *practical with doctrinal preaching* is of the
utmost importance.   Some have thought that the doctrine of
Christ crucified is of far greater moment than the details of obligation—as if the one did not necessarily belong to the other.   To inculcate Christian duty upon the basis of Christian doctrine—to
represent it as the natural exercise of gratitude for redeeming love
—to exhibit the operation of heavenly motives flowing from the
doctrine of the cross—to mark the union of the soul with Christ,
as the only source of holiness ; and to trace the acceptance of the

[1] Ezek. xxxiii. 32.   [2] See Matt. xiii. 20.   John v. 35.   Heb. vi. 5.
[3] See Matt. xxviii. 19, 20.

fruits of this union solely to his atonement and mediation—to connect all relative duties with the doctrine of Christ[1]—this was the apostolical—the only efficient—system of practical preaching; this is raising a holy fabric upon the only "foundation laid in Zion." Bishop Horsley's testimony is most decisive on this point —'The practice of religion will always thrive, in proportion as its doctrines are generally understood, and firmly received : and the practice will degenerate and decay, in proportion as the doctrine is misunderstood and neglected. It is true, therefore, that it is the great duty of a preacher of the Gospel to press the practice of its precepts upon the consciences of men. But then it is equally true, that it is his duty to enforce this practice in a particular way, namely, by inculcating its doctrines. The motives, which the revealed doctrines furnish, are the only motives he has to do with, and *the only motives, by which religious duty can be effectually enforced.*[2]

Bishop Horne has well observed—'To preach practical sermons, as they are called—i. e. sermons upon virtues and vices—without inculcating those great Scripture truths of redemption and grace, and which alone can excite and enable us to forsake sin, and follow after righteousness ; what is it, but to put together the wheels, and set the hands of a watch, forgetting the spring, which is to make them all go ?'[3] In another place he remarks to the same effect, with his happy power of illustration—one ' thing indeed we do affirm, because we can prove it from Scripture, that whoever preaches and enforces moral duties, without justification and sanctification preceding, may as well declaim upon the advantages of walking, to a man that can neither stir hand nor foot : such is the natural impotence of the soul to do any good thing, till it is justified and sanctified ! Let the declamation be ever so elegant, St. Peter's plain address, I suppose, would be worth ten thousand of them, to a cripple—"In the name of Jesus of Nazareth, rise up and walk." Such is the difference between an Ethical Divine and a Christian preacher !'[4]

---

[1] Such as the duties of husbands, Eph. v. 25—wives, 22—servants, Eph. vi. 5; Col. iii. 1. Titus ii. 10—subjects, 1 Peter ii. 13—25—evil speaking, Titus iii. 2—7. Compare also the Apostle's preaching to Felix, Acts xxiv. 21, 25. The illative particle (*therefore*) significantly illustrates this connexion and dependence. Rom. xii. 1; Ephes. iv. 1; Col. iii. 1, &c.

[2] Charges, p. 10.   [3] Bishop Horne's Essays, p. 162.

[4] Bishop Horne on preaching the Gospel, pp. 7, 8. ' A morality more elevated and pure, than is to be met with in the pages of Seneca or Epictetus, will breathe through your sermons founded on a basis, which every understanding can comprehend, and enforced by sanctions, which nothing but the utmost stupidity can despise—a morality, of which the love of God, and a devoted attachment to the Redeemer, are the plastic soul, which, pervading every limb, and expressing itself in every lineament of the new crea-

In illustration of this subject—the doctrine of the Trinity is stated in connexion with Christian worship, and with the exercise of love to God.[1] From the doctrine of the incarnation is drawn at one time an arrow of conviction ;[2] at other times it is the motive for humility,[3] love,[4] or obedience.[5] The atonement is displayed, as the principle of hatred of sin,[6] and love to the Saviour.[7] The doctrine. of election (as we have lately remarked[8]) is always linked with personal holiness, and an incentive to persevering diligence.[9] The sovereignty and freeness of grace are the principles of laborious activity,[10] not the allowance of Antinomian ease.

Thus the doctrines of the Gospel not only explain the nature and obligation, but are themselves the principles—nay the only principles—of holiness. We must live every moment by faith ; and as we live, we shall love—overcome the world—crucify sin—delight in the service of God. No mere precepts will extirpate the natural love of sin, or infuse this new bias in the heart. The doctrine of faith alone effects this mighty change, by exhibiting Christ as the source of life, and *detailing* all the exercises of holy practice, flowing from that life.[11] We say—*detailing*—because the Apostle (whose preaching in this respect is our model)—describes the new man, not only in his general appearance, but in the delineation of his every feature and movement. He follows out the general inculcation of holiness into the distinct enumeration of particular duties, and reproof of particular sins, as his knowledge of the state of his people dictated to him.[12]

The connexion of *practical with experimental preaching* is also of considerable moment. An exclusive standard of experimental preaching, and an unvaried representation of the joys of the Gospel—irrespective of practical obligations, would be a most unfaithful and sickly dispensation of our Divine commission. We must show Christian privilege to be a principle not of inactive indulgence—but of habitual devotedness to God. It is, when the man of God is realizing his interest in an heavenly portion ; when a sense of pardon is applied to his soul ; when the seal of the Spirit

ture, gives it a beauty all his own. As it is the genuine fruit of just and affecting views of Divine truth, you will never sever it from its parent stock, nor indulge the fruitless hope of leading men to holiness, without strongly imbuing them with the spirit of the Gospel. Truth and holiness are, in the Christian system, so intimately allied, that the warm and faithful inculcation of the one, lays the only foundation for the other.' Hall's Sermon, p. 39.

[1] Matt. xxviii. 19. 2 Thess. iii. 5.   [2] Ye have *killed the Holy One*. Acts iii. 14, 15.
[3] Phil. ii. 4—6.   [4] 2 Cor. viii. 9.   [5] Matt. xvii. 5. Acts iii. 22, 23.
[6] Rom. v. vi.   [7] 2 Cor. v. 14, 15.   [8] See p. 224.   [9] 2 Pet. i. 10.   [10] Phil. ii. 12, 13.
[11] See an admirable sermon on this subject preached at the Visitation of the Archdeacon of Wells. By Ralph Lyon, M.A.
[12] See Rom. xii. ; Eph. iv. v. throughout.

is impressed upon his heart ; when his soul is invigorated by " fellowship with the Father, and with his Son Jesus Christ"—then it is, that the grateful enquiry springs forth,—" What shall I render unto the Lord for all his benefits towards me ?"[1] The detail of Christian duty is the practical expression of his gratitude for experimental privileges. His relative connexions are now improved for increased activity in the discharge of every social obligation—" that he may adorn the doctrine of God his Saviour in all things." Thus (as has been beautifully observed) 'Christ is the soul *of duty, of grace, of privilege*. Christ is the light and warmth, which cheer and an imate to exertion. It is the promise, and not the precept ; it is encouragement, and not exaction ; it is grace, and not nature, which consecrates a course of moral beauty and blessing, and convinces the believer, that, whether grace is to be exercised, or duty discharged, he is eminently " God's workmanship," " the new man, which after God is created in righteousness and true holiness." '[2] Scriptural preaching will expound doctrines practically, and practice doctrinally ; omitting neither, but stating neither independent of the other, or unconnected with experimental religion. We are sometimes indeed said to deny or enervate our practical obligations, by insisting upon full statements of doctrine, distinct, but not separate, from practice. But 'how' (remarks Bishop Horne) ' we can be said to deny the existence of moral duties, because we preach faith, the root from whence they spring, I know not ; unless he that plants a vine, does by that action deny the existence of grapes. The fruit receives its goodness from the tree, not the tree from the fruit, which does not make the tree good, but shows it to be so. So works receive all their goodness from faith, not faith from works ; which do not themselves justify, but show a prior justification of the soul that produces them.'[3]

But if some be defective in their doctrinal statements, others are equally so in their practical enforcements. They withhold the details of Christian practice, lest they should entrench upon the unconditional freeness of the Gospel covenant. They expect practice to flow necessarily from the abstract exposition of doctrine, without the superfluous aid of hortatory persuasions. Yet did not the Apostles thus leave the tree to grow of itself, and put forth its leaves, buddings and fruit, without active care and nurture. They

---

[1] Psalm cxvi. 12. Comp. Isa. vi. 6—8.   [2] Budd on Infant Baptism, p. 446.
[3] Bishop Horne on preaching the Gospel, pp. 5—11. It is almost needless to remark the consonance of this view with the truly Scriptural, but deeply humbling doctrine of Article xiii. Upon this view Augustine justly denominated the moral virtues of Pagan philosophers, 'splendida peccata.' 'Per fidem venitur ad opera; non per opera venitur ad fidem'—was one of the sententious aphorisms of the old Divines.

were not satisfied with supplying their churches with a principle, and leaving them to their own search for a rule and a remembrancer. Who so minute in his detail of practical duties, as he that is most full in his statements of Scriptural doctrine? The latter chapters of St. Paul's Epistles (as we have hinted) expound the practical obligations in immediate connexion with Evangelical doctrine; so that a misguided commentator, or preacher, would find himself in considerable perplexity, either in dismissing his exposition of his Epistles at the close of his doctrinal statement, or in pursuing the practical parts with a disrelish upon his own mind. Are not the closing chapters of the Epistles component parts of the New Testament revelation? And did they not form a part of Apostolical instruction to professing churches? We fear that the restricted Ministry often shows a disrelish to vital holiness (tolerable in general statements, but revolting in detail), or at least to a close and searching scrutiny of the heart, and to the measurement of conduct by the uncompromising standard of the Gospel. Men will be Christians, so long as articles of faith are concerned.—They can "understand all mysteries and all knowledge." But to be told (even upon the authority of an Apostle) that "faith, if it hath not works, is dead, being alone,"[1]—is in their view legality, inconsistent with the freeness and simplicity of the Gospel. And yet in conformity to "the teaching wisdom given unto their beloved brother Paul," the other Apostles interwove their practical exhortations into the thread of their doctrinal instructions; and thus they raised a goodly superstructure upon the solid foundation of Scriptural truth.[2] The wholesome doctrine of Christ includes the path as well as the hope—the fruitfulness as well as the consolations—of the Gospel; so that the separation of the doctrine from the holiness of the Gospel is as defective a statement, as the disunion of holiness from the doctrine of the cross. Partial preaching will produce a luxuriant crop of partial hearers, to whom a large part of Scripture is useless; full of notions, excited in their feelings, forward in their profession; but unsubdued in their habits and tempers, equally destitute of the root, the life, activity, fruitfulness, enjoyment, perseverance, of vital religion. Nor is this tone of Min-

---

[1] James ii. 17.

[2] Upon this model ought the Ministers of the Gospel to form their preaching—Ministers are not to instruct only, or to exhort only, but to do both. To exhort men to holiness and the duties of the Christian life, without instructing them in the doctrine of faith, is to build a house without a foundation. And on the other side, *to instruct the mind in the knowledge of Divine things, and neglect the pressing of that practice and power of godliness, which is the undivided companion of true faith; is to forget the building, that ought to be raised upon that foundation once laid, which is likewise a point of very great folly.* Leighton on 1 Peter ii. 11.

istry less hurtful to the sincere professor of the Gospel. In the neglect of habitual self-examination, and a well-ordered conversation, the light of orthodox profession will partake more of the speculative than of an influential character ; and the " knowledge that puffeth up" will be often substituted for the " charity that edifieth." Let not therefore the dreaded imputation of being thought moral preachers, deter us from inculcating the requirements, as well as illustrating the doctrines, of the Gospel. Practical preaching is needed to sift the false professors of religion, and to quicken sincere Christians. The management of it is perhaps more difficult than doctrinal discussions. Yet is it consistent with the most unfettered display of Scriptural doctrine, and indeed mainly constitutes its perfection and effectiveness.[1]

IV.—APPLICATORY PREACHING OF THE GOSPEL.

BISHOP DAVENANT remarks, that 'the philosopher's maxim—that every action is done by the touch—has a principal place in the sacred action of preaching. The doctrine *generally proposed*, is occupied, as it were, in a distant object, and can never reach the soul itself; but *its specific application* comes in a manner into the very interior of the mind, and touches and penetrates it.'[2] This application forms the life and interest of preaching, and (what is more important) is the grand instrument of conviction. We pass over the lesser matters by the way, to hasten to our main design—" the saving of ourselves, and of them that hear us."[3] ' For this end we must show them' (as Archbishop Secker reminds us) ' from first to last, that we are not merely saying good things in their presence ; but directing what we say to them personally, as a matter which concerns them beyond expression. More general discourses they often want skill to take home to themselves, and oftener yet, inclination ; so they sit all the while stupidly regardless of what is delivered. Therefore we must interest them in it, by calling upon them to observe, by asking them questions to an-

[1] 'Mr. Robinson'—observes his Biographer—'was eminently a practical preacher; generally he had much of Evangelical doctrine in his sermons; sometimes he was experimental; but he was always practical. Never did he discuss a doctrine without drawing from it strict practical conclusions, and closely applying them to the conscience; never did he detail Christian experience without specifically pointing out its practical tendencies; often he entered very minutely and particularly into a full and heart-searching developement of distinct parts of duty: insomuch that some of his hearers, who did not greatly approve his doctrinal opinions, were led highly to extol his Ministry, as being replete with useful family instructions.' Vaughan's Life, pp. 309, 310.
[2] Dav. in Col. i. 21.   [3] 1 Tim. iv. 16. ' Semper ad eventum festinat.' Horace.

swer silently in their own mind, by every prudent incitement to follow us closely.'[1] Massillon's preaching is said to have been so pointed, that no one stopped to criticise or admire. Each carried away the arrow fastened in his heart, considering himself to be the person addressed, and having neither time, thought, nor inclination to apply it to others.[2]

We must not expect our hearers to apply to themselves such unpalatable truths. So unnatural is this habit of personal application, that most will fit the doctrine to any one but themselves; and their general and unmeaning commendation too plainly bespeaks the absence of personal interest and concern. The preacher must make the application himself.[3] The "goads and nails" must not be laid by, as if the posts would knock them in; but "*fastened* by the masters of assemblies."[4] To insist therefore upon general truths without distributive application; or to give important directions without clearing the way for their improvement— this is not, according to the design of our Ministry, to lay the truth at every man's door, to press it upon every man's heart, and to "give to them their portion of meat in due season."[5] That tone of preaching, that smoothes down or qualifies revolting truths— that does not cause the hearers some uneasiness—that does not bear directly upon them as individuals, but feebly illustrates the living power of the word;[6] nor will it ever "compel sinners to come in"[7] to the Gospel. It will probably only produce the heartless reply—"How forcible are right words! but what doth your arguing reprove?"[8] This palatable ministry, that blunts the edge of "the

[1] Charges, pp. 181, 182.
[2] Mr. Cecil adopted Lavater's practice—to fix on certain persons in his congregation, as representatives of the different classes of his hearers—to keep these persons in his eye in the composition of his sermons—and to endeavour to mould his subjects, so as to meet their respective cases. This rule obviously requires much judgment to avoid that personality, which—except in particular cases, (1 Tim. v. 20.) belongs to private—not to public rebukes. (Matt. xviii. 15.) Perhaps the better general rule would be to aim at that direct exhibition of truth, which would compel conscience to do its own work in individual application. Compare Dwight's Sermons, Vol. ii. 451—454.
[3] See 2 Sam. xii. 1—7. When John preached generally, "Herod heard him gladly;" when he came to particulars of application—"It is not lawful for thee to have thy brother's wife"—the preacher lost his head. 'The Minister' (as an excellent old Divine observes) 'should desire to have that knowledge of all his hearers, that he may be able to speak as particularly to every one as is possible. (Jer. vi. 27.) Though he may not make private faults public, or so touch the sin, as to note and disgrace the sinner; yet he may apply his reproofs particularly, so that the guilty party may know and feel himself touched with the reproof. We must in preaching aim as directly as we can at him, whom we desire to profit. Our doctrine must be as a garment, fitted for the body it is made for; a garment that is fit for every body, is fit for nobody. Paul saith of himself, that in his preaching he laboured to *admonish every man, to present every man perfect in Christ Jesus.*' Hildersham on John iv. Lect. lxxx.   [4] Eccles. xii. 11.
[5] 2 Tim. ii. 15, with Luke xii. 42.   [6] Heb. iv. 12.   [7] Luke xiv. 23.
[8] Job vi. 25. It was observed of Philip Henry, that 'he did not shoot the arrow of the word *over the heads* of his audience, in the flourishes of affected rhetoric, nor *under*

sword of the Spirit," in order to avoid the reproach of the cross, brings upon the preacher a most tremendous responsibility.

Personal application formed the nerve of the preaching of the Jewish prophets,[1] and of our Lord's public and individual addresses. His reproofs to the Scribes and Pharisees, to the Sadducees and Herodians, had distinct reference to their particular sins.[2] In his treatment of the young ruler,[3] and the woman of Samaria,[4] he avoided general remark, to point his instructions to their besetting and indulged sin—' talking to their thoughts,' (as a sensible writer has observed in the case of the young man) 'as we do to each other's words.'[5] Peter's hearers " were pricked to the heart" by his applicatory address.[6] Even the hardest heart—the most stubborn sinner—is made to smart under the point of the two-edged sword.[7]

Nothing of this kind is found in the instructions of the heathen sages. Plato, Aristotle, and Tully, dealt out to their disciples cold and indefinite descriptions of certain virtues and vices; but with no endeavours to impress the mind with personal conviction. Horace and Juvenal attempted something in this way; but in a spirit more likely to excite ridicule and disgust, than to produce any practical result. Their system was a mass of inert matter, without action. Such probably also were the instructions of the Jewish teachers—consisting chiefly (as the Evangelist implies) of spiritless disputations, drawn from the traditions of men, with no power to work upon the mind, affections, or conscience.[8]

Preaching, in order to be effective, must be reduced from vague generalities, to a tangible, individual character—coming home to every man's business, and even to his bosom. He goes on in a slumbering routine of customary attendance. Nothing but the Preacher's blow— the *hand not lifted towards him, but actually reaching him*—will rouse him to consideration. There is no need to mention names. The truth brought into contact with the conscience speaks for itself.[9] Even the ungodly can bear forcible sermons, without any well-directed aim. The general sermons, that are preached to every body, in fact are preached to no body. They will therefore suit the congregations of the last century, or in a

their feet by homely expressions, but *to their hearts in close and lively application.*' Life, p. 59. [1] Isaiah lviii. 1. Micah iii. 8.
[2] Comp. Matt. xxii. xxiii. [3] Matt. xix. 16—22.
[4] John iv. 7—26. Comp. Bishop of Winchester's Min. Char. of Christ, ch. 13.
[5] Benson's Life of Christ, p. 300. [6] Acts ii. 22—37.
[7] 1 Kings xvi. 20. xxii. 8. Amos vii. 9. Luke iv. 28. Acts v. 33. Rev. xi. 10.
[8] Matt. vii. 29, with Mark vii. 1—9.
[9] Compare Matt. xxi. 45. John viii. 9. Often have Ministers been accused of preaching at individuals sermons written without the slightest knowledge of their cases. What is this, but the piercing of the two-edged sword? 1 Cor. xiv. 25.

foreign land, as well as the people before our eyes. 'Such discourses' (as Bishop Stillingfleet remarks) 'have commonly little
effect on the people's minds. But if any thing moves them, it is
particular application as to such things, in which their consciences
are concerned.'[1] We must therefore preach *to* our people, as well
as *before* them. 'The consciences of the audience' should 'feel
the hand of the Preacher searching it, and every individual know
where to class himself. The Preacher, who aims at doing good,
will endeavour above all things to insulate his hearers, to place each
of them apart, and render it impossible for him to escape by losing
himself in the crowd. At the day of judgment, the attention excited by the surrounding scene, the strange aspect of nature, the
dissolution of the elements and the last trump—will have no
other effect, than to cause the reflections of the sinner to return
with a more overwhelming tide on his own character, his sentence,
his unchanging destiny; and, amid the innumerable millions
which surround him, he will "mourn apart." It is thus the Christian Minister should endeavour to prepare the tribunal of conscience, and turn the eyes of every one of his hearers upon himself.'[2]

But this applicatory mode should extend to the consolatory as
well as to the awakening exhortations of the Gospel; bringing
home the general promises of forgiveness to every distinct case of
penitence and faith; of direction, support, or comfort, to each

[1] Duties and Rights of the Parochial Clergy, p 31. 'General declarations against
vice and sin, rouse men to consider and look about them; but they often want effect,
because they only raise confused apprehensions of things, and undeterminate propen-
sions to action; the which usually, before men thoroughly perceive or resolve what they
should practice, do decay and vanish. As he that cries out 'fire' doth stir up people, and
inspireth them with a kind of hovering tendency every way, yet no man thence to purpose moveth, until he be distinctly informed, where the mischief is; (then do they, who
apprehend themselves concerned, run hastily to oppose it) so, till we particularly discern,
where our offences lie, till we distinctly know the heinous nature and the mischievous
consequences of them—we scarce will effectually apply ourselves to correct them.
Whence it is requisite, that men should be particularly acquainted with their sins, and
by proper arguments be dissuaded from them.' Barrow's Sermons. 'General discourses
do not so immediately tend to reform the lives of men, because they fall among the crowd,
and do not touch the consciences of particular persons in so sensible and awakening a
manner, as when we treat of particular doctrines and sins, and endeavour to put men
upon the practice of the one, and reclaim them from the other, by proper arguments
taken from the word of God, and from the nature of particular virtues and vices.' Tillotson's Sermons, folio, p. 491. 'The preacher who only flourishes in general notions,
and does not aim at some particular argument, is like an unwise fisher, who spreads
his net to the empty air, where he cannot expect any success to his labours.' Bishop
Wilkins's Eccles.
[2] Hall's Sermons, &c. pp. 23, 24. George Herbert's 'Parson was used to preach with
particularizing of his speech; *for particulars ever touch and wake more than generals.*'
Chap. vii.—'Let every preacher so preach, as every wise preacher ought to preach; not
only *unto men* or *unto* men's ears, but *into* men's ears, and *into* men's hearts also, if possible. It is easier to find out a sermon to preach *unto the people*, than to find out this
skill and wisdom, how to be able to distil or preach a sermon *into the people.*' More's
Wise Preacher.

particular emergency, as if they had been made for it alone. The property of a good portrait well describes a good sermon—that it looks directly at all, though placed in different situations, as if it were ready to speak to each—" *I have a message from God unto thee.*"[1]

The doctrine of the sermon requires wisdom; the application, earnestness. The one needs a clear head; the other a warm heart. The discussion of our subjects must be in a straight line. Considerable latitude is allowable in the application. Many points may be purposely omitted in the course of discussion, to be here enforced with more effect. We may here also fix upon the conscience many things, which, in the progress of the sermon, were perhaps delivered in the abstract.[2]

The application of our discourse will furnish ample field for the exercise of natural talents and eloquence, diversified according to the character of the discussion. In *historical* subjects, it may be drawn either from some prominent feature of the record, or from some collateral circumstances connected with it. In *doctrinal* subjects, it would be usually deduced in the way of inference, illustrating the practical tendency, or the experimental comfort of the doctrine. In a *practical* subject it would naturally flow from the detailed exposition of Christian duty; some searching inquiry into our influential acknowledgment of the obligation; or some clear exhibition of its reasonableness and advantage, together with the most effectual methods of overcoming opposing hindrances. In *typical or parabolical subjects* it would be sought from the anti-type or doctrine, to which the figure was related. The just application of *prophetical texts* requires much care and caution. In the prophecies *relating to Christ*, the path lies in the direct track of evangelical preaching. The prophecies *relating to the Church*

---

[1] Judges iii. 20. See Bishop Burnet's admirable remarks upon application at the close of our discourses. Pastoral Care, ch. ix. on Preaching. Also Claude's observations, with Mr. Simeon's notes appended. Mr. Alleine's preaching beautifully illustrated the 'heart and soul,' which the Bishop would bring to this point.—' So loth was he to labour in vain, and to pass from one discourse to another, as one unconcerned whether he had sown any good seed or no on the hearts of his hearers; that in the close of his applicatory part on any text, he ever expressed his great unwillingness to leave that subject without some assurances, that he had not "fought" in that spiritual warfare, ' as one that beateth the air;" when also he expressed his great fear, lest he should, after all his most importunate warnings, leave them as he found them. And here, with how much holy taking rhetoric did he frequently expostulate the case with impenitent sinners, in words too many to mention, and yet too weighty to be forgotten; vehemently urging them to come to some good resolve, before he and they parted, and to make their choice either of life or death!' Alleine's Life and Letters.

[2] Quintilian remarks, that the power of the conclusion depends upon the warmth of its appeal to the heart. To this part the highest powers of address should be reserved. Here, if ever, it is proper to open all the fountains of eloquence. Here, if we have succeeded in other parts, we may take possession of our hearers' minds.

—whether fulfilled or unfulfilled, whether referring to her present or prospective privileges and tribulations—set forth our interest in her promises, our sympathy in her trials, our anticipations of the glorious prospects of her triumphant state, or our danger from judgments impending over her. The *prophetic declarations concerning the world*, give full scope for awakening alarm and encouragement; how certain! how tremendous the danger! how instant the urgency to humble ourselves before the power of our Judge, and to seek a lot among his obedient and happy people!

These remarks, however, chiefly suppose the *application to be left to the close of the sermon*. But Dr. Doddridge's advice was— 'Remember, that the final application, reflections, or inferences, *are not the only places*, in which to introduce your addresses to the converted and unconverted.'[1] Indeed this practice is fraught with many disadvantages. The formality and routine of the address detract from its power; while sudden, well-directed appeals—naturally arising from the subject—are far more calculated to awaken the slumbering interest. Add to which—the closing address too often falls powerless upon wearied attention; or the preacher's mind, in the sight or anticipation of this, passes over the materials for conviction with undigested haste. The method of perpetual application, therefore, *where the subject will admit of it*, is probably best calculated for effect—applying each head distinctly; and addressing separate classes at the close with suitable exhortation, warning, or encouragement.[2] The Epistle to the Hebrews furnishes a most complete model of this scheme. Argumentative throughout, connected in . its train of reasoning, and logical in its deductions—each successive link is interrupted by some personal and forcible conviction; while the continuity of the chain is preserved entire to the end. Thus the superiority of Christ to the angels (the first step of the argument) is improved as a motive for attention to the Gospel, and a warning against the neglect of it.[3] His superiority to Moses next suggests an encouraging excitement to stedfastness;[4] the mention of whose name naturally introduces the history of the nation, to whom the inspired penman was addressing himself; and thus

---

[1] Doddridge's Preaching Lectures, Lect. 10.

[2] 'You have been half an hour,' (said the late Mr. Robinson to a clergyman) 'without one word directly aimed at the conscience.' Life, p. 217. His own 'Scripture Characters' (originally delivered in the form of sermons) are admirable specimens of this mode of address. See also Claude's Sermon on Phil. ii. 12—Mr. Simeon's Sermon on the Gospel Message, appended to his edition of Claude—the Sermons of Walker of Edinburgh (as for instance, on 2 Cor. vi. 1,) and Vitringa's Sermon on the history of Jabez, (1 Chron. iv. 10.) in his Methodus Homiletica. 'As much as possible, sermons ought to be carried on in a strain of direct address to the audience.' Blair's Lectures.

[3] Heb. i. ii.   [4] Ibid. iii. 1—6.

brings out solemn caution and animating encouragement, in the view of their typical character and privileges.[1] Passing onward— the display of his superior excellency to the Levitical priesthood is varied with practical exhortation, fresh views of evangelical privilege, or some new and cheering glance at the all-sufficiency of his work.[2] The exhibition of the whole system of the Jewish economy —shadowing forth the incomparably more substantial privileges of the Gospel—is intermixed with heart-stirring motives to the exercise of faith, love, and general devotedness.[3] The concluding sketch of the Old Testament history, beautifully illustrates the identity of Christian principle under both dispensations :[4] while the various practical inferences deduced from it are well calculated to instruct and enliven the sincere believer under all his trials and perplexities.[5]

This method of current application is however the most difficult form of address. The skilful introduction of suitable topics, and the decent dismissal of them severally, before they become worn out—peculiar choice of thoughts and expressions—affectionate impressiveness and animation of manner, are indispensable to give to this mode of address its full effect. Hortatory subjects are on the whole best adapted, and doctrinal subjects the least fitting, for this way of preaching. It is not necessary to analyse exery minute particle of the text; but far preferable, with due regard to textual exposition, to select the most impressive and awakening topics, forming the prominent features of the passage under consideration. This mode also, least of all, can be adopted as a system. Few men are capable of sustaining it equably, and with a suitable adaptation to the ever-varying occasions, and to the characters and circumstances of their hearers. It requires an elevated tone of excitement under judicious control, so as to be searching, appropriate, solemn, and animated throughout. Much depends, therefore, upon the preacher's state of mind. To enter in an unequal frame upon an exercise, which demands his full powers of interest and vigour, would probably end in personal discomfort to himself, and in total failure of effect.

Closeness, faithfulness, discrimination, and love, will be the characteristics of this system ; the matter of which will be gathered from an accurate acquaintance with the individual cases of our hearers, and from a full display of the infinite riches of grace and glory, and of the tremendously awful consequences of "neglecting so great salvation."

---

[1] Heb. iii. 7—19. iv. 1—11.   [2] Ibid. iv. 12—16. v.—vii.   [3] Ibid. viii.—x.
[4] Ibid xi.   [5] Ibid. xii. xiii.

V.—DISCRIMINATING PREACHING OF THE GOSPEL.

" THE discerning of spirits"[1]—including an accurate knowledge of the principles of human character and action—is a spiritual gift yet continued to the Church, for the wise and edifying discharge of our office.   Whatever natural acuteness may belong to it, yet, *as a spiritual qualification*, it is that heavenly wisdom, of which the Preacher needs a double portion, and which is " given liberally unto him"[2] that asketh.

The losing sight of the wide distinction between a credible profession and a spiritual conversion has occasioned that too frequent and most dangerous mode of accrediting all persons as Christians, upon their acknowledgment of a national creed, or external regulations.   It is as if either we had no unconverted hearers among us, or had no care about their conversion.   One great end of our preaching is, distinctly to trace the line of demarcation *between the Church and the world.*[3]   Our Lord clearly marked this line of separation at the close of his sermon on the mount.[4]   Boldness in declaring it will give a high tone of decision to our message.[5]   As ministers of the word, we recognise but two classes among men— those that " are of God—and the whole world that lieth in wickedness."[6]   They are described by *their state before God*, as righteous or wicked[7]—by *their knowledge or ignorance of the Gospel*, as spiritual or natural men[8]—by *their special regard to Christ*, as believers or unbelievers[9]—by *their interest in the Spirit of God*, " being in the Spirit, or having not the Spirit of Christ"[10]— by *their habits of life*, " walking after and minding, the things of the Spirit, or the things of the flesh"[11]—by their respective *rules of conduct*, the word of God, or " the course of this world,"[12]—by *the Masters whom they respectively obey*, the servants of God, or the servants of Satan[13]—by *the road in which they travel*, the narrow way or the broad road[14]—by *the ends to which their roads are carrying them*, life or death—heaven or hell.[15]   The line of demarcation, therefore, between these two classes, including the numerous modifications belonging to each, is like that " great

---

[1] 1 Cor. xii. 10.   [2] James i. 5.
[3] See this subject drawn out with equal power and accuracy in Dr. Chalmers' Sermons at the Tron Church, pp. 361, 362, and Watts' Humb. Attempt, p. 41.
[4] Matt. vii. 24—29.   [5] See Jer. xv. 19.   [6] 1 John v. 19.
[7] Prov. xiv. 32.   Mal. iii. 18.   [8] 1 Cor. ii. 14, 15.   [9] Mark xvi. 16. John iii. 18, 36.
[10] Rom. viii. 9.   [11] Ibid. v. 1, 5.   [12] Ps. cxix. 105. Eph. ii. 2.
[13] Rom. vi. 16.   [14] Matt. vii. 13, 14.   [15] Rom. viii. 13. Matt. xxv. 46.

gulf,"[1] which separates the two divisions of the eternal state.   There can be no more amalgamation between them, than between light and darkness—between Christ and Belial.   Nor is there any greater delusion for the consciences of the unconverted, or greater perplexity to the sincere but unintelligent Christian, than an indiscriminate application of the Gospel to them both in one general mass.[2] Nor again—is the bold tracing of this broad line sufficient for our purpose.   To many, who would not dispute its correctness, it would bring no conviction.   The painter's broad stroke is wholly insufficient to give an accurate likeness.   The sweeping terms of saint and sinner bring no intelligible discrimination, without due regard to the spiritual characteristics of each division in their more circumstantial delineation.   It is only by this minute accuracy, that each class will be brought to stand on his own side of the line laid open before him.   Misconception, indistinctness, or indecision, greatly encourages the self-deceiving of the heart on the one side, and the scrupulosity of unbelief on the other—two serious hindrances to the spiritual welfare of our people.

Nor is it less important to *separate between the professing and the true Church.*   This line also is distinctly drawn by our Lord.[3] Every part of the Christian character has its counterfeit.   How easily are the delusions of fancy or feeling mistaken for the impressions of grace !   The genuineness of the work of God must be estimated, not by the extent, but by the influence, of Scriptural knowledge—not by a fluency of gifts, but by their exercise in connexion with holiness and love.   Brainerd (than whom no man had a clearer insight into counterfeit religion) excellently remarked— ' that much more of true religion consists in deep humility, brokenness of heart, and an abasing sense of want of grace and holiness, than most, who are called Christians, imagine.'—' He spoke' (as his biographer informs us) ' with much detestation of that pretended experience of religion, which had nothing of the nature of sanctification in it ; that did not tend to strictness, tenderness and diligence in religion, to meekness and benevolence towards mankind ; and that was not manifested by modesty of conduct and conversation.'   He emphatically enforced the importance of this

---

[1] Luke xvi. 26.

[2] 'Most assuredly' (remarks Mr. Scott) 'this *undistinguishing* way of preaching is " casting that which is holy unto the dogs ;" and, I am deeply convinced, is one of the worst mistakes that a preacher can fall into ; tending most directly to stupify the consciences and harden the hearts of the ungodly, and to " strengthen their hands, that they should not return from their evil way ;" and, in proportion, discouraging the heart of the humble, broken, contrite believer.'   Letters and Papers, p. 441.   Comp. Ezek. xxii. 26.   [3] Matt. vii. 21—23.

discrimination upon a probationer for the Ministry—'Labour (said he) '*to distinguish clearly*, upon experiences and affections in religion, that you may make a difference between the gold and the shining dross. I say, labour here, if ever *you would be an useful* *Minister of Christ*.[1] We would remark the importance of giving vital and distinctive marks of the Christian character—*yet in a state of imperfection.* For to describe them in their perfect state, would be to confound the standard with the measure of attain ment, and by drawing the saint as an angel, to invalidate the titl• and confound the assurance of the humble believer. The stud₁ of the frame and moving principles of the human mind, wil¹ throw light upon many perplexing cases ; and enable us to mark the influence of bodily passions, constitutional temperament, or disordered imagination, in obscuring or counterfeiting genuine piety.

But we must also regard *the different individualities of profession within the Church*. And here again our Lord's parabol-ical description of his earthly kingdom assists us.[2] The Apostolical Ministry also, after the same pattern, marks these subdivisions in the Church.[3] And doubtless in the treatment of some, it is important to ascertain the stage of the Christian life ; the degree of strength or weakness, of faintness or overcoming in the spiritual conflict ; of advancement or retrogression in evangelical holiness ; of growing distinctness or obscurity in the apprehensions of truth ; of decided separation from the world, or remaining conformity to it ; of increasing glow or decline of the love of Christ in the soul. The Minister (as Bishop Hall remarks) 'must discern between his sheep and wolves ; in his sheep, between the sound and unsound ; in the unsound, between the weak and the tainted ; in the tainted, between the nature, qualities, and degrees of the disease and infection ; and to all these he must know to administer a word in season. He hath antidotes for all temptations, counsels for all doubts, evictions for all errors, for all languishings. No occasion, from any altered state of the soul, may find him unfurnished.'[4] 'The epidemic malady of our nature' (as has been admirably observed by a writer lately referred to) 'assumes so many shapes,

[1] See his Diary, and Letter ix. appended to his Life. It is scarcely necessary to refer to Edwards' celebrated work on the Affections—as the closest and most searching touchstone of Christian sincerity, and the most accurate detector of the diversified forms of false profession and delusive experience.
[2] See Mark iv. 26—29.
[3] Comp. St. Paul's distinct treatment of babes and adults ; and St. John's distribution of believers into the several classes of " little children, young men, and fathers." 1 Cor. iii. 1 ; Heb. v. 12—14 ; with 1 John ii. 12, 13.
[4] Bishop Hall's Epistles, Decad iv. Epist. v. Works, (Oxford Edition) vi. 221.

and appears under such a variety of symptoms, that these may be considered as so many distinct diseases, which demand a proportionate variety in the method of treatment; nor will the same prescription suit all cases. A different set of truths, a different mode of address, is requisite to rouse the careless, to beat down the arrogance of a self-justifying spirit, from what is necessary to comfort the humble and contrite in heart: nor is it easy to say, which we should most guard against, the infusion of a false peace, or the inflaming of the wounds which we ought to heal.'[1]

A defect of this discrimination must greatly impede our success. For it is not the general virtue of medicine, but its suitable application to the disease, that heals, though perhaps with painful efficacy. A practitioner, who had one sovereign remedy for every complaint, without regard to the patient's age, constitution, or habit, would be thought, as Baxter says, ' a sort of civil murderer.' Much more would we deprecate the spiritual application of this promiscuous regimen; inasmuch as the fatal result would be—not for time, but for eternity.[2]

VI.—DECIDED PREACHING OF THE GOSPEL.

THE power even of a Scriptural exhibition of truth is often materially weakened by an indecisive mode of statement. The doctrines of the Gospel appear to be allowed and set forth; but in so feeble and hesitating a tone, as evinces either a careless investigation into their character, a doubtful opinion of their truth, or an indistinct apprehension of their value and efficacy. Such a representation awakens but little interest, and produces no effect. Our people feel little obligation to receive what, from

[1] Hall's Sermons, ut supra, p. 22.
[2] Zepper speaks so admirably upon the subject of this Section, that, as his work is but in few hands, we give a quotation :—'Cujus operis difficultatem tam multiplex et varia auditorum, quibus verbi divini mysteria dispensanda sunt, diversitas sexuum, ætatum, ingeniorum, opinionum, profectuum, conditionis, institutionis, morborum et affectionum animi discrimen, imó contrarietas non parum auget: dum alii hypocritæ sunt; alii afflicti peccatores: alii flagitiosi; alii pié viventes: alii desperabundi; alii cum infirmitate et conscientiæ variis tentationibus variè luctantes; alii pabulo, quod pascua tantum, et fontes Israelis sapiat, contenti; alii delicati et nauseabundi, quorum palato nihil feré sapit, quantumvis orthodoxum, nisi carnem quoque et mundum resipiat. Quos animorum morbos, et diversam auditorum rationem, ut nosse difficile est: ita convenientia omnibus et singulis remedia, ex verbi divini pharmacopolio depromere, eaque feliciter etiam applicare, quanti, quamque immensi laboris et sudoris, quanti ingenii, quantæ spiritualis prudentiæ res est.—Unde etiam Christus Ecclesiæ suæ pastorem servo comparat prudenti et fideli, super famulitium Domini constituto, ut illis alimentum det, et quidem in tempore, hoc est, non promiscué, obiter aut perfunctorie, sed pro ratione temporum, adeoque et locorum et ingeniorum, quibuscum negotium illi est. Matt. xxiv. 45.' Pref. pp. 5, 6.

the spiritless mode of presentment, seems to be of minor importance—at least not worthy of inconvenient consideration, or expensive sacrifices. In many views of human corruption, of the grand doctrine of justification, and of the work and influence of the Spirit, it would be difficult to detect any. positive contrariety to Scripture ; while yet there is an evident deterioration from the " full assurance," with which our reformers have laid them down, as the primary doctrines of the Gospel, indispensable to˙ the character, hope, and establishment. of the Christian. There is an excessive caution in fencing and guarding the statement. The offensive spirituality of terms is covered in the garb of a more popular theology, and the distinct recognition of the cardinal points is greatly obscured : so that, though there is no actual pulling down of the house, there is a palpable want of power to build it up. This indecisive tone may be partially traced to an undue regard to human standards; in some measure taking the place of an entire submission to the word of God. For it is only when we stand upon the whole ground of Scripture, that we can make those strong and constant appeals " to the law and to the testimony," which characterize a decided view of the Gospel, and enable us to deliver it in a clear and decided manner. It is not enough for us to speak the oracles of God. We must speak *as the oracles ;*[1] " magnifying our office" by the undoubted confidence, that " the Gospel, which is preached of us is not after man"—that our message is " not the word of man, but in truth the word of God."[2] On the deeper and more mysterious points of the Gospel, (on which difference of sentiment has always existed) Christian moderation and forbearance may be required. But on the grand fundamentals, an authoritative decision of statement becomes us ; not allowing a doubt to belong to our message, any more than to our own existence. Thus did the Apostles and their fellow-labourers preach the Gospel. They had received it from the mouth of God ; they were assured of its Divine authority ; they delivered it in despite of all resistance,[3] as a *testimony*, bringing with it its own evidence ; and thus, " by manifestation of the truth, they commended themselves to every man's conscience in the sight of God."[4] The Apostle considered the charge of indecision, even in ordinary matters, to be so grave an accusation, and so injurious to his Ministry, that he˙ felt himself justified in calling his God to witness, that in no re-

---

[1] 1 Peter iv. 11. [2] Gal. i. 11, 12; 1 Thess. ii. 13. [3] See Gal. v. 2—4.
[4] Comp. Luke i. 3; 1 John i. 1—3; 2 Peter i. 16; with 2 Cor. iv. 2.

spect had his word been fickle among them ; but that his testimony had been consistent, decided, and unwavering.[1]

Such—again—was his decided conviction of the truth of his own testimony, that he hesitates not to curse himself, or even " an angel from heaven," upon the supposition, that he could " preach any other Gospel, than that which he had preached unto them."[2] To those whom he detected in undermining it, he "*would give place by subjection, no, not for an hour,* that the truth of the Gospel might continue with" the church.   Nay when he met with an opponent to the liberty of the Gospel in the person of an Apostle— " he withstood him to the face," even before the whole Church, " because he was to be blamed."[3]   Yet this was the same Apostle, who in matters of lesser moment was ever ready to "become all things to all men, if that by any means he might save some ;"[4] who would give up the use of meat to the end of his life, rather than put a stumbling-block in the way of a weak brother ;[5] and who would circumcise Timothy in condescension to the infirmities and prejudices of his brethren, to gain a more conciliating access to their hearts.[6]   This was he, who, in his own spirit, was "gentle among his people, as a nursing-mother cherisheth her children ;" who yet could not endure among them any perversion of doctrine, or laxity of practice, without the severest rebukes and most fearful threatenings.[7]   So important is it, that the character of decision should be—not our own spirit—"lording over the Lord's heritage," or " having dominion over their faith,"[8] (a spiritual exercise of the power of the princes of this world[9]) ; but " the meekness and gentleness of Christ," who, though " the servant of all," yet as the messenger of God, " spake as one having authority."   " We speak," (said he on one occasion) " *that we do know : and testify that we have seen.*"[10]   " We having the same spirit of faith," (said his chosen Apostle) " according as it is written, I believed, and therefore have I spoken ; *we also believe, and therefore speak.*"[11]

[1] 2 Cor. i. 17—20.   [2] Gal. 8, 9.   [3] Gal. ii. 5, 11, 12.
[4] 1 Cor. ix. 22.   [5] Ib. viii. 13.   [6] Acts xvi. 3.
[7] 1 Thess. ii. 7, 8, with Gal. v. 2. 1 Cor. iii. 47.   [8] 1 Peter v. 3; 2 Cor. i. 24.
[9] Matt. xx. 25.   [10] John iii. 11.   [11] 2 Cor. iv. 13.

CHAPTER V.

THE MODE OF SCRIPTURAL PREACHING.

WHAT diversity do we observe in the mode, in which our most approved Ministers exhibit the doctrines of the Gospel! Their style, their compositions, their mechanical system of instruction, have each an individual character; and something probably may be learned from all. Our tone of mind, habits, preparatory training, schemes of study, conversance with certain schools and standards of preaching—all combine to mould the character of our Ministrations. Some will adopt one mode, some another; nor can we pronounce absolutely upon the superior excellence of one of them to the rest under all circumstances. The Divine blessing evidently depends not on the discovery and practice of the best mode, but upon our simplicity in seeking for direction, and our conscientious diligence in improving the light afforded to us. Yet there are some specialities worthy our consideration, on which we shall venture to offer a few suggestions.

I.—TOPICAL AND EXPOSITORY PREACHING.

THE mode of communicating our message is either *topical,* preaching from texts and small detached portions of Scripture—or *expository,* taking large and connected portions of sacred writ, as the ground-work of our public discourses.

Our Lord's first sermon was an example of the *topical scheme.* He read his text, interpreted it, laid down the doctrine of it, began to apply it for reproof, and to illustrate it by Scripture example; and thus would have proceeded to the end, had not the madness of the people, succeeding their wonder, interrupted him.[1] The design of this scheme is two-fold. 1st. The discerning of the mind of the Spirit in the text, as connected with the context, so as to reduce it to a single and definite proposition; and then—2ndly, to lay open the view of truth, which seems naturally to arise out of it. *This* enables us to diversify our application of truth, in its place and season, and prevents a wearisome repetition of the same gen-

---

[1] Luke iv. 16—30.

eral statement. For such is the fulness of the Gospel, that there is no part or proposition of God's word, which does not admit of rich and appropriate elucidation from it. A mind acquainted with the depth of this heavenly mine, will find in every portion of Holy Writ some trace of "the unsearchable riches of Christ;" and a failure of bringing forth the fundamental doctrines from such resources, will prove, not the exhausted state of the treasure, but the want of spiritual and accurate observation of its hidden store.

The *expository* scheme, though a less impassioned exercise, yet, by a judicious mixture with the topical system, forms a most important vehicle of instruction. Comprehensive and connected views of truth are thus set forth, equally conducive to Christian intelligence, privilege, and stedfastness. It avoids the habit of building upon a text what is not authorized by the context; and enables our people to read the Scriptures with more interest, because with more understanding, and with less danger of being misled by disjointed views of truth. Thus is Scriptural doctrine confirmed, more from the general strain of the sacred argument, than from the partial citation of insulated texts.

Many subjects are also brought forward, which otherwise might probably have been omitted.[1] Matters of application to particular sins or errors occur in their course, without just imputation of parsonality; and short occasional hints, thus naturally arising from our subjects, fall with a weight of conviction, for which our hearers are often wholly unprepared. There is no time to take the alarm, and to fortify the mind against conviction; as when the main subject is directly levelled against their known sins. The whole extent of the Scripture field is also thus laid open in the length and breadth thereof. Occasions are offered of setting forth every doctrine, and enforcing every practical obligation. We are forced into an extended apprehension and application of truth. The mind of God is discovered more accurately in the precise statements, proportions, and connexions of truth. Here 'God speaks much, and man little.'[2] Without being entangled in the trammels of system, our views are both enlarged and controlled by tracing the scope, argument, and relative position of truth in its several compartments. The course of family worship would materially assist the moulding of the mind into this scheme. Large portions of Scripture drawn out within the limit of time usually allotted to this interesting ser-

[1] Perhaps instruction connected with divorce would not have occurred in a village Ministry, except in a regular course of Exposition. (Mark x. 2—12.) In this way the Writer somewhat reluctantly introduced it, but with unexpected effect.
[2] Chrysostom.

vice, would gradually train us to the successful habit of connecting the main points, rather than of analyzing the minute particles, of our subjects.

The scheme formed a prominent part of Primitive instruction.[1] Augustine, Basil, and Chrysostom dealt largely in it. The Homilies of the last father are justly considered as among the best models for expository preaching, and the most valuable relics of ecclesiastical antiquity. The course of exposition however, should not be too long; the subjects should be selected with a special regard to our own resources, and to the circumstances of our people; care should be taken to mingle conviction with instruction, to keep the heart and conscience in view in our endeavour to inform the understanding; we should watch the decline of interest in our course; and interchange the two systems for greater variety, and to obtain the advantage of both.

II.—EXTEMPORE AND WRITTEN SERMONS.

THE Writer does not attempt to settle this mooted point for his brethren. None however but enthusiasts will contend for *extempore preaching*, strictly so called. Unpremeditated speech was promised to the Aposdes in their peculiar difficulties, beyond all human resources.[2] But though their public Ministry was probably of this kind, yet no precedent can be drawn from miraculous influence, superinduced for the overcoming natural disadvantages, in an extraordinary work.

We use therefore the term in its popular reference to *unwritten* sermons, digested and arranged by preparatory meditation; the language and the filling up of the outlines only being left to the moment of delivery.

As a general rule—we must feel ourselves, in order to excite others;[3] and perhaps the passage from heart to heart is more direct, and the sympathy more immediate, with the natural flowings of the preacher's heart, than with communications through a written medium. The look, attitude, manner of address of the extemporary

---

[1] See Cave's Primitive Christianity, ch. ix.

[2] Luke xxi. 14, 15. Matt. x. 19, 20. The martyrs inherited a full and undoubted interest in this promise. But it never was intended to promise Divine inspiration in its ordinary sense without premeditation; or to imply, that preparatory study was either useless, or a bar to the reception of needful assistance. The exhortation to Timothy (1 Tim. iv. 13, referred to Part I. ch. vii. Sect. i.) evidently implies the necessity of the study of our subjects.

[3] ————Si vis me flere, dolendum est
Primum ipsi tibi.   HORACE.

Preacher, is more direct, personal, and arresting. His habit is more ready to improve passing occasions, or to introduce a striking hint to rouse his careless hearers. The reality before his eyes at the moment of action inspires a warmth, which, abstracted from the scene of work, he could never impart. The sight of his people in the presence of God—their very countenances—their attention or listlessness—their feeding interest or apparent dislike—suggests many points of animated address, which did not occur in the study; excites many visible impressions in his heart, stirs up a living energy of expression, which awakens corresponding sympathy and interest in his congregation. This is a matter of no small moment. Men are little influenced by argument; nor is conviction a matter of the intellect, but intimately connected with all the sympathies of the heart. Impressions made through this medium, and diligently cherished, are often of lasting effect. Nor needs this course exhibit less substance and thought than written composition. The time necessarily given to writing is a subtraction from what might have been improved for thinking; and though indolence or self-conceit might abuse the exemption from the pen; yet a solid mind, impressed with the responsibility of the occasion, would gladly redeem it for a more fruitful intellectual exercise.

Mr. Cecil's advice for commencing this practice was—'Begin at once, take the ease and pliancy of youth into the formation of your habit.' Mr. Robinson on the contrary recommended very cautious steps—'Let no man attempt to preach without book, till he has patiently written all, and the whole of his discourses for seven years; let him then begin sparingly and gradually.'[1] This had been the rule of the first seven years of his own Ministry; from which, he declared, only dire necessity induced him to swerve. Much, however, must depend upon the preparatory discipline of the mind; upon the extent of its stores, and its success in conflicting with, and overcoming, constitutional or spiritual hindrances. Mr. Robinson (unlike Mr. Richmond, who subsequently attained unparalleled eminence in this practice,[2]) was successful from the first, and probably would have been equally so, had his term of probation been curtailed to half its limits. A mind formed in his mould —correct and orderly in its arrangements, furnished with ample and solid materials, and trained to enlarged Ministerial exercises— might commence within a much shorter period.

Bishop Burnet acquired this gift by a fixed and constant habit of meditation upon an extended range of subjects, and by speak-

<hr />

[1] Vaughan's Life, p. 322, 325.   [2] Richmond's Life, p. 155.

ing his thoughts aloud at those times with a studied accuracy of expression.[1] A most erroneous notion prevails of the easiness of this attainment. A collection of words is often mistaken for a justly-defined sentiment ; and fluency of utterance is considered to be either indicative of solidity of thought, or a fair amends for its deficiency. Now such an extemporaneous faculty can bring no substantial instruction to our people. Our subject must be studied, till it is understood, digested, and felt. For a well-conducted habit we need—not impulse or fluency merely—but a furniture of solid knowledge—combined with simplicity of style—solid as well as animated manner—and *instar omnium*—a mind deeply enriched with the unsearchable treasure of Scripture.[2] This resource will supply the place of many secondary qualifications, while nothing will compensate for the lack of it.

Much help may also be derived from conversational habits with our people. What the moment suggests for individual use, would more or less apply collectively ; and frequent interchange of communication will gradually inspire confidence in the delivery of it.

' Smaller excursions'[3] in Cottage readings, or family exposition, also are among the best preparations. A young Minister studying a passage morning and evening, consulting commentators and expounding extempore, can hardly fail of enriching his mind, and of acquiring a Scriptural style of simplicity, and the free natural method of pouring out a full heart in ready words.

This exercise however should be combined with thoughtful and well-digested habits of composition. Dr. Doddridge, without recommending the practice of written sermons, gives detailed rules for most elaborate pulpit composition.[4] And thus the fluency of the pulpit, being the result of diligent employment in the study, has often been committed to the press with very slight variation from the public delivery. This system may therefore decisively claim the advantage, which Bishop Burnet ascribes to written sermons. It often combines ' heat and force in delivery,' with ' strength and solidity of matter ;'[5] and has produced volumes of sermons, which in all essential points will rank with the most elaborate compositions of a more mechanical system.

Yet we must admit the advantages of written composition, in avoiding wearisome repetition—defective modes of expression—a

---

[1] See his Life.
[2] Such as Jerome observed of his friend Nepotian—' that by daily reading and meditation in the sacred volume he had made his soul *a library of Christ.*'
[3] Burnet's Past. Care.   [4] See his Preaching Lectures.
[5] Burnet's History of the Reformation, Book I. year 1542.

confused arrangement of the flowing thoughts of the moment—
—(evils more or less incidental to the opposite scheme) and embodying our matter in greater compactness and solidity, in lucid
order, and correct style. So that (at the early stages at least) the
Roman orator may justly recommend ' much writing as the best
preparation to good speaking.'[1] The tyro in theology has probably
little conception of his own immature attainments, until his ideas
have been expressed on paper. At every step he finds his need of
expansion or condensation. Not having prepared his way as he
advanced, by a thorough maturing of his subject, he has to " lay
again the foundation" of what he fancied himself to have attained.
The quantum of composition will however vary according to the
natural or acquired habits of the mind ; but in few cases can a
certain proportion be omitted with advantage. Rarely do young
men unite *sound judgment* with a lively imagination ; and therefore ordinary sermons, without any pains of composition, would be
a mass of inanimate matter, deficient in apt illustration and pointed application. The *excursive* preacher needs the use of his pen
to restrain himself within the limits of an accurate and connected
plan ; without which digressive and unconnected matter would
probably form the main substance of his discourses. The *fluent,
unfurnished* preacher, without this resource to fill his shadowy
mechanism, will be wordy, declamatory, unsubstantial, and uninteresting. Indeed the gift of fluency, without furniture or application, is rather a misfortune than a desirable qualification. Besides
the personal danger of neglecting intellectual improvement, it di-
gresses from our proper subject at times of embarrassment, to irrelevant, but more agreeable points. Thus some have been spoilt
from the want of the book, as well as others fettered by the use
of it.

The primitive records furnish traces both of the written and
the extemporary form. Sermons could not then be wholly written, as they generally consisted of expositions of Scripture commonly of the lesson last read (as being most fresh in the memory of the people); and two or three sermons were often delivered successively in the same service.[2] Origen is thought to
have fully introduced the extemporary mode. Notices of this

---

[1] Caput autem est, quod (ut veré dicam) minime facimus (est enim magni laboris, quem
plerique fugimus) quam plurimum scribere. Cic. de. Orat. At the same time he observes
that, should the speaker only avail himself in part of the habit of writing, the remainder
of his address will partake more or less of the style of correct composition.
[2] After the reading of the Gospel, the Presbyters exhorting the people, one by one, not
all at once; and after all the Bishop, as it is fitting for the Master to do. Cave's Primitive Christianity.

method are found in the writings of Augustine and Chrysostom; whose frequency of preaching naturally gave them this freedom; and whose incessant Ministerial activity rendered it morally impossible, that they could have *always written* their sermons. At the same time plain notices are found in the writings of the Fathers, of sermons written—not only for the preacher's own use, but for more general advantage.[1] Burnet mentions the practice of reading at the Reformation era ; yet Latimer's honest " plainness of speech," and the memorials of some of his cotemporaries, furnish evidence of the opposite usage.[2]

Archbishop Secker, after discussing the question of written and extempore sermons, recommends written sketches, combined with extempore delivery, as ' a middle way used by some of our predecessors,'[3] and adds—' perhaps duly managed, this would be the best.'[4] The scheme, argument, and application of the discourse are given, without needless anxiety to preserve the precise letter of the composition. This indeed is adopted, when naturally occurring to the mind ; otherwise the matter is clothed in the garb, which the present moment supplies. This plan seems to combine the advantages of the two schemes—restraining within the bounds of chastised feeling and well-digested arrangement, without the shackles of a written composition. The memory is exercised without painful anxiety : while the mind is left free to the excitement of the feelings of the moment, in dependence upon Divine assistance. And this freedom must undoubtedly be claimed, of not being restricted to the letter of our premeditated sentiments. A richer unction of the spirit may reasonably be expected at the moment of preaching, after public and united prayer, while standing up in the immediate presence of God as an ambassador for Christ, beyond what had been previously vouchsafed in the study. As regards means however, ' a man cannot expect a good habit of preaching thus, without much study and experience. Young beginners should use themselves to a more exact and elaborate way. When a good style and expression is first learned by perusing, it will afterwards be more easily retained in discoursing.'[5] No lack

---

[1] Some hints in the writings of Augustine and Gregory refer to the custom of their sermons being written and read to the people, when they were prevented from preaching in person; which shows that the custom of reading was not wholly unknown.

[2] See some references in Budd on Infant Baptism, pp. 474, 475.

[3] Such as Bishop Bull. See his Life by Nelson, p. 59. Burnet gives some excellent rules for the attainment of this exercise. Pastoral Care, ch. ix. Comp. Fenelon's Dialogues. Erasmus traces the practice to the Fathers—' Tutum est capita sermonis in charta notata habere ad manum, *quod in Psalmos aliquot fecisse videtur Augustinus ; et haud scio, an in omnes, quanquam vir memoria ad prodigium usque felici.*'

[4] Charges, p. 287—291.   [5] Wilkins' Eccles. p. 203.

either of matter or expression needs generally be apprehended in a well-digested and arranged subject.[1] " Of the abundance of the heart the mouth will speak ;" 'nor will the preacher be able to repeat a tenth part of the truths which God has communicated to him, while meditating upon his text.'[2] Increasing interest, aided by practice, will also gradually remove difficulties ; and that 'vehement simplicity,' which Cecil justly defined to be 'true eloquence,'[3] will characterize our preaching, even amidst much humbling and most profitable experience of Ministerial weakness. If parliamentary or forensic speakers have attained an uninterrupted fluency of expression, even while "leaning to their own understanding ;" much more if the Lord means to employ this habit in his service may we assure ourselves of a competent measure of spiritual ability, in the use of the appointed means, and in dependence on his promised aid. And never are we better fitted for our work, than while cherishing a deep-toned recollection—" Without me ye can do nothing."[4]

After all, however, as appears to the Writer, far too great importance is often attached to this mode. Though much consideration has determined his own practice of it, he is fully persuaded, that such is the diversity of gifts among preachers of equal eminence, that the best mode is not always the best in all cases. Some have greater readiness of expression by their pen. With others, most freedom is experienced in the excitement of their feelings, by the vivid presentment of their awful responsibility. It will readily be granted, that a judicious and animated system of reading (no very infrequent case) is better than an ill-conducted and

---

[1] —————————Cui lecta potenter erit res,
Nec facundia deseret hunc, nec lucidus ordo ;
Verbaque provisam rem non invita sequuntur.
Hor. de Arte Poet.

' Whose mind soever is fully possessed with the fervent desire to know good things, and with the dearest charity to infuse the knowledge of them into others—when *such a man would speak*, his words, like so many nimble and airy servitors, trip about him at command, and in well-ordered files, as he would wish, fall aptly into their own places.' Milton.

[2] Act of Synod of Berne, ch. xl. quoted in Fletcher's Portrait of St. Paul.

[3] Cecil's Remains.

[4] John xv. 5. Professor Campbell seems scarcely to recognize this practice in the Kirk. In discussing the several advantages and disadvantages of *reading and repeating our discourses*, he justly complained of the burden of the latter usage, as interfering with important pastoral engagements. (Campbell on Pulp. Eloquence, Lect. iv. On Past. Char. Lect. ix.) We might add—in the act of delivery, it is likely to deaden the affections by the anxious process of reciting, to divert the attention from the sentiment to the word, and to produce a hurried, monotonous, or inharmonious tone of address. Indeed, upon the whole, it is no more than a schoolboy's exercise of 'most unreasonable laboriousness,' which Bishop Burnet conceives it possible few to maintain, and with which the heart has as little necessary concern, as it is often supposed to have with the pages of the book. Compare Secker's Charges, p. 291. Fenelon's Dialogues (ii.) Burnet's Pastoral Care, ch. ix. Smith on the Pastoral Office, Lect. xx.

unfurnished habit of extempore speaking[1]—not to speak of the re-excited, remembered, and digested, materials of experience, which are more advantageously brought forward on this system.[2] The preaching of Mr. Milner of Hull, and Mr. Walker of Truro, the early years of Mr. Robinson, and some of the most successful Min-istrations within the Writer's knowledge, have been formed upon the scheme of written compositions. And may we not ask on the ground of ecclesiastical consistency—Why should the book be more objectionable in the pulpit than in the desk? Why is it not possible spiritually to preach, as well as to pray, with a form? Extempore preaching is the *mode*, not the *matter*; the shell, the vehicle; not the essential substance. A sermon written or un-written may be alike the fruit of prayer, and the exercise of faith; and, according to its spirit and principles, not according to the mode of its delivery, is it accepted and honoured. In either case there is the same need of faith, and the same difficulty in its ex-ercise. In either case is the same danger of formality; nor is it easier to say, whether the dependence upon the book or upon the gift is more natural or delusive.

But it is hard to insist on advantages of one system, without an undue depreciation of the other. Many excellent divines trace the preaching of written sermons to unbelief, an undue regard to self, the fear of man,[3] or to "the spirit of the world."[4] But who, from the days of St. Paul, was less under the influence of these unevangelical principles than Luther? Yet he tells us 'that (*occasionally*, not in his ordinary custom) he preached out of the book, though not of necessity, as if he could not do otherwise,

---

[1] The following lines have much good sense in them:

> 'Should you, my friend, the important question ask—
> With or without my papers shall I preach?
> My answer hear and weigh. Your sermons write
> From end to end; and every thought invest
> With full expression, such as best may suit
> Its nature and its use; and then pronounce
> As much as your remembrance can retain.
> Rather read every sentence word for word,
> Than wander in a desultory strain—
> A chaos, dark, irregular, and wild—
> Where the same thought and language oft revolves,—
> And re-revolves to tire sagacious minds;
> However loud the momentary praise
> Of ignorance, and empty fervors charm'd.
> But never to your notes be so enslav'd,
> As to repress some instantaneous thought,
> That may, like lightning, dart upon the soul,
> And blaze in strength and majesty Divine.'
>
> Gibbons' Christian Minister.

[2] We would remark, that a written sermon, repeatedly read over before the delivery, will have much of the ease and force of an extemporaneous discourse.

[3] See Newton's Letters to Mr. Barlass.   [4] Budd on Infant Baptism, p. 493—496.

yet for example's sake to others.[1]   Mr. Milner's written compositions, in faithfulness of statement, unction of style, and closeness
of application, are exceeded—we might almost say equalled—by
no Ministry conducted on the opposite system.   Perhaps they
could not but be more justly characterized, than by Mr. Budd's description of the offensiveness of *extemporaneous preaching*.[2]

A Writer in the Christian Observer[3] (who has thrown out
some valuable hints upon the general subject) charges this practice
upon idleness.   The principle however of Mr. Baxter's reply to
the Quaker's objection bears upon this point—'You read your sermons out of a paper, therefore, you have not the Spirit'—'It is not
want of your abilities'—he rejoins—'that makes Ministers use
notes; but it is a regard to the work, and good of the hearers,'—
'*I use notes as much as any man, when I take pains;* and as
little as any man, when I am lazy, or busy, or have not time to
prepare.   It is easier for us to preach three sermons without notes,
than one with them.'[4]   This accusation was made the ground of
the celebrated mandate of King Charles.[5]   But the theological authority of this curious document, issuing from a profligate court, is
reduced to a minimum; and its universal observance at the time
when religion was at the lowest ebb among the clergy, would have
been a woeful calamity to the nation.   For how much less calculated for instruction would have been extemporary addresses from
unpracticed and unspiritual men, than written compositions, which
might have embodied some useful substance from extrinsical resources!   Besides, may not this charge be sometimes applied to
the extempore system?   May not indolence render the mind
(with a tolerable fluency of utterance) unwilling to burden itself
with the labour of thinking out important matters?[6]   In both
cases it would be admitted to be the abuse; but both systems
are evidently liable to abuse.   The same Writer somewhat boldly states, that a man incapable of preaching extemporaneously,
is 'not fit for the Ministry—being not "apt to teach."'   But

---

[1] See Edward's Preacher, i. 220.   [2] Budd on Infant Baptism, p. 497.
[3] See Christian Observer, Oct. 1828.
[4] Church History, 4to. 1680, p. 471.   Bishop Hall tells us of his own practice—'When
I preached three times in a week, yet never durst I climb into the pulpit to preach any
sermon, whereof I had not before, in my poor and plain fashion, penned every word in
the same order wherein I hoped to deliver it; although in the expression I listed not to
be a slave to syllables.'   Account of himself, p. 34.
[5] Appendix to Dr. Buchanan's Sermons on Eras of Light, and Richmond's Life,
p. 157.
[6] Bishop Stillingfleet complained in his day—'There is got an ill habit of speaking
extempore, and a loose and careless way of talking in the pulpit; which is easy to the
preacher, and plausible to less judicious people.'   Duties and Rights of the Parochial
Clergy, p. 30.

would not this supposition have disqualified Moses from his Divine commission; which, though not identical with preaching, yet comprised a considerable proportion of instruction, and would have been much commended by fluency of utterance? Yet if God had deemed it indispensable for his work, would he not have supplied the personal deficiency, instead of compensating for it by extrinsical help?[1] When therefore the heart is right, and the indications of the will of God clear, why may not the same deficiency be similarly provided for by another mode of administration?

The most common reason for the adoption of written sermons— *is concession to the temper and prejudices of our people.* It seems incurring a fearful responsibility, to repel any from our Ministry on account of an offensive mode. "The offence of the cross" —the only offence unconnected with personal guilt—respects the matter, and not the mode, of our Ministrations. The principle of "becoming all things to all men,"[2] surely extends to every particular of the *mode of address*, though not to one particle of the fundamental matter;[3] and if the Apostle Paul was accustomed to speak from the immediate impulse of his mind, it is hard to believe, that he, who felt himself "a debtor both to the Greeks and to the barbarians, both to the wise and to the unwise,"[4] would not have used a different mode, had it been at any time necessary to answer his great end. Few but would admit the spirit of Henry Martyn's concession to his Anglo-Indian congregation, on his extempore preaching—'saying, that he would give them a folio sermon book, if they would receive the word of God on that account.'[5] Nor is the propriety of conformity to established usage commonly questioned, in the occasion of *conciones ad clerum*, whether in University, Cathedral, or Visitation Pulpits. The appendage of a written composition might here be made the vehicle of statements as faithful and as important, as has been delivered by the preacher in his ordinary Ministration through a more free medium.

The writer, therefore, fully accords with Archbishop Secker's view of the question—'After all, every man (as the Apostle saith on a very different occasion) hath his proper gift of God, one after this manner, another after that. Let each cultivate his own, and no one censure or despise his brother.'[6] This was Mr. Robinson's judgment of the matter, who with a decided preference for extempore preaching, 'taught his people to relish either; and to consider

---

[1] Exod. iv. 10—16. [2] 1 Cor. ix. 22. [3] See Gal. ii. 5.
[4] Rom. i. 14. [5] Life, pp. 227, 228. [6] Charges, pp. 290, 291.

book or no book, as one of those circumstantials in the fulfilment of the ordinance, which was of secondary, or rather of no moment.'[1]—However this is one of those questions that can never be decided upon paper. The conscientious Minister will consider the nature of his situation, the temper of his people, the character and suitableness of his individual talent—which mode is most adapted to subserve his own Ministerial efficiency. It will probably be well for him to use himself to both methods—to combine the freedom and vigour of extempore preaching with that clearness, regularity, and fulness of matter, which is best secured by much reflection and writing. It might be his duty to yield to a decided preference for extempore preaching among his people; though it would be wise to avail himself of the judgment of his more discerning brethren in forming his ultimate determination.

<hr />

CHAPTER VI.

THE SPIRIT OF SCRIPTURAL PREACHING.

A THOUGHTFUL study of the Gospels and the Acts of the Apostles, will afford the best illustrations of this subject. Our Lord's Ministry furnishes the perfect exemplification, of which the Apostolic Ministry exhibited a close detailed imitation; and therefore as entrusted with the same commission, opposed by the same hindrances, and sustained by the same promises with the first Ministers of the Church, an attentive consideration of their spirit must be replete with most important instruction and support. A few leading particulars will be specified, which may be filled up with advantage, even in the most contracted sphere of the Christian Ministry.

I.—BOLDNESS—THE SPIRIT OF SCRIPTURAL PREACHING.

OUR Lord's pungent addresses to the Scribes and Pharisees[2] exhibit the boldness of a Christian Ministration. The same spirit in the Apostles—unaccountable upon human calculations[3]—confounded their judges to theirface.[4] Witness Paul before Felix—a prisoner

<hr />

[1] Vaughan's Life, p. 234.   [2] See Matt. xxiii.   [3] Acts ii. 13.
[4] Acts iv. 13.   See the power that rested upon this spirit; 29—33: xiv. 3.   St. Paul's

on his trial for life—"no man standing by him"—hated even to death ᵗby the influential body of his countrymen; yet, mean, and in peril, looking his Judge in the face, with the power of life and· death in his hands;· and—remembering only the dignity of his office—delivering to this noble sinner and his guilty partner the most personal and offensive truths.[1] · How did this splendid example of Ministerial boldness "magnify his office !" For what can be more degrading to our Divine commission, than that we should fear the face of men? What unmindfulness does it argue of our Master's presence and authority, and of our high responsibilities, as " set forth for the defence of the Gospel !"[2] The independence, that disregards alike the praise and the censure of man, is indispensable for the integrity of the Christian Ministry.

Luther would have been tolerated on many truths of general application; but his bold statements of justification could not be endured. How different from Erasmus, who, though a layman, delivered his doctrines *ex cathedrâ*, yet with an unworthy carefulness to avoid inconvenient offence ! But the question is not, how our people may be pleased; but how they may be warned, instructed, and saved. We would indeed strongly rebuke that modesty, which makes us ashamed of our grand message ; or that tremulous timidity, which seems to imply, that we are only half-believers in our grand commission.[3] To keep offensive doctrines out of view, or to apologize for the occasional mention of them, or to be over-cautious respecting the rudeness of disquieting the conscience with unwelcome truth; to compromise with the world ; to connive at fashionable sins; or to be silent, where the cause of God demands an open confession—this is not the spirit which honours our Master, and which he "delighteth to honour."*

The *reproof of sin* is an important part of Ministerial boldness. Even the courtesies of life never restrained our Lord from this office. The Pharisees' dinners were made the seasons of rebuke, and never used as an excuse for declining it.[5] The Scriptural rules and· exhortations in the Ministerial Epistles show, that it should be, when occasion required, *public*,[6] as a warning to others—*sharp*,[7]

---

deep sense of its importance. Eph. vi. 19, 20. Col. iv. 3, 4—the same spirit characterizing the Jewish prophets, 1 Kings xxi. 20; xxii. 14—25. 2 Chron. xvi. 7; xxiv. 20. Isaiah lviii. 1; lxv. 2, with Rom. x. 20. Amos vii. 10—13. Micah iii. 8. Matt. iii. 7·
[1] Acts xxiv. 24, 25.   [2] Phil. i. 17.   [3] See Jer. xxiii. 28.
[4] See some searching views, in a sermon entitled ' The Gospel Message, by Rev. Dr. Dealtry, pp. 24—26. ' Be afraid of nothing more'—said a holy Minister—' than the detestable cowardice of a selfish and unbelieving heart.' Correspondence of the late Rev. Henry Venn, p. 248. ' Lord, turn the fear of men's faces into a love of their souls'—was Mr. Walker's godly prayer.—Life, p. 356.
[5] Luke vii. 36—46; xi. 37—54.   [6] 1 Tim. v. 20.   [7] Titus i. 13.

as a means of conviction to the offender—with *authority*,[1] in our Master's name—with *love*,[2] in the hope of ultimate restoration. It should, however, be always aimed at the sin, not at the sinner. There was no need for the Apostle to make any personal allusion to Felix. Conscience told the trembling criminal—" Thou art the man."[3]

Yet it is not *every kind of boldness*, that commends the glory of our message, and the dignity of our office. It is not an affected faithfulness, that makes a merit of provoking hostility to the truth —(a temper more closely connected with a man's own spirit than with the Gospel)—not a presumptuous rashness, that utters the holy oracles without premeditation of what is most fitting to be said, or most likely to be effective. But it is a spiritual, holy principle, combined with meekness, humility, and love, and with a deep consciousness of our own weakness and infirmities.[4] This spirit is " a door of utterance"—a door shut, till the Lord opens it —a matter of special difficulty—and therefore a subject of special prayer, both with the Minister and with the people on his account.[5]

This Ministerial boldness is fenced on either side by warning and encouragement.[6] Yet many probably know, and even feel, more truth, than they have courage to preach. Want we then a further motive ? Think of the despised Saviour in the judgment hall, " *before Pontius Pilate, witnessing a good confession*"[7]— an example of fidelity enough to make a coward bold !

The deficiency of this spirit lowers us in the estimation of our people, as time-servers, whose moral and religious integrity are alike suspected. Many who love the ' smooth things' we should ' prophesy,' would despise us in their hearts for this accommodation to their sinful indulgences ; whilst Christian boldness awes the haters of our message, and secures the confidence of the true flock of Christ, and the approbation of our conscience in the sight of God.

II.—WISDOM—THE SPIRIT OF SCRIPTURAL PREACHING.

" WISDOM"—observes the wise king of Jerusalem, who had known its value in public instruction—" is profitable to direct."[8]

---

[1] Titus ii. 15, with 1 Cor. v. 4.   [2] 1 Tim. v. 1.   2 Tim. ii. 24, 25.
[3] Acts xxiv. 25.   [4] See 1 Cor. ii. 3.   [5] See Eph. vi. 19, 20.
[6] Comp. Jer. i. 17—19. Ezek. ii. 6—8. 2 Tim. iv. 16. This thought seems to have been the last prop of Jeremiah's sinking spirit, chap. xx. 9—11.
[7] 1 Tim. vi. 13.   [8] Eccl. x. 10, with xii. 10.

We may be useful without learning, but not without wisdom. This was a part of our Master's furniture for his work ;[1] to which the multitude, and even his enemies, bore ample testimony.[2] His sermons were fraught with solemn, weighty, unmingled truth, judicious appeals to Scripture, an intimate acquaintance with the heart, and a suitable adaptation of incidental occurrences to the great end of his mission ;[3] so that in every view it was the manifestation of the " wisdom of God." In the same spirit his Apostle bore testimony to his own labours ; " teaching every man *in all wisdom,* that he might present every man perfect in Christ Jesus."[4]

The wisdom of our public Ministration includes the character of our compositions—that they should be such, that the lowest may understand, and the intelligent may have no cause to complain ; that the weak may not be offended, nor the captious gratified. There must be *unity of subject,* that the minds of our hearers may not be distracted ; *perspicuity of arrangement,* that they may enter into every part of the subject ; and *simplicity of diction,* that no part of it may be concealed by artificial language. The *precise view of the mind of the Spirit in the text itself* will naturally give *unity of subject.* Discernment of its *distinct character* will facilitate *arrangement.* The infusion of its spirit (whether of an energetic or tender kind) will of itself lead to suitable *"plainness of speech."*[5]

Thus the judgment arrives at a clear perception of the subject—the will has a ready ground of assent—the affections an intelligent and practical excitement—the memory a stronger habit of retention—the conscience an awakened exercise. And, though we would not ascribe innate efficacy to the best disposition of our great subject, yet we must deal with rational man through a rational medium. On the other hand—when *the unity* is disturbed by the intermixture of different points, and the dissociation of the several parts—when the *arrangement* is filled up with general matter, without the explication of the main heads of the discussion—when there is but little *moulding of the mind into the spirit of the subject*—want of clearness, sympathy, and power of application is the result. Yet mechanical uniformity—treating all subjects in the same precise method—greatly fails in effect. Sound wisdom

---

[1] Isaiah xi. 2, 3; l. 4.   [2] Luke iv. 22. xxi. 40, with John vii. 46.
[3] This particular of the Ministry of Christ, is admirably illustrated by the Bishop of Winchester.—Minister. Char. of Christ, ch. vi.   [4] Col. i. 28.
[5] The Writer begs particularly to refer to Mr. Simeon's short but admirable rules for composition in his edition of Claude's Essay, 12mo. pp. 30—34.

will make use of the best rules, and the settled principles of composition ; at the same time taking care that their influence does not
crush the powers of imagination, or weaken the force of free and
natural address to the conscience.

" Preaching Christ in wisdom" implies *a just and connected
view of truth.* " A wise master builder" not only lays a right
foundation, but " takes heed how he builds thereupon." He marks
the different qualities of his materials ;[1] placing the doctrine at the
foundation, and building duties upon it, as a superstructure of
lively stones, growing up into a holy edifice.[2]   He will guard
equally against confounding what God has distinguished, and putting asunder " what God hath joined together ;" not halting on the
verge of truth in scrupulous timidity, nor yet presumptuously over-
leaping the sacred barrier.   He may often see reason to insist upon
some points with more detail than others ; but he will carefully
bring every part into its Scriptural prominence and connexion ; instead of rashly assaulting one part with another—(the fruitful
source of heresy)—improving the whole " for doctrine, for reproof,
for correction, and for instruction in righteousness."[3]

This wise exhibition of the Gospel is of the highest moment.
Many will patiently listen to its practical enforcements, who cannot
endure its doctrinal statements—such as the sovereignty of God—
his free election of his people—justification by the righteousness of
Christ—the utter insufficiency of works as the ground of trust—
the helplessness of man in the act of turning to God—and the indispensable need of heavenly influence to incline his heart.   Many
on the other hand gladly receive the more mysterious doctrines of
the Gospel ; while they revolt from its invitations, and stigmatize
as legal, inculcations of the law as the rule of life, or of evangelical
repentance and holiness.   Now both these extremes proceed from
the same principle—a proud determination to receive a part only
of the counsel of God.   Both need the same corrective—a full,
well-proportioned, and connected display of truth—opposing the notions of self-sufficiency, without weakening the obligations to duty ;
enforcing these obligations, without entrenching upon the Sovereignty or the freeness of Divine grace ; cutting down self-righteousness by the perfection of the work of Christ, and Antinomianism by the glory of his example.

[1] 1 Cor. iii. 10—15.
[2] Mark the statement of justification in the Epistle to the Galatians. The Apostle did
not (as some appear to think) conceive that the view of *its simplicity* (ch. i.–iv.) was in
any wise obscured by the exhibition of *its fruitfulness* (ch. v. vi.) The tree is known by
its fruits while it is distinguished from them.   [3] 2 Tim. iii. 16.

Great indeed is the wisdom required in setting forth the analogy of faith, and the connected chain of doctrine. And from a deficiency of this just distribution of truth, much and dangerous error has arisen. The foundations of holiness have been weakened, by severing the doctrine of grace from its use and end; by leading men to rest upon its notions, while they neglect its holy influence; or by insinuating a carelessness of the evil and consequenses of sin from the misconceived doctrine of forgiveness. The wise Ministration of the Gospel connects the full display of mercy with a deep and humbling sense of sin. A free pardon will be watered with tears; forgiven sin will be detested and crucified; and the Gospel will be clearly seen to be the only principle of holiness both of heart and life.[1]

The exhibition of a correct standard both in doctrine and profession belongs to this subject. *In doctrine* it should be remembered, that every truth is not of equal importance; and that no single truth, unconnected with the rest, constitutes the Gospel. The force even of important truth (such as election, imputed righteousness, or Christian assurance) is much enervated by exclusive inculcation; while the beauty of the whole system is marred by insisting upon unconnected portions. If large integral parts of Scripture (such as the several Epistles to the Churches) be studied in simplicity and prayer, we should at once discover the main subjects, that filled the minds of the inspired writers; and also the precise proportion, which our favourite views bear to the whole " counsel of God" thus laid open before us.[2] We should thus mark the difference *between Scriptural doctrines and Scriptural statements,* and observe that points—*Scriptural in their place and proportion—may become unscriptural* by their disproportioned and unnatural application. We shall thus learn also to preach cautious, and yet unfettered, truth, reverencing *Scriptural guards;*[3] but watching against those human fetters, which sometimes restrain the freeness of the Gospel from the undue apprehen-

[1] Comp. Rom. v. vi.

[2] May the Writer venture to suggest the inquiry to some of the ardent investigators of prophecy—What proportion in extent and clearness their schemes (admitting them—*for the sake of argument only*—to be correct) occupy in the systems of Apostolical instruction; and whether the prophetic views and principles there set forth are not clearly subordinated to the display of Christ crucified, as the manifestation of all the love and glory of the Divine perfections? Let not this suggestion be supposed to discountenance *the study of prophecy* (which *within its due bounds* is equally practical, enlivening, and obligatory) but only the uncontrouled extent, to which it sometimes is pursued; and the exclusive dogmatical view, in which it is too often brought before the Church. The principle of these remarks may bear a qualified reference to some other points, which unhappily divide, instead of uniting, the Church in the present day.

[3] Such as Romans vi. 1—3, compared with v. 20.

sion of consequences. Our work is not to make or to improve the Gospel ; but simply and fully to preach it. A *distinct standard of truth* in its individual application is also of great moment—not merely inculcating certain qualifications (such as regeneration, faith, repentance) as indispensable to salvation : but—like " an interpreter, one among a thousand"[1]—explaining their true character and properties, and directing to the attainment and establishment of them.

As to the standard of profession—the reality and substance of the Gospel mainly consists in its *spiritual character*, which lays open the secret ways of sin, in forgetfulness of God, neglect of Christ, quenching of the Spirit, and enmity to the law ; and inculcates holiness in all its detail in the inward parts. Yet we should here be careful not to set our standard too low, or too high ; to insist upon nothing as evidence of the Christian character, merely because it belongs to a decorous, amiable, natural disposition ; and on the other hand to bring forth the lowest germ of sincerity as a decisive evidence of the work of God ; distinguishing between the existence and the degrees of grace ; and remembering that there are babes, as well as young men and fathers, in the family of God.[2] By a deviation from the Scriptural standard on either side, we " slay the souls that should not die, and save the souls alive that should not live ; we make the heart of the righteous sad, whom the Lord hath not made sad ; and strengthen the hands of the wicked, by promising him life."[3]

We remark here also the importance of a *correct application of our message*—like a faithful and wise steward[4]—*faithful*, in " giving the portions ;" "*wise*," in the seasonable mode, time, and objects of distribution—in the discernment of the particular truth, the argument, the method, the words, and the utterance, best adapted for instruction and edification. How observable is the difference in our Lord's discourses to the Scribes and Pharisees, to the multitude, and to his disciples ; as well as in his more private treat-

[1] See Job xxxiii. 23.

[2] 'The line of demarcation is sometimes so strictly drawn, that, it would seem, as if no attainments, which fall short of a prescribed standard, were to be accounted as indicative of the existence of any religious feeling. It would be more consonant to our Lord's example, if, when appearances on the whole are favourable, those who are yet lacking one thing, were to be brought to a clearer knowledge of the way of salvation by forbearance and seasonable admonition. If the Apostle thought it necessary to exhort believers to *add to their faith* virtue, and to virtue knowledge, &c. he must have contemplated the possibility, that those, who might afterwards become *thoroughly furnished unto all good works*, had been formerly deficient in some of the Christian graces.' Bishop of Winchester's Min. Char. pp. 196—198.

[3] Ezek. xiii. 19, 22.

[4] Luke xii. 42. The extreme care, with which the Levitical sacrifices were dissected and distributed, affords an apt illustration of this Ministerial wisdom. 2 Tim. ii. 15.

ment of individual cases! How accurately also did the Apostle accommodate the method of his Ministerial application to the temper of his people! ready to "change his voice" to the occasion, and to "come to them," as their circumstances might require, with a rod, or in love, and in the "spirit of meekness."[1]   Thus must the Minister not only state his commission, but adapt it to the different temperaments of his people: though (as Dr. Campbell has well observed) 'the more mixed the auditory is, the greater is the difficulty of speaking to them with effect.'[2]   Yet most unskilful would he be, were he to apply to the humbled sinner the corrosives of the Láw, instead of the balm of the Gospel; or to spread before the desponding soul a full view of his difficulties; instead of administering the cheering cordials and sustaining encouragements of the Gospel.   This would indeed be, unlike his Master, to "break the bruised reed, and quench the smoking flax."   On the other hand, most unfaithful would he be, were he—instead of rousing slumbering sinners by "the terror of the Lord"—to lull them into deeper slumber by an exclusive display of Christian privileges; or to comfort the presumptuous professor with the stability of the Divine engagements, instead of warning him of the fearful danger of self-deception.   Perhaps a wise intermingling of the two prominent systems in the Church may be of important service to the disciples of both.   The Calvinist from the abuse of his principles may be in danger of security, and may need some wholesome exhortations to holy fear from the opposite system; while his own system may furnish to the Arminian some important views of the Sovereignty of God, and the freeness and simplicity of the Gospel, to neutralize the principles of self-dependence and self-sufficiency.   Thus 'it is possible, that the truly Scriptural statement will be found, not in an exclusive adoption of either, nor yet in a confused mixture of both, but in the proper and seasonable application of both; or (to use the language of St. Paul) in "rightly dividing the word of truth." '[3]

In his extended course, the Minister must be skilled in personating a variety of characters; becoming a Boanerges or a Barhabas—having a word for the worldly and the spiritual, for the self-righteous and the contrite, for the wise and for the unwise, for the weak and for the strong, for the presumptuous and for the

[1] Gal. iv. 20.   1 Cor. iv. 21.
[2] See his Philosophy of Rhetoric, and some striking remarks in Hall's Sermon, pp. 25, 26.
[3] Preface to Mr. Simeon's Helps to Composition—to which the Writer gladly refers, as a full, clear, and unfettered display of Evangelical truth.

doubting, for the mourner and for the rejoicing. "A word fitly spoken" for each, will be "like apples of gold in pictures" (or frame works) "of silver."[1] "Of some," that have been beguiled, he must "have compassion ; making a difference" between them and obstinate offenders. "Others" he must "save with fear, pulling them out of the fire."[2] It will not indeed be always wise to persevere in the same treatment with the same cases. Spiritual, like medical, applications, require occasional change to strengthen the system ; and thus must the applications be varied to meet the ever-varying exigencies of the several cases.[3] And here he will find, that it is not enough to cultivate his own gift—whether for the Church or for the world—(which, however valuable, grasps only half the compass of his sphere) he must set himself in diligent prayer and industry to *cultivate the opposite gift*. How successful was the Apostle John in this effort ! Who would ever have thought that his Epistles had. been written by a "Son of Thunder?"[4] We sometimes indeed hear the peal in the sound of solemn rebuke and warning. But their main characteristic is the endearing enforcement of "a Son of Consolation." Thus must we endeavour to apply our Ministry upon the broad ground of universal adaptation, maintaining a just equipoise and combination of spiritual gifts, "that the man of God may be perfect, thoroughly furnished unto all good works."[5]

Not less illustrative of the Scriptural wisdom of the pulpit Ministry is the *adaptation of instruction to the different stages of Christian progress*. The gospel is not taught by one or more lessons, so as to render further instructions unnecessary. The Apostle compares the elementary truths to "milk," the proper and necessary nourishment "for babes ;" the deeper and more mysterious doctrines to "strong meat," adapted to the adult spiritual state, when experience is more exercised, and the judgment more matured.[6] Our Divine teacher gently led his scholars from the more simple to the higher truths, "as they were able to bear them."[7]

---

[1] Prov. xxv. 11.   [2] Jude 22, 23.

[3] 'A preacher must carefully observe the manners, customs, and inclinations of those whom he would persuade, that he may gain an easier admission of the truth into their minds.' Quesnel on Acts xvii. 23.

[4] Mark iii. 17, with Luke ix. 54.   [5] 2 Tim. iii. 17.

[6] Heb. v. 11—14. 1 Cor. iii. 1—3. Si pro viribus suis alatur infans, fiet, ut crescendo plus capiat ; si modum suæ capacitatis excedat, deficit antequam crescat. Aug. de Civit. Dei. Lib. xii. 'It is a great degree of knowledge to be able to observe and follow the motions of grace, on which all depends ; and which commonly performs its work by degrees.' Quesnel on Matt. ix. 17.

[7] Compare Isaiah xl. 11.—as illustrated by the wise and tender condescension of his public Ministry, Mark ix. 33. How remarkable is the contrast between the elementary character of his sermon on the Mount and his latter discourses, evidently adapted to a

But human teachers too often fail in forbearance to the weakness of young converts.   Expecting them to learn and receive every thing at once, contrary to the Apostolical prescription, they offer "strong meat" to the "babes ;" and thus seriously injure the spiritual constitution by a course of unsuitable diet.   Yet while giving "milk to babes," we must not forget to distribute meat to adults.   The Apostle deemed it necessary to go on from " the doctrine of repentance," (the subject of his Master's early Ministry) "to perfection" —not indeed giving it up as unnecessary ; but " leaving" it, as the builder leaves the foundation, when advancing the building to completion.[1]   Dr. Owen well observed—' It is the duty of Ministers of the Gospel to take care, not only that the doctrine which they preach be true, but also that it be seasonable with respect to the state and condition of their hearers.   *Herein consists no small part of that wisdom, which is required in the dispensation of the word.*[2]

Much wisdom indeed is required for this diversified application. In our private Ministrations we can individualize each particular case ; but in public addresses to hearers of different capacities and states, when invisible agency is actively diverting the word from its course, the difficulty is painfully felt.   Frequently is the tender " reed bruised" by a word of seasonable application to the thoughtless or the backsliding ; while the promises, too hastily rejected by the self-condemning penitent, are eagerly seized by the presumptuous, to bind the spirit of slumber more strongly upon their consciences.

This mode is sometimes unjustly exposed to the imputation of unfaithfulness.   ' Some men' (as Mr. Cecil remarks) ' seem to think, that in the choice of a wise way there lurks always a trimming disposition.'[3]   There is doubtless considerable danger of adulterating the Gospel, under the cover of prudence, and in the well-intentioned endeavour to commend it to the endless diversity of cases.   But there is an important distinction between rational contrivance and Christian accommodation.   As Mr. Cecil again remarks—' It is a foolish project *to avoid giving offence ;* but it is our duty to *avoid giving unnecessary offence.*'   To seek to be

higher stage of Christian knowledge, and promising a yet more full revelation of the gospel to his Church! John xvi. 12, 13. Yet it is important to observe, that it was the same gospel in all its perfect integrity at first as at last—not modified or stripped of its native offensiveness—only more fully developed.

[1] Compare Matt. iv. 17, with Heb. vi. 1, 2.

[2] Owen on Heb. vi. 1. ' This work must be carried on prudently, orderly, and by degrees. " Milk" must go before " strong meat." The foundation must be laid, before we build upon it. Children must not be dealt with as men at age. We must not go beyond the capacities of our people, nor teach them the perfection, that have not learned the principle.' Baxter's Reformed Pastor.   [3] Cecil's Remains.

acceptable is by no means inconsistent with faithfulness. Why should not we, after the example of the royal preacher, " *seek to find out acceptable* words ;"[1] " keeping back nothing that is profitable," but with " the wise man's heart discerning both time and judgment ;"[2] avoiding an irritating and repulsive mode of statement ; and labouring to distribute unpalatable truths in the sweetness of persuasion, compassion, and sympathy ? " In doctrine," let us " show uncorruptness ;"[3] in mode, acceptableness ; like our heavenly Pattern considering, not so .much what we are able to say, as what our people are able to hear.[4] The Preacher's " acceptable words were upright—even words of truth ;" so consistent is Ministerial conciliation, *when it does not lead to compromise*, with Christian wisdom.

The state of our people will also influence the tone of our Ministrations. We must deal out *" present truth"*[5]—truth (like the doctrine of justification under the existing circumstances of the Galatian Church) adapted to the present emergency. Again— though truth itself is unalterable, its mode of presentment admits of much variation. It may be brought out in the form of doctrine, precept, warning, encouragement, or privilege. It may be set forth in statement or figure ; it may be illustrated by a parable ; deduced from a miracle ; substantiated in a Scripture character ; displayed in type or prophecy ; delivered from the mouth of the Lord or of his Apostles—and in all these different modes with equal simplicity and faithfulness. What a diversity of gifts do we observe in the Apostles ! Peter acknowledges it in the case of himself, and his " beloved brother Paul."[6] The contrast between the Epistles of Paul and James, upon the same doctrine of justification, is even more striking. In the general complexion of his Epistles, James, though less doctrinal than his brother Paul, yet wrote under the same inspiration, and could commend himself by *his* " manifestation of the truth," with equal confidence " in the sight of God." Contrast again Paul with himself—Paul at Antioch, and Paul at Athens—Paul before Felix, and before Agrippa.[7] Compare the Epistles to his Gentile churches with each other,[8] and with his

---

[1] Eccles. xii. 10. The first nine chapters of the Book of Proverbs (as Dr. Wardlaw admirably observes) ' present us with a most interesting specimen of these " acceptable words." There is in them an inimitable union of admonitory fidelity, and enticing and subduing kindness. Like Paul, he " exhorts, and comforts, and charges, as a father doth his children." The whole soul of the writer is breathed out in the earnestness of benevolent desire.' Wardlaw on Eccles. xii. 10.

[2] Acts xx. 20. with Eccl. viii. 5.   [3] Titus ii. 7.   [4] Mark iv. 33.

[5] See 2 Peter i. 12.   [6] 2 Peter iii. 15.   [7] Acts xiii. xvii.. xxiv. xxvi.

[8] With the Romans, he embraces the whole compass of Christian doctrine ; with the Galatians, he is mainly occupied with the single point of justification ; with the Corin-

Epistle to his own countrymen ; not communicating different systems of truth, but the same system in different modes ; not abandoning any point of truth, but adapting the mode of its distribution to the circumstances of the respective churches ; in all cases " according to the wisdom given unto him ;" and in all his Ministrations with Divine power and success.

We may here also refer to *the influence of our Christian temper amentupon the character of our Ministrations.* It is natural, and under due regulation important, to carry the peculiar bias of our mind into our Ministry. Every man is formed to think, and speak, and write in a manner of his own ; and he will be far more useful in preserving his own manner (improved by comparison with others, but never wholly forsaken), than by enslaving himself to some popular mode. But let it be known, watched, balanced. It has its evils as well as its advantages. A speculative mind is apt to speculate in sacred Ministration—to discuss subjects in a train of argumentation, which divests them of their heavenly unction and simplicity. An accomplished mind may be in danger, even in the evangelical field, of furnishing more food for the imagination than for the immortal soul. A doctrinal Preacher mainly confines his Ministration within his favourite chapters and class of subjects. An experimental Preacher, awakened by the terrors of the law, will imbue his preaching more with the character of alarm, than of tenderness. Or if he has been " drawn by the bands of love," he may be led almost unconsciously to omit the " persuasive" influence of " the terror of the Lord."[1] A practical Preacher, having seen the loose profession resulting from exclusive views of doctrine or experience, perhaps leaves his statements bare, or imperfectly connected with either. An applicatory Preacher may fail in giving clear and connected statements of doctrine. A discriminating Preacher may be in danger of perplexing his hearers with refined distinctions drawn more immediately from his own spiritual exercises, than from the clear system of the word of God. A decided Preacher will need a deep tincture of humility, forbearance, and love ; else his " zeal will be without knowledge," and his labour prove the occasion of almost unqualified offence. It is

thians he largely expounds questions of casuistry, matters of discipline, and general practical duty ; but all inculcated upon the foundation, and intermingled with the display, of the doctrine of Christ.

[1] See 2 Cor. v. 11. It is well that our experience should furnish materials for our Ministry ; but care must be taken that the standard of our preaching be elevated and its character formed, upon the basis of the word of God. Thus only will it be sealed with the warrant of Divine acceptance, and sympathize with all classes of Christians as well as with the wants of the ignorant and unconverted.

therefore an important exercise of Ministerial wisdom, not to frame our preaching to the bias of our own mind, without great self-distrust, much earnest prayer, and a clear persuasion, that it embraces within its range, alike the converted and the unconverted, and is equally calculated to awaken and to establish ; ·to "add to the Church," and to strengthen in the Church, "such as shall be saved."

III.—PLAINNESS—THE SPIRIT OF SCRIPTURAL PREACHING.

THE spirit of preaching consists in its adaptation to the subjects of instruction. It may be Scriptural in its statements, experimental in its character, and practical in its enforcement. It may have all the features of discrimination and decision. But if it is not intelligible in its mode of address, it must fail in application to the objects proposed. Philip Henry was deeply sensible of the necessity of plain preaching—' We study how to speak' (said he, at the commencement of his Ministry) ' that you may understand us ; and I never think that I can speak plain enough, when I am speaking about souls and their salvation.'[1] Our Lord's discourses —without any of the artificial pomp of oratory, and with a profusion of imagery—are a perfect model of simplicity. Never was there a more plain and popular Preacher. The most sublime truths are illustrated by the most familiar comparisons from the objects around him. The beautiful figures interspersed in the sermon on the Mount were probably drawn from the objects, which his elevated situation placed before him ; ' such as a city set upon a hill ; persons manuring the fields with salt ; the sun shining on all the fields without distinction ; the fowls flying in the air, and the lilies growing about him.'[2] Most of his parables also were drawn from the same natural´ sources. Even children's play was made to minister conviction to his hearers.[3] The fields, under his observant eye, were made fruitful in spiritual instruction ;[4] and wherever he moved, he was the Teacher of the people according to their way and capacity. His Apostles closely followed in his steps. They felt themselves " debtors to the unwise," as well as

---

[1] Life, p. 26. Thus also Dr. Doddridge in one of his devotional exercises, writes—' I fear my discourse to-day was too abstruse for my hearers. I resolve to labour after great plainness and seriousness; and to bring down my preaching to the understanding of the weakest.' Life, ch. ii.

[2] Gerard's Pastoral Care, p. 127. ' Can any man imitate'—asks Bishop Wilson—' a greater Master of eloquence, than Jesus Christ was, whose great excellence appears in making great truths understood by the meanest capacity?' Sacra Privata.

[3] Matt. xi. 16—;19.   [4] Ibid. xiii.

" to the wise."[1]   They would neither sink beneath the dignity of
their subject, nor soar above the capacities of their people.   They
" used great plainness of speech."[2]   Their mode of teaching, though,
with considerable difference of style, was brought down to the
reach of the lowest intelligence.   Paul dealt much in illustration,
never remote, and always on subjects with which he knew his
people to be conversant.   The Grecian games furnished useful and
pointed instruction to the churches in the neighbourhood of these
pastimes, or who were interested in them.[3]   James, in the same
style of writing, crowded together the most familiar illustrations in
the exhibition of a single point.[4]   Peter and John were plain and
didactic.   Jude, so far as we can judge from one short epistle, is
energetic and expressive.   All of them, however, in their language
and turns of sentiment, are distinguished by a remarkable perspicuity, never above the ordinary level—plainness without familiarity.
The discourses of the the Christian Fathers were generally of the
same character.   Augustine's discourses are remarked to be the
most simple of all his works.[5]   He often interrupted them, to explain what might seem to be beyond the capacity of his hearers ;
who would, on the other hand, sometimes express their intelligent
satisfaction with his meaning.   The Homilies of Chrysostom and
others of that day were so called, as being delivered in a familiar
and conversational mode.   The sermons of our Reformers (judging
from the book of Homilies and other specimens, and making allowance for the phraseology of the times) are admirable specimens
of a style equally simple, forcible, and interesting.   Luther tells
us, that when asked by Dr. Albert the best way of preaching before the elector—' I said—Let all your preaching be in the most
plain manner.   Look not to the prince, but to the plain, simple,
and unlearned people, of which cloth the prince himself is also
made.   If I in my preaching should have regard to Philip Melancthon, or other learned doctors, I should work but little good.   I
preach in the simplest sort to the unskilful, and the same giveth
content to all.'[6]

---

[1] Rom. i. 14.
[2] 2 Cor. iii. 12; Comp. 1 Cor. xiv. 19.   'Habent sacræ Scripturæ, sed non ostendunt,
eloquentiam.'   August. de Doctr. Christ. Lib. iv.—especially and most justly recommended
by Milner to the study of Ministers.   Hist. ii. pp. 441, 442.
[3] 1 Cor. ix. ; Phil. iii.
[4] See especially James iii. 1—12. and the ingenious and exquisite exposition of it in
Bishop Jebb's Sacred Literature, pp. 273—308.
[5] See quotation from his Sermons in page 281.
[6] Table Talk.   It was one of his sayings—'Optimi ad vulgus hi concionatores, qui
pueriliter, populariter, et simplissime docent.'   See a beautiful anecdote characteristic of
this great reformer, advising Bucer on this subject.   Scott's Continuation of Milner, vol.
i. 216, 217.   Adams, in his Life of Luther, has inserted some homely rhymes, which he

One of the ancient prophets was commanded—"Write the vis-ion, and *make it plain upon tables, that he may run that read-eth it.*"[1] That this command may have its due effect, we must pay attention to *style, subject-matter, and mode of address.*

A plain style is most suitable for the expression of plain things. Here probably many of us have much to learn. Education has formed our minds into a mould so different, and given us a lan-guage so remote, from familiar usage, that there must be a great, and possibly an uncongenial, change in our flow of thought and composition ; and yet without losing that vigour and liveliness, necessary to arrest attention. In fact, we must be learners among our people, before we can hope to succeed as teachers. We must " condescend to men of low estate,"[2] to study their minds, habits, and phraseology ; never use a hard word, where a plain one can be found ; giving proper words in their proper places ; short sentences, and specially simple ideas ; for many will comprehend, or success-fully guess at, the meaning of a hard word, who would be baffled by a complex idea. ' Parenthesis and circumlocution' (it is justly remarked,) ' deprive expression of its edge : and the idea, attenua-ted by frequent tropes and figures, arrives at the mind of the hear-er, like an arrow spent in its flight ;'[3] and rather serves to startle than to impress. Archbishop Secker judiciously recommends (as a means of winning the attention of our people) ' to make our ser-mons extremely clear. Terms and phrases' (he remarks) ' may be familiar to you, which are quite unintelligible to them; and I fear this happens much oftener than we suspect ; therefore guard against it. Your expressions may be very common, without being low ; yet employ the lowest (provided they are not ridiculous) ra-ther than not be understood.'[4] It is a frequent mistake to take too

composed for the common people. And ' for these beggarly ballads' (says a shrewd writer) 'Luther may receive a greater reward at the last day, than for whole shelves of learned folios. Vanity will make a man speak and write learnedly ; but piety only can prevail upon a good scholar to simplify his speech for the sake of the vulgar. Such a preacher, though his worth may be overlooked by the undiscerning now, will one day have a name above every name, whether it be philosopher. poet, orator, or whatever else is most revered among mankind.' Rev. R. Robinson's Notes on Claude's Essay—a work, not devoid of information or interest; but painfully distinguished by an unchristian, vituperative spirit.   [1] Hab. ii. 2.

[2] A Preacher is to fancy himself in the room of the most unlearned man in his whole parish ; and therefore he must put such parts of his discourse as he would have all under-stand, in so plain a form, that it may not be beyond the meanest of them. This he will certainly study to do, if his desire is to edify them, rather than to make them admire himself as a learned and high-spoken man.' Burnet's Pastoral Care, ch. ix.

[3] Budd on Infant Baptism, pp. 493, 494.

[4] Charges, pp. 273, 274. Augustine continually reverts to this subject. He did not scruple to say—'Melius est, ut nos reprehendant grammatici, quam ut non intelligant populi.' In Ps. cxxxix. 15. Thus in one of his sermons to the same purport—' Rogo humiliter, ut contentæ sint eruditæ aures vestræ verba rustica æquanimiter sustinere, dummodo totus grex Domini simplici, et, ut ita dicam, pedestri sermone, pabulum spiri-

much for granted.   Fenelon's remark is applicable to many Protestant congregations—'that there are always three quarters of an
ordinary congregation, who do not know those first principles of religion, with which the preacher supposes every one to be fully instructed.'[1]   We must remember, that our commission extends to
the explanation of the words, as well as of the things, of God.   The
meaning is hid in the word, and cannot be discovered without it.
There are many important Scriptural terms, whose meaning is little,
if at all, understood by the mass : so that a want of brief verbal explanation is often a great hindrance to edification.   We must not
judge the extent of the people's information by our own.   'Have
ye understood these things ?'[2]—would often be a seasonable inquiry ; while the expression of à wish to be understood would be attractive and engaging.   After all, a popular view of the simplest
elementary principles is the best introduction to more extended and
accurate views of truth.

Nor is this style of simplicity degrading to the most intellectual
mind.   We could do no more with "the tongues of angels," than
communicate our ideas intelligibly to one another—an exercise,
which many preachers of excellent literary endowments have found
to require considerable pains and diligence.[3]   Not, that, in our la-

---

tuale possit accipere ; et quia imperiti et simplices ad scholasticorum altitudinem non
possunt ascendere, eruditi se dignentur ad illorum ignorantiam se inclinare.'   Quesnel
remarks—' That a man need not fear stooping too low, when he considers himself as the
dispenser of the mysteries of abased wisdom.   The gospel is more for the poor and simple
than for the refined wits ; and yet a minister thereof is sometimes (as one may say) afraid
of being understood by the simple, lest he should not be admired by the learned.'   On
Mark iv. 33.   ' Affect not fine words, but words which the Holy Ghost teacheth.   Enticing words of man's wisdom debase your matter.   Gold needs not to be painted.   Scripture expressions are what people are used to, and will remember.'   William's Life of M.
Henry, p. 162.
   [1] Dialogues on Eloquence, iii.   [2] Matt. xiii. 51.
   [3] Quintilian excellently observes, that our meaning, 'like the light of the sun, should
obtrude itself upon the eyes of the ignorant, not only without any pains to search for it,
but, as it were, whether he will or not.'   Institut. Lib. viii. cap. 2.   Rollin has the same
illustration.   Belles Letters, vii.   Luther used to say—' To preach plainly and simply is
a great art.'   Table Talk.   Archbishop Usher observed—' It requires all our learning to
make things plain.—It is not difficult to make *easy things* appear *hard*; but to render
hard things easy, is *the hardest* part of a good orator and preacher.'   ' *He* is the power-
fullest preacher, and the best orator'—said Dr. South—'who can make himself best understood.'   Bishop Wilkins observes—' the greatest learning is to be seen in the greatest
plainness.   The more clearly we understand any thing ourselves, the more easily can
we expound it to others.'   Eccles. p. 168.   (The character that Photius gave of the
preaching of Athanasius will confirm this point.   ' In sermonibus ubique in locutione
clarus est, et brevis, et simplex, *acutus tamen et altus*.')   Bishop Hurd charged his clergy
to the same purport—' Your sermons cannot well be too plain : and I need not say unto
you who hear me—that to frame a discourse in this way, as it is the usefullest way of
preaching, so it will afford full scope and exercise for all the talents, which the ablest
of us may possess.'   Charges.   Archbishop Tillotson is said to have been 'in the habit
of reading his sermons to an illiterate old woman of plain sense who lived with him, and
of altering his words and expressions, till he had brought the style down to her level.'
If the story be true, 'it is' (as Professor Campbell observes) 'much to the prelate's honour ; for, however incompetent such judges might be of the composition, the doctrine, or

bour for "plainness of speech," we would strip the Gospel of its dignified terseness, beautiful figures, and heavenly elevation.   Nor would we recommend a style of naked simplicity in our addresses. Our Lord's example, as that of the simplest Preachers, seems to recommend an infusion of the illustrative style into our discourses. And indeed natural images furnish most useful elucidation of spiritual things, by their palpable exhibition to the senses.   The study of the Scripture metaphors will give a correct mode of illustration, in marking their exquisite adaptation to the subjects of reference. Remote images (from which no clear light can be obtained) should be avoided.   Every thing bordering upon the ridiculous, light, or trifling, must be discountenanced, as being utterly inconsistent with the dignity and holiness of the Sacred Volume, and 'with that Divine and powerful delivery, which becometh him, that speaks the oracles of God.'[1]   Only that which is serious has a tendency to permanent edification.

The vanity of learned preaching is proved by its unproductiveness.   The plainest preachers in a Christian spirit, are commonly the most successful.[2]   We might as well think of adding clearness to light, as hope to embellish the simplicity of the Gospel by rhetorical expression.[3]   Such embellishments, if allowed at all, should be sparingly used.[4]   King James aptly compared them in public discourses ' to the red and blue flowers, that pester the corn, when it stands in the fields ; more noisome to the growing crop, than beautiful to the beholding eye.'[5]   The Apostle laid much stress upon " words easy to be understood."   How would he then have rebuked as contemptible and most responsible trifling, the affectation of de-

---

the arguments, they are certainly the most competent judges of what terms and phrases fall within the apprehension of the vulgar, the class to which they belong.'   On Pulpit Eloquence, Lect. iii.   Compare Fenelon on Eloquence, ut supra.   Perhaps however the poet's rule—' Non fumum ex fulgore, sed ex fumo dare lucem'—expresses the whole in the fewest words.

[1] Ward's Coal from the Altar.   Compare Bowles' Past. Evang. Lib. ii. c. 10.

[2] Archbishop Leighton, after hearing a plain and homely sermon with entire satisfaction, observed—' This good man seems in earnest to catch souls.'   ' The measure of speech' (he remarked) ' ought to be the character of the audience, which is made up for the most part of illiterate persons.'   Pearson's Life, p. lix.

[3] What has been said of commentators, may apply to preachers of this character—that their subjects were plain, until they expounded them.

[4] Augustine's animadversion was—' Numquid hic ornamenta, et non documenta, quæruntur?'   De Doctr. Christ. Lib. iv. 19, ut supra.   Not that he was wholly averse to ornament.   His idea of the style of discourses was most just—' Nec inornata relinquitur, nec indecenter ornatur.'   Ib. iv. 26.

[5] Preface to his Remonstrance—'Preachers' (remarks Bishop Taylor) ' are to feed the people, not with gay tulips and useless daffodils, but with the bread of life and medicinal plants, springing from the margin of the fountain of salvation.'   ' Very fine, Sir,' (said Robert Hall, when asked his opinion of a sermon) ' but men can't eat flowers.'   ' Lord,' (said a pious old writer) ' let me never be guilty, by painting the windows, of hindering the light of thy glorious Gospel from shining powerfully into the hearts !'

livering common truths in an uncommon manner, of modernizing the language of the sacred volume, or exchanging it for classical phraseology; often "speaking in an unknown tongue," and "shutting up the kingdom of heaven against men."[1]   Such terms (as Professor Campbell remarks) 'give a learned dress to religion ; but it is a dress, that very ill befits an institution intended for the comfort and direction of all, even of the lowest ranks.'[2]   'Nothing indeed (as Jerome long since observed) 'is so easy, as to impose upon an illiterate audience, whose habit is to admire what they do not understand.'[3]   But the garb used for this purpose 'is often no other than a cloak for ignorance.   And of all kinds of ignorance, learned ignorance is undoubtedly the most contemptible.'[4] Indeed the influence of this unevangelical system, would sink the true glory and dignity of the pulpit into a stage exhibition of self-display.   'The sword of the Spirit' (to use a terse illustration of an old Divine) is 'put into a velvet scabbard, that it cannot prick and wound the heart.'[5]

Plainness in the choice of our subjects marks also the spirit of Scriptural preaching.   We may here attend to the excellent advice of the primitive Bishop Wilson—'Avoid' (says he) 'such discourses and subjects, as would divert the mind without instructing it.   Never consult your own fancy in the choice of subjects, but the necessities of the flock.   I would rather send away the hearers smiting their breasts than please the most learned audience with a fine sermon against any vice.   With what truth can it be said, that "the sheep hear your voice," when you speak matters above their capacities, or in language and terms which they do not understand?   It is too often, that preachers perplex those whom they should instruct.   There is a great deal of difference between people admiring the preacher, and being edified by his sermons.'[6]

---

[1] 1 Cor. xiv. 11—19.   Matt. xxiii. 13.
[2] On Systematic Theology, Lect. iii.   See the sensible advice that Mr. Richmond received from his College Tutor on this subject. Life, p. 152.
[3] Hieron. ad Nepot.
[4] Campbell, ut supra.   'An affected obscurity of style' (Baxter remarks) 'makes a fool admire the preacher's learning ; but it will make a wise man wonder at his hypocrisy or folly.'   Kirke White justly remarked of a preacher whom he had lately heard—'I think in particular he has one great fault, that is, *elegance.   He is not sufficiently plain.*   Remember (adds he) we do not mount the pulpit to say fine things or eloquent things. . We have there to proclaim the good tidings of salvation to fallen man, to point out the way to eternal life, to exhort, to cheer, to support, the suffering sinner: these are the glorious topics upon which we have to enlarge: and will these permit the tricks of oratory or the studied beauties of eloquence?   Shall truths and counsels like these be couched in terms, which the poor and ignorant cannot comprehend?'—See his Remains.
[5] Ward's Coal from the Altar.
[6] Sacra Privata.   'Let your performances' (said the excellent Matthew Henry) 'be plain and Scriptural.   Choose for your pulpit subjects the plainest and most needful truths, and endeavour to make them plainer.'   Williams' Life, ut supra.

Metaphysical preaching, would come under these animadversions. Dr. Dwight (a man of a strong natural bias of this character) admirably observes—'All preaching of this kind is chiefly useless, and commonly mischievous. No ordinary congregation ever understood, to any valuable purpose, metaphysical subjects; and no congregation, it is believed, was ever much edified by a metaphysical manner of discussion.'[1] We would not encourage a superficial treatment of more elaborate subjects; but let all reasoning be grounded upon the simple principles of Scripture, rather than upon inductive or excursive philosophy. All "intrusions into things which we have not seen"[2]—all questions not directly tending to edification (such as the Apostle denominates "old wives' fables," "vain babblings," "foolish questions"[3]) are to be avoided. To the weeping complaint—"Thy prophets have seen *vain and foolish things* for thee"[4]—every serious Christian must respond, when he sees Ministers 'picking straws in Divinity;'[5] substituting husks for the bread of life; scholastic or metaphysical distinctions, curious researches into antiquity, ingenious dissertations upon the fitness of things, abstract proofs of the evidences of Christianity, elucidations merely critical of the sacred text, for the simple exhibition of the truth. 'The hungry sheep look up, and are not fed.' It is not "stones turned into bread;" but rather bread turned into stones. There is more nourishment in a single plain discourse on Christ crucified, than in these shadowy discussions, misnamed sermons, or preaching the Gospel.

We might refer to *the plausible ground of dissent* arising from this preaching, as a minor consideration for Ministers of the Establishment,[6] (for our people will soon be tired of hearing what they do not understand); but a far *higher responsibility* is contracted

---

[1] Dwight's Theology, v. 209, 210. 'That which metaphysical preaching teaches' (as he elsewhere remarks) 'may be true, and the arguments used to support it may be sound; but the distinctions are so subtle, and the reasoning so abstruse and difficult, that the hearer's attention to the truth is lost in his attention to the preacher's ingenuity; his mind prevented from feeling what is intended, by the absorption of his thoughts in the difficulties of the argument; and his heart chilled by the cold manner, in which all such discussions are conducted. The metaphysician, whether aware of it or not, is employed in displaying his own ingenuity, and not in disclosing and confirming the truth of God.' Sermons, vol. ii. 461. Compare Burnet's Pastoral Care, c. ix.   [2] Col. ii. 18.
[3] 1 Tim. iv. 7. vi. 20. Tit. iii. 9.   [4] Lam. ii. 14.   [5] Bishop Hall.
[6] Dr. Johnson (see Boswell's Life) with much truth ascribes the success of the Methodists, in drawing away the members of the establishment, to their plain mode of address. King James in a curious document, entitled—'The Reason of the King's Direction for Preaching and Preachers'—traces the many defections to Popery, and Anabaptism, or other points of separation, to the 'lightness, affectedness, and unprofitableness,' of the preachers in his day, 'mustering up of much reading, or displaying of their wits,' leaving the people's mind, 'for all this airy nourishment, no better than mere table-books, ready to be filled up with the catechism of the Popish priests, or the pamphlets of the Anabaptists.'

than *dissent.* It may be that the grammarian, the critic, the theologian, approve our discourses. But to an illiterate congregation of perishing sinners, should we not use, as the grand vehicle of our communication—" words easy to be understood ?" If they do not understand their preacher, they " are destroyed for lack of knowledge." For how can they be saved by the preaching of the Gospel in an unknown tongue? And of how little account will be the reputation of an accurate logician, deep theologian, or orthodox Divine, under the weight of this awful charge !¹

A plain mode of address is also included in the spirit of preaching. A want of plain dealing with our people will inevitably betray their souls, and ours with them. We are engaged with them on subjects connected with eternity, on which mistakes are so various and so fatal. It is of far higher moment, that we should be useful than eloquent, that the watchman should blow the trumpet intelligibly than musically. Nothing is done, until we bring them into immediate contact with their imminent, unseen, unsuspected danger. Let this plainness embrace all the variety of illustration, argumentation, appeal, and entreaty. Let it include the enforcement of every motive of terror and of love, of warning and of encouragement. But let there be a careful separation from meretricious · embellishments,² a freedom from a false scrupulosity of tenderness, and an unreserved devotedness to the grand object of the Ministry ; applying always the message of the Gospel in clear and uncompromising terms; and pursuing sin and Satan in a course of unwearied warfare, until they are dispossessed of all their strong holds, and " every thought is brought into captivity unto the obedience of Christ."

IV.—FERVENCY—THE SPIRIT OF SCRIPTURAL PREACHING.

To enlighten the mind, and affect the heart, are the two main ends of the Christian Ministry. The first demands *wisdom and plainness*—the second *fervency*—as the spirit of Scriptural preaching. This combination exhibits the Minister as " a burning and shining light"—' the sun in his sphere' (as Pavillon, the celebrated Bishop of Alet, describes him) ; ' imparting the spiritual light of

---

¹ 'I had rather' (said Dr. John Edwards) ' be fully understood by ten, than be admired by ten thousand. If our words be not understood, it is of no consequence in what language they are spoken, and we cannot expect that the Holy Spirit will give a blessing on unintelligible language—I mean—unintelligible to the many, though a few of superior attainments or refinements may admire them.'

² Bishop Stillingfleet compares this mode of treatment to ' stroking the consciences of people with feathers dipped in oil.' Duties and Rights of Parochial Clergy, p. 30.

Divine truth, as well as the spiritual heat of Divine fervour.' As to fervency—if it be natural to express ourselves with earnestness upon subjects of deep and acknowledged interest—much more in the delivery of our great commission. 'Nothing' (says Baxter) 'is more indecent, than a dead preacher speaking to dead sinners the living truth of the living God.' It were surely better to subject ourselves to the misapprehension of being " beside ourselves,"[1] than not to deliver our message with some evidence of personal impression. As a matter of life and death—of eternal life and eternal death—it is connected with the most powerful motives, and acts upon the most influential principles of the heart. Charles V. remarked of one of the German Reformers—'He preached with such spirit and devotion, as might almost serve to make the very stones weep.' Such was the spirit of our Great Master,[2] and of his chosen Apostle.[3] The same spirit constituted the main power of Whitfield's Ministry. There have been men of like unction, faith, and prayer—men whose views of the gospel have been equally comprehensive, and whose love for souls has been equally fervent; but it was the picture of his whole soul pourtrayed in his countenance;[4] his expressions cast into the most awakening and penetrating forms; the solemnity of his address; the deep feeling from within, bursting forth in every word, streaming in his eyes, and breathing an energy of love throughout the effusions of his overflowing heart —this it was that convinced the listening throngs, that he was not trifling with them. They caught sympathy with his natural eloquence, and in thousands of instances, "the flint was turned into a fountain of waters;" and his Ministry was life from the dead " to his fellow-sinners." 'This faculty of moving hearers thus' (Archbishop Secker remarks) 'is a most valuable blessing. And such as have but little of it, may considerably improve it, by labouring to affect themselves more deeply with what they would say, and thinking what methods of saying it would be most persuasive.'

[1] 2 Cor. v. 13. Compare Acts ii. 12, 13. ' So long as our zeal takes not its colour from human infirmities and human passions, but is regulated by the word of God; so long as we tread in the steps of those, " who did all things decently and in order;" far from having to apologize for our zeal, we should think that we act unworthily of our cause, if we possessed it not.' The Gospel Message, by Rev. Dr. Dealtry, p. 21.

[2] John ii. 17.   [3] Acts xvii. 16.

[4] The description given of an old foreign preacher would give an accurate sketch of Whitfield in the pulpit—'Vivida in eo omnia fuerunt; vivida vox, vividi oculi, vividi manus, gestus omnes vividi.' His ingenious confessions at the close of life, of a tincture of enthusiasm, and an occasional admixture of his own spirit with his Ministry, eminently displayed Christian humility. As Fuller memorialized the celebrated Wickliff in his characteristic style—'I intend neither to deny, dissemble, defend, or excuse any of his faults. "We have this treasure" (says the Apostle) "in *earthen* vessels," and he that shall endeavour to prove a pitcher of clay to be a pot of gold, will take great pains to small purpose. Yea, should I be over-officious to retain myself to plead for Wickliff's faults, that glorious saint would sooner chide than thank me.' Church History, Book iv.

But (as he elsewhere observes) 'smooth discourses' to our people, 'containing little that awakens their drowsy attention, little that enforces on them plainly and home "what they must do to be saved," leave them as ignorant and unreformed as ever, and only lull them into a fatal security.'[1] Even Bishop Warburton decides, that 'a pathetic address to the passions and affections of penitent hearers, is perhaps the most operative of all the various speeches of instruction.'[2] George Herbert's Parson, 'when he preacheth, procures attention by all possible art :—by earnestness of speech ; it being natural to men to think, that where there is much earnestness, there is something worth hearing.'[3] Visible impression upon ourselves gives inexpressible weight to our subject. The Minister, that does not manifestly put his heart into his sermon, will never put his sermon into the hearts of his people. Pompous elocution, attempts at theatrical display, or affected emotions, are indeed most repugnant to the simple dignity of our office. A painted fire may glare, but will not warm. Violent agitations, without correspondent tenderness of feeling, will disgust instead of arresting the mind. Preaching is not (as some appear to think it) the work of the lungs, or the mimickry of gesture, or the impulse of uncontrolable feeling ; but the spiritual energy of a heart constrained by the love of Christ, and devoted to the care of those immortal souls, for whom Christ died. Yet surely the habit of realizing our Master's presence, and the awful responsibility vested in us, will find expression in something beyond the tone of tame seriousness, and the general accuracy of pulpit decorum.[4] The Country Parson finds the people 'thick and heavy, and hard to raise to a point of zeal and fervency, and needing a mountain of fire to kindle them.' He recommends therefore most beautifully, the 'dipping and seasoning all our words and sentences in our hearts, before they come into our mouths ; truly affecting, and cordially expressing all that we can say, so that our auditors may plainly perceive, that every word is heart-deep.'[5] A lively impression of interest seems the natural result of a cordial belief of the Gospel ; and therefore a want of expression of this interest conveys a plausible suspicion of the credibility of our message. For who could bring a *true* report of a

---

[1] Charges, pp. 252, 284.
[2] Directions to Students of Theology.   [3] Chapter vii.
[4] 'While I have any reverence for Scripture, or any knowledge of human nature, I shall never affect to speak of the glories of Christ, and of the eternal interests of man, as coldly, as if I were reading a lecture of mathematics, or relating an experiment in natural philosophy.' Dr. Doddridge—Orton's Life, chap. v. King James remarked of one of his chaplains—' This man preaches before me, just as if death was seated at his elbow.'
[5] Chap. vii.

fire, or of any extraordinary news, with a calm tone, gentle voice, or elegant expression ? And can we wonder, that a cold correctness in the delivery of our instructions should weaken in our people a belief of their truth, or at least of their importance ; that they should consider it to be a work of office, for which we are paid, rather than as a matter of personal concern to themselves ; and that, with such impressions, they should want the disposition necessary to give to preaching its due effect—a desire to hear ? Indeed, so unnatural is it thus to speak of weighty subjects, that they would rather attach importance to a slight matter expressed with vehemence, than to a weighty truth conveyed in a lifeless manner.[1] It has been well remarked—that 'the really useful man in winning souls to Christ is he, who is so penetrated with the value of the doctrines of the Gospel, as to persuade by the zeal and sincerity of his manners, when a less earnest mode of teaching would have failed to convince.'[2] Some Ministers indeed of phlegmatic constitutions may manifest less of warmth and animation than others of far lower faith and Christian sensibility.   All of us are orators when we feel. No eloquence can reach the energy and emotion of the language of the heart.   Increased solemnity, and energy in the delivery of the message, should supply the want of sensible excitement ; and fervent prayer should be employed to overcome constitutional languor, to quicken heavenly affections, and to bring them warm into immediate exercise for the enlivening of our people.

A want of fervency in our Ministrations is a serious hindrance to their efficiency.   For though it is the same word, however preached ; yet an earnest delivery adds to the naked truth the sensible exhibition of Divine love, and moves one of the most enlivening springs of conviction.[3] On the other hand (as a sensible writer has observed) 'the monotonous wearisome sound of a single bell may be almost as soon expected to excite moral impressions, as the general tenor of public discourses, drowsily composed and drowsily delivered.'[4] Our people want their hearts, as well as their understandings, to be addressed.   They want words flowing from the

[1] See Sir R. Blackmore's Accomplished Preacher, Sect. viii. May we not learn a lesson of conviction from Garrick's reply to a preacher, who asked—'How is it, that you who deal in nothing but fiction, can so affect your audience, as to throw them into tears; while we, who deliver the most awful and interesting truths, can scarcely produce any effect whatever ?' *Here lies the secret : you deliver your truths as if they were fictions; but we deliver our fictions as if they were truth.*

[2] Bishop of Winchester's Ministerial Character of Christ, p. 285.

[3] Cicero (De Orat.) calls this lively representation *evidence* (evidentia)—the orator not seeming so much to speak, as to show the very things themselves, as if they were before the eyes. Quintilian's term is *vision*. Instit. Lib. viii.

[4] Jerningham's Essay on the Eloquence of the English Pulpit, prefixed to a Translation of Select Sermons from Bossuet.

37

heart, giving power to argument by their piercing heat and penetrating force, and compassionate entreaty.   However this fervour may be mistaken for the false fire of enthusiasm or vain glory, it is only the expression of a heart deeply impressed with the conviction, that religion is a matter of primary, immediate and universal concern.[1] But which of us does not exhibit the inconsistency of apparent earnestness in the pulpit, with the general habit of cold and lifeless affections?   To ascend the pulpit with a heart full of life, zeal, and love, is not a matter of course : yet when "out of the abundance of the heart the mouth speaketh," what unction seems to pervade the word! what a power of sympathy affects our people !

Baxter's impassioned pleadings show what our addresses ought to be, in order to give full effect to our message. 'How thin' (exclaims he) 'are those Ministers, that are serious in this work! Nay, how mightily do the best fail in this ! Do we cry out of men's disobedience to the Gospel " in the demonstration of the Spirit ;" and deal with sin as the destroying fire in our towns, and by force pull men out of it ? Do we persuade our people, as those should, who " know the terror of the Lord ?" Do we press Christ and regeneration and faith and holiness;—believing that without these, men can never have life ? Do our bowels yearn over the ignorant, careless, and obstinate multitude ? When we look them in the face, do our hearts melt over them, lest we should never see their faces in rest ? Do we, as St. Paul, " tell them weeping," of their fleshly and earthly disposition ? and " teach them publicly, and from house to house," at all seasons and with many tears ? And do we entreat them, as for their soul's salvation ? Or rather, do we not study to gain the approbation of critical hearers ; as if a Minister's business were of no more weight, but to tell a smooth tale for an hour, and look no more after the people till the next sermon ? Does not carnal prudence control our fervour, and make our discourses lifeless on subjects the most piercing? How gently we handle those sins, which will so cruelly handle our people's souls ! In a word—our want of seriousness about the things of

---

[1] This is well borne out and illustrated by an eminent writer, who has never been suspected of giving encouragement to enthusiasm—'The chief characteristics of the eloquence suited to the pulpit, as distinguished from the other kinds of public speaking, appear to me to be these two—gravity and *warmth*. The serious nature of the subjects belonging to the pulpit requires gravity—*their importance to mankind requires warmth.*' Dr. Blair's Lectures, Lect. xxix.—On the Eloquence of the Pulpit. Again he remarks— 'Gravity and warmth united, form that character of preaching which the French call *unction*—the affecting, penetrating, interesting manner, flowing from a strong sensibility of heart in the Preacher to the importance of those truths which he delivers, and an earnest desire, that they make a full impression on the hearts of his hearers.'

heaven, charms the souls of men into formality, and brings them into this customary careless hearing which undoes them'—'I know not what others think,' (says he in another place) 'but for my own part, I am ashamed of my stupidity, and wonder at myself, that I deal not with my own and others' souls, as one that looks for the great day of the Lord ; and that I can have room for almost any other thoughts or words, and that such astonishing matters do not wholly absorb my mind.   I marvel, how I can preach of them slightly and coldly ; and how I can let men alone in their sins ; and that I do not go to them, and beseech them for the Lord's sake to repent, however they take it, or whatever pains or trouble it should cost me.   I seldom come out of the pulpit, but my conscience smites me, that I have been no more serious and fervent in such a case.   It accuses me, not so much for want of human ornaments or elegancy—but it asketh me—'How couldst thou speak of life and death with such a heart ?'   The God of mercy pardon me, and awaken me with the rest of his servants, that have been thus sinfully negligent !   O Lord, save us from the plague of infidelity and hard-heartedness ourselves ; or else how shall we be fit instruments of saving others from it ?[1]

V.—DILIGENCE—THE SPIRIT OF SCRIPTURAL PREACHING.

How instructive is the constant eyeing of our Divine Pattern, consecrating his whole heart, his whole time, in his Father's work ! His greatest diligence, however, was concentrated in his public Ministry.   "He taught," when at Jerusalem, "*daily* in the temple ;"[2] and, wherever else a concourse was gathered, he was ready to open his mouth for hortatory, didactic, or illustrative instruction.[3]   The first labourers of the Gospel, and the Fathers of the early church, closely followed their Master's example.[4]

The Apostle contemplated far greater danger from sloth, than from excessive activity in "preaching the word."   He adjures therefore his beloved Timothy by the solemn view and anticipations of the day of account—to "be instant in season and *out of season ;*"[5] not only regular in the routine of preaching seasons ; but under the guidance of an enlightened conscience, embracing every

---

[1] Reformed Pastor.   How did the fervour of this holy man exemplify his own lines—
　　I'll preach as though I ne'er shall preach again ;
　　And as a dying man to dying men !
[2] Luke xix. 47; xxi. 37; xxii. 53.　　　　　　[3] John vii. 37; Matt. v. xiii.
[4] Acts v. 42; xix. 9; xx. 18—21. xxviii. 23, and notices in the Homiletical writings of the Fathers.   Comp. Jer. xxvi. 5; Hag. ii. 10. 20.　　　　[5] 2 Tim. iv. 1, 2.

unlooked-for, and seemingly unseasonable, call to service. And what
is there in the present day, that renders this diligence less necessary, less binding, or less effectual? Is not the mass of unconverted
hearers as large with us as in the primitive church? · And how
can Christ's sheep among them " hear his voice" without a Preacher ?[1]   No other medium will supersede this appointed channel of
Divine communications.[2]

The frequency of Sabbath-preaching must depend upon physical
strength, and other circumstances, over which there can be no control.   The willingness of the devoted spirit will be in general only
restrained by the weakness of the flesh.   A double exercise of our
duty begins to be called for by the concurrent voices of our Diocesans.
A familiar repetition of one of these exercises would profitably and
popularly furnish a third service, should this addition be found either desirable or practicable. Few minds could long support the
labour and excitement of bringing forth three successive subjects.
Nor indeed could the digestive powers of our people healthfully receive so large a quantity of food ; whereas the system of repetition
assists instead of loading the digestion.

Much more is implied in this diligence, than the formal routine
of a Sabbath address.   Such a mechanical exhibition ill represents
the parental obligations subsisting between a pastor and his flock.
Would a father be satisfied with this feeble periodical admonition,
when his beloved son was in continual and most imminent
danger ?

Our Church annals furnish exciting examples of preaching diligence.   Hooper was not one of the ' unpreaching prelates,' who
excited honest Latimer's indignation and remonstrance. He would
say, 'that no Bishop ought to complain of one sermon a-day.'[3]
Probably his own custom exceeded these bounds. Foxe informs
us, that, ' being Bishop of two dioceses (Gloucester and Worcester),
he yet so ruled and guided either of them and both together, as
though he had in charge but one family. No father in his household, no gardener in his garden, no husbandman in his vineyard,
was more or better occupied, than he in his diocese among his flock,

---

[1] John x. 16, 27; with Rom. x. 14.

[2] The apostle, though keeping up intercourse with the Thessalonians by his pen, still
desired to see their face, for their better advantages of Christian instruction. 1 Thess.
iii. 10.

[3] ' Fifteen masses a day did not suffice for the priests of Baal; and yet one sermon a
day seems more than a good Bishop or Evangelical Pastor can bear.' Hooper's Confession delivered to the King and Parliament, 1550. Daily preaching was Chrysostom's rule
for a Bishop (doubtless with application to subordinate Ministers.) De Sacer. Lib. vi. 4.
If the letter of the rule be impracticable, let us at least endeavour to approximate to its
standard and spirit. See Burnet's Pastoral Care, Ch. vi.

going about his towns and villages in teaching and preaching to the people there.' Bishop Jewell's saying—' A Bishop ought to die preaching'—was strikingly confirmed in his own death, which appears to have been hastened, if not to have been caused, by the ardour of his Episcopal zeal.[1]   Of Abp. Matthew it was said, that 'it was easy to trace his journies by the churches he preached at.' The most inveterate haters of prelacy were silenced by the example of this Apostolic Bishop.[2]   Preaching he used to call 'his beloved work,' from which the government of the province of York did not discharge him ;—so that a challenge was thrown out to Popery—' That Tobias Matthew, the Archbishop of York, though almost eighty years of age, preached more sermons in a year, than you (the Popish party) can prove have been preached by all your Popes from Gregory the Great's days.'[3]

The examples of Grimshaw and Wesley, nearer to our own time, may stimulate to greater devotedness to our public employ. Twelve or fourteen preaching engagements were included in Mr. Grimshaw's idle week.[4]   Wesley is calculated to have preached upwards of forty thousand sermons (exclusive of a large number of exhortations) during an itinerantcy of nearly fifty years, and an average annual ratio of travelling four thousand five hundred miles.   Whatever irregularity or enthusiasm belonged to these unprecedented labours, the large success with which they were honoured, displayed the main-spring of their exertion—"the love of Christ constraining them."[5]   Let not our censure of their undisciplined system hinder us from transferring an impulse of their zeal, self-denial, and self-devotedness, to a more chastised course of Ministration.

But preaching diligence includes not only frequency of employ, but constant repetition of truth.   The workman is more anxious to fasten one nail by reiterated blows, than slightly to fix many upon the outward surface.   To preach " the same things is not grievous" to the Christian Minister ; and for his people it is often " safe."[6]   The fruitfulness of the earth arises from its " drinking in the rain *that cometh oft upon it.*"   The constant repetition,—not the weight—of the heavenly showers, makes impressions on the

---

[1] The motto at the bottom of a curious portrait of Jewell preserved in Salisbury Palace is—' Væ mihi, si non evangelizavero !'   This was also the motto of Usher's own selection for his Archiepiscopal seal—illustrated by his increasing constancy in preaching, subsequent to his elevation.   Augustine's views of the Episcopal office were Scriptural—' Episcopatus nomen est operis, non honoris—Intelligat se, non esse Episcopum, qui præesse dilexerit, non prodesse.'   Aug. de Civit. Dei. Lib. xix. c. 19.
[2] No mention of Archbishop Matthew occurs in Prynne's celebrated work of invective against prelates.   [3] Granger's Biog. Hist. Vol. i. p. 343.
[4] Newton's Life of Grimshaw, p. 51.   [5] 2 Cor. v. 14.   [6] Phil. iii. 1.

hardest substances. That our "doctrine" therefore may "drop as the rain,"[1] it must fall not only in the gentleness of love, but in the frequency of diligence.[2] The constant enforcement of fundamental truths is necessary for their deeper and more practical influence. Truths that have been marked out by gainsayers or seducers, must form prominent topics of our Ministry. Truths also of daily use and practice, will be sound doctrine to preach to the end of our course ; not however in the slothful repetition of our former discourses, but in waiting at our Master's feet for fresh instruction ; always learning, and teaching what we have learned.[3]

VI.—SINGLENESS—THE SPIRIT OF SCRIPTURAL PREACHING.

'The Ministerial work must be managed purely for God and the salvation of the people, and not for any private ends of our own. This is our sincerity in it. A wrong end makes all the work bad from us, however good in itself. Self-denial is of absolute necessity in every Christian ; but of a double necessity in a Minister, as he hath a double sanctification and dedication to God. And without self-denial he cannot do God an hour's faithful service. Hard studies, much knowledge, and excellent preaching, is but more glorious hypocritical sinning, if the ends be not right.'[4] The main end of the Ministry is the glory of God. It is 'the single eyeing' of this end, that 'makes all things sweet and holy.'[5] This was the purpose, that filled the heart, and directed the course, of our Great Exemplar.[6] This was also the spirit of the Apostle ;[7] the true spirit of the Minister—the result of serious self-scrutiny, and often of severe spiritual conflict. Experience (for it must plainly be more a matter of experience than of observation) assures us of the extreme difficulty of preaching with singleness of heart. How much of our study in *the very composition of our sermons*, flows from a selfish principle, and rolls on in the same corrupt channel ! Even while

---

[1] Deut. xxxii. 2. with Heb. vi. 7.   [2] Isa. xxviii. 10.
[3] The apostle exhorts to pulpit diligence by a most foreboding anticipation. 2 Tim. iv. 2, 3. Owen enumerates the following constraining motives to preaching diligence—'The command of God—the love and care of Christ towards his Church—the ends of God's patience and long-suffering—the future manifestation of his glory in the salvation of believers, and the condemnation of the disobedient—the necessities of the souls of men— the way by which God gives spiritual supplies by the Ministry of the word—the weakness of the natural faculties in receiving, and of the memory in retaining, spiritual things —the weakness of grace requiring continual refreshment—the frequency and variety of temptations—the design of Christ to bring us gradually to perfection.' He adds—'But the law of this duty is in some measure written on the hearts of all faithful Ministers ; and those who are otherwise must bear their own burdens.' On Heb. vi. 7, 8.
[4] Baxter's Reformed Pastor.   [5] Leighton.   [6] John viii. 50. v. 41.
[7] 1 Thess. ii. 6.

Christ is the text, self may be the spirit and substance of our sermon, as if we were lifting up the cross of Christ, to hang our own glory upon it. *In the pulpit* itself—in our Master's immediate presence—what is it, that sometimes gives animation to our delivery, tone to our voice, and emphasis to our words? Are we never "preaching ourselves" in the very form and act of preaching "Christ Jesus the Lord?" If in the impulse of the moment, any forcible matter falls from us; how seldom is it unaccompanied with self-complacency, expectation of present effect, or disappointment in its failure! How hard is it to preach without undue regard to the approbation of the Christian or intelligent part of our congregation! What a struggle often to repress the fear of being considered *common-place,* or the desire to be original and powerful! How difficult thus to sink our gifts in the grace of humility, and to suppress what might recommend us to men of taste and talent, in order to clothe the same sentiment in a less imposing, but more useful garb! How natural the desire rather to know whether the sermon has been approved, than whether it has been profitably applied! And when we feel that we have made but an indifferent figure, it is as if we had missed the prize of the day. Thus is the desire of usefulness selfishly connected with the honour of our own name; when we cannot bear that "our God should humble us among" our flock, and that they should think of us as vessels of inferior value—of "wood and earth"—rather than "of gold and of silver."[1]

Baxter's serious remarks are equally applicable to our own day, as to his—'Consider, I beseech you, brethren, what baits there are in the work of the Ministry to entice a man to be selfish, that is, to be carnal and impious, even in the highest works of piety. The fame of a godly man is as great a snare as the fame of a learned man. And woe to him that takes up with *the fame of godliness* instead of godliness! " Verily I say unto you, they have their reward." When the times were all for learning and empty formal-

---

[1] See Solomon's wise aphorism, Prov. xxv. 27. It is said of one of the ancient Fathers, that he would weep at the applause that was frequently given to his sermons. 'Would to God,' (said he) 'they had rather gone away silent and thoughtful!' 'Docente te in Ecclesia, non clamor populi, sed gemitus suscitatur. Lachrymæ auditorum laudes tuæ sunt.'—Hieron. ad Nepot. ' Libenter vocem audio, non qui sibi plausum, sed qui mihi planctum movet.' Bern. Serm. 59. Cantic. 'I love a serious preacher, who speaks for my sake, and not for his own, who seeks my salvation, and not his own vain-glory.' Fenelon's Letter to the French Academy, Sect. 4, p. 230. 'Surely' (exclaims Dr. Chalmers) 'it were a sight to make angels weep, when a weak and vapouring mortal, surrounded by his fellow-sinners, and hastening to the grave and the judgment along with them—finds it a dearer object to his bosom, to regale his hearers by the exhibition of himself, than to do in plain earnest the work of his Master, and urge on the business of repentance and faith by the impressive simplicities of the Gospel!' Sermons, ut supra. p. 25.

ities, then the temptation of the proud did lie that way. But now, through the unspeakable mercy of God, the most lively practical preaching is in credit, and godliness itself is in credit : and now the temptation to proud men is here, even to pretend to be 'zealous preachers and godly men. O what a fine thing doth it seem, to have the people crowd to hear us, and to be affected with what we say, and that we can command their judgments and affections ! To have the people call you " the chariots and horsemen of Israel" —to have them depend upon you, and be ruled by you, though this may be no more than their duty, yet a little grace may serve to make you seem zealous men for them. *Nay,* pride may do it without any special grace.'¹

Perhaps indeed the character of the present age is peculiarly adverse to this singleness of spirit. The love of novelty, and the idolatry of intellect, are besetting snares, by which the subtle enemy " corrupts" the church " from the simplicity that is in Christ."² It is difficult for ministers to preserve the tone of their instructions wholly uninfluenced by these temptations. There is great danger, lest we provide more food for the understanding than for the heart ; and lest the important opportunities of close application to the conscience be frittered away in prurient fancies, ingenious theories, and elaborate compositions ; than which nothing is more hurtful to the spirituality of our Ministration, in occupying our secret retirement with men-pleasing contrivances, rather than with diligent waiting upon God, for an enlarged spiritual unction upon our work. This danger of making our office a stepping-stone to selfish indulgence, is acknowledged by the most eminent Ministers. The following exercises from the diary of a late excellent Minister, strike a chord of sympathy with many of us—'I have to observe in my mind a sinful anxiety to preach well, rather than a holy anxiety to preach usefully. I fear I rather seek my own honour than God's. I confess this sin ; I trust I repent of it from my heart : I hope for its forgiveness, and its removal from my breast.' Again—' The evening spoiled with wretched pride and self-complacency—a mischievous weed, deep-rooted, which all my winter seasons have not yet killed. O may it at length be rooted

¹ Reformed Pastor. ' That which many times causes uneasiness in Pastors, is a principle of self-love, which prompts us to seek a private unwarranted delight in that change of men's minds, which we have effected. The spirit of man pleases itself with the success of its own travail ; and when we seem to propose no other aim but God's glory, the deceitfulness of self-love is less capable of discovery.' Bishop Godeau's Past. Instructions, pp. 44, 45. ' See here the perfect pattern of an Evangelical preacher—to make his reputation and the confidence of the people subservient—not to his own interest—but to the good of souls, and to the establishing of the kingdom of God.' Quesnel on Matt. iv. 23—25.   ² 2 Cor. xi. 3

out !'[1] It was therefore seasonable advice of Bishop Taylor to his Clergy—'Let no man preach for the praise of men. But if you meet it, instantly watch and stand upon your guard, and pray against your own vanity ; and by an express act of acknowledgment and adoration return the praise to God. Remember, that Herod was for the omission of this, smitten by an angel ; and do thou tremble, fearing lest the judgment of God be otherwise than the sentence of the people.'[2]

The most pernicious and debasing evil of all is, a converting our sacred office into a medium for setting forth our own excellence —prostituting the glories of the cross for the indulgence of our own pride—drawing a veil over the glories of our adorable Master—and committing a robbery against him, even in the professed business to exalt him. This is to lose sight of the great end of the Ministry—commending ourselves, instead of our Master, to the regard of our people ; rather conciliating ourselves to their good-will, than our message to their consciences. This lays the foundation for a gradual departure from the truth, and proportionally deteriorates the power of our work. 'Our business is to make men think, not of our eloquence, but of their own souls; to attend, not to our fine language, but to their own everlasting interest.[3] Our duty is, 'not to please but to feel ;' (as one of the old writers expressed it) 'not to stroke the ear, but to strike the heart.'[4] Mr. Richmond well said

---

[1] Biographical Portraiture of Rev. J. Hinton, p. 116. 'I know I ought to fit myself in the best manner I can for public service; but this is my misery—I study and prepare, that I may consume it upon my own pride and self-confidence.' Brainerd.

[2] Clergyman's Instructor, p. 108. 'Let all eloquent preachers beware, lest they fill any man's ears with sounding words, when they should be feeding his soul with the bread of everlasting life. Let them fear, lest, instead of honouring God, they honour themselves. *If any man ascend the pulpit with the intention of uttering a fine thing, he is committing a deadly sin.*' H. K. White.

[3] Smith on the Sacred Office, Lect. xviii. It was a subject of bitter regret to Augustine, that his early Ministry had been distinguished by this character—'ut placeret, non ut doceret.' Jerome complained of many in his time—'Id habent curæ, non quomodo scripturarum medullas ebibant, sed quomodo aures populi declamatorum flosculis mulceant.' 'Do not say within yourself—How much or how elegantly I can talk upon such a text: but what can I say more usefully to those who hear me, for the instruction of their minds, for the conviction of their consciences, and for the persuasion of their hearts? Let not your chief design be to work out a sheet, or to hold out an hour, but to save a soul.' Watts' Humble Attempt, pp. 19, 20.

[4] 'Pungere, non palpare'—was Jerome's direction for the Preacher's words. One among the evils of this selfish spirit, is the encouragement of a critical spirit among our hearers—a chief bane of the Ministry. Besides, 'this desire of appearing a fine speaker' (as Dr. Macgill tells his young friend) 'unfits you for attaining even that kind of excellence, which you desire. Your style, instead of presenting the just expression of thoughts and feelings suited to your objects, presents an exhibition of artificial beauties, unsuitably introduced, laboriously and affectedly pourtrayed, while the higher order of beauties in thought and language are neglected, or lost in the gaudy colouring, which surrounds them.' (Considerations to a Young Clergyman.) In thus spending our strength in the eloquence of words, we lose the eloquence of thought. We shall not become truly elo-

—' I have no wish to be a popular preacher in any sense but one, viz., *a preacher to the hearts of the people.*'[1]   Indeed the Gospel was never meant as an occasion of display, but as a treasure to dispense for the benefit of the world.   And as far as we are imbued with the spirit of our office, we shall esteem the enriching of one soul with the unsearchable riches of Christ a more durable recompense, than an investiture with the dignity and honour of an earthly crown.

Without this singleness of spirit there is no warranted expectation of success.   The matter indeed is from God ; but the manner and the dress, the principle and the exhibition, may be but ' incense thrown upon the altar of vanity.'[2]   We may preach clearly in statement, and forcibly in matter; but habitual defect in " doing all" with a single eye " to the glory of God," brings upon us the awful " woe to the idol-shepherd" (his own idol, and wishing to be the idol of his people), whose ministry is blasted, and his judgment blinded.[3]   However diligently we may be employed in his service, yet nothing is really done, done to any purpose, or with any acceptance, that is done for self—not for God.   So that a pains-taking Minister, who has been engaged in the service of God for selfish ends, may at last sink into the grave with Grotius's affecting lamentation—' Alas ! I have lost my life in laboriously doing nothing.'   Or should he be used as an instrument in the work of God, it will be only as the servant, who never tastes the provision which he dispenses to his Master's guests ; or as the physician, who heals others, but is unhealed himself.[4]   Godly simplicity is the alchemy that converts every thing it touches into gold.   The paramount desire that Christ " in all things may have the pre-eminence ;" and the corresponding expression of the heart—" He must increase, but I must decrease"[5]—will compensate for a deficiency in talent and judgment.   This is the true character of the friends of the bridegroom ;"[6] to woo for him, not for ourselves ; to seek his honour, not our own ; and to adopt an earnest tone of preaching, not as gaining more regard to ourselves, but as bringing sinners to him.   Our privilege is to wait upon the gospel, and to reflect our Master's glory through the transparent medium of Christian simplicity.   This usefulness is quite distinct from popu-

quent, until we have lost the desire to be so, and gain our elevation by rising with our subject, and giving up ourselves to it.
   [1] Richmond's Life, p. 50.   [2] Hall's Sermon, p. 45.   [3] Zech. xi. 17.
   [4] It is a solemn remark of Massillon, that ' God sometimes, in saving his elect, makes use of instruments which he afterwards casts away.'   A thought, that may well call to mind, 1 Cor. ix. 27, with deep and serious personal application!
   [5] John iii. 30.   [6] Ibid. 29.

larity. But how poor a thing is the admiration of man, compared with this success in winning souls to Christ !¹

'He that intends truly to preach the Gospel, and not himself; he that is more concerned to do good to others, than to raise his own fame, or to procure a following to himself; and that makes this the measure of all his meditations and sermons, that he may put things in the best light, and recommend them with the most advantage to his people—this man so made and so moulded, cannot miscarry in his work :—he will certainly succeed to some degree. The word spoken by him shall not return again. He shall have his crown, and his reward from his labours. And to say all that can be said, in one word with St. Paul ; he " shall both save himself, and them that hear him." '²

VII.—LOVE—THE SPIRIT OF SCRIPTURAL PREACHING.

LOVE is the grand distinctive mark of our office. It exhibits salvation flowing from the bosom of Divine mercy. It sets forth a most tender Father, a bleeding Saviour, and a faithful Comforter; so that the spirit of every discourse should be—" God is love." Thus therefore should we so cast ourselves into the mould of our commission, that we may infuse its very life and character throughout our Ministry.³

"*Speaking the truth in love*"⁴ is perhaps in few words the most complete description of our office. Some, from a false charity, would keep back offensive truth. Some again speak it in fear, from the apprehension of inconvenient consequences to themselves. Some also speak in faithfulness *only*, as if their responsi-

---

¹ Mr. Cotton preached an university sermon at Cambridge, much approved by those 'who relished the wisdom of words more than the words of wisdom;' which however, upon a clear understanding of the true principles of the Ministry, he committed to the flames. Subsequently preaching in the same pulpit in a more Scriptural tone, his sermon was attended with the Divine blessing to one of the most eminent divines of that day—Dr. Preston. Mather's New England, Book iii. pp. 15, 16. This was according to an old writer's rule, 'that the Preacher expound the sermon in a plain and common speech; not having any respect to his own commendation for his eloquence, but rather to advance the glory of God.'—N. Hemminge's Methode of preaching. 12mo. 1574.

² Burnet's Pastoral Care, ch. ix.

³ 'If a man has great and good news to tell me, he will not do it angrily, and in much heat and discomposure of spirit. It is not therefore easy to conceive, on what ground a scolding Minister can justify a conduct, which only proves, that he does not understand his errand.' Cowper's Letters. Paley has admirably illustrated the Epistle to the Romans, as characterized by an exquisite address of Christian love; mixing itself with the most unpalatable statements of truth, and conciliating a kind attention, as the most effectual avenue to conviction. See his Horæ Paulinæ. This, as an old writer observes— 'doth not only serve the affections, but also (if I may so term it) maketh the oration more sharp and witty, to the end it may altogether pierce into the minds of the hearers, and so possess the whole heart itself.' Hemminge, ut supra, p. 54.

⁴ Eph. iv. 15.

bility was simply to deliver their own souls, and not rather to win souls to Christ.

Love should pervade the whole tone of our Ministry. The cause of truth may be weakened by an inaccurate exhibition of its spirit. The Scripture marks the temper as well as the subject-matter of our Ministry. An Apostle assures us in his own case, that if he " were to speak with the tongues of men and of angels," yet without love ; he would be no better than " sounding brass, or a tinkling cymbal."[1] How delightful is it in the tone of endearing and animated instruction, to look down from the pulpit, and regard the Christian part of our congregation in the light of " mother, and sister, and brother !" Even with the unconverted, our most fruitful seasons of conversion are, when we are most yearning over lost sinners. This was the spirit of our Divine Pattern ;[2] and therefore, that which he most " delighteth to honour." Besides —who does not feel the force of such a Ministry? What power does that affecting declaration carry with it—" Of whom I tell you even weeping !"[3] The testimony that is borne on this particular respecting Mr. Brown of Haddington, is far more important than that of eloquence or originality. Though able to endure bodily or domestic afflictions without a tear (we mention this unenviable exercise of self-control, only for the sake of the contrast); yet, when warning sinners of their danger, and " beseeching them to be reconciled unto God," he is said to have been often unable to restrain his emotions.[4]

It would add considerably to effect, if this spirit be *suffered to express itself in corresponding tenderness of appellation.* The Apostles were used to address their people with language, expres-

---

[1] 1 Cor. xiii. 1.

[2] Matt. ix. 36. Luke xix. 41, 42, with Deut. v. 29. Psalm lxxxi. 13. Ezekiel xviii. 31. Hosea xi. 7—9. Compare Bowles, Lib. i. c. 21.

[3] Phil. iii. 18. ' Oh! how deep into the heart go those periods, that are sown in the unforced, uninvited tears of the preacher!' Robinson on Claude.—Calvin writes excellently on this point—' Sunt multi clamosi reprehensores, qui in vitia declamitando, vel potius fulminando, mirum zeli ardorem præ se ferunt; interea securo sunt animo, ut videantur per lusum guttur et latera exercere velle. At pii pastoris est, flere secum, priusquam alios ad fletum provocet; tacita cogitatione discruciari, priusquam indignationis signa edat; et plus retinere apud se doloris, quam aliis faciat.' In 2 Cor. ii. 4.

[4] Brown's Life, p. 22. Mr. Winter tells us of his friend Mr. Whitfield—' I hardly knew him to go through his sermon without weeping more or less; and I truly believe his were the tears of sincerity. I have heard him say in the pulpit—' You blame me for weeping; but how can I help it, when you will not weep for yourselves, though your immortal souls are upon the verge of destruction; and for aught you know, you are hearing your last sermon, and may never more have an opportunity to have Christ offered to you.' Jay's Life of Winter, pp. 27, 28. Constitutional causes will greatly vary the outward expression of love; nor would we insist upon tears, as a necessary evidence of a tender heart. But the spirit here was fully warranted to be genuine and fervent love to souls, and is well worthy of our imitation.

sive of the earnest endearment.[1]   The extant Epistles of the Primitive Fathers, the most earnest discourses of Cyprian and Augustine, and the Homilies of Chrysostom, are strongly imbued with this
character.   The amiable Fenelon observes—' I would have every
Minister of the Gospel address his audience with the zeal of a
friend, with the generous energy of a father, *and with the exuberant
affection of a mother.*'   This language obviously requires a chaste
control; but the sober expression of heartfelt tenderness would
strike many a chord of sympathy, interest, and reciprocal feeling,
such as would bring us into affectionate contact with our people.
We might also bring before them from time to time, our remembrance of them in our prayers and thanksgivings,[2] our tender interest in their welfare,[3] our devotedness to their service,[4] our ardent
longing for their Christian advancement,[5] and the strong connection of their prosperity with our own happiness.[6]   Such a spirit will
contribute most beneficially to cement the bond between us.

This *spirit of love must deeply imbue* the language of reproof.
We must " exhort," but " with all long-suffering ;"[7] bearing with
the frowardness, that will often resist the most affectionate pleading.   Meekness, gentleness, and patience must stamp our instruction of the opponents of the Gospel.[8]   We must wound their consciences as sinners, not their feelings as men : carefully avoiding
unnecessary excitement of enmity ; and showing the faithfulness
that lays open their sins, to be " the wounds of a friend,"[9] the chas-
tening to be that of a father.[10]   The recollection of our own former
state (not to speak of our present sympathy with them as their
fellow-sinners,) will give a considerate tenderness to our reproof,[11]
which, without weakening its application, will powerfully soften
the heart to receive it: so that it falls, "as a wise reprover upon an
obedient ear."[12]   Indeed it is when we most deeply feel our own

[1] Comp. Phil. iv. 1—and the Apostolic greetings of the several Epistles.
[2] Compare Rom. i. 9.   1 Cor. i. 4.   Eph. i. 6.   Phil. i. 3, 4, &c.   [5] Phil. i. 8—11.
[3] 1 Thess. ii. 7, 8.   [4] 2 Cor. xii. 15.   [7] 2 Tim. iv. 2.
[6] 1 Thess. iii. 8.   2 John 4.   3 John 4.
[8] 2 Tim. ii. 24, 25.   Circumliniatur modo poculum cœlestis sapientiæ melle, ut possint
ab imprudentibus amara remedia sine offensione potari; dum illiciens prima dulcedo acer-
bitatem soporis asperi sub prætextu suavitatis occultat.   Lactant.   Cowper's remarks and
illustration are singularly terse—' No man was ever yet scolded out of his sins.   His
heart, because it is corrupt, grows angry, if not treated with some management and good
manners.   A surly mastiff will bear perhaps to be stroked (though he will growl even
under this operation); but if you touch him roughly he will bite.'   Letters, ut supra.
See our Lord's Ministry beautifully illustrated in detail.   Bishop of Winchester's Min.
Char. ch. viii.
[9] Prov. xxvii. 6.   [10] See 2 Cor. ii. 4.   xii. 14—21.
[11] See Titus iii. 2, 3.   'I never seemed fit to say a word to a sinner, except when I had
a broken heart myself; when I was subdued and melted into penitence, and felt as though
I had just received a pardon to my own soul, and when my heart was full of tenderness
and pity.'   Payson's Life.   [12] Prov. xxv. 12.

sinfulness, that we speak most closely and powerfully to the consciences of our people.

But especially must this spirit be cultivated, in *the solemn delivery of the burden of the Lord ;* lest we mingle strange fire with
the flame from the holy altar. Some Ministers seem to combine
human passions with their zeal ; as if, in speaking of the wrath of
God, they were giving vent to their own indignation. How different this spirit from the *persuasiveness* of the Apostolic Ministry,[1]
and from the tenderness of our Divine Master, who breaks off from
his most awful strain of denunciation, as if unable any longer to
suppress the yearnings of his compassion—" O Jerusalem ! Jerusalem !"[2]

The idea of a judge compelled to pronounce the sentence of condemnation upon his own beloved son, might illustrate the combined
solemnity and affection, with which the Minister of Christ ought
ever to speak of " that place, where the worm dieth not, and the
fire is not quenched." To forbear to speak of it from a scrupulous
sensitiveness of feeling, is an act of positive unfaithfulness to God,
to our own conscience, and to our people.[3] To make it the prominent characteristic of our Ministry, is to disguise the Gospel of love
" with a covering not of God's Spirit." To point the thunder-bolts
of heaven in a light and careless spirit is to expose ourselves to our
Master's rebuke—" Ye know not what manner of spirit ye are
of."[4] To attempt to gain effect by vehemence of manner, or unnatural elevation of voice—is to look for the Lord in the wind and
in the earthquake, rather than in " the still small voice."[5] Tender seriousness commends our office as Ambassadors of a God of
love. Trembling, faltering, lips—the index of a heart touched
with the melting sympathies of Christ—best become us, as guilty
sinners speaking to our fellow-men, not more guilty than ourselves.[6]
A bold fidelity—setting at defiance the best feelings of our nature—is most uncongenial with our Master's spirit, clothes our
message in a most repulsive garb, and brings us under suspicion
of ill-temper or resentment; whereas a meek and affectionate address—having terror in the thought rather than in the language
—awakens, and commands the awakened anxiety to a deep and
serious consideration.

We are not arguing, however, for that sensitive delicacy, which
refrains to wound, when the patient shrinks. But we know not,

---

[1] 2 Cor. v. 11. Comp. Deut. xxxii. 2.   [2] Matt. xxiii. 23—37.
[3] Is not the latter clause in Mark xvi. 16, as component a part of the Ministerial commission as the former ?   [4] Luke ix. 55.
[5] See 1 Kings xix. 11, 12.   [6] See Jer. xvii. 16.

why the most energetic tone of faithfulness should not be blended
with that considerate treatment, which unquestionably, is best
adapted to the exigency of the case.   The brute creation may be
driven : but rational ,creatures require to be drawn.   The compulsion of love is the mighty lever of operation.[1]   Even the heathen
sophists insisted upon kindness in an orator as indispensable to his
success ;[2] and doubtless none will open their hearts to the Christian
orator except the tone of his instructions has impressed them with
a sincere conviction of his love to their best interests.[3]   Love is the
life, power, soul, and spirit of pulpit eloquence ; entreating rather
than denouncing the character of our office ;[4] and it is the delivery of our Master's message with the looks and language of his
own manifested tenderness, that attracts and triumphs over the
hearts of a willing people.   We wonder not at the Apostle's success,
when we read, that at Ephesus (which doubtless was an instance
of his general course of Ministry) he " ceased not for three years
to warn every *one of them night and day with tears.*"[5]   The
most honoured Ministers have been men, distinguished, not for the
brightest talents, but for an humble and affectionate spirit.   Some
eminent servants of God, from the want of this spirit, alarm rather
than persuade ; confirm prejudice rather than remove it ; and consequently the effectiveness of their labours falls below many of
their brethren, of far inferior gifts.   ' The Christian Pastor, of all
men in the world, should have an affectionate heart.   When he
preaches, it is the Shepherd in search of the strayed sheep ; the

---

[1] 'I have always been afraid' (said a late excellent young Minister) ' of driving my
people away from the Saviour. I would rather err on the side of drawing them.' Memoirs of the Rev. John Escreet, by Rev. T. Webster, p. 50. This is in accordance with
the highest pattern. Hos. xi. 4.

[2] The fabled tradition of Amphion by his music drawing stones after him for the walls
of Thebes, and of Orpheus taming wild beasts by his harp, alluded probably to their extraordinary power over insensible and unyielding hearts. Ευνοια.   Arist. Rhet. Lib. ii.
Homer introduces his hoary Nestor pleading in this insinuating spirit—ευφρονεων. Iliad.
Lib. ii. 78.

[3] ' Qui dicendo nititur persuadere quod bonum est, nihil horum trium spernat, ut scilicet
doceat, delectet, flectat ; ita enim audietur intelligenter, libenter, obedienter.'—Augustine
De Doctr. Christian, iv. 12, 17, 26. 'These three steps in this progress are intimately
connected. We should speak so, as in the first place, to instruct, and be understood ; in
the second, to please, so far at least as to attract, and fix attention ; in the third, to gain
and conquer.' Campbell on Past. Char. p. 87.

[4] See 2 Cor. v. 20.

[5] Acts xx. 31. George Herbert's description of the love of St. Paul's Ministry is exquisitely beautiful. ' How did he put the Romans into his prayers (i., 4.)! He ceased
not to give thanks for the Ephesians, (i. 16.) for the Corinthians, (1 Cor. i. 4.) ; for the
Philippians, (i. 4.) He is in contention for them, whether to live or die—to be with them
or Christ ; which, setting aside the care of his flock, it were madness to doubt. What
an admirable Epistle is the 2nd to the Corinthians ! How full of affection. He joys
and he sorrows ; he grieves and he glories. Never was such care of a flock expressed,
save in the Great Shepherd of the fold, who first shed tears over Jerusalem, and afterwards, blood. Therefore let this care be naturally learnt, and then woven unto our sermons, which will make them appear exceeding reverend and holy.' Ch. vii.

father in pursuit of his lost child.   Is it possible for a statue to perform this part of necessary duty?   As well might a marble parent
supply the place of a real one.'[1]   Though, however, every pastor
may not be equally successful in gaining upon the affections of
his people, yet " the love of Christ will constrain us" all to some
clear evidence of our tender love to his flock.   Menelaus was pronounced to 'bring nothing worthy of the priesthood, because he
had the fury of a cruel tyrant, and the rage of a savage beast ;'[2]
thus illustrating by the force of contrast, gentleness and love to be
the spirit of the priesthood, and the paralyzing influence of the
contrary spirit upon the efficiency of our Ministrations.   Fletcher
remarked despondingly with regard to himself, but most truly with
regard to the office, that 'love, continual, universal, ardent love was
the *soul of all the labour of a Minister*.[3]   The tenderness of
Ministerial earnestness is best calculated to win upon repulsive
minds, and ' to bring our people to God, and to keep them continually near to him.'   This Dr. Doddridge judged to be the
grand purpose of our work; but found, as he complained, ' that it
was, to him at least, a very hard thing.'[4]

In concluding this division of our subject we advert to Bishop
Sumner's admirable remarks—' The Scriptures contain two classes
of directions, which may be considered as referring more particularly to those who are entrusted with Ministerial functions.   The
first class includes all that relates to the discharge of the fundamental duty of their office—the message they have to deliver, and the
faithful and right division of the word ; while all such as are of
secondary importance—the manner of communicating instruction
and reproof, prudential admonitions calculated to rectify the judgment, the discretion requisite for the due management of a delicate
mission—may be properly referred to the second class.   With these
passages of scripture for a daily manual, with our Lord's own example as a commentary upon them, and with his blessing upon
their study and application, it may reasonably be expected that the
members of the priesthood " may wax riper and stronger in their
Ministry, and that they may so endeavour themselves from time
to time to sanctify the lives of them and theirs, and to fashion
them after the rule and doctrine of Christ, that they may be

---

[1] Simeon's Preface to Claude.   [2] 2 Maccab. iv. 25.   See the contrast Heb. v. 2.
[3] Cox's Life of Fletcher, p. 21.   [4] Orton's Life of Doddridge, ch. v.

wholesome and godly examples and patterns for the people to follow." [1]

In pondering therefore the deep responsibility of this department of our work[2]—the importance of due preparation for it[3]—the vast momentum of its substance[4]—the wisdom needed for selecting the best mode of its presentment[5]—the efficiency of its Scriptural Spirit[6]—all this linked with our office as the " Ministers"[7] of God —"Ambassadors for Christ"[8]—" separated by the Holy Ghost"[9]— bearing the word of life—the cup of salvation—in our hands. Oh ! can we forbear the question of anxious weakness—" Who is sufficient for these things ?"[10]   Can we conceive of an effective preacher, if he be not a man of prayer?   Was not the secret of Apostolic success hidden (as we have before hinted) in the resolution—" We will give ourselves continually unto prayer, and to the Ministry of the word ?"[11]   The man of prayer will shine forth in the pulpit with a full reflection of his Divine Master's likeness—" grace poured upon his lips."[12]   Gifted with a wise and understanding heart"[13]—he will produce clear and luminous masses of truth—putting into his sermons all that he finds in his bible in its correct harmony and proportion ; while his own spirit will be suitably moulded into the spirit of his message—bold—wise—simple—fervent—diligent—single-minded—full of love.   May every Minister of the Gospel listen with profound reverence and self-abasement to the solemn charge of the Apostle, speaking from the mouth of his great Master— *I charge thee therefore before God, and the Lord Jesus Christ, who shall judge the quick and the dead at his appearing and his kingdom ; preach the word, be instant in season, out of season ; reprove, rebuke, exhort, with all long-suffering and doctrine.*   2 Tim. iv. 1, 2.

[1] Min. Ch. pp. 48, 49. Ordination Service.   [2] Ch. i.   [3] Ch. ii.
[4] Ch. iii. iv.   [5] Ch. v.   [6] Ch. vi.   [7] 2 Cor. v. 18, 19.   [8] Ib. v. 20.
[9] Acts xx. 28.   [10] 2 Cor. xi. 16.   [11] Acts vi. 4—7. See p. 138, 139.
[12] Ps. xlv. 2.   [13] 1 Kings iii. 12. with 2 Tim. i. 6, 7.

PART V.

THE PASTORAL WORK OF THE CHRISTIAN MINISTRY.

LET us not think, that all our work is done in the study and in the pulpit. Preaching—the grand lever of the Ministry—derives much of its power from connexion with the Pastoral work; and its too frequent disjunction from it is a main cause of our inefficiency.[1] The Pastor and Preacher combine to form the completeness of the sacred office, as expounded in our Ordination services and in Scriptural illustrations. How little can a stated appearance in public answer to the lowest sense of such terms as Shepherd, Watchman, Overseer, Steward!—terms, which import not a mere general superintendence over the flock, charge, or household, but an acquaintance with their individual wants, and a distribution suitable to this occasion; without which, instead of "taking heed to the flock, over which the Holy Ghost hath made us overseers," we can scarcely be said to "take the oversight of it" at all. This interesting relation cheers our toil with a new tide of spiritual affections, and exercises our Christian wisdom and faith, in seeking of the Lord an "open door," in prudently improving opportunities of instruction, and in adapting our mode to the different classes of our people.

We shall enter into some details of this most important subject.

---

[1] Thus Dr. Doddridge remarked—'My heart does not upbraid me with having kept back any thing that may be profitable to my people. But *I fear I have not followed them sufficiently with domestic and personal exhortations.*' Orton's Life, ch. ii. Bishop Wilson recommended his Clergy to 'visit every family and soul in his parish at least once a year, that *we may all of us*' (said he, alluding probably to Heb. xiii. 17.) '*be able to give a comfortable account of our labour to our great Master.*' Stowell's Life, p. 114. Baxter's Reformed Pastor may be referred to, as placing this Ministry upon its high ground of obligation, urging the strongest motives, answering the chief objections, and suggesting most admirable directions for the work.

CHAPTER I.

THE NATURE AND IMPORTANCE OF THE PASTORAL WORK.

THE Pastoral work is the personal applicatoin of the pulpit Ministry to the proper individualities of our people—looking upon them severally as having a distinct and separate claim upon our attention, cares, and anxiety; urging each of them, as far as possible, to the concerns of eternity; and commending to their hearts a' suitable exhibition and offer of salvation. For this purpose we must acquaint ourselves with their situation, habits, character, state of heart, peculiar wants, and difficulties, that we may "give to each of them a portion in due season." The Pastor unites in himself the offices of Watchman and Evangelist. He "*watches for souls,*" lest a "root of bitterness should spring up" to the trouble and' defilement of the church—lest unchristian tempers and practices should mar the profession of Christ—lest a lukewarm spirit should paralyze exertion, or a spirit of contention hinder Christian love. All need his superintendence. The indolent are slumbering—the self-dependent are falling back—the zealous are under the influence of spiritual pride—the earnest are becoming self-righteous—the regular, formal. Then there is the enquirer, asking for direction —the tempted and perplexed, looking for support—the afflicted, longing for the cheering consolation of the Gospel—the convinced sinner, from the slight healing of his wound,[1] settling in a delusive peace—the professor, "having a name that he lives; but he is dead." These cases cannot, in all their minute and diversified forms, be fully treated in the pulpit. It is therefore in his Pastoral character, that the Minister "watches for souls, as one that must give account."[2] But he "watches also *in all things.*" There *are seasons* peculiarly suited for specific instruction, or for the enforcement of particular duties—special opportunities (such as providential visitations) for conviction or consolation—seasons that should find the Minister "doing the work of an Evangelist,"[3] in the instant and due improvement of them; and which, without the constant oversight of our people, would be neglected and lost.

Not pretending to lay down a complete scheme of the Pastoral work, we shall illustrate its general principles by slight sketches of

---

[1] Jer. vi. 14.   [2] Heb. xiii. 17.   [3] 2 Tim. iv. 5.

detail. In order that plans may be useful, they must be suitable to their intended sphere—not only really, but relatively, good—formed by the character, circumstances, and habits of the people—as they are scattered or congregated, educated or illiterate, or a mixture of both; according to their state of ignorance or knowledge—whether the ground has been previously cultivated, or neglected—whether it has been occupied by Dissenters, or left wholly waste—whether the disposition of the people is prepared for the Gospel, or opposed to it. These and many other considerations, though they would not alter the system of our Ministry, yet would mould its several parts to a more close and definite adaptation.

The importance of this system is evident from the nature of the case. The husbandman does not rest, when he has committed his seed to the earth. He watches its growth with constant anxiety, and toils incessantly for its preservation from impending dangers, until he has safely gathered his fruit. And are not our people the field of God ? Are not we the husbandmen, to sow the imperishable seed, and instrumentally to gather the harvest ? And are our fields more secure from injury, or in less need of constant and anxious superintendence ?[1] Every other view of our work illustrates the same point. As physicians, how can we prepare the proper medicines, without a knowledge of the individual disease ? As stewards, how can we make our distribution, if unacquainted with the respective objects of our attention ? As nursing-mothers, how ineffective our care and tenderness, if it be not regulated according to the known strength or weakness of our people !

We cannot but advert to the necessity of a systematic adherence to this Ministry. It must not be left to the humour or convenience of the moment; or subject to worldly interruptions. Fixed hours of the day (portioned with a due regard to all other Ministerial claims) should be devoted to it with the same conscientious determination as to pulpit preparation. Our instruction should be solid, searching, and lively; aiming to draw out the minds of our people in confidence, to mark the baneful influence of wrong principles, and to infuse the holy and active operations of the fundamentals of the Gospel. An affectionate attention to the young is closely connected with the present encouragement and future prospects of our work, and will open many successful avenues to the hearts of the parents. It may sometimes be necessary to hear of our people through some correct medium of information ;[2] though much dis-

[1] Zepperi Ars. Concion. Lib. iv. Bowles, Lib. i. c. 20.
[2] See 1 Cor. i. 11. Phil. ii. 19. 1 Thess. iii. 1—5. 3 John 3. Bowles, Lib. i. c. 20.

cretion is required, to avoid the evils of jealousy and suspicion, and to apply to the best use the materials thus furnished to our hand.

This system is most strongly inculcated from the highest authority. "*Searching and seeking out the sheep*" is marked by the Great Shepherd, as the difference between himself and hirelings ; against whom the neglect of this Pastoral care formed a main article of indictment.[1] Indeed his own Ministry was of this character. With his disciples, it was that of the Good Shepherd, who "calleth his own sheep by name, and leadeth them out."[2] With the world, it was the constant wakefulness to improve every opportunity, as well of private as of public and general instruction.[3] The Ministry of his Apostle was framed after the same pattern.[4] During the three years, that he was the resident Pastor of a Church, he combined pastoral with public instruction.[5] " He *ceased not to warn every one of them night and day with tears ;*" and the testimony of his conscience on this particular, seems to have been his rejoicing under the overwhelming pressure of Ministerial responsibility.[6] Indeed his intimate knowledge of the spiritual state of a vast number of individuals in the churches, is evident from his multiplied salutations, as well as from the relative appropriateness of his instructions given in the exact line of exhortation, reproof, or encouragement, to which he knew the personal distinctness of their experience would instantly respond. His readiness in " changing his voice"[7] to his people, could have been the result only of an accurate and diligent inspection of their state.

The documents of the early ages furnish abundant testimony to the Pastoral work, as a constituent part of the Primitive Ministry. Ignatius is said to have known almost every individual in his flock.[8] Cyprian frequently gives us his judgment and practice on this subject.[9] Gregory wrote a serious treatise on this department

---

[1] Ezek. xxxiv. 6, 8. with 4, 11.   [2] John x. 3.
[3] Comp. Luke xiv.   [4] Acts v. 42.
[5] Publicly and from house to house, Acts xx. 20.—'as if he perceived that his public doctrine would vanish into air, except it were assisted by private admonition and conference.' Bowles, lib. ii. c. 6. See Calvin, Grotius, Hammond, in loco, Beza on Acts v. 42. and Secker's Charges, p. 246. Comp. also the Apostle's Ministry at Colosse and Thes-salonica, Col. i. 28, 29. 1 Thess. ii. 11, 12. 'If false teachers "creep into houses," for the purposes of seduction from the truth, (2 Tim. iii. 6.) should not the orthodox pastors show at least equal diligence?' Bowles, ib.
[6] Acts xx. 31. with 26, 27.   [7] Gal. iv. 20.
[8] He gives a useful parochial hint—not to forget servants in our ministrations. Epist. ad Polycarp. No class of our people are generally more removed from individual instruction. Sometimes however, they have been assembled on the Sabbath, with consent of their employers, for an expository and catechetical reading of Scripture. Several Tracts may be recommended for popular application. 'Ruth Clark'—'Eliezer, the Faithful Servant'—(Hatchard and Son.) 'My Station and its Duties'—'The Eye-servant and the Servant of Christ contrasted.'—(Seeleys).
[9] Quid est enim major aut melior curâ præpositorum, quam diligenti solicitudine et

of the Ministry. The questions and exhortations in our own Ordination services are evidently formed upon this model.[1] The episcopal instructions of Taylor, Hort, Burnet, Leighton, Secker, and
Wilson,[2] (not to mention other names of more recent date) have
solemnly charged it upon our consciences. The obligation of our
Ordination vow—to "take heed *to all the* flock, over which the
Holy Ghost hath made us overseers"[3]—evidently implies (as Baxter
observes) that 'each individual member of our charge must be
taken heed of, and watched over by us in our Ministry. To which
end it is supposed necessary, that (unless where *absolute necessity
forbiddeth it*, through the scarcity of Pastors, and greatness of
the flock) we should know every person that belongeth to our
charge.' 'I confess' (says Bishop Burnet), 'that this way of parochial visitation is an increase of labour ; but that will seem no
hard matter to such, as have a right sense of their Ordination
vows, of the value of souls, and of the dignity of their function.
If men had the spirit of their calling in them, and a due measure
of flame and heat in carrying it on, labour in it would be rather a
pleasure than a trouble.'[4]

Calvin often lays down the Scriptural obligation to this work,
and reports the fruitful harvests reaped at Geneva, when the ministers and elders went from house to house, and dealt closely and
individually with the consciences of the people. Kidderminster,
'before Baxter's coming there, was like a piece of dry and barren
earth ; but by the blessing of heaven upon his labours, the face of
Paradise appeared there in all the fruits of righteousness.'[5] On his
first coming, scarcely a worshipping family was known in the

---

medela salubri fovendis et conservandis ovibus providere; cum Dominus loquatur et
dicat.—Ezek. xxxiv. 4. Cum ergo pastoribus talibus, per quos Dominicæ oves negligen-
tur et pereunt—si Dominus comminatur—quid nos aliud facere oportet, frater carissime,
quam colligendi et revocandi Christi ovibus exhibere diligentiam plenam? Cyp. Epist.
lxviii.

[1] See Comber on the Ordination of Priests, and Secker's Charges, pp. 192, 193. Burnet remarks on the question respecting the use of private as well as public admonition—
to the whole, as well as to the sick—'This is as plainly personal and constant, as words
can make any thing: and in this is expressed the so much neglected, but so necessary
duty, which incumbents owe their flock—in a private way, visiting, instructing, and ad-
monishing them, which is one of the most useful and important parts of their duty.'—
Past. Care, ch. vi. See also Stowell's Life of Bishop Wilson, p. 133.

[2] Clergyman's Instructor, pp. 109, 110, 365. Burnet's Past. Care, ch. viii. Secker's
Charges, p. 25, 229, 245. Leighton's Works, ii. 445, 447. Often would Leighton com-
miserate the London Clergy, (how would his sympathy have been enlarged in our own
day beyond the precincts of the metropolis) whom the extent of their cures disabled
from individual attention to their flock. 'Were I again' (said he in his last retirement)
'to be a parish Minister, I must follow sinners to their homes, and even to their ale-
houses.' Life, lv. lvi. Ostervald expresses his surprise, that a Christian Minister can
satisfy his own conscience, without a diligent parochial Ministration. Lectures on the
sacred office, pp. 242—245.

[3] Acts xx. 28.   [4] Pastoral Care, ch. viii.   [5] Dr. Bates' Funeral Sermon.

place. When he left it, but few families were living without this daily acknowledgment of God, or were unwilling to submit to his private catechizings and personal conference. Six hundred communicants attended the Lord's Table. Alleine often did bless God for the great success he had in these exercises, saying, that God had made him as instrumental of good to souls this way, as by his public preaching, if not more.'[1] Cotton Mather, while ' he looked upon this work as laborious as any in all his Ministry,' yet 'set a great value upon his pastoral visits. He not only did, but got good in his conversations with all sorts of persons, and thought he never walked more in the Spirit, than thus walking to his flock, to serve and seek their best interest.'[2]

The *uses of this Pastoral system to ourselves* are of the highest moment. By a judicious improvement of this intercourse, we may receive instruction from the meanest of our flock. Teachers must be constant learners ; and much is here learned consciously or unconsciously. It is at once the seal to the testimony of the preceding, and the treasure-house, which furnishes the most valuable materials for the ensuing Sabbath.[3] Perhaps there is no better way of filling up interesting subjects for the pulpit, than to draw them out in familiar contact with cases, to which they might be adapted. The sermons thus made in our parishes differ from those that are thought out or collected in the study. If they are less

[1] See his Life—'I never knew Ministers' (as Baxter remarks, speaking of Alleine's parochial diligence) 'who *prudently and diligently* took that course, to be unprosperous in their work : but by them, that have wisely and faithfully used it, I have known that done, that before seemed incredible.'

[2] See his Life, p. 37. and his Essays to do good. See also the Life of Pliny Fisk, pp. 31, 32. Dr. Doddridge's exercises on this subject, on his return from an ordination, are most deeply interesting—'I have many cares and troubles ; may God forgive me, that I am so apt to forget those of the Pastoral office! I now resolve, 1. To take a more particular account of the souls committed to my care. 2. To visit, as soon as possible, the whole congregation, to learn more particularly the circumstances of them, their children, and servants. 3. Will make as exact a list as I can of those that I have reason to believe are unconverted, awakened, converted, fit for communion, or already in it. 4. When I hear any thing particular, relating to the religious state of my people, I will visit them, and talk with them. 5. I will especially be careful to visit the sick. I will begin immediately with inspection over those under my own roof, that I may with the greater freedom urge other families to the like care. O my soul! thy account is great: it is high time that it be got into better order. Lord, I hope thou knowest I am desirous of approving myself a faithful servant of Thee and of souls. O watch over me, that I may watch over them; and then all will be well.' Orton's Life, ch. v.

[3] See pp. 202, 265, 266. 'Acquaint yourselves' (was the excellent advice of Matthew Henry) ' with the state of your people's souls—their temptations—their infirmities. *You will then know the better how to preach to them.'* Life, p. 124. 'Rely on it, he who hopes to discharge the duties of the pulpit ably, appropriately, seasonably, and to the greatest advantage of his flock, *without being much with them,* entertains a hope, which is perfectly unreasonable, and will certainly be disappointed.' Professor Miller's Letters. The parcelling out of our country into parishes under their several Ministers, obviously tends to facilitate this pastoral system. So fully sensible was Philip Henry of this—"that he often wished and prayed for the opening of a door, by which to return to that order again." Life, pp. 47, 48. On this point see much valuable remark and discussion in an 'Essay on the Parochial System,' by Rev. H. W. Wilberforce.

abstract, they are more pointed and experimental. We mark the precise evil requiring caution, the deficiency calling for exhortation, the circumstances needing 'advice, the distress or perplexity looking for consolation and encouragement : and thus the Pastoral preaching gives a local and instructive application to our pulpit Ministry.

Medical skill is gained much more by practical experience, than by the abstract study even of standard works. However valuable therefore is an accurate and well-directed course of reading, (and the Writer will not be suspected of depreciating its value[1]) yet he is persuaded, that the study of the human heart—of our own hearts most especially—is far more important.[2] Without that experience, which can be obtained only in Pastoral practice, the most scriptural statements, like the promiscuous application of medical science, will be inapplicable, and proportionably ineffective.

Nor is this *system less important to our people.* Some points of private or personal application are scarcely suited or expedient for the pulpit. Many persons also, in great need of instruction, are hindered by bodily infirmity from attendance on the public means. Many, from their awful indifference, require to have the word brought to their own doors. And with regard to many that do hear—every parochial Minister is conversant with the fact, how very little our pulpit discourses are comprehended, retained, or applied by them. There is a ,sort of mental deafness among the mass : so that, except the word is brought to them in the smallest parcels, and with the most direct application, the sound only is heard ; while the meaning is never fixed upon the mind with an intelligent or permanent apprehension.

---

[1] See Part I. Chap. vii. Sect. I.

[2] An old divine used to say, that a preacher had three books to study—the Bible, himself, and the people. Gillies' Hist. Coll. Bishop Burnet remarks it, as 'the capital error in men's preparing themselves for the sacred Ministry, that they study books more than themselves.'—History of his Own Times. 'While a minister is engaged in composing and preaching, he is giving out to others; but whilst he is occupied in familiar conferences, he is taking in for himself. One half hour's practical study of the human heart in personal visits, gives an impulse to ten hours' speculative meditation from men and authors.' Bishop of Calcutta's Essay to Baxter's Reformed Pastor, p. xliii. 'I was fond enough of books' (said Halyburton, on his death-bed); ' but what the Lord let me see *of my evil heart,* and what was necessary against it, was more useful to me in the course of my Ministry than all my books. This is the best pulpit I was ever in. I presume, in the case I am now in, (on his death-bed,) to suggest this advice: that it may not only be your care to be diligent in composing sermons : but above all, examine your own hearts ; and make use of what discoveries you get there, to enable you to dive into consciences, to awaken hypocrites, to separate the precious from the vile, and to do it with that accuracy and caution, as not to make sad the hearts of those, whom God has made glad. This is the great point in religion, and in the management of your Ministry, that you may obtain the testimony of the great Shepherd, when he shall appear.' Halyburton's Memoirs. The aphorism (Prov. xxvii. 19.) proves the habit of self-inspection to be the most valuable means of knowing and addressing the hearts of our people.

40

*The preservation of our people from schism, and the main-
tenance of Christian unity among them,* is one of the many
blessings resulting from this system.   The converts of preaching,
left destitute of this fostering superintendence, become like " children tossed to and fro, and carried about with every wind of doctrine."[1]   If the fold be tended only on the Sabbath, we must not
wonder, if sectarianism makes progress—if " grievous wolves enter
in among them, not sparing the flock ;" or if even among the flock
should " arise men speaking perverse things, to draw away disciples after them."[2]   Evangelical preaching (as distinguished from
modern ethics, or cold orthodoxy) naturally excites a spirit of inquiry and interest ; which, important as it is, except it be carefully
directed and controlled, lays our flock more open than before, to
" the sleight of men and cunning craftiness, whereby they lie in
wait to deceive."[3]   Vast indeed is the responsibility of what Hooker
calls—' the greatest blot or blemish of notable ignorance—uncon-
scionable absence from the cures whereof men have taken the
charge[4]—(absence however that will now be checked by the late
legal restrictions upon pluralities) depriving our people of the influence of example, and of seasonable counsel, encouragement, and
reproof.   Yet we are persuaded, that the mere residence, and even
the faithful preaching, of the servant of Christ, without his watchful fatherly care, will be comparatively of little avail.   Erroneous
doctrines or practices will take root, before he is aware of their
existence.   We cannot blame the Apostle (entrusted as he was
with an universal commission) for not fixing himself as the stated
Pastor of the Galatian Church.   Yet the ascendancy of the Judaizing teachers was the evil of his non-residence, which led him to
express his earnest " desire to be present with them ;" feeling that

[1] Eph. iv. 12—14.
[2] This danger is expressly marked as an incentive to pastoral care, Acts xx. 29, 30,
with 28.   Comp. Bowles, Lib. i. xiv. xvi.   Burn. Past. Care, ch. iii.
                                    Nunquam, custodibus illis,
        Nocturnam stabulis furem, incursusque luporum,
        Aut impacatos a tergo horrebis Iberos.—Virg. Georg. iii. 406.

[3] Eph. iv. 14.
[4] Book v. 81.   Quesnel, in his sketches of the Minister's character, marks the following—' To love residence—to absent himself but little, and that out of necessity—never
to be absent in heart—to return to his flock as soon as possible—to try all means of sur-
mounting the obstacles which keep him from it—and to look upon non-residence as the
most grateful thing imaginable to Satan, and which he promotes with all his power, as a
source of the perdition of souls.'   On 1 Thess. ii. 17, 18.   The term προϊσεδρευοντες
implies a constant residence and sitting at our charge.   1 Cor. ix. 13.   In this spirit a
change of sphere will not be lightly entertained.   Circumstances of health—the shutting
of the present door, an unsought-for interposition of providence—or a clear prospect of
more suitable adaptation or enlarged usefulness—may indeed warrant and even dictate
the step.   But great care will be needed to watch the inclination of the will, and to guard
against the influence of worldly or self-pleasing motives, an unsettled spirit, or the disposition to flinch from a painful cross.

his personal inspection would be more useful than his letters could be.[1] Thus the prevention or cure of evils will be found, under the blessing of God, in the exertions of a Pastor, steadily devoting himself to his people, cementing the bond of union and confidence " by the mutual faith both of him and them ;"[2] they looking unto him as their affectionate Minister, and he living for them as his beloved charge.

This leads to another advantage of this system—*the gaining the confidence and affection of our people.* The orbit of the Preacher, however regular, sheds but a scanty light over the poor man's dwelling. A pulpit Ministration may command attention and respect ; but except the preacher convert himself into a Pastor, descending from the pulpit to the cottage, and in Christian simplicity " becoming all things to all men ;" there will be nothing that fastens on the affections—no " bands of love." The people cannot love an unknown and untried friend, and confidence without love is an anomaly. The unintelligent, more influenced by impulse than by judgment, will probably unite themselves with Teachers upon their own level, with whom they live as fathers, brothers, and friends, in all the reciprocity of daily fellowship. We must therefore constantly aim at nearer contact, and closer interest with them ; winning their hearts, as the way to win their souls—living among them in the interchange of those kindly offices, which (as Bishop Gibson admirably observed) 'are the means of endearing Ministers to their people, and of opening a passage into their hearts for spiritual instruction of all sorts.'[3] It was by thus combining the office of Missionary and Pastor, that Eliot ' was indeed' (as his Biographer tells us) ' the father of his people. By holding frequent intercourse with them, he greatly endeared himself to them, and became acquainted with the extent of their knowledge of Divine things, with their trials and difficulties, with their joys and sorrows. He was in this manner enabled to act as their instructor, counsellor, and comforter.'[4] A congregation thus used to see their Minis-

---

[1] See Gal. iv. 19, 20. The Shepherd's absence from the flock forty days, opened the way for the entrance of the wolf into the fold. Exod. xxxii. 1.
[2] Romans i. 12. [3] Clerg. Instructor, p. 325.
[4] See his Life. ' I am too backward' (said the celebrated John Rogers of Dedham) 'to *private visiting of neighbours at their houses, which neglect is very injurious ; for from this cause their love to me cannot be so great as it would be,* nor am I so well acquainted with their particular states, and therefore cannot speak so fitly to them as I might.' Archbishop Secker remarks—' A chief reason why we have so little hold upon our people is that we converse with them so little as watchmen over their souls.' After alluding to the influence, which the Foreign Protestant pastors, the Romish priests, and the dissenters gain over their people by this means, he adds—' Why should not we learn from them ?'— Charges, pp. 246, 247. Mr. Hall observes—' The more frequently the pastor converses with his people, provided his conversation be properly conducted, the more will his per-

ter in private, is like a family listening to a father's instruction. When, after the example of our Great High Priest, we are "touched with the feeling of their infirmities," and tenderly enter into the details of their several trials, a mutual sympathy is excited; their confidence is encouraged; they readily apply for more personal counsel and consolation; and they bring to us their cases, doubts, and perplexities, that we may make them our own. Thus moulding our Ministerial counsel in the endearing form of brotherly sympathy, we can say—"Who is weak, and I am not weak?"[1] And how else can we ascertain the real state of religion among us, its progress or decline, the drawbacks, or the means of advancement, or the besetting temptations of our people, so as to provide them "with the armour of righteousness on the right hand and on the left?"

The *character of this pastoral intercourse* is therefore a conciliating, close, affectionate, and spiritual contact with our people, combining the dignity with the condescension and humility of our office—as "the messengers of the Lord of Hosts;" and yet "their servants for Jesus' sake."[2] Thus we at once invite confidence, and repress familiarity. Without sinking our dignity, we clothe it in the garb of a friend; entering (not with prying curiosity, but with kindly interest) into their circumstances of family difficulty, their temporal wants, habits of living, and connections (if among the poor) with their masters and neighbours. Prudent advice may here be given to the heads of families on the management of their expenses, the education and the government of their children, family worship, and instruction, and whatever else makes up their little world.[3] Christian instruction may be grafted upon these particulars, such as could not enter into our pulpit Ministrations with sufficient distinctness for practical utility.

Social visits to our people for the purpose of spreading a general spiritual atmosphere, are also a highly important part of the Pastoral work. What Dr. Watts aptly calls "parlour preaching"[4]—

son be endeared, and his Ministry acceptable.' Sermons, p. 29. For this purpose Bishop Wilson, (Stowell's Life, p. 114, 143.) Dr. Doddridge, (Life, ch. v.) Sir James Stonehouse, (see his letters to a Young Minister,) Ostervald, Dr. Stearne, (Clerg. Instruct. p. 384,) and Dr. Watts, (Humble Address, p. 91,) recommend a Ministerial register, to note, as may be practicable, the individualities of character and circumstances among our people. [1] 2 Cor. xi. 29. [2] Mal. ii. 7, with 2 Cor. iv. 5.

[3] George Herbert, speaking of parochial inquiries into the spiritual economy of the house, decides—'If the parson were ashamed of particularizing in these things, he *were not fit to be a parson*,' Ch. xiv. It would be well to furnish our people, and especially the poor, with a system of family worship. Sixteen short sermons; Short prayers for every day in the week; Cottager's Companion (from the Religious Tract Society,) stitched together in a cover, would form a complete manual for a family at a trifling cost. Scripture Reading must however be always inculcated as an essential part of their worship.

[4] Humble Attempt, pp. 90, 91.

that is, the ability to introduce the subject of religion seasonably and acceptably into social intercourse—is one of the most valuable talents to the Church. If it be in part a natural gift; yet its lowest exercise is capable of unlimited improvement; and they who have attained the highest excellence in this way, are not those, who were most richly endowed by nature, but those who have "stirred up this gift of God that is in them" with the most assiduous diligence. We do not indeed recommend that sententious and authoritative tone, which carries with it the air of solemn affectation. Let the great subject rather blend with the habit of Christian cheerfulness: only taking care not to diverge from the main object, so as to preclude a natural and graceful return: and remembering that seriousness is as essential to unction, as unction is to edification. Nor would we always open the subject formally, or in the way of abrupt commencement. If no direct method offers itself, an intelligent readiness of address, and the expression of a glowing heart, will turn some incident or topic of conversation to good account. When the obligation is deeply felt, opportunities generally will be found, or a watchful spirit of love will make them; and if the character of the preacher is put off, the man of God will engage himself in close, affectionate, vigorous conversation upon matters of eternal moment.

An adaptation of topics is, however, necessary to give effect to the exercise of this talent. Matters of general interest will always afford subjects of instruction. In mixed society, two or more real Christians, interchanging their sentiments on any interesting topic, will furnish a vehicle of profitable communicatian with the rest. Intercourse with the higher classes is often attended with considerable difficulty. Yet even here the introduction of truth "in the meekness of wisdom" will accomplish much; and the Pastor never appears in greater dignity, or speaks with greater effectiveness to the rich, than when his mild decision of heavenly character exhibits the determination to "obey God rather than man," and to honour the authority of his commission with pre-eminent regard. We must not forget the strict account that will be required of this weighty burden of the souls of the rich; and with an eye to this account, we must wisely and diligently search out the avenues, by which to convey to them the most enduring treasure.

For the improvement of this conversational intercourse, a store of materials, drawn from an acquaintance with the best practical writers, or from our religious biographies, will prove of essential service. A readiness to produce the circulating medium—added to a recollected habit for the most suitable disposition of the topics, for the study of proper variety, and above all, for exercising our dependence upon Almighty aid—will be most important. In this spirit of consideration, diligence, and faith, the feeblest efforts will be abundantly honoured ; while the best-ordered conversation, in our own spirit, will prove ineffectual for the desired ends.

We would suggest also a monthly meeting at the parsonage, of the higher or middling females, for the purpose of working for the poor, or some other definite object. This has been found a kindly and conciliatory means of drawing together inaccessible young persons within the sphere of the parochial Ministry. The introduction of a suitable book, easily shuts out unprofitable conversation, and gives opportunity to intersperse matter of more direct application and interest.

The system of Bible classes, embracing all divisions of our charge, is making way among us with considerable effect. The present Bishop of Ohio mentioned, when a Pastor at New York, (1830) that he knew not a Minister of Christ in America, who had not a Bible class, in which, not merely the young, but the married, and persons of all classes gladly received instruction at the feet of the Pastor. There can be no greater preservation against error, no more assured means of Christian stedfastness and consistency, than an enriching study of the sacred volume ; and to direct and encourage the minds of our people in this investigation is one of the most interesting and important exercises of Ministerial responsibility.

On another department, we may advert to our Lord's example in combining kindness to the body with love to the soul.[1] We are often reminded in our Pastoral employ, that " a man's gift maketh room for him."[2] Christian sympathy doubtless gives great weight to our instructions ; and thus our means combine with our labours for the most important objects. We must however well ascertain the character, lest this system should encourage a false profession. And indeed in all cases, the want of a wise discrimination of the objects, seasons, and measure of assistance, makes well-intentioned charity one of the greatest evils. Our benevolent fund must be regulated by personal means, calculated in the spirit of prudence and *self-denial*, and applied to the relief of want—not (except in cases of sickness) to the procurement of indulgence. Its Scriptural extent thus regulated, is universal, with a special regard " to the household of faith."[3] Respectability with distress has the

[1] Matt. ix. 1—6.　　　[2] Prov. xviii. 16.　　　[3] Gal. vi. 10.

next claim, according to the gradations of character and want. As a general rule, partial assistance—giving a stimulus to their own exertions—is more efficient as well as more œconomical, than a complete deliverance from their difficulties.[1] The opportunity of combining spiritual with temporal charity, will not be forgotten. A tract may often convey an useful lesson, where personal conversation had not been found practicable of seasonable.

Yet in every point of contact with our people, we must feel that we are Ministers, and they must feel and receive us as such. We cannot therefore dismiss our parochial visitation without some more or less direct message from God. Even the mention of common affairs should be connected with a spiritual purpose,[2] while at the same time room must be found for some more pointed application. Thus Cotton Mather would leave some awful questions with his people—as—' What have I been doing ever since I came into the world, about the great errand, upon which God sent me into the world? If God should now call me out of the world, what would become of me throughout eternal ages? Have I ever yet by faith carried a perishing soul unto the Lord Jesus for both righteousness and salvation?'[3] So again—' Do you trust wholly in Christ? Do you love him? Do you enjoy him? Do you give him your whole heart?' Answer these questions to yourselves—to your consciences—to your God. If we cannot grapple thus closely with them; yet the value of the soul, the evil of sin, the love of the Saviour, the study of the word, the influences of the Spirit, the privilege of secret, family, and public prayer, the importance of personal and family religion, and its intimate connexion with every day's employment, the comfort of the Gospel, and the work of preparation for eternity—all these will furnish topics of conversation with them, of common interest and inexhaustible fulness. Yet, however animated and impressive our exhortations, we must not forget the main object of imparting intelligent doctrinal views of the Gospel. Our familiar intercourse therefore, no less than our public Ministry, should be conducted on the principle, that truth is the

---

[1] Mr. Thomas Gouge (a rich and liberal non-conformist Divine) used to employ the poor at his own charge, furnishing them with the materials, and giving them the full profit of their work. Thus he indulged the flow of his own charity with the best encouragement to honest industry. Clark's Lives, vol. iii. p. 203. Clothing, rent, or shoe Societies (adding a certain ratio to the weekly contributions of the poor) have materially contributed to their comfort, by enabling them to meet anticipated demands; by fixing habits of providence and economy; and showing the fruitful results of the smallest efforts of self-denial, and of a well-directed use of their straitened resources. These points belong to what George Herbert well calls ' the Parson's completeness,' and are equally connected with the well-being of our people, and with the effectiveness of our Ministrations. Country Parson, Ch. xxiii. and Bishop of Winchester's Charge, 1829, p. 49.

[2] See Eph. vi. 22.   [3] See his Life, and Essays to do Good.

only medium of Divine influence. The connexion between suc-cessive visits may be usefully kept up by means of a text, left for consideration, which, even if it could not be read, might be re-peated, till learned by heart. Thus a word from God would be left behind for practical application ; bringing to mind in our next visit the prominent tone of our last conversation ; and directing us to continue in the same track, or to strike out a new path, as circum-stances might dictate.

The form of pastoral intercourse admits of considerable variation. While it may often be wise to combine sympathy in temporals with our Ministerial instruction ; at other times our contact with our people should be purely upon spiritual principles. Let them be alone with us in the presence of God. The delicacy and weakness of early impressions need this intimate intercourse. The awa-kened enquirer—filled, and often confounded, with the engrossing subject—wants a guide, a confidential counsellor, a tender and ex-perienced friend. He must be taken aside, and made to feel him-self the object of exclusive solicitude. Others again in a hesi-tating suspense need this tender confidence—to have their convic-tions cherished, retouched, deepened, and directed more immedi-ately to the Saviour, as the charm that dispels the allurements, and as the power that breaks the chains, of this world. The se-rious, humble, and perplexed, through the same medium, 'open their grief, and receive the benefit of ghostly counsel and advice.'[1] In these confidential communications, affectionate catechetical en-quiry will bring out their individual perplexities, and thus furnish the most valuable materials for a more suitable adaptation of our instruction.

But the Minister must carefully equalize his communion with his flock. He must shew himself equally the friend, the father, the Pastor, of all—" a debtor to the wise and to the unwise"—

---

[1] See exhortation in Communion Service. 'We could wish to transplant ' the Confes-sional,'—this mighty engine of power—most harmlessly and most beneficially into every Protestant Ministration. We would not have the Pastor stand upon ground too high for his people's reach. We would guard the people against any degree of Popish super-stition. But with a Scriptural measure of authority on one side, and reverence on the other (Heb. xiii. 17.) this mode of Ministry we conceive to be of the highest importance. In private conference alone will our people state their difficulties freely, open their trials, and ask for further information. Here we shew them our true sympathy in their troubles, we can solve cases of conscience—we can give them individual directions for their per-sonal and family duties. Here it is that we see the state of their minds—their degrees of knowledge and experience—any distinct indication of tenderness and awakening concern for their souls. Here also we learn how to preach with more distinct application—how to analyze character—to feel and to reach the heart—to touch the right chord—to be able to advise and reconcile differences. We are persuaded that this method of conference brings with it advantages, of which it is hard to say, whether they preponderate on the side of the Minister or the people.' Author's Preface to the Life of Martin Boos, pp. xlv. xlvi.

" without preferring one above another, doing nothing by par·tiality."[1] He should be to his flock—as the soul to the body—as the head to the members—invigorating every part of the body—the lowest as well as the highest ; and contributing to the benefit of every member alike. The suspicion of favouritism invariably fosters a spirit of pride in its objects, and of envy in the rest, most destructive to the unity and prosperity of the flock. In this confidential character there will be as little occasion to enforce relative rights and obligations, as to fix the precise boundaries of authority and obedience between man and wife, where the spirit of the marriage-relation is maintained. How far however this intercourse should extend to Dissenters in our parishes may be a question of some difficulty. Those who wilfully reject our Ministry, have no claim upon our official responsibilities. Yet so far as time and strength will allow, as they manifest a Christian Spirit, we would not decline *that open, candid, winning intercourse*, which might bring them to a conviction of their error, to a closer conformity to the Scriptural rule, and to the will of our Divine Master. This appears to be the principle to be carried out as far as we can, though localities must have their influence in shaping the precise mode of our Ministrations.

This department of the Ministry is deficient in that excitement, which makes it so delightful to preach to a congregation hanging upon our lips. It presents great demands for patience, self-denial, and severe exercises of faith, the cost of which has not always been duly calculated. Henry Martyn confessed, that at times he was ' tried with a sinful dislike of his parochial work,' and seemed frequently ' as a stone speaking to stones.'[2] The writer was struck with the observations of a local preacher, who has subsequently relinquished his work for secular engagements—that from his experience he considered a Minister's life to be the happiest in the world, and that he had never known such enjoyment, as when in the act of preaching the Gospel. This judgment, though correct, was yet incompetently formed, because grounded upon the knowledge of only one half of our work. For *the preacher's delight* in proclaiming the glad tidings of the Gospel to his fellow-sinners is chastened with the heavy responsibility of *the watchman's commission*. The " necessity laid upon us"[3]—the " watching for souls,

[1] Rom. i. 14. 1 Tim. v. 21.
[2] Life, p. 60. Dr. Witherspoon observes, on the testimony of conscience to this Ministry—' We may gratify our vanity by preaching ; but diligence in private can scarcely arise from any thing but a sense of duty.'
[3] 1 Cor. ix. 16.

as they that must give account"[1]—the darkness—thick as night, and alas! the presage of eternal night—so often attendant upon death-beds—the wisdom and tender faithfulness, which such scenes imperiously demand—the " travailing in birth" for souls once and " again, until Christ be formed in them"[2]—the disappointments on account of professed Christians, and the weeping over the falls of real ones—the daily contact with sin, obstinacy, and impenitence— and finally, the conflict with the powers of darkness—all these combine in our sacred employment, wakening emotions of the most opposite character, and yet issuing at length in the triumph of faith ; " as sorrowful, yet always rejoicing."

This general view of the Pastoral work will shew at once its la- boriousness, and its importance. To acquaint ourselves with the various wants of our people ; to win their affections ; to give a seasonable warning, encouragement, instruction, or consolation ; to identify ourselves with their spiritual interests, in tender sympathy, and Ministerial obligation ; to do this with the constancy, serious- ness, and fervid energy which the matter requires, is indeed a work of industry, patience, and self-denial. And yet how else can we " make full proof of our Ministry," but by ready obedience to the injunction—" watch thou in all things ; do the work of an evangelist ?"[3]

The true portrait of a Christian Pastor, is that of a Parent walk- ing among his children—maintaining indeed the authority and reverence, but carefully securing along with it the love and confi- dence, that belongs to this endearing relation. He is always to be found in his own house, or met with among the folds of his flock— encouraging, warning, directing, instructing—as a counsellor, ready to advise—as a friend to aid, sympathize, and console—with the affection of a mother to lift up the weak—" with the long-suffer- ing" of a father to " reprove, rebuke, and exhort." Such a one— like Bishop Wilson in the Isle of Man, Oberlin in the Ban de la Roche—or the Apostolical Pastor of the High Alps[4]—gradually bears down all opposition—really lives in the hearts of his people, and will do more for their temporal and spiritual welfare, than men of the most splendid talents and commanding eloquence.

---

[1] Heb. xiii. 17. ' Let the pastor, who trembles not at these words, tremble at least at his own blindness and insensibility.' Quesnel in loco.
[2] Gal. iv. 19.   [3] 2 Tim. iv. 5.
[4] Gilly's Life of Felix Neff, a most exciting piece of Biography. See also a new Life of this devoted Pastor, by M. Bost, with large and most interesting correspondence, lately published by Messrs. Seeley.

CHAPTER II.

TREATMENT OF CASES IN THE PASTORAL WORK.

THE many subdivisions of the two grand classes which divide the world, offer a great variety of cases,[1] the just treatment of which is a matter of the greatest moment. We venture a few hints on some of the most important of them—chiefly drawn from the observation of the New Testament ministry, as illustrative of the several specialities of our Ministrations.

I.—THE INFIDEL.

MANY of us come in contact with infidelity in its most malignant and popular forms—impatient of all moral restraints—breaking with a bold hand all social bonds, and defying the authority of the government of God. There is *the sensual infidel.* His belly or his money is his god. He wants to be persuaded that there is no God, because he wishes there were none : and because he is afraid, lest there should be. This class are not thinking men ; but they " have heard the blasphemy of some :" they try to believe a doctrine, which they trust will quiet their consciences, and prove the warrant, encouragement, and refuge of sin. They " beseech us to depart out of their coasts"—" saying—Let us eat and drink, for to-morrow we die."[2] Our Lord traces this infidelity to its source—not the want of evidence, but the love of sin ; and teaches us to deal with it, by aiming at the conscience ; setting forth the sentence of condemnation ; convincing of sin ; exhibiting the correspondence of the heart with the declarations of God ; and contrasting with it the holy character of the work of God.[3]

There is also *the imitative infidel,*—such as those who are often in infidel society. They dare not confess a cause, which is a standing jest with men of wit. They cannot endure their scorn. They are overpowered by their bold assurance. They hear plausible arguments advanced, or some witty speech uttered against re-

---

[1] Gregory treats of no less than thirty-six cases (chiefly relative situations, or moral dispositions;) but with very scanty exercise of spiritual discrimination. De Cura Past. Part iii. c. 1. Bucer enters into detail with more accurate and instructive distinctness. Scripta Anglicana. De Animarum Cura. pp. 293—350.
[2] Matt. viii. 34. 1 Cor. xv. 32. [3] John iii. 19—21.

ligion. They take it up as their own. The ambition of being thought a little above their own class makes them retail it. This is common among young men, just advancing into all the pride and pruriency of self-conceit. We can only expose their foolish pride, inculcate a teachable spirit, and bring before them the simple authority of the Divine testimony, which to candid minds will come with more powerful conviction than all the witty sayings of wise fools.

There is also *the shrewd infidel*,—such as Hume, Gibbon, and Paine. Here we find the love of sin gathering strength from the pride of reasoning. Refusing to believe what they do not understand (a palpable proof of inconsistency and ignorance; for upon this principle they must reject the works as well as the word of God); they degrade revelation by the supposition, that a system within the grasp of the puny intellect of man could be worthy of God, or proceed from God. How can their principles account for prophecy, miracles, the establishment of the Gospel in the world by such weak instruments in opposition to all the power and learning of man, its civilizing and new-creating influence? Let them be pressed with their own difficulties—far greater than those of the Gospel. Let them be convicted of credulity, in being constrained to believe the greatest improbabilities, in order to make way for their disbelief of Revelation. Let them be shown the cruelty of their scheme—" despoiling"[1] men of their only hope—excluding every glimmer of light in the vista of futurity—offering nothing for the present distress—promising nothing but doubt, anxiety, and despair. Can a system so dark and gloomy have proceeded from a God of love? Is there not a far stronger motive to embrace, than to reject, the Gospel? If it be false, believers are as safe as unbelievers. If it be true (and has the unbeliever no misgiving here?), where is his lot for eternity?

St. Paul's Ministry at Athens teaches us to set forth Christ to infidels of every class and character.[2] And indeed this—as a remedy commensurate with every distress—is the strongest testimony for the Gospel. The prevalence of this poison should lead us to inculcate upon all, especially the young, the study of the evidences of Christianity, that they may " be ready always to give an answer to every man that asketh them, a reason of the hope that is in them, with meekness and fear."[2]

---

[1] Col. ii. 8.   [2] Acts xvii. 22—34.   [3] 1 Peter iii. 15.

II.—THE IGNORANT AND CARELESS.[1]

SUCH were the multitude in our Lord's time. The spirituality and requirements of his law—the most searching developments of the heart, mingled however with the strongest encouragement;[2] the nature and immediate duty of faith in himself;[3] the awful consequences of rejecting his salvation;[4] uncompromising exhibitions of the terms of the Gospel;[5] the most unfettered invitations to all that were willing to accept them[6]—these formed the prominent topics of his general instruction. In individual cases he dealt closely with the conscience by tangible points of conviction.[7] The exhortations of the Apostles were of course more explicit. Their arrows of conviction were dipped in the blood of Christ; and the display of the cross was the ground of their successful pleadings of love.[8]

This, like every other class, must be treated according to character. The principle of unbelief needs to be laid open to them, as the source of all the proud reasonings against the fundamental truths of the Gospel, and of the awful contempt of its gracious offers; and issuing at length in hardness of heart, and stupidity under the means of grace. Let them be charged solemnly upon the inexpressible sinfulness and danger of their state, especially in the aggravated guilt of the rejection of the Saviour. We must picture before us men asleep in the immediate neighbourhood of fire, "saving them with fear, pulling them out of the fire."[9] A solemn statement has often been owned with an awakening blessing. The man also should be brought, if possible, to a point, and some appeal fastened upon his own declarations. He thinks but little of eternity; yet he hopes to go to heaven, *because he wishes to go thither.* Here is ground to work upon—the folly of making his indolent wishes the ground of his hopes. He would give every thing on a death-bed to be assured of his safety: why is he not in earnest now? He knows Christ as a Saviour, but has no personal interest in him—no sense of want, no spiritual exercise of faith. He needs instruction, like a babe or a heathen, upon the elementary truths of the Gospel. The hardened of this class must be treat-

[1] Baxter's practical treatises contain the most arresting addresses to the unconverted, that probably have ever come from the pen or heart of man. A more clear exhibition of evangelical doctrine and motive would however have added much to their power. His method also of Christian establishment greatly fails in the display of the freeness, fulness, and simplicity of the Gospel.   [2] Matt. v.—vii.   [3] John vi. 29—65.
[4] Matt. xi. 20—24.   [5] Ibid. xiii. 44—46. Luke xiv. 25—33.
[6] Matt. xi. 28—30. John vii. 37.   [7] Luke vii. 40—50; xii. 13—21. John iv. 5—26.
[8] Acts ii, iii, iv, xiii. with Zech. xii. 10.   [9] Jude 23.

ed with the greatest mildness;[1] speaking to their condition with the most compassionate regard,[2] and with the most "beseeching" entreaties—"Be ye reconciled to God."[3] Let them not suppose, that by denouncing the judgments of God, we seal their condemnation; but rather that we endeavour to awaken them to escape from it—that we "shut them up under" wrath, only as the means of "bringing them to Christ."[4] Let us connect every exposure of wilful infatuation with the invitations of the Gospel.[5] Many, who are repelled by remonstrance, and proof against reasoning, have been overpowered by love. The cross of Calvary has arrested the attention of the most ignorant;[6] wrought irresistibly upon the most stubborn;[7] and displayed the vanity and wretchedness of the world to the conviction of its most determined votaries.[8] The exhibition of the Saviour in his all-sufficiency, suitableness, faithfulness, and love, affords ample warrant for enlivening hope in the most desperate cases.

III.—THE SELF-RIGHTEOUS.

THE young ruler exemplifies our Lord's treatment of this case.[9] Conviction was wanted, and the law was the medium employed. Ignorance of the law is the root of self-deception. An acquaintance with its spirituality unveils the hidden world of guilt and defilement, brings down self-complacency, and lays the sinner prostrate before the cross.[10] In another case, he made the necessity of an entire change of heart the instrument of conviction.[11] He denounced the enmity or hypocrisy of this spirit, as the wilful rejection of his gospel, and as making a "stumbling-stone and rock of offence" of the foundation laid for the trust, glory, and salvation of his people.[12] The Epistles to the Romans and Galatians exhibit this principle, entrenched in a system of external religion, without faith, love, contrition, separation from the world, or spiritual desires; or depending on the mercy of God, even in the rejection of the ordained means of its communication; of which the man has no other notion, than as a help to supply deficiencies, upon the condition of future amendment.

What makes the case of the self-justiciary so affecting, is, that

---

[1] 2 Tim. ii. 24, 25.   [2] Comp. Jer. iv. 19.   Micah i. 7, 8.
[3] 2 Cor. v. 20.   [4] See Gal. iii. 23, 24.
[5] 1 Sam. xii. 20—22.   Ezra x. 2.   Isaiah lv.   Acts ii. 23, with 37—39.
[6] Matt. xxvii. 54.   [7] Acts ix. 4—6.   [8] Gal. vi. 14.
[9] Matt. xix. 16—21.   [10] Rom. vii. 9.   [11] John iii.
[12] Matt. xxi. 42—44.

we have no gospel message to deliver him. Our Master "came not to call the righteous, but sinners to repentance."[1] The righteous need him not, seek him not, and have no interest in him. Our commission is to sinners ; and, judging from this man's own account of himself ; of the goodness of his heart ; the correctness of his conduct ; and the multitude and excellency of his meritorious actions—we should conceive him not to belong to that "lost" race, whom "the Son of man came" expressly *and exclusively* "to save."[2] Indeed his spiritual ignorance presents a difficulty, at the outset, in dealing with him. We have with all simplicity and plainness proved to him the fallacy of his expectations. We have "judged him out of his own mouth." Yet the next conversation finds him as far as ever removed even from the comprehension of the gospel ; expressing the same dependence upon his own performances, as if no attempt had been made to undeceive him, and no confession extorted of the weakness of his foundation.

To pursue the self-justiciary into all his "refuges of lies," and to sweep them away before his face, is a most laborious task. When disturbed in his first refuge of his own righteousness, he flies to repentance. Half-distrusting his security, he strengthens it by the merits of his Saviour, by the delusive substitution of sincerity for perfection, or by the recollection of his best endeavours, as a warrant for his hope in the mercy of God. But place him on his death-bed : is he sure that his works are not deficient in weight, that he has attained the precise measure, commensurate with the full and equitable demands of his holy and inflexible Judge? What if "the hand-writing" should then be seen "upon the wall," "against him, and contrary to him ?" Let sin, the law, and the Saviour, be exhibited before him, fully, constantly, and connectedly ; let the pride, guilt, ingratitude, and ruin of unbelief, be faithfully and affectionately applied to his conscience ; let him know, that the substitution of any form of doctrine, or course of duties, in the place of a simple reliance on Christ, turns life itself into death, and hinders not only the law, but even the Gospel, from saving him.[3] Who knoweth, but thus he may be humbled, enlightened, and accepted, in the renunciation of his own hopes, and the reception of the Gospel of Christ ?

There is another form of spiritual self-righteousness requiring different treatment. When the sinner is held back from the gospel by a sense of unworthiness, his worthiness is *the implied ground*

---

[1] Matt. ix. 12, 13. [2] Luke xix. 10. with xviii. 9—13.
[3] Matt. xxi. 33—46. Comp. Acts xiii. 38—41.

of his coming to the gospel—his work—not Christ's. When the Christian longs for a deeper view of sin, and love to Christ, and forgets, that, when attained, he will have the same need as before of the blood and righteousness of Christ—this is again to put spiritual self in the place of Christ. To such the Apostle would say —" Christ is become of no effect to you ; ye are fallen from grace. Having begun in the Spirit, are ye made perfect in the flesh ?"[1] If our ground be sure in Christ, let this be our only confidence in our highest frame ; and it will be a satisfactory stay in our lowest. And under all variations, let us give glory to God by simply believing.

IV.—THE FALSE PROFESSOR.

This is the man, who has listened to the Gospel—who has been " persuaded of these things," but not " embraced them." He gives us his words. He exhibits " the form of godliness." His lusts are either restrained by conviction, or dormant from the absence of temptation, or overcome by some dominant propensity ; or he is frightened into hypocrisy by the dread of imminent danger ; or perhaps he has relinquished some outward evils. But what is the amount of the work accomplished? Instead of " the axe being laid to the root of the tree," the branches are pruned, only to sprout again with fresh luxuriance. The birds, instead of being driven away, are only chased from bough to bough. Instead of the fountain being dried up, only the course of the stream is changed. Sin is not touched in its principles. The heart is unrenewed. It is of little use to sweep away the open viciousness, when the seeds of the evil lie within in active operation.

Let us mark the scriptural treatment of this character. Our Lord sifted him, by applying to his conscience the spirituality of his doctrines,[2] the extent of his requirements,[3] the connection between the heart and conduct,[4] and the remembrance of the different standards of God and the world.[5] The Apostle convicts him in the proof, that union with Christ, and consequent renewal of the heart—not outward attainments or privileges—show the real Christian.[6] The Epistle of St. John brings him mainly to the test of love, as the presiding and animating principle of the heart and conduct.

---

[1] Gal. v. 4; iii. 3.   [2] John vi. 60—66.   [3] Luke xiv. 25—33.
[4] Matt. vii. 15—23. xii. 33—35.   [5] Luke xvi. 15.
[6] Rom. ii. 17—29. ix. 6, 7. 2 Cor. v. 17. Col. iii. 11.

But the false professor is a very Proteus, evading our grasp by a constant change of form. Yet if *he speaks of his comforts,* how unlike the awakening and serious consolations of the Christian! There is no dread of self-deception, no acquaintance with his own sinfulness, no assault from Satan, because there is no real exercise of grace, or incentive to diligence. *If he speaks of his state before God,* can he abide the test of the holiness of God, of the "exceeding breadth" of his law, with its fearful disclosure of his utter depravity and defilement? Can he bear to have the detailed evidences of a radical change, the indispensable importance of an interest in Christ, and the solemn alternative, of "having the Spirit of Christ," or "being none of his"[1]—closely pressed upon him? Has the awful consideration—that if "Christ is not in him," "though he speak with the tongues of men and of angels," he is a "reprobate"—ever led him to "examine himself, whether he be in the faith, and to prove his own self?"[2] *If he speaks of his love,* he owns his obligations; but what are his views of the Divine excellency of the Saviour? Where is his readiness to bear his cross, the proof of delight in his word, or of union with his people?[3] How often is the Saviour's merit made—whether avowedly or not—a support for a bold confidence in insensibility to all spiritual affection and Christian deportment! And therefore, as the sum of the whole inquiry—"Every one that loveth is born of God, and knoweth God. He that loveth not, knoweth not God; for God is love."[4]

This case is sometimes beyond the reach of ordinary discernment. Notwithstanding all our vigilance, some counterfeit coin will pass for gold. Judas among the Apostles, and Ananias and others in the Primitive Church, are standing mementos, that it is not our prerogative to search the heart. The form of godliness may be maintained accurate in every feature, and complete in every limb. Generally speaking, however, there will be some inconsistency betraying the self-deceiver, and affording a handle of conviction in dealing with him. Dislike to spiritual religion, and to conversation connected with it;[5] prevalent love of the world;[6] and unsubdued inveterate tempers,[7] indicate his insincere reception

---

[1] Rom. viii. 9.　　　　　　　　[2] 2 Cor. xiii. 5.

[3] Maclaurin admirably observes, 'that the lively and vigorous exercise of love must be judged of by a better standard, than the natural outward signs of inward emotions, depending upon constitution and other causes; that a main thing, in which its true strength consists, is its influence on universal holiness in practice, which is a matter of great importance for the discovering the delusions of self-deceivers.' Essay on Divine Grace, sect. v.　　　　　　　　　　　　　　　　　　　　　　[4] 1 John iv. 7, 8.

[5] Cant. v. 7.　　　　　[6] 2 Tim. iv. 10.　　　　　[7] Gal. v. 24.

of the truth. The love of holiness, and the desire of conformity to his Saviour, were never in his aim. The truth was received as a speculative dogma; " not in the love of it." Being loosely held, it was therefore ineffectively applied, and (when inconvenience was threatened) readily surrendered. Such persons are the great stumbling-blocks to the unestablished Christian—and not less so to the world. Their discovery should make us cautious and slow in forming our judgment of characters; at the same time not treating the sincere with coldness and suspicion.

V.—NATURAL AND SPIRITUAL CONVICTIONS.[1]

THE power of conviction was strongly and variously exhibited under the New Testament Ministry. The thundering discourses of John pierced the conscience. Many were interested, and partially reformed.[2] Under our Lord's first sermon, and in the cases of " the sorrowful young man," and " the chief rulers,"[3] there must have been strong conviction; yet (as the want of universal obedience proved) without Divine influence. The practical effects in the sons of Zebedee, Matthew, and Zaccheus on the other hand,[4] exhibited spiritual and permanent conviction. Under the Apostolic Ministry, Peter's hearers, Cornelius, Sergius Paulus, Lydia, the jailor, the Gentile hearers at Antioch and other places,[5] showed the fruits of spiritual conviction, in faith, love, and universal holiness; while the frantic Jews under Stephen and Paul, and trembling Felix,[6] displayed the power of conscience, overcome by the natural enmity and the love of sin. Few cases more peculiarly need (not, of course, miraculously) the gift of "discerning of spirits," to distinguish between awakenings and humiliation—between a sight of sin, and a loathing of its sinfulness; and thus to determine the character of the conviction, in order to its safe and successful treatment. Its unsoundness or sincerity will be determined—whether it rest in general acknowledgment, or brings out detailed exercises of contrition; whether it respects the misery, or the defilement of sin;[7] its consequences merely, or its character;[8] whether it springs from fear of wrath, or regard for the honour of God;[9] whether it

---

[1] Halyburton's Memoirs may be referred to, as giving the most graphical delineation of the diversified and conflicting exercises of conviction.
[2] Matt. iii. 1—6. Luke iii. 10—14. John v. 35. Mark vi. 20.
[3] Luke iv. 22—28. Matt. xix. 22. John xii. 42, 43.
[4] Matt. iv. 18—22; ix. 9. Luke xix. 1—10.
[5] Acts ii. 37—46. x. xiii. 12. xvi. 14, 15, 30—34. xiii. 44—48. xiv. 1, &c.
[6] Ibid. vii. 54. xiii. 45. xxiv. 25.   [7] Gen. iv. 13, 23. with Ezra ix. 6.
[8] Exod. ix. 27, 28, with Luke xv. 18.   [9] 1 Kings xxi. 27—29, with Psalm li.

extends to some sins, or to all;[1] whether it is consistent with the love of sin, or producing abhorrence of and separation from it ,[2] whether its influence is temporary or abiding ;[3] whether it repels us from Christ in despondency, or leads us to him in the exercise of faith.[4] In the early stages of sincerity, it is often a mixture of legal and evangelical principle, resulting more from sense of sin, than from apprehension of Christ, and productive rather of alarm than of contrition—of terror than of tenderness and love.[5] Self-deceitfulness never shows itself more than in a state of conviction. Some are neither at ease in their sins, nor heartily seek for deliverance. Perhaps they will yield partially to the Gospel; but they rest short of a full restoration. In such cases we must be most careful, that we do not heal the wound, before it has been searched, and probed to the bottom.[6] A slight healing is the prelude to the most fatal delusion. Much wisdom however is requisite to discriminate the true work of God. If, indeed, the excitement be merely the irritation of natural conscience by the law,[7] it will rest in sullen dissatisfaction, or in " a form of godliness" without the power. It must therefore be kept alive, deepened, alarmed, and enlightened by close statements of the danger of yielding to the entanglements of unbelief—of the urgency of an immediate application to the Saviour— of the self-delusion and certain ruin of abiding under present convictions; and at the same time of the assured acceptance of the weakest act of faith. ' Contrition'—as an old writer observes—' is of no force, unless there be also faith in Christ.'[8] The reception of the Saviour is a proof of spiritual life in conviction, and the spring of its continued exercise. Thus both Peter's and Stephen's hearers were pierced—the former only spiritually changed. Whatever feeling, therefore, brings us to Christ, heartily weary of sin, sensible of danger, thirsting for mercy, and anxious to walk by the rules of the Gospel, is the convincing power—not of conscience, but of the Spirit of God. But what tenderness is required, lest we " break the bruised reed !" Let the wide distinction between the indwelling

---

[1] Matt. xxvii. 4, with 1 Cor. xiv. 24.   [2] 1 Sam. xv. 30, with 2 Cor. vii. 11.
[3] John v. 35, with Acts ii. 37—47.   [4] Matt. xxvii. 5. with Acts xvi. 30—34.
[5] Comp. Acts ii. 37, with Zech. xii. 10, as marking the difference between legal and evangelical conviction.   The one precedes, the other follows, faith.
[6] Nothing can be more judicious than Calvin's remarks on this point—' Ubi homines senserint, quam graviter deliquerint, illic non statim curandus est dolor, quemadmodum impostores deliniunt conscientias, ita ut sibi indulgeant, et se fallant inanibus blanditiis. Medicus enim non statim leniet dolorem, sed videbit, quid magis expediat; forte magis angebit, quia necessaria erit acrior purgatio. Sic etiam faciunt prophetæ; cum vident trepidas conscientias, non statim adhibent blandas consolationes; sed potius ostendunt, non esse ludendum cum Deo, et solicitant, sponte currentes, ut sibi proponant terribile Dei judicium, quo magis ac magis humilientur.' In Joel ii.
[7] See Rom. vii. 8, 11.   1 Cor. xv. 56.   [8] Hemminge's Method of Preaching, p. 31.

and the indulgence of sin—between its occasional prevalence and its habitual dominion—be accurately marked : nay, even the over-ruling of its lamented incursions in deepening the contrition, estab-lishing the watchfulness, exercising and strengthening the faith, of the afflicted penitent. Let him view the strong encouragement to repeated applications to Christ. If he be really mourning over his guilt, and desiring the pardon and love of the Saviour (a frame of mind inconsistent with the least indulgence of sin), he has his promise for the rest of his soul.[1] In bringing his wants and desires to the Gospel, he will find increasing light, consolation, and strength, for the maintenance of the spiritual conflict, until judgment " be brought forth unto victory."[2]

VI.—THE YOUNG CHRISTIAN.

JUDGMENT, experience, tenderness, and acquaintance with the natural character, circumstances, and habits of the individual, must direct the treatment of this most important case. The young Christian is awakened and excited, but very imperfectly enlightened. There is much self-deception and self-righteousness. *His repentance* is sincere, but partial; more exercised from the trouble, than from the sinfulness of sin ; but slightly connected with faith ; and with little consciousness of the habitual back-sliding of the heart from God. His *faith*, though genuine, is confused ; rather a feeling or a train of feelings, than an influ-ential principle ; associated with comfort rather than with holiness ; its principle confounded with its exercise, or different exercises mistaken for each other. There is but little of " knowledge and judgment"[3] in *his love ;* so that, though pleasing in its impres-sions, it is not that uniform and powerful energy of self-denial and devotedness, which characterizes the adult Christian. He has many infirmities to exercise our forbearance ; and many difficulties to excite our sympathy. Glad should we be, could he reach at one flight the summit of perfection. But mean-while, let us not, in vi-olation of our Master's instructions,[4] insist upon his maturity.

As the general rule, he must be " fed with milk, not with meat."[5] Yet this must include a *full and explicit exhibition of the Saviour* in His personal dignity, in His Mediatorial character,

---

[1] See Matt. xi. 28.
[2] Ibid. xii. 20. For some most discriminating views, and encouraging directions, rela-tive to these cases, consult Bowles' Past. Evan. Lib. ii. c. 19, 20.
[3] See Phil. i. 9.   [4] Matt. ix. 14—17. and Calv. in loco.   [5] 1 Cor. iii. 2.

and in His relation to His people, that in the simplicity of the Gospel he may continually come to Him, "that he may have life more abundantly."[1] Our Lord advanced the progress of his disciples by the gradual revelation of himself :[2] for doubtless to "grow in the knowledge of" Him, is the most efficient means of "growing in grace."[3]

The conflict of faith is a subject of suitable instruction for this case. The perplexities of our Lord's disciples arose from their indistinct perception of the character• and power of faith. They knew nothing of its power in realizing unseen help ; and, connecting it only with the sensible comfort of their Master's presence, they were utterly unprepared for any emergency in his temporary absence from them.[4] And thus the young Christian wants to be correctly informed in the nature of faith, as an habitual dependence upon Christ, grounded upon the sense of need, and• the Scriptural warrant of his power and love. This principle is perhaps most vigorous in a state of conflict,[5] when striking its roots deeper in the heart, in humility, contrition, and self-abasement ; so that spiritual depression, (when not directly arising from the indulgence of sin) is the trial of its reality, and the peculiar season for its exercise.

The true nature of experience must be also set out—its ground —the testimony of the word, not an impression on the mind—*its principle*—faith, not feeling—*its evidence*—holiness, not profession. It is not excitement, which, originating in self, can never be permanent ; but the active. exercise of dependence on Christ. Faith is the habit of dependence—Experience is the consequent habit of enjoyment ; faith instrumentally the life of experience. As the ground therefore is wholly independent of feeling, and fixed upon the perfect work and office of Christ ;[6] so no set of feelings, whether bright or clouded, must• be suffered to remove the eye from the grand object—the soul from the one sure foundation. The changes however in the Divine dispensations, are needful for the trial of the young Christian's grace, and for his establishment in Christ. Let him therefore *in his happy experience* be directed to be thankful, but watchful ; lest it become the occasion of his pride, rather than the matter of his praise ; his security rather than his encouragement ; his rest rather than his enjoyment. *In*

[1] John x. 10.
[2] See Matt. xvi. 21 ; xvii. 22, 23 ; and John xiv.—xvi. and the Bishop of Winchester's work, Ch. v. [3] 2 Peter iii. 18.
[4] Comp. Matt. xiv. 24—26, and Mark ix. 14 ; with Matthew xvii. 19, 20.
[5] Job xiii. 15. [6] See Heb. x. 19—22.

clouded experience, let him ask his heart—" Is there not a cause ?"
Let him be humbled, not discouraged—quickened to prayer, not
hindered by unbelief. Let him suspect his heart, not the promises
of God. Let him see his own weakness and unworthiness, without forgetting the power and love of his Saviour. Let him expect to
realize his confidence only in humility, self-denial, love, separation
from the world and general consistency; the absence or deficiency of
which would cast a shade over the genuineness of his faith in his
most elevated enjoyment.

The nature, certainty, and requisites of the cross, were the
subject of our Lord's *early* instructions,[1] that his disciples might
wisely calculate the cost of impending trials—an admirable pattern
for us, now that the profession of the Gospel is so often taken up in
the dream of a flowery path ! as if the crown were easily won,
or ever could be won, without the daily cross ; or as if there could
be a moment for the young Christian, when the denial of his own
will, wisdom, or lust, will not be imperatively called for. No outward circumstances of the church can alter these requisitions. He
is not forced into the service of Christ ; but if he will be a follower,
these are the terms.[2] He has no reason to complain of their strictness. The subjugation of his mind to the wisest regulations ; the
loosening of his heart from the world ; the support of his Gracious
Master ; and a closer conformity to his spirit and example ; will
be the happy and permanent fruits.

" *The Spirit of a sound mind*" must also be strongly inculcated.
A defect in judgment is a frequent attendant upon the early stage
of profession. The mind loses its balance under the first influence
of a strong excitement. The affections are tumultuous rather than
rational. Like " the crackling of thorns under a pot," they blaze
furiously, but with little heat, and speedy extinction. Comfort
rather than truth is the object of search. Feeling is mistaken for
faith—animal sensations for religion, which is too often estimated
by their depth and variety, rather than by their connection with
the holy character of Scriptural truth. In various ways, enthusiasm, delusion, foolish and unjustifiable practices, often spring up
with serious personal injury, and much to the hindrance and discredit of the Gospel. Hours are sometimes wasted, even over the
Bible, in a superficial and irregular course, under the mistaken
conception, that not only vain pleasures, but solid pursuits, and
even relative obligations, are inconsistent with the exclusive claims
of God upon the heart. Thus one set of graces is exhibited to the

[1] Matt. x. 34—39.   [2] Matt. xvi. 24.

exclusion of others of a different character, but equal importance; presenting a mis-shapen figure in the place of the symmetry of graces in "the beauty of holiness." The watch needs a regulator as well as a main-spring, to maintain that uniform, harmonious, and subservient motion, which accurately represents the succession of time. Holiness in its first motions may be full of heat and joy. But we must give it time to settle into temper and habit—the gospel acting upon the whole man; regulating every disposition by its authority, and exercising it in its due proportion and combination; thus introducing its subject into the high privilege of "adorning the doctrine of God our Saviour in all things."

We must also enforce *the importance of inculcating subjection and conformity to superiors (whether in age or relative connection) in all things consistent with the paramount authority of God.* Young Christians (those particularly who are young in age) often offend here. Untempered zeal brings needless offence upon religion, and (as they afterwards discover) difficulties into their own path. With a yielding character, firmness in withstanding worldly compliances should be urged. On a naturally firm temperament, submission—especially to parents—should be pressed; else a warm zeal for God will prove to be the indulgence of self-will, and impatience of restraint. Let it be ever recollected, that nothing but the positive obligation of a Divine command can set aside the deference so justly due to parental authority. To preserve the just equilibrium in this exercise, as well as to assist the progress towards maturity, the counsel of a friend of tried sympathy, experience, and consistency, would be of material service.

But after all—our watchword of counsel, admonition, and encouragement is—"*Press forward.*" Let not the novice satisfy himself with being a sincere Christian. Let him seek to be an advancing Christian. Let him remember, that his present attainments are but the commencement, and not the finishing, of his work. Let him constantly examine and exercise his faith. Let him guard against neglecting his own heart in remissness or security; against needless fellowship with the world; inordinate enjoyment of lawful pleasure; neglect of the Word of God; formality in duty; and the power of besetting sins and temptations. Let him enter upon the course of holy violence, in the assurance that the fruit of his conflict will abundantly recompense his toil.[1] Let him know, that the privileges, which he had anticipated at some indefinitely distant period, were his portion from the earliest dawn

[1] Matt. xi. 12.

of his faith, as being not attached to its degree, but to its sincerity; and that his more full apprehension and enjoyment of them, so far from giving license to indolence, will furnish a fresh stimulus for renewed and increased exertion. Forgiveness of sin is his present possession;[1] union with Christ is the direct source of his spiritual life[2]—"springing up," by the power of the Spirit in his heart, "unto everlasting life."[3] Thus receiving the promise, the Author, the earnest, and first-fruits of salvation—he "receives salvation" itself, as "the end of his faith."[4]

VII.—THE BACKSLIDER.[5]

WHAT Minister is not conversant with this most affecting case; connected with unsoundness of doctrine, love of the world, the indulgence of sin, or the neglect of prayer? Perhaps also, the power of unbelief, and the want of Christian establishment, are causes, less obvious, but not less frequent or injurious. The unsettled professor, unable to plead a *certain* title to the promises of support, is paralyzed in prayer, and left to his own unassisted weakness. His comforts (if indeed he could speak of them) not being built upon a personal interest in the Gospel, were feelings, fancies, delusions—not faith—no solid ground of support.

Sometimes we find the *backslider in a hardened state*—flinching from close dealing—advancing rapidly on the high road to apostacy. Solemn recollections (such as "Where is the blessedness that ye spake of?"[6]—Are the thoughts of eternity peaceful?)—the awful declarations of Scripture,[7] or (as in David's case) a sudden and unexpected self-accusation—may however produce conviction.[8] Yet until the man begins to feel restless and miserable, the case is hopeless.

The *convinced backslider* should be treated as if we really grieved over him—not spared, but yet felt for—his conscience probed, yet with tender recollection—-the depth of his departure pointed out, yet himself "restored in the spirit of meekness."[9] Thus was the incestuous Corinthian first handled with severity, in order to produce conviction; when convinced, sustained and confirmed in the most tender regard, "lest haply such a one would be swallowed

---

[1] 1 John ii. 12.   [2] John xv. 1—5.   [3] Ibid. iv. 14.   [4] 1 Peter i. 9.
[5] The reader is referred to a tract by the late Andrew Fuller, for the most full and instructive description of this case, and of the best mode of treatment. Compare also Blackwell's Method. Evan. pp. 212—223. See also an admirable letter in Sidney's Life of Walker, pp. 286—294.   [6] Gal. iv. 15, also iii. 1—4.
[7] Such as Prov. xiv. 14.   [8] 2 Sam. xii. 1—13.   [9] Gal. vi. 1.

up with overmuch sorrow," and Satan should get advantage of the church.[1] Let him be exhorted to a diligent use of means, and a resolute abandonment of the ways which had drawn him aside. Let him be guided afresh, as if he had never known the way, to the foot of the cross, there to "look on him, whom he has pierced, and mourn :"[2] in the assurance, that the same love that pardons sins, "heals backslidings."[3] Peter's case illustrates the tenderness employed at once to deepen conviction, and to complete the restoration.[4] The power of this love will mark the subsequent character with a deeper hatred of sin—a more contrite abasement in the recollection of guilt—a more careful circumspection of conduct,[5] combined with a constant attention to the means of grace, and with a higher estimation of the Saviour.

VIII.—THE UNESTABLISHED CHRISTIAN.

THE *sincerity* of our Lord's disciples was not more evident than their *want of establishment* in faith and knowledge. We often remark a similar defectiveness among our people. Grace is more in the seed than in the operation. It wants exercise to draw it out into practical influence, that love may be more fervent; faith more active; prayer, if not more frequent, yet more spiritual. The Apostle did not treat this case with the soothing tone of sympathy, but with the strong stimulants of conviction and reproof.[6] And indeed such professors, if they do not actually—at least "*seem to*— come short."[7] If they are alive, it is a bare sickly existence, with little power of exertion, or capacity for enjoyment. If they did not undervalue even their scanty measure of progress, they would reach forth for higher attainments and more aspiring hopes. True grace sets an edge upon the appetite, rather than satisfies it. But where unbelief is faintly resisted; indolence substituted for exertion; and they are "lying on their faces," instead of exercising painful diligence in their work;[8] "the things that remain," for want of being "strengthened," will be "ready to die."[9] Hence we see a narrowness in their charity, an unconcern for the spiritual

---

[1] 1 Cor. v. 1—7, with 2 Cor. ii. 1—11.   [2] Zech. xii. 10.
[3] Micah vii. 18. Hosea xiv. 4. The whole book of Hosea, together with Jer. ii.—iv. 1, deserves most careful study for the treatment of this case.
[4] Luke xxii. 61, 62. Mark xvi. 7. John xxi. 15—17.
[5] Comp. Isa. xxxviii. 15. Ezek. xvi. 63.   [6] Heb. v, 11—14.   [7] Ibid. iv. 1.
[8] Josh. vii. 18, with 2 Pet. i. 5—10.   [9] Rev. iii. 2.

wretchedness around them, and a lack of interest and exertion for perishing souls and the grand cause of Christ.

Possibly the first impressions may have been made rather by the novelty than by the direct power of truth. Hence the impulse to shape a religion after our own fancy, instead of embracing the true revelation of God—to live upon the continual excitement of novelty, in preference to the old established truths. This naturally results in an imperfect apprehension of the Gospel, that fully accounts for defects of Christian temper,[1] as well as for an unsteady resistance to the world.[2] The neglect also of the Ministry (the institution expressly ordained for the prevention of this evil[3]) issues in a feeble and inconstant profession. Perhaps the most effectual discipline for this case is the inculcation of an accurate comprehension of the whole compass of Scripture, as the grand means of arriving at Christian perfection.[4] Favoritism in Scripture is the grand parent both of heresy and instability of profession. The word of God loses its power, when displayed from its position, dissevered from its practical connexion, or when a part, however important, is taken for the whole. It would be well also to set forth the full glory of evangelical privileges, not only for the consolation of the established, but for the excitement and conviction of the indolent. For, what do they know of being "filled with all joy and peace in believing?" How little comprehension have they "*with all saints*, what is the breadth, and length, and depth, and height of the love of Christ," as the medium of being "filled with all the fulness of God!"[5] Should we not warn them against resting in the perception of truth without realizing its experimental and practical influence? And should we not labour to stir up a close self-inquiry, an earnest habit of prayer, deep self-acquaintance and self-abasement, increasing activity in obedience, and a stronger excitement to ascend the elevated stations of faith, that they might gain more extensive, animating, and heavenly prospects? Especially should we not quicken them to a more habitual contemplation of Christ, as the means of more complete conformity to his image,[6] and a more steady and enlightened profession of his name.[7] Oh! let them remember also, that it is only in the persevering exercise of faith and diligence that our Christian privileges can be enjoyed, or our Christian confidence assured.[8]

---

[1] Gal. v. 1—8, 15, 26. vi. 14. 1 John v. 4, 5.   [2] Ibid. vi. 14.
[3] Eph. iv. 8—14.   [4] 2 Tim. iii. 16, 17.   [5] Eph. iii. 17—19. with Rom. xv. 13.
[6] 2 Cor. iii. 18.   [7] Heb. iii. 1.   [8] Ib. iii. 6, 14.

IX.—THE CONFIRMED AND CONSISTENT CHRISTIAN.

HERE we find the combination of Scriptural doctrine, holy privilege, and consistent practice. The sum of the prayers and exhortations of the Apostles for their converts, was, that their views of doctrine might be enlarged;[1] their sense of obligation more deep and active;[2] their standard of profession more elevated;[3] their enjoyment of privileges more exciting;[4] their fruitfulness more abundant;[5] their course of obedience more complete.[6] The Apostle's example directs us to substitute instruction in the deepest and most solid truths, in the room of the elementary principles of the Gospel;[7] entering largely into the counsels of God concerning his people—the security of his covenant on their behalf—the more full exhibition of his perfections in the work of their redemption, of the office and work of Christ, and of the Divine life derived from him.[8] By this system of "strong meat" the adult Christian is "nourished up in the words of faith and of sound doctrine," and "his senses" will be yet further "exercised" in spiritual discernment. The same acts indeed belong to the young and to the old Christian; but in the latter they are more grounded and solid. The ordinances of God are attended by the young with greater ardency, but from the old with deeper principle. The affections in the young are more vigorous and lively. But what is gradually lost in the natural decay of their sensible operations, is abundantly compensated in the improvement of their understanding, resolution, and judgment. Spiritual subjects have changed their seat in the soul. If they are less sensibly exercised in the affections (though here it might sometimes be well to kindle excitement) they are more permanently fixed in the mind. The choice is more settled, intelligent, and uniform. If there be less of spiritual excitement, there is a deeper insight into spiritual corruption, a deeper fixedness of habit in the Gospel.

Apart from affliction (a most important means of grace to the Christian[9]) the active operation of spiritual life and joy strengthens and establishes his daily progress heavenward. His release from the dominion of sin; his fellowship with Christ in his sufferings, death, and resurrection,[10] his continual view and application of the

---

[1] Eph. i. 17, 18.   Heb. v. 12.   [2] Phil. i. 9.   1 Cor. vi. 19, 20.   1 Pet. i. 14—19.
[3] Col. i. 9—12.   Phil. iii. 12—17.   [4] Eph. iii. 14—19.   Heb. vi. 11.
[5] Phil. i. 11.   1 Thess. iv. 1.   [6] Heb. xiii. 20, 21.   2 Cor. xiii. 9—11.
[7] Heb. v. 14, vi. 1—3.   [8] Ib. vi.—x.   [9] See John xv. 2.   1 Peter v. 10.
[10] Rom. vi. 1—11.

cross, constrain him with irresistible and most delightful influence. " The beholding, as in a glass, the glory of the Lord" prostrates his soul in admiring, adoring, and transforming contemplation.[1] Sinking in humility, he rises higher and higher in knowledge, holiness, and love. His esteem of his Lord more deeply impresses his heart. He glows with increasing fervour, with more constant and assured delight, with more wakeful and animating gratitude. And thus every exercise of love brings out a growing conformity to the Divine image. It is difficult to turn to human writings for a full exhibition of this heavenly glory. Mr. Romaine has drawn, so far as it extends, a simple and beautiful portrait; imperfect however, as wanting the practical features of the Scriptural sketch. Baxter has thrown out its features with much fire, force, and power of enchantment; but he has often so disguised his figure with his own constrained feelings and metaphysical trammels, that it seems like an angel in fetters. Perhaps Leighton may be said to have given the full portrait, both in his writings and in his character, with as little touch of human infirmity, as can be looked for, till the brighter days of the church.

Yet with this love, as the grand material and means of edification, must be combined a positive enforcement of Evangelical warning. David expressly acknowledged the value of this Scriptural discipline;[2] nor did the fear of legality deter the Apostles from connecting it, as a part of the Gospel, even with the fullest view of the glories of their Great Master.[3] The warnings of Scripture have indeed each their own meaning; yet applying to both classes of our people. Those threatenings, which to the ungodly "work wrath" in the dread of their enemy and judge— with the righteous, produce a wholesome fear of a "jealous God," love for the holiness of his dispensations,[4] a godly fear of sin, and a quickening stimulus to the use of the appointed means of preservation.[5] A prominent display indeed of " the terror of the Lord" would savour of the covenant that "gendereth unto bondage;" but an exclusive ministration of the promises of the Gospel, blotting out all enforcement of its threatenings, would not only incur the guilt of mutilating the word of God, and failing to " warn the wicked of his way;" but would deprive the believer of a Divinely-ordained means of his preservation and establishment.[6]

[1] 2 Cor. iii. 18.   [2] Psalm xix. 11.
[3] See Heb. ii. 2—4, with chap. i.   Col. i. 28.
[4] See Psalm cxix. 119, 120.   [5] Heb. iv. 1. with iii. 18, 19.
[6] ' Let not men think themselves more evangelical than the Author of the Gospel—more skilled in the mystery of conversion and edification of the souls of men than the

The Apostle's exhortation to the Hebrews, furnishes an admirable pattern of this mixed mode of address. Though he styles them —"holy brethren, and partakers of the heavenly calling," he does not spare to "rebuke them sharply," as "dull of hearing;" even setting before them the doom of their rebellious forefathers, and of miserable apostates among themselves, as an incentive to that holy fear, which is always a necessary part of the grace of perseverance; while he concludes with expressing his good opinion concerning them, and setting out the "strong consolation," arising from the immutable certainty of the foundation of their hope.[1] Thus the dark ground occupies so large a portion of the canvass, evidently with a view of displaying more vividly the attractive glory of love shedding its beams over the gloom. Thus also the Christian equipoise is maintained. The balance of faith with fear preserves each principle in its due sphere of operation—restrains the former from presumption, the latter from bondage and unbelief.

The Writer feels deeply impressed with the responsibility of this individual and discriminating Ministry. The recollection, that every word we speak to the several classes has a bearing upon their eternal state—clothes it with inexpressible importance, as it respects themselves, our own consciences, and the Church of God. Our office acts *ultimately* upon the conscience,[2] the various perplexities of which require the most skilful treatment. For the right interpretation of the mind of God, we *must not only have learning in Divine things, but we must ourselves be Divinely learned.* For how can we know the mind of God, but by the unction and teaching of his own Spirit?[3] To qualify ourselves therefore for this anxious service—we need much acquaintance with the human heart, and with our own heart in particular—a deep-searching knowledge of Scripture—a careful study of the best works on casuistical, and experimental divinity[4]—most of all—a spirit of hum-

Apostles: in a word, more wise than God himself; which they must do, if they neglect this part of his ordinance. The hearts of believers are like gardens, wherein there are not only flowers, but weeds also; and as the former must be watered and cherished, so the latter must be curbed and nipped. If nothing but dews and showers of promises should fall upon the heart, though they seem to tend to the cherishing of their graces, yet the weeds of corruption will be apt to grow up with them, and in the end to choke them, unless they are nipped and blasted by the severity of chastenings. And although their persons, in the use of means, shall be secured from falling under the final execution of comminations; yet they know there is an infallible connexion signified in them between sin and destruction (1 Cor. vi. 9—11); and that they must avoid the one, if they would escape the other.' Owen on Heb. ii. 2—4.

[1] Heb. iii.—vi. [2] 2 Cor. iv. 2. [3] Caryl on Job xxxiii. 23. Comp. 1 Cor. ii. 10, 11.
[4] In this respect the study of the Puritan and Nonconformist Divines—Such as the

ble and importunate prayer for constant and increased supplies of " the wisdom which is from above." Add to this—a knowledge of the constitutional temperament of the individuals is obviously most important. A sanguine mind would give a delusive character of ardour and intensity to religious impressions. A constitutional depression would obscure the symptoms even of a genuine work of faith. An undue confidence, or backwardness, would need a different tone of address—to be restrained, cautioned, or encouraged, " as the matter should require."

The Writer does not pretend to have given in this detail a complete Ministerial directory. So diversified are the features both of sin and grace, that no human sources have ever furnished him with rules, which did not leave many cases unprovided for. He has aimed only to sketch a few broad lines and traits of conversation, which might in some measure meet the prominent difficulties, and be readily filled up under Divine teaching at the moment of emergency. Experience shows us, that often the most difficult work remains when we have come down from the pulpit, needing special direction of prayer, study, and careful regard to our Master's ministration for its effectual discharge. On one particular, however, we cannot mistake; that to all, of every class and at every stage, the attractions of the cross must be unfolded, and its heavenly glory made intelligible, for every purpose of conviction and conversion, of instruction and sanctification; for the establishment, comfort, and eternal salvation of all who are willing to receive it. It is a grand specific, applicable to every variety and complication of disease, equally powerful to break the hard heart, or to heal the broken heart. The timid or mistaken exhibition of it, is but a feeble instrument of conviction : while the wilful disguise and misapprehension of it will be blasted with ineffectiveness.

"Morning Exercises," Owen's and Flavel's Treatises, Baxter's Christian Directory, Perkins, Hildersham, Bolton, Greenham, Gurnal—will be invaluable. 'Pike and Hayward's Cases of Conscience' will be interesting to Ministers, who conceive with Philip Henry—' That the true learning of a Gospel Minister consists not in being able to talk Latin fluently, or to dispute in philosophy, but in being able to speak a word in season to weary souls.' Life, p. 207. Compare a small work—' Philip on Christian Experience,' also Walker's Life, pp. 22—46.

CHAPTER III.

THE VISITATION OF THE SICK.

THIS Divinely-appointed work[1]—often the only kind office that we can do for our people—is a Ministry of special responsibility. God himself is the Preacher, speaking more loudly and directly to the conscience than the mere voice of man. Our work therefore, is to call attention to the speaking voice of this Divine rod.[2] Again, in the sinner's contact with 'Death—that terrible and thundering Preacher,'[3]—a deeper impression is sometimes made in the sick chamber, than in the pulpit. Most of all at this crisis, the conscience is more or less awakened—the need of a Refuge is acknowledged—the prospect of eternity without it is dreaded. How golden the opportunity to set forth our Saviour, in every office suitable—in every offer of his grace so free, so encouraging!

Neglect or error therefore in this Ministration, involves consequences far more responsible than medical inattention or unskilfulness—the trifling with the salvation of immortal souls. 'This intolerable defect in Ministers' (as an old Writer observes) 'never shows itself more shamefully, or with greater hurt, than when men have need of spiritual help, at the hour of death, or in the time of great affliction.'[4] 'Opiate divinity'[5] is too often administered to slumbering souls, instead of the awakening excitements of anxious alarm. Perhaps no where are our faith and seriousness more painfully exercised; and no where do we realize more sensibly the importance of "rightly dividing the word of truth." The temper of the individual (who sometimes hates the remedy more than the disease,) and the fearful mischiefs, which might result from a small error in his treatment,[6] add much to the difficulty; so that (as seems to be intimated) it is "one among a thousand," that may peculiarly excel in this work.[7]

The promiscuous use of a general form cannot be recommended.[8] The 67th Canon determines the use of the appointed service, 'as

---

[1] James v. 14.   [2] See Micah vi. 9.   [3] Bishop Hopkins.
[4] Marbury's Exposition of Psalm xxxii. 5. Augustine calls such Ministers *desolators*, instead of *consolators*. The strict law of the Scotch Kirk punishes habitual negligence in his visitation by deposition. Smith's Lectures, xxiv. We need scarcely observe, that this obligation includes—'not visiting barely, when one is sent for: he is to go as soon as he hears that any of his flock are ill.' Burnet's Past. Care, ch. viii. Compare Ezek. xxxiv. 24.   [5] Winchester's Ser. p. 81.   [6] In medicina nihil exiguum est. Galen.
[7] See Job xxxiii. 22, 23.   [8] See Isaiah xxviii. 27.

the Preacher shall think most needful and convenient'—a wise and necessary discretion, since (whatever be its excellence) it partakes of the disadvantage of ' not being particular enough for each several occasion.'[1]

It would be impossible to give general rules for difficult cases ; of which, when they come before us, we can scarcely judge with any certainty, and our judgment is determined by a very small matter. We only mention a few hints ;—as first—*The duty of weighing our words, with much previous meditation and prayer.* The case too often meets us in the regular routine, and is counselled only by the suggestions of the moment. ' It is rather strange' (as Ostervald remarks) ' that Ministers should take so much pains to prepare their discourses for the pulpit, and take so little pains to prepare for what they should say to the sick, or how to conduct their visits to them, though it is one of the most difficult and important offices in the Ministry.' Habitual readiness, without much considerate and prayerful exercise, will afford no warranted expectations of the Divine blessing.

We must approach the sick in the garb of a friend. Our aim (unlike that of the medical attendant,) is often unconnected in his mind with any definite prospect of benefit. It is more necessary, therefore, that we should enter fully into his case—that our spirit, manners, and voice should exhibit manifest sympathy—like our Master, when he stopped the bier at the gate of Nain, and wept at the tomb of Lazarus.[2] Nothing more successfully engages confidence, than when the official garb shows "a brother, that is born for adversity."[3]

We should endeavour to obtain an accurate knowledge of the case. And here the vast variety of cases (each of them having some distinguishing characteristic) and the great mixture and combination found in each, even when its proper individuality is ascertained, present no small difficulty. This establishes the importance of general visiting, in order to gain the necessary knowledge. The

---

[1] Bishop Wilkins' Gift of Prayer, p. 12. Indeed the service, as presuming the sick person to be a penitent, is obviously inappropriate to the melancholy multitude of cases of an opposite description; so that (as Bishop Barrington justly observed) 'in many cases the funeral service might be used with almost as much propriety as the office for the sick.' Charge, 1797, p. 31. Bishop Horsley gives the same judgment on the exclusive use of the service. Charges, p. 153. Much edifying use may however be made of it, where suitable. The Absolution in this service appears to be a matter of unreasonable objection. As connected with confession of sin, it is restricted to sincere penitents. *In the letter* therefore it is the authoritative declaration given on earth in our Master's name, and which, *so far as it is given according to his mind,* will be ratified in heaven. See John xx. 22, 23. 2 Cor. ii. 10. αφεθησεται. James v. 15. *In substance,* it is only the solemn judgment by which we are accustomed *in the name of Christ* to assure the confidence of many doubtful and fearful believers.

[2] Luke vii. 12, 13. John xi. 35.   [3] Prov. xvii. 17.

physician cannot prescribe without feeling the pulse, and enquiring concerning the diet and habits of life. He takes pains to converse with friends, and gains his information from every quarter. Thus must we prudently gather from the best—and, as far as possible, from Christian sources.

In the treatment of the case, we should endeavour to bring out some of the diversified applications of Scripture according to the symptoms evolved for our direction. The Psalms are peculiarly suitable from their simplicity of language and sympathy of feeling; and especially as furnishing matter and moulding for prayer, both for and with the sick person. Our Lord's conversation with Nicodemus embraces the two main points for the instruction of the ignorant and careless—the necessity of the change of heart, and faith in Christ—the work of the Spirit, and the work of the Saviour.[1] His subsequent discourse to the multitude is universally applicable, as marking the freeness of the Gospel, for the encouragement of the sinner; and its spirituality, for the conviction of the self-righteous.[2] His closing discourses to his disciples are fraught with consolation and support to the penitent and established Christian.[3] The Epistles furnish equal variety of suitable instruction. Sometimes it may be advisable to take a whole book, or several connected chapters, to give a comprehensive view of evangelical truth. If this become too general and pointless, we might combine some detached portions, that admit of a more close and particular application. Every passage brings out some exhibition (more or less direct) of Christ. He is the centre of all—"the way, the truth, and the life," in all and in each. We may, therefore, easily, from him, put the several parts together, and enlarge on each separately to any extent; aiming to appropriate suitable texts to the main features of the case. The Creed, or some other part of the Service of the Visitation of the Sick, might be drawn out into a simple and detailed system of instruction and examination. Something from the person's own mouth will give the most pointed ground of our address; while a few kind and confidential enquiries often will engage his confidence, and draw out some close and awakening recollections on the state and prospects of his soul. In doubtful cases we may profitably advert to these enquiries; adding our plain and serious view of his state; and leading him to earnest prayer for increasing self-acquaintance.

The treatment of cases will often exercise "long patience." A cold unmeaning assent may meet us from day to day—perhaps

[1] John iii. 1—21. [2] Ibid. vi. 25—65. [3] Ibid. xiv.—xvi.

from month to month. Here we must vary—not the truth, but the medium of its presentment—such as a word casually dropped —a tract left behind us—occasional visits rather of a familiar than of an official character. Yet the constant effort to "bring forth new things" may partake too much of human wisdom. The unvarying repetition of the "old" statement has generally proved as "the waters, that wear the stones."[1] Legal expressions in common use must often be tried by the standard of their own imperfect mode of communication, rather than by the rules of strict accuracy.

No regulations can prescribe the precise measure of attendance upon the sick. Imminent danger demands our constant care. The nearness of eternity gives an infinite moment to every opportunity of instruction. Yet in other cases, frequent visits should not ordinarily be long. In cases of peculiar repulsiveness, some intermission would be advisable—watching however unexpected openings, and important emergencies. The time also of visiting may vary. Sometimes regularity is desirable, often inexpedient; customary attendance usually losing something of its impressiveness. A system without a system is generally to be preferred—perseverance and watchfulness rather than exactness— under all circumstances, however, considering the convenience of the sick. None of us, we presume, will restrict our attendance to cases of spiritual indulgence and refreshment. The more unfavourable cases, if less exciting, will eventually be found not the less profitable department of our visitations, in the exercises of compassion, self-denial, and dependence on Divine aid ; and in the cheering encouragement of the proffer of a free salvation to those, who are " ready to perish."

The *importance of Ministerial faithfulness* cannot be too highly estimated. This is not a time for common-place topics of trifling, or for "prophesying smooth things." The emaciated countenance of the sufferer, the symptoms of death, mourning relations around, call indeed loudly for tenderness. But love to the immortal soul, and intense interest in its eternal destiny, call louder still for fidelity of treatment. Our first concern must be, to be plain, and studiously faithful in our exhibition of truth. We have a great temptation from the sufferer's willingness to be deluded, his greedy desire for comfort, and from the false tenderness of his misguided friends.[2] But unfaithfulness is to undo our own souls no

---

[1] See Job xiv. 19.

[2] 'Our chief danger in the present age seems to be in erring on the side of candor and complaisance, and not dealing with mankind with sufficient plainness and fidelity. Many

less than his.[1] Silence is cruelty. For the knowledge of his real condition either way is for his advantage—that he may enjoy the comfort of his soundness, or be saved from the certain ruin of his own delusion. 'While you are tender, therefore,' (Mr. Mason charges us) 'be sure to be faithful, and have respect to the approbation of your conscience afterwards. Remember that you are a Minister of the Gospel; and must not sacrifice the cause of truth and godliness to a false shame or tenderness.'[2] We must, however, like skilful physicians, mingle emollients with corrosives:[3] labouring to work a solid, not a sudden cure: and never causing pain, but from the necessity of the case, and with the purpose of effecting a radical cure. The charge of harshness will then reflect upon our message,[4] not upon the delivery of it; while our full display of the encouragement and invitations of the Gospel, will prove, that we only pointed out the danger, to save the sinner from ruin; and to set before him a sure and everlasting refuge.

Nor must we forget to *insist upon the love of him that afflicts*. Here we see that clear view of that paternal character of God,[5] which sustained the Redeemer's soul in his bitterest moments of suffering.[6] It is a Father's love that strikes, in order to humble his rebellious child; and that supports his humbled child with such sustaining peaceful joy, that he kisses the rod, while it is in the act of smiting him; and feels that comfort in the endurance of affliction, which he had anticipated in his removal. Here then we must *point out the reason of affliction*—"not without necessity"[7]— "coming not from the ground," but from the good providence of God[8]—*its end*—for the trial of faith, and the glory of the Saviour[9] —*its duties*—self-inquiry,[10] watchfulness,[11] faith,[12] submission,[13] and thankfulness[14]—*its fruits*—the removal of sin,[15] the humbling of the soul,[16] the loosening of the heart from the world,[17] a larger spirit of supplication,[18] the establishment of Christian assurance,[19] and joy-

---

of my people have died, with whom my conscience has afterwards accused me of not dealing so plainly as I should.'—Orton's Letters to Dissenting Ministers, i. 59, 60. Melius est cum severitate diligere, quam cum lenitate decipere. Augustine.

[1] Ezek. xxxiii. 8.

[2] Student and Pastor. By the author of the celebrated treatise on Self-Knowledge, p. 114—a work with many serious hints upon the ministry. Its scanty and defective views of Christian doctrine have been lately Socinianized by the editorial labours of Dr. Toulmin.

[3] For specimens of this healing exercise of faithfulness, see 1 Sam. xii. 20—22. Ezra x. 2. See some valuable hints in Cecil's Remains—'On visiting Death-beds.'

[4] See Mark ix. 44; xvi. 16. Comp. Lam. iii. 22—33.

[5] Psalm ciii. 13, with Heb. xii. 5—11.　　[6] Matt. xxvi. 39, 42. John xviii. 11.

[7] 1 Pet. i. 6, 7.　　[8] Job v. 6. Matt. x. 30.　　[9] 1 Pet. i. 7.

[10] Job x. 2.　　[11] Hab. ii. 1.　　[12] Job xiii. 15.

[13] Lev. x. 3. 1 Sam. iii. 18. 2 Kings xx. 19. Psalm xxxix. 9.　　[14] Job i. 21.

[15] Isaiah xxvii. 9.　　[16] 2 Chron. xxxiii. 12.　　[17] Eccles. i.

[18] Psalm l. 15.　　[19] Zech. xiii. 9.

ful anticipation of the heavenly inheritance.[1]   " In a weanedness of soul" and a cheerful suffering spirit, the full blessing of this visitation of love will be realized.

It is of infinite *moment to make Christ the sum of our instructions to the sick*.   This indeed is the specific object of our commission ; as the " Interpreter" of these painful dispensations, to exhibit the " uprightness of God" in punishing and pardoning sin —" having found a ransom ;" and thus, as in the camp of Israel, to lift up the brazen serpent, with the warrant and inscription— " Look and live."[2]   This is the only gospel for the sick chamber. To tell the impotent man to labour for heaven by his own works, is like mocking the misery of the wounded Israelite, by calling him tō his work.   He *now*, perhaps, for the first time, feels his impotence.   To work therefore, is to despair.   But point his eye to the pole—and it is " life from the dead."   And here the simplicity of our work greatly assists us.   Unlike the physician, we have only one remedy of diversified application, but equally adapted to all, for conviction, life, consolation, holiness.   We use indeed the law—not as Ministers of the law--but as " a schoolmaster to bring to Christ"[3]—not however, keeping back the Gospel till the law has fully done its work ; but setting out the Divine physician, in order to show the sinner his desperate disease, and to excite his desires, and soften his heart for an immediate application for healing. Thus we proclaim an open door under the most desponding circumstances[4]—invitation to all—discouragement to none—security to the people of God.[5]   All instruction is *essentially defective*, that is not grounded upon this free and full display of the Gospel, which furnishes the only effectual principle of holiness, in bringing us into union with God, and conformity to his image.

We cannot forbear to remark *the comfort of going to the sick only as the Lord's instruments*.   This is the warrant of our commission—" Messengers"—sent by God for this express purpose. What a relief from that excessive anxiety, which often hinders the freedom and cheerfulness of our spirit !   And what a warrant to pray in faith for God's power in his own ordinance ; which, like every Divine institution, carries a promise with it ; the pleading of which, and the benefit resulting therefrom, are hindered only by our own unbelief !

---

[1] Ps. lv. 6—8.   2 Cor. iv. 17, 18; v. 1, 5.   See Archbishop Laud's Manual of Prayers in Stearne's Tractat. de Visit. Infirm.   Clergyman's Instructor, p. 392.   Cradock's Knowledge and Practice (ch. xxix.) gives a full and edifying view of this subject.
[2] Job xxxiii. 23, 24.   John iii. 14, 15; xii. 32.   Isaiah xlv. 22.   [3] Gal. iii. 24
[4] See Acts viii. 22.   Isa. xliii. 24, 25.   Hos. xiii. 9.   [5] See John vi. 35—37.

We recommend, as a general rule, to conclude our visits to the sick with short but solemn prayer, moulding the precise petitions most suitable to his circumstances and spiritual condition. His case may not always admit of the act of prayer. Sometimes however, Scripture prayerfully expounded, or ejaculatory petitions mingled in the course of conversation, will be an acceptable means of supplication according *to the spirit* of the Scriptural rule, and with a promise of spiritual, if not of temporal benefit.[1]

We need scarcely observe the peculiar caution requisite in administering the sacrament to the sick. While to the Christian pilgrim it may be the true viaticum for the last stage of his journey ; by formalists, and even by the careless, ' it is desired, as the passport on the road to heaven, which they expect will answer their purpose at once.'[2] A familiar exposition of John vi. is the best preparation for its reception ; not as enforcing the obligation of the commemorative command (to which there was no immediate reference ;) but as illustrating the nature and operations of that faith, which alone qualifies the communicant to "discern the Lord's body."

We must not forget the instruction of the attendants,[3] which indeed is often a most important medium of indirect address to the sick. How impressive is the scene before their eyes, in the vivid picture of the consequences of sin, the vanity of the world, the nearness and unspeakable importance of eternity, and of an instant preparation for it ! We must inculcate their immense responsibility, to add the care of the sick man's soul to the care of his body ; to keep off the too successful diversion of impertinent topics ; to improve seasonable opportunities of reading or instruction : and to seek in special prayer a permanent blessing both upon him and upon themselves.

Nor must we omit the convalescent in our consideration. Bishop Burnet advises to exact from the sick solemn promises of renovation of life in the event of their restoration.[4] Our future Ministry to them will be setting home these sick-bed engagements

---

[1] See James v. 14—16.

[2] Stonehouse's Sick Man's Friend—a work of defective Christian doctrine, but of much valuable practical detail, chiefly compiled from Doddridge, Mason, and others.

[3] In every thing that a Minister says to a sick person, he ought to keep three things steadily in view ;—the influence which it may have on the person, if dying—the influence which it may have on him, if he recover—and the influence it may have on persons in health who are about him.' Gerard's Pastoral Care, p. 168—a sensible and serious work ; but for the most part unconnected with an elevated standard, and with Evangelical motives.

[4] Past. Care, ch. viii. Compare Stearne's Tractatus, ut supra—a treatise with most admirable systematic rules ; but with an almost total destitution of enlivening views of the gospel. –Clergyman's Instructor, p. 408.

for their constant remembrance, but yet in the deepest sense of their utter helplessness, and entire dependence on the strength of Christ. To each of them we might say—"Behold, thou art made whole ; sin no more, lest a worst thing come upon thee."[1] To all we should recommend daily application of the lessons which they have learned in this school ;[2] daily prayer to keep alive the teaching of the Spirit in their seasons of affliction ;[3] daily recollection of their peculiar trials ;[4] daily renewal of their sick-bed vows ;[5] and daily "remembrance" of "them that are in adversity, as being themselves also in the body."[6]

CHAPTER IV.

PASTORAL MINISTRY OF THE YOUNG.

To the intelligent Christian, anxiously rejoicing in the growing prospects of the Church, no sight is more full of life and promise, than that of the Pastor folding the lambs of the flock in the "green pastures, and beside the still waters" of the Gospel of peace. ' My first and greatest success' (says Baxter) ' was upon the youth ; and so it was that when God had touched the hearts of the young with the love of goodness, and delightful obedience to the truth ; in various instances their friends, their fathers, and their grand-fathers, who had grown old in an ignorant and worldly state, did many of them fall into a liking and loving of piety, induced by their love to their children, who now appeared so much wiser and better, and more dutiful to them.'[7] So sensible was Dr. Doddridge of the importance of this work, that he resolved at his entrance into the Ministry—' I will often make it my humble prayer, that God would teach me to speak to children in such a manner, as may make early impressions of religion upon their hearts.'[8] The peculiar encouragement of this " morning seed-time" is thus beautifully set forth—' This is perhaps the most delightful of all the Minister's labours.   He has indeed ignorance to contend with ; but ignorance is more easily overcome, than that worse knowledge of " the counsels of the ungodly," which commonly belongs to more

[1] John v. 14.
[2] Psalm xcii. 12. cxix. 67, 71, 75.
[3] Isaiah lxiii. 15—19; lxiv. 1.
[4] Lam. iii. 19—21.
[5] Psalms ciii. cxvi.
[6] Heb. xiii. 3.
[7] Introduction to his Compassionate Counsel to Young Men.
[8] Orton's Life of Doddridge, ch. v.

advanced years. He has evil to encounter; but it is the evil of nature, not yet rendered obstinate by habit; of vicious propensities, not yet strengthened by indulgence, till the attempt to eradicate is nothing less than the "plucking out a right eye, or the cutting off a right hand."—All reason, all experience, all Scripture, concur in this—"*In the morning* sow thy seed." Often has it sprung up, and brought forth the fruits of grace, when it had seemed to outward eyes to have been choked with tares.'[1]

The general responsibility of this Ministry is of the highest moment. It concerns the parents of the next generation; and—according to the profound remark of Bishop Butler—'every successive generation is left in the ordinary course of Providence to be formed by the preceding one.'[2] 'Knowledge' in the present age indeed is 'power'—of the best or the worst character, according to the direction and controul given to it. Truly are "the children of the youth" in this eventful day ". as arrows in the hands of a mighty man"[3]—instruments of the most important good, or of the most frightful evil. For their beneficial direction, all the schemes of human wisdom (such as mechanic institutes, or schools for useful knowledge, *dissevered from Christian principles*) are palpably inefficient. The only knowledge that tells upon the mass of our population is that which is impregnated with the doctrine of the Gospel. All besides is morally powerless as a skeleton to start into life and motion, and perform the exercises of a man.

But the Ministers of the Establishment have a special responsibility in this matter. Well does it become them to look carefully to their anxious work—lest haply "the arrows" just alluded to should be hereafter misdirected with mighty influence against their own walls. Public Education—dissociated from the Church—would be a machine of powerful opposition. Without a concentrated and vigorous effort, we may live to see the next generation formed upon the principles of Dissent—the most valuable part of our charge cut asunder from us, and growing up in separation from our communion, if not in hostility to our constitution. Then indeed would the Establishment lose all her hold on the affections of the people, all her moral influence, and all respect in common estimation; and in the disruption of these bonds of mutual interest, she would soon be considered as an expensive and useless encumbrance on the land. We have been well reminded therefore, 'that it is out of the younger branches of their parochial family—the

---

[1] Bishop of Chester's Sermons on the Christian Ministry, pp. 23—26.
[2] Sermon before the Schools. Works ii. 335.   [3] Psalm cxxvii. 4.

lambs of their flock, that the clergy must provide for the progressive renovation of the strength of our national and Apostolical
Church.'[1] Under a deep sense of this responsibility, we proceed to
investigate some of the most interesting points of detail.

<h2>I.—CATECHIZING.</h2>

A CATECHIZING Ministry—so far as local circumstances will
admit of it—demands a high place among the means of bringing
our people into an early, conciliating, and instructive contact with
ourselves as their spiritual instructors. Comber[2] defines the work
from one of the old Fathers, to be ' the knowledge of religion first
delivered to the ignorant by the Catechist, and then by them repeated over and over again,' first giving—then extracting the information given ; or, according to the familiar illustration of an eminently practised Catechist—' pumping knowledge into the children,
and then pumping it out again.' For the completeness of the
system, there should be reciprocity of interrogation between the
catechumen and the instructor—the former not merely repeating
lessons, or answering questions, but asking further explanation of
questions either imperfectly apprehended, or capable of further elucidation. This however cannot form a component part of public
catechizing, consistent with a due regard to the reverential order of
the Sacred services.

Whether the Apostolic Ministry included this exercise, is not
fully demonstrable. The term descriptive of the Christian education of some of the early converts,[3] combined with the diversity of
terms employed to describe the New Testament Ministry, seems to
have some reference to this familiar mode of instruction.[4] The authority and practice of antiquity is undoubted.[5] Men of the highest rank in the church appear to have exercised themselves in this
work. Origen's close mode of Catechetical Ministry was blessed to
the conversion of many heathen bystanders of influence. Cyril
and Augustine—two of the shining lights of the ancient church—
have left their strong testimony of its importance. All the great

---

[1] Bishop of Winchester's Primary Charge, pp. 30, 31. 'It is to these seminaries that
we are to look for a succession of youthful branches, which, having been grafted into the
body of Christ's Church at baptism, may here imbibe the sap of holy principles, and be
prepared by culture under the gracious influence of the Holy Spirit, sought for in prayer,
to become "trees of righteousness, the planting of the Lord." ' Bishop of London's Primary Charge, 1830.   [2] Comber on Catechism.
[3] Luke i. 3, 4.   Acts xviii. 25.   Comp. Rom. ii. 18.   1 Cor. xiv. 19.   Gal. vi. 6.
[4] Acts v. 42.   2 Tim. i. 11.   See Hooker, Book v. 18, and Herbert's Country Parson.
ch. xxi.   [5] See Bingham's Antiquities, Book x.

names of the Reformation are on the same side. Luther's Catechism still forms the standard in many of the Reformed Foreign Churches.[1] The judgment of our own Church is manifest, from the strong language of her canonical legislation, from the valuable Catechism which forms a part of her Liturgy, and from the two others, (Nowell's and King Edward's,) which she has always accredited by her authority. Few of her great divines, but have set their seal to the value of this exercise, many by their valuable expositions of her Catechism, many (as Bishop Burnet) by their personal engagements in the work. The Romanists seem to have been well aware of the value of this ministry, and of its use as a weapon against themselves—giving as one reason for the imperative obligation—' the mischief which the Protestants have done the Catholic church, not only by their tongues, *but especially by their writings called Catechisms.*'[2]

The use of this practice to ourselves is most important. It gives us a plain, familiar, affectionate mode of address. It leads us to study simplicity of thought and illustration ;[3] for we cease to be catechists when we cease to be intelligible to the lowest capacity. The breaking up of Scripture—needful for this mode of instilling knowledge by little and little—supplies us with much valuable material for our Pulpit Ministry. We are thus also enabled to give much familiar personal instruction, growing out of circumstances, which would be needlessly offensive in our public Ministry, or otherwise inconsistent with the dignity of the pulpit.

To our young people—also this system is most useful. The palpable evidence which this important intercourse gives of our office, as the nursing fathers of their souls, tends to cement a ' cord that will not be quickly broken,' far more effective than argument to attach them to ourselves, to our Ministry, and to the Church. Added to which, the imbibing of milk gradually strengthens them for the more wholesome digestion of "strong meat," so that they grow up, ' having their senses exercised to discern both good and

---

[1] See also the authorities in Gilly's Horæ Catecheticæ.

[2] Preface to Catechism published by Council of Trent.

[3] This made Bishop Hall complain—'No one thing I regret so much, as not having given more time to the public exercises of Catechizing. 'Oh!' (said Dr. Doddridge,) 'could I spend more of my time in *catechizing children*, in exhorting heads of families, and *addressing young people!*' Chap. viii. Mr. Brown of Haddington observes of himself—'I lament, that I have not been more diligent in catechizing and exhorting the children in my congregation. I am persuaded, that these exercises are some of the best means, which Ministers can use for promoting the welfare of souls.' Life and Remains, p. 28. Dr. Owen remarked to the same effect—that 'more knowledge is ordinarily diffused, especially among the young and ignorant, by one hour's catechetical exercise, than by many hours' continued discourse.' Mr. Charles of Bala declared, ' Catechizing children has taught me more divinity than any other human means.'

evil.' On all this account we wonder not that the charges of our Ecclesiastical Rulers have often and earnestly called our attention to this subject.[1]

The variety of tact and local circumstances, make it difficult to give practical hints on this subject. The Catechism of our Church should of course form a primary substance of instruction, not as a matter of rote, but as broken into questions, illustrated by Scripture, and brought forth in lively and well-directed application. To render this familiar and interesting, will require careful study and consideration. The system however should be extended to the Scriptural field, engaging our young people to learn a portion of Scripture, whether from the service of the day, or in any more regular course, and requiring answers, either in the explanation of the passage, or its illustration by parallel passages. Examination of one or more of the Sermons might vary the course, or form the regular course, as circumstances might suggest. The time after the afternoon service is perhaps the most convenient for Catechizing, where a large part of the congregation would probably share the benefit of the instruction. Should however the Rubrical interval after the second lesson be preferred, it will be necessary to prepare the children with answers to the questions proposed (in order to prevent the awkwardness which would result from eliciting answers without preparation,) or to confine the questions to those of the children, from whom we can calculate upon ready and intelligent answers.[2]

When answers cannot readily be obtained, we must be satisfied with our children carrying away the substance of our instruction, conveyed in as familiar a manner as possible. A wide and diversified sphere is most desirable for the full operation of this system, while at the same time, those who can only make the experiment upon a limited scale, will feel the value of that experiment as an encouragement to persevere.

II.—THE SUNDAY SCHOOL—ITS IMPORTANCE—CONSTITUTION—
AND SUPERINTENDENCE.

THE establishment of Sunday Schools may be considered as an era of moral light to our country. No difference of opinion can exist on their importance.[3] The system enters into almost every de-

---

[1] Charge of Archbishop of Canterbury to the Diocese of London, 1822. Charge of Bishop of Chester. Primary Charge of Bishop of Winchester. Archdeacon Bayley's Charge, London, 1826, and a detailed Charge of Archdeacon Bather, 1835.

[2] This part of Mr. Walker's Catechizing was most encouraging. Life, ch. iv. Gilly's Horæ Catecheticæ will furnish many valuable hints as the result of actual experience.

[3] Many of our Episcopal Charges have pointedly insisted upon it. Bishop Law re-

partment of our Ministry. It is often instrumentally *an adult school*. Parents have been taught to read by their instructed children. The Scriptural lessons also of the school have been retailed at home with interesting simplicity and suitable application. And thus we speak through this attractive channel, with extensive and most powerful interest. In many cases also the palpable happy fruits of teaching put the ignorance of parents to shame, and excite a sincere and active desire to partake of the advantage. And thus the School is a medium of family instruction, and becomes the lever, whose force is felt over the whole parish. 'No one' therefore ' can have been long entrusted with the care of a parish, without observing, that it is through the agency of his school, directly or indirectly, that he will best win his way to the hearts of his people, as their spiritual Minister and friend, for their souls' good.'[1]

On all accounts, therefore, the instruction of the young is of the highest moment : and though, like every other Ministry, it will be the occasion of deeper condemnation in the neglect or misimprovement ; yet many now on earth, and many more in heaven, will remember this important advantage in their songs of everlasting praise.[2]

Often is it the seed-time for the future harvest. As the immediate result, the pulpit Ministry becomes more intelligible and interesting.[3] In many cases of subsequent reception of the truth, (as with Timothy,[4]) the advantages of a previously enlightened mind are sensibly felt ; while in less decisive instances, its restraints operate with wholesome effect. There is also much preparatory work

marked—' There are few means, by which a Minister of our church can more effectually promote the cause of order and religion. A Sunday School is an easy, cheap, and unmixed good.' (Primary Charge, 1825.) Bishop Blomfield enforced the necessity of a Sunday School ' *in every place*—taught, in the failure of other resources, by the Clergyman himself, or some part of his family.' (Primary Charge at Chester, 1825.) We need scarcely refer to Bishop Porteus' earnest recommendations on this subject.

[1] Bishop of Winchester's Primary Charge, p. 31.

[2] Cotton Mather mentions Eliot's prayers, when the question of Ministerial inefficiency was discussed in their synod—' Lord, for schools everywhere amongst us! that our schools may flourish! that every member of this assembly may go home, and procure a good school in his town! that, before we die, we may be so happy as to see a good school encouraged in every plantation of the country.' See some interesting details of the effects of Sunday Schools in Wales, under the instrumentality of the late Mr. Charles, connected with the revival and extension of religion. Life of Rev. T. Charles, (p. 237—258) a most edifying piece of Ministerial Biography.

[3] Should not the plan, arrangement, and illustration of our sermons have a specific reference to the children's apprehension, and to a subsequent enquiry of their intelligence? Not to speak of the advantages to ourselves in the cultivation of a more simple mode of address, the benefit to the children would be most important, in forming and fixing their habit of attention in the house of God, &c. Still further—if the Scriptural lesson in the school were to form the subject of one of the sermons of the day, the unity of the system about to be detailed would be complete, and the school be most advantageously connected with the Pulpit Ministry.

[4] 2 Tim. iii. 15.

of subordinate but most important benefit—much material for the operation of converting grace in a mind stored with Scriptural truth. For though the teaching heart is exclusively the work of God, yet an uninstructed mind—speaking after the manner of men—presents an additional difficulty to the reception of the Gospel. There is also supply of food for adults in the destitution of a living voice. Besides these spiritual benefits, the moral influence of this system is apparent. A village with or without a Sunday School, presents to the most casual eye a difference in sobriety and quietness. Many respectable servants, apprentices, and even parents, have also been produced. And thus even in the deficiency of the main success, much valuable result is produced. Add to this—the teachers, in watering others, have often themselves been watered ; and have realized in their interesting official engagements impressions of religion hitherto unknown.

The constitution of the school is the course of instruction adapted to the taste and capacities of children—varying from the first rudiments to the highest parts of the system, but ever keeping the main object in view—the intelligent and saving knowledge of the Scriptures. The mere repetition even of the best selected Scriptural lessons, offer no satisfactory assurance towards this object. For if the memories of children be stored, while the intelligent powers remain wholly dormant, no interest can be excited—no permanent impression can be made. In the routine of mechanical instruction, small classes with a competent supply of teachers are preferable. Each teacher might be provided with a bag, containing a copy of the books used in the class, and a card ruled by the superintendent for a quarter of a year—marking on one side the names of the children, with their conduct, attendance, and lessons ; and on the other side, the Scriptural, catechetical, and other exercises for the quarter.

The two main points of the external routine are *œconomy of time and order of arrangement*—aiming to give as much instruction as possible within the very limited time allowed. A quarter of an hour is sufficient for a devotional opening of the schools. Five minutes more should include the disposition of the classes—so that in twenty minutes the whole system should be in regular operation. Due regard should be paid to proper division of time allotted to the several exercises. The hearing the lessons from the whole class in one voice ; or, if this be impracticable, the distribution of it in successive verses or parts in rotation—will effect much saving. An arbitrary division of the parts to each child would prevent any collusion, and secure the learning of the whole lesson. By this mode, the time requisite for each child is given to the whole class at once, while the attention of each is engaged in the whole lesson, without listlessness or disorder. The importance of insisting upon perfect lessons cannot be too strongly inculcated. Imperfect lessons are only transient; while instruction solidly acquired has been retained through life, and even formed (as the Writer can testify from his own observation) the viaticum on a death-bed—the food and nourishment of eternal life.

Too often however from the disproportionate size of the classes —the length or number of the lessons—or the imperfect manner of their repetition—little or no time is left for catechetical instruction. In reading, one or more chapters of the Bible are gone through: attention is paid to a correct mode of reading; but still, no time is given to explanation. The Church Catechism, or a hymn, is repeated after the same mode, without the infusion of one intelligent idea of their contents. Now this want of connected and expository instruction deprives it of interest and profit. The plan wants simplicity—a less variety of books, with greater unity of system. Provide *for the elder classes some good catechetical exercises* on the Catechism; breaking each part into the simplest questions, and requiring the children to supply the answers. Thus not only their memories (as where the answers are subjoined and learned by rote) are employed, but their minds are exercised. The explanation of difficult words or terms, with Scripture proofs of the doctrines, might be added. From the want of this system, probably the learning of the Church Catechism by rote, seldom brings an intelligent apprehension of this most admirable formulary of doctrine. Some *preparatory similar exercises on some easier catechism* might gradually train the younger classes for an accurate understanding of our own Catechism.[1]

---

[1] This system has been well applied to the national catechisms of the Kirk. Initiatory catechisms have been prepared for the younger classes, containing a more simple statement of the truths found in the Established formularies; thus preserving the children's minds from the distraction of a multiplicity of books and catechisms, and at the same time gradually preparing them for ascent into the more intelligent classes. The same simple and minute analysis has been successfully applied to Scripture exercises. The principles (though some parts of the machinery might easily be dispensed with) are well deserving the consideration of parochial Ministers. Their full development may be seen in an Essay entitled 'The End and Essence of Sabbath School Teaching, &c., Gall, Edinburgh; Nisbet, London.' We might suggest here the importance of introducing into our system, *where practicable*, catechisms upon the evidence of Christianity, and upon the principles of our own Church. In these days of shaking and controversy it is highly desirable, that our children should "be ready to give a reason of the hope that is in them" —both as respects their faith in the Gospel, and their adherence to the Church. The publications of the Bristol Tract Society, and the *new* list of the Christian Knowledge Society, will furnish some assistance on both these subjects.

Next—Let *the lessons consist of a system of Scriptural exercises.* Each doctrine or precept, supported by one or more obvious and popular texts, might be written on the back of the teacher's card, and be distributed in the classes as one of the lessons. Portions of Scripture connected with it might be read, and in part committed to memory for the succeeding Sunday.[1] Those who cannot read, might have the portion read to them, and be questioned upon it. The mode of oral teaching might here be most usefully applied ; a mode, which (though little more is learnt by it than one or two verses on the Sunday) yet has many advantages, of curtailing the expensive demands for books, of fixing a habit of attention, and of ensuring perfect lessons. By means of this unity of system, the Minister examines the whole school with far greater facility, than he could have gone through the examination of the several classes. And this official inspection is of the highest moment, ' as an intelligent, presiding mind of authority, to rebuke and check ; of knowledge to inform and counsel; of spirituality to communicate that true wisdom, which is really valuable ; of vigilance, to observe the first dawn of light upon the soul ; and of patience, to watch and foster its progressive increase.'[2] Add to this, the influence of this superintendence in cementing the bond, which ought ever to subsist between the Minister and the younger members of the parochial family. And surely nothing can be an object of higher interest with us, than thus early to secure the affections

---

[1] With teachers of piety, judgment, and sufficient cultivation of mind, the following somewhat similar scheme of instruction has been tried. The Minister has fixed upon a course of subjects, (such as the principal histories of the Bible; or the Miracles, Parables or Life of Christ,) sketching out for the teachers the plan which he wishes them to pursue in questioning and explaining the subject in their several classes. This scheme admirably prepares the children's minds for his examination, and directs the general course of Scriptural instruction throughout the School. Take as an illustration one of the first and most important events of Scripture—The Fall of Man, Gen. iii. I. As it regarded Satan. 1. His object—To shew his enmity against God—To make man as miserable as himself. 2. His subtilty in accomplishing his object, 1.—Undermining Eve's confidence in God, 1, 3,—Appealing to her weakest part—her appetites—her senses, 5, 6. II. As it regarded man—The inability even of perfect Adam to keep himself—The gradual effect of the poison, 2, 3, 6. Eve tempted, becomes the tempter—The instant fruit of shame, 7,—fear—sense of guilt, 8—10,—prevarication—laying the fault upon the other, 12, 13. III. As it regarded God—His law broken—his love slighted—his justice called into exercise, 14—19—himself separated from his creatures, 24—his wisdom—contriving a marvellous way of recovery, 15, &c. Learn to dread being left alone in temptation—Eve was weak—much more are we. Watch against hard thoughts of God's commands or prohibitions. Suspect all that falls in with the lusts of our own hearts. Remember the constant need of self-denial. When you fall into sin, beware of keeping from God—as Adam did—of hiding or excusing sin—of throwing the blame upon others. Humble yourselves before God—The way to come to God is more plainly revealed, than it was to Adam. Improve it for obtaining pardon. See here all the principles of sin, in disobedience—rebellion—and unbelief. Learn to trace all the sin and misery in your heart, and in the world to this source. Learn to adore the plan, that restores and raises the sinner, and glorifies God.

[2] Bishop of Winchester's Primary Charge, pp. 37, 38.

of so important a portion of our charge. They will listen to our public instructions with intelligence and advantage, if we have accustomed them in the school to our mode of presenting Christian truth ; and especially, if we have taught them to look up to us as their nursing-fathers and their friends. No character therefore is more consonant to our grand designs than that of "a teacher of babes"—the affectionate instructor of children. If however the various demands on our time and strength restrain our personal direction of the school, we might at least open or close the day, or both, with some short catechetical exercise or address, concluding with singing and prayer. Every contact with this most interesting part of our flock will qualify us for a more apt and effective distribution of the truth.

The *Hymns* of the school should be simple and evangelical—but not too experimental. They form an interesting part of the system, and often fix upon the memory with peculiar power of retention. In order ever to keep in view the book of God as the basis of instruction, the children might be questioned upon them, and Scripture proofs required of their main doctrines.[1]

Yet must this course of exercises always leave room for Scripture reading. Perhaps small portions are often preferable to larger ; answering the end of improvement in the letter, while a catechetical examination would expound the spirit and application. The reading lessons should be selected from the simplest parts of the Bible. The narrative part of the Gospels might be chosen for the younger classes, and indeed, at the commencement, for all. Then the New Testament might be read through in its course. As the time would not allow of a regular progress through the Old Testament, a slight outline might be taught orally, and a portion of school-time well employed in reading at length the important chapters connected with its successive parts.[2]

Upon the whole—it is expedient to diversify the details *as far as is consistent with the unity of the system*—'to drop the truth into narrow-mouthed understandings ; and thereupon to graft exhortations, which may draw the catechumen into declared resolutions of piety, which is one of the things, where an abundance of

---

[1] The Sunday School Union Hymn Book, and one for St. James's School, Leeds, may be recommended. Every child should learn Watts's Divine Songs, and be questioned upon them. For the use of such teachers as may need help, a set of Questions and Answers has been published by Westley, London. Miss Taylor's Hymns, though exquisite in their kind, are inferior to Watts's, both in fulness and simplicity of doctrine, and in the tone of Scripture language ; and hence are less suitable for Sunday Schools.

[2] 'Outline of Old Testament History' (Seeleys) might be recommended. It would be well, after the routine of instruction, to read some of the most interesting Scripture narratives (such as the history of Joseph, &c.) to the class, as a reward for good behaviour.

wisdom and prudence may be demonstrated.'[1] Throughout it is implied, that religion stands alone in the system of this consecrated day, without partnership or competition with secular instruction.

The full prominence of Scriptural instruction is, however, necessary to secure an implicit reverence of the Sacred Book. Youthful obituaries, however interesting, should be introduced but sparingly even into the unoccupied moments of the school. They often tend to the excitement of a fictitious taste, which indisposes the mind to solid and didactic instruction, as if the simple reading of the book of God was rather a task than a privilege. Such narratives will find their more suitable place in a Sunday School Library. Every way the fearful spread of infidel poison deepens the responsibility of grounding children in Scriptural knowledge—thus providing them, as far as in us lies, "with the armour of righteousness on the right hand and on the left." We should not *willingly* allow a child to leave our schools, without some general idea at least of the Divine authority of the Bible, and without the testimony of our own conscience, that we have carefully endeavoured to educate his heart, no less than his mind, in the fundamentals of the Gospel.[2]

But the improvement of the school mainly depends upon its *efficient superintendence*. The direction of the mechanism, the system of instruction, and the choice of teachers, should be under the supervision of the Ministry. The selection and controul of the teachers requires much prayer and consideration. They should be marked by readiness and intelligence, general good conduct, and, *if possible*, by consistent godliness. The discretion allowed to

---

[1] Mather's Student and Pastor, pp. 197, 198.

[2] Nothing is more important in this system than a clear and interesting view of Christian doctrine. Perhaps the miracles illustrated by doctrinal proofs, might be the well-known and effective plan of teaching the young by pictures. Instance the leper, Matt. viii. 1—4. I. His leprosy—a picture of sin. Compare Num. xi. 44—46, with Psalm li. 2, 7. Isaiah vi. 5. II. His application to Christ—an illustration of faith, in his sense of need, and dependence on Christ. Matt. xi. 28. John vii. 37. III. His healing—a representation of the power of faith. Isaiah lxi. 1. John vi. 37. Heb. vii. 25. Some of the most obvious types, (as the brazen serpent, Num. xxi. 6—9, with John iii. 14, 15,) might well admit of this simple and interesting mode of doctrinal illustration. Dr. Beattie has indeed ventured the opinion (equally unchristian and unphilosophical), that it is of no use to teach children the doctrines of the Gospel, '*because they cannot understand them.*' But is it desirable that they should know them at all? If we wait for intelligence as the commencing era of instruction, shall we not find, that *while we slept*, another instructor and another system have preoccupied the ground? See Matt. xiii. 25. Compare also xxi. 16. We do not expect children to understand all that they learn. Much that we teach ourselves is upon the principle of faith more than of intelligence: assured, that though there are "many things" in Revelation "hard to be understood," there are none, that we are not bound to believe. We may therefore safely accord with the inspired rules of the wisest and most experimental philosopher—" *Train up a child in the way he should go.*" (*Set a child right at the entrance of his way.* Heb.) " *In the morning sow thy seed.*" Prov. xxii. 6. Eccles. xi. 6.

them must vary according to their qualifications. Considerable license may be given to piety, education, judgment, and experience. But piety with an unfurnished or undisciplined mind; or steadiness and good intention without Christian principle, require more immediate and minute controul. The real power, however, should be vested in the superintendent·director, under whom all should act upon a regular system.[1]

An inefficient agency materially impedes the best schemes. The instruction of the teachers is therefore often necessary tò give a spring to the working of the system. Want of habit and intelligence often hinders their clear perception of our plans; so that they either shrink from a hearty concurrence, or they are awkward in their attempts to co-operate. They must not therefore be left to their own resources. Books must be supplied to them,[2] and their precise routine of instruction distinctly marked out. They must be urged to take pains with themselves at home, making the Bible their constant study, endeavouring to obtain from thence solid materials, simple modes of communication, and persuasive and cheerful earnestness of address. Nor let them suppose that these are matters of easy attainment; or that a mechanical system, conducted without this furniture, can be efficient. A monotonous tone of gravity and continued exhortation only produces listlessness. There is a difference between teaching and preaching. Sermons are out of place in a Sunday School. Here we want something brief, lively, expository, addressed to the conscience. The catechetical mode is decidedly the most effective to maintain attention, elicit intelligence, convey information, and most of all, to apply the instructions to the heart. Without this mode, 'the Bible will be read, not as the book of Life, but as a class-book, or Scripture lesson. The child may become a good textuary, but continue wholly ignorant of experimental religion, and of its blessed influence on the character of man.'[3] We must inculcate also the primary importance of bringing before children clear and simple statements of the Gospel; the want of which, may probably have restrained a large measure of Divine influence upon our Schools. We must in-

---

[1] The Hints published by the Irish Sunday School Society, furnishes admirable suggestions on all subjects connected with the mechanism of Sunday Schools. On the department of Teachers, 'James' Sunday School Teacher's Guide,' 'Lloyd's Sunday Teacher's Manual,' and 'Todd's Sabbath School Teacher,' 'The Scythe Sharpened' (Seeleys) may be consulted with advantage.

[2] The following works will furnish most valuable assistance—'Helps to the study of the Gospels,' (Nisbet, London)—'Fuller's (of Bristol) Child's Examiner'—'Judson's Scripture questions,' (Religious Tract Society)—'The Bible Teacher's Manual,' (Holdsworth)—'Clark's Bible Exercises, and Teacher's Questioning Book on the New Testament for the use of the Royal Military Asylum.' 'Glenrock Sunday School,' (Seeleys.)

[3] Bishop of Winchester's Primary Charge, p. 35.

struct our Teachers also *in the difficulties of their work,* as a
" work of faith, and labour of love." They are our " fellow-workers with God"—as truly labouring for God, as the most eminent
Minister in the church.   In fact, they in a measure take our place,
whose oppressive burden hinders us from the full devotedness to
this great work—the place also of parents, who, either cannot or
will not instruct their children.   Like us, they are living for the
conversion of the world.   They have the soul of each child committed to their trust.   Their work therefore calls for the exercise
of steadiness, punctuality, perseverance, kindness, meekness, patience, faith.   Instead of being finished with the school-hours, it
needs constant recollection, in order to furnish the. *daily* practical
exhibition of their Sabbath instruction.   Thus they learn to sympathize with their Pastor, labouring with intense anxiety for the
conversion of every child in their class, instead of resting with delusive satisfaction in their external attention and progress. Thus
the heart is disciplined by prayer, faith is called into exercise, and
" patience has her perfect work."   They will feel that they are doing a great work.   They will be looking for present fruit, and yet,
if they " see not their tokens" of success, they will continue
" stedfast, unmoveable, always abounding in the work of the Lord ;
forasmuch as they know, that their labour *is not in vain in the
Lord.*"[1]

Where, however, the teachers (as it often happens) are selected
from the elder children, or from young persons who have left the
school, they must be formed into a class, practised in the best modes
of suiting the taste of children, commanding their attention, gaining their confidence, and drawing out their measure of natural capacity and information.   We must lend them books for their own
improvement, (such as those just mentioned); take them under
our personal inspection ; and direct the turn of their mind to the
most efficient exercises for their important work.   In general, young
teachers are far preferable to old, as being more easily instructed
and managed ; and having that full spring and elasticity, which
act promptly on the varying exigencies of the moment, and enliven
serious instruction with cheerfulness and interest.   Their general
conduct must however be a subject of especial pastoral vigilance ;
needing frequent counsel, caution, encouragement, or reproof
grounded upon their voluntary obligations.

Periodical meetings of the teachers are among the most important

[1] 1 Cor. xv. 58.

parts of the Sunday School system.[1] We thus ascertain the progress of the school; investigate the hindrances to its advancement,
the many little trials and vexations that belong to it, and suggest
means for their removal; recommend the adoption of new plans;
or encourage perseverance in the old frame-work. By comparing
each other's notes, many profitable questions are started, and many
improvements are made. We mark where we have failed in prayer, faith, perseverance, or interest; while the discovery of any
points of success brings with it fresh energy and encouragement
under more humbling recollections. These meetings are also most
valuable, as a bond of union with the teachers, strengthening the
influence of evangelical motives, awakening a spirit of mutual inspection and provocation,[2] and, joining in special prayer for increasing energy, faith, and patience in the work, and a larger effusion
of Divine influence upon it.

The system of rewards and punishments requires judicious regulation. Rewards might be distributed monthly in small books :[3]
or annually in books of greater value, or in useful articles of clothing, making some additions to weekly deposits for this purpose.
We should however be careful, that the excitement of reward encourages real rather than comparative excellence. Emulation,
awakened by competition, is the principle of selfishness; and therefore must be as much as possible repressed. As to punishment,
the teachers should never be permitted to strike the children, nor
the master to use any corporal correction, except by the express appointment of the superintendent. In most cases it is desirable to
resign this needful discipline over to the parents. Confinement beyond the hours of school is often found most efficient correction.
Yet we should characterize our system rather by rewards than by
punishments, never using restraint, until milder means have been
tried in vain. Children are much more powerfully influenced by
encouragement than by repulsion.[4]

[1] The obvious form of conducting them appears to be, commencing with prayer; then
proceeding to the business of the school, by examination of each teacher's card: raising
the children to higher classes: discussing their conduct; make such alterations in the
classes or in the rules of the school, as may be requisite (in which each teacher is considered to have a voice); throwing out suggestions or hints, as they may occur; mentioning new books, that may be wanted: general inquiries as to the progress of the children
in reading, learning, intelligence, steadiness, or seriousness of deportment. After the
routine of business is finished, endeavour to promote general conversation upon the importance of religious instruction, or particular points of detail. Then finish with exposition and prayer. Where the teachers are of nearly equal rank with ourselves, it is desirable to make it a social meeting of kindly Christian intercourse.
[2] Heb. x. 24, 25.
[3] Such as the Friendly Visitor, Children's Friend, or the Monthly Publications of the
Religious Tract Society.
[4] Where practicable, a Sunday School Library would operate as a useful stimulus to

But if the mechanism of a Sunday School—however admirably regulated and amply provided—forms the quantum of spiritual instruction for the young, it will only add further proof of the comparative inefficacy of a *mere Sabbath ministration.* For can we forget, how much that is learned at school is unlearned at home— either from the habits of "childhood and youth," which, by an infallible judgment, are pronounced to be "vanity;"[1] or by the neglect and bad example of those who ought to be their instructors? It is no common miracle, that one day's struggle against the stream should overcome the bad habits of the other six, falling in, as they do, with the natural bias of the heart. Even if the evils at home do not destroy the fruits of the school, yet the ground lies fallow; weeds grow; the boy that follows the plough all the week with no home or evening school instruction, is like the iron, which, though heated in the furnace in order to be softened, has only received one blow, and has been suffered to grow cold. We scarcely discern the traces of the hammer. The iron must be heated again. The Day and Evening Schools, connected with the Sunday Schools, give the repeated blows of the hammer. If therefore we cannot fasten this connection in an organized system, we must bring to bear some increased force from the general Pastoral Ministry. We must investigate the influence of the school upon the daily conduct of the children—upon their habits of obedience, seriousness, industry, and truth; inculcating an affectionate and judicious application of Christian discipline, as the basis of the domestic economy. Where circumstances allow, the children should be collected during the week. Habits of intercourse, familiar instruction in private, combined with a general readiness to unbend towards them, so that they might look upon us in the light of parents or friends—all this will materially assist to open the avenues of confidence—that most successful medium of approach to the heart. Great encouragement will be found to persevere in these exercises; though parochial hindrances restrain much of their energy and effectiveness.

The elder children also, who either have left, or are about to leave, the school, furnish a most anxious Ministration. This period is usually the crisis in their lives.[2] If no power of restraint or

improvement, enriching the mind with a valuable store of Christian principles. This library might be readily furnished from the Publications of the Religious Tract Society, and from the Youth's and Nursery Library in Bickersteth's Christian Student—a work, which needs not the Writer's recommendation, for its adaptation to Ministerial and general usefulness.   [1] Eccles. xi. 10.

[2] A fixed period for leaving the school, (giving full permission to remain after that time) operates as a restraint and encouragement upon the better children, and secures a decent dismissal to those, who would shortly, by breaking the yoke, separate themselves wholly from all kindly communication with us. The friends of education at Glasgow a

conviction has been produced, it is too frequently the era of their complete declension in conduct. The restrictions of the school are removed; they become disencumbered of an irksome yoke : they join light and trifling companions; and we have the grief of finding, that their instruction, instead of becoming a blessing, has proved the awful means of hardening them in sin. Two remedies suggest themselves to prevent this melancholy issue. *First*—increasing pains to make our teaching interesting to their minds; and to cultivate that love, which will rarely fail to engage their confidence or respect. *Next*—that we provide some means of linking them with us, after they have left the school. Some of them might be engaged as teachers under our vigilant superintendence ; themselves—if we can prevail upon them—still continuing with us as learners—formed into a class at some separate time, either on the Sunday evening or during the week. Of course the lesson system, as a *compulsory* engagement, should be relinquished. Portions of Scripture, with the parallel proofs or illustrations ; the principal events in a book of Scripture ; or the doctrines, precepts, and promises contained within a certain compass; the comparison of prophecy with its fulfilment ; or Scripture Proofs of the Catechism, the Articles, or other formularies of our church, might profitably exercise and interest their minds. Intercourse with them should be encouraged in every possible way, by employing them at our houses; interesting ourselves about their temporal concerns; lending them useful books; endeavouring to place them in respectable and serious families ; enquiring respecting them of their masters; inviting them to see us in their periodical visits to their friends ; thus maintaining affectionate sympathy and communication with them. Some of these ways may appear almost too minute and trifling for suggestion ; but in practical experience, they are found to bear upon the accomplishment of the most desirable ends.

III.—INFANT SCHOOLS.

THE Infant School system *regulated by Christian discipline and instruction,* is one of the most valuable and successful experiments on the theory of Education. The bending of the twig some years sooner than it was used to be bent, has gained a considerable advantage over the dominion of darkness and error ; an

few years since formed an association, called—' The Glasgow young men's society for religious improvement'—the grand object of which was, by meeting at stated seasons, to keep up the remembrance of their Sabbath-school instruction.

advantage however, which will turn against us, except the early.
intelligence is controuled and directed to the great end of life.
'The first seven years' (as has been accurately observed) 'are the
seed-time of life'[1]—only the two or three last years of which had
hitherto been cultivated ; while the earlier years had been lost to
the child and to the Church.

The importance of this system is now universally acknowledged.
Yet it may be well to enumerate some of its specific advantages,
and to glance at some of its general principles. *It is no small
benefit to the Parochial Ministry.* It forms a nursery for the
Sunday and Weekly School. Children taken immediately from
their families into these Schools, cost much time and pains to form
their habits. But entering from the door of the Infant School,
habits of order and attention have already commenced. The
drudgery of the alphabet also is passed through, which (in the Sunday School especially) interposes a serious hindrance to the present
results of Scriptural instruction. *The advantages to parents*
(*particularly mothers*) are of no small value ; giving them time,
quiet, ability to learn, and to do the work of the house : with the
comfort of knowing, that their children are safely and kindly provided for. The separation of children from their natural guardians
(as likely to encourage parental negligence) might be a plausible
objection, if most mothers exercised a wise and effective discipline.
But observation of the poor proves, that their children are generally
unrestrained till the age of five or six, (often where their mothers
might attend to them) ; and that the school-habits bind the children happily to their parents by the early improvement in temper,
subordination, and cheerfulness. *The advantage also to the
children* is equally great—*negatively*, in their deliverance from
filth, bad company, and mischief; and *positively*, in cleanliness,
order, obedience, attraction to what is useful, formation of good
habits, correction of bad tempers, real learning, storing the mind
with the elements of Scripture, early impressions of religion,
&c. &c.

It is desirable to conduct infant Schools with as much simplicity, and as little excitement as possible. Great injury arises
from bringing the children forward into notice. As little as possible
should be taught that is useless. Amusement and play in instruction, however needful, *must not be carried too far*. 'The
idea of teaching every thing as play or entertainment,' (as has

[1] Manual for Instruction of Infant Schools, by the Rev. W. Wilson, Walthamstow,
p. 149.

been well remarked) even if the project could be accomplished, 'would sacrifice the great moral benefits of education.' What indulgence could compensate for the loss of the early habits of appiication? The main object of the school is not to amuse, but to instruct; to direct the mind to the word of God, as the standard of right and wrong, and as the guide to the knowledge of ourselves, of our present happiness, and of our eternal hopes. This design will admit of much variety of illustration, such as objects, pictures, conversation, narrative, reading, &c.—in each of which departments the Scriptures open an abundant field. Nor is it at all correct to conclude, that the elementary principles of religion are beyond the intelligence of a child. For—not to speak of their perfect simplicity—the light and dictates of conscience materially assist the comprehension.

In country parishes some of the children come or remain older at the school, than in large towns, where other weekly schools are ready to receive them. But as soon as the children are capable of it, a useful employment (such as knitting and platting for boys, and sewing for girls) must be found: and Scripture stories or Scriptural knowledge be taught orally in the midst of these occupations.

In many respects several small schools are preferable to one large one. There is less display and excitement. The main difficulty is to obtain efficient superintendence. True piety must ever be a primary requisite. Combined with this, "aptness to teach," decided fondness for children, quickness in marking their character and habits, and in gaining their affections, condescension to their amusements, good health, active habits, patience, kindness, correcting without passion, to effect the desired end in the mildest mode— in the general system ruling by love, not by fear. Kind management however must be moderated by discipline; or it will foster a softness of character, rather than a solid and strengthened habit of mind.

Should want of funds, room, co-operation, or other causes, prevent the regular system, much may be done by improving the Dame Schools already in existence. Occasional visits, supply of books, suggestions of improvement in their plan of instruction, some small increase made to the income of the mistress by addition to her scholars; these trifling attempts might secure influence, and be productive of much good. In all cases it is desirable that the children should make some payment, however inconsiderable.

In general however we observe, that unless Christian instruction and discipline be the governing principles of this system, it must be viewed as a scheme of uncertain prospect of usefulness, or even of probable overbalancing evil.[1]

IV.—WEEKLY SCHOOLS.

On this subject we can do little more than lay down general principles. Local circumstances must at once furnish and direct the detail. Much that is simple and easy in practice does not admit of description; and experience alone can determine its expediency. Much attention has been lately given to improve the National system; chiefly to counteract the infidel projects now afloat of dissevering education from religion. Many valuable subsidiary suggestions might, however, be added to it (the result of experiments upon the principles of education) for more local adaptation; so that in establishing or re-modelling a weekly School, it will be highly desirable to improve all the helps that are afforded, and to inspect different experiments in actual progress and efficiency. The design of the Weekly School is to provide cheap and solid instruction for every child in the parish. In Village Schools, the variety of ages, and the great difficulty of ensuring regular attendance, are more sensibly felt. Indeed the enforcement of attendance is often scarcely just or expedient; where the absence of the children is occasioned by their early training to industrious work, necessary for their livelihood. Yet as the licence is frequently abused both by children and parents, some trifling reward to regular attendance at the end of the quarter, often marks the difference between necessary and unnecessary absence. The children's payment of a penny (more or less), connected with this system of rewards, by giving a personal interest in the school, helps to insure regularity. It is obvious, how much depends upon effective superintendence. Undoubted piety, firmness, judgment, system, alacrity, strict probity, and real love for the employment, are requisites, which every Minister would desire to see combined in the Master or Mistress. They should gain the respect, in order to secure the obedience of the children. Yet it is not desirable that they should be vested with much discretionary power. The

---

1. It is almost needless to refer to Rev. W. Wilson's admirable development of the whole machinery, in his 'System of Infant Schools,' and 'Manual of Instruction for Infant Schools.' Should the expensiveness of some of his plans be objected to (where the strictest economy was required); yet his works abound in valuable hints upon the general principles. Some of the small publications of the Home and Colonial School Society are admirably adapted to this system.

parents are better satisfied, when they are bound by a regular course marked out for them by authority. The assistance of visitors, maintaining the rules of the School, and the regularity of all its minute arrangements, should be thankfully received. The value of rewards is of far less moment, than their just distribution ; so that the children may see them proportioned to their conduct and exertion. In punishments, certainty is much more to be considered than severity. Disgrace or forfeiture of reward will generally supply the place of corporal punishment; which at least ought not to be resorted to, until milder measures have been ineffectually tried. In the circulating classes (a method first adopted in the Islington Schools) the circles gained by the children may be of a given value, and periodically redeemed for books, or clothes, or other articles of reward—accurate registers being kept of the progress and conduct of the children. This system excites the natural impetus of advancement; while it possesses the high advantage of repressing *personal emulation*. The child is not bent on taking the place of another ; but only on securing a place for himself. Each may exert himself to the utmost, and be rewarded accordingly. Eight or ten in the same class may receive the same reward, and in every respect be considered equal. Before, the children were taught to consider the top place in the class as the highest station of honorary distinction, and the last place as the lowest point of degradation. But on this system, all places, considered *as places*, are alike honourable ; and the movement is unlimited according to merit. The child is perpetually rising or retrograding. If attentive, he finds an unceasing motive to exertion ; while even the dull are enlivened, in not standing at the bottom of the class in hopeless despondency.[1]

Change of occupation—carefully preserving the order of their employment—is very necessary to keep up the interest of the children. Equally necessary is it, that, *as far as possible*, they should be made to understand every thing which they learn or read. A periodical examination on all their lessons—whether by the Minister, or some delegated and competent inspector—is most important. This applies specially to the religious instruction, which constitutes the main power of the system ; without which, even under the most orderly regulations, it is a lifeless mechanism. The Master may be competent for the official arrangements ; but either from ignorance of religion, want of spiritual apprehensions,

---

1 For a full description, see a small work published by John Stoat, late Master of the Islington Parochial School. Rivingtons.

or of intelligent and affectionate mode of communication, he is seldom efficient, at least for the entire direction of this primary responsibility. To make it the employment of the first hour, may serve
to impress the children's minds with a sense of its pre-eminent
importance. Oral teaching of the Scripture, Catechism, or Hymns,
before the other books are distributed ; would (when this plan can
be adopted) spread a serious atmosphere over the whole subsequent
course. So powerful a machinery as schools, requires in every
part the controul of the principles of the Gospel, to render them
efficient to the desired ends.

V.—THE TREATMENT OF THE YOUNG IN A HOPEFUL STATE OF IMPRESSION.

WITH the exception of special cases in the Visitation of the Sick,
this may be considered as the most difficult part of the Pastoral
office. No peculiar talent, originality, or Ministerial fluency, is
requisite ; but the "spirit of power, and of love," combined with
"the spirit of a sound mind."[1] Our youthful flock are readily
melted by an affectionate address ; while too often the conduct
proves their consciences to be unawakened, and their hearts unimpressed. Their very susceptibility of religious impressions has a
strong influence to foster self-deception, mistaking natural impulse
for the exercise of the spiritual life, conviction of sin for conversion
of heart, feeling for principle, attachment to their minister for love
to their Saviour, interest in the mechanical form of instruction for
interest in the Gospel. Hence the desire for comfort is often independent of any vigour or even principle of holiness. We must be
equally careful therefore to instruct as to impress, and to strengthen
the judgment with a tone of manly and intelligent seriousness,
which may control any irregular exercise of the feelings. Christian
experience must be cautiously exhibited (lest, almost unconsciously,
we form the character either to hypocrisy or self-delusion) ; much
close personal application of the Gospel to the several cases is
needed ; together with a clear separation between natural and
spiritual excitement ; and a watchfulness against every influence
that does not distinctly act upon the conscience. Even the love
of Christ should be set forth in its glory and sublimity, as well as
in its expressible tenderness and endearment; that, while the wax
is warmed and softened by the lively glow of feeling, a deep, com-

[1] 2 Tim. i. 7.

plete, and permanent impression may be made ; and the judgment, conscience, and habits may be connectedly influenced.

Not that we would deprecate that legitimate excitement, which may often, under God, awaken the exercise of spiritual affections, producing, in their turn, a most important reaction. But let not the character and progress be measured by excitement, which, if not connected with Scriptural truth, is delusion—not edification. It may move without *moulding the heart.* Sympathy may work by a kindly earnestness of address, or (as in the history of the sufferings of Christ) by the tenderness of sacred truths, without any spiritual principle, perception, or practical influence. The will—the sovereign power in the soul—may be disturbed and restrained by the light of the mind and the working of the conscience ; and yet may still shew its natural bias to sin. There may also be a work of illumination without spiritual light, complacency, rest, or transformation.[1] Natural conviction may awaken the conscience to a greater quickness and sensibility ; but without that penitent abhorrence of sin, turning to the blood of Christ, that it might be "purged from dead works to serve the living God."[2] The affections may be also touched ; yet not fixed, nor filled with the things of God. The impression therefore is transient and uninfluential.[3] The love of the world is not wholly thrust out ; nor is its place filled with holy love and delight. "The house is swept and garnished" with outward reformation ; but, being "empty" of Christ, and not inlaid with Divine grace, it is ready for the re-entrance of Satan with more established power.[4]

To distinguish the true and hidden life from amiable dispositions, warm affections, and evangelical correctness of profession, is often a special gift of "the manifold grace of God." Spiritual principles as well as external duties, may be fearfully counterfeited ;[5] and therefore their evidences must be carefully sifted, and tried by consistent conduct. Admitting their sincerity, these young persons require much cautious treatment. Quiet means sholud be used to check their effervescence. Let them be kept employed—whether for themselves or for others—to prevent a sickly excitement, and an engrossing analysis of their own feelings. Let us direct their reading of Scripture, that it may be regular, not desultory ; and yet that its paramount obligation does not interfere with immediate

---

[1] See Heb. vi. 4, 5.   [2] Ibid. ix. 14.   [3] Hosea vi. 4.   Matt. xiii. 20, 21.
[4] Matt. xii. 43—45. This is especially the case with the unconverted children of Christian parents.
[5] Such as Repentance, 1 Kings xxi. 27—29 : Faith, Luke viii. 13. Acts viii. 13 : Joy, Matt. xiii. 20. John v. 35. Holiness, Phil. iii. 6.

duties. Let us keep solid truth—scriptural views of Christ—revolving before them ; drawing out their own state rather from conversation on suitable topics of the Gospel, than from direct and
immediate enquiry. We must also narrowly watch their conduct,
strictly, but tenderly, pointing out inconsistencies ; bringing every
part to bear upon the standard of the Gospel—not *necessarily*
inculcating a change of duties, but of principles—the same, relative
duties—only now performed "after a godly sort"—" as untc
Christ ;" with a constant reference to his example—with a single
eye to his glory.

This system will bring encouragement without excitement, and
produce a sure rather than a rapid progress. And this is the true
wisdom in this case—rather to *seem* to keep back the youthful
converts, than by an indiscreet confidence to hazard a forward and
doubtful profession. As the happy heralds of the Gospel, we are
charged with a special commission respecting them, grounded upon
the most endearing motives.[1] We have messages to them of peculiar encouragement, and of generous and munificent love, warrant-
ing the largest anticipation of lasting happiness.[2] Yet must we
restrain confidence in a new excitement of interest irrespective of
a spiritual apprehension of Christ, a lowly, and consistent walk in
him, and an experimental acquaintance with themselves and their
besetting temptations. Sincerity, instead of being cast down by
this *apparent* (for it is only apparent) discouragement, will eventually be strengthened in a more self-suspecting scrutiny. The
prevailing defect in the religion of young persons is, that their
views of the Saviour are too slightly connected with this self-inquiry, and therefore, are more connected with feeling than with
faith—more with their own resources, than with the cross of Christ.
Hence they fail in producing a deepened work of Christian humility, love, and consistency. ' Young persons will grow happily, and
fight valiantly, who firmly hold Jesus Christ as their Head, receive
their strength and courage from Him, and " put on the whole armour of God." '[3] Let this exercise of faith be connected with a
" still communing with the heart ;"[4] which, if it seems to check
the forwardness of the plant, will only make it strike its root deeper in the soil for more abundant fruitfulness. This retarding system, therefore, (so to call it) is eminently useful in separating the
chaff from the wheat. If it disappoints a bold profession, it will
cherish and preserve the germ of trembling simplicity. Young

[1] John xxi. 15.   [2] Such as Prov. viii. 17. Jer. iii. 4.
     [3] Hottinger. Typus Pastor. Ev. p. 33.   [4] Psa. iv. 4.

trees, even of " the Lord's planting," require diligent care and watering : but any attempt to force the fruit would materially injure the vital principle. Indeed they cannot be *accurately distinguished*, until their budding and blossoms have ripened into fruit. Many a hard frost nips the bud ; many an eastern blast threatens the blossom : and therefore the result of winter and spring can alone determine the life of " the incorruptible seed." A gradual, kindly warmth, without a too indulgent treatment, will be the most safe temperature for these tender plants in an unkindly soil.

VI.—YOUNG MEN.

THE breaking in of " the wild asses' colt," demands extreme management and patience. The trite French proverb aptly applies —' A drop of honey will catch more flies than a pint of vinegar.' All means—change of means—every effort, must be tried in succession, to discover what treatment is most likely to produce effect. Substantial expressions of interest in their employments—intelligible kindness of manners, and accessibility of address—the improvement of apparently accidental opportunities of intercourse—the use of suitable books, with a cast of seriousness more or less deepened according to their temper—friendly suggestions upon their temporal concerns, at the same time carefully guarding against meddling interference—these and other plans, adapted to our knowledge of their dispositions and habits, may possibly effect some good. And let it be remembered, that something must be at least attempted for them. They are in some respects the most important part of our flock ; and in their day will form the great body of influence among us. While the few imbued with the spirit of the Gospel are our most powerful support ; those who are restrained neither by education, attachment, personal respect, nor religious principle, generally become (the Writer speaks from experience) the thorns in our side —the very pests of the parish.

Steady, well-conducted young men may, however, by good management, be brought under a course of Bible instruction. The minister's invitation to join them in a searching of the Scriptures might perhaps allure them. A chapter read in rotation, and afterwards verse by verse broken into questions, illustrated by references, and concluded by short and pointed application, would present the concentrated substance of truth in an interesting form. The instruction must however be carefully adapted to the varied capacities and seriousness of the catechumens, such as will engage their confidence, in the act of informing their ignorance. An answer not altogether pertinent must be allowed so far as it goes, while its more full and definite meaning is explained. When a backwardness to reply to doubtful questions is discovered, we should propose those admitting of a more certain answer; taking care that each individual receives distinct consideration and appropriate instruction. This exercise must be enlivened with as much variety as is consistent with the main purpose, avoiding tedious and monotonous arrangement, which will soon weary those, whose hearts are but slightly, if at all, moulded into a spiritual character.[1]

In many cases the utter disrelish for religion renders such plans impracticable. The most affectionate controul, acting upon pride and self-will, often produces the most violent reaction. Like " the horse and the mule, their mouths must be held in with bit and bridle, lest they come near unto us."[2] So that, when we have failed in taming their untractableness, nothing remains but to endeavour to preserve others (and especially the elder lads of our Sunday Schools) from the contagion of their society or example.

Sometimes, however, their popular institutions may open a distinct Ministry. We may obtain important influence in their Benefit Societies. Or we might organize a Society under our immediate superintendence, by the transfer of the alehouse money to the public fund, affording higher pecuniary advantage at the same ratio of payment. And by holding out this attraction to the considerate, we might form their rules to a Christian standard, and enforce a decided regard to moral obligations.[3] The line would thus be drawn between the steady and the irregular; and, though the more fearful might hesitate to join a society bearing a pecu-

---

[1] A plan of engaging the interest of elder lads and young men, on the Sunday evenings, was successfully tried in a large sphere. All who could read well were invited without limitation of age. The classes were divided with as much regard as possible to age; the Minister himself taking the first and largest class. About an hour was spent in repeating a portion of Scripture, which had been selected on the preceding Sunday, and which the teachers explained in the several classes, requiring the lads to bring their own parallels, as an evidence of their diligent study and interest. There was no compulsion. The lessons were set before them as subjects of interest, rather than as a task and duty. In the next division of time, the whole school was arranged before the Minister, who questioned, illustrated, and applied the subject which had been set before them in their classes; requiring an answer of Scripture proof, sometimes from a lad, sometimes from a class, sometimes from the whole school. A short sketch of Christian Biography, or serious address, was then given (unless, as was sometimes the case, the interest of the catechetical subject employed the whole time); the subject for the ensuing Sunday was made known, and singing and prayer ended the evening. The attendance of the lads was regular and voluntary. A bond of union was cemented with their Minister and with each other. The power of restraint was extensively felt; and in many cases a permanent and practical influence was manifested.

[2] Psalm xxxii. 9.

[3] Friendly Societies on Mr. Becher's system are well known. Interesting details of similar Societies, grounded upon different, though, probably, not insecure principles, may be seen in Richmond's Life, pp. 116—130.

liar stamp of reproach ; yet its slow progress towards general acceptance will be attended with considerable indirect advantages.
The monthly meetings might be improved for reading the Scriptures and for prayer ; or by directing each member to contribute
a text, which, with the rest, might be recapitulated at the close of
the business with personal application. Such an attempt to engraft
spiritual intercourse upon friendly advice, might be found acceptable.[1] Perhaps also to the more ignorant—not wholly beyond controul—an Adult School for reading—holding out the promise of a
large Testament, when they should be able to use it—might be a
pleasing temptation. Others might be allured by an invitation to
an Evening Writing or Cyphering School, appending Christian
counsel, as they might be able to bear it. With the more intelligent, instruction in some branches of useful knowledge might be a
bond of valuable restraint and interest.

But after all, this Ministry is too often marked with peculiar discouragement. We have the respect of our young men, not their
confidence. In other instances, we almost feel, that the means
used only increase the evil; and that it is more wise to maintain a
degree of reserve and distance, labouring at the same time with
more intensity to spread their case before the Lord. Yet under all
trials this Ministry should bear the stamp of peculiar tenderness—
the "nursing mother cherishing her children."[2] Let us guard
against the rising of our own spirit, when they turn their backs
upon our repeated admonitions.[3] While we "rebuke them sharply," let us "instruct them in meekness ;" shutting out despondency
by the "*peradventure*, that God will give them repentance."[4] Let
successive disappointments exercise faith, deepen humiliation,
quicken prayer, increase anxieties—not induce a sullen, indolent
heartlessness. We have a solemn responsibility on their account ;
nor must we readily exclude them, as "the dogs and the swine,"
from our commission.[5] However humbling may be our want of
sensible encouragement, our rule must be—'Sow in faith, and have
long patience ; wait on and for the Lord.' Fruit will be found under the most unpromising appearances ; but we must expect to
wait for it. "The patience of hope" is the preparation for the "as-

[1] For an interesting plan of 'young men associated' upon Christian principles, see
Mather's Essays to do Good, pp. 92—96; and Dr. Woodward's account of the rise and
progress of Religious Societies, chap. ii. iii. One of the excellent rules in Dr. W.'s Societies was, that each member should endeavour to bring at least one other into their
Christian fellowship,—a resolution which was often honoured with the Divine blessing.
[2] 1 Thess. ii. 7.
[3] 'Quicquid lacerato animo dixeris, punientis est impetus, non charitas corrigentis.'
August. in Gal. vi.
[4] Tit. i. 13. with 2 Tim. ii. 25.   [5] See Matt. vii. 6.

surance of hope." "Through faith and patience, we shall inherit the promise."

Another point of great moment in the Ministry of the young, regards those incautious connections, formed even under a religious profession. The power to throw in a seasonable warning, before the die is cast, on which perhaps depends eternity, is among the many advantages of confidential intercourse. Incalculable havoc has Satan ever made in the church, through these fatal unions. How many hopeful blossoms have been withered! How many apparently promising converts, thus sifted, have proved but chaff! How many sincere, but hesitating Christians, have been shaken by *the infatuated* attempt to unite "the temple of God with idols!"[1] And yet to choose the moment, and to discover the safe extent, of interference: and for this purpose to combine the influence of confidence, and our knowledge of their character and circumstances, demands extreme delicacy, tenderness, and prudence. Indeed, there is no Ministry, which requires more anxious consideration, than the development of the sophistries and self-indulgent delusions of this moment, and the application of the touch-stone of the Gospel to the spiritual system. The blessing upon wise and faithful counsels at this crisis, is a special token of our Master's favour and help; and even cases of failure bring with them much advantage, in a deeper insight into the devices of Satan and the self-deceit of the heart.

VII.—PRACTICAL SUGGESTIONS ON CONFIRMATION.[2]

THIS exercise of the Ministry of the Young, brings with it peculiar encouragements, anxieties, and responsibilities. Never perhaps are the Pastor's affectionate yearnings more drawn out towards his beloved flock, than at the season of Confirmation. Then, if ever, he meets them with the intensity of parental interest—"My little children, of whom I travail in birth again, until Christ be formed in you."[3] The rite of Confirmation, if not of express Apostolical origin, was at least derived from Apostolical practice. We cannot indeed identify it with that imposition of hands,[4] which appears to have been invariably followed with miraculous influence;

---

[1] 2 Cor. vi. 14, 15.
[2] The substance of this Section appeared in the Christian Observer, February and March, 1829.
[3] Gal. iv. 19.   [4] Acts viii. 17; xix. 6.

but the concurrent testimonies of antiquity afford strong presumption that it was the continuance of this rite, as an ordinary means of grace, and for a purpose and object somewhat varied from its original institution.[1] Calvin admits it to have been the custom of the ancient church, and wishes that it had been preserved in its simplicity in his own church, before the Papacy unduly exalted it into a sacrament.[2] The Waldensian church retains the substance of it as an Apostolical institution.[3] The most eminent lights of the Reformed Churches, (Peter Martyr, Rive, Peter des Moulin, &c.) and the Bohemian and Lutheran Churches, give it the weight of their authority. Indeed it is (as Archbishop Secker has observed) ' of such acknowledged usefulness, that in the times of confusion, when Bishops were rejected, some of their adversaries took upon them to perform this part of their function ; and within these few years (1741) the Church of Geneva hath restored it in the best manner their form of church government will admit, and added an office for it to their Liturgy.'[4]

This rite is the complement and seal of infant baptism. Then a sponsorial profession of the child's faith, requisite for the act of covenanting with God, had been made. This was sufficient for the infant covenant : when the infant was received into the Church, not on its own account, but as a part of its parent, having a covenant interest in the promises to the seed of believers.[5] But in the adult covenant, personal benefits are claimed, and consequently personal obligations are involved. And hence without a personal profession—as a visible investiture of the Church privileges sealed at Baptism—the infant title to these privileges is invalidated. The

[1] See the authorities in Wheatly and Comber, and the Rev. B. Woodd's and the Bishop of Calcutta's valuable tracts on the subject. Comp. Bishop Hall's Polem. Works, vol. ix., and an excellent treatise by the Rev. T. H. Kingdon. Dr. Hammond's View of the Directory, and Calvin's Institutes, (Christian Observer, 1829, pp. 71, 72, 143, 144,) give some important statements from very opposite schools of divinity. A scarce but satisfactory treatise, by Jonathan Hanmer (1658), besides the ancient authorities, gives the approving judgment of Baxter, Calamy, Venning, and others of the Puritan Divines. Archbishop Leighton strongly recommended to his clergy the substance of the rite; though the turbulent spirit of his times did not allow him to introduce the ceremony. Works, ii. 450. It is difficult to conjecture any reasonable objection to the form—consecrated as it is by the frequent usage of the Old Testament Church, by the example of our Lord; and being (as Calvin remarks) ' the ordinary rite among the Jews, in commending any one to the blessing of God.' Calv. in Acts xiii. 3.

[2] Calv. Instit. lib. iv. cap. xix. 4. 13; and on Heb. vi. 2; which text he conceives fully sufficient to prove the apostolical origin of the present institution. Chrysostom expounds the passage to the same purport.

[3] See their Confession and Apologies, quoted in Hanmer's Exercitation, pp. 37—40.

[4] Secker's Charges, p. 52. The professors of Theology at Leyden, having with Calvin expressed their wishes for its restoration in the Church, add—' Cujus substantia in Ecclesiis nostris religiose servatur.'—Synopsis Purioris Theologiæ, Lugd. 1625. Disput. xlvii. sect. 13, a work deservedly of high estimation. Compare also Baxter's Infant's Church Membership.

[5] See Gen. xvii. 7—10; Deut. xxix. 10—12; Acts ii. 39.

profession made at the Eucharist by no means answers this design ; having no distinct reference to the title, on which we claim to be admitted complete members of the visible church.

The Church manifestly has a right to demand a profession. She cannot judge of what she does not know. She does not pretend to be a searcher of hearts. She can only therefore determine by outward signs. The Apostles even hesitated to receive Saul into their company, (though with the strongest evidence of sincerity) until the Church had received a voucher of the credibility of his profession.[1] Indeed without this profession, what hinders the infidel from advancing a claim, on the ground of his infant baptism, to the full privileges of the Church, and the Church herself from being thus virtually unchurched ? Every church, therefore, practising infant baptism, insists upon a confession of faith, as indispensable for full communion with the visible body : and, this being admitted, we decide, (forbearing with those who conscientiously differ from us) that the profession of confirmation is more conformable to the practice of the Apostolical churches and primitive usage, than any that prevails.

In fact, while it secures all the privileges of *infant baptism,* and certifies God's favour and gracious goodness to our children—it includes also the substance of *adult baptism*—" the answer of a good conscience towards God."[2] Here the grace that had been faithfully prayed for in baptism is publicly acknowledged, and its increase sought and expected by the renewed exercise of the same faith. So far therefore as it is sincere, it exhibits profession converted into principle—the outward sign of the cross as the mark of the true spirit of the cross, imbuing the heart, and manifested in the consistency of the Christian character.

The character of this engagement is distinctly spiritual. What else is the baptismal covenant between God and the infant ? Are not the preface, question and answer, and the prayer in the Confirmation service eminently spiritual ? Is—" *I do*" *renew the solemn promise*—any thing less than a purpose of the heart ? Can that be solemn, which is mere lip-profession ? Our Church regards the confirmed as ready for the communion ; and does she not insist upon spiritual qualifications for the reception of that holy sacrament ?[3] Consider our spiritual catechism on the one side, and our peculiarly spiritual Communion Service on the other ; and we cannot conceive this intermediate Service to be of a less spiritual mould.

[1] Acts ix. 26, 27.   [2] 1 Peter iii. 21.
[3] Compare the answer to the last question in the Catechism.

As the preliminary however for Ministerial instruction, the debasing rubbish of superstition and ignorance must be cleared away. Many of us have elicited notions in the course of catechetical inquiry, which, had not familiar intercourse brought them to light, would have been deemed traditionary relics of the dark ages. Some will come for the bishop's blessing, with no idea, desire, or expectation of the blessing of God; others, to relieve their sponsors of the burden of their sins and duties; as if personal responsibility were not coeval with the earliest " discernment between our right hand and our left hand ;" or as if we, who are utterly unable to answer for ourselves, could answer for one another ; or as if any one could be found to answer for one of us, but Him, " who his own self bore our sins in his own body on the tree." The true candidate for Confirmation will come in self-renunciation and faith—not to take his sins upon himself, but to lay them upon Christ; and to take his yoke upon him, in the simple devotedness of a pardoned and accepted sinner. With the more intelligent, who yet are ignorant of the spiritual requisitions of the service of God, errors are prevalent, less palpably absurd, but scarcely less dangerous. It is often expected to operate as a charm, to make the path-way to heaven from henceforth more easy. Resolutions are connected with the ordinance itself, with more or less of sincerity, but the natural fruit of ignorance and self-deception. From that day a new era will begin ; a more serious course of life will be commenced ; the world, if not wholly forsaken, will be restrained within more measured limits. And all this is anticipated, without any distinct feeling of helplessness, perception of the need of a change of heart, or dependence on Divine grace. They are soon however reminded, that, while the heart remains unchanged, the difficulty must remain in full force; that the world will be as ensnaring, Satan as tempting, and sin as powerful as before ; that, if there is not at the present moment a sincere and humble desire of self-dedication to God, the day and service of Confirmation possess no innate power to give a new bias to the heart.

But we have also to contend with the gross misconceptions of parents. Confirmation is with them a respectable church form, with no meaning, and linked with no obligations. Their children are come to a proper age. They must receive the sacrament—fit or unfit; and therefore as a preliminary, it is decent that they should be confirmed ; that is, that they should solemnly promise, in the presence and in the house of God, what they have no desire or intention to perform ; and the performance of which would often be in direct opposition to their parents' wishes, instructions, and example.   Thus does the rash heedlessness—we might say—the profane trifling—of parents—encourage their children in the profession of a wilful falsehood ; striking a blow at the root of all moral obligations, Christian integrity, and even common honesty.

. The course of Confirmation instruction naturally includes a clear exposition of the nature and obligation of the baptismal vow ;[1] which is as strictly bound upon every professing Christian, as if he had made it in his own person.   It was made on his account ; from a regard to his best interests ; and to bring him early into covenant with God, and into fellowship with Christ.   As therefore his baptismal obligation bound him only for his good in the way of privilege ; and to nothing in the way of duty, to which his relation to God had not previously bound him from his first moment of accountableness ; he has every reason, when come to competent understanding, to set his own hand to it.   He comes therefore now in Confirmation, to affix his seal to his infant baptism by his own act and deed ; and to dedicate himself to God in that engagement, in which he had been dedicated to him in infancy.

He now makes the declaration, not of what he wishes to do, but of what he does ; not of what he would be, but of what he is. The grace here prayed for is, not that he may devote himself to God ; but that, having devoted himself, and now making the profession of it, he may be faithful to the end. .Indeed, upon the ground of the faith professed in his baptism, he has already called himself " a member of Christ," and has acknowledged his obligations to God, " who *hath called* him unto this state of salvation." He is now come to confess before the church his humble and sincere readiness, according to the terms of the baptismal covenant, to renounce the service of his spiritual enemies ; to accept the Gospel as his hope of salvation ; and to determine by God's help, sought and obtained in earnest prayer, to continue in the way to his life's end.   Upon this credible profession, the Bishop, as the Minister of God, lays his hands upon him, with prayer, as the sign of the Holy Spirit already vouchsafed, and as an assurance, on God's behalf, of its confirmation and increase.

This is the meaning of the rite, upon the supposition of the sincerity of the confirmant.   But we cannot shut our eyes to the lamentable fact, that a vast majority of our candidates are alike. ignorant of the nature of this ordinance, and unimpressed with its

---

[1] The Writer ventures to refer to his own Tract upon Confirmation, for a system of Pulpit and Private instruction.

obligations. Some remember the profane merriment of the last occasion ; and wish to have their holiday, like others, in the mock ery of the service of God. Some think to please their parents by this blind profanation : forgetting, how unable they will be to shelter them from the awful consequences of their wilful falsehood ; and that the plea of parental obligation will be of no avail, when the heavy indictment appears against them at the bar of their Judge. Some think with their parents, that Confirmation is proper for every young person, and that is a reproach not to be confirmed ; and therefore, though they have no more intention of leaving the world for Christ, than of quitting their country for a foreign land, they have no objection to the mere ceremony of a promise ; and, for decency's sake, they wish to be confirmed.

Now for young persons under these or similar misconceptions, a customary course of Pulpit Ministry is clearly inefficient. They need the simplest elementary instruction, conveyed to their minds in an interesting and arresting form.[1] They need to be awakened from their ignorance or carelessness, in order to be informed and encouraged. They require a close as well as a familiar and affectionate address ; an adaptation of the broad outline of instruction, (such as the detail of the baptismal vow) to their several tempers, habits, pleasures, temptations, and general conduct ;[2] together with frequent enquiry into their intelligent and experimental apprehension of truth. Texts, or short courses of reading, might be marked for special examination and prayer—such as brief statements of the fundamental doctrines, practical exhibitions of Christian duty, affecting views of the Saviour's love, portions for prayer, and encouraging illustrations of the character and happiness of devotedness to God.'[3] We should enforce the constraining motives of the Gospel

[1] See Rev. J. Bickersteth's Short Catechism on Confirmation.

[2] Bishop Butler insists upon personal conference, as an indispensable part of preparation for confirmation. See his Charge to the Diocese of Durham. Works, ii. 422. Compare also Bishop Wilson's Parochialia. Works, iv. 16—34. Bishop of Winchester's Primary Charge, p. 39.

[3] Take an example from the interesting memoir of Rev. J. Escreet—' Mr. E. was excited to labour as much as possible to prepare his young parishioners for the ordinance, to which they were invited. He employed such time and labour in explaining the institution, expounding suitable passages of Scripture, and impressing upon their minds the spirit, and temper, and disposition, which they should cultivate. He addressed to them a series of discourses upon the subject, pointing out, from 1 Sam. i. 28, the blessedness of an early devotion to God ; from Josh. xxiv. 15, the duty of choosing God's service ; from 1 Peter v. 8, the importance of resisting our great adversary ; and from Heb. vi. 2, the grounds and utility of the institution, by the effect produced on the minds of the confirmed, and on the minds of others.' Again : 'Mr. Escreet earnestly called upon his young people, seriously to consider the nature of the ordinance, and carefully to examine themselves ; to sit down and count the cost ; to remember their obligations to Almighty God, that they must either serve him, their rightful Lord and Master, or join themselves to his enemies ; and that therefore it was their true interest, as well as their bounden duty, to devote themselves entirely to God's service ; and to pour out their souls

with tender seriousness, combined with strong remonstrances upon the reasonableness of the service of God, and the ingratitude and rebellion of resisting his love. ' Can you,'—we might say to them —' hesitate to give your hearts to such a Saviour ? How ungrateful, how inexcusable, this reluctance to so blessed a service ! Had he been as reluctant to die for you, as you are to live for him, would he have emptied himself of his heavenly glory for your sakes ? Think of the Son of God becoming a man of sorrows for you : and can you turn away from his command of love, which seems to come from his cross—" My son, give me thine heart ?"'

We can only however broadly sketch the course of private communication with catechumens. Its shaping into a more distinct and applicatory form will vary, more or less, in every instance. We come into contact with minds cast into different moulds, or minds similarly constructed, but passing before us, in different stages of ignorance or of enquiry, of resistance or of yielding, to the influence of the Gospel. In large numbers, where it would be nearly impracticable to insulate each particular case, we might form classes with advantage, after short individual converse ; and thus retain, in a great measure, the familiar mode of instruction.[1] With educated minds perhaps the use of the pen might supply an useful medium of communication, in requesting written replies to a series of explicit and searching enquiries.

Many of us feel some difficulty in ascertaining the precise qualification intended by the church for this holy, but, alas ! too often profaned, rite. The sixty-first canon is express—that we take especial care that none be presented, but such as we know are fit.[2] Now, if this canon be explained according to the letter of the

---

in fervent prayers, that he would accept the sacrifice, and receive and keep them for his own.'

[1] This was the plan of Mr. Robinson of Leicester, in his extensive sphere. His ' Confirmation season' (his biographer informs us) ' was one he particularly valued, and had reason to esteem as his choicest seed-time. He prepared his congregation for it by sermons : he collected the young people, arranged their names, insisted upon their regular attendance, as a condition of giving them a certificate, and addressed a sort of family lecture to them on the Church Catechism, which he accompanied with solemn and earnest prayer, during five or six weeks before the bishop appeared. In this interval he would talk with some of them familiarly, but seriously, in small parties ; with some separately in his study ; to all he made a present of his excellent little tract on the subject : to all he gave special and appropriate exhortations from the pulpit ; to all he showed himself the faithful shepherd, leading his flock with great solemnity on the morning of the service, praying, exhorting, and at length presenting them, with his own hands, to his superior, and to his superior's Lord.' Life, pp. 335, 336.

[2] Thus Abp. Secker gives the spirit, not the letter of the canon, (Charges, p. 55.) The words of the canon are, ' that none shall be presented to the bishop, for him to lay his hands upon, but such as can *render an account of their faith*, according to the catechism in the said book contained.' The rubric in the Catechism respecting Confirmation, more accords with the *letter* of the archbishop's words, and probably was in his mind—' All such as *he shall think fit* to be presented to the bishop to be confirmed.'

mandate to the sponsor in the baptismal service, the fitness for Confirmation would seem only to imply an acquaintance with and instruction (*whether influential or not*) in, the Catechism. This
line would include every species of the ungodly, while living in the
habitual indulgence of wilful and flagrant sin. But that our
church, in requiring ' an account of the candidate's faith,'[1] combined
with a capacity to ' answer to the questions of the Catechism,'[2]
a practical acknowledgment of the baptismal obligation, is sufficiently evident, both from the fearful profanation, which must
result from a literal adherence to the mandate, and from the judgment of some of her most accredited authorities. ' I must entreat
you,' (as Secker charged his clergy) ' to endeavour, that none be
brought, but those who (to speak in the language of the Rubric,)
are come to years of discretion, who have learned, not the words
only, but in a competent degree, the meaning of what was promised for them in baptism; who can say with *seriousness and truth,*
(*what surely else they ought not to say at all,*) that ' in the presence of God and the congregation, they ratify and confirm the
same in their own persons.' Bishop Burnet speaks most plainly
and admirably to the same point.[3]

This concurrent decision of these authorized guardians of our
church, deservedly of great name among us, must be deemed satisfactory. It needs only be added, that the compliance with the
letter of the mandate gives plausible ground to the objections of Dissenters; is utterly inconsistent with the spiritual character of our
church, and the spiritual engagements she requires from her members; and reduces the ordinance of Confirmation to an empty ceremony, productive of no possible benefit to the persons confirmed,
and bearing only the stamp of wilful falsehood and solemn mockery, insulting to the presence and house of a holy, jealous God.

The difficulty however that is often and painfully felt, of com-
plying with the literal requisition of the Church, will be materially
diminished, by a decided course of applicatory instruction. As the
affecting result of this experiment—At the commencement of the
course, all the catechumens were constant in their attendance;
but, as the subject gradually opened before them, and was brought
into individual and grappling contact with their consciences, the
numbers gradually diminished, (as in Gideon's army, though indeed not in the same fearful proportion,) until they had dwindled
down to one half of their original body. The " mixed multitude"

---

[1] See the words of the canon quoted above.
[2] Preface to Confirmation Service, and rubric appended to the Catechism.
[3] Secker's Charges, p. 53. Pastoral Care, chap. viii.

began to find the gate too strait, and the way too narrow, for their pleasures, self-indulgence, and habits of sin; and retired from the course. They perceived that they had altogether mistaken the matter; and that, what they had conceived to be only a decent form, or perhaps a day of mirth, involved a profession, which, in common honesty, they dared not make, and obligations which they had neither desire nor purpose to acknowledge. And though they were repeatedly warned, that the declining of the public profession still left these obligations in their full force; yet they had not the hardihood to venture upon the solemn aggravation of hypocrisy in the profession, without any possible benefit to be expected from it. They were often indeed assured of the earnest desire of their Minister for their Confirmation; while he felt it incumbent upon him to explain to them its real nature and importance—as the ratification, 'with their own mouth *and consent*, openly before the Church,' of their baptismal engagement of renunciation, faith, and obedience. If they were willing 'to confirm this promise in their own persons,' it was equally his duty and privilege to encourage them. But if they were in *heart and life* unwilling, would they dare to present themselves to the bishop with a falsehood in their mouths; the guilt of which would be in no degree diminished by the awful fact of a multitude uniting with them in it; but rather would be aggravated by every circumstance of the occasion, by the light and knowledge which made it wilful; and by the presence of God in his own house, with the Minister and representatives of his church? This close dealing with their consciences would need little exercise of our prerogative. Though we should admit indeed the imputation of discouraging their wishes and intentions: yet the responsibility of declining the profession will be entirely their own.

Yet our system would be widely different, not only with the more encouraging cases, but also with the first dawn of hope upon discouragement. Here we would imitate our Master's merciful tenderness to "the bruised reed and the smoking flax." But with the careless, the more respectable (still remaining unintelligent or unimpressed) and even with many of the doubtful, this treatment may be pursued in perfect consistency with Ministerial tenderness, though not indeed, (in some instances more especially,) without some personal conflict, and probably some Ministerial cross. We would ever hold out invitation to the last stage of enquiry, lest we seem to prescribe limits to the grace of God, and hinder, as far as men can do, the operation of his own work, by want of consideration, patience, and love.

The difficulties however in the right treatment òf Confirmation are often exceedingly great. They begin in our own bosoms; they belong to the various motives operating with catechumens, their different states of mind, the conflicting opinions in our parishes, especially among Dissenters, and perhaps also among our own brethren; and even if none of these things embarrass us, there is the pain of possibly dismissing any, that may possess the latent germ of true piety; and of admitting *neutrals*—those of whose cases we can form no decided judgment. Truly the season calls for special prayer; that power and wisdom may be given to us to lay bare the heart of the candidate to his own eyes; and that, seeing our path clearly, we may act to our satisfaction, and to his conviction.

The proper age for Confirmation has been variously determined. In England, during the reign of Popery, it was five years of age. The Council of Trent appointed between seven and twelve years. Another Council at Milan forbad the confirming of any under seven. This requisition was consistent with the true genius of popery. It was, like their six other sacraments, an *opus operatum* upon passive agents. Calvin determined the age of ten, an age usually far too young for intelligent sincerity or profession. Our church has more wisely marked the time indefinitely—'come to the years of discretion,' an era, which must vary in some degree according to natural capacity, and opportunities of instruction and preparation. Few reach this era before the age of thirteen, and not many so early.

We ·must deeply regret, that Ministerial unfaithfulness should give plausible pretext for Dissenting misconceptions, as to the nature and value of this ordinance. But that "eye" must "be evil" indeed, that cannot distinguish between a rite, diligently improved as a sign and means of self-dedication, and the same rite left to its own nakedness, unconnected with Christian instruction or Christian motives; and therefore—*from Ministerial neglect—not from unscriptural superstition*—made an occasion of affronting mockery to God under the shadow of a reasonable service. Is there no difference between a promiscuous multitude, gathered—like the assembly at Ephesus, "the more part of whom knew not wherefore they were come together"[1]—and between a "little flock," duly instructed in the nature of their obligations; and coming to the

---

[1] Acts xix. 32.

house of God to testify their public and willing surrender to the service of their Saviour? Methinks candour would forbear to condemn, where it could not wholly accord, and would forgive the mode in the approval of the end, and would be ready to say —" The blessing of the Lord be upon you; we bless you in the name of the Lord."[1]

We add a suggestion on the importance of keeping alive the impressions of the season in our subsequent Ministry. Much anticipated blessing has often been lost from the neglect of " stirring up the minds" of the confirmants, from time to time, " by way of remembrance." Would it not be desirable occasionally to address them from the pulpit; to probe and encourage them in private conference; and to assemble them periodically for the pupose of a renewed, systematic, and self-examining exhortation, to an habitual and consistent fulfilment of their obligations?

As *a mere ceremony*, nothing can be more unmeaning, or we may say, more profane, than Confirmation. As an *ordinance*, seriously considered, and conscientiously improved—its successive eras add living members to our churches. But if not a single instance of visible blessing had been vouchsafed, yet the opportunities then specially afforded, of exciting a spirit of prayer for the rising generation; of bringing the grace and mercy of the Saviour into more immediate contact with their understandings and affections; and of detailing before them a more explicit exhibition of their solemn and unchangeable obligations, cannot be wholly unproductive of a blessing to our own hearts; and may be confidently expected to produce an ultimate and abundant harvest in many unpromising cases.

A memorandum book to enter minutes of conversation with catechumens would afford many useful and interesting recollections. —The following may furnish a sample:—

The approach of A. B. to Confirmation gave me from the beginning unmixed uneasiness. My conversations with him, from time to time, elicited no satisfactory evidence of true penitence. The character and habit of his mind were decidedly, though not grossly, worldly; and therefore the profession of renunciation of the world in entireness and sincerity was probing, the specific application of the baptismal vow to his individual case. He professed increased seriousness of mind, and a readiness to give more consideration to the subject of religion; but the intention of buying " the pearl of great price" at the cost of " selling all that he had,"[2] I fear,

---

[1] Psalm cxxix. 8.   [2] Matt. xiii. 45, 46.

had never found a place in his heart. I entered into the subject with him in close conversation, entreaty, and prayer. 'Are you willing to stand to this profession to renounce all that this world offers for Christ?' He was afraid—not all: he was willing to give up some things, but he could not say more. I told him that some, and not all, meant nothing : that an unreadiness to forsake all made it doubtful, whether there was a real desire and sincere intention to yield any thing ; as that " faith," which alone could enable him *cheerfully* to make one sacrifice for Christ, was " the victory that overcometh the world"[1] in every form of temptation in which it could present itself. I should have spoken to him differently, allowing hesitation and conflict in his mind, had I felt any reason for hope, that the germ of Christian sincerity, even in its weakest influence, was hid in the ground of his heart. He hoped indeed that he might be different some future day ; but at present he was not prepared to come up to the requisitions of the Gospel. Either he had not counted the cost ; or he was not willing to abide it. His faint resolutions derived all their strength from his own resources ; and were wholly unconnected with a sense of helplessness, and dependence upon strength from above. It was therefore easy to determine their character, and to predict their failure.

Another case (of the same character, and with the same melancholy issue) was that of C. D. a wild and careless lad, whose mind had hitherto been undisturbed with the most cursory thought of religion. The world was every thing with him ; all his care, all his employ, all his delight. Eternity, with its infinite momentous stake, had been wholly disregarded. Confirmation, in his view, was a thing of course. Several of his family had gone to the last Confirmation ; and he was old enough for the present; and the repetition of his catechism was all that he conceived would be required. I endeavoured to impress serious conviction upon his conscience ; but could only obtain a promise, that he would turn the matter over in his mind. Some slight impressions however were made by repeated conversations. As the time drew near, I endeavoured to bring his mind to a crisis. He told me, that he was willing to be confirmed ; to which I replied—' I am glad to hear it, if it be really true that you wish to confirm your baptismal vow, and really to renounce the devil, the world, and the flesh. But you must understand the meaning and seriousness of this determination. Confirmation is a promise you are going to make—or rather to renew —to God. You are going to promise great things—things, which,

[1] John v. 4, 5.

if you perform them, will make the world wonder. You are going to promise the great, holy, heart-searching God, that you will, from this time forth, for ever renounce, forsake, and abhor the devil and all his works; sin of every kind, of every degree, whatever your conscience tells you to be wrong; and that you will resist with all your might whatever temptations have hitherto overcome you. These are great things for you to promise.' 'I doubt,' (said he) 'I am not fit: I had rather not go.' Not at present taking notice of his hesitation, I proceeded—'You are in the world from morning to night; Satan puts every temptation in your way—sin, the neglect of God, the neglect of his word and prayer; your companions draw you as far as they can from every serious thought about your soul, your Saviour, or eternity. Now you are going to promise, that, when you meet them to-morrow, you will strive against them as far as you can; and, if they will not hear you, that you will turn away from them. This is a part of the meaning of Confirmation. Is this your meaning?' 'I think,' (said he) 'I had better not go.' 'I do not wholly discourage you from going. If you can go without telling a falsehood, it will be a blessing to you. But to profess and promise to God in his own house what you do not mean to perform, would be the most wicked falsehood you could utter. Did you know that it meant all this?' 'Nothing near so much.' 'Now' (said I) 'I do not wish to frighten you, but it is so dreadful, to go blindfolded, and ignorant of the promise you are about to make. In your business you never promise in this thoughtless way; and this is by far the most serious business you ever took in hand.' 'Yes indeed, I begin to see it is; and I think I had better give it up.' 'I do not recommend you to give it up to-night. You have not asked God to teach you. He is waiting for the first turn of your heart to him, if you will but seek him. Let me show you in the parable of the prodigal a picture of God's love and readiness to welcome you.' He listened with considerable attention, and at length said—'I should like to go; but I think I had better not, if I am not fit.' 'I think so. Only remember, that unfitness for Confirmation is unfitness for death. And how awful to be called into eternity in this state of unfitness! How awful to be growing more unfit every day by neglecting these things! Do not despise this precious gift. It is worth all that you have in the world—it is the pearl of great price—worth ten thousand worlds, if you had them to buy it.' 'Yes, but it is such a very strict thing.' 'And you must expect to find it so. You never can be religious without a hard struggle. Could you bear what the world will say? to have all your old companions joining the laugh against you?' He gave me no answer, and I continued—'Let me tell you, how much happier it is to serve God than to run after the world: at least let me persuade you to make the trial. God has more to give you than the world; and if you will but ask him—"He giveth liberally, and upbraideth not." Now have you really ever asked him?' 'I think I have prayed lately; but I doubt, not with all my heart.' I continued at some length, showing him his state of guilt, helplessness, and unbelief—his need of a Saviour to bring him to God—the only way to give up the world, and choose the service of God, by faith in Jesus Christ. His conscience was evidently under the temporary power of conviction; but he could not make up his mind to the cost. The chains of sin and Satan were too strong to be broken by faint and unproductive convictions.

E. F. in the Sunday School. Happily for herself—not gifted with fluency of utterance: but the little that was elicited by patient questioning, seemed to bear the genuine stamp of the language of the heart. 'How do you feel now about being confirmed?' 'Not by a great deal, as I could wish.' 'I suppose you feel it a great thing to do: would you wish *not* to be confirmed?' 'No—I wish to serve God.' 'And what good do you expect it will do you?' 'None at all, except I go with a true heart.' 'What does Confirmation mean?' 'The giving up of the heart to God.' 'But were you not given up to God soon after you were born?' 'Yes, when I was baptized.' 'Then why do you want to be confirmed?' '*To give up myself to God.*' 'It will cost you a good deal: there is so much to be given up first. Would you give your heart wholly to God?' 'I will try.' 'Is there nothing in the world that you love so well as God?' 'I do not think there is.' 'But can you ever perform these great things that you are going to promise?' 'Not without God's help.' 'But to whom does God give his help?' 'To them that ask him.' 'But what hope have you of God's help?' 'Because he has promised.' 'And why did God promise it to you?' 'Because Jesus Christ died for sinners.' 'Now you will promise to renounce all that the devil, the world, and your own wicked heart tempt you against following the word of God; which of these three do you find to be 'the hardest?' 'I think I find my heart the greatest trouble.' 'And how do you expect to overcome?' 'By faith, by believing in Jesus Christ so as to love him.' 'What are the Articles of the Christian faith?' 'All that the Bible tells me of Jesus Christ.' 'And do you really believe all that you read about him?' 'I hope I do, but not enough.' 'Do you believe in him, so as to try to seek him?' 'I hope I do, but not enough: I wish I did.' 'What do you think of God's commandments? Do you think you can keep them?' 'By God's grace I will try: I find them very comfortable.'—There was little enlargement of mind, but hopeful signs of the guidance of the Spirit of truth. Monosyllables, however, that in other instances betoken only a cold and unmeaning assent, in her case evidenced at once the timidity of her character, and the sincerity of her profession.

We have only to recommend the sealing of Confirmation engagements at the Sacramental Table; not always as an immediate consequent, but as connected with a due preparation, and a competent judgment of Christian intelligence and sincerity. Nothing indeed can be more injudicious or more injurious, than hurrying young persons, immediately after Confirmation, to the Lord's Table; as if we might dispense with all scrutiny of their profession, and all intelligent preparation for that solemn ordinance. Where their consciences are not benumbed in formality or indifference, this rash decision has usually issued in a heartless profession, characterized by indolent unavailing regret. We would not indeed wilfully err on the other extreme, and expect *every thing to be quite satisfactory*—"We wish their perfection," but we must not wait for it; nor should we debar them in almost the lowest gradation of sincerity (for what more had the Apostles at the original institution of the supper?) from an ordinance, which, by fixing them in communion with the Church, is most helpful to their establishment in the Gospel.[1]

CHAPTER V.[2]

SACRAMENTAL INSTRUCTION.

THE Dispensation of the Sacraments must be considered as one of the most important parts of our Ministry. For its efficient administration however we need sound and Scriptural apprehensions of their nature and uses, of the privileges and obligations connected with them, and of the medium by which their grace is received

---

[1] See an interesting view of Confirmation, connected with attendance at the Lord's table in the memoir of Rev. G. T. Bedell, D.D. Philadelphia. On the admission of serious young porsons to the sacrament. Comp. Philip Henry's Life, pp. 11, 84, 195, and also Scott's Life, pp. 619, 620—and an excellent Catechism by Rev. J. Bickersteth.

[2] This chapter is published separately in an enlarged form.

and applied. Our Homily well states their distinct character—'In prayer we beg at God's hands all such things as otherwise we cannot obtain. In the Sacraments he embraceth, and offereth himself to be embraced of us.'[1] In opening a more full discussion, we advert to their primary object; which is, to exhibit Christ in all the rich treasures of grace and salvation. For, 'Christ being taken away,'—as Bishop Davenant admirably observes—'there remains nothing in the Sacraments but an empty show.'[2] In this view we cannot but acknowledge the full love of our God in these gracious ordinances—so fraught with encouragement to our faith, and so eminently conducive to our holiness. For while they bring our Great Redeemer vividly before our eyes, they at the same time, 'serve as bonds of obedience to God, strict obligations to the mutual exercise of Christian charity, provocations to godliness, preservations from sin, memorials of the principal benefits of Christ.'[3] It is indeed a melancholy instance of the perverseness of the human mind, that these enriching blessings should from their misuse or neglect be so unfruitful to the church—that these ordinances—intended to cement the body of Christ in one fellowship[4]—should be the matter of ceaseless controversy and division. For Hooker's statement is beyond question, that 'Sacraments, are more diversely interpreted and disputed of, than any other part of religion besides.'[5]

In order to arrive at some accurate view of the subject, we will expound the comprehensive definition of a Sacrament, which our Church has given for the instruction of her younger members. She explains it to be an 'outward and visible sign of an inward and spiritual grace given unto us; ordained by Christ himself, as a means whereby we receive the same, and as a pledge to assure us thereof.'[6]

The Ordination of Christ himself—the Divine Head of the Church—is justly laid as the ground of this ordinance. Who besides has the prerogative to ordain?—"Go ye, and teach all nations, baptizing them—This do in remembrance of me"[7]— here is his "image and superscription" stamped broad and clear upon the Sacraments of the Church. And so sacred is their authority and entireness, that to add to their number, and to violate their integrity, is the high treason of altering the royal seal—the defilement of setting "up our threshold by God's threshold, and our post by

---

[1] Homily on Prayer and Sacraments.   [2] On Col. ii. 11.
[3] Hooker, Book v. lvii. 2.   [4] 1 Cor. x. 17. xii. 13.   [5] Ib. ut supra.
[6] Catechism.   [7] Matt. xxviii. 19. Luke xxii. 19.

God's 'posts.'"[1] The Church indeed rightly claims the liberty of prescribing the mode and circumstantials of their celebration.[2] But she never places her own requisitions upon a Divine basis. She maintains the strictest regard to the spirit of the Apostolic rules,[3] and carefully preserves both the substance and form of the elements, and the representation of the inestimable blessings which they shadow forth.

Our definition next proceeds to the more distinct description of a Sacrament, considering it *as a sign—a means—and a seal—of grace.*

It is obviously *a sign*—'a sign of profession, and a mark of difference, whereby men are discerned from others :'[4] 'a mark of distinction, to separate God's own from strangers.'[5] Thus *the sign* of circumcision[6] distinguished the Jews from the Heathen around them ; and the Christian Sacraments are the open 'badges of Christian men's profession' before the world.[7] Thus also their outward parts are *the signs* of their inward and spiritual grace[8]— 'visible signs of invisible grace.'[9] Indeed they may be called ' the visible words,'[10] as representing to our eyes what the word speaks to our ears. ' In the word we have the promises of God. In the Sacraments we see them.'[11]

Yet they are far from being empty signs, or naked representations. ' It greatly offendeth'—says our great writer—'that some, when they labour to show the use of the holy Sacraments, assign to them no end but merely to teach the mind by other sources that, which the word doth teach by hearing. For where the word of God may be heard, which teacheth with much more expedition and more full explication any thing we have to learn ; if all the benefit we reap by Sacraments be instruction, they which at all times have opportunity of using the better means for that purpose, will surely hold the worst in less estimation. There is of Sacraments undoubtedly some other more excellent and heavenly use.'[12]

This 'more excellent and heavenly use' our Church defines to be a ' means, *whereby we receive the grace given to us.*' They are ' visible signs, expressly commanded in the New Testament,

---

[1] Ez. xliii. 7.   [2] Art. xx.   [3] 1 Cor. xiv. 26, 40.
[4] Art. xxvii.   [5] Hooker, Book v. lvii. 2.   [6] Rom. iv. 11.
[7] Art. xxv.   Comp. Acts ii. 37—46.   [8] Art. xx. xxv. xxvii. and Catechism.
[9] Homily on Prayer and Sacraments. Hooker v.1.3.   This is also the Definition of the Council of Trent.   Sess. xiii. c. iii.
[10] Augustine calls them 'verba visibilia.'   Hooker's MSS. note v. lvii. 3.   (Keble's Edit.)
[11] Bishop Jewell on the Sacraments, Edit. 1611. p. 261.
[12] Hooker v. lvii. 1.   See also his remarks on 'the Christian Letter' Appended to Book v. ii. 703. (Keble's Ed.)

whereunto is annexed the promise of free forgiveness of our sins, and of our holiness and joining in Christ.'[1] 'Sacraments ordained of Christ be not only badges or tokens of Christian men's profession ; but rather they be *effectual* signs of grace and of God's goodwill towards us, *by the which he doth work invisibly in us.*'[2] This is in strict accordance with the Scripture testimony. In reference to one Sacrament—'We are born of water and of the Spirit—buried with Christ by baptism unto death. Christ sanctifieth and cleanseth his Church with the washing of water. God hath saved us by the washing of regeneration, and the renewing of the Holy Ghost. Baptism doth now save us.'[3] In individual instances—the baptized Apostle was manifestly strengthened by the holy ordinance.[4] The baptized eunuch—the jailor also—"went on his way rejoicing."[5] If the references to the other Sacrament are not equally full, they are not less decided. "The cup of blessing which we bless, is it not the communion of the blood of Christ? The bread which we break, is it not the communion of the body of Christ?"[6] How largely the Pentecostal converts were refreshed by this communion, their brief history fully testifies.[7] We cannot, therefore, doubt that the Scripture designates 'these heavenly ceremonies'[8] as a means of rich and special grace. They exhibit the blessings of the Gospel to all. But to the faithful receiver they convey to his very bosom the blessings which they exhibit.

We complete our exposition of the Sacrament by setting it out, not only as a means of grace, but a *pledge to assure us thereof.* Thus "*the sign* of circumcision was *a seal* of the righteousness of the faith."[9] The corresponding Sacrament of baptism is also a seal of the remission of sin to the worthy recipient.[10] "This cup," spake our Lord at the sacred supper, "is *my blood of the New Testament*," 'representing his blood as shed to make way for the new covenant, and to *ratify it as valid for their benefit*'[11]—not making the covenant more valid in itself, but 'certain sure witnesses, strengthening and confirming our faith[12] to apprehend and apply it. 'God's gift'—as Archbishop Sandys excellently remarks

[1] Homily on Prayer and Sacraments. [2] Art. xxv.
[3] John iii. 5. Rom. vi. 4. Eph. v. 26. Tit. iii. 5. 1 Pet. iii. 21.
[4] Acts ix. 18—20. Yet—as our Church accurately expressed it—'faith is confirmed and grace increased *by virtue of prayer* to God. Art. xxvii. Comp. verse 11. xxii. 16, also the Baptism of our Divine Master. Luke iii. 21, 22. iv. i. Compare also Cyprian's description of the comfort of his Baptism quoted by Mr. Faber. Primit. Doctr. of Regeneration, pp. 37—39.
[5] Ib. viii. 38, 39. xvi. 33, 34. [6] 1 Cor. x. 16. [7] Acts ii. 42—47.
[8] Hooker v. lvii. 3. [9] Rom. iv. 11.
[10] Acts ii. 38; xxii. 16. Compare Nicene Creed, Art. xxvii.
[11] Matt. xxvi. 28. Scott in loco. Compare Bishop Hopkins' Works, ii. 440.
[12] Art. xxv. Hooker v. lvii. 2.

—' without sealing is sure, as he himself is all one without changing.   Yet to bear with our infirmity, and to make us more secure
of his promise, to his writing and word he added these outward
signs and seals, to establish our faith, and to certify us that his
promise is most certain.'[1]

Thus far we have endeavoured to set out what, according to the
definition of the Church and in strict harmony with Scripture,
forms the sum and substance of a Sacrament.   The statement of
the Foreign Reformers, as embodied in their public confessions, or
as they can be elicited from a careful study of their writings, seem
to be marked with some variation ; nor do the most sound of them,
in the writer's judgment, come up to the completeness of the Anglican exposition.[2]

We next advert to the medium, by which sacramental grace is
conveyed.   Let it *never be supposed, that there is any innate
grace in these holy ordinances.*   They are what they are, not by
inherent efficacy, but by Divine institution.   They are—as our
Church most accurately defines them—*means* only, not sources of
grace. · The blessing is not *in them*.   But it flows *through them*
from the Great Fountain Head.   Nor let this be thought to be a
mere verbal distinction.   To make them—as some appear to do—
sources of grace, is to put them in the place of Christ.   To acknowledge them as means, is to depend on Christ in them, to look
for his grace imparted by them, to honour his appointment in their
diligent improvement, and thus to ensure his gracious acceptance.
We ascribe nothing to the instruments : all belongs to him, who
condescends to work by them.   Eminently clear and evangelical
is the statement of Bishop Ridley—' Every sacrament hath grace

---

[1] Sermons, Parker Society Ed. pp. 303, 304.—'Sweeter it is unto us than honey,
where we are certified by this outward sacrament of the inward grace given unto us through
his death, when in him we are assured of remission of sins and eternal life.   Better food
than this thy soul can never feed upon.'   Ibid. p. 89.

[2] Zuingle's views of the sacrament were far short of the truth.   He speaks of them
as 'signs, by which the receiver gives to the Church a pledge of his faith' (Fol. Works
ii. 198; also 202, 204.   See Bishop Hall's judgment of his doctrine.   Christian Moderation, Book ii. Rule viii.)   Calvin's systematic statement goes further, but not far enough,
—'testimonies of Divine favour to us, confirmed by outward signs, combined with the
pledge of our piety to him.' (Instit. iv. xiv. 1.)   In his free and later communications
with his friends, however, he rises to a more full and enlarged view.   He speaks of
'agreeing with Luther, that the sacraments are not empty signs—that in baptism the
power of the Spirit is present to wash and regenerate us; and that the sacred supper is a
spiritual feast, in which we truly feed on the flesh and blood of Christ.'   Epist. p. 82.
Bucer's views of baptism appear to have been generally sound.   (On Matt. xix. et De vi
baptismi in his 'Scripta Anglicana.')   On the Lord's Supper he exhibits spiritual apprehensions.   (' We are taught,' he says, 'that the body and blood of Christ are received by
faith.'   Tetrapol. Confess.) though his mind was much clouded by the Lutheran dogma.
Bullinger's Sermons on the Sacraments lately edited from his Decades, by the Norrisian
Professor at Cambridge, have the general imprimatur of the Anglican Church.   Luther's
views on Baptism are full, though of course their weight is somewhat weakened by his
mystical and unscriptural theory of the other Sacrament.   See on Gal. iii. 27.

annexed to it instrumentally.   It hath not grace included in it ; but
to those that receive it well it is turned to grace.   After that manner, water in baptism hath grace promised, and by that grace the
Holy Spirit is given ; *not that grace is included in water, but that
grace cometh by water.*[1]   To the same purport writes the judicious Hooker—' Sacraments really exhibit, but for aught we can
gather out of that which is written of them, they are not really,
nor *do they really contain in themselves, that grace, which with
them or by them it pleaseth God to bestow.*[2]

Bishop Ridley—let it be observed—limits the promise of grace
in the sacrament to *them that receive it well.*   And indeed, while
our Church clearly insists upon the unworthy administration as no
bar,[3] she clearly sets out a *worthy reception* as an indispensable
mean, to the blessing, ' The sacraments were ordained, that we
should *duly use* them.   And in such only as *worthily receive* the
same, they have a wholesome effect and operation.   But they that
receive them unworthily, purchase to themselves damnation, as St.
Paul saith.'[4]   To presume that they would work alike when they
are improved or profaned, is indeed the essence of Romish superstition ; contravening the Divine rule expressly given to preserve the
purity of worship—" Them that honour me I will honour, and
they that despise me shall be lightly esteemed."[5]   ' The real presence of Christ's most precious body and blood'—as Hooker most
accurately states—' *is not therefore to be sought for in the Sacrament*, but in the worthy receiver of the Sacrament—in the heart
and soul of him which receiveth.'[6]

Our Church justly points out faith as the principle of a worthy
reception, and the only medium through which the blessing is applied.   To such alone, as ' rightly, worthily, *and with faith* receive
the same,' does she conceive the ordinance to be a real and spiritual
participation.[7]   And this is in strict harmony with Scripture.   If
we are " buried with Christ in baptism," we " are risen with him
from this burial *through the faith of the operation of God.*"[8]
The " baptism that doth now save us," is expressly stated to be—
" *not* the putting away of the filth of the flesh,"? the mere external
ceremony—" but the answer of a good conscience toward God"—
the act and profession of faith.[9]   The unworthy partaking of the

[1] Works, Parker's Society Ed. pp. 240, 241.
[2] Book v. lxvii. 6.   Compare lvii. 4.   [3] Art. xxvi.   [4] Art. xxv.
[5] 1 Sam. ii. 30.   [6] Book v. lxvii. 6.   Compare Waterland, chap. v.
[7] Art. xxvii. xxviii.   [8] Col. ii. 12.
[9] 1 Peter iii. 21.   ' It is not the water, but the faith,' (saith good Bishop Hall, alluding
to this text) ' for " who takes baptism without a full faith,"—saith Jerome—" takes the
water, takes not the Spirit."   Baptism therefore without faith cannot save a man, and by
faith does save him.'—Ep. Dec. v. Ep. iv.

holy supper is—"not discerning the Lord's body."[1]   The due reception therefore must be in the exercise of that intelligent *faith*,
which discerns the great end, substance, and blessing of the ordinance.

Indeed we cannot but bless God for the singular wisdom, which
guided the general statements of our Reformers on this important
subject.   They took up their position in the true mean between
Rationalism and Romanism.   They expounded high and glowing
views of sacramental grace.   But they avoided the Patristic and
Romish error, by grounding it on the promise of the covenant, and
linking it with the instrumental agency of faith.   We need only
refer to the Baptismal services, where the prayers are little more
than the promises taken hold on by faith, and the exhortations encourage an undoubting confidence, grounded upon the manifested
work and love of the Saviour.   We are aware indeed, that statements have been produced from their writings, on the side of exag-
gerated views of the Sacraments.   But we are persuaded that a
careful comparison will exhibit these statements as connected with
the grand principles of the Gospel, and with a more precise limitation than is often given to them.   Nor must it be forgotten, that
they are applied to *the whole ordinance*—not to the bare external
ceremony—reminding us (with our Homily) ' that faith is a necessary instrument in all these holy ceremonies, for that, as St. Paul
saith, "without faith it is impossible to please God." '[2]   Indeed to
insist upon the efficacy of the Sacraments without this necessary
mean, is ' basely to bind ourselves to the elements and the creatures'[3]—to make the ordinances matter of idolatrous dependence
rather than of warranted scriptural improvement—as if the Sacrament itself gave and did every thing by its innate grace.

It seems necessary, in order to complete our view of this part of
our Ministry, to advert, as briefly as possible, to some principal
errors on the right hand and on the left.   That there should be
errors—diversified and important errors—connected with so much
difference of judgment and corruption of heart, is no marvel.   The
ordinances themselves are holy.   Yet man's perverseness makes

---

[1] 1 Cor. xi. 29.

[2] Homily on Sacrament, Part i.   Take an example from Cranmer, who perhaps may
be considered to have spoken most strongly on the subject of the Sacraments.   Speaking
of baptism—' Some will say, ' How can water work such great things?'   To whom I answer—That it is not the water that doeth these things, but the almighty word of God
(which is knit and joined to the water,) *and faith*, which receiveth God's word and
promise.   For *without the word of God, water is water, and not baptism.*'   Catechism,
1548.

[3] Homily ut supra.   Bishop Hopkins gives very valuable views of the necessity of
faith, as the mean of spiritual efficacy in the use of the Sacraments.   Works, ii. pp. 434,
—445.

them the occasion of sin and fearful provocation even in the profession of a sound faith.[1] Who needs not the warning—" Let him
that thinketh he standeth take heed lest he fall ?"[2]

Archbishop Leighton admirably remarks upon the two extremes
of Sacramental error—' First, of those that ascribe too much to
Sacraments, as if they wrought by a natural inherent virtue, and
carried grace in them inseparably. Secondly, of those who ascribe
too little to them—making them only signs and badges of our profession.'[3]

To the first of these *errors of excess* we have already adverted.
Others not less momentous we would briefly notice—such as
making the Sacraments the casual ground of our justification,
which the Apostle distinctly states to be subverting the foundations
of the Gospel[4]—*connecting the grace inseparably with the sign*
repugnant to the testimony of Scripture[5]—of the Church[6] and of
fact—*making these ordinances the exclusive means of grace,*
when the Scripture sets forth the preaching of the word as the
grand instrument of salvation[7]—*insisting upon them as absolutely—and not as our Church—only ' generally* necessary'[8]—to salvation. These are errors of no small magnitude, which change
the character, obscure the glory, and paralyse the influence, of the
Gospel of the grace of God. They are characteristic of " another
Gospel,"[9] not worthy of the name.

Yet we must not forget to guard against *errors of defect,* which
work every way to the deterioration of our Ministry. Bishop
Hoadley's Sacramental views were in consistency with the heretical
school, to which he unhappily belonged. We should however
deeply regret to mark any tendencies to his Rationalistic Theory
connected with a sounder creed. Those symbols, which are employed to represent and to convey such inestimable blessings, are
far beyond naked signs. They claim our reverence, and they
should exercise our faith. Animated as they are with life, let us
honour them as a means, by which our gracious God ' doth not
only quicken, but also strengthen and confirm our faith in him.'[10]
Unbelief is no less dishonourable to God, and paralyzing to his
work, than formal superstition.[11] If the Sacraments are means of
grace, ought we not to be looking for grace through them ? And
may not their barrenness be too often explained—" Ye have not,
because ye ask not ?"[12] To call to mind the rich and free promises

1 1 Cor. x. 1—5.   2 Ib. verse 12.   3 On 1 Peter iii. 21.
4 Gal. v. 2—4.   5 Comp. Rom. ii. 28, 29.
6 Which limits the blessing to the worthy recipient. Art. xxv.
7 1 Cor. i. 21.   8 Catechism.   9 Gal. i. 6, 7.
10 Art. xxv.   11 Matt. xiii. 58. xvii. 19, 20. Mark vi. 5.   12 James iv. 2.

here sealed to us, to lay hold of them by faith—to consider the seals as the earnests of the blessings to be applied in God's best time—this would establish a confidence fraught with life and energy, hope and joy to our Christian profession. 'Where they are not either through contempt unreceived, or received with contempt, we are not to doubt, but that they really give what they promise, and are what they signify. For we take not baptism, nor the eucharist for *bare resemblance* or memorials of things absent neither for *naked signs* and testimonies, assuring us of grace re ceived before ; but (as they are indeed and in verity) for means ef fectual, whereby God, when we take the Sacraments, delivereth into our hands that grace available unto eternal life, which grace the sacraments represent or signify.'[1]

The great importance of this subject, as a component part of the Christian Ministry, has appeared to the Writer to demand this ex tended discussion upon the general question of the Sacraments. We now proceed to advert to the specific character, privileges, and obligations connected with each of them separately.

I.—BAPTISM.

"What mean ye by this service"—might be asked of us by many, who bring their children to baptism only as an ecclesiastical rite—the custom of the place—and the ordinary mode of giving them their name. Baptismal instruction is therefore—as Bishop Burnet reminds us[2]—most important. Our people need for the most part, very full and clear expositions of the nature of this Sacrament, in the three-fold definition which our Church has given —*as a sign—a seal—a means—of grace.* As *a sign*, it marks our original guilt and impurity ; and our cleansing by the blood of Christ, and the regenerating influence of his Spirit. As *a means* —it encourages the prayer of faith for the communication of his favour and grace. As *a seal* of the covenant of grace, by which we are mutually engaged to God, and God to us—it assures our faith of the manifested favour of God to His believing people and their seed.

That there should be any controversy as *to the subjects of Bap- tism*, is a matter of some marvel. There was none in the Apos- tolic, or in the Primitive Church. The circumcision of infants, and the substantial identity of circumcision with baptism[3]—the

---

[1] Hooker, book v. lvii. 5.   [2] Past. Care, ch. viii.   [3] Col. ii. 11, 12.

covenant promises of God extending to the believer's seed[1]—the clear encouragement of the. Saviour in admitting children into his kingdom[2]—the unfettered baptismal commission extending to "all nations"[3]—to infants therefore as a corporate part of nations—in conformity with this command, the Apostolical records of the baptism of whole households[4]—the acknowledged practice of the early Christians—these particulars combine to strengthen and confirm the declaration of our Church, that ' the baptism of young children is in any wise to be retained in the Church, as most agreeable with the institution of Christ.[5] If we are called upon for a plain command, we are ready to adduce it. God charged his people upon the strictest penalty, to bring their children into covenant with himself —*and that by the seal of the Gospel.*[7] Until therefore the repeal of the statute, and the sentence of their exclusion be produced, we will thankfully hold to the judgment of Bishop Hall —' children are the blessing of parents ; and baptism is the blessing of children and parents.'[8]

The Divine institution of this Sacrament of admission sufficiently attests its spiritual character. *Its privileges* are therefore accordant with this character—an investiture with all the blessings of the Christian covenant.[9] *The grace* connected with this ordinance is " a death unto sin, and a new birth unto righteousness"[10]— a real, not a relative change.

Yet experience and observation too plainly prove, that its priv-

---

[1] Gen. xvii. 7. Acts ii. 39. See Calvin Instit. iv. 16 ult.   [2] Mark x. 13—16.
[3] Matt. xxviii. 19.   [4] Acts xvi. 15, 33. 1 Cor. i. 16.   [5] Art. xxvii.
[6] Gen. xvii. 9—14.   [7] Rom. iv. 11.   [8] Epist. Dec. v. 4.
[9] Comp. Rom. ix. 4, 5. These privileges belonged to the Lord's visible people—*not as converted* (for the contrary was their palpable character, verses 3, 6.) *but as circumcised.* Comp. Deut. xiv. 1. Thus our Lord gave the same investiture to those. who had manifestly no true and personal interest in the blessings (Luke xv. 2. 31). Our Church therefore, upon the assumed identity of circumcision and baptism, not doubting that the privileges under a more enlarged dispensation were at least equally full—details the Jewish privileges as the substantial appendage of Christian baptism (Catechism). The title in both cases was the admission into covenant with God ; though, unless when it was pleaded and brought out in faith, it was virtually a title without possession. We may observe also in connexion with this subject, the *distributive individuality* with which the Apostle invested *the several members* of the visible Church with baptismal privileges—"as many *of you*" (not some—or as elsewhere (Phil. i. 7,) *all, en masse,*) "as have been baptized into Christ have put on Christ." (Gal. iii. 27). Would the Apostle have hesitated in making this investiture a matter 'of thanksgiving? Wherein would this differ from the thanksgiving severally pronounced in our service respecting baptized infants ? If this were warranted in the case of Judaizing, backsliding professors (iv. 19, 20. v. 4, 15) much more is it in the case of infants, where no open ground of exclusion can be shown. We conceive this fully to justify *the letter* of our service, as applied to the visible church. *The spirit* of the service, as applied to the true church, is to be explained upon the general consistent principle of spiritual and acceptable worship. But we cannot forbear to admire the precise Scriptural accuracy of our Liturgical service. The difficulties, which after all may remain upon some minds, belong not so much to the church as to the Scripture, to an imperfect apprehension of the popular language and statements of the inspired writers.
[10] Catechism.

ilege and grace are not *necessarily and in all cases* connected with the external administration. We surely can only expect the blessing where God is honoured in the improvement of the ordinance, and where the *ends* for which he appointed it are duly regarded. The design is, that the child of Abraham—the only true member of the Church—may here plead and make good his children's interest jointly with his own in the favour and grace of God. It is not merely *a dedicatory*[1]—but chiefly *a covenanting* service[2] —pleading and embracing for his child the promises of grace. In affixing therefore the seal of God's own covenant in his appointed ordinance, we give thanks, *as in duty bound,* for the child's interest in this large expanse of mercy. For whether the grace be vouchsafed at the moment, or at some future period; as confirmed to our faith by God's own seal, it is alike in both cases a just ground of present confidence, *and therefore* of grateful acknowledgment.

In reply to the difficulty, which here meets us, arising from the indiscrimination of baptism, we reply—We are Ministers by Divine appointment in a mixed Church.[3] Yet we can only administer spiritual ordinances in a spiritual frame. To conceive of acceptable ordinances for hypocrites and unbelievers is an anomaly—To accommodate the service of the Church to the temperament of " the mixed multitude," would be to rob the true Christian of his warranted and enlarged confidence in " the promises of God" applied "by us,"[4]—and to approach God with a worship that could not be pleasing to him.[5] If therefore the ordinance be profaned, as doubtless it is most fearfully—on whom lies the responsibility? Not on us, who—as the Ministers of Christ—can only administer ordinances suited to his own spiritual Church and Service, but on those who make his spiritual service a mockery. Doubtless it is the duty of unbelievers, now as under the old dispensation, to present their children to God in solemn worship and professed covenanting.[6] But it is their sin that they perform this bounden duty in an ungodly and unacceptable manner.

In conformity therefore with the general character of acceptable worship, our Baptismal service is framed—*not,* as some would have it, *upon the principle of charity, but of* faith. The ordinance is " the seal of the righteousness of the faith"[7]—" that is, of Gods way of acceptance pleaded and applied by faith. The seal therefore only confirms the promise in the exercise of faith. In the

---

[1] 1 Sam. i. 26—28.   [2] Gen. xvii. 9, 10.
[3] Matt. xiii. 30, 47. xxv. 1, 2.   [4] 2 Cor. i. 20.
[5] See Heb. xi. 6.   [6] Hooker v. lxiv. 5.   [7] Rom. iv. 11.

case of the adult, personal faith is the indispensable requisite. In the case of the infant, faith on its behalf, such as was honoured in similar cases of helplessness[1]—will here be equally encouraged.[2] The child thus "*brought* to Christ" will be counted as if he "*came* to him"—a welcome subject of his heavenly kingdom.[3]

Hence it is obvious that a doubting spirit, or positive unbelief, substitutes uncertainty and suspicion in the place of the appropriate act and thanksgiving of faith. And can this be honourable to God? Does it not of itself, according to the rule of his kingdom,[4] nullify the desired blessing? So far as "faith is made void, the promise is made of none effect."[5] On the other hand a Christian, bringing his child to the font for the sign and seal of spiritual regeneration, in the assurance of his joint interest in the promises of the covenant: the sponsor at the same time, in dependence on the promises, engaging in the child's name to renounce the service of his enemies, 'to believe in God, and to serve him,' and joining in prayer for the confirmation of those privileges to the child; such a sight exhibits a clear and animating warrant of faith, most honourable to the sacred ordinance. God honours his own name—his sovereignty in the gift of faith—his faithfulness in the acceptance of his own gift.

How enlivening and practical is the constraint of this Sacrament! The child in his first dawning intelligence finds 'his name put into the gospel grant'[6]—himself therefore a dedicated child—taken out of the evil world, and pledged to the service of God. To encourage his faithfulness, he feels himself surrounded with the special guardianship of a covenant-keeping God, introduced into his family, commended to the prayer and sympathies of every member of the household, brought under the blessing of all the means of grace—specially under the teaching of "the Holy Scriptures, which are able to make him wise unto salvation, through faith which is in Christ Jesus."[7] *But he must not sleep insensible of his obligations.* His responsibilities are now commenced. 'The sign of the cross' on his forehead will never be effaced from the eye of God; nor the day of his Baptismal consecration blotted out of his book. In the obligations and privileges of the covenant into which he has entered, are contained all the quickening motives to personal devotedness. And therefore his unfaithfulness will not be judged as the heathen, who "knew not his Lord's will," but as "the servant,

---

[1] See Matt. viii. 6. 10. ix. 2. xv. 22—28. Mark ix. 23—27.
[2] Compare Matt. xxi. 22. James i. 6, 7.   [3] Mark x. 13, 14. '
[4] Matt. ix. 29.   [5] Rom. iv. 14—17.
[6] Matthew Henry's Treatise on Baptism, p. 120.   [7] 2 Tim. iii. 15.

who knew his Lord's will, neither did according to his will, and who shall be beaten with many stripes."[1]

The office of Sponsors—though *in the letter* an human ordinance—yet *in the spirit of it*, seems an essential appendage. Baptism is not merely an office of dedication, but of covenanting with God. If therefore the infant be a party in the contract, he must appear by his Surety, who may represent in his own person the child's fidelity to his engagements. Hence the canons require communicants for this office, as the accredited pledge of sincerity. Nor is this Christian standard less necessary as respects the child. We must here "know no man after the flesh"—no consideration of convenience, relationship, or worldly advantage. The one principle of our choice is—'Who will be most helpful in training the child for God?' The difficulty of obtaining satisfactory Sponsors may often delay baptism, sometimes even remove the children wholly from us. Yet the very difficulty often brings conviction of an unchristian life, which makes Christian interference uncongenial and nugatory. We would, however, invite our communicants to step in, where needful, for this office of love, diligence, sympathy, prayer and helpfulness. We would explain the difficulties which hinder their engagement in this sacred proxy; as if it involved them in the wilful responsibility of the child; or this misconception being removed, as if it were only an empty and fruitless vow. We must not expect the ordinances of the church to change. It is much more important to maintain their due tone and dignity by a Scriptural discipline, than to draw a promiscuous multitude within our external pale, at the expense of all the sacredness of the sacraments, and to the serious injury of religion.

We must remind Parents and Sponsors that the dedication of a child to God, though an acceptable, is a most solemn and responsible service. How awful the profanation of "offering the blind for sacrifice !"[2] Let them understand *what they do*—binding them-

---

[1] Luke xii. 47, 48. Thus P. Henry 'in dealing with his children about their spiritual state, took hold of them very much by the handle of their infant baptism; and frequently inculcated upon them, that they were born in God's house, and were betimes dedicated and given up to him, and therefore were obliged to be his servants.' Life, p. 83. Compare Psalm cxvi. 16. Thus his son bears his personal testimony to the value of this ordinance. 'I cannot but take occasion' (said he) 'to express my gratitude to God for my infant baptism; not only, as it was an early admission into the visible body of Christ; but as it furnished my pious parents with a good argument (and as I trust through grace a prevailing argument) for an early dedication of my own self to God in my childhood. If God has wrought any good work upon my soul, I desire with humble thankfulness to acknowledge the moral influence of my infant baptism upon it.' Treatise on Baptism, p. 118. 'As to the *real influence of baptism*,'—he adds, however, in another place—'when the children grow up, we are sure that their baptismal regeneration, without something else, will not bring them to heaven: and yet it may be urged in praying to God to give them grace, and in persuading them to submit to it.' Matthew Henry on Baptism, pp. 130, 131.   [2] Mal. i. 8.

selves and their children to the service of God—*and why they do it*—in conformity to the appointment of God, and to the terms of the covenant, which is the ground of this Baptismal dedication. Let them know, that by this sacred act they profess their personal consecration to his service, (for who can give his child freely and sincerely, except he had " first given his own self, to the Lord ?") and give their pledge, that their children shall be the Lord's for ever—trained for his service and glory. Let them be reminded of the great honour of this most responsible trust, and of the fearful guilt of neglecting it. *Where it is practicable,* no sponsors or parents should present themselves at the font without previous Ministerial instruction ;[1] that they may, under the Lord's blessing, attend upon this ordinance with a penitent, upright, believing, and thankful spirit—presenting an " holy, and acceptable," as well as a " reasonable service."

Nor should we forget to inculcate the *improvement of the baptismal engagements.* Much use may be made of them as a restraint from sin[2]—an excitement to duty—a support to faith—and an encouragement to prayer ; while the remembrance of the investiture of privileges may animate to press for a real participation of them ; as living members of a living Head—in spiritual communion with a spiritual church.[3]

II.—THE LORD'S SUPPER.

OUR course of instruction naturally passes from the initial sacrament to that, which marks the complete privilege of Church membership—the one marking the commencement, the other the support of, the spiritual life.

This sacrament connects itself with the great doctrines of the Gospel. Man as a sinner was condemned under the everlasting curse of the broken law. God accepts the vicarious death of his

---

[1] Address to Parents and Sponsors on Baptism, by the Rev. P. Booth, B. D., Norwich. For a full view of the whole subject, the writer refers to a ' Treatise on Baptism,' by his friend and brother the Rev. E. Bickersteth—a work fraught with useful information and sound practical instruction.

[2] Luther mentions a Christian woman—' Quæ quoties tentabatur, *non nisi baptismo suo repugnabat*—dicens brevissime—Christiana sum.' ' Intellexit enim hostis'—adds Luther—' statim *virtutem baptismi, et fidei, quæ in veritate promittentis pendebat, et fugit ab eo.'*

[3] In some of the American churches the baptized children are assembled periodically in the church, with their natural and spiritual guardians, and addressed by their pastor upon the obligation of their vow. We could wish that similar ecclesiastical assemblies might be transferred into our Established system; or at least, that the spirit of this interesting ceremony would imbue our ordinary Ministrations with a more frequent and affectionate enforcement of baptismal responsibilities.

own Son as his surety. The great Sufferer himself upon the eve of his death appointed this ordinance as a perpetual memorial of his acceptable sacrifice, and as a seal of the covenanted blessings, which it obtained for his Church.

This memorial eminently illustrates the spiritual character of the ordinance. 'The remembrance which is thus ordained' (to use the beautiful language of Bishop Ridley)—'as the author thereof is Christ—both God and man ; so by the Almighty power of God it far passeth all kinds of remembrances that any other man is able to make, either of himself, or of any other thing. For whosoever receiveth this holy sacrament thus ordained in remembrance of Christ, *he receiveth therewith either death or life.*'[1] Cherishing this spiritual remembrance, we shall be preserved from the snare— 'lest of the memory, it be made a sacrifice ; lest of a communion, a private eating ; lest of two parts, we have but one—instead of a heavenly refection, a gross carnal feeding.'[2]

The distinctness and singular value of this ordinance is, that it appears to combine much of the real blessing of the other means. If preaching is to represent Christ crucified, to " do this in remembrance of him" is to " show forth his death till he come."[3] 'Thus also, (as Dean Comber justly remarks) 'that which is more compendiously expressed in the conclusion of our prayers *through Jesus Christ our Lord*—is more fully and more vigorously set out in this most holy sacrament; wherein we intercede on earth in imitation of, and in conjunction with, the great intercession of our High Priest in heaven—pleading here in the virtue and merits of the same sacrifice, which he doeth there for us.'[4]

The sacramental table is therefore equally precious and honourable as a command to be obeyed, and a privilege to be enjoyed. It is an exercise of faith—a remembrance of love—a covenant of dedication. Here our Divine Master's *real and spiritual* presence is specially vouchsafed. ' His body and blood are verily and indeed taken and received *by the faithful.*' And in this participation their souls are strengthened and refreshed, and their acceptance visibly sealed and established.[5] Here also we enjoy fellowship with the Lord's people as members of the same body, and partakers of the same privilege.[6] The sacramental graces (repentance and faith, hungering and thirsting for Christ, thanksgiving and brotherly love[7])

---

[1] Brief Declaration of the Lord's Supper. Works, Parker Society's Ed. p. 8.
[2] Homily on Sacrament, Part I.   [3] Gal. iii. 1. with Luke xxii. 19. 1 Cor. xi. 26.
[4] Introd. to Communion Service.
[5] Catechism and Communion Service—Prayer in Post-Communion.
[6] 1 Cor. x. 17.   [7] Communion service throughout.

are excited by the contemplation of the Great Author of the ordinance in the wondrous act of his dying love.

We insist upon these graces as qualifications for communion, and the profession of them is an intelligent and credible, though not always a satisfactory, profession of faith. We can warn hypocrites, but we cannot exclude them. The king's eye only can infallibly see the unwelcome guest, and he will not fail to put him to shame.[1] Our duty is to set out the awful guilt of this profanation,[2] connected as it often is—not only with utter ignorance and hardness—but with a formal or self-righteous customary attendance, and with the neglect of the exercise of these graces, which alone can realize an acceptable or profitable improvement of the ordinance.

Generally speaking—our instruction should be directed by Philip Henry's admirable rule—so ' to manage it, that the weak may not be discouraged, and yet that the ordinance might not be profaned;'[3] neither raising the standard too high for the humble, contrite, or even scrupulous ; nor lowering it to the generality of a formal profession ; using only the alluring compulsion of evangelical motive.[4]

Our instruction must obviously vary according to the character of the recipient. *To the ignorant,* the spiritual character and the solemn obligations, of the ordinance ; the hypocrisy of uniting in the deep-toned abasement and elevated exercises of our mode of administration ; and most of all, the awful condemnation of unworthy participation, are subjects of direct and awakening conviction. For how affecting is the consideration, that the "table" of the Lord (to accommodate the prophetic imprecation) will " become a snare before them, and that, which should have been for their welfare, will become a trap !"[5] *To those who wish to commence their attendance in this unsatisfactory* state, we should strongly recommend delay, with much self-enquiry and earnest prayer for Christian sincerity and Divine illumination. *Many persons in a state of conviction* regard this ordinance as an end—rather than as a means to an end—they put it in the place of Christ, instead of using it as a means of coming to Christ. They have a strong impulse to come to the ordinance, but without any intelligent perception of its meaning. They must be taught, that the sacrament is not life, but food to support life ; food, which nourishes the living,

---

[1] Matt. xxii. 11—13.   [2] 1 Cor. xi. 27—29.   [3] Life, p. 43.
[4] Luke xiv. 23. The exclusion of the ungodly, under every form, from this ordinance, seems to be directly implied, if not commanded—Ezek. xliv. 6—9. Comp. 1 Cor. x. 16 —21, also Ex. xii. 43, 48.   [5] Psalm lxix. 22.

but cannot quicken the dead.   Christ—not the ordinance—is life. *Faith in him—not in the means—*will ensure acceptance.   *To the sincere, but scrupulous,* we must shew, that there is the sin of unbelief as well as of presumption—sin in refusing to come, as well as in coming unworthily—the guilt of disobedience to the dying command of our best and dearest friend—the neglect of the privilege of a heavenly feast, of an open confession of the cross, and of brotherly communion with the followers of Christ.   The early stage of awakened tenderness and concern needs special instruction and encouragement.   The weakest disciple has an equal right to this ordinance with the most established.   Perfect assurance is not required ; rather the want of it is supposed.   The seal is given in confirmation of what was before a matter of doubt.   Let *the solemnity* of the ordinance enforce preparation, and *its simplicity,* encourage faith ; and so let him come with humility and reverence ; and who can doubt of his acceptance ?[1]

The Sacrificial character and efficacy of this Ordinance— though supported by some names of note, have in the writer's judgment no warrant from Scripture, which often calls the death of Christ a sacrifice—nowhere the memorial of his death.   Indeed the contrast drawn between the one offering of Calvary, and the continual remembrance and offering of the Jewish sacrifices seems clearly to contravene this view.[2]   The studied substitution of the table for altar in the Sacramental service shews the judgment of our Reformers ; and though they have retained the name of Priest, yet it evidently is in reference to its etymological derivation (Presbyter) which has no connection with sacrificial institution. Her language is in perfect accordance with the original command[3] —' *a perpetual memory* of that his most precious death.'   It is this memorial and representation of the sacrifice, that constitutes its profitable use as a means in the exercise of faith of receiving its inestimable blessings.   We commemorate (as Waterland justly observes) the grand sacrifice, but do not reiterate it—*no, not so much as under symbols.*   ' The whole substance of our Sacrifice, which is frequented of the Church in the Lord's Supper, consisteth in prayer, praise, and in giving of thanks, and in remembering and

---

[1] Mr. Robinson, on one occasion in his early Ministry, being surprised by the ardent and determined wish of a stranger to attend his sacrament, and having in vain recommended delay, at length asked him—'Do you cordially grieve for sin ?   Is your dependence simply upon Christ ?   Is your mind fully bent upon serving God in holiness ?'   The man answering satisfactorily, was desired to listen to the service, to look for Divine direction, and if his heart were still inclined, to come with assurance of welcome.   Strength and consolation were given ; and he went on his way rejoicing.'   Life, pp. 45—47.

[2] Heb. x. 2, 3, 11.

[3] 1 Cor. xi. 25, 26, with Exhortation in the Communion Service.

shewing forth of that Sacrifice offered upon the altar of the cross.'[1] Any other view is a retrograde movement to the bondage of Judaism.

It is important also to view this sacrament in conformity with the true spirit of the dispensation as—Augustine well reminds us— to 'venerate these ordinances, not with carnal bondage, but with spiritual liberty.'[2] To invest the holy table, as some appear to do, with a cloud of awful mystery, is as if we were living under " the covenant that gendereth unto bondage."[3] Whereas we are not come to the dark gloom of the Mount that burned with fire, affrighting the heart even of the holy mediator. We are come to the Mount of light and love—to the joy of communion with our God. Instead of being debarred—as of old—from a near approach, we " have boldness to enter into the holiest."[4] Deeply let us cherish the godly reverence in his service—remembering that " even our God is a consuming fire."[5] But never let us forget that the holy ordinance is a means of acceptance to a rejoicing heart. And if under the dispensation of shadows, much more we, under the sunshine of the joyous gospel should " go unto the altar of God, unto God *our exceeding joy*."[6] To cloud our sunshine is to cramp our privilege, and to palsy our strength.

It is also most important to connect this sacrament with all its high practical obligations—both to our Divine Master, and to his church—*to our Lord*—as the public profession of his name[7]—as the soldier's oath of fidelity and devotedness—*to his Church*, as uniting us in holy brotherhood[8]—one with the body, ready to join in every helpful exercise of love, in all the offices of spiritual relationship[9]—meeting in " his banquetting house," with " the banner of love over us,"[10]—the spirit of this union shedding all its radiance over our daily profession.

Much profitable use may be made of the ordinance previous to express and immediate invitation. Under an early impression, it presents the most full and simple view of the blessed atonement. The palpable exhibition of the sufferings of the Lord is well calculated to deepen spiritual sensibilities, to lead the young Christian to contemplate a positive obligation, to count the cost of the consequent engagements, and to anticipate the enjoyment of its attendant privileges. Sacramental meetings preparatory to the ordinance, form a most interesting Ministry to the Church. The familiar

---

[1] Works vii. 378. Bishop Ridley's Works ut supra, p. 211.
[2] De Doctr. Christ. c. iii. 9.   [3] Gal. iv. 24—26.   [4] Heb. xii. 18—24, with x. 19.
[5] Ib. xii. 28, 29.   [6] Ps. xliii. 4.   [7] 1 Cor. xi. 26.
[8] Ib. x. 16, 17.   [9] Ib. xii. 25.   [10] Can. ii. 4.

exposition of the institution, or of subjects connected with it,[1] makes these meetings specially valuable for Catechumens, as a medium of conveying intelligent as well as tender impressions, and thus removing much perplexing hindrance to " the discerning of the Lord's body." Individual instruction also is of great service in restoring the sacrament to its high dignity among Christian ordinances, and thus of instrumentally " adding to the Church such as should be saved."

The more deeply we consider the Sacramental Ministry, the stronger is our conviction of its great moment upon our whole work. A full, free, and Scriptural exposition conduces much to the fruitfulness and establishment of our people. But divest our system of its pure simplicity—it loses its Christian character and solid usefulness. It ministers to self-righteousness, not to self-abasement —" to bodily exercise"—not to evangelical godliness. It exalts ordinances—not Christ ; the Church—not his glorious Head. There can be no life in our Ministrations, if Christ be not the Sun of our system. The dim cloudy glimpse of light which we catch through the reflection of the Church is but a feeble compensation for the loss of the invigorating glow of his direct rays. Let us honour our Divine Saviour fully, and largely will he honour us.

CHAPTER VI.

CLERICAL AND CHURCH COMMUNION.

" THE communion of saints" is a high and holy privilege, without which the body of Christ—if it exists—cannot thrive. The extension therefore of the spirit by which it is maintained, is a

---

[1] In this view the Bishop of Winchester has recommended them. Charge, pp. 42, 43. Short and *applicatory illustrations of the Communion service*, will give the most intelligent view, both of the ordinance, and of its mode of administration, the want of which is often found a serious hindrance to edification. The *grand subject of Christ crucified* naturally leads us to explain the nature of the ordinance, the qualifications of worthy participants, both to awaken conviction upon the sin of unworthy receiving, and to grapple with the various perplexing scrupulosities of the young Christian. See 1 Cor. xi. 23—32. More generally the *great doctrines connected with the knowledge of Christ;* such as—union with him, the free offer of his salvation, the blessings and practical obligations flowing from it —these are in the spirit of our Lord's discourses and prayer connected with the ordinance (John xiv—xvi.) and will draw forth the sacramental graces of faith and love, for the conviction of the professor, and the excitement of the believer to more habitual and elevated devotedness. Matthew Henry's well-known and excellent work on the Sacrament will suggest a considerable variety of subject for these edifying meetings. An interesting account of them, and of a general system of instruction relative to the Lord's supper, is given in Rev. Dr. Bedell's Life, pp. 98—106.

grand means of spiritual prosperity to the Church. As it consists, and becomes " effectual, by that which every joint supplieth"[1]—by the links which connect every Member and Minister with his own society, the same means and materials are at hand for all circumstances. Shall we not find, that, a close union with our great Head, and a more connected harmony among the several members, would produce a larger supply of spiritual gifts and grace : and effect the salvation of the Church in God's own way, by uniting the several members as one body, and making each a medium for the communication of Divine life to the rest ?

We shall consider this subject in reference to ourselves and our people.

I.—CLERICAL COMMUNION.

DOCTRINAL differences have greatly marred our brotherly communion. Even the grand uniting doctrine of the expectancy of our Lord's coming has set brother against brother, when uncertain speculations have diverted the mind from the heavenly glory of the event.[2] Great indeed are the advantages of Ministerial fellowship —such as elucidation of practical difficulties—instruction in the different cases of Christian experience—the correctings of the errors of our own inexperience—obtaining more enlarged views of Scriptural doctrine—communication of Ministerial plans and successful experiments—encouragement of brotherly sympathy, and general interchange of kindly intercourse—mutual excitement to increased exertion—directing a combined effort to any weak or threatened quarter of the church, or to any newly-formed object for the promotion of our Master's kingdom. Yet we must in this fellowship carefully consider the best means for profit—such as meeting in the spirit of prayer, and under a sense of our responsibility—avoiding doubtful disputations—drawing with most interest to those subjects, that more directly lead to Christ—and keeping our main object in view in our social intercourse. Stated Clerical Meetings upon these principles are most edifying. The routine however generally needs to be wisely regulated ; disciplined, not fettered. They should embrace the two grand divisions of our work—the Pulpit and the Pastoral Ministry—treated in separate

---

[1] Eph. iv. 15, 16.

[2] Had all the discussions on this subject been conducted in the spirit of Mr. Stewart's Sermons on the Advent, what a glow of Christian love and heavenly anticipation would have pervaded the church! But would ' brethren grudge one against another' on account of the time and circumstantials of the event, did they *really believe*—"Behold the judge standeth before the door ?" James v. 9.

exercises—the former generally filling up the more regular discussions—the other drawing out supplemental and more free communication.   Each member shall be expected to give in rotation the result of matured consideration of the proposed subject—*extempore in form (if he pleases), but deliberate in substance.*   Collateral points, naturally arising out of the treatment of the subject, had better be reserved under the direction of the chairman for the close of the meeting, in order to restrain desultory discussion, and to give each member the full opportunity of delivering his own sentiments. Meetings of a holy and pastoral character—thus prudently conducted, would naturally both open and close in the spirit of Eliot's suggestion to his brethren on a similar occasion—' The Lord Jesus takes much notice of what is done and said among his Ministers, when they are together.   Come, let us pray before we part.'[1]   Massillon characterizes such meetings as ' those holy assemblies, so calculated to maintain a sacerdotal union among the Ministers, a sacred harmony, in order to animate us individually to the uniform observance of the duties of the Ministry of the Church, and a support in order to clear up, or remove the doubts, or obviate the difficulties of it.[2]   Such were Archbishop Grindal's ' preaching exercises,' which Lord Bacon pronounced ' to be the best way to frame and train up preachers to handle the word of God as it ought to be handled, that hath been practised.[3]   Upon the whole—we may

[1] Mather's Life of Eliot.

[2] Charges, pp. 224, 225.   The meetings to which he alludes were held in some religious house, called the Retreat, and the time devoted to meditation, prayer, exposition of Scripture, and mutual conference.   In taking his leave of Massillon, the Writer has been much affected to observe his impressive and awakening truths often connected with most erroneous statements, or with a total deficiency of Christian doctrine.

[3] Full particulars are given in Strype and Fuller.   They seem to have consisted of meetings of Clergy within large districts, under the presidency of some experienced Minister, to discuss seriatim passages of Scripture previously proposed—always commencing and ending with prayer.   Lord Bacon (Treatise concerning the Church) recommends their adoption in the Universities.   Queen Elizabeth, influenced by her favourite, the Earl of Leicester, put them down by an arbitrary enactment, and in opposition to a most noble and Christian protest from Archbishop Grindal.   They were, however, partially revived in the next reign by the connivance or encouragement of Archbishop Matthew.   Archbishop Tenison enlarged and improved the design.   His circular letter, April 6, 1699, (quoted by Dr. Woodward—account of Religious Societies, ch. iv.) gives the following excellent advice.   ' It were to be wished, that the Clergy of every neighbourhood would agree upon frequent meetings to consult for the good of religion in general, and to advise with one another about any difficulties that may happen in their particular cures—as, ' By what methods any evil custom may most readily be broken ?   How a sinner may most effectually be reclaimed ?   And in general, how each of them in their several circumstances may contribute most to the advancement of religion ?   ' Such consultations as these, besides the mutual benefit of advice and instruction, will be a mutual means to excite the zeal of some, and reduce the over-eagerness of others to a due temper, and to provoke all to a religious emulation in the improvement of piety and order within their respective parishes.'   Bishop Burnet (Past. Care, ch. viii.) and in our own time Bishop Burgess have sanctioned these meetings.   Herman of Cologne had combined Archbishops Grindal's and Tenison's plans in his system of Reformation.   See his work, ut supra, fol. 273. Would not periodical or occasional meetings of Christian Ministers for social prayer *ex-*

conclude, that Ministerial union in confidence, counsel, prayer, and service, by every practicable means, will always operate with most beneficial energy upon our work.

II.—CHURCH COMMUNION.

THE Scriptural idea of the Church is that of one body animated by one soul in the fellowship of the Gospel.[1] Its strength lies in the union of its members. This union naturally embraces the whole body of Christ with affectionate interest and constant prayer. Its more definite sphere will be the distinct community, of which the Christian is a member. The means of promoting it among our people, are of diversified, though sometimes of difficult, application.

One point of great delicacy and importance is to *set forth the unscriptural principles of separation.* No supposition is more harassing to the conscience, than that of a complete Ecclesiastical model given in the New Testament. A Christian finds a want of precise Scriptural authority for certain canons of his Church. He joins therefore some other body, *on the first aspect* more exactly conformable to the sacred rule. He soon discovers a similar defect in his new system. He looks in vain for a pure and perfect model among the different communities of the visible body; and, after wearying himself with fruitless labour, he is driven at last to form a Church after his own mind—to become a Church to himself. The New Testament gives indeed the general principles of a Church; but nowhere (as in the case of the tabernacle[2]) its minute points of detail. No communion therefore can be formed upon the exclusive basis of the letter of Scripture; because no Church can produce Divine authority for every precept. In fact, we leave the print of our fingers upon every thing we touch—upon those institutions, which are essentially founded upon a sound basis. The " Jerusalem which is above—the Mother of us all"—is the only " Church, not having spot, or wrinkle, or any such thing."[3] It is therefore the mark of a restless theorist, rather than of sober practical wisdom, to insist upon a perfection, unwarranted by Scripture, and manifestly inconsistent with the character of the present dis-

clusively, and with a special reference to the outpouring of the Spirit, command a blessing upon their work? Matt. xviii. 19, 20.

[1] See Acts ii. 41—47; iv. 32. It was one of Pastor Oberlin's questions to his parishioners, ' Do you so love and reverence our Lord and Saviour Jésus Christ, as to feel united in the bonds of Christian fellowship with that flock, of which he is the Pastor?' See his Life.

[2] Heb. viii. 5.   [3] Gal. iv. 29. Eph. v. 27.

pensation. To separate therefore from a Church, *in the main Scriptural*, on account of adhering corruptions—is *true schism*—contrary to the example and inculcations of Christ[1]—a rent in his mystical body; connected—if at all with conscience—yet with a scrupulous, rather than with an enlightened conscience: and grounded upon self-will and self-conceit, rather than upon forbearance, humility, and love.[2] Equally wrong is it to make a movement on the ground of expediency, or some problematic theory of usefulness. If it be lawful to remain, it must be sinful to depart. Scripture insists upon the necessity of union. Schisms are justly numbered among the works of the flesh ;[3] obedience to ministers is strongly inculcated,[4] together with the awful guilt of slighting or neglecting them ;[5] and a solemn mark is set upon those, who, in the indulgence of the flesh, seek a name and party for themselves, instead of " forbearing one another in love" to win souls to Christ.[6] And yet the vague apprehensions upon the question of church-membership and union, give a strong advantage to the separatist, and makes it important to compact the spiritual body, as well as to instruct the several members. 1 Cor. xii. clearly marks the fixed office of every member of the body, and their connexion and dependence, both with each other, and with their common Head. The subsequent chapter shews " the more excellent way of the bond

---

[1] John x. 23, with Matt. xxiii. 1—3. Our Lord never sanctioned, much less directed, separation from the Apocalyptic Churches, though defaced with serious, and *even tolerated*, corruption. Rev. ii. 13—15, 20.

[2] Admitting that conscience is concerned—is no regard due to the consciences (possibly equally intelligent) of our brethren, and to the unity of the Church? If every point of difference *remotely connected with conscience* must be made a ground of separation, what room exists for the exercise of Christian forbearance? Besides, 'it is far from sufficient in all cases to act upon conscience—having professed to commit the matter to God. Has the individual who professes to be following his conscience, taken due care to clear it from morbid scrupulosity, and to inform it upon the full and practical principles of the word of God? Has he improved all the resources within his reach of obtaining satisfactory light upon his perplexities? Has he been conversant with those—whether the living or the dead—who have pondered over these difficulties with greater advantages than himself, and who have communicated, or are ready to communicate, their results for the benefit of their sensitive and exercised brethren? Has he duly considered the responsibility of secession—an influence reaching far beyond himself, in the rending of the body of Christ, and the unsettlement of many sincere and godly minds? Without much preparatory painful exercise, this course carries with it the mark of impulse—morbid temperament—precipitation—sometimes we fear of disappointment, self-will, self-conceit, with but a small portion of mental furniture, self-discipline, or forbearance. Hence, what seemed at the crisis to be obedience " to the heavenly vision," ultimately proves, when repentance comes too late for amendment, to have been an evil moment of the tempter's advantage to contract or paralyze ministerial efficiency, and to canker the principles of Christian peace, consistency, and establishment. It would be well to remember that as much care and responsibility is due to give intelligence to the conscience, as to preserve its tenderness: else its very tenderness will degenerate into scrupulosity, and become the source of serious evil both to the individual and to the church.' Author's Preface to Life of M. Boos, pp. xv. xvi.

[3] Gal. v. 20. Gr. with 1 Cor. iii. 1—3. Jude 19.   [4] 1 Thess. v. 13. Heb. xiii. 17.
[5] Luke x. 16.   [6] Rom. xvi. 17, 18.

of perfectness." The connexion of the two chapters teaches us to combine decision in fundamentals, with forbearance in non-essentials—the true spirit of that Church union, which is a grand subject of our Lord's intercession, and a chief means of conviction to the world.[1]

Faith and love are the two primary principles of Church communion and Christian stedfastness—the one drawing us all to a common centre—the other uniting us with each other[2]—like the magnet, bringing the several particles to each other, by attracting them to itself. With more definite bearing upon present circumstances—we would recommend *the inculcation of practical religion* in meekness, humility, and self-denial. This will silently operate, if not in active opposition, yet in impeding the progress of the evil. It is the practical exercise of our principles, which "maketh increase of the body to the edifying of itself in love."[3]

Popular expositions of our services may be suggested—'not with a view to extol them immoderately, much less to provoke wrath against those who dissent from us; but mildly to answer unjust imputations upon our Liturgy: and chiefly to show the meaning, the reasons, the uses of each part, that the congregation may, as the Apostle expresses it, "pray with the understanding."[4] The unmeaning cry—" The temple of the Lord are we"[5]—excites the ridicule of enemies, without bringing conviction to our friends; but illustrations of the spiritual character, ordinances, and worship of the Establishment, furnish a sound warrant for enforcing a steady adherence to her communion. Such a course of liturgical exposition would produce a style of religion clothed in the beautiful costume of the Church—an exquisite pattern of Scriptural simplicity, holiness and consistency. It may be doubted, whether the obligations to instruct our people in and through our Church ordinances is sufficiently considered. Yet how much might be effected for their settled unity, by expounding their admirable adaptation for their respective ends, by marking the identity of their language with the Bible, thus framing Churchmen and Christians by the same process in the same mould! A more full recognition of our fasts, festivals, and commemorative seasons, would be an edifying means of grace. For this or some collateral purpose, the weekly lecture might often be made available. Such a Ministry would disqualify our people for Dissent, and make the attempt to force it upon them an act of

[1] See John xvii. 21.   [2] See Col. ii. 1, 2.   [3] Eph. iv. 16.
[4] Secker's Charges, pp. 293, 294. For most exquisite specimens of this exposition—see Life of Geo. Herbert. Life of Rev. S. Walker, ch. v. vi.
[5] Jer. vii. 4.

unsuccessful violence.   Whereas a course of instruction, equally appropriate to the Meeting as to the Church—though not necessarily unsound—is yet defective.   Our fold—having no church-barrier, is exposed to the inroads of all kinds of separatists.   Our sheep, having no private mark, are easily withdrawn from "the footsteps of the flock."[1]

Let our *mode of administration also be dignified with the consciousness of our high employment.*   Let it be marked by a solemn, intelligent, devotional reading of our services ; fixing on them all the interests of our mind, and throwing into them all the exercise of our hearts.   Who does not feel the difference between reading, and praying, the prayers ?   Often from organic deficiencies, or from moral causes, we see the Liturgy of our church lying under the feet of one, who is unconsciously treading upon pearls. A good understanding, correct taste, and most of all a prayerful spirit, is needed to do it justice.   The form then, enlivened by heavenly unction, ceases to be mere form ; our congregations not only hear, but with edification ; they are enabled not *only to attend* to the service, but also *to unite in it.*

Frequent communion at the Lord's table tends much to unite our people together in the constant remembrance, that they, " being many, are one body and one bread, and partakers of that one bread ;"[2] and therefore are bound to each other by the most endearing engagements.   Sacramental meetings strengthen this bond ; embracing (as in all intelligent Christian congregations they ought to do) the main objects of Church communion ; uniting in prayer for our personal progress in the Divine life—for our families, unconverted friends, or Christian friends in affliction—for our congregations, in their different states of ignorance, indifference, or of awakening interest, and consistent profession and enjoyment of the gospel—for our immediate neighbourhoods—for the general spread of the kingdom of Christ throughout the world—and for a holy and joyful anticipation of his second coming.   These social meetings embody the exercise of church unity, in its most spiritual, enlivening, and practical operations.   As an appendage, stated meetings for united, though separate, prayer for the prosperity of the

   [1] 'The result of Church principles being kept out of the view of our congregations is— that many members of our church have no distinct consciousness of the church to which they belong.   They lose all the benefit of church-union, church-spmpathy, church-discipline.   They are isolated and independent beings, instead of parts of a body, linked in a holy partnership with fellow-pilgrims, "every one members one of another."   Their hearts are not "comforted, being knit together in love."' Bishop of Winchester's Charge, 1837.   Robert's Call to the Church, p. 52.   Some admirable remarks from Bishops Spratt and Bull on this subject, may be found in the Clergyman's Instructor, pp. 246, 309.
   [2] 1 Cor. x. 17.

church, and special remembrance of afflicted members, have a strong cementing influence.[1]

The *full preaching of the Gospel* is however the grand cementing bond. Many dissent, not from choice, but *from what appears to them* to be necessity. It is a sharp trial to the sincere but unintelligent Churchman, should he mark more holiness of doctrine or life in dissenting communities than in his own sphere. Nor will the strongest arguments against separation have any force against his appetite for Christian instruction, or convince him that he is wrong in seeking out of his church what he sometimes may fail to find within. Efficiency and purity of Ministry are therefore a . main barrier against schism. 'Feed your people better, and they will not stray'—was a Nonconformist's reply to the complaint of a neighbouring Minister, that he had drawn away his people.[2] The enemy indeed is too successful, even in the most Scriptural churches, in "beguiling unstable souls from the simplicity that is in Christ;" yet the standard of the Gospel is a wall of defence against any material injury.

We may say of our candid and orthodox Dissenters,—"Give them of the fruit of their hands, and let their own works praise them in the gates."[3] Admitting them however to be conscientious, we are not bound to hold them to be right; nor must we compromise with them important differences, *because they are not fundamental.* We would not deny the work of God among them. But we do not by this admission accredit their authority. "Send, I pray thee, by the hand of him whom thou wilt send."[4] Our Lord did not *forbid* the man who was casting out devils, but he evidently had not given to him—*as he had to his apostles*—a commission for this work.[5] And thus, though *as a Sovereign* he may employ his own instruments according to his own will, yet this does not deteriorate the weight or value of that transmitted commission, which, *as the Head of his Church*, he has ordained and delegated with his special authority and promise.[6] We would not therefore

---

[1] See Author's Pastoral Address upon united prayer. (Seeleys.)

[2] Eloquence may dazzle, and argument may compel the homage of its intellectual admirers; but it is only, if armed with the panoply of Scriptural truth, that there will *gather and adhere* to the preacher a people, who hunger for the bread of Life, and make a business of their eternity. To *fill the church well, we must fill the pulpit well.*' Chalmers' Sermons at St. John's Church, Glasgow, p. 392.

[3] Prov. xxxi. 31. Some admirable views may be found in Burnet's Preface to Pastoral Care. 'Recollect that it is possible to defend your own fort, without storming another's battery. Maintain by Scriptural argument your own principles and practices with modest confidence—but rail not; insinuate no reflection on your opponents; name them not, unless with respect.' Such was the wise advice of a truly Christian Non-conformist to his pupil. Jay's Life of Winter. [4] Ex. iv. 13.

[5] Mark ix. 38—40, with Matt. x. 5—8.   [6] Matt. xxviii. 16—20. 2 Tim. ii. 2.

lower the just claims of an accredited Ministry in comparison of one, whose credentials do not appear—to our perception at least— equally warranted. Yet we would be careful to combine the decision of our own standard, with a forbearing consideration of others. And should we be constrained to *oppose them as Dissenters,* we would *cease not to love and pray for those among them,* whom (whatever be their prejudices or misconceptions) we cordially believe to be *true servants of Christ.* It is best to combine with hearty good-will to other communions[1] a strict adherence to our own pale, and a diligent and thankful improvement of its privileges. Some indeed, as a proof of their expansive love, or rather latitudinarian indifference, would follow all. But this was not the rule of Christ,[2] or of his Apostles ;[3] nor is it recommended by the experience of its own disciples, who are usually found at the extreme point from Christian stedfastness, and distinguished rather by "itching ears," than by teachable hearts :[4] hearing all, and learning from none : driven forward with zeal, but with no judgment to direct their course ; pretending to "prove all things," yet wholly neglecting to "hold fast that which is good."[5]

But the rise and progress of the evil should be a matter of self-inquiry. Baxter exclaims—'O that the Ministry had been more guiltless of those errors and schisms that they talk against ! But it is easier to chide a sectary in the pulpit, and to subscribe a testimony against them, than to play the skilful physician for their cure, and do the tenth part of the duty that lieth upon us, to prevent and heal such calamitous distempers.[6] The tares were sown, *"while men slept."*[7] And might we not ask for our own conviction, whether these victims of delusion had been invited, encouraged and cherished with parental confidence ; and (while we were jealous of our Ministerial prerogative) whether we laid ourselves out to conciliate their affections, and to condescend to their infirmities ? Some indeed, after all, in the heat of their zeal, and the infancy of their understanding, "will turn away their ears from the truth, and be turned unto fables." Concession to their conceits would bring woeful confusion among us. The most forward would become the governors of the church. One step yielded for peace

---

[1] Eph. vi. 24.
[2] See Mark ix. 38—40, ut supra. Though our Lord would not have his disciples *forbid the man,* he did not intimate, that they should leave their own master, and follow him. Comp. Prov. xxvii. 8.
[3] "Order" combined with "stedfastness," formed the beauty of the Church of Colosse, and the Apostle's joy on their account. Col. ii. 5.
[4] 2 Tim. iv. 3, 4.   [5] 1 Thess. v. 21.
[6] Reformed Pastor. Comp. Hos. ix. 8.   [7] Matt. xiii. 25.

would constrain us to advance, to the grievous discredit of our Ministry, the wounding of our conscience, and the dishonour of our Master's name. Baxter well remarks—'A sinful humouring of rash professors is as great a temptation to godly Ministers, as a sinful compliance with the great ones of the world.'[1] Redoubled watchful diligence is the Scriptural rule for these trying circumstances.[2]

But apart from this sectarian spirit—there is often a want of that 'mutual society, help and comfort, that Christians ought to have of each other,' as members of one body ; and which would promote the general interests of the Church, as well as the establishment, consistency, and "joyfulness" of her individual members.[3] Each, in this spirit, would impart to the other the support of brotherly help, counsel, and prayer ; " looking not every man on his own things, but every man also on the things of others ;" "bearing one another's burdens ;" " the strong bearing the infirmities of the weak," and all in their several relations "receiving one another, as Christ also received them, to the glory of God."[4]

The Old Testament saints, as well as the Primitive Christians,[5] diligently improved this fellowship for mutual edification.[6] The distribution of gifts and graces was for this purpose.[7] This mutual commerce (as between different countries) would enable Christians to enrich each other. Seduction and error would be more successfully resisted. If the enemy's watch-word is—' Divide and conquer,'—ours should be—' Union is invincible.' The church is ' terrible'—not in its single members, but " as an army with banners."[8] Brotherly love would be much increased in this system of reciprocal inspection and provocations,[9] by a better knowledge of each other's state, progress, trials, and consolations. The maturity of the experienced would confirm the weak ; each individual would enjoy the advantage of union to the whole body ; and the Minister would have his warmest sympathies awakened, cherished, and enlarged by this fresh medium of acquainting himself with the spiritual state of the members.

Most important is the cultivation of suitable graces for this mutual fellowship ; such as sobriety of judgment ; lowliness of mind ; readiness to acknowledge each other's gifts and graces ; forbearance and encouragement to the young ; godly plainness and sincerity ;

---

[1] Cure of Church Divisions, p. 394. Some valuable remarks will be found on this subject in Cecil's Life of Cadogan. [2] 2 Tim. iv. 4, 5.
[3] Union of spirit was the apostle's great desire for the church of Colosse, as the means of their spiritual consolation. Col. ii. 1, 2.
[4] Phil. ii. 4. Rom. xv. 1, 7. [5] See Psalm xxxiv. 2, 3. Psalm lxvi. 16. Mal. iii. 16.
[6] See Acts ii. 42, 45. [7] See 1 Pet. iv. 10. 1 Cor. xii. 7.
[8] Cant. vi. 10. [9] See Heb. x. 24.

a careful guard against a censorious or controversial spirit : and anxiety to impart only what will advance true knowledge, holiness, and love.

Yet even in the age of primitive simplicity, a harvest of tares sprung up, where better seed had been sown. " Spots there were in their feasts of charity,"[1] which made it too evident, that they " came together, not for the better, but for the worse." The recollection of this abuse even in the best times, recommends the balance of Ministerial superintendence, to maintain godliness in connexion with due order, and to preserve brotherly love and unity on the solid basis of genuine humility. Mr. Robinson decidedly discountenanced the principle of unrestrained communion in his extensive sphere ; and ultimately relinquished the plan of mutual conference, as being *under his circumstances* unnecessary and injudicious.[2]

But after all, our want of Church communion operates as unfavourably upon the mass, as the want of Christian communion upon individuals. It affords also plausible ground for separation. The social stimulus of pastoral and fraternal meetings in Dissenting bodies is a strong principle of excitement. An awakened enquirer is too timid to apply to his Minister. Here he is taken by the hand, as if to be " instructed in the way of God more perfectly." He joins their communion, and is lost to the Church. In our body there is too often a want of what Dr. Owen justly calls ' charitative episcopacy'[3]—that kindly oversight, which obtained among the Primitive Christians.   There is nothing to compact the several parts together ; to give strength to the weaker joints, to gather out the spiritual from the visible Church ; and to unite the spiritual members together, so that they might (like Jonathan and David in the wood) " strengthen each other's hands in God"[4] And therefore the entrance of any irregular or unscriptural excitement proves a sifting time, drawing away the weak and unstable from us. To the system of dissenting communion, we feel decided—though not uncharitable—objections. It seems to forget—that the Minister— not some officer of the church—" is the messenger of the Lord of Hosts,"—that *his* lips must keep knowledge, and at his mouth they should seek the law."[5] As " the communion of saints" is the reciprocal intercourse of the body under the influence of their Great Head : so is Church communion the interchange of sympathy

---

[1] Jude 12.
[2] Vaughan's Life of Robinson, pp. 85—88. Compare also Scott's Life, pp. 494—498.
[3] επισκοπουντες. Heb. xii. 15. Hence επισκοπος.
[4] 1 Sam. xxiii. 16.   [5] Mal. ii. 7.

among the several members, under the direction, more or less immediate, of him, who stands to them in the place of their head.
But why should we not gather, under our affectionate superintendence, assemblies of our people, ready and willing to learn of one another, to exhort one another, and to lift up one another's hands in
humility and love? The test of admission should be—not doctrinal knowledge, gifted or sounding profession, or fervid zeal—but
(so far as they can be ascertained) "simplicity and godly sincerity"
of heart and conduct. Circumstances would regulate these meetings within due restraint, yet so as to encourage unreserved communication. The members might propose any subject for consideration, or ask any question concerning Scriptural difficulties, the worship of God, their own experience, their family trials, their duties to
their relations and neighbours, books to read—and in short how
they may best advance the work of God in their own souls, and in
those around them. In small parties, the plan might profitably
combine the formality of a religious service with somewhat of a
conversational mould.[1] Perhaps however the discussion will be
best directed rather to Scriptural subjects than personal experience.
Experience may be delusive. Scripture is solid substance. The
one belongs to us—the other more generally to God and his
Church. While therefore conversation on the latter will always
be profitable—discussions on the former—*unless wisely introduced
and controuled*—may be injurious alike to speakers and hearers.
Generally speaking, such matters belong rather to Christian confidence, or secret communion with God, than to meetings of a
larger and diversified temperament.

Selection, however, in these meetings is of much importance. It
elevates the tone of religion in our parishes, by exhibiting the broad

[1] When the Writer first offered this suggestion, he was not aware, that it was a
Puritan practice. According to their plan—The question was given out, and answers
were required; from whence arose a free and unreserved conversation; in the course of
which the Minister would help, as he saw occasion; restraining the parties in the path
of the discussion from encroaching upon his office. At the conclusion of the conference,
he gathered in their scattered sentiments, confirmed and applied them by suitable Scriptures and remarks. See Life of Mr. T. Wilson in Clark's Lives, Vol. iii. p. 33. His
own Life, prefixed, states the advantages of these meetings. Pref. 4, 5. Interesting
specimens may also be seen in Philip Henry's Life, pp. 41, 42, 349—351. His excellent
son introduced them also into his congregation, for the use of his young people, himself
always presiding. He appears to have had a similar but less restricted meeting among
the older members of his Church. One of his prayers before the sacrament proved his
interest in these meetings—'That which I desire particularly to receive from the Lord at
his table to-morrow, is wisdom for personal conference about matters of religion.' Life,
pp. 134, 135. Mather also gives an interesting sketch—Essays to do Good, pp. 87—91.
Baxter remarks the necessity of social meetings to preserve unity among our people; but
seems to insist on the necessity of Ministerial controul. Reformed Pastor. Where,
however, these meetings cannot be systematically held, occasional gatherings of our Church,
as circumstances might suggest, for special prayer and exhortation, would strengthen the
mutual bond.

line of separation between the Church and the world.   The exclusion also of unworthy members shuts out a large mass of inconsistency, which would be readily transferred to the collective body; while the union with those, whom in judgment as well as in charity we acknowledge as brethren, spreads a truly delightful atmosphere of love and sacredness over the assemblies.   Such Societies are well calculated to enlarge our interest in the sympathies and prayers of our people.   Nor will they be less profitable to the several members, as a bond of union and wholesome restraint : exciting them to watch over each other with brotherly love, and over themselves " with godly jealousy," recollecting the responsibility of their character before the Church and the world, as members of a Christian body.   Yet if a society, so fenced in, be thought to endanger the humility of its members on one side, and their charity on the other ; the same system might substantially, *and less offensively*, be formed upon the principles of more open communion. A general invitation to our communicants would exclude no credible professor.   Yet the spiritual character of these meetings will generally preclude the attendance of unspiritual professors ; while their non-attendance will be self-exclusion, and consequently without any plausible ground of offence.   And even the few, who might intrude to preserve their name in the church, though they will partially interrupt harmony and confidence, yet may hear much for their personal conviction, their forwardness being repressed by firm and judicious restraint.   The more *spiritual and practical*, however the tone of these meetings, the less will they accord with their taste, and the more speedily will it hasten their retirement.

Mr. Walker of Truro organized Societies for Church communion, after Dr. Woodward's pattern, upon this principle of fostering controul, with admirable wisdom and effectiveness.[1]   The objects however

[1] Mr. Walker's object was, to excite among the serious members of his congregation a particular interest in each other's spiritual welfare; that they should watch over each other, exhort, reprove, encourage, as brethren and sisters in the faith of the Gospel.   He formed a weekly meeting of communicants, of tried religious profession ; separated into two classes; one of unmarried men; another of married men with their wives, and other females of the Society.   They met alternately every other week.—The whole society was under his own superintendence as Director—regulating all their business (such as the admission and exclusion of members; making new rules, &c.) presiding in the meetings or prescribing for them a form of proceeding, when unavoidably absent.   They began their meeting with a form of prayer, exhortation, and singing.   Connected with this, were smaller assemblies at their own houses in rotation, for more free communion with the same separation of unmarried and married members.   For the direction of these meetings Mr. Walker drew up most admirable regulations.   He described the general objects of these Societies in his first address to be—1. To glorify God. 2. To be quickened and confirmed themselves. 3. To render them more useful among their neighbours.   The members were pledged to faithful mutual superintendence; each to consider himself as "his brother's keeper;" to be bound not to " suffer sin upon each other," nor to allow it

of these associations (details of which are given below) being distinctly spiritual, it was evident that they could be preserved only by the spirituality of the members under the prompt vigilance of

in themselves; to be strictly circumspect in their lives; separate from worldly custom and practices; walking in humility, meekness, heavenly-mindedness, and love; and often considering it as a motive to holiness, that they belonged to a society, whose avowed object was the promotion of the glory of God.

The rules of these Societies were formed upon the true principles of the Gospel. Their strict separation from worldly amusements was inculcated upon the ground of their being disciples of a crucified Saviour. Their watchfulness over each other was directed to spring from watchfulness over their own hearts, lest there should be 'the least decay of love to Christ, or of zeal for his honour and the good of souls there. The obligation and privilege of mutual intercession were inculcated. They were warned against disgust at those, who exercised towards them the duty of Christian faithfulness and love. And the remembrance, that their very fellowship with a Society professedly Christian would tend to foster spiritual pride, suggested strong and repeated exhortations to humility and self-abasement.' See the valuable Life of Mr. Walker, prefixed to his Lectures on the Catechism, pp. xxv.—xlviii. Sidney's Life, chap. iii. Comp. also his excellent Collection of Tracts entitled 'Practical Christianity.' To give this work a practical character, we add a digest of Mr. Walker's rules, simplified for more general application. I. That these meetings be under the direction and superintendence of the Minister present. II. That all the members pray especially for their Minister, and for the Divine blessing on his preaching, and on all the means of grace, as well as on these meetings. III. That, besides these meetings, the members endeavour to meet in smaller numbers as early as possible on Sunday morning, to pray for the special outpouring of the Holy Spirit. IV. That the heads of families adopt family prayer in their own houses; without which no Church unity or Christian love can be expected. V. That they depend solely on the Holy Spirit through the mediation of Christ, to excite, advance, and perfect all good within themselves and others. VI. That they be particularly kind to each other, as fellow-members of the same family, and united to the same Divine head; and that they cultivate the spirit of wisdom, forbearance, and love to Christians, who differ from them in smaller matters; as also to those, who may oppose the Gospel or themselves. VII. That all prying curiosity into their neighbour's affairs be avoided; but that all be encouraged to mention any hopeful sign they may see in them. VIII. That in the spirit of meekness and humility, "each esteeming other better than themselves," they do freely and affectionately warn each other of their faults; and that they be ready also to "confess their faults one to another." IX. That all do consider the solemn responsibility of being communicants at the Lord's table, and earnestly endeavour to "adorn the doctrine of God their Saviour in all things"—in life, temper, and conversation. X. That no conversation passing at these meetings be disclosed elsewhere, except to the members of the Society, who may have been unavoidably absent. XI. That these meetings may answer the intended purpose of Christian fellowship, each member should attend constantly, and be present precisely at the hour of meeting. From the Rules of a religious Society, (which appears to have worked well upon more exclusive principles), we extract the following—chiefly relating to its administration—'That the object of this meeting is to promote a spirit of decided piety in its members, and to unite them closely to each other in Christian affection and fellowship—That the principal means proposed be the singing of a Psalm or Hymn, offering up prayer, and expounding the Scriptures; which two last exercises shall be conducted solely by the Minister. The members shall however severally be at liberty in succession to select the Scripture for exposition at the next meeting—That the member, whose turn it may be to name the subject for the next exposition, shall also be at liberty to put any question for advice in any case, or for information on any subject, whether connected with the individual soul, or with the general cause of God, which question shall be answered after the exposition at the next meeting; and at the close of the meeting, any member may request through the medium of the Minister a special interest in the prayers of the other members, when particular circumstances seem to require it —That in case a member should wish the subject not to be made a topic of conversation elsewhere, it must be introduced as confidential, and the members will be expected not to betray the confidence so reposed in them—That any member wishing to propose a candidate for admission, shall make such proposition privately to the Minister after the meeting is over; when any of the members may also stay for the purpose of consulting him on any private matter, which could not have been introduced with propriety in the presence of the meeting—That, should a member be guilty of any scandalous offence, his name shall be erased from the Register book of the Society at the time of meeting; the

the Director.   Without this constant security the form only would remain.   Yet under Mr. Walker's wise and efficient care, their influence was maintained with much edification in a large sphere, and for many years after his Scriptural doctrines had, unhappily the people, ceased to be delivered from the pulpit.[1]   While the importance of mutual confidence and help cannot be denied ; yet to secure the advantages without the attendant temptations and inlets to evil, is a matter often of most perplexing exercise.   Sound judgment is indeed greatly needed for the management and effective application of this social system.   The junction of Ministerial controul with confidence offers, upon the whole, the best promise of attaining that " Christian communion," which (as a Puritan Minister 'justly remarked) " *keeps our religion in breath, and without which it will be ready to die.*"

CHAPTER VII.

THE OFFICE AND USES OF HELPERS.

It was never intended, that the Minister should sustain the whole weight of the service of God.   Moses was assisted in his work by seventy elders, in tender consideration of his overwhelming responsibility.[2]   And thus the office of " helpers" in the Primitive Church appears to have been of efficient service to the Ministry.[3]   And as one of the most important results of the Pastoral work—the confidence with our people, and our insight into their individual character enable us to employ them in subservient but most valuable labour.   Few exercises however, require more of that " wisdom that is profitable to direct."   The " differences of administration" among us, and the different temperament of the Church from the Primitive times; a spirit of independency; the

Minister notifying it to the other Members—That a member, accused of any inconsistency, which may be grievous to the rest, shall first be admonished by the Minister in private; and, should he persist in the inconsistency, the evil shall be pointed out to the offender in the presence of the meeting; and if no signs of compunction be shown, he must be expelled from the Society.'—Christian Guardian, January, 1830.

[1] Mr. Richmond in his early Ministry established an interesting Church-meeting, mainly, though with less formality, upon these principles.   It included the explanation of the Scriptures, Prayer Book, and other useful books; friendly and Christian exhortation according to their circumstances; questions of Scriptural or experimental difficulties; and united prayer for a blessing upon themselves, their families, their neighbours, their country, and the whole Church of God.   See his Life, pp. 43, 44. note.

[2] See Numbers xi. 10—25.   Comp. also Jethro's wise advice to Moses, Exod. xviii. 13—26.   [3] Rom. xvi. 9, 12.   Phil. iv. 3.

excitement of spiritual pride ; the introduction of the baneful mischief of " many masters ;"[1] and the consequent diminution of the
just influence of the Parochial Head, are serious evils incident to
this system.   But yet, with strict subordination to the Ministry,
and with a large share of humility and forbearance, localized lay-
agency, portioned out according to the " diversities of gifts," might
actively co-operate.

Dr. Chalmers has fully pointed out the relative advantages to
Ministers and people from this subordinate employment of the
laity.[2] If at first it may be more easy to do the work ourselves,
they will ultimately be found in many cases to be more effective
labourers.   The appropriate employment of the members of our
Church is probably, the most profitable use of human agency ; and
from the neglect of it many are often drawn from us, by those,
who unduly avail themselves of their assistance, and elevate them
to an importance, most injurious to Christian simplicity and lowliness.[3]

The various parochial plans will furnish suitable work. Sunday Schools—superintendence of adult schools—the management
or promotion of religious Societies—the diligent and sympathizing
inquiry into the wants of the poor,—the administering to their
temporal, and much more to their spiritual, necessities—the visitation of the sick—these, and similar plans, will give as much engagement for our people, as a conscientious regard to their secular
callings will generally allow.

The responsibility of this work, with a due consideration of
their private circumstances, should be inculcated upon every Christian.   Ministers are the primary—not the exclusive instructors.
They are the principal directors of the system, but not the sole
agents.   Their office is to set many lesser wheels in motion, in
subservient harmony with the grand movements of the machine.

---

[1] James iii. 1.   [2] See his Christian and Civic Œconomy.
[3] Baxter wisely recommends an active and orderly use of the gifts of our people under
our own superintendence, lest they should use them in a way of division against us. He
remarks to Ministers, as one of the causes of schism—'a desire not to make use of the
gifts that God hath given them for their assistance;'—and adds, 'I am persuaded, if Ministers had thus made use of the parts of their ablest members, they might have prevented
much of the divisions, and distractions, and apostacies that hath befallen us: for they
would then have found work enough upon their hands for higher parts than theirs, without invading the Ministry. Experience would have convinced and humbled them more
than our words can do. A man may think that he can stir up a block, or pluck up a
tree by the roots, that never tried; but when he sets his hand to it, he will come off
ashamed. And see that you drive them to diligence in their own works, and let them
know what a sin it is to neglect their own families, and their ignorant miserable neighbours ; and then they will be kept humble, and have no such mind to be running upon
more work, when they feel you spurring them on to their own, and rebuking them for
the neglect; nor will they have any leisure for schismatical enterprizes, because of the
constancy and greatness of their employment.'

Men cannot seek their own edification too fervently : but they may be occupied in it too selfishly. Many appear to have no more concern for the unconverted around them, than if there were no such beings in the world. Or they are content to leave their souls to the superintendence of the Parish Minister, with the same indifference as they leave their bodies to the care of the Parish Apothecary. This inaction is ruinous to themselves no less than to the Church. They seem to forget that they are " called out of darkness into marvellous light," that they might " arise and shine" —that they are bound therefore, to strengthen our hands, not only by the light of their example, but by personal labour and activity. We were destitue of helpers : and God has converted them, that they might be our " helpers in the Lord."[1]

The *individual advantages,* also of this service are of the highest importance. Active devotedness to the wants of our fellow-sinners is one of the best stimulants to personal religion. Thus the additional benefit resulting from the agency renders the employment of helpers more effective than our own exertion. Graces are called into exercise, which otherwise might have been dormant; while their fellowship with our burdens and our privileges, our sorrows and our joys, brings a sensible relief to our work. With this view, and with a due regard to relative duties (which must upon no account be superseded), it is important to bring young Christians to work. They are apt to be absorbed in the new world of interest that surrounds them. They want to be drawn forth into the practical habits of religion—to have their sympathies excited, their sense of obligation deepened, and their view of the realities of the Gospel established, by a close contact with the spiritual distresses and supports of those around them. Some departments indeed demand matured experience, wisdom, and patience— qualities, however, that gather strength and establishment by prayerful diligence. But the simple work of private instruction falls within the sphere of the lowest spiritual capacity ; needing only an acquaintance with the value of the soul—the lost estate of man —the need of a Saviour—the power of his love—the work of his Spirit—the hope of his glory. These, when really felt, will be readily explained—not indeed with eloquence, or perhaps with systematic accuracy ; but yet with that earnestness of simplicity, which characterizes the Gospel, honours God, and is honoured of God. And this active training in the most limited sphere qualifies

[1] See 1 Pet. ii. 9. with Is. lx. 1. Matt. v. 14—16.

the novice for a more extended and defined labour,—"He that is faithful in that which is least, is faithful also in much."[1]

Not less is the advantage also of this system to the Minister himself. It has been well observed—' Lay agency is of incalculable moment. A Minister cannot undertake every thing himself. He must not fritter away his time. He must not widen too much his field of personal effort. He must concentrate, he must influence, he must be the centre to a hundred hands and minds moving around him. This is more especially the case in populous places; where the actual efforts of any one or two Ministers would be lost in detail, and his public instructions would be hasty and undigested effusions, if he attempted individual instruction. Wisdom therefore must be exercised. Others must be set to work, and a machinery be erected, of which he takes only the general guidance.'[2] Indeed how else can a Minister in a wide field of labour acquit his own conscience of the responsible charge of thousands of perishing immortals, except he do *per alium,* what it is impossible that he can do *per se ;* and set in motion a machinery, whose influence, directly emanating from himself, is felt throughout every part? How manifestly unequal is our mere personal strength to make a palpable impression upon the great mass? If we want to extend our aggressive operations, we must bring our whole disposable force into the field. We must not only discharge ourselves the functions of agency ; but we must create an agency under wise, delicate, confidential·control. We must wield the power of our people, or we shall soon exhaust our own strength. The Minister must indeed use the word of command, and take the lead. But he must not be taking all the offices of the army upon himself. He must drill his subalterns into regimental discipline and effective service. And if in some cases activity becomes bustle—forwardness—conceit—neglect of personal or relative obligations ; he must be careful in controling the pruriency of the principle, not to check its healthful circulation. When all are alive and always at work—the Minister in devising, and the Church in executing plans of usefulness—the machinery will germinate an influence of indefinite extent and effectiveness.

There are few Christian congregations in a large sphere, but would afford an organized system of Helpers, to "supply" the Min-

---

[1] Luke xvi. 10.

[2] Prefatory Essay to Baxter's Reformed Pastor, by the Bishop of Calcutta, p. xliv. For a clear, important, and practical statement upon this interesting subject—the Writer would refer to the Bishop of Chester's Primary Charge (pp. 21—26) and to his Sermon before the Pastoral Aid Society—a Society, which commends itself powerfully to the prayers and assistance of all the true friends of our Church.

ister's necessary "lack of service on behalf of" his people. Let him only impress their minds with the love of Christ, and the love of souls, as the principles of their personal responsibility. Let him suggest the most suitable exercise of their obligations. Let him from time to time direct, encourage, or control their operations. Let him excite them to take only one step towards the attainment of their object—to spread, if it were only a luminous spot, over their several districts—to be in constant motion, in the routine of regular distributiveness; and they will become his most useful coadjutors. The system of Tract distribution under the Pastor's superintendence, has been found an important means of evangelizing many dark places of our land. Monthly or Quarterly Meetings for prayer and conference should however be appended to this system.[1]

[1] The System of District Societies is working under the sanction of our Hierarchy in some of our large spheres. It is the most likely means of diffusing instruction among masses of immortal beings, that could not otherwise be reached. The nucleus of the system is a Christian congregation, and the strength of it—Christian Visitors, well-exercised in all its duties of patience, compassion, and self-denial. The London Society has entered upon the work with an organized system of operation, and with admirable perseverance. They thus forcibly state their case, in language of extensive application—
'Some parishes have gradually become so thickly peopled, that an acquaintance, either personal or through the medium of his clerical assistants, with the majority of his parishioners, is beyond the reach of the most active and laborious incumbent. With the utmost zeal on his part, thousands may yet be left comparatively to themselves, without even the moral restraint, which in a smaller parish the frequent intercourse between the clergyman and his people often imposes on the most careless and unconcerned. Extensive districts are to be found, where a mass of ignorance, vice, and superstition, is untouched, or nearly so, by the ordinary and prescribed means of preventing '*error in re-ligion and viciousness in life.*' Their inhabitants live in the undisturbed practice of ungodliness, by the force of mutual example confirming each other in the disregard of every religious duty. Places of worship are unfrequented by them. They will not go in search of the means of spiritual instruction, these means must be brought home to them. If an impression is to be made, they must be invited, nay, "compelled" to attend to their eternal interests, by the earnest, persevering, long-suffering labours of individuals, willing to penetrate the abodes of misery and vice, to go from door to door, and to encounter frequent disappointment in their benevolent object.'
'The appointment of Visitors' (as the London Committee judiciously observe) 'is of the highest moment; they may be obtained from every rank of society, and many of them will be Members of Local Committees. It is however essential, that they should be impressed with the importance of eternity—persons who earnestly desire, that their fellow creatures may walk in a right course, and who will interest themselves, not only in the relief of the body, but in the spiritual welfare of those whom they undertake to visit.
'In order that they may have time for the performance of such serious duties, care should be taken not to devolve too much upon one individual; in general from twenty to thirty families will be found sufficient for the most active Visitor! and for female Visitors a number still more limited may often be desirable. If however two Visitors act together (a course which will frequently be found expedient, particularly in their early labours) a large section may be allotted them.
'But there is no point, which the Central Committee would more strongly urge on Local Committees, than that of confining their own and their Visitors' exertions within a practicable compass; a small space effectively visited is infinitely preferable (whether in reference to the good that is really done, or to the example which it affords) to a large district, only partially occupied.'
Their instructions to the Visitors are most admirable—'You will visit the families comprehended in your section, as often as time and other circumstances may render expedient, with the view of promoting their temporal and spiritual improvement.—You will make it your first object to gain their attention, and secure their confidence, by convin-

One valuable use of this office is to discover cases of religious impression in the several districts, and to encourage free communication with the Minister, gladly introducing them, as Barnabas,

cing them, that you are actuated solely by motives of Christian charity and kindness, and have no other end in view than their welfare.—Many topics of friendly conversation and enquiry will readily suggest themselves to you; and in the selection of these, much will depend on your own good sense and discretion.'

'The Committee, however, would suggest the following hints:—

1. Your first enquiries should relate to those subjects, which afford the greatest interest to the poor; such as the number of which the family consists—the ages of the children—whether they attend any school, or can read—whether the family possesses a Bible or any other religious books; and, where you find a disposition to answer your inquiries, you will endeavour to ascertain whether the persons you visit attend Public Worship, and where—their occupation—means of subsistence—whether by parochial relief, by labour, charity, or otherwise—the period of their residence in the district—amount of rent paid—and manner of spending Sundays and leisure hours.—2. You will gently and prudently lead their attention to religious subjects, endeavouring to impress their minds with a sense of the importance of their immortal souls and of the value of the Holy Scriptures as a message of mercy from God to sinful man. You will urge on them the duty and privilege of observing the Sabbath, of prayer, and of attending Public Worship. You will point out to them, as occasion may require, their relative duties; and avail yourself of suitable opportunities of reproving open vice. You will pay particular attention to the young, the sick, and the aged. You will encourage parents to send their children to Day and Sunday Schools, and recommend grown up persons, who cannot read, to attend adult evening schools. You will inform those who are without a Bible, how they may obtain one, and suggest weekly subscriptions for this purpose; and you will transmit their names and residence to the nearest Bible Association, or to the Society for Promoting Christian Knowledge.—3. It will be necessary, that you should be provided with information as to the Places of Worship, Adult, Day, Sunday, and Infant Schools in the neighbourhood; and where there is any obstacle to the attendance of the persons you visit, from want of accommodation or distance, you will make this circumstance known to the Local Committee of the District.—4. You will not fail to inculcate habits of industry, and cleanliness both of rooms and persons. Where practicable, employment should be suggested to persons out of work, and in many cases it will be desirable to point out the advantages of Savings' Banks, and encourage weekly deposits for rent.—5. In cases of sickness and want, you will endeavour to ascertain, whether there is any medical or other attendance, whether relief is afforded by any benevolent society, and what charitable assistance is required.—6. The Committee recommend that relief should be administered (where practicable) through the medium of some existing Society or Institution: and it will be very desirable, that the Visitors should be provided with recommendations of Subscribers to such Societies, and to the nearest Dispensary, to be used as occasion may require.—7. It may in some cases be advisable to release the tools and clothes of mechanics from pawn; but, except in instances of pressing and immediate want, it is strongly recommended, that no pecuniary aid be afforded from the funds of the Society, before the case has been submitted to the Local Committee.—8. It will be necessary to bear in mind the prevalence of fraud and imposture; and it is hoped that the frequency of your visits will gradually facilitate their detection. While you will avoid all appearance of harshness, or want of feeling for the misery which meets your notice, you will use every precaution to guard against the misapplication of charitable aid upon objects of merely pretended distress, or upon those who are receiving adequate relief from other sources.—9. You will avoid as far as possible encroaching on the necessary occupations of families and individuals; and with this view it will be very important, that you should ascertain the time, when visits are most acceptable, and put persons the least out of the way.—10. You will not attempt to force yourselves on those, who shew a determined aversion to your visits; but you will express to them in a friendly manner your readiness to call upon them again, should they become more disposed to receive you.—11. It will generally be desirable, that the Visitors should go two and two, although they may frequently be engaged at the same time with different families under the same roof.—12. You will be provided with a journal, in which you will enter the name, residence, &c. of the persons visited; with answers to certain queries suggested, which should be submitted to the Local Committee of your district, at each meeting, accompanied with a notice of any particular occurrences tending to illustrate character, shew improvement, call for particular advice, &c., and with such general observations on the state of your Section as may appear useful.—13. The Committee would only further entreat you to remember the Master whom you serve;

when certified of the conversion of Saul,[1] to the fellowship of the Church. This is at once a most important benefit to the individual, and a real support to the Pastor; enabling him to combine with his solemn warnings to the unconverted, his delightful commission to "comfort the people of God,"[2] and establish them in the faith of the Gospel.

It must however be remembered, that *helpers are not Ministers.* There is an essential difference between Lay Agency and Lay Preaching. The Ministry of the New Testament stands upon the same authority as the Priesthood of the Old. No entrenchment must be allowed upon the consecrated office. Laymen may exhort with love, meekness, entreaty, but not with authority. Their work is rather brotherly admonition than fatherly teaching. They have no special commission. They must "speak as the oracles of . God, and as of the ability which God giveth;"[3] but they cannot speak as "ambassadors for Christ." They may speak in his name (in dependence upon him as their Head) but not "in his stead"— as having a message and commission from him. They need at once to be excited, directed, and controuled; and under this discipline, we may cherish the "hope, when their faith is increased, that we shall be enlarged by them according to our rule abundantly."[4] They will indeed be to us "instead of eyes;"[5] their "work and labour of love" will powerfully act, as one of the wheels in the great machine of perpetual motion; and their reward of grace will be with "Urbane and the beloved Persis," with "Clement and with other fellow-labourers, whose names are in the book of life."[6]

But we must not forget, that the meanest member of the Church sustains this useful character of a helper. How cheering is it to enter the pulpit (as the Apostle spoke of coming to Rome) not only to "impart to our hearers some spiritual gift;" but with the hope of being "comforted by their faith!"[7] When faith glistens in the eyes of an attentive congregation, how does it quicken our energies, interest, and love; producing from the impulse of the occasion thoughts far more striking than had been the result of the contemplation of the study! We need scarcely remark upon the daily help we derive from the power of a consistent example, sometimes even more forcible than the Pulpit Ministry.[8] None can gainsay

and in cases of opposition or insult, to govern your temper—to return good for evil— blessing for cursing—to be patient towards all men, "in meekness instructing those who oppose themselves."'
[1] See Acts ix. 27.   [2] See Isaiah xl. 1, 2.
[3] 1 Peter iv. 11.   [4] 2 Cor. x. 16.   [5] Numb. x. 31
[6] Rom. xvi. 9, 12: Phil. iv. 3.   [7] Rom. i. 11, 12.   [8] See 1 Peter iii. 1, 2.

or resist this visible "seal of our Apostleship." As confirming every word of instruction, invitation, and encouragement; and as exhibiting the strait ways of the Gospel to be "paths of pleasantness and peace," this testimony is above all price.

Least of all, must we forget (though it has been before alluded to) the help we obtain from the prayers of our people. So sensible was the Apostle of the value of this help, that, distinguished as he was for eminence of grace, experience, and services, he pleads for it with the earnestness of a beggar requesting alms.[1] Bishop Davenant justly traces the allowance of so many ignorant Ministers in the Church to the want of hearty supplication.[2] And indeed a praying people will be sure *eventually* to be blessed with an edifying Ministry. We are far more in the power of our people than we are always conscious of. Humanly speaking—our personal graces, the spiritual character of our Ministrations, and the consequent consolation and fruitfulness with our people, very materially depend upon their secret labours on our behalf. We are the conduits by which the living water flows into the Church. The Church therefore must pray for the continual supplies to be poured into those conduits; or they will return (like the nobles of Judah) " with their vessels empty ; ashamed and confounded, and covering their heads."[3] It will doubtless be found, that the Gospel is promoted by the prayers as well as by the Ministry of the Church. Christians therefore should be reminded, that they owe this exercise of love to their fellow-sinners, as redeemed by the same blood—to us, as in some degree probably the instruments of their salvation—and still more to our great Master, as the undoubted and sole Author of it. Let therefore the blessing, through our instrumentality be sought in this way—" ye also helping together in prayer to God for us; that for the gift bestowed upon us by the means of many persons, thanks may be given by many on our behalf."[4] And while we realize the delightful enjoyment of being raised on the wings of our people's prayers ; they will not be without their recompence. For never is supplication sent up for a blessing upon the Minister, but it returns with tenfold blessing upon the supplicant's head.[5]

At all events therefore, let us expose the fallacy of the indolent notion, that Ministers are to do every thing. The best answer to give to the adversaries of our Establishment, is to set in motion

---

[1] See Rom. xv. 30.   [2] Daven. in Col. iv. 3.   [3] Jer. xiv. 3.   [4] 2 Cor. i. 11.

[5] Specific remembrance of the Minister in secret and social worship, on the mornings of the Sabbaths especially (not of course forgetting his daily claim upon their remembrance) might be inculcated with the greatest, though perhaps unconscious, advantage to ourselves and to our Ministry.

every wheel of the great machine. Reminding therefore our people of our immense burden—" besides" the weight of personal trial—" that which cometh upon us daily—the care of the churches"[1]—let us call out our resources for active service, as the matter may require.   Let us inculcate expansive and energetic diligence—making our people generally useful to each other—parents to their families—neighbours among one another—promising young persons to the rising generation.   They often look to the Pastor to suggest plans of practical usefulness.   Almost every sphere furnishes work for every Christian under the Minister's direction and controul.   Each will find a large blessing in laying himself out for the interests of his fellow-sinner—not to speak that his office—working with his Minister—necessarily invests him with a public character, and consequently furnishes a strong incentive to personal piety.   Conscious helplessness brings with it special encouragements. The pride of Satan is humbled by being vanquished by worms; while Christ is glorified in the manifestation of his "strength made perfect in weakness."[2]

If then our people can do any thing, let them help us in winning souls to Christ. Let them spread the influence of the sacred leaven around them, " till the whole be leavened ;" so that, while our doctrine is perverted, misunderstood, or opposed on all sides, we may be able to point to their lives and tempers, in illustration of its holy tendency and happy effects—" Ye are our epistle, known and read of all men—manifestly declared to be the epistle of Christ, ministered by us."[3]

CHAPTER VIII.

MISCELLANEOUS.[4]

A few particulars, which have not hitherto found a place in our work, may be here specified, such as—*The importance of Adult Schools.*   These are indeed the complement of the School System.

---

[1] 2 Cor. xi. 28. "Cometh unto me"—rushing like a torrent, one after another, ready to bear me down. For the illustration of the peculiar emphasis of the term, Beza and Doddridge may be consulted, or perhaps a better commentator than either—at particular seasons of trial—*experience.*

[2] 2 Cor. xii. 9.   [3] Ibid. iii. 2, 3.

[4] Some useful hints on various miscellaneous departments of the Ministry, may be found in "The Country Clergyman's Advice to his Flock." By Rev. William Mudge. (Hatchards and Seeleys.)

It is difficult to retain boys in the weekly school long enough to ground them in the principles of useful instruction. The Sunday School also is left, without any other means of preserving the knowledge which they have acquired. The utility of adult schools —as an indefinite continuance of instruction—is therefore of the highest consideration. The knowledge of the word of God is equally valuable to adults as to children ; while their capacity of understanding it (though much hindered by inability to read) is far greater. Shame indeed will sometimes restrain from stooping to the first elements of instruction ; yet on the other hand, experience even of the temporal disadvantages of ignorance (where the spiritual deprivations are not apprehended) supplies a constant stimulus for exertion. Here is useful employment for helpers, though some ministerial superintendence will be usually needed. The smallness of numbers must not discourage. It is a great matter to persuade a person in the middle or decline of life, that in commencing his alphabet, he may be able by a few months of patient application to read his Testament. In a village therefore, but few may be sometimes found willing to attend. But an assembly of three or four is well worth our regular pains. If sufficient numbers of different ages can be collected to form into classes, the lads and adults should, as far as possible, be separated. The Scripture lessons will furnish an interesting course of questioning, and personal application. Where confidence has been gained, and opportunities are favourable, a Sunday class might be formed for more direct instruction, either between the hours of service, or at any more convenient time of the day. Employment of this leisure hour for spiritual instruction (which otherwise might have been spent in idleness or sin) ; and the advantage to the domestic œconomy from a more intelligent acquaintance with relative duties and obligations, render this system peculiarly important. The general success, especially where the love of the sacred volume is the principle of perseverance, is highly encouraging. Many, whose scanty knowledge of its contents had flowed from the uncertain kindness of others, have thus found an immediate and most happy access to this unsearchable treasure.[1]

A Parochial Library, where practicable, is an excellent appendage to the Pastoral system. The capacity of reading, communicated to old and young, lays upon us a weighty responsibility, to give a right direction to this new medium of intelligence, which

[1] We recommend the Bristol Adult Spelling Book, (Mason, Paternoster Row,) from its excellent type, and selection of Scripture Lessons.

otherwise will become a channel of vain curiosity and idleness— probably also of infidelity and sin—a field for the agency of Satan, rather than for Christian usefulness. 'But' (as Mr. Newton observed) 'one proposes to fill a bushel with *tares;* now if I can fill it first with wheat, I shall defy his attempts.' A store therefore of valuable instruction, adapted to the different gradations of intelligence and seriousness, would be an useful preservative from deleterious poison, and an excitement of profitable interest. With the admission of a few works of general information, the complexion of the library should however be distinctly evangelical, practical, and popular—formed upon the basis of the Divine aphorism—" One thing is needful."[1] A payment of a penny, or at most of two-pence, a quarter, would not be felt by the poorest of our people : while it would give them a sort of interesting property in it, and accumulate a trifling fund for fresh additions to the catalogue, which should be widely made known. A ledger should be kept for the entry of the names of the books and subscribers, and of the period, when their subscriptions become due or are paid. The times of exchange and distribution, and the limit of the detention of the books, should be definitely fixed, and strictly observed. Sunday distribution is objectionable ; as, besides the time that would be employed in the arrangements, it would be the means of circulating works of too light a cast for Sabbath edification, as well as others, excellent in their kind, but unsuitable to the sacredness of that holy day. The books, well covered with brown paper, will sustain for a considerable time the rough handling to which they will be exposed ; while a forfeit should be exacted for injury or loss, as well as for unreasonable detention beyond the fixed bounds.

The advantages also of Cottage Readings must not be omitted in this detail. Our Lord's public Ministry extended beyond the precincts of the synagogue, to every concourse of people. Familiar opportunities for collective instruction are therefore in strict conformity with the spirit of this example. In every parish, bodily infirmity or other causes, exclude many from the sphere of the pulpit Ministry, who need, not merely general or individual conversations upon spiritual subjects, but distinct expositions of the word of God. This free and popular instruction—scarcely consistent with the dignity of the pulpit—gives a powerful excitement to the unintelligent mind. 'No one,' (as has been justly observed by a most competent judge) 'but those accustomed to question the

[1] Luke x. 42. Bickersteth's Christian Student (ch. xv.) will furnish a valuable selection for this purpose.

poor, or to be questioned by them, can form an idea of what by way of explanation they require. It is not only "line upon line, and precept upon precept" they need; but it is almost word by word, and letter by letter."[1] This mode of Ministry will admit of considerable diversity of application. The catechetical form has been found well adapted to an advanced state of knowledge or mutual confidence. In a less matured state, exercises in the sacred field—proposing subjects for successive readings, and illustrating them by Scripture parallels, have proved interesting and instructive. In more ordinary cases, familiar reading and exposition of a course of Scripture (perhaps preferable to unconnected portions), commenced and concluded with prayer, will furnish the plan, and fill up the outlines. The evenings only allow the attendance of men upon these meetings. Women (except in the manufacturing districts) may be collected during the day. The time, however, should be fixed with all possible consideration of convenience, and should be considered on our part as a regular and paramount engagement. One hour of this system includes the work of many hours of individual visitation; while its orderly formality shuts out many interruptions, which belong to domiciliary visits. Care however must be taken, that the attendance upon these readings does not compensate for the self-indulgent neglect of the house of God; instead of sharpening the appetite for the Sabbath Ministrations. The freedom of these simple assemblies of the poor, (often attended with a special blessing) render them an appropriate work and labour of love for the Minister's wife. The Sabbath might furnish an useful appendage to them, gathering before the afternoon service in the vestry, or some suitable place, those who, whether from habit, or want of some employment, come to church half an hour before the service commences. The desire for instruction would induce others to join this little assembly.

We would mention as the last particular in this lengthened detail, *the excitement of an interest in the promotion of the Redeemer's kingdom.* Missionary and Bible Associations, especially the former, deal much in affecting and encouraging facts; though in the latter case it too frequently happens (unless the claims of the heathen are strongly pressed) that the subscription proceeds no further than the purchase of a good Bible at a cheap cost. The principles of these Associations are—the imparting of interesting information, and the inculcating of evangelical motives. For the former, the monthly publications of the Societies will furnish ample

---

[1] Rev. H. C. Ridley's Parochial Duties Illustrated, pp. 16, 17.

materials. The latter will be drawn in rich abundance from the word of God. The positive command of Christ[1]—his dying love —the value and perishing condition of the soul—the nearness of eternity—the "sure word of prophecy," as indicative of the purposes of God respecting his church—and the high privilege of being "fellow-workers with him"—these are motives of powerful constraint. The regularity of system should be introduced as far as possible into these Associations, especially in the collecting department ; which generally should be managed weekly, or monthly at most, and used as a medium of distributing information, and maintaining the tone of interest.[2] Monthly, or at least quarterly meetings, must be considered a component part of the system. Singing, prayer, select reading from the best sources of information—personal application and excitement grounded upon it—concluding with Scripture reading or exposition, and prayer, will assemble our people, with much advantage to themselves, as well as with effective influence upon the cause of Christ.[3]

In these institutions the elements of vital religion are cherished, in the subjugation of the natural selfishness to that "charity, that seeketh not her own ;" in the awakened spirit of self-denial, pity, and intercession ; and in a deepened sense of privileges, obligations, and responsibilities ; so that the offering cast into the sacred treasury, (though by no means to be despised) constitutes but a small proportion of the benefit derived : and thus the endeavour to diffuse the Gospel abroad is closely connected with its enlarged blessing at home.

In concluding this extended Pastoral survey, the Writer would guard against attaching too much to the mere mechanism of the work, and would strongly insist, that, whatever be our diligence in this department, we can only be blessed, as we are faithful in delivering, according to the light given to us, the whole message of God. He would however at the same time express his strong conviction, that the combination of Pastoral labour with the full exhibition of a Scriptural Ministry, is the medium, through which the Spirit of God will produce among us an extension of true religion, which for explicitness, durability, and consistency, will abide the day of trial, and cause even the enemies of the Gospel to " see, and know, and

---

[1] Mark xvi. 15.

[2] A Collector once gave a most satisfactory explanation of her success—ascribing it to her conscientious adherence to two rules—regularity of collecting, and commencing her work periodically with prayer—the one marking the mechanism, the other forming the living principle of the system.

[3] For a beautiful specimen of these meetings, long before they were known among us, see Memoirs of Oberlin, pp. 178, 179.

consider, and understand together, that the hand of the Lord hath done this, and that the Holy One of Israel hath created it."[1]

It is not however an exclusive interest in any department that is recommended, but a combined regard and concentrated attention to the whole work ; making it our study and prayer, that we be not inwardly satisfied without earnest longings, and constant advance towards the full Scriptural standard. In every department we may confidently expect, that our labours will be instrumentally blessed, wherever faith is the principle, and prayer the spirit, of our work ; and where the moving principle is acted out in self-denial, diligence, simplicity, and perseverance. We must not indeed suffer our energies to stagnate. We must be always on the watch to improve fresh openings for enlarging our work, and ready to apply and appropriate every instrument that can be made to subserve it. But with all this we must be careful not to attempt too many plans at once—not more, than we have a reasonable hope of sustaining ; and especially not more, than is consistent with a primary devotedness to communion with God, and preparation for our public work. Yet by regularity ; doing one thing at a time ; allowing a pause ; by short exercises ; and by such prudence as is consistent with zeal, (not letting a variety of exercises carry us beyond our strength,) much more may be done than is commonly imagined.

EN ΤΟΥΤΟΙΣ ΙΣΘΙ.—1 Tιm. iv. 15.

[1] Isaiah xli. 20.

PART VI.

RECOLLECTIONS OF THE CHRISTIAN MINISTRY.

It may be useful to shut up this immensely momentous and interesting subject with an attempt to concentrate some of its serious recollections in fixed and permanent impressions. Habitually to realize just views, both of the gospel, and of the sacred office, tends most profitably at once to excite, support, and direct us. Thus while the Minister's views of responsibility—*if indeed he be under divine teaching*—will fill him with the deepest humiliation; yet the contemplation of the Saviour's glory and love inspires him with hope and joy. Often will the cheering recollection present itself—'Where should I have been, if I could not look to Him, whose "blood cleanseth from all sin?"' In this spirit he will tenderly plead with his people respecting their sins; and be ready to sit at the feet of the least and lowest of them, while he executes his solemn commission towards them. And how will he speak of the Saviour? Like one who feels his own need of mercy, and who sees the sufficiency of his adorable Lord for the chief of sinners, and the glorious work that he has undertaken for him; he will set forth this enlivening subject with a richness, fulness, confidence, and joy, which, if he has learnt from the Scriptures, he has learnt no less from his own experience. Thus is he humbled, but not discouraged; and while he lies low, he is lifted up by a " grace" that " is sufficient for him," and sustained by a "strength that is made perfect in" his " weakness."[2] Thus he is weeping, yet rejoicing—encouraged, thankful, devoted, happy.

However partial views of the Christian Ministry may, by eclipsing the prospects of faith, make our "hands hang down," we are persuaded, that the sober calculation and enlarged apprehension of faith, will substantiate before us the full support of the Gospel; will enliven our present gratitude; and result in fresh and unceasing excitement in the world of everlasting praise.

[1] To maintain these recollections, the Writer recommends Shuttleworth's 'Christian Minister's Pocket Companion'—a valuable compilation. (Holdsworth.)

[2] See 2 Cor. xii. 9.

But to maintain abiding and deepening convictions of our responsibilities, the Writer has ventured to expand a few questions, which the course of this survey has suggested for his own use, and which he would respectfully submit for the consideration of his honoured and beloved brethren.

I. *Do we honour our work?* 'One of the mistakes'—said the late Mr. Venn,—'that I have cause to regret, is, that from fear of pride, I never paid due regard to the numberless passages of Holy Writ, which so plainly point out, and extol, the high dignity of our office. Had I given but a little consideration to these passages, I indeed believe, I should have had much more comfort in my own soul, and more success both in public and private addresses to my people.'[1] When God would allure his people to return, by the richest prospect of blessing, he sets before them—not the promise of temporal prosperity and aggrandisement (this had been found ineffectual)—but the *gift of "pastors according to his heart, who should feed them with knowledge and understanding."*[2] How high then is our obligation—as the most important gift of God to his Church, in the deepest personal humiliation—to "*magnify our office!*"[3] And this we do—*when Christ is the inspiring principle of our Ministrations*—not one subject among the rest, but that which involves the rest, and gives to them their proper life and interest. "The truth *as it is in Jesus*"[4]—as he is the centre of every line—is the glory and substance of our office.[5] 'Let Jesus Christ' (said the excellent Matthew Henry) 'be All in All. Study Christ—preach Christ—live Christ.'[6] Let us sink ourselves to exalt our Master.[7] It was said of Ignatius, that he carried Christ about with him in his heart; 'and this I will say—if to represent a glorious Christ to the view, the love, and the admiration of all people, be the grand intention of your life—if you are exquisitely studious, that the holiness and yet the gentleness of Christ may shine in your conversation—if in your public discourses you do with rapture bring in the mention of Christ in every paragraph, and on every occasion where he is to be spoken of—and if, in your private conversation, you contrive to insinuate something of his glories and praises, whenever it may be decently introduced—final-

---

[1] Life, p. 516.   [2] Jeremiah iii. 12—15.
[3] Compare Eph. iii. 8.   Rom. xi. 13.   [4] Ephesians iv. 21.
[5] 'Christ crucified—the great pervading theme of the Christian Ministry, judiciously expanded, and closely applied—is itself a complete system of doctrines, a connected succession of duties, an unfailing supply of motives, an unexhausted treasury of hopes.' Young Pastor's Guide. Sermons before the University of Cambridge. By the Rev. Thomas Dale.
[6] Life, p. 122.   Compare Sermon on John xiv. 1.   Miscellaneous Works, pp. 581—583.   [7] See John iii. 30.

ly, if, when you find, that a glorious Christ is the more considered and acknowledged by your means, you exclaim—'Lord! this is my desired happiness'—truly you then live to good purpose.'[1] 'If'—said a dying Pastor—'Ministers only saw (especially in their public exercises) the preciousness of Christ, they would not be able to refrain from clapping their hands with joy, and exclaiming—'I am a minister of Christ! I am a Minister of Christ!' '[2]

We "magnify our office" also by an *exhibition of its spirit*. An inconsistent, worldly, or self-indulgent Minister, trifling with his sacred obligations—as an old writer strongly remarks—' is the pest of the Church.'[3] Even if his Ministry should enlighten, it will not sanctify his people. Far less injurious are the open attacks of our avowed and most bitter adversaries. Oh! that the Ministers of the Church may be kept from destroying the Church! Let it be remembered, that the high honour to which we are called, is to give a just representation, not only of the doctrine, but of the person of Christ. Whatever talents be not made subservient to this grand purpose of expressing the dignity and humility, " the meekness and gentleness," the self-denial, zeal, and love of our Divine Master will bear the awful stamp of unprofitableness at the day of account. Like our Heavenly Pattern therefore, let us display before the world a manifest elevation above it, uninfluenced by its smiles—unmoved by its frowns. Let it be seen and read of all men, that we " seek not theirs, but them"[4]—that " in all things we approve ourselves as the Ministers of God"[5]—having our souls animated, excited, and filled with our work—making it the one absorbing concern—feeling the insignificance of every thing in comparison with it—giving it the lead in every pursuit—concentrating upon it the best and most steady efforts of self-denial and love

[1] Mather's Essays to do Good, 113, 114.
[2] Memoir of Dr. Payson. 'I love to live preaching Christ, and I love to die preaching Christ.' Halyburton. 'Happy the Christian Minister,' says Bishop Horne—'who, like St. John, lives only to point out this Saviour to his people!' On John Baptist—'That preacher'—as one observes—'shall have *most comfort*, who preaches most of Christ.'
[3] Nich. Hemmingii Pastor.   [4] 2 Cor. xii. 14.
[5] 2 Cor. vi. 4. The following lines exhibit the primitive simplicity of their well-known Author.

' Give me the priest these graces shall possess—
Of an ambassador the first address—
A father's tenderness—a shepherd's care,
A leader's courage, which the cross can bear—
A ruler's awe—a watchman's wakeful eye—
A pilot's skill, the helm in storms to ply—
A fisher's patience—and a labourer's toil—
A guide's dexterity, to disembroil—
A prophet's inspiration from above—
A teacher's knowledge—and a Saviour's love.'--BISHOP KENN.

—and manifesting that sympathizing tenderness of heart, which bespeaks a sense of its responsibility. This high tone of Ministerial character, grounded upon personal consistency, will never fail to command respect. Thus Mr. Nelson truly remarked—'He knows but little of the dignity of the Priesthood, who is content with ordinary attainments.' Nor can we calculate upon extended usefulness, unless we magnify our office so as to count it worthy of all our pains. This was George Herbert's spirit, when dissuaded from the Ministry, as a degrading employment—'Though the iniquity of the times has made the sacred name of *priest* contemptible, yet I will labour to make it honourable, by consecrating all my learning, and all my poor abilities, to advance the glory of that God that gave them.'[1] Such also was Henry Martyn's holy exultation. 'Blessed be God'—said he—'*I feel myself to be his Minister!*' Tremendous, yet blessed feeling! laying us in the dust, yet lifting us up to heaven.

II. *Do we feel the responsibility of our work?* The Minister of the Gospel is not an isolated individual, nor is his influence bounded by parochial limits. The character of his profession gives a tone, not to the Church only, but to the nation at large. Entrusted as he is with the eternal interests of the world, with all its countless population, and successive generations to the end of time —Surely he may well say—"*I am doing a great work!*"[2] And indeed an affecting, though not an overwhelming, conviction of its dignity and difficulty, is eminently serviceable to check a vain, indolent, and careless mind; to excite us to the improvement of all necessary gifts and graces; to call forth earnest supplications in a matter so plainly above human strength; to exercise our entire dependence on Christ for guidance, assistance, and success; to preserve us against impertinent diversions from our work;[3] and to make us deeply solicitous about its success. As a ground of encouragement also—it argues high thoughts of our Great Master; a firm belief of the truth and weight of our message; a freedom from secular ends; an humble, serious, tender, and prepared heart; a readiness to acknowledge our deficiencies, to improve our helps, to be earnest in prayer, to wait in expectation of heavenly influence, to watch against all hindrances, and to render to God the honour of all our success—and even of all due preparation and diligence.

May we not then inquire—*What is our personal sympathy with this awful sense of responsibility?* How are we affected

[1] Walton's Life of Herbert.   [2] Neh. vi. 3.   [3] Ibid. vi. 3.

by the Scriptural warnings—enough to "make both the ears of every" watchman "that heareth them to tingle?"[1] How by the spirit of our Ordination service? than which (as Bishop Burnet justly remarks) 'nothing in any office is so serious and so solemn'[2] —exhibiting us in both parts of our mighty business—as the mouth of God to the people, and the mouth of the people to God. Do we feel this *responsibility in regard to our care and diligence?* Is not Ministerial diligence as necessary for our salvation, as Christian diligence for our people? The most regular course of external service or irreproachable conduct will not meet the emergency, without a deep sense of the "necessity laid upon us." The ransom found for immortal souls shows at once their infinite value, and their solemn charge. What could be purchased only by the blood of the Son of God must be worth the labours of a thousand generations. Nor can the murder of a fellow-creature bear any comparison with "the voice 'of the blood of our brother's" soul "crying" for vengeance "from the ground." What fervent exercises of holy sympathy—the clear evidences of our Divine call—flow from a just sense of the weight of our office! Mr. Brown was often deprived of a night's rest by his tender and oppressive anxiety;[3] and, did young Ministers cherish this impression, they would have deeper views of their awful engagements; and instead of desiring extensive spheres of service, they would be more sensible of the solemn charge of a single soul.[4]

How do we feel *with regard to our talents?* They were given to us on account; neither to waste on sin, nor to slumber in indolence, not to concentrate in selfishness—but to "occupy" in our Master's service.[5] As in our soul's salvation, so in our Ministry, the freeness of the gift is the quickening motive to its active energy.[6] But are our "gifts stirred up," our graces exercised—our opportunities improved to the uttermost? To think of talents being specially given to us for the object dearest to the heart of our Divine Master—that of feeding his own purchased church—and yet that

[1] Ezekiel iii. xxxiii. xxxiv. Zech. xi. 17.
[2] Past. Care, ch. vi. Compare Bishop Porteus' Charges, 1790. Comber mentions a prayer for a Minister in an old Gallican form of ordination—'that he may tremble for all the people committed to his care; remembering that all their souls are to be required at the watchman's hand.'
[3] Life and Remains, p. 28. 'When a man is sensibly affected with the value of souls, with the manner of their redemption, and with the price paid for them; and is well acquainted with the New Testament, in which all this is plainly set forth; as he will never want matter for the best sermons, so he will never want arguments sufficient to convince his hearers of his own heart being touched with the importance of the subject.' Bishop Wilson's Parochialia.
[4] Bishop Andrews engraved on his episcopal seal the memorable words—"Who is sufficient for these things!"
[5] Luke xix. 13—26.   [6] Comp. Phil. ii. 12, 13, with 2 Tim. i. 6, 7.

they should so often be spent in our own indulgence, or in the
empty acquirement of a name in the church of God! Even on
moral grounds we are convicted of dishonesty. Are not our wages
the compensation for time and talents faithfully devoted to our
work? If the abuse of the public money of the state be censura-
ble, much more the waste of the treasury of the Church.

How do we feel *respecting the completeness* of our Ministry?
"not preferring one" part "above another"—or at least not engaged in one to the neglect of another. We want combination
with concentration. To confine our attention to the Pulpit, is to
leave uncultivated a vast sphere of sympathetic and aggressive
influence. On the other hand to give ourselves *exclusively* to
the Pastoral work, would endanger our bringing into the Pulpit
slight exercises—words without matter—fluency without substance
—such as would command no weight or respect with our intelligent people.

*How, again, do we feel the responsibility of our pulpit prepa-
ration?* Most beautiful was the spirit of M. Boos—'spending
whatever time he could spare in his Church before the altar, until
he was able to comfort his congregation;' judging rightly, that
'those are not the best sermons, which we have laboured over with
difficulty, but which we have, as it were, supplicated from the Lord
with tears and prayers.' This was connected with a searching
Scriptural habit. 'We must'—he said—'dig very deep to discern
the treasure'—adding, 'it is when we feel our weakness most, that
we dig the deepest.'[1]

This spirit is a cover from the snare of mechanical preparation,
which evaporates the Christian glow in chalking out artificial arrangement; while at the same time it is the spring of prayerful industry—far more valuable than talents, improving the highest, and
supplying many deficiencies of the more moderate. It will lead us
away from the love of novelty, which fills the mind with fancies;
instead of seeking after originality, pressing home the common but
primary truths of the Gospel—taking the same ground-work, though
with enlarged and diversified illustration, with our fathers and prophets of old. Thus will the people "seek the law at the mouth of the
priest"—when he lives upon the level of his high obligation, his mind
treasuring up—and *therefore* his "lips keeping—knowledge."[2] We
ask—*how is this responsibility felt as regards the substance of
our preaching?* Admitting our Ministry to be exclusively occupied with the one subject,[3] yet are we labouring to compass the

---

[1] Life, p. 428. Comp. p. 14. Pref. xlv.   [2] Mal. ii. 7.   [3] 1 Cor. ii. 2.

whole extent, setting it forth *in its integrity*—concealing no doctrine, nor bringing any into undue proportions—*in its purity*—
without the intermixture of human traditions or authority[1]—*in its
simplicity*—opening an instant way for the contrite sinner without previous safe preparation—*in its connection*—giving life and
substance to every part by a clear exhibition of the Saviour, seeing
that every point inclines to the magnetism of the great centre—
combining the doctrine of salvation with the statement of the penalty and defilement of sin—the work of the Spirit in all his perfections and Divinity with the work of Christ; thus through the Spirit
raising the whole edifice of faith and godliness upon the true foundation.[2] Again—*If our Ministry be thus Scriptural, is it advancing?* As Christians we are led to search, "what is the
breadth, and length, and depth, and height, and to know the love
of Christ, which passeth knowledge."[3] Ought not then our Ministry to exhibit the results of this exploring, in a more comprehensive, unctional, endearing display of our grand subject? If
our office be to open a mine of "unsearchable riches,"[4] should we
not plant our steps deeper into this golden storehouse, and thence
draw out more enriching treasures for our Sabbath Ministrations?
Those of us, who have most reason, and (what goes with it) most
readiness, to acknowledge our Divine Master's grace upon our
work, are most sensible of their need of this experience, and most
earnest in their desires and efforts to attain it. If we insist upon
growth in our people, must we not shew it in our Ministry? The
same motto is for Minister and for people—"*Not as though I have
already attained, either were already perfect: but I follow after.*"[5]

What need have we of a deep sense of the responsibility of the
pulpit; like the great Apostle—to be deeply penetrated with the
subject of our commission—with the object in view—with the recollection of the Omniscient witness of our conduct,—*Truth—conscience—the presence of our God*[6]—thoughts so weighty and impressive! enough to fill our whole soul! Well would it be for us
thus to realize our true character—as not the magistrate—the
statesman—the legislator—the wise or prudent man—the moralist
—the poet—the man of feeling—or even the Minister of the law
—but the ambassador of Christ, 'sent to man, the sinner—not
the partial, but the total sinner—not the impoverished, but the
ruined—not to man hurt by sin, but to man dead in sin—not

1 See some discriminating remarks, Bowles, Lib. ii. c. 9.   2 Eph. ii. 20—22.
3 Ibid. iii. 18, 19.   4 Ibid. verse 8.   5 Phil. iii. 12.   6 See 2 Cor. iv. 2.

man to be repaired, but to be made—not to be rectified, but to
be created.'[1] How important is the recollection, that we bring to
man nothing that is truly valuable, without an acquaintance with
his true character, his lost condition, and his only solid hopes for
eternity !

How *does our example speak*—a most responsible part of our
office ? Spirituality is a main qualification of the Ministry. A
faithful Pastor is a living witness, bearing a powerful testimony in
the great controversy between God and the world. His life is
vocal—like Chaucer's Parson—'a living sermon of the truth he
taught.' Indeed it is only where the life preaches, that the pulpit
will be effective. Unless we are men of God out of the pulpit, we
shall never be honoured Ministers in it. Our people look at us
narrowly in the week, to see what we mean—whether we mean
any thing—on the Sabbath. We may teach, warn, exhort, but
there will be no movement without the holy walk—unless we act
the faith we preach. While we preach faith, we must live works,
to put to shame the charge of licentiousness, and to put away a
stumbling block out of the path of the world. For " though we
should speak with the tongues of men and of angels," we should
fail to charm our people into a love of the Gospel, without an exhibition of its spirit. Our obligation every way is most strong to
be what we preach. And there must be some defect, unless we
bring our own atmosphere of holiness, more or less immediately
felt. ' What Bishop' or Pastor ' can forbear trembling, seeing himself engaged by Jesus Christ himself to be like an " *angel*"—pure,
spiritual, in a constant application to men by labour, and to God
by prayer ; and like a " star" full of light, elevated above the earth,
fixed to his sphere which is his " church," incessantly moving in it,
and continually diffusing his influences below !'[2] Do we realize
the responsibility of our office, as " the salt of the earth ?"[3] Alas !
sometimes do we not rather seem to assist the putrefaction, than
preserve from it? Do we consider the delicate exactness belonging
to our function—like the female character, requiring not only restraint within strict propriety, but the most remote distance from
the bounds even of suspicion[4]—a restriction, which, however burden-

1 Budd's Sermon before the Church Missionary Society.
2 Quesnel on Rev. i. 19, 20. ' Vouchsafe, Lord,' (adds this pious expositor) ' to send
such "angels," and cause such "stars" as these to shine in thy church.'—' So holy is our
employment, that were our souls as pure as cherubs, as zealous and active as the blessed
spirits that are above, we should yet have reason to cover our faces, and to be swallowed
up in a deep sense of our own insufficiency for these things.' Scougal's Sermon on the
Importance and Difficulty of the Ministerial Function.   3 Matt. v. 13.
4 The Ministerial qualifications are ανιπιληπτος, to take hold of (1 Tim. iii. 2.)—not
to be apprehended—nothing ανεγκλητος (1 Tim. iii. 10. Titus i. 6, 7.)—not liable to be

some it may appear, is a most constraining obligation, and effectual support of our work? Christian consistency alone can shield our office from contempt.[1] Negative holiness is of little avail for influence. We must be "*examples*"—not to the world—but '*to believers*—an example of holiness and purity among the holy and pure.'[2]

The responsibility of the temporal concerns of the nation, or even the holding up of the pillars of the earth, bears no proportion to the tremendous weight of the charge of immortal souls. Ministers are not "visited after the visitation of all men." Nothing is distributed to them, either in judgment or in mercy, upon the common scale of calculation, or according to the general balance of the Divine dispensations. "We are made a spectacle to the world, and to angels, and to men."[3] The eternal interests of others are so bound up with us, that we are denied the comparative privilege of perishing alone. Nor indeed can we singly save ourselves; or save ourselves at all, except (as Bishop Wilson reminds us) 'by labouring to save others.'[4] What means then the frequent caution or charge of excessive zeal, when our own consciences must tell us, that—did we but realize the value of the soul—were we suitably impressed with the love of the Saviour, or with the sense of our obligations, we should not minister in the cold and indifferent manner that we do—that we have reason to be ashamed of every sermon we preach—and perhaps to tremble in the very best of them, lest we be convicted of pouring contempt upon the truth of God, and of the guilt of the blood of our people? And are there none of us, whose consciences might present the fearful prospect of hearers dropping successively into the arms of death through the Minister's negligence, unwarned as well as unprepared; and of going down to the grave after them—with their hands deeply dyed with the blood of their souls—and themselves overwhelmed in their eternal damnation?

Oh! how infinitely awful and mysterious is the appointment, which has thus laid upon us so sinking a burden; and what are the bitterest of earthly sorrows—what the curse of an ungodly world—what the torture of the martyr's stake—compared with the unutterable, eternal sting of unfaithfulness to these perishing—yet imperishable—souls? The anticipation of the day of account—solemn to all—is inexpressibly so to us. How awful the peal, which

arraigned—both implying not only freedom from blame, but beyond any suspicion or ground of it.
[1] See 1 Tim. iv. 12.　　　　[2] Nicholson's Call upon the Church, p. 43.
[3] 1 Cor. iv. 9.　　　　[4] See his Sacra Privata. Comp. 1 Tim. iv. 16.

the passing bell—that useful memento of the great judgment—rings in our ears !   Another account is carried in before the bar of our Judge—an account linked with our own, and crowded with sins of Ministerial omission and unfaithfulness !   And then to think of the last meeting with all that have died under our charge—to suppose ourselves interrogated concerning our obligations to them. .—Oh ! can we forbear the impassioned deprecation of guilt—" Deliver me from blood-guiltiness, O God."[1]   An external performance of our duty will easily screen us from Episcopal censure.   But to answer to the *Chief Bishop* for our diligence, at his judgment seat—this is the trembling prospect.   Can we forget, that the Minister is the man of all others, who needs the superabounding mercy of God, and continual application to the cleansing blood of Calvary ?   Have we then no sympathy with the thrice-repeated flight of Ambrose from the Episcopate—the compulsory ordination of Gregory Nazianzen—the deprecation of the Apostolic Bishop of Hippo (Quid ! vultis ut peream ?)—and the deep distress of Chrysostom, counting his elevation a judgment upon the Church ?[2]   If there was a mixture of superstition with this shrinking humility—"forgive them the wrong ;" and let us condescend to learn something of them, which they are well able to teach—to temper our more enlightened views of faith with a portion of that " weakness, and fear, and much trembling,"[3] which they so vividly pourtrayed.[4] To feel our responsibility in the spirit of dependence[5]—to confess

---

[1] Psalm li. 14. '*Alienas mortes addimus, quia tot occidimus, quot ad mortem ire quotidie tepidi et tacentes vidimus,*'—is Gregory's awakening exposition of this text. Chrysostom's words on this subject (Scougal declares) 'are so terrible, that I tremble to put them into English; and yet'—adds he with a deep-toned impressiveness—'if a man should speak fire, blood, and smoke; if flames should come out of his mouth instead of words; if he had a voice like thunder, and an eye like lightning, he could not sufficiently represent the dreadful account that an unfaithful pastor shall make.' Scougal's Sermon, ut supra. See also some striking thoughts in Dwight's Sermons, Vol. ii. 444.

[2] 'In the first and most blessed times of Christianity, those only were then judged worthy the Ministry, whose quiet and meek spirit did make them look upon that sacred calling with an humble adoration, and fear to undertake it; which indeed requires such great degrees of humility, and labour, and care, that none but such were then thought worthy of that celestial dignity; and such only were then sought out, and solicited to undertake it.' Walton's Life of Donne.   [3] 1 Cor. ii. 3, with 2 Cor. xii. 9.

[4] The celebrated Rutherford, when petitioning the Assembly against his removal from Anworth, the beloved sphere of his parochial labours, to the Divinty chair, used as one plea—'Let it be considered, if one, who dare not be able to answer to Christ for a lesser charge, should be burdened with a more weighty.' Murray's Life of Rutherford, p. 153.

Leighton assigns as one reason for his resignation of the see of Glasgow—' The sense I have of the dreadful weight of whatsoever charge of souls, and all kind of spiritual inspection over all people, but much more over Ministers; and there is'—added he—' an episcopal act, that is above all others formidable to me—*ordaining Ministers*.' Pearson's Life, cxv. Compare Burnet's Pastoral Care, ch. vi. The toil of sleepless nights seems to be implied in the Apostle's emphatic term, αγρυπνυσιν (Heb. xiii. 17.) Were not the Apostle's " watchings often" (εν αγρυπνιαις 2 Cor. vi. 5.) probably connected with his deep intensity of Ministerial anxiety ?

[5] Compare 2 Cor. ii. 16, with iii. 5, 6. .

our deficiencies and defilements with unfeigned self-abasement—and, under this sense of shame, to prize more highly, and apply more constantly, the blood of atonement for our acceptance—this is the frame we should desire—not oppressed with legal despondency ; but humbled, sustained, rejoicing, fruitful, under the influence of the faith, and hope of the gospel.

III. *Do we earnestly desire and expect success in our work ?* The merchant fails, when he loses his cargo—the statesman, when the kingdom suffers loss—the Minister, when the soul perishes. And what failure in its ruinous consequences can compare with his ? His desire therefore for success is spiritualized humanity. Yet who of us prays, or stirs up his people to pray, for success, as if he suitably realized its unspeakable importance ? And what hope can there be of success without an anxious concern for it ? ' If you would prosper in your work,' (says Baxter) ' be sure to keep up earnest desires and expectations of success. If your heart be not set upon the end of your labours, and you long not to see the conversion and edification of your hearers, and do not study and preach in this hope, you are not likely to see much fruit of it.'[1] "The ostrich" indeed " leaveth her eggs in the earth," careless what may befal them, " *because* God hath deprived her of wisdom, neither hath he imparted unto her understanding."[2] But what husbandman would sow the seed without some anxiety and expectation of the harvest ? And who can help admiring the conduct of faithful Eliezer, who would neither eat nor drink, until he saw how his master's business would speed ?[3] Yet how often are we satisfied with a creditable performance of our duties, without a deep concern for the success of our work, and yearning compassion for the multitudes, hardening themselves under the sound of the Gospel ![4] A Ministry devoted to the salvation of souls ; aiming intensely and simply at this main object ; counting every soul a kingdom ; and more delighted to save a soul than to win a crown—this is love for perishing immortals—this is the true spirit of our office. This was the mind of our Great Master—the satisfaction he anticipated from " the travail of his soul"—" the joy that was set before him."[5] This also was the sustaining desire of the Apostle under his wearisome labours.[6] Oh ! then, let us, like men and

---

[1] Reformed Pastor and his Life of Alleine.
[2] Job xxxix. 14—17, with John x. 12, 13.   [3] Gen. xxiv. 33.
[4] Mr. Ottee, ejected from Beccles, Suffolk, if he preached ,five or six sermons without hearing of any good effect upon some or other of his hearers, was greatly dejected and very fervent in prayer for further success.   [5] Isaiah liii. 11. Heb. xii. 2.
[6] See Rom. i. 13. Bishop Patrick informs us, in his interesting account of the learned John Smith—'that he had resolved (as he one day told me) very much to lay aside other

Ministers of God, thirst insatiably for the conversion of souls. We must be utterly dead to any high sense of our calling, if we can roll along a course of years in the responsible relation of Pastor, without enquiry or concern, whether our people thrive or decline under our Ministry. Let us not be satisfied with evidence of personal attachment to ourselves, without one beating pulse of love to our Master. Acceptance with man is an empty bubble—success in conversion is every thing. Let nothing therefore content us, short of real fruit. Some outward restraint or reformation may be wrought; but while the heart is uninfluenced, the principle of sin remains in full vigour, and no real or permanent advantage is gained. The *main design* of our work is left unaccomplished. One soul converted to God is better than thousands merely moralized, and still sleeping on in their sins. Our primary and absorbing object is to have fellowship with the angels in " gathering together the elect of God "[1]

Though it is true, that the seed buried is not lost, yet we must not tamely acquiesce in the admission of our results not being always visible.[2] Nor must we live upon undefined hopes; or too indulgently console ourselves in the event of a total failure, with the assurance of personal acceptance. For, though the reward is measured by labour, not by success, and is still " with our God, though Israel be not gathered;"[3] yet the promises, pleaded and waited for in the diligence and perseverance of faith, warrant the

studies, and to *travail in the salvation of men's souls*, after whose good he most earnestly thirsted.' Alleine ' was infinitely and insatiably greedy of the conversion of souls; and to this end he poured out his very heart in prayer and in preaching. He " imparted not the gospel of God only, but his own soul." His supplications and his exhortations many times were so affectionate, so full of holy zeal, life, and vigour, that they quite overcame his hearers. He melted over them, so that he mollified, and sometimes dissolved, the hardest hearts.' Mr. Ward of Ipswich, an eminent Puritan divine, asks—'If God were to say to a Minister, as he said to Solomon—" Ask what I shall give thee !"—what should he desire, either before, or more than this—namely, a large portion of that magnetical virtue, whereby Peter and Paul, and other primitive preachers, drew many thousand souls to the knowledge of Jesus?' 'How many faithful Ministers' (says Baxter in his Preface to Alleine's Alarm) ' have I lately known who have lived in pining poverty and want; and yet, if they could but have truly said'—' Lord, ' *the sermons which I privately and in danger have preached have won many souls to thee*'—it would have made their burden easy. ' In my preaching' (said Bunyan) ' I could not be satisfied, unless some fruits did appear in my work. If I were fruitless, it mattered not who commended me; but if I were fruitful, I care not, who did condemn.' 'I would think it a greater happiness' (said Matthew Henry, in the view of his ordination) ' to gain one soul to Christ, than mountains of silver and gold to myself,' adding, in his *dread of the misery of Ministerial unfruitfulness*—' If God suffers me to labour in vain (though I *should get hundreds a year by my labour*,) it would be the constant grief and trouble of my soul; and if I do not gain souls, I shall enjoy all my other gains with very little satisfaction, and *I would rather beg my bread from door to door, than undertake this great work.*' Dr. Doddridge wrote thus to a friend—'I long for the conversion of souls more sensibly than any thing besides. Methinks I could not only labour, but die, for it with pleasure—The love of Christ constraineth me.'

[1] Matt. xxiv. 31.   [2] See Part ii. chap. i.   Mark iv. 26—29.
[3] See 1 Cor. iii. 8.   Isaiah xlix. 4, 5.   Comp. Quesnel on John xxi. 1—3.

expectation of a *measure at least of apparent fruit*. Mr. Robinson of Leicester solemnly reminded his brethren—*The want of Ministerial success is a tremendous circumstance, never to be contemplated but with horror.* 'Search, ask'—added he—'if there be nót a cause, when your seals are not broad and visible.'[1] Acquiescence without enquiry is the slumber of indolence, not the quietness and resignation of faith. The Sovereignty of God must indeed be fully acknowledged, but not pleaded in excuse for inertion ; nor rested upon, except as a sustaining encouragement in conflict and difficulty. The Apostles, while they were ever ready to bow to this deep and mysterious exhibition of the divine character, yet were full of distress and activity, or joy and praise, according as their Master's work was retarded or advanced. While their faith was tranquil, their efforts were incessant.

IV. *Are we laying ourselves out for our work ?* At this busy moment, inactivity is fatal to the best interests of the Church. The irregular movements on every side of her are enough to keep all her watchmen in active motion. We have "put our hands to the plough," from which there is no "looking back."[2] In fact—as with the husbandman, there is little ór no vacation from our daily labours. The end of one work is but the beginning of another, as the season brings it round. But in the strongest emphasis of the term, does the Pastoral labourer " eat his bread in the sweat of his face."[3] There is an eternity of rest before us. But here we must not expect a life of indolence ; and if we are the Lord's servants, we shall not desire it. But to be successful labourers, we must bring the spirit of the Gospel into our work. There is sometimes a heartlessness about us, most paralyzing to the activity of faith, and quenching to the faint spark of Ministerial zeal and Christian love. Mr. Scott warns us against it, as ' very dishonourable to the

[1] Visitation Sermon, pp. 36, 37. 'To see no better fruit of our employment than merely to have a benefice to live upon, and some reverence from the people, is a poor encouragement. The first thing to be done in this sad case, is to search whether the fault be not in ourselves—whether we choose the most suitable subjects, study plainness, yet the love of our hearers, deal with them privately and personally, as well as publicly— whether our lives preach to them as well as our tongues, &c. If any of this be amiss, it must be amended.' Baxter on Obedient Patience.—' When a man is in earnest, nothing will satisfy him but this. Others may be satisfied without success: they may go through a formal set of observances, and be contented; instead of examining their Ministry, and saying—"Shew me wherefore thou contendest with me." If any thing but usefulness will satisfy us, I do not wonder that we are nót useful. We must thank God for this and that thing: but nothing must satisfy us but the conversion of sinners. The least success in our profession is better than the greatest in any other.'—Scott's Sermon on Rom. xv. 29. We must not, however, confine Ministerial success to the grand work of conversion. See Part. ii. chap. i. ut supra. Comp. Eph. iv. 12—16, illustrated by Acts xiv. 22. xvi. 5. 1 Thess. iii. 2, 10. [2] See Luke ix. 62.
[3] Gen. iii. 19. 'Nihil est in hac vita difficilius, laboriosius, periculosius Presbyteri vita.' Aug.

mercy and grace of the Gospel, and to his name, who commands his servants to *rejoice in hope.*[1] Weariness of our work, when it seems at a low ebb, is much to be deprecated ; still more so—the readiness to seek relief from present discouragement in self-indulgent studies or recreations. The disappointed fisherman sits not down in despondency—much less does he direct his mind to any other employment—but he sets himself to enquire into the causes of his failure, and the best mode of obviating them ; and girds himself for the next opportunity with the same glistening expectation. Thus must we, like the disciples, " at our Lord's command," continue to " let down the net," even though " we have toiled all the night, and have taken nothing."[2] But is it ever too long a time to wait ? Discouragement realizes most fully the blessedness of our work. Its supports do not spring from sensible excitements. We work " by faith, not by sight,"[3] not acted upon by a temporary and adventitious impulse, but constrained by the love of our unseen adorable Saviour. Our failure, therefore (as has been well observed) should ' not be a cause for relaxation in diligence, or for despondency in spirit, or for remission in prayer. Let it rather be an argument for renewed energy, for greater zeal and earnestness.'[4] Like the ancient servants of God, let our discouragements enflame weeping tenderness of intercession before our God.[5] But let us remember, that prayer without exertion will subject us to his reproofs —" Wherefore criest thou unto me ? Get thee up ; wherefore liest thou upon thy face ?"[6]

The axiom—' Duties are ours—events are God's'—is precisely that mixture of Arminianism and Calvinism, which constitutes the true Ministerial habit. It is, however, a maxim for rest in unvarying effort—not in slumbering supineness. Philip Henry tells us— ' The more we do, the more we may do, in the service of God.'[7]

[1] Scott's Life, p. 344.
[2] Luke v. 5. See Dr. Whitby's valuable note on John xxi. 6.   [3] 2 Cor. v. 7.
[4] Bishop of Winchester, p. 526. 'To relinquish or intermit parochial labour, because it is not attended with success, would be terribly inexcusable. Labour on; commit the matter to God; wait patiently; get a feeling of the bowels of Christ; and die, praying, Lord! pity the people.' Adam's Private Thoughts. 'Our business is only to 'declare the whole counsel of God'—to live the life of a Minister—and not to cease praying. Our reward is sure; our record is on high.' Venn's Life, p. 380. 'Not the Minister who has most success in his preaching shall stand highest in the day of the Lord; but the Minister, whose eye has been single; whose prayers have been fervent; whose bowels of mercies have been yearning over "the ignorant, and those who are out of the way;" and who has most readily sacrificed his own will and temporal interest. Such are comfortable to Christ; and upon such he will put the greatest honour.' Ibid. p. 365.
[5] Exod. xxxii. 19. Acts xiv. 14. xvii. 16. Lam. i. 4. Joel ii. 17.
[6] Exod. xiv. 15. Josh. vii. 10.
[7] Life, p. 53. The account of Rutherford's personal diligence is a stimulating record. ' He was accustomed to rise every morning at three o'clock. The early parts of the day he spent in prayer, meditation, and study ; and the remainder of it was devoted to his more public duties; to the visitation of the sick, the afflicted, and the dying, and to the

We may perhaps have to guard against a temptation to bustling activity, or a restlessness of mind, because our plans do not advance as we had hoped. But in good health, and in an equable state of mind, as a late diligent parochial Minister observed—'I am always happiest, when I have most to do.'[1] Let us therefore satisfy ourselves, that we are using all the means, and with all the earnestness, in our power—like men, filled with what Lord Shaftesbury was pleased to call—'the heroic passion of saving souls'—a passion, which will not confine its impulse to the pulpit. Let us enquire throughout our whole course of Ministry—Is nothing done defectively, or in a wrong spirit? Can we think of nothing more that might be done? Does "the trumpet give" either "an uncertain," or a feeble "sound?"[2] What weekly provision is there for our flock—for those of them especially, who feel the intervals between the Sabbaths to be long? What is there, that shews our readiness to be "out of season," as well as "in season, to watch in all things, to endure afflictions, to do the work of an Evangelist, to make full proof of our Ministry?"[3] Do our people mark, in our going in and out before them a *daily* renewal of our Ordination vow, without reservation for our own ease and interest? Are we "offering ourselves" up joyfully upon the service of souls *in the spirit of a sacrifice?*[4] Do we guard against a prevalent danger of wasting our time and strength upon matters of inferior moment? And do we count the day lost, when something has not been either written, or said, or done, in our Master's service? The fisherman, when not actually engaged in his employment, is mending his nets, or more or less exercised in preparation for his business. And thus might the intervals between our immediate work be filled up with the relaxation of study, conversation, or Christian intercourse, bearing directly at least, upon our great object. 'Indeed' (as Bishop

examination and encouragement in godliness of the different families of his congregation.' Murray's Life, p. 43. Dr. Payson's (of America) Memoir (Seeleys) gives a similar and most interesting sketch of one, who was ready to labour even to faintness in his Master's service. We read indeed of an eminent Minister, who "for the work of Christ was nigh unto death." (Phil. ii. 30.); yet (as a general rule) we must regard it as a temptation of Satan, when a legal dread of unfaithfulness, and the undisciplined fervour of zeal incites the servants of Christ to a prodigal expenditure of health, strength, and spirits; thus wasting the candle immoderately while it burns, and extinguishing its light before the time. Their ends indeed are so sincere, their work so delightful, and their hearts so overflowing, that the discovery is often made too late of the advantage, which the kingdom of darkness derives from this premature removal of the candlestick from its place. At the same time a chastised transfusion of this burning zeal into our temperament would prove of essential service; and though we would dissuade from that overstretched exertion, which in most cases is a speedy suicide; yet authentic records of extraordinary devotedness to the work are eminently calculated to resist the encroachments of self-indulgence, and to elevate our own Ministerial standard.

[1] Methuen's Life of Rev. R. P. Beachcroft.   [2] 1 Cor. xiv. 8.
[3] 2 Tim. iv. 2, 5.   [4] See Phil. ii. 17.

Davenant justly remarks) ' a good Minister is never less at leisure, than when he seems to be so. Our people may think, that we have whole days for ease and indulgence, and that we have nothing to do, when we have left the house of God. But if we are what we ought to be, the conflict—I had almost said—the perpetual—but at least the daily and diligent—conflict of prayer, meditation, and study, lies upon us.'[1]

We may indeed go through our outward routine with respectable but heartless regularity—sometimes perhaps blaming the greater earnestness, which it would be inconvenient to imitate. But how different is this from " doing the work of an Evangelist," which alone " makes full proof of our Ministry !"[2] How different from that self-denying self-devotedness, which spiritualizes even our most cursory, and much more our stated, employment ; which, instead of waiting for favourable opportunities (that from men's indisposition to the Gospel may never occur) is endeavouring to make them ; constantly devising some plan for the benefit of our flock ; and primarily aiming to raise them to a higher standard of obligation and of privilege ! It is the holy, humble, and laborious exercise—concentrating doctrine, spirit, example, intensity of interest, and entire endeavour ; and " striving therein according to the mighty power" of God,[3] that is the appointed instrument for the fulfilment of the Divine purposes. Mr. Scott well observes, that ' Satan prevails as much by persuading Ministers to sit still, or merely to go on in the beaten round, without attempting any thing more, as in any other way.[4] For indeed, present qualifications, however great, can never annul the " necessity laid upon us," as debtors to our flock, and as " scribes instructed unto the kingdom of heaven," to acquire greater skill, richer stores, and more heavenly unction, for its all-important engagements. An aged Minister, when exhorted to be more sparing of himself, once observed—' When a man has loitered the best part of his day, and the even-

---

[1] Dav. in Col. ii. 1. 'I may say to him that snatches at the Ministry, as Henry IV. did to his son, that hastily snatched at the crown—'He little knows what a heap of cares and toils he snatches at.' . The labours of the Ministry will exhaust the very marrow from your bones, hasten old age and death.' Life of Rev. J. Flavel.

[2] 2 Tim. iv. 5.

[3] Col. i. 29. Scarcely one word in our translation of this verse seems to answer the emphasis of the original, in marking the apostle's determined devotedness to his work—κοπιῶ—ἀγωνιζομενος—κατα την ενεργειαν αυτη—ενεργυμενην εν εμοι—εν δυναμει—I labour even to weariness. I strive as in a conflict. I struggle according to the inward operation of Christ, working effectually in me with great and exceeding power. It seems (as Dr. Hammond remarks) as if ' all the agonistical phrases in use among the ancient Grecians were culled out and scattered among his Epistles ; fetched from Olympus to Zion, from Athens to Jerusalem ; and all little enough to express the earnestness of the holy violence of his soul in this καλος αγων.' Sermon entitled, The Pastor's Motto.   [4] Life, p. 213.

ing draws on, he had need double his strokes.' And surely, all of us—had we a livelier impression of the near conclusion of our work ; and did we ponder its importance according to the worth of souls—would be more active in discovering, inventing, and improving from time to time, some fresh point of contact with the souls dropping into eternity before our eyes—some new medium of more accurate acquaintance with their individual condition[1]—some closer intimacy with their false refuges—some nearer access to their affections—some sharper edge for the piercing of their consciences— that ultimately the Saviour might be honoured and reign in them, as his redeemed people. Many schemes might be devised for the purpose, of valuable efficiency, but little outward display. As ministers of the Establishment, our framework is ready to hand. Our influence, as the accredited instructors of the land, added to the authority of our parochial oversight, is much to our advantage. But how will also our talents and opportunities increase the awful balance at the day of account, if they be not sanctified to our great work ! As men specially consecrated to God, we must labour, as if our life was one continued moving on in the course of the Ministry, and our sweetest rest was found in his service. As a beloved friend of the Writer once observed, (exemplifying unconsciously his own character,)—' The true pastor is so devoted to his parish, that his parish is to him in some sense the whole world. He should have no heart, as it were, for any thing else. His invention, and every faculty of the mind, should always be upon the stretch to discover and execute means for benefitting his parish.' Indeed without this entire devotedness of mind and powers, how can we be said practically to listen to the Divine message—" Take heed to the Ministry which thou hast received in the Lord, *that thou fulfil it ?*"[2]

---

[1] Dr. Doddridge set down in his memorandum book hints, as they occurred to him, of what might be done for the good of his congregation. At the close of the year he took a large and distinct view of its state, wrote some remarks upon it, and laid down rules for his future conduct in his relation to it.—Orton's Life, ch. v. 'Were the Lord to make me young again' (said Mr. Brown on his death-bed), 'I think I should study to devise some other means for the gaining of souls, than those which I have used, and to prosecute them with more activity than ever I did.'—Life and Remains, p. 287. 'If an angel' (says Cotton Mather) 'were in the flesh, as I am, and in such a post as mine, what methods would he use to glorify God!' One of Plato's qualifications for his disciple— φιλοπονος—(De Repub. Lib. vi.) illustrates the industry, interest, and labour of the whole heart concentrated in the work of God. 'The Devil in the last day shall rise against us in condemnation, for that he hath been more careful to gain souls, than we to save them.' Bernard.

[2] Col. iv. 17. See Chaucer's picture of the 'Poor Parson of a town;' (supposed to refer to Wickliff)—

'Wide was his parish, and houses far asunder;
But he ne left nought, for ne rain ne thunder;

V. *Does the Spirit of love characterize our Ministrations?*
Let us enquire *generally, as to our interest in our work.* " Not
by constraint" is the spirit of our office ; at least by no other constraint than " the love of Christ."[1] Irksome indeed must it be to
him, who only makes it subservient to his own selfish purpose.
But under Christian constraint, our duty will be our delight—our
work our wages.[2] Indeed, even under depressing circumstances,
the obligation of standing up as a witness for Christ, and the excitement to set forth his excellence to sinners, bring a sensible refreshment to our own souls, so that our labour of love is a most
blessed service. Yet it may be often well to ask—What fellowship
have we here with the delight, which faithful servants of God have
always experienced in their Master's work[3]—a delight strongly connected with its effectiveness ? For it has been truly remarked—
that ' justice can never be done to any profession, which is pursued
with aversion or indifference.. *Without loving his profession, no*

In sickness and in mischief to visite,
The ferrest in his parish, moche and light
Upon his fete, and in his hand a staff.'
Prologue to Canterbury Tales.
Dryden versified these lines into more intelligible English—
Wide was his parish; not contracted close
In streets, but here and there a straggling house;
Yet still he was at hand, without request,
To serve the sick or succour the distrest.
Tempting on foot alone, without affright,
The danger of a dark, tempestuous night.

[1] 1 Peter v. 2, with 2 Cor. v. 14.

[2] ' I may conscientiously take the wages for the work, when I have a distinct consciousness, that I would do the work without the wages,'—Adam's Private Thoughts.

[3] The expectation of solid happiness is thus held out in our path—' A faithful Minister
ought to be the happiest and most cheerful of human beings.'—Bishop Jebb's Charge. ' A
clergyman *who has his heart in his work,*' (not only ought to be, but) ' is the happiest of
men.'—Bishop of Chester's Primary Charge. Let us mark this happiness realized in persevering self-devotedness—' I do not wish for any heaven upon earth, besides that of
preaching the precious gospel of Jesus Christ to immortal souls. I wish for no service but
the service of God, in labouring for souls on earth, and to do his will in heaven.'—Henry
Martyn. ' I esteem the Ministry the most desirable employment in the world; and find
that delight in it, and those advantages from it, which I think hardly any other employment on earth could give me.' Dr. Doddridge—' There is nothing out of heaven, next to
Christ, dearer to me than my Ministry.' Rutherford—' Now after near forty years'
preaching of Christ, I think I would rather beg my bread all the labouring days of the
week, for an opportunity of publishing the gospel on the Sabbath, than without such a
privilege to enjoy the richest possessions on earth.' Brown—' Were God to present me'
(said this excellent man on his death-bed) ' with the dukedom of Argyll, on the one hand,
and the being a Minister of the gospel, with the stipend which I have had, on the other,
so *pleasant hath the ministry been to me, notwithstanding all my weakness and fears of little
success,* that I would instantly prefer the last.' ' After nearly thirty-five years' engagement as a Minister of the gospel, I can declare to the honour of the Master whom I serve,
that no moments, next to those of private communion with my God, are to be compared
with those, in which I am preparing to bring before others the truths which I have enjoyed myself.' Memoirs of Rev. W. Kingsbury. ' My employments, which I have always loved, win upon me with fresh charms every day. I think the work of a Minister,
where he can know his people, the very happiest while it is the most anxious, on this side
heaven.' Methuen's Life of Beachcroft.

one can become an able and faithful Minister of the Gospel of Christ. But to such, the love which David had for the priesthood, for its occupations and duties, will become the living principle of conduct. A faithful Minister will love his profession, for the sake of Him who founded it; for the sake of the church and brethren, for whom Christ died; and for the invaluable advantages, which it possesses towards the acquisition of happiness here and hereafter.'[1] 'A Minister'—observes a serious writer—'who dislikes the business of his calling—who has not *even an ardent love for it*, must lead a very unpleasant life. He saunters away life in listlessness; he turns to his own proper functions with reluctance: he toils through them with distaste; he performs them ill, and is dissatisfied with himself, and, from this dissatisfaction, again performs them worse, and is more uneasy in his own feelings and reflections.'[2] It is not necessary, that he should be distinguished by talent, or by ecclesiastical dignity or preferment; but that love should be the main spring of his work is of the first moment.[3]

Let this enquiry also be more specific, with *regard to our love to our people.* The exercise of this love is one of the most valuable Ministerial gifts. It regards each individual committed to our charge in connection with his capacity for the eternal happiness of the gospel—the infinite value of his soul—his perishing condition—the ransom found by God—and his consequent redemption by the application of this ransom to his soul. According to our perception of these important details will be the enlargement of our loving anxiety on his behalf. This Pastoral connection, in its full extent of interest and responsibility, is, we fear, too little considered and felt among us. A general concern on one side, and a respectful regard on the other, convey a very inadequate expression of the sacred and affectionate character of this cementing bond.[4] But we cannot conceive of a Minister's usefulness—at least of his extensive usefulness—without a cordial love to his people. His powerful

[1] Bishop Burgess' Primary Charge to the Diocese of St. David's, pp. 23—25.
[2] Gerard's Pastoral Care, p. 93. See some excellent remarks in Burnet's Pastoral Care, chap. vii.
[3] See Witsius, 'De Vero Theologo.'
[4] Bowles gives some judicious rules for the forming of this interesting bond. 1. Kindness of speech and manners, Eccl. x. xii. 2. Sympathy with the trials and perplexities of our people. 2 Cor. xi. 29. 3. Readiness to communicate to their necessities. Acts x. 38. 4. Condescension to their infirmities. 1 Cor. ix. 19—22; x. 33. 5. Social habits of intercourse, *with a strict regard to the main designs of our office.* Luke v. 30: xv. 2, 3, 6. Watching against incidental occasions of irritation. Further, to maintain this union, he recommends—1. To avoid, as much as possible, worldly connexion or business with our people, as a fruitful source of contention. Jer. xv. 10. 2. In the necessary intercourse of this world with them, to have a careful guard over our own spirit. 3. To bury all remembrance of any ill-natured speeches or injuries, in giving an ear or thought to which, we may broil ourselves in endless and most hurtful disputes. Lib. i. c. 22.

mind or fine imagination may command their admiration; but love is the magnet, that will draw them to himself. Let him bear them therefore upon his heart, as did the High-Priest on his breast-plate.[1] Let him live with them as a father with his children. *'Bishops'* (as Jerome reminded his friend) are *'not Lords, but Fathers.'*[2] The Pastoral work, without the habitual influence of this princi- ple, is indeed a most severe task; while its privileges are either wholly unknown or misconceived; and the reciprocal affection of our people is considered as a relic of Popish veneration, or the effect of interested motives or enthusiastic feelings. But, in truth, none but those who "watch for souls, as they that must give an ac- count," can know our painful anxiety, "until Christ be formed in our people, the hope of glory;" or understand our intense interest in superintending the various stages of their "growth unto the per- fect man."[3] They cannot be safely left to grow up without food and instruction, on the strength of some supposed innate principle of life. Nor do they ever arrive at that state, which does not re- quire our concentrated watchfulness and care. They need exhor- tation, not only in a careless and backsliding state, but as the ap- pointed means of maintaining their stedfastness,[4] and of "going on unto perfection." All the kindly offices of neighbourly consider- ation are valuable 'means of endearing Ministers to their people, and of opening a passage into their hearts for spiritual instruction

---

[1] Exod. xxviii. 29.   [2] Jer. ad Nepot.

[3] The following interesting and accurate sketch will touch many a chord of Ministerial sympathy. 'How beautiful and holy in all its perfectness of obligation is the spiritual connexion, which subsists between a faithful Minister of Christ and the flock, which he is appointed to feed with the pure word of God! How many are the methods, by which that bond of affection may be more closely drawn! How various are the ways, in which a faithful and vigilant Pastor may apply himself to the conscience of men and promote their spiritual welfare; administering instruction, reproof, consolation; "becoming all things to all men, that he might by all means save some;" always on the watch for oppor- tunities of seasonably interposing the great truths and warnings of the gospel; anxiously alive to the symptoms of religious improvement in his flock; and looking at that, as his strong encouragement and rich reward! Many an anxious care does he experience for the welfare of those, who are endeared to him by the sacred sympathies of spiritual affin- ity; many a sorrow for failures, in which the world thinks he has no interest; many a joy also for blessings, which he alone perceives descending upon the heads of those whom he loves in the Lord. And such a shepherd is not without recompence, even in this world: "the sheep follow him, for they know his voice." Such, my brethren, were the Apostles; such were the first pastors and teachers of the church of Christ; such have been many holy fathers of that church, who imbibed the true spirit of that gospel, which it is intended to uphold and propagate; and in proportion as all its Ministers, by the aid of that spirit, which is promised to them as an abiding and sanctifying Spirit, can assimilate themselves to that perfect model of self-devotedness and disinterestedness, of ardent zeal for the salvation of mankind, and of singleness of intention, as preachers of the gospel only; in that proportion will they be "burning and shining lights" to illuminate and pu- rify the world; and in that proportion will the kingdom of Christ on earth be set forward, and his great designs of mercy carried on towards their accomplishment.' Bishop Blom- field's Lectures on the Acts, pp. 114—116. Another beautiful sketch may be found in the Bishop of Winchester's Primary Charge, pp. 56—58.

[4] See Part V. c. ii. sect. ix.

of all sorts.'[1] It will not then be necessary for them to be told, that we love them. This condescension to all their sympathies—this interest in their trials, their comforts, and their families—will constrain them to feel it. Indeed, we hesitate not to say, that there is no feeling of the parent, with which the experience of the Christian Minister does not sympathize.[2] Even needful reproof will be conveyed in parental language;[3] and the exhortation of the true Pastor will differ as widely from mere official advice or remonstrance, as the tender counsel of a loving father from the accurate tuition of a well-principled instructor.[4] If indeed, on looking round upon our flock, we can see no one, who, in the language of the Apostle, "owes to us his soul,"[5] we can have no conception of that endearing bond of attachment, that unites a faithful shepherd to his deeply indebted flock. But to prove the existence of such a bond would be a most superfluous task. Every parochial visit reminds the affectionate Minister of its happy influence; binding him a willing servant to his Divine Master, and to the church for which he died.[6]

Now let us apply the Apostle's description of his own Ministerial feelings to ourselves. His Epistles to the Philippians and Thessalonians present a most exciting picture of Pastoral endearment, in his thankfulness for his people, his prayers for them, and delight in them. Mark his continual "longings to see" his different flocks, for their mutual enlargement and comfort. "Taken from them," sometimes "in presence, never in heart," his return to them is the subject of his constant prayers, in which he entreats them to unite with him.[7] Nor could he meanwhile be satisfied, without sending messengers to hear of their state and progress; as if good tidings of them were the life of his own life, and an excitement to his

[1] Bishop Gibson's Directions to the Clergy of London.
[2] Ambrose could say to his people—'Non minus vos diligo, quos genui ex Evangelio, quam si suscepissem conjugio.' De Offic. Lib. i. c. 5. The record of this faithful Pastor is of the same spirit—Jacere eum putes cum jacentibus; lachrymari cum lachrymantibus; gemere cum gementibus. Vir clementissimus in omnem formam se transformavit, ut homines diaboli faucibus ereptos Christo lucrifaceret. In the same spirit, the primitive Bishop Wilson remarks—'He that considers himself as the Father of the flock, will not forget, with what mildness, tenderness, and love, a Father treats his children.' Stowell's Life, p. 286.
[3] See 1 Cor. iv. 14. [4] See 1 Cor. iv. 15, 16. [5] Philemon 19.
[6] Rutherford's Pastoral Life furnishes a beautiful illustration of this subject. He could assure his flock, that they 'were the objects of his tears, care, fear, and daily prayers—that he laboured among them early and late'—and (to use his strong language) 'my witness is above, that your heaven would be two heavens to me, and the salvation of you all as two salvations to me.' Letters, part i. sect. 2. They, in their turn, in petitioning against his removal from them, declared, that 'it has pleased God so to evidence his calling here, by his blessing on his labours amongst us; the consequence whereof we find to be a mutual union of our hearts betwixt him and us.'—Murray's Life, ut supra, Appendix, F.
[7] Rom. i. 9—12; xv. 30—32; 1 Thess. ii. 17.

continual thankfulness.[1] He could not forbear telling them, how
his "mouth was opened," and "his heart enlarged" towards them
—that he was looking with a father's expectations to be "somewhat filled with their company"—and (as if a father's tenderness
was inadequate. to convey the overflow of his heart) that he was
ready to "cherish them, as a nursing-mother her children ;" being
" affectionately desirous to impart not the Gospel of God only, but
also his own soul to them."[2] His habit of carrying them always
" in his heart, to die and live with them ;" his anxiety during his
imprisonment, employed more on their welfare than on his own
life ; nay, even his readiness to be detained from the immediate
presence of his Redeemer for their sakes ; and the joy with which
he anticipated the offering of his life " upon the sacrifice and service of their faith,"[3] are far beyond our standard of Ministerial sympathy. He was ever willing, for the more effectual attainment of
his object, to wave the right of command for the language of entreaty.[4] His disinterested love forgot all personal injury, and all
occasion of resentment, in the grand object of his people's restoration to the simplicity of the Gospel.[5] Nay, he is willing to lose
their hearts for himself, if he could but win them to Christ ; overcoming ungrateful returns with the continued overflowing of affection ; "seeking not theirs, but them ; very gladly spending and
being spent for them, though the more abundantly he loved them,
the less he was loved."[6] "Glad was he even of his own weakness,
if only they were strong," having his mind absorbed with one great
desire—" their perfection."[7] Whether or not the Apostle was raised
up as a Pastoral model to his successors in the Ministry—this at
least is the true spirit of the office, embodied, and moulded to real
life and experience. For be it remembered, that this care, solicitude,
and tenderness expressed in prayers, tears, continual sacrifices of
personal ease and indulgence, and frequent exposure to imminent
peril[8] were not the effect of direct miracle or inspiration, but the effusions of a heart, lamenting over the miserable condition of perishing sinners ; yearning over his own children in the faith ; glowing
with the love of Christ, and filled with his Spirit.

[1] Phil. ii. 19 ; 1 Thess. iii. 1—11.
[2] 2 Cor. vi. 11.   Rom. xv. 24.   1 Thess. ii. 7, 8.
[3] 2 Cor. vii. 3; Col. ii. 1, 2; iv. 7, 8; Phil. i. 21—24; ii. 17.
[4] Philemon 8, 9.   [5] Gal. iv. 11—15.
[6] 2 Cor. xii. 12—15. 'This motto of an Apostle ("I seek not yours, but you") is transmitted to us with his Apostleship, to be transcribed, not into our rings and seals of orders,
but into our hearts; there, if you please, to be engraven with a diamond; set, as the
stones in our ephod, the jewels in our breast-plate, gloriously legible to all that behold us.'
—Dr. Hammond's Pastor's Motto, ut supra.
[7] Ibid. xiii. 9.   [8] Ibid. vi. 4, 5 ; xi. 23—27.

The Writer knows not when he has felt more sensibly his almost infinite distance from the Scriptural standard of obligation, than while sketching out this imperfect outline of what a Minister ought to be, *and what he might be.* For let it not be supposed, that these are graces and duties peculiar either to the Apostle or the Apostolic age. They mark the standard, which all, who have pledged themselves to the sacred function, would do well habitually to contemplate; and the practical influence of which constitutes the life of our Ministrations. 'He who has not this solicitous care and Apostolic tenderness, knows not what it is to be a father and a Pastor.' But 'happy is that Pastor, to whom his life, his labours, his zeal, and the testimony of his conscience, give the just confidence to say, that he loves the flock of Christ; and that he loves it only for and in Christ, only by his charity, and in his spirit.'[1] That he should have a shepherd's eye and a shepherd's heart, is equally important for his acceptance with the flock and with the chief Shepherd. The former will often bear the most repulsive truths in such a spirit;[2] and if the Pastor is not in every one's mouth, he is at least in the hearts of the people of his charge. The latter expects to see in him the image of his own tenderness and love—" feeding his flock like a shepherd; gathering the lambs in his arms, and carrying them in his bosom, and gently leading those that are with young."[3]

But if this love to our people is the spring of success, it is equally certain, that the principle of this love to souls is love to Him that purchased them. Hence flow all our pains, patience, and care: from the delight of " spending and being spent" in the service of one whom we supremely love. Under this constraint we cannot be loiterers. There are many tracks of life before us of far greater temporal indulgence. But the recollection comes with power— " He is worthy, for whom we should do this." The awful immensity of our obligation enlivens the endurance of the Ministerial cross, and makes us feel, that all that we have attempted scarcely expresses even the consciousness of our infinite debt. This love 'is the great endowment of a shepherd of Christ's flock.' He says not

[1] Quesnel on Phil. ii. 19; 1 Cor. xvi. 24.
[2] 'Dilige, et dic quicquid voles.' August. in Gal. vi. 1. 'Scarce can the harshest reproofs be thrown back, that have upon them the stamp of love.'—Leighton on 1 Peter ii. 11 In illustration of this—a Minister of a remarkable spirit of love, sharply rebuked, in the presence of a clerical friend, a parishioner for gross misconduct. The severity of the reproof astonished his friend, who could not help declaring, that in his own case, with one of his people, he should have expected an irreconcilable breach. The answer was the result of Christian wisdom and experience—'O my friend, when there is love in the heart, you may say any thing.' See also Dwight's Theology, Sermons cliii. cliv. and Bishop of Winchester's Min. Cha. of Christ, pp. 396—398.
[3] Isaiah xl. 11.

to Peter—'Art thou wise, or learned, or eloquent?' but "lovest thou me?" "Then feed my sheep"[1]—as if he would not trust them with one who did not love him. And surely the under-shepherds cannot forget the attractive influence of that thrice-repeated command,[2] enforced as it is by the power of his example, and by the constraining motives of his love. Our whole charge must then be our "dearly beloved and longed for;" many of them doubtless will be our "joy and crown;" and the prospect of meeting them as such "in the presence of our Lord Jesus Christ, at his "coming," is an auxiliary joy belonging to our anticipation of that glorious consummation.[3]

VI. *Do we pray for our flock?* It is of little use to be devoted to labour for our people, if we are not equally devoted to prayer on their behalf. God make us Ministers of much prayer! For without this devotional spirit, we possess only that negative existence, which will eventually cut us off from the Church, as an useless incumbrance, instead of an instrument of good. A Ministry of power must be a Ministry of prayer. Thus Moses, Aaron, and Samuel,[4] stood in the gap. Jeremiah's intercession seemed as if it could restrain the execution of the Divine purposes.[5] This was the Apostle's chief mode of expressing his "longing after" his people, "in the bowels of Jesus Christ." He seems as if he never bowed his knee before his God without expressing his interest on their behalf.[6] Could such a spirit fail of "having power with God, and prevailing?" Without this prevalency with God, we can never hope to prevail with men. 'The Minister of the Gospel should indeed be as the angels of God, going betwixt him and his people; not only bringing down useful instructions from God to them, but putting up earnest supplications to God for them. And without this, there can be little answer of success in the other; little springing up of this seed, though Ministers sow it plentifully in preaching, unless they secretly water it with their prayers and tears.'[7]

---

[1] Leighton on 1 Peter v. 2. 'Christ might have said to Peter—If you love me, fast, lie on the naked ground, be in watchings, defend the oppressed, be the father of the orphan, and the husband of the widow. But, passing by all these—what does he say?— Feed my sheep.' Chrys. De Sacerd. Lib. ii. Comp. Bowles. Lib. iii. 29. and Wits. de Vero Theologo. It was a high commendation of the late Dr. Gillies of Glasgow from a Deist —'that he believed, that he would be glad to carry all mankind in his bosom to the kingdom of heaven.'

[2] John xxi. 15—17.   [3] Phil. iv. 1. 1 Thess. ii. 19, 20.
[4] Exod. xxxii. 11, 31. Numb. xvi. 46—48. 1 Sam. xii.
[5] See Jer. vii. 16.   [6] See Eph. i. 16. Phil. i. 4. 2 Tim. i. 3.
[7] Leighton on 1 Peter v. 10. Such prayers as Eph. i. 17—19; iii. 14—19. Phil. i. 9—11. Col. i. 9—12, &c. are well deserving of study, as models for enlarged and profitable Ministerial intercession. It was well observed by an old divine, that 'the Minister, who is more before his people in *public*, than he is before God for them in *private*, has little reason to expect a blessing on his labours.' 'No man ever rose from his

Our *constant need of this duty* is most palpable. Our responsibilities on behalf of our people are great and awful. The consciousness of the dangers which surround them—the multitude of eyes that are upon them—their helplessness, discouragements, and perplexities—all demand our remembrance before God. More affecting and stimulating excitements may be found in their too frequent insensibility to our glad tidings, and determined opposition to their reception. And indeed here we may ask—Why do we so seldom mark any signal displays of Almighty power—any extended awakening of souls, but because that spirit of intercession is straitened within us, which is at once the preparative and forerunner of enlarged success? Why is it, that our words—instead of bringing our Master's message from heaven—often seem to die in our mouths, or drop and die between us and our people—that we seldom speak as if we hoped to prevail—that we are ready to despond under protracted unfruitfulness—but because our secret exercises on behalf of our people are so cold and infrequent? Do we not complain of a spirit of formality with our people? Time was, when we worked together upon new ground, when sin crouched under us, when our machine from the impulse of excitement seemed to move of itself. Perhaps now the attendance on our lectures has fallen short. Our churches are less crowded. The restraints of our early Ministry are worn out. Indifference has crept in. Even Christians have waxed cold. Our former plans have lost their interest. The edge of ardour is blunted. But has not the main-spring of the machine been weakened? Has not pleading intercession been neglected? If the emergency demands increase of faith, how much better is it to rejoice in the promised strength, than indolently to mourn over the increase of difficulty! Whatever variation of system may be attempted, (and some occasional variation will be necessary,) nothing will permanently maintain the real interest among us, when the excitement of novelty has subsided, but increased energy and faith in Ministerial prayer.[1] Revivals in our congregations must be expected to com-

knees after praying for his parish, without experiencing an increase of love for his Ministerial work, and of ardour in its prosecution. He returns to his flock with something of that holy light shed around his head, which shone on the face of Moses, after talking with the Lord on the Mount; so that all men may know by the consistency of his walk and demeanour, and the concentration of every thought on the one great and absorbing object—that he too has been with Jesus.' Bp. of Winchester's Charge, 1837. Bowles. Lib. i. 22.

[1] Dr. Doddridge felt this so strongly, that it was his custom to set apart days of public prayer, when the work of religion seemed to be at a stand in his congregation.—Orton's Life, ch. v. Most interesting memorials are preserved of the hours (golden hours doubtless for his people as well as for himself) which he used to spend in his vestry, in personal humiliation and Ministerial intercession. Ib. ch. viii. sect. viii.

mence with ourselves. The declining or prosperous state of the Church may be estimated by the standard of our own religion. Larger supplication for the outpouring of the Spirit would bring increased power to the lever of the pulpit. Our sermons would be manifestly sent down from heaven. Our word would come "*with much assurance*"[1]—with immediate authority—with a distinct message from God. Such a Ministry—connected with enlarged expectations of faith, a higher standard of devotedness, a richer unction of spirit—would "add to the Church *daily* such as shall be saved."[2] The Lord hasten his promised blessing.

Oh for a due impression of our vast responsibility in this matter![3] What is the most Evangelical Ministry without this heavenly influence, but battering the wall of China with our breath? What avails any completeness of Ministration, except every atom that forms this completeness be impregnated with Divine life? How else can we maintain that affectionate self-denying devotion to the service of our people, which is one of the master-springs of our work? Thus we learn how to preach to them; we endure their discouragements; and the spark or flame of love is kept alive under successive provocations and disappointments.[4] Individual cases, whether of temptation, perplexity, or obstinacy, should be carried with special earnestness and particularity "to the throne of grace." 'Without the ability to spread the cases of the people before God on all occasions'—Cotton Mather tells his Pastor and Student—'I should not judge you qualified for an ordination to the pastoral care of a flock among the churches of God, but worthy to have an ΑΝΑΞΙΟΣ cried out upon you.'[5]

The encouragement to this duty is full and explicit. It was when Daniel was presenting *supplication for his people*, as well as for himself—"*whiles he was speaking in prayer*" at the beginning of his supplication, "the commandment came forth."[6] And

---

[1] 1 Thess. i. 5.   [2] Acts ii. 47.

[3] Fleming mentions Mr. Welch—often in the coldest winter nights, found weeping on the ground, in wrestling prayer, for his people. When his wife, pressed him for an explanation of his distress—'*I have*—said he—*the souls of 3000 to answer for, while I know not how it is with many of them.*' Fulfilment of Scripture, p. 183. The following record of a late excellent Pastor is well worthy to be preserved—'So deeply concerned was this good man for the salvation of his people, that he was often heard by his beloved partner, ere the morning light had scarcely appeared, recounting the names of those inscribed upon his Christian list, and offering such ejaculatory petitions in their behalf, as their respective cases seemed to call for.' Memoir of Rev. T. Lloyd.

[4] See Law's exquisite portrait of Ouranius.—Serious Call, ch. xxi. Comp. Davenant's description of Epaphras in Col. iv. 12. Mr. Allport's Translation with copious illustrative notes, has made this valuable exposition more fully the property of the Church.

[5] Student and Pastor, p. 202. His own ability in prayer was most remarkable. On his days of special intercession, he is stated to have individualized with more or less minuteness the case of each member of his church—amounting to upwards of four hundred persons. See his Life.   [6] Dan. ix. 16—20.

if prayer was substituted for complaint—if instead of mourning—
"There is none that calleth upon thy name"—we were to send up
the cries—"Oh that thou wouldst rend the heavens, that thou
wouldst come down, that the mountains might flow down at thy
presence!"—our gracious Lord could not "*long* be angry against
the prayer of his people."[1] Surely in penitent returning to him,
and faithful waiting upon him, "after two days will he revive us;
on the third day he will raise us up, and we shall live in his
sight."[2]

But *constancy* in this *work* is indispensable to the full receipt of
its blessings. Well is it for us, if in the midst of our discouragements we can appeal to our flock—"God forbid that I should sin
against the Lord in ceasing to pray for you!"[3]—if our return from
concluding the service of the temple is—not the interruption of the
course of our work—but a transition only to another part of it—if
the seed just sown is secretly followed and watered with prayer.
But is it with us, as it was with the Apostle—*an unceasing employment*—"giving account with joy," or "with grief;" as our
"watching for the souls"[4] of our flock, has shown the progress or
decline of the work of God among them? *The subjects of our
intercession* should have respect to the success of the work of God,
in the awakening, enlightening, strengthening, and consoling influences of his Holy Spirit; to his presence in our congregations (upon
which—as we have just observed—not upon the ability and fervour
of the Ministrations, our efficacy supremely depends); to the supply of unction, life, and comfort proportioned to the weakness, and
wants, and temptation of each of our people: and finally to the
general effusion of his Holy Spirit upon the Church, to consummate the glory of the latter days; to "establish the mountain of
the Lord's house in the top of the mountains," that "all flesh may
see the salvation of God," and the voice of Zion may be heard,
"lifted up with strength, saying unto the cities of Judah, Behold
your God."[5] This spirit of Ministerial prayer is as necessary to
form the character of a Pastor, as the spirit of personal prayer to
form that of a Christian. Nor can there be hope of acceptance
for diligence in every department of our momentous labour, unless
it be constantly cherished.[6] Let us therefore exhibit our character,

[1] Isaiah lxiv. 7, 1, with Psalm lxxx. 4.   [2] Hosea vi. 2.   [3] 1 Sam. xii. 23.
[4] Comp. 1 Thess. iii. 9, 10. Rom. xi. 2, 3. with Heb. xiii. 17.—where the Apostle
is primarily referring—not to the solemnity of the final account—but to a continual rendering of account to God in the manner here intimated. See Owen, Doddridge, and
Scott in loco. The examples of the disciples suggests also this most important habit of
rendering a daily account of our Ministry to our Divine Master. Mark vi. 30.
[5] Isaiah ii. 2; xl. 5, 9.
[6] 'That Ministration of the word, which is not accompanied with continual prayer

as "watchmen set upon the walls, who shall never hold their peace day nor night; giving our God no rest, till he establish, and till he make Jerusalem a praise in the earth."[1] The blessed influences of this spirit of intercession upon our public work will be manifest to all men.   While habitually praying for our people, we shall find our people praying with us and for us, so that "for the gift bestowed upon us by the means of many persons, thanks will be given by many on our behalf."[2]

In fine—let us sow in faith, water the seed in prayer, wait for the fruit in patience ; and we shall reap in joy.   We must not expect to advance *per saltum ;* but "in due season, we shall reap, *if we faint not.*"[3]   Let us aim at great things, but be thankful and encouraged by "the day of small things ;" never allowing despondency ; quietly waiting for greater results, and expecting them in the full assurance of faith and hope.   *Our whole work* is the display of Divine "strength made perfect in weakness," so as to make it abundantly manifest, "that the excellency of the power is of God, and not of us."[4]   *Its obligations* call the life of faith into practical exercise, and can only be maintained by the daily habits of that life. *Its difficulties*—scripturally viewed—are "the trials of faith"— operating as incentives to effort, and encouragements to perseverance. This makes it a means of grace to our own souls, as well as a grand medium of exalting our Blessed Master, and building up his Church. *Its object* is no less than to gather the revenue of God's glory from the world, to "complete the number of the elect," and to prepare the Bride for her Husband.[5] *Its recompence* will be—a cross from the world,[6] and a crown from our Master.[7] And we know but little of the character, privilege, and glory of our work, if we look for any other recompence.

What remaineth then, but to honour our great commission by a high standard and completeness of Ministry—and, for the accomplishment of its grand results, to plead with that most eminent servant of God—Moses—for a more full display of the Divine power and glory in the Church :—"Make us glad according to the days wherein thou hast afflicted us, and the

---

for its success, is not like to have any very great blessing to go along with it. For a Minister to preach the word without constant prayer for its success, is a likely means to cherish and strengthen secret atheism in the heart, and very unlikely to work holiness in the lives of others.' Owen on Apostacy, p. 441—one of his most searching and important treatises.

[1] Isaiah lxii. 6, 7.   [2] 2 Cor. i. 11.
[3] Gal. vi. 9.   How wisely does the Apostle mark as the foremost sign of a Minister— *much patience!* 2 Cor. vi. 4.
[4] 2 Cor. xii. 9. with iv. 7.   [5] Ibid. xi. 2.
[6] Ibid. vi. 4—9.   [7] Dan. xii. 3. 1 Peter v. 4.

YEARS WHEREIN WE HAVE SEEN EVIL. LET THY WORK AP-
PEAR UNTO THY SERVANTS, AND THY GLORY UNTO THEIR
CHILDREN. LET THE BEAUTY OF THE LORD OUR GOD BE UPON
US; AND ESTABLISH THOU THE WORK OF OUR HANDS UPON US;
YEA, THE WORK OF OUR HANDS ESTABLISH THOU IT."[1]

[1] Psalm xc. 15—17.

59

APPENDIX.

〜〜〜

THE SUBSTANCE OF

AN

ADDRESS

MADE TO ABOUT THREE HUNDRED AND FIFTY OF THE

IRISH CLERGY,

(AFTER AN EARLY BREAKFAST TOGETHER)

AT THE ROTUNDA, IN DUBLIN,

ON FRIDAY MORNING, APRIL 14, 1837;

BEFORE THE ANNUAL MEETING OF THE HIBERNIAN AUXILIARY
CHURCH MISSIONARY SOCIETY.

THE Author sends out this Address with much reluctance, and only in deference to the kind and earnest expression of those who were most interested in it. He has made a few additions, which time did not allow him to give in the delivery ; and he begs his dear brethren to receive it, as deprecating all assumption of authority, and dictated only by an affectionate desire to " stir up" his own mind and theirs, " by way of remembrance," upon a few matters of primary importance to those, who are charged with the high responsibility of the Christian Ministry.

OLD NEWTON VICARAGE, MAY 3, 1837.

ADDRESS.

BELOVED FATHERS AND BRETHREN,

"I AM with you in weakness, and in fear, and in much trembling." I cannot but feel, that I am standing before many, at whose feet I should most gladly sit; I can only thank you for the strengthening sympathy of your prayers. I have longed these many years to see you, not as though I could "impart unto you any spiritual gift;" but trusting "that we might be comforted together by our mutual faith" and love. And now that we are "come together with joy by the will of God, may we with each other be refreshed!"

We have looked upon you as a Church in the fellowship of the sufferings of our common Lord. We have viewed you in the consecrated furnace, stamped with the special seal of God's election,[1] the cheering badge of fatherly love;[2] and having "the Spirit of Glory, and of God resting upon you."[3] We come, therefore, not to sympathize with your sorrows, but to join in your songs of praise—"Thou causest men to ride over our heads; we went through fire and through water, and thou broughtest us into a wealthy place."[4]

Bear with me, however, dear brethren, while I bring before you one practical recollection connected with the Lord's dispensation with you. "The Refiner purifies the sons of Levi, and purges them as gold and silver, that they may offer unto the Lord an offering in righteousness."[5] We look therefore to see in you the shining of the furnace, the character of our God visibly reflected in you. We look for this manifestation mainly in the grand object of your ministration—the exaltation of Christ. This is the object for which we are to live; to set up Christ, and none beside him, before our people; Christ for us, the ground of our faith; Christ in us, the life of our souls; his blood and righteousness, the matter of our trust; his Spirit, the quickening principle of our souls; Christ, "the way, the truth, and the life;" Christ, the refuge and consolation, the present and eternal salvation of his people. Ah! when we look at the hopes of a fallen world centering in him, this fixes our purpose, not to "know anything but Jesus Christ, and him crucified;"[6] this gives to us our text, this furnishes the materials of our sermon; this brings out

---

[1] Isaiah xlviii. 10.   [2] Heb. xii. 6.   [3] 1 Peter iv. 14.
[4] Psalm lxvi. 10.   [5] Mal. iii. 3.   [6] 1 Cor. ii. 2.

the commanding truths of the Gospel before the Church, in a more vivid apprehension of the person, glory, and work of Christ.

In adverting, however, to this point, I would state two features essential to a complete ministration of the Gospel.

First, that it *should be a continually advancing ministration.* Though the whole substance of our message is contained in the single sentence —"Christ Jesus came into the world to save sinners"[1]—yet who does not know that in this compass is included the infinite and eternal love of God—"the height, and depth, and length, and breadth, of that love which passeth knowledge?"[2] If we might be satisfied with having a family of little children, "begotten in the Gospel;" instead of training up young men as the strength, and fathers as the stay, of the Church; then it may be sufficient to deal out the elementary truths of God. But if our souls grow, our Ministry will grow. If we regard the real welfare of our people, we shall "go on to perfection;" in the exercise of the work, "not laying again the foundation,"[3] so as to stop there; but "building up" our people "upon their most holy faith." We are to "speak to them the wisdom of God in a mystery;"[4] that they may not only "receive Jesus Christ the Lord;" but that they may "walk in him, rooted and built in him, and stablished in the faith;" adding to their "faith, knowledge;" "forgetting the things that are behind, and reaching forth," in the path of heaven, "to the things that are before."[5] This, my dear friends, I feel to be a matter of very primary moment. The exercise of it must lead us from Sabbath to Sabbath, and from year to year, to advance from general statements to more detailed and enlarged expositions; to descend into a more minute contact with the sympathies of God's people; to describe not merely the person of Christ, but, as in the book of Canticles, his very feature; as in the Epistle to the Hebrews, all the Office characters connected with him. I cannot allude to this point without the deepest humiliation before God. Often have I been tempted to commit the Ministrations of the last few years (though I believe them to be scripturally accurate in their character) to the flames. But I have felt the preservation of so humbling a memorial of scanty knowledge to be useful to me. I have thought it also important by this means to mark continual progress, or otherwise, in thought and experience. I have looked also prospectively to make a valuable use of it in future time, by filling up the mechanism with richer moulding; the result of more deep in-wrought influence of Divine teaching. But, be that as it may, the real responsibility belonging to us is, not merely to preach, but "*to fulfil* the word of God;" to be going on in a course of expansion and enlargement, "warning every man, and teaching every man in all wisdom"—not satisfied

[1] 1 Tim. i. 15.   [2] Eph. iii. 18, 19.   [3] Heb. vi. 1, 2.
[4] 1 Cor. ii. 7.   [5] Col. ii. 6, 7; 2 Peter i. 5; Phil. iii. 13, 14.

with the early stage of the Christian life—but "that we may present every man perfect in Christ Jesus."[1]

Secondly, I would suggest the importance of a complete ministration of the Gospel. This would include three points, suited to the complex character of man. There is doctrine for the head, experience for the heart, practice for the life and conversation. Take one or two of these things separately, and what a poor, starving, ineffective Ministration it is! What are *doctrines* without experience, but dry, abstract notions? What are they without practice, but Antinomian ungodliness? What, again, is *experience* without doctrine? It is a religion of feeling; a religion of delusion; fostered by excitement, instead of connected with principle; a mere *ignis fatuus*, instead of the "light of life;" inducing a spiritual "confidence in the flesh," instead of a "rejoicing in Christ Jesus." What is experience without practice? It shows only the power of impulse, instead of permanent habit, and leaves the man the wretched victim of his own delusions. Thus, again, what is *practice* without doctrine, but "the body without the spirit, which is dead?" without experience—mere external formality, wholly destitute of the "joy and peace of believing in Christ?" We bring the matter to a very simple point, when we connect every feeling, and every obligation with a continual contemplation of Christ, and an entire dependence on him, "rejoicing with joy unspeakable and full of glory," that "all our springs are in him."

I am led to dwell upon this point, because, so far as my own observations have gone, I have uniformly marked instability of profession to be combined with partial views of Scripture, a sort of favouritism of Scripture. Sometimes it may be doctrines, or some particular doctrines. Sometimes it may be the prophetical parts of the Word—those parts that give occasion to the indulgence of speculation, or which act more directly upon the imagination, than upon the conscience and the conduct. It is very difficult to preserve a well-balanced mind in the reception or dispensation of the Gospel. Where no positive error is introduced, important truths are too often misplaced, or stretched beyond their scriptural dimensions. It matters little which be the favourite point. A partial exhibition must be ineffectual. We can never uphold a steadfast consistency of conduct, except as connected with a whole Christ, and a whole revelation of God.

I add one further responsibility on this point. We "beget our children in the Gospel;" but we do more; we educate our children in the Gospel, and we must expect our children to show the character of their education, whether it be a wise and sound; or a defective, or eccentric, education. In the former case, we may expect them to set out the adorning of Christian perfection; in the latter case we shall observe the absence, or, at least, the imperfect development, of some feature

[1] Col. i. 25, 28.

of godliness, if not some spiritual deformity in the profession of the Gospel.

Does not this view—slight as it is—bring out the practical conviction, that it is no light or trifling matter to preach the Gospel ? See how it exercised all the wisdom[1]—all the energy[2]—of the great apostle ! " Who is sufficient for these things ?"[3]

I cannot but hope, dear brethren, that our minds are deeply impressed with the grand moment of this matter—that it does command the best feelings and the warmest glow of our hearts. But it calls for much more than this. It involves the responsibility of the cultivation of all our tal-ents, the enriching of our minds, the concentration of every power of man, the redemption and improvement of all our time, to be consecrated to this primary work. Those who feel that less than this entire all is needed—that preparation, and thought, and exercise are matters of small concern, have never realized those views of the sacred office, which (speaking for myself) I desire daily to impress more vividly upon my own mind.

There is often much delusive misconception on this point, arising from natural causes. Fluency of utterance, for example, stands with some ministers as a welcome and indolent substitute for more laborious work. This, indeed, when it opens the communication with a well-stored mind, is a most valuable gift. But, apart from this resource, it is a most seri-ous evil to the individual, and a starving injury to the Church. It leads to the habit of saying a great deal, when we have very little to say. It leads us to mistake a flow of words for solid instruction. It exhibits a library of duplicates, instead of a well-assorted stock of theology, or an ill-furnished house, crammed with a multitude of articles, but most of them of the same kind. Now the results can obviously never stretch beyond a little temporary interest and excitement, while there is nothing here of permanent edification to feed the Church of God. An eminent minister relinquished for a while the practice of extempore preaching, because he often detected himself to be speaking without thought, know-ledge, experience, or judgment ;[4] and though I do not see it necessary to follow his example, yet the spirit of it is greatly to be cherished. My heart trembles under the recollection, that the mischief of one crude sentence in the pulpit may spread throughout eternity. What is deliv-ered, therefore, as from the mouth of God, needs to be weighed and ex-amined with the most deep and considerate study. As to myself, I con-fess that I should as soon think of building an house from the result of my own unassisted labour, or a navy from the oaks of my own planting, as of furnishing myself for the diversified cases of my people without any enlargement of my own resources, and without a well-digested use of

---

[1] Col. i. 28.   [2] Ibid. 29.
[3] 2 Cor. ii. 16.   [4] Life of Rev. T. Thomason, p. 169.

them in previous preparation and study. "How," asks an old writer, "can the people grow, if the minister does not grow—and how can the minister grow without study—if he does not daily drink in more than he pours out? If the nurse does not feed, and that more than another, she will soon bring both herself and her child into a consumption."[1] As, therefore, we would not have the souls that are hanging upon our breasts languish for want of nourishment, and ourselves faint in the work, let us endeavour to recruit ourselves for the expenditure laid upon us. The distinguishing mark of "the pastor according to God's own heart" is, that he "shall feed his people with knowledge and understanding."[2] The "scribe well-instructed unto the kingdom of heaven" has a "storehouse," from whence he "brings out things new and old."[3] I would, therefore, that we might bind it as a responsibility resting upon us all, to study and pray, to pray and study again; to labour and work; to concentrate mind, as well as heart and soul, in our great and glorious object—saving souls—feeding souls—winning souls, and rearing families for heaven. In this way only I hope to establish my people solidly in the ways of heaven, and to anticipate a joyous meeting with them in the presence of our God.

But we come now to an obvious inquiry—Whence are the necessary stores for our work to be obtained? And here, of course, we first of all have recourse to the sacred Book. This is indeed the *liber sacerdotalis*, to which we may well apply the rule of the ancient critic—*Nocturnâ versate manu, versate diurnâ*. This is our grand material for solidity, sobriety, clearness of adaptation. No study is so enriching as the deep, diligent, accurate, and meditative study of the Word of God. All other studies—be they ever so valuable in themselves—are utterly unfruitful to us, if this book, with all its rich unction and Divine influence, be not the ground, substance, and foundation of all. But oh! how barren is even this Book of God, if it be not read and studied on our knees! How utterly uninstructive it is to us, except as we are living in fellowship with our Lord and Saviour! It is only when we are walking with him, and he with us, "opening to us the Scriptures," that "our hearts burn within us."[4] But on this point, I would observe, that it is no trifling matter to sit down to the study of this holy volume. Much time is frittered away, even in Scriptural reading. I feel deeply the value of this rule—"*Let the Word of Christ dwell in you richly in all wisdom*"[5]—as directing to a profitable study of the Word. In the neglect of this rule, I have known sermons full of scripture, yet most unedifying. The sacred treasury was largely drawn upon; but they were "profitable" neither "for doctrine, nor for reproof, nor for correction, nor for instruction in righteousness." The power of the Word depends not upon its careless and promiscuous use,

---

[1] Gurnal.   [2] Jer. iii. 15.   [3] Matt. xiii. 52.
[4] Luke xxiv. 32.   [5] Col. iii. 16.

but upon its suitable and practicable application. I would advert especially to the study of the Apostolical epistles, as forming the moulding and full character of our ministry. The epistle to the Romans marks a complete and connected ministry ; to the Galatians, a controversial ministry ; to the Thessalonians, a loving ministry ; to the Hebrews, an advancing ministry, well balanced between the awful and enlivening views of the Gospel ; the epistle of James, a practical ministry ; the epistle of John, a searching ministry to professors, shewing the different features of heart-religion, grounded upon the grand doctrines, and connected with the high privileges of the Gospel ; the epistle to the Corinthians will throw frequent light upon the treatment upon many cases of casuistry in our parochial ministry, dealing with backsliders or conceited professors. The Ministerial epistles I need scarcely commend to most careful and constant meditation. In thus marking out some parts of the sacred volume, I would, however, add my deep conviction of the need of a diligent experimental study of the *whole Book*, in order to " make full proof of our ministry," and to maintain and strengthen the life of God in our own souls.

I trust that I shall not be supposed to derogate from the entire sufficiency of the Word of God, if I inculcate the high importance, to the extent of our opportunity, of pursuing a course of sound theological reading. I feel that, in so doing, I am only admiring that " manifold wisdom of God," by which he hath made man a helper to his fellow-man. I feel that part of the delightful privilege of " the communion of saints," is the fellowship with that world of valuable Christian mind which is embodied in the writings of the servants of God—a fellowship that extends to generations long since past. For, though " dead, they yet speak" with us, and we commune with them. I feel that our store is increased ; our conceptions obtain an enlargement, a simplicity, a more vivid power of interest and attraction, by the help we receive one from another in a simple dependence on God, a careful distrust of man, and in the habit of the soul to " try every spirit" by the infallible standard.

I would not burden your minds upon this subject. I would only suggest the importance of an acquaintance with the writings of our Reformers which are now placed within the reach of most of us.[1] The foundations of our Church should be carefully examined in Hooker's invaluable work. The Popish controversy may be carefully studied in the Disputations of the Grand Confessors given in full by our great Martyrologist.[2] Sound theology will be always brought out in the works of your own Usher, Downham, and Hopkins ; not to speak of Bishops Hall and Reynolds in our Church, and the writings of Owen, Charnock, Flavel, and Howe, in the Puritan school. The field of prophecy may be

[1] We are happy to observe that select portions are now publishing by the Society for Promoting Christian Knowledge; and the writings themselves more fully by the Parker Society (1844).

[2] See especially the valuable Edition of Foxe published by Messrs. Seeley and Burnside.

traversed with the light of the profound and pious Mede—with the ac. curate information of Bishop Newton; adding much that is intrinsically valuable—though mixed with a portion of doubtful hypothesis—in the elaborate interpreters of the present day—Faber, Cuninghame, &c. &c. I would observe, in general, that the neglect of the Apostolical rule— "Give attendance to reading"—has often stamped the mark of unprof. itableness upon minds of considerable power; while we have often pow. ers of a more limited range concentrated by habits of application, so as to bring forth valuable stores for the enriching of the Church of God. I would observe, also, the imprudence of neglecting the responsibility of this work. The man who is living upon his capital without increasing it, is plainly on the high road to bankruptcy. The demands that are dai. ly made upon us for knowledge and wisdom, to direct and to control, to establish and to uphold, to comfort, reprove, exhort, are drawing upon our present resources, and call for increasing supplies to be poured in to meet the prospective and increasing exigencies. It is also a weighty con. cern to keep pace with the improving knowledge of the day. Any fail. ure here will be quickly discernible, and will greatly diminish one main instrument of influence with our people; in the lack of which, ' knowl. edge will be power' of the most frightful character and threatening evil.

But in speaking of the importance of study, we obviously allude—not to the posture of study, or to the time given to it, but to the steady and fixed habit of mind. We can conceive of sitting at the study-table with. out thought; or with our thoughts " wandering to the ends of the earth," for want of the power or habit of concentrating them. The time of study is often frittered away in preparing for study; while indolence chains down every decided effort of application, and vagrancy equally repels every successful attempt to direct it to any useful purpose. This re. minds us of the high value of intellectual habits, as the medium of an effective communication of truth. In this view, I have thought of rec. ommending to my brethren a small work, perhaps uninviting in its char. acter, but full of principles of active usefulness—*Locke's Essay on the Conduct of the Understanding*—or, if I could relieve the unexercised mind from the dryness of this book, I would advert to *Watts's Improvement of the Mind*, in which, in the judgment of Dr. Johnson, its princi. ples are ramified and brought out with a glow of illustration more suited to Irish minds. I remember when I was a child, one who knew me best, and saw prospectively what would be the needed discipline of my mind, put this book into my hands. And I never expect to live so old, or to attain such maturity in judgment, as not to be able to derive new and increasing benefit from the perusal of this inestimable book. I feel more deeply as I advance in my ministry, the importance of disciplining the mind to exercises of connected thinking, as strengthening the habit of meditation upon the Word of God, and thus enriching the inner man with far deeper and more profitable interest in these " treasures of wisdom and knowledge hid," in the sacred store-house. Some of us, I fear, have little conception of the personal loss from this neglect. For what employment can be conceived so rich in privilege and so fruitful in blessing, as a combined intellectual and spiritual exercise on the deepest book in the universe ! Here is a field at once, for the expansion of the most splendid intellect, and for the warmth of the most glowing heart. In this spirit our Ministry will combine, what ought never to be separated —*instruction with impression.*

It is probable, that my dear younger brethren may feel difficulty in persevering study. I will for a moment advert to a natural, and probably not very infrequent way, in which this difficulty presents itself. We have been led, we will suppose, to choose a text for our Sabbath Ministration. Upon a slight consideration it does not answer our anticipations—or, in other words, it requires more labour and activity of mind than we are at the moment disposed to give it. Hence, before the close of the week, a change of text and subject is acted upon—something that presents a richer surface and a more easy treatment. Now, I conceive this habit is to be watched and checked with the most determined resistance. The Scripture selected—as a Minister ought to select it, as the result of prayer—should be considered God's text—not ours—God's appointed means of feeding our people on the next Sabbath. If the materials of this text are not readily producible, it only proves that the " iron of our spade" is somewhat " blunt." But the Scripture rule is— not to lay aside the spade, but to " put forth more strength."[1] Never shall we fail in this, or in any other exigency in the minute detail of our work. When shall we come to the throne of grace, and not " find grace to help in time of need ?" Shall we ever go to our Master's feet, and seek his Divine light and counsel in vain ? And when we have gone *first* to him, and found some light reflected upon our textual difficulty, we may go next to our people, and break up the groundwork in a simple application to a few suitable cases. And how will our wonder kindle in the view of the richness of the soil now laid open—so full of matter— so full of mind—and that mind, the mind of God ! Whereas, on the other hand, the indulgence of this changeable spirit makes serious inroad into the habit of mental perseverance—one of the most valuable ministerial habits, for the establishment of our own souls, and of the temperament of our ministry.[2]

[1] Eccles. x. 10:

[2] We extract the following notice from the Diary of an excellent foreign Minister, lately published—' I find that I always go on best in the business, when I keep close to the first text or truth, which the Lord makes important to me. This is at the time as it were only as a small lighted taper which beams into my heart, and commonly soon disappears. But if I take care not to let it go, but meditate it thoroughly as a word sent from God, and do not care for the dryness and obscurity which re-appears, then I easily

In concluding these remarks upon pulpit considerations, a brother tells me, that he has found himself greatly encouraged, when he has made little or no preparation, and on the other hand much straitened, when he has been diligent in this exercise. The natural inference therefore to his own mind is, that it is better to make no preparation at all. Now this is indeed judging by feeling and sense, instead of by the standard of the Word of God. We are to " walk by faith." Faith is an active principle of diligence. As concerns ourselves—" the soul of the diligent is made fat."[1] As concerns our people—"the hand of the diligent maketh rich."[2] Without diligence therefore, we shall impoverish both ourselves and our flock. Again—God is a God of means ; we trust God, therefore, in the use of means ; and we tempt him in the neglect of means. To judge of the results of our work by uncertain impressions upon our minds and feelings, would be a lamentable proof of misconception and self-delusion. And I confess in plain words my own conviction, that habitually to neglect a careful preparation for my work, is to insult both my God and my people ; my God, by serving him with " that which hath cost me nothing"—my people, by treating them always as children, and stunting their " growth in grace, and in the knowledge of their Lord and Saviour." I would add, however, that in all that has been thrown out —I suppose the mind to be in a spiritual habit and atmosphere ; else, while chalking out the work with accuracy of judgment, the vital principle may be paralyzed, and the healthful glow evaporate in the intellectual process. We cannot make unctional and edifying sermons, while the heart is slumbering, or diverted from its main and single object.

Let me briefly allude to some of the serious evils resulting from the want of a well-disciplined mind in the Ministrations of God. I will hint at *a crude exposition of Scripture.* Oh ! there is one responsibility that presses upon me more heavily than all—sitting down as *" an interpreter,"* with the Word of God before me. It would seem, from the incidental allusion in the Book of Job, that this is a very difficult and rare character—*" one of a thousand."*[3] Yes, indeed, it is a matter of deep and anxious moment to expound the mind of God—not to show what the Bible may be made to mean, but what it was intended to mean—not to exercise imagination, but faith, prayer, humility, simplicity, in setting forth the Divine testimony. How often is the undisciplined mind indulging fancy and figures, instead of being engaged in active, reverent, self-instructing meditation ! Hence that system, miscalled spiritualizing of Scripture, by which one set of opinions is ingeniously, but most wrongly,

come to the point. Whereas, if I begin to change my subject, and think there is really nothing at all clear, or of concernment to me in the one I am engaged upon; and that I must get upon something which is more to the purpose, then I am drifted upon my own choosing and selecting, and miss the Lord's aim.' Memoir of Hilman Rauschenbush— an interesting piece of Biography (Seeleys) 1844.

[1] Prov. xiii. 4.   [2] Ibid. x. 4.   [3] Job xxxiii. 23.

engrafted upon another set, even the most opposite. One rule may stand in the stead of all—"If any man speak, let him speak as the oracles of God."[1]

Again, let us illustrate the wrong treatment of some of the doctrines of Scripture—as, for example, that doctrine of the most exciting interest in the Church, *the Second Advent.* Oh! who of us does not know the transcendent glory and joyous anticipation connected with this holy doctrine? Every day is cheerless, that is not illumined with the sunshine of this grand consummation. Every exercise of practical obligation—every endearment of Christian privilege—every enlivening hope of the Gospel is linked with this blessed coming. And yet how has this doctrine been marred by the subtlety of the enemy, acting upon the undisciplined mind and imagination of man! So that the bond of union has become an occasion of discord; and "brethren are grudging one against another," in the profession that "the coming of the Lord draweth nigh?"[2] The proselyte of a lively fancy pencils the circumstantials of the day, as if from the truth of God. The calculating mind finds the dates as decisive as Daniel's weeks. The mind of active interest concentrates all upon the mode,—whether it is to be a spiritual or a personal reign: or the time—whether a pre-millennarian or post-millennarian advent. These points, I fully admit, have their relative importance. Nothing can be unimportant connected with this event. But I strongly feel that they have engrossed an absorbing interest—that by a disproportionate stress upon the circumstantials, the spiritual contemplation of the glory of the event has been in some measure overlooked; that too much dogmatism has been exercised upon non-essential points—too little discrimination has been shown in marking the matter of forbearance, and the matter of faith. Thus the pure and practical influence of the doctrine has been diverted into a speculative channel. Curiosity has been fed, instead of faith and love, to the great injury of the Church. Let it be considered, that the real power of this great doctrine flows, not from its appurtenances, but from the believing apprehension of the event itself. Much care is needed, lest, in resting upon uncertain calculations, we loosen our foundation from the simple resting upon the testimony of God. The early Christians realized the nearness of the event even in the distant horizon, and that in the most safe and simple assurance. "Faith," was to them "the substance of things hoped for, and the evidence of things not seen."[3] This faith sees, as with the eye of God, "with whom a thousand years are as one day." In the same faith we rejoice, that "now is our salvation nearer than when we believed,"[4] and, in the posture of constant readiness and "lively hope," we are loosed from earth; we have "our conversation in heaven, from whence we look for the Saviour, the Lord Jesus!"[5]

[1] 1 Peter iv. 11.   [2] James v. 9.   [3] Heb. xi. 1.   [4] Phil. iii. 20.   [5] Rom. xiii. 11.

Allow me to close with two or three practical recollections, which I pray God may enable me to apply to myself. There is no one among you that needs a word from God more than I do; and I never could stand up before you, if I did not look that God would speak to me the word that I am enabled to give to you. Well then, my dear friends, let us remember, *The importance of living in the spirit of our Ministry.* For, how clear is it, that, if we are living in this spirit, we must grow in grace, and in the knowledge of Christ! Our work is to study Christ, in order that we may preach Christ. And, "beholding, as in a glass, the glory of the Lord, we are changed into the same image, from glory to glory."[1] If, therefore, we are at a stand-still in our Ministry—if our statements are not marked by increasing fulness and unction, I fear that there is a neglect of the study of Christ; because we can never study him without having the moulding of his Spirit in our souls, and communicating a rich mould upon our Ministrations. In the spirit of our work we should be like Moses, going up to God; receiving our message afresh from Him; and then, surely, when we stand up before our people, our faces would shine before them. Receiving much from God, we should impart more and more to our people, and thus we should grow and rejoice together. This is not the work of a single Sabbath, but of a whole life; and happy, indeed, is that life spent under the teaching of the Holy Spirit; learning to preach with more unction, love, more full and direct application to our people. The power of our Ministry is its simplicity, having only one object, living for this alone, subordinating every thing to it—*Exalt Christ.* All our privilege, dignity, happiness, centre here. This is the object for which we were separated, to which we were consecrated; the work in which we live, and in which we hope to "finish our course with joy." All our personal spirituality, all our ministerial effectiveness, depends, not upon talents, not upon adventitious endowments, not upon exemplary diligence and conscientiousness, but upon the singleness with which we devote every exercise of our mind, every feeling of our heart, every pulse of our soul, to this great object. A Divine influence will always be manifested on our character and message, only when we are simply devoted to exalt our Master. But this is not pulpit work, though it ought to be the work of every pulpit. It must be the exhibition of our characters before our people. We must be living epistles of our Ministry. Our people cannot understand our pulpit expositions, except as they are explained by our daily professions; and then, when they see the reflected holiness and happiness of the Gospel, what a mighty means will it be to draw them to the Saviour, and to bring them into union with him! But this is a spirit we cannot maintain, except as we are separate from the world. And here, I doubt not, you are involved in special difficulties. Obliged as you are, in the ex-

[1] 2 Cor. iii. 18.

ercise of your rights (connected as they almost seem to be with the pres-ervation of religion), to adhere to a party ; what special care and watchfulness need you, to be separated from the spirit of party! As to the selfish politics of this world,—" Let the potsherd strive with the potsherds of the earth."[1] Our Master's message is,—" Let the dead bury their dead ; but go thou, and preach the kingdom of God."[2] Ignorance of this country forbids me entering into detail, as to the spirit of your parochial Ministry. All that I would say is, that the Minister who is most full of tenderness, of yearning sympathy for the young, of affectionate confidence, self-devotedness to the interests of his people, is the Minister, who will make them one with himself, and win them most successfully to his Master.

I venture to add the importance of steadily *prosecuting our work upon our own platform.* One object of my desiring to see you was, under God to link myself with you in affectionate, increasing, intelligent attachment to our own Church. If a somewhat different system of discipline should open a door for Missionary preaching to our benighted countrymen, in consistency with canonical obedience and Christian consideration, I pray God to bless you a thousand-fold. Yet must you expect your love and ardency to be disciplined by many painful trials, and much patient waiting upon God. " He openeth, and no man shutteth ;"[3] and I doubt not, but in diligently waiting upon Him, many a door that is now closed will be opened, and many stumbling-blocks that now hinder, will be removed. Meanwhile it is yours to listen to the word of wisdom, and the Word of God—" He that believeth will not make haste."[4] Yet I cannot forbear reminding you of the importance of due " order" in a Christian Church. The sight of this was a matter of " joy" to the great Apostle, and with good reason ; for his own reflecting mind connected it with " stedfastness of faith in Christ."[5] I feel there is great need of caution, lest a relaxation of discipline should produce a relaxation of the whole system. And, if you have greater liberty than your English brethren, you have so much greater need of watchfulness, lest it degenerate into disorder. I would entreat you to consider the importance of joining, with the full preaching of the Gospel, the distinct principles of your own Church—in the instruction of the young—in the circulation of proper tracts —and in imbuing your sermons with the spirit and exposition of our formularies. In the defect of this, a generalized ministry in a country of political turmoil and hostility to the Church, may leave the next generations unpro-

---

[1] Isaiah xlv. 9.　　　　[2] Luke ix. 60.　　　　[3] Rev. iii. 7.
[4] Isaiah xxviii. 1.　　　　　　　　[5] Col. ii. 5.
[6] I name a few from the *new list* of the Christian Knowledge Society :—No. 51, " Our Protestant Forefathers ;" No. 71, " Oxford Catechism ;" No. 424, " Wilks's Dialogues ;" No. 448, " Nicholl's Sunday-School Exercises ;" No. 464, " Hey's Authority of a Three fold Ministry ;" No. 500, " The Church, the Nursing Mother of her People." " The Homilies." I add, also, a popular tract, to be obtained at Messrs. Curry and Co's.—" I am a Churchman," for the use of the younger and unlearned members of the Church, by the Rev. Hugh Stowell.

vided with any intelligent principles of attachment to the Establishment, and exposed to all the tossing instability and errors of Dissent. Be as_sured you will never be fettered in preaching Christ, with such a system of doctrinal Articles as the foundation of your Gospel Ministrations. You need never fear your love to souls, or to the Saviour, being deadened, while you connect your specific ordination responsibilities, as Ministers of the Establishment, with the general dispensation of preaching the Gospel. I want no broader or more scriptural platform for preaching the Gospel, than the platform of the Church of England. I feel most thankful to my God for this definite ground. It saves me from wander-ing on the wide field of unsettled error, and affords the privilege of iden-tifying myself with all the sympathies of my dear brethren in this coun-try, who are living and working, serving God, and exalting Christ in the same interest with myself.

One more consideration, and I have done. I cannot forget to add a few words upon the special trials of your Ministry. *As a Church*, you are in the furnace, "heated" perhaps, "seven times more than it is wont to be heated." But, be that as it may, "the Son of God is walking with you in the midst of the furnace," and "not a hair of your heads shall perish." You are in the front of the fight, and you are called upon to descend from your lesser conflicts to the great battle of the Lord. You must stand on your principles—Love to Romanists, but no peace with Rome. Here you are prepared to suffer, yea, even to "resist unto blood, striving against sin."[1] But though the conflict is awful, the victory is sure. The field is spread with the marks of defeat ; but you are on the conquering side. The mystical "seed of the woman shall bruise the ser-pent's head." Meanwhile, let me remind you that an enlarged Mission-ary spirit would greatly invigorate the principles, and strengthen the foundations of your own Church. Smyrna was the Church of Ireland in the primitive era.[2] This was the Church, that, in the midst of her afflic-tions, sent her little band of martyrs across the Atlantic into Gaul. And this is the single Church of the Apocalyptic seven, that remaineth unto this day. Let the Church of Ireland read the lesson, and "go and do likewise."

As to your more individual trials, live as Christians, and you will not be much discouraged as Ministers. "The life of faith on the Son of God" will strengthen you to "fight the good fight of faith." Every thing min-isters to humiliation—nothing to despondency. We have such a Min-istry, and we have received such mercy, that how can we faint ?[3] Re-member, it is our privilege to rejoice in hope. Trials will come, but they will issue in a rich and abundant harvest. They will cast us off from ourselves upon our God. They will bring us nearer to God. They will become the riches and glory of our people. We are carrying now

[1] Heb. xii. 4.   [2] See Rev. ii. 8—10.   [3] 2 Cor. iv. 1.

a little flock to heaven. If they burden us with anxiety by the way, they will be at the end " our crown of rejoicing, in the presence of our Lord Jesus Christ at his coming."[1] Meanwhile, all our trials, personal and ministerial, strengthen our joyous expectation as " partakers of the sufferings of Christ, that when he shall appear, we may be glad also with exceeding joy."[2]

[1] 1 Thess. ii. 19, 20.   [2] 1 Peter iv. 13.

INDEX.

Preaching of the Law. See Law
Preston, Dr. 140 n. 299 n.
Pride, spiritual, 140—144, 295—299
Primitive Ministry, 258, 262, 310, 352
Pupillizing system, 134
Prophecy, study of, 58, 272 n. 474, 475
Prynne's Invective against Prelates, 293 n.
Puritan Divines, study of, 46, 67, 341 n. 474

Q

Qualifications for the Ministry. See Ministry
Quesnel, 16, 25 n. 28 n. 33, 39 n. 54, 65 n. 88 n. 90 n. 91, 94, 103, 106, 109 n. 113 n. 115, 116, 120 n. 135, 136 n. 137 n. 142, 143 n. 150—154, 164 n. 192, 275 n. 281 n. 296 n. 314 n. 321 n. 443, 448 n. 459
Quintilian, 247 n. 282 n. 289 n.

R

Raikes, Rev. H. on Clerical Education, 57 n. 179 n.
Ranschenbush, Life of, 476, 477 n.
Recollections of Ministry. See Ministry
Reformers, writings of, 45, 462
Reformed Churches, judgment on Confirmation, 377
Relaxation, 129, 130
Religious Tract Society, 45 n. 121 n. 198 n. 316 n. 363 n. 462
Repetition of Sermons recommended, 292
Reproof, Ministerial, 268, 269, 301, 459 n.
Residence, importance of, 106 n. 314, 315
Retirement, importance of, 136—141
Revival of Religion, 461
Reybaz quoted, 183 n.
Reynolds, Bishop, quoted, 149 n. 180 n. 216, 229, 229 n. 233, 234
Richmond, Rev. Leigh, 48, 53 n. 55 n. 69 n. 91, 104 n. 109 n. 111 n. 125 n. 128 n. 155, 157 n. 226, 237, 259, 265 n. 284 n. 298, 374 n. 422 n.
Ridley, Bishop, quoted, 227 n. 394, 395, 404
——— Rev. H. C. Parochial duties, 157, 433
Riland's, Rev. J. Antichrist, 115 n.
Roberts's Call upon the Church, 414 n.
Robinson's, Rev. R. Notes on Claude. See Claude
——— T. 44, 86 n. 175 n. 185 n. 243 n. 248 n. 259, 264, 266, 382 n. 406 n. 418, 449
Rogers of Dedham quoted, 213, 315 n.
Rollin referred to, 282 n.
Romaine, Rev. Wm. 218 n. 340
Romans, epistles to, 211, 225 n. 277 n. 299 n. 326, 474
Rutherford, 446 n. 450 n. 454 n. 457 n.

S

Sacrament, invitation of the young to, 390

Sacramental instruction, 390—408
——— meetings, 408 n. 414
Sanderson, Bishop, quoted, 37 n. 139 n. 193 n.
Satan, power of, 83—85
Saurin, referred to, 187
Schism, nature and evil of, 411, 412
——— preservation from, 314, 412—416
Schools, Adult, 354, 375, 430, 431
——— Infant, 365—368
——— Sunday, 165, 354—365
——— Weekly, 364, 368—370
Schwartz's Life referred to,
Scott, Rev. T. 31, 40 n. 48, 53, 57, 58, 59, 60, 65 n. 73, 86, 98 n. 103, 103 n. 108, 109 n. 114 n. 116, 125, 127, 132 n. 134, 149, 160, 161 n. 172 n. 196, 214 n. 226 n. 251 n. 390 n. 393 n. 418 n. 449, 449 n. 450, 452, 462 n.
——— J. Continuation of Milner, Pref. viii. 41 n. 57 n. 88 n. 122 n. 134 n. 135 n. 209 n. 217 n. 280 n.
Scougal quoted, 20 n. 443 n. 466 n.
Scriptural preaching of the Gospel. See Gospel
——— of the Law. See Law
Scripture, exposition of, 180, 181, 184, 387
——— study of, 55—64, 185, 473, 474, 476
Secker, Archbishop, 51, 56, 108 n. 110 n. 111, 120 n. 127, 128 n. 132 n. 140 n. 154 n. 158 n. 222, 243, 244, 263 n. 266, 281, 287, 288, 310 n. 311 n. 315 n. 377 n. 382, 413
Self-denial, importance of, 120—130
Selfishness, sin of, 144
Self-righteous, treatment of, 326, 327
Seneca, quoted, 49, 51, 130
Sermons, composition of. See Composition
Servants, qualification of, 311 n.
——— Tracts for, Ibid.
Shaftesbury, Lord, referred to, 451
Shepard, Rev. T. 23, 24 n. 50 n. 147 n. 190 n. 196 n.
Shuttleworth's Ministry, Pocket Companion, 437 n.
Sick, visitation of, 67, 68, 165, 343—350
——— Service for, 343, 344, 345
Simeon's Works, 182 n. 247 n. 248 n 270 n. 274 n. 304
Singleness in preaching, 294—299
Skelton quoted, 218 n.
Smith's Lectures on the Sacred Office, 263 n. 297, 343 n.
——— J. referred to, 447 n.
Social meetings, 418, 419
——— visits, 316, 317
Sound mind, spirit of, 334, 335, 422
South quoted, 41 n. 288 n.
Southey quoted, 198 n.
Spanheim's Annals, 43 n.
——— Wright's, Rev. E. translation of, 43 n.

SCRIPTURES ILLUSTRATED

CPSIA information can be obtained
at www.ICGtesting.com
Printed in the USA
BVHW08s1444060618
518369BV00009B/352/P